Dictionary of First Names

A good name is better
than precious ointment

ECCLESIASTES 7.1

DICTIONARY OF
First Names

Adrian Room

CASSELL

FOR

Claudia Lucienne Alexandra Louise,
with love

First published in the UK 1995 by Cassell
Wellington House, 125 Strand, London WC2R 0BB

This edition 2002

Copyright © Adrian Room 1995, 2002

The right of Adrian Room to be identified as author of this work
has been asserted by him in accordance with the Copyright, Designs
and Patents Act 1988.

Distributed in the United States by
Sterling Publishing Co. Inc. 387 Park Avenue South, New York,
NY 10016, USA

British Library Cataloguing-in-Publication Data

A catalogue record for this book is available from the British Library

ISBN 0-304-36226-3

Printed and bound in Great Britain by
Bookmarque Ltd, Croydon, Surrey

CONTENTS

Introduction

The names that we now know as first names (or forenames, or given names, or Christian names) were originally the only names that people bore. When in medieval times it became necessary to distinguish people of identical names from one another – this John from that John, that Mary from this one – surnames arose to specify a particular person's family or ancestry.

Where did the names actually come from? The mention of John and Mary indicates a prime source: the Bible. And not only the historical or fictional characters of the Bible who bore the names, but the early saints (again, historical or fictional) who were the first to adopt, or be given, the biblical names.

Bible characters bearing names that are still current and in active use today include *Abigail, Adam, Anna, Benjamin, Chloe, Claudia, Clement, Daniel, David, Deborah, Diana, Elisabeth, Esther, Eve, Felix, Gabriel, Hannah, Jacob, James, Jason, Jemima, Jeremiah, Joanna, John, Jonathan, Joseph, Julia, Luke, Mark, Martha, Mary, Matthew, Michael, Miriam, Naomi, Paul, Peter, Philip, Priscilla, Rachel, Rebekah, Rhoda, Rufus, Ruth, Samuel, Sarah, Simon, Stephen, Susanna, Thomas* and *Timothy*.

True, a few of these names are now more familiar in a slightly altered form or spelling, such as *Elizabeth* for Elisabeth, *Jeremy* for Jeremiah, *Rebecca* for Rebekah and *Susan* for Susanna, but they are all in the Bible even so. *Hannah*, although still existing in this form, is more familiar today as *Ann* or *Anne*.

Most of these names are Hebrew in origin and in many

cases had a meaning that related in some way to its bearer or was specifically devised to do so. The prophet *Jeremiah* thus has a name appropriately meaning 'appointed by God', and *Samuel*, king and prophet, has a name meaning 'asked of God'. His mother, Hannah, had asked God for a son, and named him accordingly when he was born. In the New Testament an angel tells Mary with regard to the child she is carrying: 'Thou shalt call his name JESUS: for he shall save his people from their sin' (Matthew 1.21). His name thus means 'saviour', and is of the same origin as *Joseph*.

In some cases the Bible text explains how a name is altered to give it a special meaning. *Abram*, with a name meaning 'high father', was thus renamed *Abraham*, meaning 'father of a multitude', and *Sarai*, whose name means 'contentious', was renamed *Sarah*, 'princess', to denote her special favour with God. The actual naming or renaming often forms part of the narrative. In the latter case, for example, we read: 'And God said unto Abraham, As for Sarai thy wife, thou shalt not call her name Sarai, but Sarah shall her name be' (Genesis 17.15). In fact, however, *Abram* and *Abraham* are merely variants of the same name, and both *Sarai* and *Sarah* mean 'princess'.

Unless the literal meaning, or supposed meaning, of the Hebrew name is known, the textual comment often made on its first mention will be lost on most English readers. For example, we are told that 'Adam called his wife's name Eve; because she was the mother of all living' (Genesis 3.20). This is because Eve's name derives from Hebrew *havvā*, 'living'. In other cases, a person is named (or renamed) without any explanatory text. Thus, when Joseph is in Egypt, Pharaoh renames him *Zaphnath-paaneah* (Genesis 41.45). The name probably means 'the god speaks, he lives' .

Some biblical names derive from the Hebrew words for

plants, animals or insects, and have a less specific reference to the bearer. Thus *Deborah* means 'bee', *Jemima* means 'dove', and *Rachel* means 'ewe'.

Not all biblical names are Hebrew in origin, of course, and the listing above includes some names that come from Greek and Latin words. *Chloe, Peter, Philip* and *Rhoda* are Greek in origin, while *Claudia, Clement, Felix* and *Paul* derive from Latin.

While it is true that some biblical names, especially the true 'Christian' names of the New Testament, have been in use since medieval times, many biblical names, notably those of the Old Testament, and including several no longer in use, were adopted by Puritans in England in the 16th and 17th centuries and by evangelical sects in later years. It was the Puritans, in fact, who introduced many such names to America. They took up the names not simply because they were biblical but because of their literal religious meaning. For the Puritans, *Obadiah* was not simply an Old Testament character (a praiseworthy prophet) but someone whose name meant 'servant of God'. The name was therefore desirable, and accordingly approved and adopted. (Puritans tended to avoid New Testament names that were saints' names, since these were associated with the Roman Catholic Church.)

The biblical names quoted above are a reminder that classical names themselves have been drawn on for individual adoption, whether they originated as names of mythological characters or of individual Romans or Greeks. *Diana*, included in the listing, is a good example of such a name, although it was taken up in the English-speaking world only in the 16th century, and then initially as a learned or 'bookish' name. It did not really become popular until the 19th century.

Other first names of Greek or Latin origin include *Adrian,*

Agatha, Alexander, Amanda, Anthony, Bernice, Candida, Cassandra, Celia, Christopher, Clare, Crispin, Delia, Dorothy, Flora, George, Helen, Hermione, Hilary, Julian, Lawrence, Luke, Margaret, Mark, Nicholas, Pamela, Patrick, Penelope, Phoebe, Phyllis, Sebastian, Sophie, Terence, Timothy, Ursula, Victoria and *Zoe.* However, it should not be assumed that these are all 'classical' names. Many are, but *Amanda,* although representing a Latin word, is a 17th-century literary coinage, and *Pamela,* although Greek, was devised in the 16th century by the Elizabethan pastoral poet Sir Philip Sidney.

The names of many saints will be recognized in the list just quoted. Other saints of early or relatively recent times whose names have inspired adoption include *Agnes, Andrew, Barbara, Benedict, Bernard, Bridget, Catherine, Denis, Francis, Giles, Hilda, Joan, Leonard, Martin, Monica* and *Veronica.* Some of these names, too, are Greek or Latin in origin. But names such as *Bernard, Francis* and *Hilda* are Germanic, and represent another important strand of names that have passed into English.

Many Germanic names were introduced to England by the Normans in the 11th century. Examples are *Albert, Frederick* and *William.* Some Germanic names already existed in Britain before the Norman Conquest in their Anglo-Saxon (Old English) forms. Examples are *Edward* and *Harold.* (In the latter case the Old English name was reinforced by Norse settlers, whose own form of the name was *Haraldr.*) Sometimes a name introduced in this way displaced its Anglo-Saxon equivalent. *Albert,* for instance, ousted Old English *Æthelbeorht* (which is closer to modern German *Albrecht*).

Because the Normans came to England from France, the Germanic names introduced by them will often also have their counterpart in France today. There are, therefore, names that correspond in modern English, German and French, such as English *William*, German *Wilhelm* and French *Guillaume*, or English *Henry*, French *Henri* and German *Heinrich*. In the case of *Richard*, the names are identical in spelling (but not pronunciation) in all three languages.

The popularity of many Germanic names resulted from their adoption by royalty, not only in Germany itself but in England, France and other European countries. France's eighteen kings named *Louis* constantly promoted this name, which became similarly familiar in Germany as *Ludwig*. For some reason, the English equivalent, *Lewis*, was not taken up by royalty. But England's eight kings *Henry* and three kings *Richard* bore a Germanic name introduced by the Normans. (The eight kings *Edward*, as mentioned, bore a Germanic name that already existed in England before the Conquest.) *Charles*, on the other hand, although a Germanic name, was not introduced by the Normans but by Mary, Queen of Scots in the 16th century, when she gave it to her son *Charles James*, the future James VI of Scotland and James I of England.

The sole non-Germanic name favoured by English royalty is thus *George*, although George I himself came to England from Germany in the 18th century and in doing so reinforced the name.

Whereas many biblical Hebrew names have a meaning that represents either a single word or a complete phrase or even sentence, most Germanic names, including Old English and Norse names, consist of two elements that may or may not together make logical sense. *William*, for instance, represents a combination of the Germanic words *wil*, 'will', 'desire' and *helm*, 'helmet', 'protection', which can be understood to mean 'one who desires protection', otherwise 'defender'. Similarly *Edward* represents a blend of Old English *ēad*, 'prosperity', 'fortune', and *weard*, 'guard', so that it can be understood as 'one who guards wealth'. But although such names are meaningful, they were often given for family reasons, not for their sense. That is, a child was given a name that repeated one element of the father's name, and sometimes also one of the mother's. This is fine for an Anglo-Saxon girl whose father (in modern terms) is *Edward* and mother is *Æthelgyth*, since the *ēad* ('prosperity') of her father's name can combine with the *gȳth* ('strife') of her mother's to give *Eadgyth*, in other words *Edith*, with an overall sense 'rich in strife', otherwise 'one who brings booty in war'. This very name was in fact borne by a daughter of Edgar, king of the Mercians and Northumbrians. (She was born in 961 and died aged twenty-two, a virgin saint. Her mother was Wulfthryth.)

But what of a child named in this way who turns out to be *Frithuwulf*, 'peace wolf', or *Wigfrith*, 'war peace'? These are clearly names with nonsensical literal meanings.

Even so, a compound name often does make sense, and its literal meaning is noted in the Dictionary accordingly.

English names that arose on home ground, so to speak, as distinct from imported biblical names or Germanic names, are those that are Celtic in origin. Many names that are today traditionally thought of as typically Scottish, such as *Donald* and *Duncan*, or typically Irish, such as *Bridget* and *Kevin*, are Gaelic in origin. Familiar Welsh names belong here, too, such as *Dylan* and *Gwyneth*. *Jennifer* is also a Celtic name, a Cornish form of *Guinevere*, familiar as the name of the beautiful wife of King Arthur.

Some of the obviously Irish names are actually Gaelic equivalents of familiar English names. Thus *Séamas* is *James*, *Seán* is *John* and *Siobhán* is *Jane*. Similarly the Scottish name now usually spelt *Sheena* is also *Jane*. A few Celtic names have lost their original 'Celticness', so that *Sheila*, for instance, is no longer felt to be a Gaelic name. Yet it represents the Irish name *Síle*, which is the equivalent of English *Cecily*.

The interrelationship between first names and surnames is fairly close. Many surnames, for example, derive from first names. Obvious examples are the *-son* names, such as *Jackson* and *Johnson*, although sometimes the original name appears in an unfamiliar form. (*Addison* is 'Adam's son', and *Anderson* is 'Andrew's son'.) Some surnames are in fact 'neat' first names, such as *John*, *Peter* or *Richard*. But surnames can in turn be adopted for first-name use, especially when they have favourable or prestigious associations. *Clifford*, *Dudley*, *Sidney* and *Stanley* are examples of such names, each representing an illustrious English family.

It by no means follows that all surnames-turned-first names honour a particular family, and many people with a name of this type have simply dropped their true first name and adopted their second or middle name (often their mother's maiden name) for first-name use. Others have simply taken on a surname from elsewhere as a first name. The American writer Carson McCullers, for example, adopted her second name in place of her original *Lula*, while the American actress Sigourney Weaver dropped her original *Susan* in favour of the surname of an admired fictional character.

Most regular or traditional first names have generated a number of derivatives over the centuries. Such derivatives are mostly of two types: alternative forms or spellings of the name; and diminutives of the name. In some instances these categories can merge, since the diminutive of one name may be the alternative form of another. *Jerry*, for instance, can be either a diminutive of *Jeremy* or an alternative spelling of *Gerry* (which is itself a diminutive of *Gerald*).

Examples of alternative forms are Latin *Anna* and French *Anne* for English *Ann*. These are all basically one and the same name, and in turn derive from the biblical (Hebrew) *Hannah*. Equivalents of names in languages other than English frequently form alternatives in this way. Other examples are Latin *Marcus* and French *Marc* for English *Mark*, or old-style German *Carl* for English *Charles*.

Sometimes a name has come down in several forms and spellings, any of which may be adopted for present-day use. A classic example is *Catherine*, which has variant forms *Katharine*, *Catharine*, *Kathryn* and *Cathryn*, to name just a few. This is to say nothing of related forms such as Scottish *Catriona* and Irish *Caitlin*, or the Danish equivalent, *Karen*, which is now regarded as a distinct name.

Both *Ann* and *Catherine* have diminutives, which are typically formed for most names by shortening or by adding the diminutive ('pet') suffix *-y* or *-ie*. (As used in this book, *diminutive* denotes a 'pet' or friendly form of the name, which may or may not actually be shorter than the original name.) When the name is itself short, as *Ann* is, it usually forms a diminutive by adding the suffix. For *Ann* this produces *Annie*. When the name is longer, as *Catherine* is, the diminutive is usually formed from the accented (stressed) syllable alone, with or without the addition of the suffix. *Catherine* thus produces both *Cath* and *Cathy*, among other forms. (*Cath* could equally be a shortened form of *Cathy* itself.)

Many names that started life as diminutives have now gained independent status in their own right. This is true of the many diminutives of *Elizabeth*, deriving not only from the accented syllable (*Liz*) but the second half of the name (*Beth*). The first half has thus produced *Eliza* and its own diminutive *Liza* as well as *Liz* and its diminutive *Lizzie*. The second half has produced *Bess, Bessie, Bet, Beth, Betsy* and *Betty*, among others.

In modern times the diminutive suffix -*y* or -*ie* has often modishly given way to -*i*, especially for female names. Thus *Judy* (a diminutive of *Judith*) is now often *Judi*, and *Jackie* or *Jacky* (a diminutive of *Jacqueline*) is frequently *Jacqui* or even *Jakki*.

Jacky could equally be a diminutive form of the male name *Jack*, and the androgynous or ambisexual nature of many names is a feature of modern times. Names that can thus be male or female include *Ashley, Aubrey, Beverley, Billie, Chris, Evelyn, Hilary, Jamie, Jan, Jo, Jody, Kelly, Kerry, Kim, Laurie, Lee, Leslie, Lindsay, Lynn, Morgan, Noel, Pat, Patsy, Robin, Sandy, Shane, Stacey, Terry* and even *Tracy*, although this last is now much less common as a male name. Where the final -*y* of such names has become -*i*, however, the bearer will almost always be female. *Teri* and *Traci* are examples. The phonetic re-spelling of a female name in general is also a characteristic of the 20th century, and frequently occurs with an androgynous name of this kind. An example is *Linzi* for the ambiguous *Lindsay* or *Lindsey*.

Some familiar variant forms and diminutives have become established in a spelling different from that of their source name. The altered spelling usually involves the change of a single letter. *Sally*, for example, is an altered form of *Sarah*, with *r* changing to *ll*, and the same alteration applies for *Molly* as a variant form of *Mary*. Many diminutives formed from the first syllable of the original name have altered the first letter. *Bob* thus represents the first syllable of *Robert*. In some cases, a letter has been *added*, so that *Ned* and *Ted* have respectively added *n* and *t* to the first syllable of *Edward*.

Changes like these occur for various linguistic reasons. The letters *l* and *r* are interrelated, and the substitution of one for the other is found in other names, such as the diminutive *Tel* from *Terry*. In the case of *Ned* and *Ted*, the initial *n* and *t* came from the final consonant of a preceding word in a common phrase such as *mine Ed* ('my Ed'). (*Mine* was at one time the regular form of *my* before a word beginning with a vowel.) A similar interrelationship explains the evolution of *Bill* from *William*. *W* changes regularly to *b* in Gaelic words, for example, so that the Irish and Scottish Gaelic word for *wall* is *balla*.

Certain female names have come to be regarded as more or less standard equivalents for a particular male name, whether etymologically related to it or not. This is a valuable attribute for parents waiting to name an as yet unborn child, especially when it is planned to pass down the father's name. If a boy, the child can have the same name as his father, as was formerly frequently the custom. If a girl, she will need a female name but one that reflects that of her father. *Jane* will thus serve as a female equivalent of *John*, and *Geraldine* as the counterpart of *Gerald*. Where an obvious equivalent does not exist, parents may give a similar sounding name, or one with a similar spelling. The comedian *Arthur* Askey named his daughter *Anthea*, since his own name has no female equivalent.

Examples of male and female equivalent names are as follows:

MALE	FEMALE
Adrian	Adrienne
Albert	Albertina
Alexander	Alexandra
Andrew	Andrea
Anthony	Antonia
Augustus	Augusta
Bernard	Bernadette

Bert	Bertha
Brendan	Brenda
Carl	Carla
Carol	Carola
Cecil	Cecily
Charles	Charlene
Christian	Christina
Clement	Clementine
Daniel	Danielle
Dean	Deanna
Denis	Denise
Dominic	Dominique
Edwin	Edwina
Eric	Erica
Ernest	Ernestine
Eugene	Eugenie
Eustace	Eustacia
Francis	Frances
Fred	Frieda
Frederick	Frederica
Gabriel	Gabrielle
George	Georgia
Gerald	Geraldine
Harry	Harriet
Henry	Henrietta
Ivan	Ivana
James	Jacqueline
Joe	Jo
John	Jane
Joseph	Josepha
Julian	Julia
Laurence	Laura

Leonard	Leonie
Lewis	Louise
Luke	Lucy
Martin	Martina
Maurice	Maureen
Michael	Michaela
Nicholas	Nicola
Oliver	Olivia
Patrick	Patricia
Paul	Pauline
Peter	Peta
Philip	Philippa
Robert	Roberta
Samuel	Samantha
Stephen	Stephanie
Terence	Teresa
Theodore	Theodora
Thomas	Thomasina
Victor	Victoria
Vivian	Vivien
William	Willa

Of course, there are possibilities other than the single name quoted. A female *John* could just as well be *Joan*, a female *Paul* could be *Paula*, and a female *Robert* could be *Robin*. As mentioned, some of the equivalents may correspond in sound or spelling but not in sense. *Luke*, for example, originates from the place-name *Lucania*, whereas *Lucy* derives from Latin *lux*, genitive *lucis*, 'light'.

Many of the names in the above list, especially the male ones, are now hardly fashionable and are a reminder that names themselves are very much subject to the vagaries of public taste. The name that was popular fifty years ago may be out of favour today. However, there is some truth in the principle that a name that was fashionable a *hundred* years ago may well have become popular again today. This is certainly true of some female names, in particular *Amy, Charlotte, Chloe, Emma, Hannah, Jessica, Laura, Lucy, Rebecca* and *Sophie*.

Not all names, however, are as traditional as these, and there are many names, male and female, that have become popular only since the mid-20th century. They include *Bryony, Carla, Charlene, Charmaine, Cheryl, Craig, Damian, Darren, Debbie, Faye, Fiona, Gareth, Gary, Gemma, Hayley, Jade, Jenna, Joanne, Jodie, Katrina, Kayleigh, Kelly, Kirsty, Kyle, Lauren, Leanne, Leigh, Lisa, Lynne, Michaela, Michelle, Natasha, Nikki, Ricky, Robyn, Ryan, Samantha, Sharon, Siobhan, Tamsin, Tania, Tracey, Vicky, Wayne* and *Zara*. Almost all these, it will be noticed, are female names. But this is simply because women, rather than men, have always been in the forefront of fashion, and it is generally more important for a girl to have a fashionable name than a boy. That is, it is important that she should not have an outmoded one. Few baby girls are these days named *Agnes, Audrey, Bertha, Doreen, Enid, Eunice, Flora, Gertrude, Ida, Ivy, Joan, Mabel, Margery, Maud, Mildred, Nellie, Noreen, Norma, Pansy, Rita, Thelma, Una, Vera* or *Winifred*, but boys may be named *Arthur* or *Thomas* with no great concession to fashion or favour.

Some names have been constantly popular throughout the 20th century. They include *Alan, Alexander, Andrew, Anthony, Catherine, Charles, Christopher, David, Edward, Elizabeth, George, Helen, Ian, James, Jane, John, Joseph, Mary, Michael, Patrick, Peter, Richard, Robert, Ruth, Sarah, Stephen, Thomas* and *William*. Here, it will be noticed, the 'regular' names are mostly the male ones.

This is not to say, even so, that the level of popularity for each name has itself remained constant. *Mary* has tailed off in recent years, and even *John* has shown a decline. *Michael* was much more popular in the 1950s than it is today, and *Jane* had its heyday in the 1920s and again in the 1960s. But all these names are as actively alive now as they were at the turn of the 20th century.

Some of the old-fashioned female names above are those of flowers and plants. These came into favour in the late 19th century but are now little used. However, as always, there are names that break the general rule, so that *Poppy* still has its appeal, and *Daisy* is also now making a comeback. Names of gemstones are similar. *Beryl* and *Pearl* are at present rarely found, but *Coral* still has its allure, *Amber* is actively adopted, and *Jade*, as mentioned, is a welcome newcomer to this particular ornamental category.

The literal, original sense of a name is today not often taken into account when it comes to the practical task of giving or adopting a name. It may not matter that *Giles* comes from a word meaning 'young goat' or that *Nicholas*, and therefore *Nicola*, means 'victory of the people'. Names are given for a variety of reasons: because one of the parents has it, because a godparent has it, because an admired popular celebrity has it, because a favourite fictional character has it, because it is fashionable, because it 'sounds right', or simply because the child has to have a name. One name may well suggest another, especially when it sounds similar or is close in spelling. There are whole clusters of names beginning with the same letter that interact and interrelate to suggest a child's name. One such letter is *J*, with male names such as *Jack, Jacob, James, Jan, Jason, Jay, Jeremy, Jim, Joe, John, Jon, Jonathan, Joseph* and *Justin*, and female names such as *Jackie, Jacqueline, Jane, Janet, Janice, Jasmine, Jayne, Jean, Jeanette, Jemma, Jennifer, Jessica, Joan, Joanna,*

Joy, Joyce, Judy, Julia, Julie, June and *Justine.* Meanings and origins (and even genders) have become even more blurred in recent times with the many names beginning *K*, among them *Karen, Karin, Kate, Kathy, Katy, Kay, Kayleigh, Keeley, Kelly, Kelsey, Kerry, Kim, Kirsty, Kyle* and *Kylie.* With such proliferation, people feel free to invent some new combination of letters, such as *Keely* or *Kyleigh*, and who can then say what the origin of the name is, let alone its 'meaning'?

In the English-speaking world, the British generally stick to names acceptable for their particular social grouping, while Americans, and especially black (African) Americans are much more innovative. This means that in Britain the traditional names usually go to the 'ordinary', while the more exotic or rarefied ones go to the offspring of aristocrats. Once again, it is usually the female names that illustrate this best, as any society diary or record will show. Names of women listed in Compton Miller's *Who's Really Who* ('the essential guide to who's in and who's out'), published in 1987, include *Susannah* Constantine, *Katya* Grenfell, *Christobel* d'Orthez, *Camilla* Cotterell, *Ivana* Citkowitz, *Horatia* Lawson, *Artemis* Cooper, *Tamsin* Jay, *Pandora* Mond, *Cressida* Bell, *Miranda* Leatham, *Phoebe* Manners, *Arabella* Bossom, *Natasha* Kenyon-Slaney and *Tania* Kindersley. The equivalent males, however, have much more prosaic names, and the twelve so-called 'high-society walkers' are respectively named *Jeffrey, James, Michael, Robin, Nicholas, John, Rupert, Michael, David, Billy, Derek* and *Bill.*

Some newspapers publish annual lists of the 'top ten' names of children whose births are announced in their pages, but because the newspapers themselves (especially *The Times* and *Daily Telegraph*) tend to be class-oriented, the record is not truly representative. A more realistic representation can be obtained from a 'grass roots' survey, and one not just of the names of newly born children but of adults, who have settled into their everyday names, with their diminutives and variant spellings.

An unusual advertisement placed in *The Times* of 12 December 1990 listed over 10,000 employees of Eastern Electricity plc by alphabetical order of first name. It showed that the ten most frequent names for each sex respectively were: (men) *John, David, Peter, Paul, Brian, Alan, Dave, Tony, Steve* and *Mark*; (women) *Sue, Julie, Karen, Linda, Margaret, Jean, Janet, Jackie, Ann* and *Susan*. Of course, some of these employees would have been middle-aged, and even approaching retirement. But they are the *real* top names of a large workforce, and are the names that we regularly encounter in our everyday lives. They may not be fashionable names, but they are the names that were predominant in 1990. If the company were to repeat the exercise in 2010, *Brian* and *Margaret* may no longer feature in the top ten. But who will have taken their places? (It is interesting that both *David* and its diminutive, *Dave*, appear in the male top ten, just as *Susan* and *Sue* do in the female list.)

Clearly, it would be impossible to include *every* current first name in this book, let alone all known variants and diminutives. Similarly, the lists of well-known name bearers are obviously very selective, and readers will doubtless think of other famous people with a particular name. But, as always, there may be a reason for a name's apparent omission from the list. It may simply not belong there. The US actress Andie McDowell (b.1958), for example, has a first name that is a diminutive of *Anderson*, originally her middle name. Her agent requested her to change her first name, *Rosie*, to something more androgynous. So her *Andie* is not a variant of *Andy* as a diminutive of *Andrée* or *Andrea*.

Arrangement of the Entries

Each name has its own entry, with the commonest names having the most detailed information. At its fullest, the information itself usually consists of the following: the language of origin of the name and its literal meaning; the period when it was generally adopted by English speakers; its recent and current popularity history; examples of famous or influential historic bearers of the name (kings or queens, for example); fictional bearers of the name in literature from Shakespeare to modern times; examples of variant forms and diminutives, especially when they have become independent names (and will thus have their own entries); and examples of familiar bearers of the name in recent times (that is, from the 19th century to the present). Ambisexual or confusingly similar names are usually designated (m.) or (f.) for ease of identification.

Names of biblical origin are stated to be such at the beginning of the entry, and a brief identity of the biblical character who bore the name will usually also be given, together in some cases with an appropriate quotation relating to the literal meaning of the name. The original Hebrew form of the name is given as if it were a proper name – that is, with a capital letter – although the Hebrew alphabet has no capitals.

Names of Latin origin are sometimes described as deriving from a 'Roman clan name'. For example, *Emily* came from the Latin name *Aemilia*, which was the feminine form of the clan name *Aemilius*. A clan name was the name borne by a Roman *gens* or clan – that is, by a group of families. (It is sometimes referred to in other literature as a 'family name', although this can be misleading in modern terms.) The 'clan name' itself was known to the Romans as a *nomen*, as distinct from a personal name, which was a *praenomen* or 'forename', or a *cognomen* or 'nickname', describing its bearer's personal characteristics. Some modern English names similarly derive from these other types of name. *Mark*, for example, came from the *praenomen Marcus*, and *Rufus* from the identical *cognomen* meaning 'red'.

Authors of literary works are usually given their full name (first name and surname) unless they are exceptionally well known (such as Shakespeare and Byron) or unless their compound surname is enough to identify them (as for Conan Doyle, rather than Arthur Conan Doyle).

Information regarding the popularity of a name – for example when it 'peaked' – relates to its UK adoption unless otherwise specifically stated (usually with reference to the US).

The final item of the entry, listing recent and current bearers of the name, is placed separately (in smaller type) for ease of reference. Each name bearer is identified by nationality, by occupation or status and by year of birth and, if appropriate, death. If the person concerned originally had an entirely different name, this is supplied. If a person came to be known by a different first name (but kept the original surname), this is similarly given. If a person adopted a new surname, but kept his or her first name, this is not noted. The listing is thus not a comprehensive record of pen names or stage names.

The individuals listed are those who have generally 'made a name' for themselves, but they may be less widely known when their prominence is in a more specialized area of activity, such as a particular type of music or sport. Probably the least familiar to the general public will be the names of aristocrats, whose fame will be mostly restricted to those of similar social status, but a few such individuals have been intentionally included to show that, in this rather rarefied world, names such as *Camilla* and *Serena* continue to be popular in titled families.

Most of the name bearers are British or American, and as such are identified respectively as UK or US. For people born before 1801, however, when the United Kingdom officially came into being, the nationality will state 'English' (or otherwise) accordingly. For people closely associated with Scotland, Wales or Northern Ireland, their land of origin will sometimes be given even after 1801. It is thus 'Scottish golfer Sandy Lyle', not 'UK golfer', implying that Lyle is a native Scot and bears a typically Scottish name.

Occupations are given mostly in general terms, but for arts and sports celebrities, who gain the greatest fame, some more specific detail is often given. A person may be a 'novelist' as distinct from simply a 'writer', for example, or a 'jazz musician' as distinct from a 'concert pianist' or 'opera singer'. Types of sport are similarly specified, for example as 'cricketer' or 'tennis player', although the individual field and track events that go to make an 'athlete' are not detailed. For the same reason, 'actor' or 'actress' could apply to the stage, screen or television. (Many performers appear in more than one medium anyway.) Further, occupations generally relate to the one in which the particular individual made his or her name. Many formerly famous footballers, for instance, went on to become football managers. But they made their name in prowess on the field and are specified as such. Sportswomen may make their name before or after marriage (or both), and the surname under which they appear here may thus be their maiden name or their married name. For the purposes of their first name, of course, this is irrelevant. Even so, it is important to have a description that properly identifies the particular individual.

It will be noticed that the representation of sports personalities is mostly restricted to younger name-bearers, at the end of the listing. This is for obvious reasons: it is mostly the young who make their names in sport. Their 'fifteen minutes of fame' is briefer than for most celebrities (actors, writers, politicians) but has, if anything, a greater impact. This means that although their names are brought before the public for a limited period, they reach a large and enthusiastic audience and have considerable impact. The same is true to a lesser extent of pop and rock stars, whose hour of fame is sometimes short, but who equally may well be in the public eye for a number of years.

The year of a person's birth is, naturally, significant for the particular name, assuming that it is a name given at birth or baptism, and not one adopted in later life. The years of birth (and death) have been checked as carefully as possible. Some personalities, however, are reluctant to divulge their actual ages and either substitute an approximate (and favourable) birth year or suppress it altogether, like an ex-directory phone number. In the latter case it has been necessary to resort to an estimate. Some such estimates will undoubtedly be 'out', and apologies are due to any whose year of birth is wrongly stated in consequence.

As mentioned, it can usually be assumed that a celebrity's name will become familiar when the person is first in the public eye. For actors and actresses, this often means when they are in their early twenties. (They may by then already have acquired a stage name. This does not affect the adoption process, however, since it is the name by which they are generally known.) Thus the American dancing and singing star Marilyn Miller first became a hit in the 1920s, when she was herself in her twenties, and that was when the name *Marilyn* first took off in the USA. Similarly the American film actress Janet Gaynor (original first name Laura) gained fame on the screen from 1926, when she was twenty, and the popularity of *Janet* in the 1920s and 1930s was largely due to her.

It is not always easy to determine to what extent a particular name's diminutives have become genuinely independent. That is, to what extent they are given to a new-born child in the first place as well as being taken up by adults later in life. There cannot be many girls who began life as *Sue*, even though many a *Susan* subsequently comes to be known by this name among friends, colleagues and family. On the other hand, some diminutives have undoubtedly become firmly established in their own right, such as *Alex* (from *Alexander*) and *Danny* (from *Daniel*). But because the naming of a child is a fairly formal business, it is usually the full name that is given, at least initially, even if it is instantly abandoned. Babies and toddlers, as diminutive human beings, are often more appropriately addressed by a diminutive name rather than by a full-blown formal one.

When a variant or diminutive of a name is noted but does not have its own entry, an example of a well-known bearer of the name may be included in the main entry itself. *Barbra*, for example, as the name of the American singer and actress Barbra Streisand, is included in the main entry for *Barbara*, and *Lysette* is instanced under *Lisa*. Most alternative spellings and diminutives are cross-referenced to the main entry. Readers not finding a variant spelling or a diminutive under its own heading should look for it in a likely entry for its source name, which will often be not too far removed alphabetically.

A word should finally be said about the meaning of the name, as given in the main part of the entry. When the meaning has (or formerly had) a direct relevance to the name, as for the biblical names mentioned, it is stated. When a name derives from a surname or place-name, however, the literal meaning of that surname or place-name has at best only an indirect relevance to the name, so it is not stated. Moreover, some surnames adopted for first-name use are themselves derived from a place-name, which makes the original meaning of the name even more remote. The fact that *Winston*, for example, is a first name adopted from a surname that itself derives from a place-name meaning 'Wine's village' has no relevance for the bearer of the name. The fact that the surname-turned-first name was taken up by the Churchill family, however, *is* relevant and is duly noted. The same goes for *Stanley*, which was adopted by some not because it has its origin in a place-name meaning 'stone clearing' but because the surname that came from that place-name was borne by an illustrious family (the earls of Derby) and by the famous 19th-century explorer Sir Henry Morton *Stanley*.

First names are thus both stable yet infinitely variable. While some, like *John* and *Mary*, retain their popularity for years or even centuries, others (the majority) are subject to the vagaries of fashion. New names, meanwhile, continue to appear, for the 'name game' is one that anyone can play, and first-name creation is a living and organic process.

The Dictionary

A

Aaron The name is of biblical origin, from Hebrew *Aharōn*, perhaps with a root meaning 'bright'. It has been taken up by English speakers from the 17th century and has suddenly grown increasingly popular from the 1970s. In the Bible Aaron is the brother of Moses and the first high priest of the Israelites. In Shakespeare's *Titus Andronicus* (1590–94) Aaron is the Moor loved by Tamora. James Fenimore Cooper's novel *The Chainbearer* (1845) has Aaron Thousandacres as a surly squatter, and in George Eliot's novel *Silas Marner* (1861) Aaron Winthrop is the wheelwright's son who marries Eppie Cass. Spelling variants of the name are often Yiddish, such as *Aaran* and *Arn*.

US vice-president Aaron Burr (1756–1836); US composer Aaron Copland (1900–90); US painter Aaron Douglas (1900–79); US TV producer Aaron Spelling (b.1923); US country musician Aaron Tippin (b.1958); US tennis player Aaron Krickstein (b.1967).

Abbey (f.) An independently adopted diminutive of ABIGAIL, in select use among English speakers from the 19th century but rare in the 20th century. In literature Miss Abbey Potterson is hostess of the Six Jolly Fellowship Porters in Charles Dickens's novel *Our Mutual Friend* (1864–5). The variant forms *Abbie* and *Abby* exist, the latter as for the US actress Abby Dalton (b.1932). This same form of the name is also familiar from the regular 'Dear Abby' column by the US writer Abigail Van Buren (b.1918) (real name Pauline Philips), who adopted the source name as her pseudonym with witty reference to David's words to Abigail in the Bible: 'And blessed be thy advice' (1 Samuel 25.33).

US actress Abbey Lincoln (b.1930) (original name Anna Marie Woolridge).

Abdullah The Arabic name, one of the most familiar in the Muslim world, is properly *'Abd-Allāh*, meaning 'servant of Allah'. Although it existed before the rise of Islam, the name is best known as that of the father of Muhammad, Islam's founder. Converts to Islam have adopted the name in recent times.

South African jazz musician Abdullah Ibrahim (b.1934) (original name Adolph Johannes Brand).

Abe The name, in select use among English speakers from the 19th century, is an independently adopted diminutive of ABRAHAM, ABRAM or, in some cases, ABEL.

US popular musician Abe Lyman (1897–1957); US lawyer Abe Fortas (1910–82); US actor Abe Vigoda (b.1921).

Abel The name is biblical in origin, from Hebrew *Hebel*, 'breath', 'vapour', implying vanity. It was adopted by English-speaking Puritans in the 16th century, and taken by them to the US, where it is now in select use, as it is in the UK. In the Bible Abel is a shepherd, the younger son of Adam and Eve, who is murdered through jealousy by his brother Cain. The English poet Abel Evans (1679–1737) is now remembered for his epigrams and epitaphs. In Ben Jonson's play *The Alchemist* (1610) Abel Drugger is a tobacconist. In later literature the name occurs for Abel Handy, an inmate of Hiram's Hospital in Anthony Trollope's novel *The Warden* (1855), and for Abel Whittle, a minor character in Thomas Hardy's novel *The Mayor of Casterbridge* (1886), among others. The name's regular diminutive is ABE.

Abigail A name of biblical origin, from Hebrew *Abīgayil*, '[my] father rejoices'. It was first adopted in England by Puritans in the 17th century. It then fell from favour in the 19th century but revived sharply from the 1970s. In the Bible Abigail is the name of the wife of Nabal of Carmel and, after his death, of King David, and also that of David's sister. In Beaumont and Fletcher's play *The Scornful Lady* (1616) the name is used for the 'waiting gentlewoman', alluding to the first of these, who in the Bible frequently refers to herself as King David's 'handmaid'. As a result, *abigail* became a general term for a lady's maid. By coincidence, Queen Anne's lady-in-waiting was Abigail Masham (1680–1734). The name was also borne by Abigail Adams (1744–1818), wife of the US president John Adams and mother of president John Quincy Adams. The name's subsequent fall from favour was partly because of the association with the maid and partly because Abigail Masham was unpopular. The main character of Christopher Marlowe's play *The Jew of Malta* (1633), the rich Jew Barabas, has a daughter named Abigail, whom he poisons after disposing of her Christian lover (among others). In Arthur Miller's play *The Crucible* (1952), which is set in Salem in 1692, Abigail is the mischief-making niece of the Rev. Parris. Diminutive forms of the name include ABBEY and GAIL, both in independent use.

Abner The name, which is biblical, derives from Hebrew *'Abnēr*, 'father of light' (that is, God). It has been in select use among English speakers from the end of 16th century but is hardly common. In the Bible Abner is the cousin and army commander of Saul, the first king of the Israelites. In later literature Abner Bush is a character in James Fenimore Cooper's novel *The Prairie* (1827); Abner Power is the uncle of Paula Power, the central character in Thomas Hardy's novel *A Laodicean* (1881); and Abner Small is a character in Eugene O'Neill's play *Mourning Becomes Electra* (1931). In recent times the name has become popularly associated, especially in the US, with 'Uncle Abner', the Bible-quoting backwoods detective in mystery fiction by Melville Davisson Post (from 1911), and with 'L'il Abner', the handsome hillbilly in Al Capp's cartoon strip (from 1934). The musical

L'il Abner (1956) was based on the latter. The diminutive ABE is sometimes found in independent use.

US actor Abner Biberman (1909–77).

Abraham A familiar biblical name, from Hebrew *Abrāham*, popularly understood as representing *av hamon* (*goyim*), 'father of a multitude [of nations]'. The name was taken up by Puritans in the 17th century and was in fairly steady English-speaking use until the early 20th century, when it declined in popularity. In the Bible Abraham is the first Jewish patriarch and father of the Hebrew nation. (His earlier name was ABRAM.) Literary bearers of the name include the Rev. Abraham Adams, a curate in Henry Fielding's novel *Joseph Andrews* (1742); Sir Abraham Haphazard, a lawyer in Anthony Trollope's novel *The Warden* (1855); and Abraham Brown, a lodging-house keeper in Thomas Hardy's novel *Desperate Remedies* (1871). A Yiddish variant spelling is *Avrom*. The name's usual diminutive is ABE, which is in independent use, although *Bram* is also sometimes found, as for Bram Stoker (1847–1912), the Irish author of *Dracula* (1897).

US president Abraham Lincoln (1809–65); US film director Abraham Polonsky (1910–99).

Abram The name is of biblical origin and is now generally regarded as a variant of ABRAHAM. It represents Hebrew *Abrām*, 'exalted father', and it is still occasionally found in English-speaking use. In the Bible Abram is the original name of Abraham, who becomes the 'exalted father' of the whole world when he enters into a covenant with God that he is to be the ancestor of all the Israelites: 'Neither shall thy name any more be called Abram, but thy name shall be Abraham; for a father of many nations have I made thee' (Genesis 17.5). (The Hebrew character *hē*, the symbol for God, was added to Abram's name when Abraham accepted one God rather than many.) In Shakespeare's *Romeo and Juliet* (1595) Abram is a servant of Montague.

Absalom A name of biblical origin, from Hebrew *Abshālōm*, 'father of peace' (that is, God), it was in regular English-speaking use from medieval times to the 19th century but is now rare. In the Bible Absalom is the favourite son of King David. In literature Absalom is one of the two central characters in Dryden's poem *Absalom and Achitophel* (1681), in which he represents the Duke of Monmouth, the illegitimate son of Charles II. William Faulkner's novel *Absalom, Absalom!* (1936) has no character of the name; its title reflects the biblical lamentation of King David (2 Samuel 18.13) on learning of the death of his son.

Achilles A well-known Greek name, traditionally said to mean 'lipless', from *a-*, 'without', 'not', and *kheile*, 'lips', referring to the fact that the famous Achilles of Greek mythology had never been suckled. The true source of the name is probably pre-Greek, however. It is only rarely found among English speakers. The mythological hero of Homer's *Iliad* appears as a Grecian commander in Shakespeare's *Troilus and Cressida* (1602).

Ada The name has its origin in the first element, *adal*, 'noble', of an Old German name such as *Adalheit* (English ADELAIDE), while perhaps also being influenced by the biblical name ADAH. It was taken up by English speakers in the 19th century, although it is now rare. In Charles Dickens's novel *Bleak House* (1852–3) Ada Clare, a ward of Mr Jarndyce, marries Richard Carstone. Ada Byron (1815–52), a mathematician who married the Earl of Lovelace, was the poet Byron's first daughter. Diminutives include *Ad*, *Addie* and *Adie*.

UK novelist Ada Leverson (1862–1933); UK actress Ada Reeve (1874–1966).

Adah The biblical name has its origin in Hebrew *Ādāh*, 'ornamented', 'decorated', but it was subsequently associated with ADA. It has been in select English-speaking use from the 19th century, although it is now rare. In the Bible Adah is the wife of Lamech, a descendant of Cain, and is the first woman's name to be mentioned after Eve. In Byron's poem *Cain* (1821) Adah is the wife of Cain.

US actress, poet Adah Mencken (1835–68).

Adam This famous biblical name, that of the first man, from Hebrew *'Ādām*, 'human being', 'man', has been in general use among English speakers from medieval times, with its popularity steadily increasing from the 1970s. Literary characters of the name include: Adam, a clerk in Chaucer's *The Canterbury Tales* (*c*.1387); Adam, Oliver's loyal old servant in Shakespeare's *As You Like It* (1599); and Adam Bede, the carpenter who is the central character of George Eliot's novel *Adam Bede* (1859), in which he is a model of diligence and propriety. The Scottish diminutive *Adie* is sometimes found.

UK actor Adam West (b.1929) (original name William Anderson); UK pop singer, actor Adam Faith (b.1940) (original name Terence Nelhams); Irish rock musician Adam Clayton (b.1960); UK actor Adam Woodyatt (b.1968); Australian actor Adam Willits (b.1972).

Addi see **Adeline**.

Addie see **Ada**, **Adrian**.

Addy see **Adeline**.

Ade see **Adrian**.

Adela Like ADA, the name derives from Old German *adal*, 'noble' as in *Adalheit* (modern English ADELAIDE). It was introduced to England by the Normans in the 11th century but is now only in very select use. William the Conqueror's youngest daughter was Adela (1062–1137). In recent literature Adela Quested is a young Englishwoman in E.M. Forster's novel *A Passage to India* (1924), while Adela Chester is a character in Agatha Christie's short story 'Problem at Pollensa Bay' in *The*

Regatta Mystery (1939). Variants of the name include *Adella* and the independently adopted ADELE.

UK pianist Adela Verne (1886–1952).

Adelaide The name is the English form (through French) of the Old German name *Adalheit*, formed from *adal*, 'noble', and *heit*, 'state', 'condition', hence 'woman of noble estate'. It has long been popular in continental Europe but is found in general English-speaking use only from the 18th century. It is now rare. It was popularized by Queen Adelaide (1792–1849), wife of William IV, for whom Adelaide, Australia, was named (1837). In Thomas Hardy's novel *Desperate Remedies* (1871) Adelaide Hinton is engaged to Edward Springrove (but marries Farmer Bollens), while in Agatha Christie's short story 'The Herb of Death' in *The Thirteen Problems* (1932) (US title *The Tuesday Club Murders*) Adelaide Carpenter is a companion to the murdered Sylvia Keene. Many diminutives and variants of the name have gained independent use, especially ADA, ADELA, ADELE and ADELINE. ALICE and HEIDI are directly related names.

US poet Adelaide Crapsey (1878–1914); US-born UK jazz singer Adelaide Hall (1901–93).

Adele The name is an independently adopted (French) diminutive of ADELAIDE or some similar name beginning with the Old German element *adal*, 'noble'. English speakers have adopted the name from the 19th century, with a slight increase in its popularity taking place since the 1980s. To some extent it was popularized by Adele, Eisenstein's maid in Johann Strauss's operetta *Die Fledermaus* (1874). The main variant is *Adèle*, with the accent, as borne by Adèle Feste, who marries 'Boy' in Dornford Yates's novel *Berry and Co.* (1920). The spelling *Adelle* is also occasionally found.

US actress, dancer Adele Astaire (1898–1981); US writer on nutrition

Adele Davis (1904–74); UK actress Adele Dixon (1908–92); US actress Adele Jergens (b.1922); US poet Adele Kenny (b.1948).

Adeline Like Adelaide, the name is a French form, influenced by ADELE, of the Old German name *Adalheit*, meaning 'woman of noble estate'. It was introduced to England by the Normans in the 11th century but is now rare. In Byron's poem *Don Juan* (1818–23) Lady Adeline is the wife of Lord Henry Amundeville, while in William de Morgan's novel *It Never Can Happen Again* (1909) Adeline Fossett is the sister of the Rev. Augustus Fossett. Diminutives and variant spellings include *Addi*, *Addy*, *Aline* and the Italian form *Adelina*, this last popularized by the Italian concert singer Adelina Patti (1843–1919).

US actress Adeline de Walt Reynolds (1862–1961).

Adella see **Adela**.

Adelle see **Adele**.

Adie see **Ada, Adam, Adrian**.

Adlai A biblical name, from an Aramaic form of the Hebrew name '*Adlaī*', 'my adornment', the name has found only very select favour among English speakers from the 19th century. In the Bible Adlai is the father of Shaphat, commissioner for cattle in the valleys under David (1 Chronicles 27.29).

US vice-president Adlai E. Stevenson (1835–1914); US politician, his grandson, Adlai E. Stevenson (1900–65).

Adolph The name derives from the Old German name *Adal-wolf*, itself from *adal*, 'noble', and *wolf*, 'wolf', so 'noble wolf'. It has been in English-speaking use from the mid-19th century but always selectively, even rarely. In literature Adolph is the Negro dandy who is the majordomo to St Clare in Harriet Beecher Stowe's novel *Uncle Tom's Cabin* (1852). The variant *Adolf* is the modern German spelling, notorious from (and hardly inspired by) the Nazi dictator Adolf Hitler (1889–1945).

The French variant is *Adolphe*, made familiar by the French-US actor Adolphe Menjou (1890–1963). ADOLPHUS is an independently adopted variant, and the diminutives *Dolly* and *Dolph* are sometimes found, the latter as for the US basketball player Dolph Schayes (b.1928).

US journalist Adolph Ochs (1858–1935); US lyricist, librettist Adolph Green (b.1915); US swimmer Adolph Kiefer (b.1918); US actor Adolph Caesar (1932–86).

Adolphus A Latin-style variant of ADOLPH that has been adopted independently and that has been in rare English-speaking use from the 19th century. The Rev. Adolphus Irwine is a character in George Eliot's novel *Adam Bede* (1859), and Adolphus (Dolly) Cusins is the fiancé of Barbara, the central character, in George Bernard Shaw's play *Major Barbara* (1905). The diminutive *Dolly* exists.

US Arctic explorer Adolphus W. Greely (1844–1935).

Adonis A Greek name, from Phoenician *adon*, 'lord'; compare *Adonai*, 'my lord', the Judaic title of God. The name is very occasionally found among English speakers. In Greek mythology Adonis was the beautiful youth loved by Aphrodite. A character of the name appears in Edmund Spenser's *The Faerie Queene* (1590, 1596), and it was used for the title of Percy Bysshe Shelley's lament on the death of Keats, *Adonaïs* (1821).

Adrian The name is an English form of the Latin name *Hadrianus*, meaning 'man of Adria' (the town in northern Italy that gave the name of the Adriatic Sea). The name was not really common among English speakers until the mid-20th century, and it reached a peak in popularity in the second half of the 1960s. It is historically familiar from the only English pope, Adrian IV (c.1100–59) (original name Nicholas Breakspear). In literature it is found for Adrian, a minor character in Shakespeare's *Coriolanus* (c.1608) and *The Tempest* (1611), and for Adrian Singleton, a friend of Dorian, the central character in

Oscar Wilde's novel *The Picture of Dorian Gray* (1891). The name's most common diminutives are *Addie*, *Ade* and *Adie*, the first of these as for the US baseball player Addie Joss (1880–1911).

UK lyricist, librettist Adrian Ross (1859–1933) (original name Arthur Reed Ropes); UK conductor Sir Adrian Boult (1889–1983); UK film director Adrian Brunel (1892–1958); US costume designer Adrian (1903–59) (original name Adrian Adolph Greenberg); US jazzman Adrian Rollini (1904–56); US film director Adrian Scott (1912–77); Australian tennis player Adrian Quist (b.1913); UK photographer Adrian Flowers (b.1926); UK poet, playwright Adrian Mitchell (b.1932); UK poet, painter Adrian Henri (1932–2000); UK film director Adrian Lyne (b.1941); UK radio DJs Adrian Love (1944–99), Adrian Juste (b.1947); UK actor Adrian Edmondson (b.1957); UK swimmer Adrian Moorhouse (b.1964).

Adrienne The name, the French female equivalent of ADRIAN, has been in modestly increasing use among English speakers from the early 20th century. Variant forms include *Adriana*, *Adriane* and *Adrianne*, with this last perhaps influenced by ANN and familiar from the UK actress Adrianne Allen (1907–93).

US actress Adrienne Ames (1909–47); US poet Adrienne Rich (b.1929); UK actress Adrienne Cord (b.1930); US actress Adrienne Barbeau (b.1945); UK actress Adrienne Posta (b.1948).

Aeneas A Greek name, traditionally derived from *ainein*, 'to praise'. It is found only rarely in English-speaking use. In Greek mythology, Aeneas was the Trojan hero who founded the Roman state, as told in Virgil's *Aeneid* (30–19BC). He appears in the same role in Shakespeare's *Troilus and Cressida* (1602). In Thomas Hardy's novel *Desperate Remedies* (1871) Aeneas Manston marries Cytherea Graye.

Agatha The name derives from Greek *agathē*, the feminine of *agathos*, 'good'. It was quite widely adopted in continental Europe in medieval times, then declined in popularity until it enjoyed something of a revival among English speakers in the 19th century, since when it has become much less common. It was originally famous from the 3rd-century virgin martyr, St Agatha. Literary uses of the name include Lady Agatha Carlisle, daughter of the Duke of Berwick in Oscar Wilde's play *Lady Windermere's Fan* (1892), and the almost stock Aunt Agatha in various early 20th-century stories, such as those by 'Saki' (H.H. Munro) and P.G. Wodehouse. A diminutive *Aggie* exists, as for AGNES.

UK detective fiction writer Agatha Christie (1890–1976).

Agnes The name comes from Greek *hagnos*, 'pure', 'chaste', but it has been also influenced by Latin *agnus*, 'lamb', with an association of meaning as well as of words. The name was popular in England in medieval times but went out of fashion for a time after the Reformation because it was not biblical in origin. Its fortunes revived in the 19th century, but it is now once again uncommon. It was first made familiar from the 4th-century virgin martyr, St Agnes, who is often pictured holding a lamb. Later it was made known by Agnes Sorel (1422–50), mistress of Charles VII of France. In literature it occurs for the central character in Anne Brontë's novel *Agnes Grey* (1847). Diminutives include *Aggie*, NESSIE and NESTA, the last two gaining independent use.

US actress Agnes Ayres (1896–1940); US ballerina, choreographer Agnes de Mille (1905–93); US actress Agnes Moorehead (1906–74); Estonian-born ballerina Agnes Oaks (b.1970).

Ahmed This common Muslim name, one of the best known in the English-speaking world, is from Arabic *aḥmad*, 'more praiseworthy', itself from *ḥamida*, 'to praise'. (Compare MUHAMMAD.) The variant spelling *Ahmad* is sometimes found.

US jazz musician Ahmed Abdul-Malik (b.1927).

Aidan This is an anglicized form of the Irish name *Aodán*, a diminutive of *Aodh*, the name of a Celtic sun god meaning 'fire'. The name has been in occasional use in the English-speaking world in the 20th century, mostly in Ireland, although its popularity began to spread more generally in the 1990s. It is the name of various early Irish saints and is particularly connected with St Aidan, who evangelized Northumbria in the 7th century.

UK politician, TV executive Aidan Crawley (1908–93); UK children's writer Aidan Chambers (b.1934); US actor Aidan Quinn (b.1959).

Aileen see **Eileen**.

Ailsa A Scottish name, probably from the rocky islet of Ailsa Craig in the Firth of Clyde, but influenced by (and popularly regarded as a variant of) ELSA. It is still mainly in Scottish use, but occasionally found elsewhere in the English-speaking; world. The UK actress Ellen Terry is credited with the remark: 'Ailsa Craig! What a magnificent name for an actress!'

Aimée The name, which represents French *aimée*, 'beloved', is the equivalent of English AMY. It has been in select English-speaking use from the late 19th century, increasing in popularity somewhat from the 1980s. Aimee Griffith is a character in Agatha Christie's novel *The Moving Finger* (1943). A variant spelling is *Aimi*, as for the Scottish-born actress Aimi MacDonald, on TV in the 1960s. The accent is frequently omitted.

Canadian-born US evangelist Aimee McPherson (1890–1944).

Al An independently adopted diminutive of ALBERT, ALEXANDER, ALFRED, ALVIN or any name beginning *Al-*. It has been in English-speaking (mostly US) use from the 19th century. Diminutives *Allie* and *Ally* exist.

German-born US entertainer Al Shean (1868–1949); US singer, actor Al Jolson (1886–1950) (original name Asa Yoelson); Mozambiquan-born jazz singer Al Bowlly (1899–1941); Italian-US gangster Al Capone (1899–1947); US nightclub comedian Al Ritz (1901–65); US cartoonist

Al Capp (1909–79); UK radio comedian Al Read (1909–87); US jazz musician Al Cohn (1925–88); US actor Al Pacino (b.1939).

Alan A Celtic name, traditionally derived from *alun*, 'harmony', 'concord', which was first taken up in the Middle Ages, when it was introduced to England by Breton followers of William the Conqueror, and in particular Alan, Earl of Brittany. In the 19th century the English-speaking world generally took to it, and the name is still in regular use, although it is now less common after enjoying a peak of popularity in the 1950s. In Walter Scott's novel *Redgauntlet* (1824) Alan Fairford is the friend of Darsie Latimer, and in Robert Louis Stevenson's novel *Treasure Island* (1883) Alan is a crew member on board the *Hispaniola*. Variant spellings *Allan* and *Allen* exist, the former as for the Australian actor Allan Cuthbertson (1920–88) and UK athlete Allan Wells (b.1952), while the Welsh form, ALUN, is in independent use. The diminutive AL is also found independently.

UK composer Alan Rawsthorne (1905–71); US actor Alan Ladd (1913–64); UK TV sports commentator Alan Weeks (1923–96); UK TV presenter Alan Whicker (b.1925); UK actors Alan Dobie (b.1932), Alan Bates (b.1934); UK playwright Alan Bennett (b.1934); US actor Alan Alda (b.1936); UK actor Alan Rothwell (b.1937); UK humorist Alan Coren (b.1938); UK playwright Alan Ayckbourn (b.1939); UK gardener, broadcaster Alan Titchmarsh (b.1949); UK actor Alan Davies (b.1966).

Alana see **Lana**.

Alastair The name is an English form of Gaelic *Alasdair*, itself a form of ALEXANDER. It has been in regular but mainly Scottish use among English speakers from the 19th century. The variant spelling ALISTAIR exists in its own right, and *Alister* is also found. The diminutive *Aly* exists.

Scottish actor Alastair Sim (1900–76); Canadian-born UK naval officer, writer Alastair Mars (1915–85); UK TV newsreaders Sir Alastair Burnet (b.1928), Alastair Stewart (b.1952).

Albert The name derives from Old German *Adalbert*, itself composed of *adal*, 'noble', and *beraht*, 'bright', 'famous', hence 'nobly famous' (or 'famously noble'). It has been in general use among English speakers from the mid-19th century, when it was made widely known by Prince Albert (1819–61), the German husband of Queen Victoria. Margery Allingham's fictional detective Albert Campion made his first appearance in *The Crime at Black Dudley* (1928). The name has sharply declined in popularity from the 1920s, however. Its two best-known diminutives in independent use are AL and BERT.

French missionary Albert Schweitzer (1875–1965); German-born US physicist, mathematician Albert Einstein (1879–1955); UK actors Albert Finney (b.1936), Albert Welling (b.1952).

Alberta The feminine form of ALBERT has been in select use among English speakers from the 19th century but is very rare today. It was popularized historically (and geographically) by Princess Louise Caroline Alberta (1848–1939), fourth daughter of Queen Victoria. (The princess married the Marquess of Lorne, governor general of Canada from 1878 to 1883, who named the province Alberta for her.)

US blues singer Alberta Hunter (1895–1984).

Aldous A name probably based on Old German *ald*, 'old', which has been in rare use among English speakers from the 19th century.

UK writer Aldous Huxley (1894–1963).

Alec This independently adopted diminutive of ALEXANDER has been in regular if modest use among English speakers from the mid-19th century, with a slight popularity peak in the first half of the 20th century. Compare ALEX.

UK writer Alec Waugh (1898–1981); UK yachtsman, world circum-navigator (1968), Sir Alec Rose (1908–91); UK actor Sir Alec Guinness

(1914–2000); UK cricketer Alec Bedser (b.1918); UK actor Alec McCowen (b.1925); US actor Alec Baldwin (b.1958).

Alethea The name has its origin in Greek *alētheia*, 'truth'. It is also sometimes associated with ALTHEA, although that name has a different derivation. It has been in English-speaking use from the early 17th century and is now fairly popular with black Americans. The name may have been initially made known by Maria Aletea, the young daughter of Philip III of Spain, who was offered in marriage to Charles I of England. In literature Alethea Pontifex is the aunt of Ernest Pontifex, the central character of Samuel Butler's novel *The Way of All Flesh* (1903). Variant forms of the name *Aleta* and *Aletha* occur, and the usual diminutive, LETTY, is in independent use.

UK literary biographer Alethea Hayter (b.1911); UK actress Alethea Charlton (b.1932).

Alex An independently adopted diminutive of ALEXANDER, which has been in select but regular use among English speakers in the 20th century, with a sharp increase in popularity in the 1990s. It is found in literature for Alex, the anti-hero of Anthony Burgess's novel *A Clockwork Orange* (1962), played by Malcolm MacDowell in the movie (1971) based on it. Its own diminutive LEX or *Lexie* also occurs. Compare ALEC.

US popular composer, conductor Alex North (1910–91); US actor Alex Nicol (b.1919); US writer Alex Comfort (1920–2000); US writer Alex Haley (1921–92); US actor Alex Karras (b.1935); Scottish footballer Alex Totten (b.1946); Northern Ireland-born UK snooker player Alex Higgins (b.1949); Scottish footballer Alex McLeish (b.1959).

Alex (f.), **Alexa** (f.) see **Alexandra**.

Alexander The name combines the two Greek words *alex-ein*, 'to defend', and *anēr*, genitive *andros*, 'man', so has the overall meaning 'defender of men'. It has been in regular use from medieval times in the English-speaking world and has been specially favoured in Scotland. In Greek legend it was the by-name of Paris, son of King Priam, while historically it gained worldwide fame through Alexander the Great, King of Macedon (4th century BC). Many Scottish kings had the name, beginning with Alexander I in the 12th century. In Shakespeare's *Troilus and Cressida* (1602) Alexander is Cressida's servant. In more recent literature the Rev. Alexander Mill is a curate in George Bernard Shaw's play *Candida* (1894). The diminutives ALEC, ALEX, SASHA and SANDY are all in independent use, while *Alick* is also found. A much rarer diminutive is *Xan*, as for the UK journalist and traveller Xan Fielding (1918–91).

Scottish-born US inventor of the telephone, Alexander Graham Bell (1847–1922); UK discoverer of penicillin, Sir Alexander Fleming (1881–1955); US writer, drama critic Alexander Woollcott (1887–1943); US film director Alexander Mackendrick (1912–1993); US Army general, politician Alexander Haig (b.1924).

Alexandra The feminine form of ALEXANDER has been in regular use among English speakers from medieval times and was particularly fashionable in the 19th century. The name then tailed off but gained renewed popularity from the 1970s. Its chief associations are with royalty, beginning with Princess Alexandra (1844–1925), eldest daughter of Christian IX of Denmark, whom Prince Albert (the future Edward VII) married in 1863. Subsequent royal bearers of the name include Empress Alexandra of Russia (1872–1918), granddaughter of Queen Victoria; Queen Alexandra of Yugoslavia (1921–93), great-great-granddaughter of Queen Victoria; and Princess Alexandra (b.1936), cousin of Queen Elizabeth II. The Queen's own second name is Alexandra, and Princess Alexandra's daughter Marina (b.1966) has it as her third name. There are many variants, mainly as shortenings or diminutives, such as *Alex*, *Alexa* and *Alexia*, with ALEXIS in independent use. Further established diminutives are SANDRA, SASHA and ZANDRA, the first two of which are more common in Scotland than in England.

Canadian actress Alexandra Stewart (b.1939); UK actress Alexandra Bastedo (b.1946); US actress Alexandra Hay (1947–93); UK fashion editor Alexandra Parnell (b.1952); UK magazine editor Alexandra Shulman (b.1957); UK writer, artist Alexandra Connor (b.1959); UK actress Alexandra Pigg (b.1963) (original name Sandra McKibbin).

Alexis (m.) A borrowing of the Greek name *Alexios*, a short form of ALEXANDER or of some similar name based on *alexein*, 'to defend', the name is now mainly in female use.

UK pop musician of Austrian and Greek parentage, Alexis Korner (1928–84); UK actor Alexis Kanner (b.1942).

Alexis (f.) Originally a female adoption of the male name ALEXIS, but now regarded as a short form of ALEXANDRA, the name has been in general but modest English-speaking use from the mid-20th century. It has been recently popularized by Alexis Carrington Colby, a leading character, played by Joan Collins, in the US TV soap *Dynasty* (1981) and its sequel *Dynasty II: The Colbys* (1985).

US actress Alexis Smith (1921–93) (original first name Gladys).

Alf The independently adopted diminutive of ALFRED has been in general English-speaking use from the late 19th century, and in recent times it has become familiar from the chauvinistic UK TV character Alf Garnett, played by Warren Mitchell from the mid-1960s. The name has a diminutive AL, in independent use, while *Alfie* also exists, as for the UK comedian and actor Alfie Bass (1921–87).

UK athlete Alf Shrubb (1879–1964); UK footballer Alf Ramsey (1920–99).

Alfonso see **Alphonse**.

Alfred The name is the modern form of the Old English name *Ælfræd*, formed from *ælf*, 'elf', and *ræd*, 'counsel', so having the overall meaning 'elf counsel' – that is, 'inspired advice'. It has been in regular use from medieval times to the 18th century, when it grew in popularity until the earliest years of the 20th century, after which it gradually declined. It was first made widely known by Alfred the Great, the 10th-century king of Wessex. In literature it occurs for Alfred Jingle, the strolling player in Dickens's novel *Pickwick Papers* (1836–7), and for Lord Alfred Rufford, a character in Oscar Wilde's play *A Woman of No Importance* (1893). (Lord Alfred Douglas (1870–1945) was a close friend of Wilde himself.) The diminutives AL, ALF and FRED are in independent use.

UK poet Alfred, Lord Tennyson (1809–92); UK film director Alfred Hitchcock (1899–1980); UK actors Alfred Marks (1921–96), Alfred Molina (b.1953).

Alfreda A name that is properly a variant form of *Elfreda*, meaning 'elf strength', but that has come to be regarded as a female equivalent for ALFRED. It found some favour among English speakers in the last quarter of the 19th century and first quarter of the 20th century but is now most frequent among black Americans. FREDA would be its independent diminutive.

UK opera singer Alfreda Hodgson (b.1940); UK ballerina Alfreda Thorogood (b.1942) (mother is Alfreda).

Algernon The name is of Norman French origin, from *als gernons*, 'with whiskers', arising as a nickname for a moustached or bewhiskered man. It has been in regular English-speaking use from the 19th century, although it is now not common. The name's adoption by aristocratic families in the 15th century (referring to a distinctively bewhiskered ancestor) gave it a 'superior' connotation, which has persisted. In Oscar Wilde's play *The Importance of Being Earnest* (1895) Algernon Moncrieff marries Cecily Cardew. The usual diminutives are *Algie* or *Algy*.

UK poet Algernon Charles Swinburne (1837–1909); UK writer Algernon Blackwood (1869–1951).

Ali see **Alice**, **Alison**.

Alice Like ADELAIDE, this is a French form, much 'smoothed', of the Old German name *Adalheit*, 'woman of noble estate'. The name has been common in England from medieval times, but declined in popularity from the 18th century. In the 19th century until the early 20th century it underwent a revival, but then again fell from favour until the 1990s, when it once more began to pick up. Literature has Alice as the name of various 'lowly' characters, such as the attendant on Katherine of France in Shakespeare's *Henry V* (1599); the maid to Countess Czerlaski in George Eliot's novel *Scenes of Clerical Life* (1858); the maid to the Deane family in Eliot's novel *The Mill on the Floss* (1860); the maid to the Knowles family in A.A. Milne's play *The Romantic Age* (1920); and even the nurse to Christopher Robin in Milne's poems *When We Were Very Young* (1924). In Lord Lytton's novel *Alice* (1838), however, the name is that of the central character. Its best-known literary bearer is the little girl heroine of Lewis Carroll's *Alice's Adventures in Wonderland* (1865) and *Through the Looking-Glass* (1872), based on an original tale told (1862) to the real-life Alice Liddell, then aged ten. The name was further popularized by the song 'Alice Blue Gown' in the musical *Irene* (1919). Variants include ALICIA, in independent use, *Alisa*, *Alissa* and *Alyssa*, the last as for the US actress Alyssa Milano (b.1972), with ALISON a diminutive also adopted independently. The diminutive *Ali* is common, as for the US actress Ali McGraw (b.1938).

UK archer Alice Legh (1855–1948); US writer Alice B. Toklas (1877–1967); US socialite Alice Longworth (1884–1980); US actress Alice Brady (1892–1939); Princess Alice, Duchess of Gloucester (aunt of Queen Elizabeth II) (b.1901); UK tennis player Alice Marble (1913–90); US actress Alice Faye (1915–98) (original name Alice Jeanne Leppert); US writer Alice Walker (b.1944).

Alicia A Latinized form of ALICE, in modest vogue among English speakers throughout the 20th century.

US magazine editor Alicia Patterson (1909–63); UK ballerina Dame Alicia Markova (b.1910) (original name Lilian Alice Marks).

Alick see **Alexander**.

Aline see **Adeline**.

Alisa see **Alice**.

Alison The name, a French diminutive form of ALICE, has been popular in Scottish use from medieval times but was adopted more generally in the English-speaking world only from the 1920s, when it virtually superseded Alice, reaching a popularity peak in the second half of the 1960s. In literature, Alison Breck is a fishwife in Walter Scott's novel *The Antiquary* (1816). Variants include *Allison* and *Alyson*, with the usual diminutive *Ali*.

UK actress Alison Skipworth (1875–1952); UK children's writer Alison Uttley (1884–1976) (original first names Alice Jane); US writer Alison Lurie (b.1926); Scottish poet Alison Fell (b.1944); UK actress Alison Steadman (b.1946); UK hockey player Alison Ramsay (b.1959); UK rock singer Alison Moyet (b.1961); UK golfer Alison Nicholas (b.1962); UK mountaineer Alison Hargreaves (1962–95); Scottish artist Alison Watt (b.1965); US bluegrass musician Alison Krauss (b.1971).

Alissa see **Alice**.

Alistair A variant of ALASTAIR, taken up generally by English speakers in the early 20th century and of equal popularity with its source name from the 1960s.

Anglo-US radio journalist Alistair Cooke (b.1909); UK novelist Alistair MacLean (1922–87); UK TV presenter Alistair Divall (b.1956).

Alister see **Alastair**.

Allan see **Alan**.

Allegra The name, in very select use among English speakers from the 19th century, is the feminine form of the Italian word *allegro*, 'merry', 'happy'. It first became known from Allegra Byron (1817–22), Lord Byron's illegitimate daughter, and the poet may even have devised it.

US ballerina Allegra Kent (b.1938); UK writer Allegra Taylor (b.1940).

Allen see **Alan**.

Allie see **Al**.

Allison see **Alison**.

Ally see **Al**.

Alma The origin of the name is in Latin *alma*, 'kind', 'nurturing', but it later became associated with Italian *alma*, 'soul'. It was rare in English-speaking use until 1854, when, during the Crimean War, Anglo-French forces defeated the Russians at the Battle of Alma, so bringing the name before the public in general. It is now mostly out of favour.

US actress Alma Kruger (1868–1960); US opera singer Alma Gluck (1884–1938) (original name Reba Fiersohn); US actress Alma Bennett (1889–1958); UK actress Alma Taylor (1895–1974); US actress Alma Rubens (1897–1931); UK screenwriter Alma Reville (1900–82); UK popular singer Alma Cogan (1932–66).

Almira A name that may derive from Arabic *amīri*, 'princess' (related to English *emir* and ultimately *admiral*), which has been in rarish adoption among English speakers from the 19th century, mostly in the US.

US actress Almira Sessions (1888–1974).

Alois see **Aloysius**.

Alonso A 'smoothed' form of the Spanish name *Alfonso* (English ALPHONSE), which has been in very selective use among

English speakers from the 19th century. In Shakespeare's *The Tempest* (1611) Alonso is the King of Naples and father of Ferdinand. The variant form *Alonzo* exists, and the diminutive AL is in independent use.

Aloysius The name perhaps evolved as a Latinized form of LOUIS. It has been in select English-speaking use from the 17th century but has never been common. St Aloysius (1568–91), a famous early Jesuit, prompted the adoption of the name by Roman Catholics. The German variant *Alois* is sometimes found, with the diminutive AL in independent use.

Alphonse The name is the French form of the Spanish name *Alfonso*, itself of Old German origin, formed from *adal*, 'noble', or *hild*, 'battle', and *funs*, 'ready', so meaning 'nobly ready' or 'battle-ready'. It has been in select use among English speakers, especially black Americans, from the 19th century, although it has never been widely adopted. It came to be used as a stock name for a Frenchman. *Alfonso* is a variant spelling, and the usual diminutive, AL, is in independent use.

Althea The name has its origin in the Greek name *Althaia*, itself from Greek *althein*, 'to heal'. It is popularly associated with ALETHEA, but that name has a different origin. In Greek mythology Althaia was the mother of the hunter Meleager. The name has found some favour among English speakers since the 17th century, and Richard Lovelace's poem (or song) *To Althea* (1642) popularized the name.

US tennis player Althea Gibson (b.1927); UK children's writer, illustrator Althea Braithwaite (b.1940).

Alun A Welsh form of ALAN, popularly associated with (or even suggested by) the name of the river Alun in north Wales. It has been in select English-speaking use from the early 20th century, mostly, but not exclusively, among the Welsh.

UK playwright, screenwriter Alun Owen (1925–94); Welsh composer Alun Hoddinott (b.1929); UK actor Alun Armstrong (b.1946).

Alva (m.) A biblical name, from Hebrew *'Alvāh*, 'height', which has been in rarish use among English speakers from the 19th century. In the Bible Alvah (as the name is spelt) is one of the leaders of Edom.

US scientist, inventor Thomas Alva Edison (1847–1931).

Alva (f.) Apparently a female adoption of the male name ALVA, but popularly regarded as the feminine equivalent of ALVIN. The name has been in select use among English speakers from the 19th century.

US socialite, suffragist Alva Belmont (1853–1933).

Alvin The name is the modern equivalent of the Old English name *Ælfwine*, composed of *ælf*, 'elf', and *wine*, 'friend', so giving the overall meaning 'elf friend', implying supernatural support. It enjoyed only slight favour among English speakers until the 20th century, when it was widely adopted in the US. In literature Alvin Belknap is the defending counsel for Clyde Griffiths in Theodore Dreiser's novel *An American Tragedy* (1925). The US soldier Alvin C. York (1887–1964), a hero in the First World War, may have initially boosted the name. Later, it was popularized by Alvin Chipmunk, the mischievous leader of the novelty singing trio the Chipmunks from the late 1950s. The usual diminutive is AL, which is in independent use.

US athlete Alvin Kraenzlein (1876–1928); US actor Alvin Childress (1907–86); US ballet dancer, choreographer Alvin Ailey (1931–89); Canadian-born UK TV and theatrical director Alvin Rakoff (b.1937); UK pop singer Alvin Stardust (b.1942) (original name Bernard Jewry).

Aly see **Alastair**.

Alyson see **Alison**.

Alyssa see **Alice**.

Amabel An English derivative of Latin *amabilis*, 'lovable' (compare AMANDA), which has been in English-speaking use from medieval times but was rare until revived in the 19th century and is now again uncommon. In Harrison Ainsworth's novel *Old St Paul's* (1841) Amabel Bloundel is the daughter of the grocer Stephen Bloundel, while the short story by 'Saki' (H.H. Munro) 'Reginald's Choir Treat', in *Reginald* (1904), has Amabel as the vicar's daughter. (Her name was 'the vicar's one extravagance'.) Later, in Angela Thirkell's *Barsetshire* novels (from the 1930s), Amabel Rose Adams is the daughter of businessman Sam Adams, while Amabel Pierce is a nursery governess in Agatha Christie's novel *Appointment with Death* (1938). The name's best-known diminutive, MABEL, has long been established in its own right.

UK writer, journalist Lady Amabel Williams-Ellis (1894–1984) (original first names Mary Annabel Nassau); UK daughter of Earl of Hardwicke, Lady Amabel Lindsay (b.1935).

Amalia The name is a Latinized form of the Germanic name *Amal*, itself from the Old German word *amal*, 'industrious', which gave names such as *Amalberta* amd *Amalfriede* and which partly gave modern AMELIA. The name, while not common among English speakers, is occasionally found.

Greek-born UK physician, political activist Lady Amalia Fleming (1909–86).

Amanda The name ultimately derives from the feminine form of the Latin saint's name *Amandus*, grammatically a gerundive meaning 'fit to be loved'. It was first taken up by English speakers in the 17th century, when classical names were fashionable in literature. In recent times it reached its peak of popularity in the second half of the 1960s. Colley Cibber's play *Love's Last Shift* (1696) has a character Amanda, and she is also in its sequel, Sir John Vanbrugh's play *The*

Relapse (1696), in which she is the wife of the reformed libertine, Loveless, so that her name puns on his. Later, Richard Brinsley Sheridan again has Amanda as the wife of Loveless in his short comedy *A Trip to Scarborough* (1777), based on Vanbrugh's play. In recent literature Amanda Prynne appears in Noël Coward's play *Private Lives* (1930). In the 1980s the name was popularized by Amanda, the European princess in the US TV soap opera *Dynasty*. The name's usual diminutive is MANDY, which is in independent use.

US actress Amanda Blake (1929–89) (original name Beverly Louise Neill); UK actresses Amanda Barrie (b.1939) (original name Shirley Ann Broadbent), Amanda Burton (b.1956), Amanda Redman (b.1958); UK journalist, critic Amanda Craig (b.1959); UK actresses Amanda Pays (b.1959), Amanda Bairstow (b.1960), Amanda Donohoe (b.1962), Amanda Whitehead (b.1965); UK opera singer Amanda Roocroft (b.1966); UK TV presenter Amanda de Cadenet (b.1972).

Amaryllis A Greek name, perhaps from *amarussein*, 'to sparkle', as of flowing water, referring to a person with sparkling eyes. It occurs in English literary use from the 17th century but is rare in general adoption. English pastoral poets used the name for a typical country girl, as the classical writers had done. An example is Amaryllis in John Fletcher's tragi-comedy *The Faithful Shepherdess* (*c*.1609). Earlier, Amaryllis in Edmund Spenser's pastoral *Colin Clouts come home againe* (1595) represented a real-life Alice Spencer, with whose family Spenser claimed kinship. In Richard Jefferies's last novel, *Amaryllis at the Fair* (1887), Amaryllis, daughter of the farmer Iden, is a central character.

UK cellist Amaryllis Fleming (b.1920).

Amber The name, from the jewel, has been in select English-speaking use from the late 19th century. In literature Amber Darke is the daughter (with sister Ruby and brother Jasper) of Solomon Darke in Mary Webb's novel *The House in Dormer*

Forest (1920), while the Restoration beauty Amber St Clair, so named for the colour of her eyes, is the central character in Kathleen Winsor's historical novel *Forever Amber* (1944).

UK writer Amber Reeves (1887–1981).

Ambrose The name is the English form of the Latin name *Ambrosius*, itself from Greek *ambrosios*, 'immortal' (hence *ambrosia* as the food of the gods). It has enjoyed modest use among English speakers from the 19th century. In Conan Doyle's novel *Rodney Stone* (1896) Ambrose is the valet to Sir Charles Tregellis, Rodney's uncle.

US writer Ambrose Bierce (1824–c.1914); UK dance bandleader Ambrose (1897–1971) (original name Albert Ambrose).

Amelia This is probably a blended name, partly from the Roman clan name *Aemilius*, which gave EMILY, and partly from the first element, *amal*, 'industrious', of an Old German name, which gave modern AMALIA. It was popularized in England by royalty in the 18th century and is still in select use, with an increase in favour from the 1990s. The first name of Queen Adelaide (1792–1849), wife of William IV, was Amelia, and Princess Amelia (1783–1810) was the youngest daughter of George III. In literature Amelia is loved by Celadon in the second book, 'Summer' (1727), of James Thomson's poem *The Seasons*, and the name is that of the central character, the virtuous and devoted wife Amelia Booth, in Henry Fielding's novel *Amelia* (1751). Later, William Makepeace Thackeray's novel *The Luck of Barry Lyndon* (1844) has Amelia Kiljoy as an Irish heiress, and in the same author's *Vanity Fair* (1847–8) Amelia Sedley is a friend of the central character, Becky Sharp. In Agatha Christie's novel *Why Didn't They Ask Evans?* (1934) (US title *The Boomerang Clue*) Amelia Cayman is the wife of Leo Cayman. Variants include the independently adopted EMILIA, and diminutives MILLIE and MILLY.

English writer Amelia Opie (1769–1853) (mother was Amelia); US feminist Amelia Bloomer (1818–94); UK writer, traveller Amelia Edwards (1831–92); US aviator Amelia Earhart (1897–1937); UK actress Amelia Bullmore (b.1964); Russian-born UK actress Amelia Frid (b.1975).

Amey see **Amy**.

Amias see **Amyas**.

Amie see **Amy**.

Aminadab The name is of biblical origin, from Hebrew *'Ammīnādāb*, 'my people (are) generous', and has been occasionally adopted by English speakers from the 17th century. In the Bible Aminadab owned the house from where David and his people took the Ark of the Covenant. In William Makepeace Thackeray's story *The Great Hoggarty Diamond* (1841) Aminadab is a sheriff's officer.

Aminta see **Araminta**.

Amos A biblical name, from Hebrew *Āmōs*, 'borne' (that is, by God), and in regular use among English speakers from the 17th to the 19th century, after which it became much less common. In the Bible Amos is an 8th-century BC prophet whose sayings form the book named for him. The Rev. Amos Barton is a leading character in George Eliot's *Scenes of Clerical Life* (1858), and Amos Graye is an architect in Thomas Hardy's novel *Desperate Remedies* (1871). The name has 'rustic' connotations in the UK, as exemplified by the popular character Amos Brearly, the rural pub landlord in the TV soap *Emmerdale* (from 1972), played by Ronald Magill.

US American football coach Amos Stagg (1862–1965); US R&B singer Amos Milburn (1927–80); Israeli writer Amos Oz (b.1939).

Amy The name represents Old French *amee* (modern *aimée*), 'beloved' (compare AIMÉE, AMANDA). It has been in use among English speakers from the 18th century, gaining considerably in popularity from the 1980s. In Daniel Defoe's romance

Roxana (1724) Amy is Roxana's faithful maid. In later literature the name is often that of a young girl, such as Amy Dorrit,
the central character in Charles Dickens's novel *Little Dorrit*
(1857); Amy March, one of the daughters of the army chaplain Mr March in Louisa M. Alcott's novel *Little Women*
(1868–9) and its sequels; and Amy Lawrence, a school friend of
Tom in Mark Twain's novel *The Adventures of Tom Sawyer*
(1876). Variant spellings are *Amey* or *Amie*, the latter often
being associated with French *amie*, '(female) friend'.

US poet Amy Lowell (1874–1925); UK actresses Amy Veness
(1876–1960), Amy Dalby (1888–1969); UK aviator Amy Johnson
(1903–41); UK opera singer Amy Shuard (1924–75); US actress Amy
Madigan (b.1951); Chinese-US writer Amy Tan (b.1952); US actress
Amy Irving (b.1953); US singer Amy Grant (b.1960); daughter of US
president Jimmy Carter, Amy Carter (b.1969).

Amyas The name seems to have evolved from the Latin name
Amatus, 'loved', influenced by French *aimé* in the same sense.
It has found only infrequent adoption among English speak-
ers from the 19th century. Its most familiar literary bearer
is Captain Sir Amyas Leigh, the central character of Charles
Kingsley's novel *Westward Ho!* (1855). A variant spelling is *Amias*.

Anastasia This is the feminine form of the Greek name *Anas-
tasius*, itself from *anastasis*, 'resurrection'. The name has
enjoyed only moderate English-speaking use from the 19th
century. It was first made familiar by the early Christians, who
adopted it to symbolize a spiritual 'resurrection' or rebirth.
Literary bearers of the name include Anastasia Rugg, the landlord's daughter in Charles Dickens's novel *Little Dorrit* (1855–7),
and the actress Anastasia Dewsbury (later Richmond) in George
Meredith's novel *The Adventures of Harry Richmond* (1871). In
recent times the name has been popularized by the US pop
singer Anastacia (b.1973) (original name Anastacia Newkirk)
and the UK pop group Anastasia (formed 1992). A regular
diminutive is STACEY.

Russian princess, youngest daughter of Tsar Nicholas II, Anastasia (1901–18).

Anatole This is a French name, from the Latin name *Anatolius*, itself in turn from the Greek word *anatolē* , 'sunrise', 'east' (hence the geographical Anatolia). It has found some favour in the English-speaking world since the 19th century. In William Makepeace Thackeray's novel *Pendennis* (1848–50) Anatole is a valet to Henry Foker, while Theodore Dreiser's novel *The Genius* (1915) has the character Anatole Charles.

French writer Anatole France (1844–1924) (original name Jacques-Anatole-François Thibault).

Andie see **Andrea**.

André This is the French form of ANDREW, which has been adopted by black Americans, among other English speakers, from the 19th century. The name is often used without its accent, as for the US tennis player Andre Agassi (b.1970).

French writer André Gide (1869–1951); Russian-born US conductor André Kostelanetz (1901–80); German-born Anglo-US conductor André Previn (b.1929) (original name Andreas Priwin).

Andrea The name has come to be regarded as a standard feminine form of ANDREW, perhaps under Italian influence. It has been in English-speaking use from the 17th century but did not become common until the 20th century, reaching a peak of popularity in the 1970s. Diminutives include *Andie* or *Andy*, as for ANDREW, with the French variant, *Andrée*, found almost as frequently.

US actress Andrea Leeds (1914–74) (original name Antoinette Lees); French-US actress Andrea King (b.1915) (original name Georgetta Barry); US skier Andrea Mead Lawrence (b.1932); UK novelist, TV dramatist Andrea Newman (b.1938); US feminist writer Andrea Dworkin (b.1946); UK actress Andrea Allan (b.1946); UK playwright

Andrea Dunbar (b.1961); US tennis player Andrea Jaeger (b.1965); Nothtern Ireland TV presenter Andrea Catherwood (b.1968); UK table tennis player Andrea Holt (b.1970).

Andrew A well-known biblical name, representing the Greek name *Andreas*, from *anēr*, genitive *andros*, 'man', so meaning 'manly', 'brave'. It has been in fairly regular use among English speakers from medieval times and became especially popular in the 1960s and 1970s, although it has since declined somewhat. In the Bible Andrew is one of the twelve apostles and the first disciple to be called by Jesus. He is venerated as St Andrew, the patron saint of Scotland, Russia and Greece, countries where the name is still popular today. In Shakespeare's *Twelfth Night* (1601) Sir Andrew Aguecheek is a famously foolish knight. In later literature William Makepeace Thackeray's novel *The Newcomes* (1853–5) has Andrew Smee as a portrait painter, while George Bernard Shaw's play *Major Barbara* (1905) has Andrew Undershaft as the father of Barbara, the central character. The French version of the name, ANDRÉ, exists in independent use, as does its Scottish diminutive, DREW. A regular diminutive is ANDY, also in independent use.

US president Andrew Jackson (1765-1845); Scottish-born US philanthropist Andrew Carnegie (1835–1919); Scottish actor Andrew Cruickshank (1907–88); UK actor Andrew Sachs (b.1930); UK writer Andrew Sinclair (b.1935); UK son of Queen Elizabeth II, Prince Andrew, Duke of York (b.1960).

Andy An independently adopted diminutive of ANDREW, which has been in select English-speaking use from the 19th century. A famous literary character of the name is Andy Rooney, the central character of Samuel Lover's comic novel *Handy Andy* (1842). In recent years the name has become popularly associated with the cloth-capped, working-class cartoon character Andy Capp, in the *Daily Mirror* from 1957. (As such, he bears a standard nickname for a cap wearer, the name punning on *handicap*.)

US actors Andy Devine (1905–77), Andy Griffith (b.1926); US pop artist Andy Warhol (1926–87); US popular singer Andy Williams (b.1928) (original first names Howard Andrew); Scottish popular singer Andy Stewart (1933–93); UK cricketer Andy Stovold (b.1953); Cuban-born US actor Andy Garcia (b.1956); UK sculptor Andy Goldsworthy (b.1956); UK radio DJ Andy Kershaw (b.1959); UK water skier Andy Mapple (b.1962); UK footballers Andy Townsend (b.1963), Andy Sinton (b.1966).

Aneurin A Welsh name, perhaps from Welsh *an*, 'all', and *eur*, 'gold', with the diminutive suffix *-in*, so essentially meaning 'very precious little one'. (The middle syllable of the name is pronounced 'nigh'.) Its usage is still chiefly Welsh. In A.J. Cronin's novel *The Citadel* (1937) bank manager Aneurin Rees marries Blodwen Page. The older spelling, *Aneirin*, is still current. The usual diminutive is *Nye*.

Welsh politician Aneurin (Nye) Bevan (1897–1960).

Ange see **Angel** (f.), **Angela**.

Angel (m.) The name comes from the Latin name *Angelus*, itself from Greek *angelos*, a word meaning literally 'messenger' but used in New Testament Greek to signify 'messenger of God', so therefore 'angel'. (See also the female ANGEL.) It has enjoyed very occasional English-speaking use from the 17th century and is now usually superseded by ANGELO. In literature Angel Clare is the central male character in Thomas Hardy's novel *Tess of the D'Urbervilles* (1891).

Angel (f.) The name had its origin either as a female adoption of the male name ANGEL or as a direct borrowing of the standard word. It is usually felt to represent a nickname, however, as given to (or describing) a sweet-looking little girl, and it has been selectively adopted by English speakers, especially black Americans, from the 19th century. Diminutives *Ange* and *Angie* exist.

Angela A feminine form of the male name ANGEL was in gradually increasing use among English speakers from the 18th century to the mid-20th century but then gradually declined. In the Gilbert and Sullivan comic opera *Patience* (1881) Lady Angela is a languishing, aesthetic maiden. One of the name's best-known variants, ANGELICA, is now in independent use, as also are ANGELINA and ANGELINE. Usual diminutives are *Angie*, *Angy* or *Ange*.

UK writer of schoolgirl stories Angela Brazil (1869–1947) (mother was Angelica); UK novelist Angela Thirkell (1890–1961); UK actress Angela Lansbury (b.1925); UK tennis player Angela Mortimer (b.1932); UK actresses Angela Thorne (b.1939), Angela Douglas (b.1940); UK writers Angela Carter (1940–92), Angela Lambert (b.1940); UK TV presenter Angela Rippon (b.1944); US militant scholar Angela Davis (b.1944); UK ballerina Angela Demello (b.1959).

Angelica The name is ultimately from the feminine form of Latin *angelicus*, 'angelic', but is now regarded as a diminutive of ANGELA. It was introduced to England from Italy in the 17th century and has been in select English-speaking use from the 19th century. In the poems by, respectively, Matteomaria Boiardo and Ludovico Ariosto, *Orlando Innamorato* (1487) and *Orlando Furioso* (1532), Angelica is the object of Orlando's love and the cause of his madness. Shakespeare has Angelica as Juliet's nurse in *Romeo and Juliet* (1595), which is, of course, set in Italy. Later, Angelica is the central character of William Congreve's play *Love for Love* (1695) as well as of William Makepeace Thackeray's fairy story *The Rose and the Ring* (1855). Variant spellings are French *Angelique* or *Angélique*, as well as the fairly recent *Anjelica*, as for the US actress Anjelica Huston (b.1952). ANGELINA is a directly related variant.

Angelina A Latin-style form of ANGELICA, which has been in English-speaking use mainly from the 17th century to the 19th century but is now rare. In literature Angelina is the sister of Don Rhodorigo in Dryden's tragi-comedy *The Rival Ladies* (1664) as well as the chief female character in the ballad 'Edwin and Angelina', which Burchell reads in Oliver Goldsmith's novel *The Vicar of Wakefield* (1766). A variant form is ANGE-LINE, with a common diminutive *Angie*.

Angeline The name is an English adoption of the French equivalent of ANGELINA, in select English-speaking use from the mid-19th century. The US actress Angie Dickinson (b.1931) was originally Angeline Brown. A popular boost was given to the name by a song of the 1930s, 'Little Angeline'. The usual diminutive is *Angie*.

Angelique see **Angelica**.

Angelo In origin the name is an Italian or Spanish form of the Latin name *Angelus* (see ANGEL). It has found some favour among English speakers from the 19th century, replacing the earlier Angel. In Shakespeare's *A Comedy of Errors* (1594) Angelo is a goldsmith, and in *Measure for Measure* (1604) he is Lord Deputy to the Duke of Vienna, betrothed to Mariana. As a literary name, Angelo was popularized to some extent by Eric Linklater's novel *Private Angelo* (1946).

Angharad A Welsh name composed of the intensifying particle *an* and the word *câr*, 'love', so having the overall meaning 'much loved'. The approximate pronunciation of the name is 'An*har*ad'. It is found in 12th-century Welsh history and was revived in the 20th century, even though still chiefly adopted by those with a genuine Welsh connection.

Welsh actress Angharad Rees (b.1949).

Angie see **Angel**, **Angela**, **Angelina**, **Angeline**.

Angus This is an English form of the Gaelic name *Aonghus*, formed from *aon*, 'one', and *ghus*, 'choice', so meaning 'sole choice', implying uniqueness. Although still chiefly a Scottish name, it has been in general, if modest, use among English speakers from the late 19th century. In Shakespeare's *Macbeth* (1606) Angus is a nobleman of Scotland, and in Walter Scott's novel *The Legend of Montrose* (1819) Angus McAulay is Laird of Darnlin-Varach. The regular diminutive GUS is in independent use, although *Angie* (pronounced with a hard 'g') is also sometimes found.

UK theatrical photographer Angus McBean (1904–90); Scottish writer Angus McVicar (b.1908); UK novelist Sir Angus Wilson (1915–91); UK husband of Princess Alexandra, Sir Angus Ogilvy (b.1928); UK TV personality Angus Deayton (b.1956).

Angy see **Angela**.

Anita A Spanish diminutive of *Ana* (English ANN), in select English-speaking use from the 19th century and originally in the US. The name's peak of popularity in the UK was in the second half of the 1960s. The usual diminutive is *Nita*.

US writer Anita Loos (1888–1981); US actresses Anita King (1889–1963), Anita Stewart (1895–1961) (original first names Anna May), Anita Louise (1915–70); US jazz singer Anita O'Day (b.1919); US singer, record producer Anita Kerr (b.1927); Swedish actress Anita Ekberg (b.1931); Indian writer Anita Desai (b.1937); UK novelists Anita Burgh (b.1937), Anita Brookner (b.1938); US pop singer Anita Bryant (b.1940); UK swimmer Anita Lonsbrough (b.1941); UK popular singer Anita Harris (b.1942); UK businesswoman Anita Roddick (b.1942); UK actress Anita Dobson (b.1949); US soul singer Anita Baker (b.1957).

Anjelica see **Angelica**.

Ann This is the English form of the biblical name HANNAH, so, like that name, it means 'grace', 'favour'. The name became popular in Europe, including England, in medieval times and is still fairly common in English-speaking use today. It was overtaken in popularity in the mid-20th century, however, by its French form, ANNE, and many famous names are still associated with that form of the name today (which see for variants and diminutives).

US actress Ann Sothern (1909–2001) (original name Harriette Lake); UK actresses Ann Todd (1909–93), Ann Davies (b.1934); Welsh politician Ann Clwyd (b.1937); UK tennis player Ann Jones (b.1938) (original first name Adrianne); UK actresses Ann Beach (b.1938), Ann Bell (b.1940).

Anna The name represents the Greek or Latin form of HANNAH (which gave the English ANN), and it is now common in many European languages, including among English speakers from the 19th century, with a modest popularity peak in the 1980s. An early literary bearer of the name was Anna, sister of Dido in Virgil's *Aeneid* (30–19BC). Later, Anna Howe is the recipient of letters from Clarissa Harlowe in Samuel Richardson's novel *Clarissa* (1748). It was further popularized by the heroine of Tolstoy's novel *Anna Karenina* (1877). Variants of the name are mostly as for ANN itself.

UK writer Anna Sewell (1820–78); Austrian-born UK child psychologist Anna Freud (1895–1982); UK actress Dame Anna Neagle (1904–86); Chinese-US actress Anna May Wong (1907–61) (original name Wong Liu Tsong); UK actresses Anna Wing (b.1914), Anna Massey (b.1937), Anna Quayle (b.1937); UK gardener Anna Pavord (b.1940); UK actress Anna Carteret (b.1942); UK newsreader Anna Ford (b.1943); UK actresses Anna Calder-Marshall (b.1949), Anna Keaveney (b.1949); Anglo-US opera singer Anna Steiger (b.1960); UK actress Anna Friel (b.1975); US actress Anna Paquin (b.1982).

Annabel The name is probably an alteration of AMABEL, the *-bel* being associated with French *belle*, 'beautiful'. It is now sometimes felt to be a compound name with ANN or ANNA as the first part. At first it was mainly in Scottish use, but from the 20th century was more widely, if selectively, adopted by English speakers, with a slight increase in popularity in the 1990s. In literature it was made famous by Edgar Allan Poe's ballad *Annabel Lee* (1849). In recent times the name has gained a superior social cachet, as typified by Annabel's, London's disco and nightclub, itself named for Lady Annabel Burley, wife of its founder, Marcus Burley. The main variants of the name are ANNABELLA and ANNABELLE, both in independent use.

UK daughter of Marquess of Londonderry, Lady Annabel Goldsmith (b.1934); UK TV presenter Annabel Giles (b.1959); UK tennis player, TV presenter Annabel Croft (b.1966).

Annabella This is a Latinized form of ANNABEL, perhaps influenced by ARABELLA. It was formerly popular in Scotland and was made known by the Scottish queen Annabella Drummond (1350–1402), mother of James I. It went on to become the more common form of the name, but the shorter form is now the one generally preferred.

US actress Annabella Sciorra (b.1964); Burmese-born UK pop singer Annabella Lwin (b.1966) (original name Myant Myant Aye).

Annabelle A French-style spelling of ANNABEL, with the *-belle* emphasizing the 'beautiful' aspect of the name. It has been taken up by English speakers since the 19th century but has never been as popular as the shorter name or as its Latinized form ANNABELLA.

Australian politician Dame Annabelle Rankin (1908–86).

Anne The French form of ANN has been in use among English speakers since medieval times. It has long been associated with European royalty, notably Queen Anne of England (1665–1714); Anne of Austria (1601–66); the second wife of Henry VIII, Anne Boleyn (1507–36) and his fourth wife, Anne of Cleves (1515–57); the wife of James I of England, Anne of Denmark (1574–1619) and many others. In Shakespeare's *The Merry Wives of Windsor* (1597) 'sweet Anne Page', the daughter of Mistress Page, is wooed by three suitors. The name is historically famous from Shakespeare's own wife, Anne Hathaway (1557–1623), but it was never widely adopted until the mid-20th century, when it may have been helped by the birth of Princess Anne (b.1950). It is now much less common. In recent literature the name became popularly associated with Anne Shirley, the little girl who is the central character of the novel *Anne of Green Gables* (1908) by the Canadian writer L.M. Montgomery. (When introduced to the elderly couple who adopt her, Anne says: 'But oh, please call me Cordelia ... Anne is such an unromantic name.') The diminutives ANNIE, NAN, NANA and NANCY are in independent use, as are many continental European diminutives, such as Spanish ANITA, Swedish ANNEKA and French ANNETTE. *Anne-Marie* (*Annemaria*) is a common French (German) combination, which for Catholics links the name of the Virgin Mary with that of her mother. The name also occurs as the second half of a dual name such as *Jo Anne* and *Mary Anne* (also with a hyphen), and it is sometimes felt to be a separate element in names such as JOANNE or MARIANNE.

US actress Anne Baxter (1923–85); Australian actress Anne Haddy (1927–99); US actress Anne Bancroft (b.1931); Northern Ireland TV presenter Anne Gregg (b.1940); UK radio DJ Anne Nightingale (b.1943); UK TV presenters Anne Robinson (b.1944), Anne Leuchars (b.1953), Anne Diamond (b.1954); UK actress Anne Kirkbride (b.1954).

Anneka This Swedish diminutive of ANN has been in select English-speaking use from the 1950s. The variant forms *Anneke* and *Annika* are also found, the former as for the Dutch-born UK actress Anneke Wills (b.1941). The diminutive is usually ANNIE.

UK TV personality Anneka Rice (b.1958) (original first name Annie).

Annette A French diminutive of ANNE (English ANN), adopted selectively by English speakers from the 19th century and peaking in popularity in the 1950s. The name is found in literature for Annette Bycliffe in George Eliot's novel *Felix Holt* (1866). Variant forms of the name are *Annetta* or *Annett*.

UK TV children's programme presenter Annette Mills (1894–1955); UK ballerina Annette Page (b.1932); Scottish actress Annette Crosbie (b.1934); US actresses Annette Funicello (b.1942), Annette O'Toole (b.1953), Annette Bening (b.1958).

Annie An independently adopted diminutive of ANN, which has been in popular use among English speakers from the mid-19th century, with a peak in the early years of the 20th century, although it is now much less common. It became well known from the 19th-century Scottish song 'Annie Laurie', which was based on a real Annie Laurie (d.1764), the youngest daughter of Sir Robert Laurie. A more recent boost to the name came from the musical *Annie* (1977), based on Harold Gray's sentimental comic strip 'Little Orphan Annie'. The spelling *Anny* is sometimes found, as for the Irish actress Anny Tobin (b.1945).

UK socialist, religious campaigner Annie Besant (1847–1933); US mountaineer Annie Peck (1850–1935); US markswoman Annie Oakley (1860–1926) (original first names Phoebe Anne); UK theatre manager Annie Horniman (1860–1937); UK suffragist Annie Kenney (1879–1953); UK jazz singer, actress Annie Ross (b.1930) (original name Annabelle Short Lynch); Scottish rock singer Annie Lennox (b.1954); UK actress Annie Miles (b.1958) (original name Anne Miller).

Anona A name of uncertain origin, but perhaps a blend of names such as ANN and FIONA, in modest English-speaking use in the 20th century.

Australian-born UK radio singer, band-leader, panellist Anona Winn (1907–94).

Anselm The name represents the Old German name *Anshelm*, formed from *ans*, 'god', and *helm*, 'helmet', so 'divinely protected'. It is rare in English-speaking use but has been adopted by some Roman Catholics, mainly as a compliment to St Anselm (1033–1109), Archbishop of Canterbury.

Anthea The English name comes from the Greek name *Antheia*, itself the feminine form of the word *antheios*, 'flowery'. The name was adopted in 17th-century literary use, then more generally taken up by English speakers in the 20th century, enjoying a popularity peak in the 1950s. It was the pastoral poets who first favoured the name, as in Robert Herrick's poem *To Anthea* (1648).

UK actress Anthea Askey (1927–99) (father was Arthur); UK TV hostess Anthea Redfern (b.1951); UK TV presenter Anthea Turner (b.1960).

Anthony The name is an English form of the Roman clan name *Antonius*, itself of uncertain origin, with *h* inserted from the association with Greek *anthos*, 'flower'. In the 20th century the name reached its peak of popularity among English speakers in the 1950s. It is familiar from various saints, especially the 3rd-century St Anthony. In literature Uncle Anthony is the uncle of the central character, Clarissa Harlowe, in Samuel Richardson's novel *Clarissa* (1748), while Sir Anthony Absolute is a character in Richard Brinsley Sheridan's play *The Rivals* (1775). Charles Dickens's novel *Martin Chuzzlewit* (1843–4) has Anthony Chuzzlewit as the brother of old Martin Chuzzlewit, grandfather of the title character. The variant spelling ANTONY is often regarded as an independent name, and the Spanish or Italian variant *Antonio* is also in occasional English-speaking use, especially in the US. The regular diminutive of the name, TONY, is used independently.

UK prime minister Sir Anthony Eden (1897–1977); UK novelist Anthony Powell (1905–2000); UK actor Sir Anthony Quayle (1913–89); Mexican-born actor Anthony Quinn (1915–2001); UK novelist Anthony Burgess (1917–93); UK actor Anthony Newley (1931–99); US actor Anthony Perkins (1932–92); UK actors Sir Anthony Hopkins (b.1937), Anthony Valentine (b.1939), Anthony Andrews (b.1948).

Antoinette The name is the French feminine diminutive of the French male name *Antoine* (English ANTHONY), which is familiar in French history from the ill-fated queen of France, Marie-Antoinette (1755–93). It has enjoyed modest favour among English speakers from the 19th century, with a slight increase in popularity from the 1960s.

UK composer Antoinette Kirkwood (b.1930); UK ballerina Antoinette Sibley (b.1 939).

Antonia The name, the feminine form of male ANTHONY or ANTONY, occurred mainly as a continental European name before its selective adoption in the 20th century by English speakers. A fairly common diminutive in independent use is TONI, with *Tonia* or *Tonya* also occurring.

UK writers Antonia White (1899–1980), Lady Antonia Fraser (b.1932), Antonia Byatt (b.1936).

Antony An independently adopted variant spelling of ANTHONY, less common than its source name (which historically developed from it), but in recent times following its popularity curve.

UK-born US ballet dancer, choreographer Antony Tudor (1908–87) (original name William Cook); UK composer Antony Hopkins (b.1921); UK photographer Antony Armstrong-Jones, Earl of Snowdon (b.1930); South African-born UK actor Antony Sher (b.1949).

April The name is that of the month, one of the most attractive of the year, implying rebirth and flowering. It enjoyed a modest popularity peak among English speakers in the second half of the 1970s. P.G. Wodehouse's novel *Young Men in Spats* (1936) has a character named April Carroway. AVRIL is an independently adopted variant, but AVERIL is really a distinct name with a different origin.

UK opera singer April Cantelo (b.2 April 1928); UK actress April Olrich (b.1941)

Arabella The name is probably an alteration of *Annabella*, an early form (now a variant) of ANNABEL, although one school of thought proposes a derivation in Latin *orabilis*, 'entreat-able', because *Orabilis* was an early doublet for some women named Arabella. The name has been in English-speaking use from medieval times and today has the aristocratic cachet that Annabel has. One earlier bearer of the name was Lady Arabella Stuart (1575–1615), niece of Mary, Queen of Scots. Later, Arabella Fermor was the subject (and dedicatee) of Alexander Pope's famous poem *The Rape of the Lock* (1712), in which she is represented as Belinda. In later literature Arabella Harlowe is the central character's elder sister in Samuel Richardson's novel *Clarissa* (1748), and Mrs Arabella Hunt is a character in Henry Fielding's novel *Tom Jones* (1749). Examples of the name in more recent fiction include Arabella Allen, the attractive brunette in Charles Dickens's novel *Pickwick Papers* (1836–7); Arabella Briggs, companion to Miss Crawley in William Make-peace Thackeray's novel *Vanity Fair* (1847–8); Arabella, Duchess of Berwick, in Oscar Wilde's play *Lady Windermere's Fan* (1892); and Arabella Donn, false wife of the central character Jude Fawley in Thomas Hardy's novel *Jude the Obscure* (1894–5). Variants are mainly spelling alterations such as *Arabel* or *Arabell*, but the diminutives BELLA and BELLE also exist and are now in independent use.

UK pianist Arabella Goddard (1836–1922); US lawyer Arabella Mans-field (1846–1911); UK food writer Arabella Boxer (b.1934); UK health writer Arabella Melville (b.1948); UK fashion designer Arabella Pollen (b.1961).

Araminta A name of uncertain origin, perhaps a blend of ARABELLA and the rare name *Aminta*, with a very modest adop-tion among English speakers from the 17th century. In liter-ature it occurs for the leading female character in William Congreve's comedy *The Old Bachelor* (1693); for Moneytrap's wife in Sir John Vanbrugh's comedy *The Confederacy* (1705); and, much more recently, for Araminta Brown, mother of the central character, Velvet Brown, in Enid Bagnold's novel

National Velvet (1935). The name is also that of the central character in Jilly Cooper's novel *Araminta's Wedding* (1993). A diminutive *Minta* exists.

Archibald The name, has its origin in the Norman French name *Archambault*, itself from an Old German name formed from *erkan*, 'genuine', and *bald*, 'bold', so overall meaning 'truly brave'. It was introduced to England by the Normans in the 12th century and adopted soon after by English speakers, especially in Scotland, who took 'arch' to imply *archbishop* and 'bald' to refer to a monk's tonsure. The name was thus regarded as the English equivalent of *Gillespie*, itself from Gaelic *Gille Easbaig*, 'bishop's servant'. Archibald Reeves is a character in Samuel Richardson's novel *Sir Charles Grandison* (1753–4). From the 1920s the name acquired an aristocratic or 'silly ass' image, which probably deterred its popular adoption from then on. The regular diminutive, in use in its own right, is ARCHIE.

UK military leader Archibald Wavell (1883–1950); US poet Archibald MacLeish (1892–1982).

Archie An independently adopted diminutive of ARCHIBALD, in select use among English speakers from the 19th century. The name is found in literature for Archie Osbaldistone, son of Frank Osbaldistone, the central character in Walter Scott's novel *Rob Roy* (1817). It was given a humorous boost by the 1950s UK radio comedy series *Educating Archie*, in which Archie Andrews was the puppet of the ventriloquist Peter Brough. The variant spelling *Archy* is also found, as for the Scottish politician Archy Kirkwood (b.1946). The name never acquired the 'upper class' overtones that its source name had.

UK cricketer Archie McLaren (1871–1944); UK bassoonist Archie Camden (1888–1979); US film director Archie Mayo (1891–1968); US country comedian Archie Campbell (b.1914); US boxer Archie Moore (1916–98).

Aretha The name arose as a form of the Greek name *Arete*, representing *aretē*, 'excellence' (compare ARETHUSA, of which it could also be a diminutive). It has found a very select adoption among English speakers in the 20th century.

US soul singer Aretha Franklin (b.1942).

Arethusa The name, that of a wood nymph in Greek mythology, and perhaps based on *aretē*, 'excellence', has found some favour among English speakers from the 17th century. In Beaumont and Fletcher's play *Philaster* (*c*.1609), Arethusa is the king's daughter loved by Philaster. Later, Arethusa is one of Harold Skimpole's three daughters in Charles Dickens's novel *Bleak House* (1852–3).

Ariadne A name of Greek origin, perhaps deriving from the intensive prefix *ari-* and *agnos*, 'pure', 'chaste', so meaning 'very pure'. It occasionally occurs among English speakers even now. In Greek mythology Ariadne was famed for using thread to lead Theseus out of the Minotaur's labyrinth. The name's adoption for use as a Christian name was helped by its association with the 2nd-century St Ariadne. Ariadne Oliver is a sleuth in Agatha Christie's detective fiction and is presumably so named for her ability to unravel the thread in various mysteries. Christie also has Lady Ariadne Grayle in her short story 'Death on the Nile' in *Parker Pyne Investigates* (1934) (US title *Mr Parker Pyne, Detective*).

Russian-born UK writer Ariadne Nicolaeff (b.1915).

Ariel The name is of biblical origin, from Hebrew *Arī'ēl*, 'lion of God', and it has enjoyed occasional adoption among English speakers. In the Bible Ariel is the messenger of Ezra. In Shakespeare's *The Tempest* (1611) Ariel is 'an airy spirit', his name being directly associated with *air*. The name is occasionally found in female use, as for the US historian Ariel Durant (1898–1981) (original first names Ida Ariel Ethel) and the UK daughter of Viscount Stonehaven and Countess of Kintore, Lady Ariel Keith (b.1916).

Arlene The name probably evolved from a name such as CHARLENE or MARLENE, minus their initial consonants. It has been in regular but limited English-speaking use, especially in the US, from the early 20th century. Variants include forms such as *Arlena*, *Arline* or *Arleen*, the last two for, respectively, the US actresses Arline Judge (1912–74) and Arleen Whelan (1916–93), and the US opera singer Arleen Auger (1939–93).

US actresses Arlene Francis (1908–2001), Arlene Dahl (b.1924); US mountaineer Arlene Blum (b.1945); US country singer Arlene Harden (b.1945).

Arlette A French name of uncertain origin, but perhaps a derivative of CHARLOTTE, minus its initial *Ch-*. It has enjoyed select English-speaking use from the mid-19th century, with a modest popularity peak in the mid-20th.

French actress Arletty (1898–1992) (original name Arlette-Léonie Bathiat).

Arline see **Arlene**.

Arn see **Aaron**, **Arnold**.

Arnold The name has its origin in the Old German name *Arinwalt*, formed from *arn*, 'eagle', and *wald*, 'ruler', so 'eagle-ruler'. It enjoyed select but gradually increasing adoption among English speakers from the 19th century to the early 20th century, since when it has declined. The name may have owed its initial popularity to the surnames of two respected Englishmen: the educationalist Dr Thomas Arnold, Arnold of Rugby (1795–1842), and his son, the poet Matthew Arnold (1822–88). Diminutives are usually *Arn* or *Arnie*.

UK economist, social reformer Arnold Toynbee (1852–83); UK novelist Arnold Bennett (1867–1931); UK composer Sir Arnold Bax (1883–

1953); UK historian Arnold Toynbee (1889–1975); UK playwright, actor Arnold Ridley (1896–1984); UK ballet critic Arnold Haskell (1903–80); US golfer Arnold Palmer (b.1929); UK playwright Arnold Wesker (b.1932); US actor Arnold Schwarzenegger (b.1947).

Art The independently adopted diminutive of ARTHUR, which has been in select English-speaking use from the late 19th century, mostly in the US. Its own diminutive is usually *Artie*.

US cartoonist Art Young (1866–1943); US actor Art Acord (1890–1931); US jazz pianist Art Tatum (1909–56); US actor Art Carney (b.1918); US writer, journalist Art Buchwald (b.1925); US jazz saxophonist Art Pepper (1925–82); US actor Art Metrano (b.1937); US popular singer Art Garfunkel (b.1941); Canadian actor Art Hindle (b.1948).

Artemis The name is that of the Greek goddess of the moon and the hunt, the equivalent of the Roman goddess DIANA. The name itself has been linked with Greek *artemia*, 'safety', referring to the goddess's virginity. It is very occasionally found among English speakers.

UK writer Artemis Cooper (b.1953) (grandmother was Lady Diana Cooper).

Arthur A Celtic name of uncertain origin, but linked with *art*, 'bear'. The name was adopted irregularly by English speakers until the 18th century, when it increased in popularity to reach its peak in the late 19th century, since when it has gradually declined. It was given its initial impetus by the semi-legendary 5th- or 6th-century King Arthur, whose own name has been closely associated ever since with the familiar characters of the Arthurian romances, especially the Knights of the Round Table. In Shakespeare's *King John* (*c*.1596) Arthur is the king's young nephew. Military support for the name in the 19th century came from Arthur Wellesley, Duke of Wellington (1769–1852), and this was continued by Queen Victoria's third son, the soldier Prince Arthur (1850–1942). The name's regular diminutive is ART, in independent use.

UK composer Sir Arthur Bliss (1891–1975); UK comedian Arthur Askey (1900–82); UK novelist Arthur Calder-Marshall (1908–92); UK writer, broadcaster Arthur Marshall (1910–89); UK actor Arthur Lowe (1915–82); US playwright Arthur Miller (b.1915); UK writer, astronomer Arthur C. Clark (b.1917); UK actor Arthur English (1919–95); US tennis player Arthur Ashe (1943–93).

Asa A biblical name, from Hebrew *Āsā*, 'healer' (originally a nickname). It was taken up by Puritans in the 17th century and has been in select use since among English speakers. In the Bible Asa is an early king of Judah. James Fenimore Cooper's novel *The Prairie* (1827) has Asa Bush as the eldest son of Ishmael Bush, the central character, and Theodore Dreiser's novel *An American Tragedy* (1925) has Asa Griffiths as the father of the main character, Clyde Griffiths.

UK historian Asa Briggs (b.1921).

Asher A name of biblical origin, from Hebre *Āshēr*, 'happy', and in modest English-speaking use from the 17th century. In the Bible Asher is the son of Jacob by Zilpah, serving woman to Leah: 'And Leah said, Happy am I, for the daughters will call me blessed; and she called his name Asher' (Genesis 30.13).

Ashley (m.) From the surname. The name was taken up by English speakers in the mid-19th century and has gradually grown in popularity since. In Margaret Mitchell's novel *Gone with the Wind* (1936), the aristocrat Ashley Wilkes, loved by the central character Scarlett O'Hara, marries his cousin, Melanie Hamilton. The name may have gained some impetus from the widely respected UK social reformer, Anthony Ashley Cooper, Earl of Shaftesbury (1801–85).

UK gardening correspondent Ashley Stephenson (b.1927); Australian tennis player Ashley Cooper (b.1936); UK artist Ashley Jackson (b.1940); UK ballet dancer Ashley Page (b.1956); UK cricketer Ashley Metcalfe (b.1963).

Ashley (f.) A female adoption of the male name ASHLEY, taken up by English speakers, especially in the US, from the 1940s.

US opera singer Ashley Putnam (b.1952).

Aspasia A name of Greek origin, meaning 'welcomed one', which was taken up on a very selective basis by some English speakers from the 19th century. Historically, Aspasia was the mistress of Pericles in the 5th century BC. In literature Aspasia Fitzgibbon is a character in Anthony Trollope's novel *Phineas Finn* (1869), while Agatha Christie's short story 'The Dead Harlequin' in *The Mysterious Mr Quin* (1930) (US title *The Passing of Mr Quin*) has a character named Aspasia Glen. A variant is *Aspatia*, as for the central character, betrothed to Amintor, in Beaumont and Fletcher's play *The Maid's Tragedy* (1610).

Asta see **Astrid**.

Astra A name either based on Latin *astrum* or Greek *astēr*, 'star', or evolving as a variant of some name with a similar meaning, such as ESTHER or STELLA. It has found some select favour among English speakers from the late 19th century.

UK opera singers Astra Desmond (1893–1973), Astra Blair (b.1932).

Astrid The name derives from the Old Norse name *Astrithr*, formed from *ans*, 'god', and *frithr*, 'fair', so overall means 'divinely beautiful'. (To English ears it may suggest 'star', however, from an association with Greek *astēr*.) Although it was adopted by some English speakers in the 20th century, it is best known as a European royal name, such as that of Princess Astrid of Norway (b.1932), youngest daughter of King Olav V; and of Queen Astrid of Belgium (1905–35), wife of Leopold III and niece of the king of Sweden. A frequent diminutive is *Asta*.

Swedish-US actress Astrid Allwyn (1909–78).

Athelstan The name represents the Old English name *Æthelstān*, formed from *æthel*, 'noble', and *stān*, 'stone', hence 'nobly strong'. It has found some favour among English speakers from the 19th century and is historically familiar from the 10th-century king of Wessex and Mercia. Athelstane of Coningsburgh is a character in Walter Scott's novel *Ivanhoe* (1819), and Athelstan Athelny is one of the many children of Thorpe Athelny in Somerset Maugham's novel *Of Human Bondage* (1915).

Aub see **Aubrey** (m.).

Auberon The name is perhaps a variant of AUBREY, influenced by *Oberon*, king of the fairies in Shakespeare's *A Midsummer Night's Dream* (1595–6). It has enjoyed irregular adoption among English speakers from the 19th century. Its usual diminutive is *Bron*.

UK journalist, critic Auberon Waugh (1939–2001) (grandfather was Aubrey).

Aubrey (m.) The name is a French version of the Old German name *Alberich*, formed from *alb*, 'elf', and *rīchi*, 'power', so meaning 'supernaturally powerful'. It has been recorded among English speakers from medieval times, but from the late 19th century it has been adopted rather more generally. In literature Aubrey Greene is an artist in John Galsworthy's novel *The White Monkey* (1924), while the Hon. Aubrey Bagot is a character in George Bernard Shaw's play *Too True to be Good* (1932). AUBERON may be a possible variant. A diminutive is *Aub*, as for the Australian speedway rider Aub Lawson (1916–77).

UK artist Aubrey Beardsley (1872–98); South African cricketer Aubrey Faulkner (1881–1930); UK actor Aubrey Mather (1885–1958); UK horn player Aubrey Brain (1893–1955); Welsh politician Aubrey Jones (b.1911); UK broadcasting executive Aubrey Singer (b.1927); UK actor Aubrey Woods (b.1928).

Aubrey (f.) A female adoption of the male name AUBREY, in rarish use among English speakers from the 19th century. In literature Aubrey Bronson is the wife of Captain Scott Bronson in John Dos Passos's novel *Chosen Country* (1951).

Audrey The name is a much 'smoothed' variant of the Old English name *Æthelthryth*, which is composed of *æthel*, 'noble', and *thrȳth*, 'strength', so 'noble strength'. In its current form it has been generally popular among English speakers from the early 20th century, although it fell fairly rapidly from favour from the 1920s. It was originally familiar from St Audrey (earlier known as St Etheldreda), the 7th-century queen of Northumbria and abbess of Ely, who died aged around 50 from a throat tumour, said to have been a punishment for her love of necklaces when young. (Cheap silk necklaces sold at St Audrey's Fair, Ely, held annually on her feast day, came to be known as 'St Audrey's lace', or colloquially 'Tawdry lace', and this gave the modern word *tawdry* meaning 'cheap' or 'shoddy'.) In Shakespeare's *As You Like It* (1599) Audrey is a country wench. Variants and diminutives include *Audrie, Audry, Audie, Audi* and *Aud*.

Irish-born UK radio broadcaster Audrey Russell (1906–89); US actresses Audrey Christie (1912–89), Audrey Meadows (1926–96); Belgian-born US actress Audrey Hepburn (1929–93) (original first name Edda); Canadian writer Audrey Thomas (b.1935); UK politician Audrey Wise (1935–2000).

Augie see **Augustus**.

Augusta A feminine form of AUGUSTUS or AUGUSTIN. Roman emperors assumed the title *Augustus* ('venerable', 'august') on their accession, and *Augusta* was the title of honour then given to their wives, daughters and other female relatives. The name was introduced to England in the 18th century by Princess Augusta of Saxe-Coburg-Gotha (d.1772), wife of Frederick,

Prince of Wales, and mother of George III. Its popularity increased in the 19th century but has since sharply declined. Variants include the French form *Auguste*, while diminutives are *Augustina* or *Augustine*, as well as the short forms *Gus* or *Gussie*. The latter became familiar through the US tennis player Gussie Moran ('Gorgeous Gussie') (b.1923) (original first names Gertrude Augusta).

US ballerina Augusta Maywood (1825–76); Irish playwright, folklorist Lady Augusta Gregory (1852–1932).

Augustine An English form of the Latin name *Augustinus*, itself a diminutive of AUGUSTUS. It has found irregular use among English speakers from medieval times but gained greater prominence in the 19th century. It was historically made famous by the great teacher and doctor St Augustine of Hippo (354–430), and subsequently by his namesake, the 6th-century Roman monk St Augustine (d.604), who became the first Archbishop of Canterbury. Father Augustine is a character in Richard Brinsley Sheridan's play *The Rivals* (1775). A spelling variant is *Augustin*, while AUSTIN is a contracted form of the name in independent use. The regular diminutive is GUS.

Augustus A name of Latin origin, from the standard word *augustus*, 'great', 'august', adopted as a title by Roman emperors. It has enjoyed English-speaking use from the 18th century, although it is now much less common. It was historically made famous by the Roman emperor Augustus, who as Octavian (and the adopted son of Julius Caesar) took the name as a title in 27BC. It then passed to successive emperors. In Charles Dickens's novel *Pickwick Papers* (1836–7), Augustus Snodgrass is a member of the Pickwick Club, while Augustus Richmond is the central character's father in George Meredith's novel *The Adventures of Harry Richmond* (1871). In George Bernard Shaw's play *Augustus Does His Bit* (1916) the name is that of the central character, Augustus Highcastle. AUGUSTINE is a related name, as is AUSTIN. The usual diminutive is GUS, in independent use, and *Augie* also exists.

UK painters Augustus Egg (1816–63), Augustus John (1878–1961).

Aurelia This is the feminine form of the Latin clan name *Aurelius*, itself ultimately from *aurum*, 'gold'. The name has found select English-speaking favour from the 17th century. In John Marston's play *The Malcontent* (1604) Aurelia is the dissolute duchess wife of the central character, Altofronto, Duke of Genoa, and in John Dryden's comedy *An Evening's Love* (1668) Aurelia is a pretty but affected flirt. In later literature Aurelia Darnel marries the title character in Tobias Smollett's novel *Sir Launcelot Greaves* (1762).

Auriol The name has its origin in the feminine form of Latin *aureolus*, the diminutive of *aureus*, 'golden'. It is also linked with the Roman clan name *Aurelius*, as for AURELIA. English speakers began to adopt the name selectively from the 19th century. The variant spellings *Auriel* and *Auriole* exist, with diminutives as *Aurie* or *Aury*.

UK educational writer, broadcaster Auriol Stevens (b.1940).

Aurora The name of the Roman goddess of the dawn, meaning 'dawn' itself, was first found at all widely in 19th-century English poetry. Aurora Raby is a character in Byron's poem *Don Juan* (1819–24), while Aurora Leigh is the heroine of Elizabeth Barrett Browning's romance of this name (1856).

Austin The name was originally a contracted form of AUGUSTINE, but it is now often an adoption of the surname. It has been in use among English speakers from medieval times. In fiction Dr Austin Sloper is the father of Catherine Sloper, the central character in Henry James's novel *Washington Square* (1880). A spelling variant is *Austen*, as borne by the UK politician Sir Austen Chamberlain (1863–1937), half-brother of prime minister Neville Chamberlain. (It was originally his second name, the first being Joseph.)

UK actor Austin Trevor (1897–1978); UK politician, broadcaster Austin Mitchell (b.1934); US actor Austin Pendleton (b.1940).

Ava The name probably evolved from EVA, an independent variant of EVE, but it has become popularly associated with Latin *avis*, 'bird'. It is not found in English-speaking use until the 20th century.

Italo-US actress Ava Gardner (1922–90).

Avaril see **Averil**.

Aveline A name that is probably a French diminutive of *Avila*, itself a name of Old German origin related to AVIS. (See also EILEEN.) It has found very selective favour among English speakers from the 19th century. In recent times it was to some extent popularized by Aveline Boswell, a character in the UK TV comedy series *Bread* (from 1986).

Averil The name may have developed as a variant of AVRIL but could also have evolved from the Old English name *Eoforhild*, which is formed from *eofor*, 'boar', and *hild*, 'battle', so 'boarlike in battle'. It has enjoyed limited English-speaking use from the early 20th century. St Averil (or Everild) was a nun in the north of England who became a minor 7th-century saint. Variants are mainly spelling alterations, such as *Avaril* or *Averill*.

UK writer on needlework Averil Colby (1900–83).

Avery From the surname, itself from a medieval form of ALFRED, the name has found sporadic English-speaking use from the late 19th century.

US Olympics administrator Avery Brundage (1887–1975).

Avice An independently adopted variant of AVIS, pronounced with a short 'a', as in 'Alice', with a select English-speaking use from the 19th century. A literary occurrence of the name is that of Avice Caro, the central character in Thomas Hardy's novel *The Well Beloved* (1897).

UK actress Avice Landone (1910–76).

Avila see **Aveline**.

Avis The ultimate origin of the name is uncertain, but it may relate to the German name *Hedwig*, both parts of which mean 'struggle'. It is now associated with Latin *avis*, 'bird', and is usually pronounced with a long 'a', as in 'Mavis'. The name has found some English-speaking favour from the early 20th century. In Jack London's novel *The Iron Heel* (1908), Avis Cunningham, the narrator, marries Ernest Everhard. Its better known variant is AVICE.

UK actress, entertainer Avis Bunnage (1923–90).

Avril The name either comes from French *avril* (English APRIL) or, like AVERIL, developed from the Old English name *Eoforhild*. It has enjoyed some popularity among English speakers from the early 20th century, achieving a modest peak in the 1950s. In literature, Avril is the name of Basil Stoke's mistress in Sean O'Casey's play *Purple Dust* (1940).

UK comedienne Avril Angers (b.1922); Irish-born UK TV music controller Avril MacRory (b.1956).

Avrom see **Abraham**.

Aylmer The present form of the name comes from the Old English name *Æthelmær*, formed from *æthel*, 'noble', and *mære*, 'famous', so 'nobly famed'. It has also been adopted from the surname. The name has occasionally found favour among English speakers from the 19th century. Aylmer is the prior of Jervaux Abbey in Walter Scott's novel *Ivanhoe* (1819), and Sir Aylmer Aylmer is the subject of Tennyson's poem *Aylmer's Field* (1864).

UK translator of Tolstoy, Aylmer Maude (1858–1938).

Azalea A flower name, taken up by some English speakers from the late 19th century. O. Henry's short story 'A Municipal Report' in *Strictly Business* (1910) has Azalea Adair as a poverty-stricken writer.

Azariah A biblical name, from Hebrew *'Azaryāh*, 'helped by Yah' (that is, by God), in selective English-speaking use from the 19th century, but rarely found today. The name is borne by several people in the Bible, including the head of King Solomon's prefects, the prophet who exhorted King Asa to undertake religious reforms, and as an alternative name for Uzziah, King of Judah.

B

Bab, Babs, Babette see **Barbara**.

Baldwin An adoption from the French form of the Old German name *Baldawin*, formed from *bald*, 'bold', 'brave', and *wine*, 'friend', so 'brave friend', 'comrade-in-arms'. The name has found some favour among English speakers from the 19th century, and it is familiar in history from various medieval rulers, including several counts of Flanders and the first king of Jerusalem, Baldwin of Boulogne (d.1118). Christopher Marlowe's play *Tamburlaine the Great* (1587) has a character of the name. Its Welsh equivalent is MALDWYN.

Balthazar The name, traditionally that of one of the Three Wise Men who brought gifts to the infant Jesus, is a form of *Belshazzar* (as for the biblical king), itself from Babylonian *Bēl-sharra-usur*, 'Bel protect the king' (Bel being the supreme deity). It is found frequently in Shakespeare: in *The Merchant of Venice* (1596–8) Portia disguises herself as the lawyer Balthazar, in *A Comedy of Errors* (1594) Balthazar is a merchant, and in *Romeo and Juliet* (1595) and *Much Ado About Nothing* (1598–9) Balthazar is a servant. The name is now not common but has been popularized by the main character of J.P. Donleavy's novel *The Beastly Beatitudes of Balthazar B.* (1968). The variant spelling *Balthasar* also exists.

US actor Balthazar Getty (b.1975).

Barbara The name is the feminine form of Greek *barbaros*, 'strange', 'foreign', a word (representing stammering) originally used of a person who did not speak Greek. It has been in English-speaking use from medieval times, gradually gaining in popularity until the 17th century, when it fell from favour as not being a biblical name. It revived sharply in the first half of the 20th century but has since steadily declined. It was first familiar as the name of the 3rd-century virgin martyr, St Barbara. In Charles Dickens's novel *The Old Curiosity Shop* (1840–41) Barbara is a maid to the Garland family, and in William Makepeace Thackeray's novel *Vanity Fair* (1847–8) Miss Barbara Pinkerton is head of Pinkerton's Seminary for Young Ladies. A more familiar literary bearer of the name is the central character of George Bernard Shaw's play *Major Barbara* (1905). The name's many diminutives include *Bab*, *Babs*, the French *Babette*, *Bar*, *Barbie* (popular from the doll) and *Barbar*. The folksong 'Barbara Allen' has added to the name's popularity. A variant spelling *Barbra* has become familiar through the US singer and actress Barbra Streisand (b.1942).

UK novelist Barbara Cartland (1900–2000); US actress Barbara Stanwyck (1907–90) (original name Ruby Stevens); UK animal trainer, TV personality Barbara Woodhouse (1910–88); UK politician Barbara Castle (b.1911); UK novelist Barbara Pym (1913–80); UK actress Barbara Lott (b.1920); US actress Barbara Bel Geddes (b.1922); UK-born US novelist Barbara Taylor Bradford (b.1933); UK actresses Barbara Leigh-Hunt (b.1935), Barbara Knox (b.1938); UK popular singer Barbara Dickson (b.1947); UK actress Barbara Flynn (b.1948).

Bardolph The name represents the Old German name *Bartholf*, consisting of *beraht*, 'bright', or *barta*, 'axe', and *wolf*, 'wolf', so 'famous wolf' or 'axe wolf', the latter implying ferocity. It has enjoyed regular but modest use among English speakers from medieval times, although it is not common today. In Shakespeare's *Henry IV* (1597), *Henry V* (1599) and *The Merry Wives of Windsor* (1597) Bardolph is the friend, follower and drinking companion of Falstaff.

Barnabas A biblical name, from Aramaic *Barnĕbhū'āh*, 'son of consolation', found in regular but modest use among English

speakers from medieval times, although now usually superseded by BARNABY. In the Bible Barnabas is the companion of
St Paul, 'a good man full of the Holy Ghost and of faith' (Acts
1.24). The diminutive BARNEY is in independent use.

Barnaby The name is a spoken form of BARNABAS, which
evolved in medieval times, finding select favour among English
speakers from the 19th century. Charles Dickens made it
familiar from the central character of his novel *Barnaby Rudge*
(1841). In Richard Aldington's novel *Death of a Hero* (1929)
Barnaby Slush is a novelist. The diminutive BARNEY exists
independently.

Barney The independently adopted diminutive of BARNABAS
or BARNABY, in regular if modest use among English speakers
from the late 19th century. It was popularized by the US racing
driver Barney Oldfield (see details below) and by the classic
silent movie in which he appears, *Barney Oldfield's Race for Life*
(1912). In literature it occurs for Barney Coles, cousin of Jesse
Piggot in Mrs Molesworth's novel *The Oriel Window* (1896).
The form *Barny* is sometimes found.

US motor-racing driver Barney Oldfield (1878–1946) (original first
names Berna Eli); US film executive Barney Balaban (1888–1971); US
jazzman Barney Bigard (1906–80) (original first names Leon Albany);
US boxer Barney Ross (1909–67) (original name Barnet Rosofsky); UK
radio producer Barney Colehan (b.c.1920).

Barrie Either from the (Scottish or Irish) surname, or an independently adopted variant of BARRY, current among English
speakers from the 1920s and in greatest favour from the 1930s
to the 1950s. The original stimulus for the name may have
been that of the Scottish writer J.M. Barrie (1860–1937), whose
immensely popular play *Peter Pan* was first staged in 1904.

UK actor Barrie Ingham (b.1932); UK footballer Barrie Meyer (b.1932);
UK playwright Barrie Keeffe (b.1945); UK actor Barrie Rutter (b.1946).

Barry The name is either an English form of the Irish name *Barra*, a short form of *Fionnbarr*, itself formed from Irish *fionn*, 'white', 'fair', and *barr*, 'head', or else comes direct from Irish *bearach*, 'spear'. It was taken up by English speakers from the mid-19th century, reaching a popularity peak in the 1950s. In fiction the name is familiar as that of the Irish adventurer who is the central character in William Makepeace Thackeray's novel *The Luck of Barry Lyndon* (1844). A variant spelling in independent use is BARRIE. Diminutive forms are often *Baz* or *Bazza*, especially in Australia, where the name has long been popular.

English songwriter Barry Cornwall (1787–1874) (original name Bryan Waller Proctor); Irish actor Barry Fitzgerald (1888–1961) (original name William Shields); UK actor Barry Jones (1893–1981); US actors Barry Sullivan (1912–94) (original name Patrick Barry), Barry Atwater (1918–78); UK broadcaster Barry Took (b.1928); Australian comedian Barry Humphries (b.1930); UK actor Barry Foster (b.1930); Australian-born UK horn player, conductor Barry Tuckwell (b.1931); UK race-horse trainer Barry Hills (b.1937) (original first name Barrington); UK writer Barry Hines (b.1939); US soul singer Barry White (b.1944); US popular singer Barry Manilow (b.1946); UK racing motorcyclist Barry Sheene (b.1950) (original first names Stephen Frank); Irish boxer Barry McGuigan (b.1961) (original first name Finbar).

Bartholomew A biblical name, from an Aramaic formation meaning 'son of Talmai'. (The latter is also a biblical name, from a Hebrew phrase meaning 'abounding in furrows'.) The name was long favoured among English speakers from medieval times but today is rarely used. In the Bible Bartholomew is one of the twelve apostles. Ben Jonson's comedy *Bartholomew Fair* (1614), set in London on St Bartholomew's Day (24 August), has Bartholomew Cokes as a rich simpleton. The usual diminutive is *Bart*.

Baruch A name of biblical origin, from Hebrew *Bārūk*, 'blessed' (compare BENEDICT), but found only rarely in

English-speaking use. In the Bible Baruch is a companion to the prophet Jeremiah.

Basil The name derives from the Greek name *Basileios*, 'royal', itself from *basileus*, 'king'. It has enjoyed fairly regular use among English speakers from the 19th century, reaching a modest popularity peak in the 1920s, since when it has fallen from favour. It is historically famous from St Basil the Great, 4th-century bishop of Caesarea. Wilkie Collins's novel *Basil* (1852) has the name for its central character. In recent times it has been humorously popularized by Basil Fawlty, the manic hotel keeper played by John Cleese in the TV comedy series *Fawlty Towers* (1975, 1979). Diminutives *Bas* and *Baz* exist.

UK conductor Basil Cameron (1884–1975); UK theatrical producer Basil Dean (1888–1978); UK publisher Basil Blackwell (1889–1984); UK actors Basil Rathbone (1892–1967), Basil Radford (1897–1952); UK poet Basil Bunting (1900–85); UK architect Sir Basil Spence (1907–76); UK Roman Catholic prelate, Cardinal Basil Hume (1923–99) (original first name George); South African cricketer Basil D'Oliveira (b.1931).

Bathsheba A biblical name, from Hebrew *Bathsheba'*, meaning either 'daughter of the oath' or 'seventh daughter'. It was taken up by 17th-century Puritans but is found only rarely today. In the Bible Bathsheba is the wife of Uriah who committed adultery with King David before marrying him. In literature Thomas Hardy's novel *Far From the Madding Crowd* (1874) has Bathsheba Everdene as its central character. The regular diminutive is SHEBA, which is in independent use.

Baz see **Barry, Basil, Sebastian**.

Bazza see **Barry, Sebastian**.

Beatrice The name comes from Latin *beatrix*, genitive *beatricis*, 'she who makes happy', itself from *beatus*, 'blessed', 'lucky'. It was adopted by English speakers in the 19th century and continued to be popular until the early 20th century, since when it has sharply declined. It was first made familiar by Princess Beatrice (1857–1944), the youngest daughter of Queen Victoria, and by her identically named near contemporary, Princess Beatrice (1884–1966), the youngest child of Prince Alfred and Grand Duchess Maria Alexandrovna of Russia. A century on, the name was chosen for another Princess Beatrice (b.1988), daughter of Prince Andrew, the son of Queen Elizabeth II. The most famous literary Beatrice occurs much earlier, as Dante's heavenly guide through Paradise in his *Divine Comedy* (1309–20). She was a real person and Dante's beloved, the Florentine noblewoman Beatrice Portinari (1266–90). They first met when he was nine and she was eight. Shakespeare also had a Beatrice as the niece of Leonato who marries Benedick in *Much Ado About Nothing* (1598–9). A later fictional bearer of the name is Beatrice Gresham in Anthony Trollope's novel *Doctor Thorne* (1858). The most common variant is BEATRIX, in independent use. A common diminutive is *Bea*, as for the US popular singer Bea Wain (b.1917).

Irish traveller, writer Beatrice Grimshaw (1871–1953); Canadian-born revue artiste Beatrice Lillie (1894–1989); US actress Beatrice Arthur (b.1923) (original name Bernice Frankel); UK actress Beatrice Campbell (1923–80).

Beatrix A direct adoption from Latin *beatrix*, 'she who makes happy', which also gave BEATRICE. The name has occurred in English-speaking use since medieval times but is now rarely found. In literature Beatrix Esmond is the second cousin of the central character in William Makepeace Thackeray's novels *The History of Henry Esmond* (1852) and *The Virginians* (1857–9). The diminutive TRIXIE gained independent use.

UK children's writer, illustrator Beatrix Potter (1866–1943) (originally second name, first being Helen); UK actress Beatrix Lehmann (1898–1979); UK feminist writer Beatrix Campbell (b.1947).

Beau An adoption of the standard nickname, from the French word for 'handsome'. The name has found some favour among English speakers in the 20th century, especially in the US. It gained considerable fame from the English dandy Beau Brummell (1778–1840) (original first names George Bryan), but was more popularly made known by the central character of P.C. Wren's novel *Beau Geste* (1924), in which the name was that assumed by Michael Geste, a bold young Englishman who joins the French Foreign Legion. The novel was followed by more stories about the three Geste brothers, Beau, Digby and John: *Beau Sabreur* (1926), *Beau Ideal* (1928) and *Good Gestes* (1929), all of which continued to keep the name before the public. Later, Beau Wilks is a character in Margaret Mitchell's novel *Gone with the Wind* (1936).

US actor Beau Bridges (b.1941).

Becky An independently adopted diminutive of REBECCA, which has been in regular English-speaking use from the 18th century but has been much rarer in the 20th century, although picking up in popularity from the 1980s. Its best-known literary bearer is Becky Sharp, the central character in William Makepeace Thackeray's novel *Vanity Fair* (1847–8).

Belinda The name perhaps ultimately derives from the Old German word *lint*, 'snake', alluding to cunning, but otherwise it is of uncertain origin. It could be a blend of Italian *bella* or French *belle*, 'beautiful', and a name such as LUCINDA, but it is now more obviously associated with BELLA and LINDA. It was current in medieval times in continental Europe but hardly in England until the 17th century. It is now found fairly generally if selectively in the English-speaking world. The name was first familiar from literature, such as Belinda in William Congreve's play *The Old Bachelor* (1693), Sir John Vanbrugh's play *The Provok'd Wife* (1697), Arthur Murphy's play *All in the Wrong* (1761), and especially as the central character in Alexander Pope's poem *The Rape of the Lock* (1714), in which Belinda represents the real-life Arabella Fermor. (Pope may have deliberately chosen a name with *bel* to link the two names.) Maria Edgeworth's novel *Belinda* (1801) has the name for its central character, while in William Makepeace Thackeray's novel *Pendennis* (1848–50) Belinda Smirke is a curate's wife. The main diminutive is *Bel*, as for the UK writer Bel Mooney (b.1946).

UK actress Belinda Lee (1935–61); US actress Belinda Montgomery (b.1950); UK actress Belinda Lang (b.1953); Australian actress Belinda Bauer (b.1956); US pop singer Belinda Carlisle (b.1958); UK actress Belinda Davison (b.1964); New Zealand tennis player Belinda Cordwell (b.1965).

Bella The name is both a derivative of names such as ARABELLA and ISABEL and an adoption of the word for 'beautiful' in a Romance language (such as Spanish *bella* or French *belle*). It is found in select English-speaking use from the 18th century. In literature Bella Wilfer is the central character in Charles Dickens's novel *Our Mutual Friend* (1864–5), while in Theodore Dreiser's novel *An American Tragedy* (1925), Bella is a daughter of Samuel Griffiths, uncle of the central character Clyde Griffiths. The main variant is the French equivalent, BELLE.

US playwright, screenwriter Bella Spewack (1899–1990); US politician, feminist Bella Abzug (1920–98); UK actress, comedienne Bella Emberg (b.1937); Togolese 'highlife' singer Bella Bellow (1946–73); UK fashion designer Bella Freud (b.1961).

Belle This name is either an independently adopted variant of BELLA, exactly reflecting French *belle*, 'beautiful', and in select US and Canadian use from the 19th century, or an independently adopted diminutive of a name such as BELINDA or ISABELLA. In recent times the name has been popularized by the song 'Belle, Belle, My Liberty Belle' (1951). The male equivalent is BEAU.

US outlaw Belle Starr (1848–89); US actress Belle Bennett (1891–1932); UK actress Belle Chrystall (b.1911); Scottish golfer Belle Robertson (b.1936).

Ben An independently adopted diminutive of BENJAMIN or (less frequently) BENEDICT, in regular English-speaking use from the 19th century and gradually gaining popularity in the 20th century. In literature the name has become familiar from the wheelwright Ben Winthrop in George Eliot's novel *Silas Marner* (1861) and from the castaway Ben Gunn in Robert Louis Stevenson's novel *Treasure Island* (1883). BENNY is a diminutive in its own right.

UK playwright Ben Travers (1886–1980); UK painter Ben Nicholson (1894–1982); US science fiction writer Ben Bova (b.1932); UK actor Ben Aris (b.1937); Anglo-Indian actor Ben Kingsley (b.1944) (original name Krishna Banji); UK comedian Ben Elton (b.1959).

Benedict An English form of the Latin name *Benedictus*, 'blessed', which has been in select use among English speakers from medieval times and especially favoured by Roman Catholics, who honour St Benedict, the 6th-century founder of the Benedictine monastic order. The name gained in popularity from the 1980s. The usual diminutive, BEN, is in independent use.

Irish writer Benedict Kiely (b.1919); UK actor Benedict Taylor (b.1960).

Benedicta The feminine form of BENEDICT, in very modest English-speaking use, but still sometimes found. The name has been borne by some obscure saints or holy women, the latter mostly in the Benedictine order.

Benita An adoption of the feminine form of the Spanish name *Benito* (English BENEDICT), in select favour with English speakers from the early 20th century, mostly in the US but also occasionally found in the UK.

UK actress Benita Hume (1906–67).

Benjamin A familiar biblical name, from Hebrew *Binyāmīn*, 'son of the right hand', implying a favourite. The name was taken up by Puritans in the 17th century and has been in regular use since, especially among Jews, with its popularity increasing from the 1960s. In the Bible Benjamin is the youngest of the twelve sons of Jacob and Rachel, the brother of Joseph, and one of the founders of the twelve tribes of Israel. (In this connection, some biblical scholars interpret the name geographically, so that it refers to a southern tribe. 'Right hand' means 'south' if one faces east, or the rising sun.) Sir Benjamin Backbite is a scandalmonger in Richard Brinsley Sheridan's comedy *The School for Scandal* (1777). Diminutives include BEN and BENNY, which are in independent use, and *Benjie* and *Benjy*.

UK prime minister Benjamin Disraeli (1804–81); US paediatrician Benjamin Spock (1903–98); UK composer Benjamin Britten, Lord Britten of Aldeburgh (1913–76); UK actor Benjamin Whitrow (b.1937).

Benny An independently adopted diminutive of BENJAMIN or BEN, in regular English-speaking use from the early 20th century. The spelling *Bennie* is also found, as for the US jazzman Bennie Green (1923–77).

US comedian Benny Fields (1894–1959); US boxer Benny Leonard (1896–1947); US bandleader, clarinettist Benny Goodman (1909–86); UK comedian Benny Hill (1925–92) (original first name Alfred); UK writer on jazz, theatre Benny Green (b.1927).

Berenice The former usual form of BERNICE, still very occasionally found among English speakers.

US photographer Berenice Abbott (1898–1991).

Bernadette A feminine form of BERNARD, in select English-speaking use from the 19th century and especially favoured by Roman Catholics and the Irish, who adopted it in commemoration of the French visionary St Bernadette (1844–79) (original name Marie-Bernarde Soubirous). Her name was more widely popularized by the film about her, *The Song of*

Bernadette (1943). A diminutive *Detta* is sometimes found.

Irish actress Bernadette O'Farrell (1924–99); French actress Bernadette Lafont (b.1938); Northern Ireland political activist Bernadette Devlin (b.1947); US actress Bernadette Peters (b.1948).

Bernard The name has its origin either in the Old English name *Beornheard*, formed from *beorn*, 'man', 'warrior', and *heard*, 'brave', or in the Old German name *Berinhard*, formed from *ber*, 'bear', and *hart*, 'bold', 'stern'. It was introduced to England by the Normans in the 11th century and has been in regular English-speaking use since. It is historically famous from three churchmen: St Bernard of Menthon, 10th-century founder of the Alpine pass hospices; St Bernard of Clairvaux, the 12th-century Cistercian reformer; and St Bernard of Chartres, the 12th-century scholastic philosopher. The name's regular diminutive is *Bernie*, with BUNNY also sometimes found in independent use.

Irish-born UK playwright George Bernard Shaw (1856–1950); UK actor Sir Bernard Miles (1907–91); Canadian radio and TV host Bernard Braden (1916–93); UK columnist Bernard Levin (b.1928); UK actors Bernard Cribbins (b.1928), Bernard Bresslaw (1933–93), Bernard Hill (b.1944).

Bernice A name of biblical origin, ultimately from the Greek name *Pherenike*, 'bringing victory'. It was formerly believed to be a variant of VERONICA, but that is a different name. It occasionally occurs in English-speaking use from the time of the Reformation but was not widely adopted until the 19th century, since when it has declined considerably. In the Bible Bernice is the sister of King Agrippa. The best-known variant is BERENICE, the former usual form of the name. Diminutives include *Bernie*, *Berry* and the independently adopted BINNIE and BUNNY.

UK novelist Bernice Rubens (b.1928).

Bernie see **Bernard**, **Bernice**.

Berry see **Bernice**, **Beryl**.

Bert An independently adopted diminutive of ALBERT or (less commonly) BERTRAM and LAMBERT, in regular use among English speakers from the 19th century but much less frequent after the 1920s. Bert Smallways is the central character of H.G. Wells's novel *War in the Air* (1908). The variant spelling BURT exists, while a common diminutive is BERTIE, both these being adopted in their own right.

US actor Bert Lahr (1895–1967); US journalist, writer Bert Bacharach (1898–1983) (original first name Bertram; son is musician Burt Bacharach); UK pop guitarist Bert Weedon (b.1920).

Berta see **Bertha**, **Roberta**.

Bertha The name derives from the Old German name *Berahta*, itself from *beraht*, 'bright', 'famous'. It occurs only occasionally in English-speaking use before the 19th century and has declined considerably from the early years of the 20th century, probably through the undesirable association with 'Big Bertha', the nickname given by the French to German howitzers in the First World War (for Frau Bertha Krupp of the famous armament firm, although the guns were actually made by the Škoda works). As a literary name it is that of the first wife of Edward Fairfax Rochester in Charlotte Brontë's novel *Jane Eyre* (1847). Later, Bertha is the central character in Fannie Hurst's novel *Lummox* (1924). The French form of the name, *Berthe*, is sometimes found, otherwise *Berta*, *Bertie* or *Bertina* are variants, as well as the simple diminutive *Bert*.

UK comedienne Bertha Belmore (1882–1953); US religious leader Bertha Lindsay (1897–1990) (original first names Goldie Ina Ruby).

Bertice The name, probably a blend of BERTHA and BERNICE, has found occasional use among English speakers from the early 20th century.

US blues singer Bertice Reading (1933–91).

Bertie (m.) An independently adopted diminutive of BERT or of its source names, ALBERT or BERTRAM. It came into vogue among English speakers from the late 19th century but is now much less common. The name was made familiar by the music-hall song 'Burlington Bertie from Bow' (1915) and given a popular boost by the dandy wit Bertie Wooster, the central character (with his manservant Jeeves) of the stories by P.G. Wodehouse (from 1915). In the UK royal family 'Bertie' was the nickname of King George VI (1895–1952), from the first of his full names, Albert Frederick Arthur George.

Scottish-born US journalist, founder of *Forbes Magazine*, Bertie Forbes (1880–1954); Irish prime minister Bertie Ahern (b.1951).

Bertie (f.) see **Bertha**.

Bertina see **Bertha**.

Bertram The name comes from the French form of the Old German name *Berahtram*, which is formed from *beraht*, 'bright', 'famous', and *hramn*, 'raven', so 'famous raven', implying a wise person. It has been in select use among English speakers from medieval times, with increasing popularity from the mid-19th century to the 1930s, since when it has sharply declined. Bertram, Count of Roussillon, is a character in Shakespeare's *All's Well That Ends Well* (1603–4). BERTRAND is a variant in its own right, while diminutives are the independently adopted BERT or BERTIE.

UK circus proprietor Bertram Mills (1873–1938).

Bertrand An independently adopted variant of BERTRAM, taken up by English speakers in medieval times and used very selectively since. The diminutive BERTIE is also in independent use.

UK philosopher Bertrand Russell, Earl Russell (1872–1970).

Beryl The name, from the precious stone, has been in vogue among English speakers from the late 19th century but has declined considerably following a popularity peak in the 1930s. Noël Coward's play *Brief Encounter* (1945) has Beryl as an assistant to the refreshment room manageress, Myrtle Bagot. The usual diminutive is *Berry*.

UK actress Beryl Mercer (1882–1939); UK aviator Beryl Markham (1902–86); UK jazz singer Beryl Bryden (1920–98); UK actress Beryl Reid (1920–96); UK artist Beryl Cook (b.1926); UK ballerina Beryl Grey (b.1927); UK writer Beryl Bainbridge (b.1933); UK cyclist Beryl Burton (1937–96).

Bess One of the independently adopted diminutives of ELIZABETH, in English-speaking use from the 17th century but now much less common. The name was popularized by the nickname for Queen Elizabeth I, 'Good Queen Bess'. In recent times it has also been brought before the public by one of the main characters, the ex-prostitute Bess, in George Gershwin's opera *Porgy and Bess* (1935), which was adapted from DuBose Heyward's novel *Porgy* (1927). The main diminutive, BESSIE, is in independent use.

US first lady, wife of president Harry S. Truman, Bess Truman (1885–1982); US scriptwriter Bess Meredyth (1890–1969) (original name Helen McGlashan); US actress Bess Flowers (1900–84).

Bessie The independently adopted diminutive of BESS or of its source name, ELIZABETH. It is found in English-speaking use from the 17th century. In Charlotte Brontë's novel *Jane Eyre* (1847) Bessie is the nurse to the Reed children, and Bessie Burgess is a street fruit-vendor in Sean O'Casey's play *The Plough and the Stars* (1926). The UK left-wing politician Mrs Elizabeth Braddock (1899–1970) was always known as Bessie Braddock. The spelling *Bessy* is also sometimes found.

US blues singer Bessie Smith (1894–1937); US actress Bessie Love (1898–1986) (original name Juanita Horton); South African writer Bessie Head (1937–86).

Bet An independently adopted diminutive of ELIZABETH, or a variant of BETH, in occasional English-speaking use from the 19th century. Bet (or Betsy) is an accomplice of Fagin in Charles Dickens's novel *Oliver Twist* (1837–8). BESS and BESSIE are directly related names.

Beth An independently adopted diminutive of ELIZABETH, which has been in select English-speaking use from the 19th century, with a slight revival in the 1990s. Beth March is one of the four daughters who are the central characters in Louisa M. Alcott's novel *Little Women* (1868–9) and its sequel *Good Wives*. The name frequently forms the second part of a compound name such as *Jo Beth* or *Mary Beth*, as for the US actresses JoBeth Williams (b.1953) and Mary Beth Hurt (b.1948). The variant BET is in independent use.

UK gardener Beth Chatto (b.1923); UK actress Beth Morris (b.1949); US playwright Beth Henley (b.1952); UK pop singer Beth Orton (b.1970).

Betsy An independently adopted diminutive of ELIZABETH, blending BET or BETH and BESS or BESSIE, which has been in select English-speaking use from the 19th century. In Charles Dickens's novel *Pickwick Papers* (1836–7) Betsy is a maid to Bob Sawyer. The variant spelling *Betsey* occurs, as for Betsey Trotwood, David's great-aunt in Dickens's novel *David Copperfield* (1849–50).

US actress Betsy Blair (b.1923) (original name Elizabeth Boger); US children's writer Betsy Byars (b.1928); US actress Betsy Palmer (b.1929) (original name Patricia Brumek); US golfer Betsy King (b.1955).

Bettina see **Elizabeth**.

Betty An independently adopted diminutive of ELIZABETH, in fairly regular English-speaking use from the 18th century, but declining quite sharply after a marked surge in popularity in the 1920s. In literature Betty Gulliver is the daughter of Lemuel Gulliver, the central character of Jonathan Swift's novel

Gulliver's Travels (1726). Variants include the spelling *Bettye*, as for the US actress Bettye Ackermann (b.1928), the French form *Bette*, adopted by the US actress Bette Davis (1908–89) (specifically from Balzac's novel *La Cousine Bette* (1847)) and the US entertainer Bette Midler (b.1944), and the Italian diminutive *Bettina*, as for the US sociologist and feminist Bettina Aptheker (b.1944).

UK comedienne Betty Jumel (1901–90); UK actress Betty Warren (1907–90) (original name Babette O'Hogan); US popular writer Betty MacDonald (1908–58); US actress Betty Grable (1918–73); UK actress Betty Driver (b.1920); US actresses Betty Hutton (b.1921), Betty White (b.1924); UK politician Betty Boothroyd (b.1930); UK pop singer Betty Boo (b.1970) (original name Alison Clarkson).

Beulah The name originates from the Bible, in which it is that of a place, not a person, from Hebrew *Be'ūlāh*, 'she who is married', referring to the new Israel: 'Thou shalt no more be termed Forsaken; neither shall thy land any more be termed Desolate: but thou shalt be called Hephzibah, and thy land Beulah: for the Lord delighteth in thee, and thy land shall be married' (Isaiah 62.4). It is found in select English-speaking use from the 17th century, and is still favoured by black Americans. In recent years it has been humorously popularized by the catch-phrase 'Beulah, peel me a grape!', first spoken by Mae West to a maid in the film *I'm No Angel* (1933). It was later brought before the public by the US TV sitcom *Beulah* (1950–53). The title role was that of a pert cook (played by Ethel Waters).

US writer Beulah Dix (1876–1970); US actress Beulah Bondi (1889–1981).

Beverley (m.) From the surname, itself from the English town in East Yorkshire. (Compare the female name BEVERLY.) The male name has enjoyed modest use among English speakers from the 19th century. Its usual diminutive is *Bev*, as for the Welsh rugby player Bev Risman (b.1937).

Canadian-born UK writer, editor Beverley Baxter (1891–1964); UK writer Beverley Nichols (1898–1983); UK playwright Beverley Cross (b.1931).

Beverly (f.) A female adoption of the male name BEVERLEY. The name was widely adopted in the US from the early 20th century, following in the UK from the late 1920s and reaching a peak of popularity in the 1960s. The glamorous associations of Beverly Hills, famous for its film stars, undoubtedly boosted the name in the US, as also did G.B. McCutcheon's romantic novel *Beverly of Graustark* (1904). The variant spelling *Beverley* is also widely found, especially in the UK. The most common diminutive is *Bev*.

US actress Beverly Bayne (1894–1982) (original name Pearl von Name); US children's writer Beverly Cleary (b.1916); US actresses Beverly Tyler (b.1924), Beverly Garland (b.1926), Beverly Michaels (b.1927); US opera singer Beverly Sills (b.1929) (original name Belle Miriam Silverman); Canadian-born US actresses Beverly Adams (b.1945), Beverly D'Angelo (b.1954).

Bevis From the surname (now more commonly Beavis), this name, which is pronounced with a short or long 'e', has been in selective English-speaking use from the 19th century. It was familiar in early times from the 13th- or 14th-century verse romance *Bevis of Hampton*, and in later literature from the country boy who is the central character of Richard Jefferies's novel *Bevis* (1882). (An introduction to the 1930 edition recommends a short 'e'.)

UK writer, authority on antiques Bevis Hillier (b.1940).

Bianca An adoption of the Italian name *Bianca*, 'white', itself a translation (like French BLANCHE) of the Latin name CANDIDA. The name has enjoyed judicious English-speaking adoption from the 16th century, and Shakespeare used it for two characters in plays with an Italian setting: Katharine's sister in

The Taming of the Shrew (*c*.1592) and a Venetian courtesan, Cassio's mistress, in *Othello* (1602–4).

Nicaraguan-born model, charity worker, ex-wife of rock star Mick Jagger, Bianca Jagger (b.1945) (original name Blanca Pérez Mora Macías).

Biddy An independently adopted diminutive of BRIDGET, in select use among English speakers from the 19th century. Biddy Gargery is the second wife of Joe Gargery in Charles Dickens's novel *Great Expectations* (1860–61). The name came to be used for 'Irishwoman' and for 'woman' in general, the latter in a derogatory sense (especially as 'old biddy'). This does not, however, seem to have affected its use, limited as it is.

Bill The best-known diminutive of WILLIAM, adopted independently and in regular use among English speakers from the mid-19th century. In Oliver Goldsmith's novel *The Vicar of Wakefield* (1766) Bill is one of six children of the central character, Dr Charles Primrose, while Charles Dickens's novel *Oliver Twist* (1837–8) has Bill Sikes as a burglar and murderer. Its own usual diminutive, also in independent use, is BILLY.

US tennis player Bill Tilden (1893–1953); Scottish footballer Bill Shankly (1913–81); UK actors Bill Owen (1914–99), Bill Waddington (1916–2000), Bill Dean (1921–2000), Bill Travers (1922–94); US rock-and-roll musician Bill Haley (1926–81); UK actor Bill Maynard (b.1928); UK cartoonist Bill Tidy (b.1933); US actor Bill Bixby (1934–93); US actor, comedian Bill Cosby (b.1937); UK rock musician Bill Wyman (b.1936); UK comedian, conservationist Bill Oddie (b.1941); Scottish actor Bill Paterson (b.1945); US president Bill Clinton (b.1946); UK rugby player Bill Beaumont (b.1952).

Billie (f.) Either an adoption of the male name BILLY (or *Billie*) (a diminutive of WILLIAM), intended as a female equivalent, or a diminutive of *William* itself when this is (now rarely) a female name. It has been selectively taken up by English speakers from the early 20th century, and is sometimes combined with a second short name, such as *Billie Jo* or *Billie Jean*, as for the US country singer Billie Jo Spears (b.1937) or the US tennis player Billie Jean King (b.1943).

US actresses Billie Burke (1885–1970) (original name Mary William Ethelbert Appleton Burke), Billie Dove (1904–97) (original name Lilian Bohny); US blues singer Billie Holiday (1915–59) (original name Eleonora Fagan); UK actress Billie Whitelaw (b.1932); UK pop singer Billie Piper (b.1982).

Billy (m.) An independently adopted diminutive of WILLIAM (and later of BILL), in select use among English speakers from the 19th century and slightly increasing in popularity from the 1980s. It was historically made familiar by the nickname 'King Billy' for William of Orange (1650–1702). In Samuel Richardson's novel *Pamela* (1740–41), Billy is Pamela's son, and a more recent literary instance of the name is found for the central character of Herman Melville's novella *Billy Budd* (written 1891, published 1924). The nickname 'Billy the Kid' was widely known for the youthful US murderer William H. Bonney (1859–81). (The name puns on *billy goat* and *kid*.) The UK writer Keith Waterhouse made his name with his first novel *Billy Liar* (1959), its central character being the compulsive dreamer Billy. The variant spelling *Billie* also exists.

US film cameraman Billy Bitzer (1874–1944) (original first names George William); UK bandleader Billy Cotton (1899–1969); Austro-Hungarian US screenwriter, movie director Billy Wilder (b.1906) (original first name Samuel); US actors Billy Benedict (1906–99); Billy De Wolfe (1907–74); US popular singer Billy Eckstine (1914–93); US evangelist Billy Graham (b.1918); UK entertainer Billy Dainty (1927–86); UK pop singer Billy Fury (1941–83) (original name Ronald Wycherley); Scottish comedian Billy Connolly (b.1942); US comedian Billy Crystal (b.1948); US rock musician Billy Joel (b.1949); US actor Billy Moses (b.1959); Irish-UK actor Billy Geraghty (b.1963); US actor Billy Zane (b.1966).

Bina see **Sabina**.

Binnie An independently adopted diminutive of BERNICE or formed from, or suggested by, the ending of a name such as *Albina* or *Robina*, which was in vogue among English speakers from the mid-19th century but is now rather rare.

UK actresses Binnie Hale (1899–1984) (original name Beatrice Mary Hale-Munro), Binnie Barnes (1905–98) (original first name Gitelle).

Birgit see **Bridget**.

Blake From the surname, and in select use among English speakers from the 19th century or even earlier. It may initially have been adopted as a tribute to the English admiral Robert Blake (1599–1657), who won several engagements against the Dutch and Spanish fleets in the Civil War.

US film producer, director Blake Edwards (b.1922) (original name William Blake McEdwards); UK poet, literary editor Blake Morrison (b.1950) (originally second name, first being Philip; father's second name was Blakemore).

Blanche A direct borrowing of the French name *Blanche*, 'white', itself a translation of the Latin name CANDIDA, familiar as a saint's name. It was already in use as a royal name in France by the 12th century, when it was brought to England by Blanche of Artois (d.1300), wife of Henry I. It occurred only rarely in English-speaking use until the end of the 19th century, when it enjoyed a modest vogue before suffering a decline, so that it is now rare again. Blanche is one of the children of Talbot Twysden in William Makepeace Thackeray's novel *The Adventures of Philip* (1861–2), and the name is that of the central character, Blanche Sartorius, in George Bernard Shaw's play *Widowers' Houses* (1892). Later, Blanche Du Bois is a character in Tennessee Williams's play *A Streetcar Named Desire* (1949), while Agatha Christie's short story 'The Golden Ball', in the identically named collection (1971), has Blanche Amery as the daughter of the Earl of Rustonbury. The Italian equivalent, BIANCA, is still selectively found.

UK tennis player Blanche Bingley (1863–1946); US actresses Blanche Ring (1871–1961), Blanche Friderici (c.1875–1933); Czech-born US actress Blanche Yurka (1887–1974); US actresses Blanche Sweet (1895–1986) (original name Daphne Wayne), Blanche Baker (b.1956).

Blodwen A Welsh name, formed from *blodau*, 'flowers', and *gwen*, 'white', and itself said to be a translation of the French name *Blanchefleur*. It has been in use in Wales from the late 19th century but has not enjoyed much wider adoption. In A.J. Cronin's novel *The Citadel* (1937), Blodwen Page marries bank manager Aneurin Rees, and in Richard Llewellyn's novel *How Green was My Valley* (1939), Blodwen Evans marries Owen Morgan. *Blodwyn* is an occasional variant spelling, familiar in the early 1970s from the name of the UK rock group Blodwyn Pig.

Blondie (f.) An adoption of the nickname for a fair-haired person, occasionally found in the 20th century. The name was popularized by Blondie Bumstead, the central character in Chic Young's strip cartoon *Blondie* (1930–50). More recently, the name was put before the public by the US pop group Blondie (formed 1974), in which it was individually identified with the group's blonde singer Debbie Harry (although she herself never adopted the name).

Blossom A borrowing of the ordinary (but rather poetic) word for a flower, in rather irregular first-name use from the late 19th century.

US nightclub entertainer Blossom Seeley (1891–1974); US cabaret singer Blossom Dearie (b.1926).

Blythe Either an adoption of the surname or, more likely, a borrowing of the word *blithe*, meaning 'happy', 'carefree', with a suggestion of 'bonnie, blithe and gay'. (BONNIE and GAY are, in fact, names similarly created.) The name has enjoyed select favour from the 1940s and may have been initially popularized by Noël Coward's play *Blithe Spirit* (1941), in which the ghost of a husband's first wife returns to tease him and her successor. (The name is not that of a character, and the title is a quotation from Shelley: 'Hail to thee, blithe Spirit!').

US actress Blythe Danner (b.1944); UK actress Blythe Duff (b.1965)

Boaz A biblical name of Hebrew origin, perhaps meaning 'swiftness', and in rare English-speaking use from the 17th century, mainly among Jewish families. In the Bible Boaz is the husband of Ruth.

Bob An independently adopted diminutive of ROBERT, which has been in regular use from the mid-19th century. Captain Robert Singleton, the central character of Daniel Defoe's novel *Captain Singleton* (1720), is usually named as Bob in the book. In Richard Brinsley Sheridan's play *The Rivals* (1775), Bob Acres is the suitor of Lydia Languish. The name's own diminutive is usually BOBBY, which is also in independent use.

UK actor Bob Todd (1922–92); UK comedian, TV presenter Bob Monkhouse (b.1928); South African-born UK TV presenter Bob Holness (b.1928); UK actors Bob Hoskins (b.1942), Bob Peck (1945–99); West Indian reggae musician Bob Marley (1945–81); US athlete Bob Beamon (b.1946); Irish-born rock musician Bob Geldof (b.1954).

Bobbie (f.) An independently adopted diminutive of ROBERTA or (less often) BARBARA, regarded as a female counterpart to the male name BOBBY, and in irregular use in the 20th century.

US writer Bobbie Ann Mason (b.1940); US popular singer Bobbie Gentry (b.1944) (original name Roberta Streeter).

Bobby (m.) An independently adopted diminutive of BOB or of its source name ROBERT. The name has enjoyed modest use from the 18th century, with a slight increase in popularity from the 1980s. In Laurence Sterne's novel *Tristram Shandy* (1759–67), Bobby Shandy is Tristram's elder brother. The 18th-century Irish song 'Bobby Shafto' may have helped to popularize the name. The spelling variant *Bobbie* also exists, as for the UK rugby player Bobbie Goulding (b.1972).

US comedian Bobby Clark (1888–1960); US golfer Bobby Jones (1902–71); South African golfer Bobby Locke (1917–87) (original first names Arthur D'Arcy); US tennis player Bobby Riggs (1918–95); US singer, dancer Bobby Van (1930–80); US country singer Bobby Bare (b.1935); US bandleader Bobby Vinton (b.1935); US actor Bobby Driscoll (1937–68); UK footballers Sir Bobby Charlton (b.1937), Bobby Moore (1941–93); US pop singers Bobby Goldsboro (b.1941), Bobby Vee (b.1943) (original name Robert Velline); US chess player Bobby Fischer (b.1943); US soul singer Bobby Womack (b.1944); UK comedians Bobby Ball (b.1944), Bobby Davro (b.1958); UK footballer Bobby Mimms (b.1963).

Bonita The feminine form of the Spanish word *bonito*, 'pretty', although not itself a Spanish name. English speakers have selectively adopted the name from the 1930s.

US actress Bonita Granville (1923–88).

Bonnie An adoption of the Scottish word meaning 'pretty', 'healthy-looking', in general English-speaking use from the mid-20th century. One fictional character of the name is Bonnie Birdie Twist, the music-hall artiste who marries Herbert Duckie in E.V. Lucas's novel *Over Bemerton's* (1908). But the true literary promoter of the name, especially in the US, was Bonnie Butler, daughter of Rhett Butler and Scarlett O'Hara in Margaret Mitchell's novel *Gone with the Wind* (1936). (The character's original name was Eugenie Victoria but she was nicknamed for her eyes, 'as blue as the bonnie blue flag'.) Later prominence was gained from the US movie *Bonnie and Clyde* (1967), based on the exploits of the real-life Bonnie Parker (see below), daughter of the intended victim of her accomplice, bank robber Clyde Barrow. The spelling *Bonny* also exists.

US bank robber Bonnie Parker (1911–34); US fashion designer Bonnie Cashin (1915–2000); US country singers Bonnie Owens (b.1932),

Bonnie Guitar (b.1934); US children's writer Bonnie Pryor (b.1942); US actress Bonnie Bedelia (b.1946); US blues singer Bonnie Raitt (b.1949); UK pop singer Bonnie Tyler (b.1953); UK actress, dancer, singer Bonnie Langford (b.1964) (original first name Bonita).

Boris A well-known Russian name, popularly derived from the Slavic root *bor-* meaning 'fight', 'struggle', but possibly in origin a Tartar nickname meaning 'small'. It has enjoyed some favour among English speakers from the 19th century and became widely known from Mussorgsky's opera *Boris Godunov* (1868–9, 1871–2).

US horror film actor Boris Karloff (1887–1969) (original name William Pratt); Russian poet Boris Pasternak (1890–1960); Bulgarian opera singer Boris Christoff (1918–93) (famous for title character in *Boris Godunov*); Russian president Boris Yeltsin (b.1931); Russian chess player Boris Spassky (b.1937); German tennis player Boris Becker (b.1967).

Boyd From the (Scottish) surname and long familiar in Scotland, the name was, from the early 20th century, adopted more generally by English speakers. Boyd Tarleton is a character in Margaret Mitchell's novel *Gone with the Wind* (1936).

UK musician Boyd Neel (1901–81) (originally middle name, first being Louis); US bandleader Boyd Bennett (b.1924).

Brad An independently adopted diminutive of BRADLEY, used mainly in the US and Canada from the 1950s.

US actors Brad Davis (1950–91), Brad Dourif (b.1950); US tennis player Brad Gilbert (b.1961); US actor Brad Pitt (b.1964).

Bradley From the surname, and in select use from the 19th century, first in the US, then in the UK, with a growing popularity from the 1980s. In Charles Dickens's novel *Our Mutual Friend* (1864–5) Bradley Headstone is a murderous schoolmaster. The name may have been given a subsequent boost by the US general Omar N. Bradley (1893–1971), commander of the 12th Army Group in the Second World War. The usual diminutive, BRAD, is in independent use.

UK boxer Bradley Stone (1971–94).

Bram see **Abraham**.

Brandon From the surname, but doubtless influenced by BRENDAN. The name has enjoyed modest support from the 19th century. A diminutive *Brandy* exists.

UK-born US actor Brandon Hurst (1866–1947); US actors Brandon Cruz (b.1962), Brandon Call (b.1976).

Branwen see **Bronwen**.

Brenda The name may ultimately come from the Old Norse word *brandr*, 'sword', although it is felt by some to be the feminine equivalent of the Celtic name BRENDAN. It was taken up early in Scotland, and was in popular English-speaking use generally down to the mid-20th century, when it quite sharply declined. Walter Scott has the name for Brenda Troil, one of two sister-heroines in his novel *The Pirate* (1821). Another literary Brenda is the teenage daughter of the adventuress the Hon. Mrs Boldero in William Makepeace Thackeray's novel *The Adventures of Philip* (1861–2). The most common diminutive is *Bren*.

UK landscape architect Brenda Colvin (1897–1981); UK actress Brenda de Banzie (1915–81); US actress Brenda Marshall (1915–92) (original name Ardis Ankerson Gaines); UK actresses Brenda de Banzie (c.1916–81), Brenda Bruce (1918–96); US actress Brenda Joyce (b.1918) (original name Betty Leabo); US socialite Brenda Frazier (c.1920–82); US actress Brenda Vaccaro (b.1939); US pop singer Brenda Lee (b.1944); Irish actress Brenda Fricker (b.1944); US soul singer Brenda Holloway (b.1946); UK actress Brenda Blethyn (b.1946).

Brendan This is the English form of the Irish name *Bréanainn*, based on a Gaelic word meaning 'prince'. The name has found selective favour among English speakers from the early 20th century. It was first made widely known by the 5th-century Irish saint Brendan the Voyager, who set up monasteries in Ireland and Scotland.

UK politician Brendan Bracken (1901–58); US writer Brendan Gill (1914–97); Irish playwright Brendan Behan (1923–64); Irish poet, playwright Brendan Kennelly (b.1936); UK artist Brendan Neiland (b.1941); UK athlete Brendan Foster (b.1948); Irish actor Brendan Gleeson (b.1955).

Brent From the surname, perhaps influenced by BRETT. The name has been in select use from the 1930s, initially in the US. In Sinclair Lewis's novel *Dodsworth* (1929) Brent Dodsworth is the son of the central character, the American automobile manufacturer Samuel (Sam) Dodsworth, while in Margaret Mitchell's novel *Gone with the Wind* (1936) Brent Tarleton is a twin son (the other is Stuart) of Jim Tarleton.

UK TV reporter Brent Sadler (b.1950); US rock musician Brent Mydland (1952–90).

Brett From the surname, as a name in modest vogue from the mid-20th century. Awareness of the name may have been initially created by the US writer Bret Harte (1836–1902) (original name Francis Brett Harte).

US actor Brett Halsey (b.1933); Australian painter Brett Whiteley (1939–92); UK actors Brett Usher (b.1946), Brett Fancy (b.1964).

Brian The name is an English form of an Irish name, which was itself perhaps based on the Celtic word *brigh*, 'strength', 'power' (compare BRIDGET). It became generally popular in the English-speaking world from the 1920s but is now in slow decline. Its first important historic bearer was Brian Boru, 10th-century high king of Ireland. In literature Brian Fitzpatrick is a character in Henry Fielding's novel *Tom Jones* (1749). The variant spelling BRYAN has gained independent use, while the usual diminutive is *Bri*.

UK-born US actor Brian Aherne (1902–86); UK sports commentator

Brian Johnston (1912–94); UK radio presenter Brian Redhead (1929–94); UK cricketer Brian Close (b.1931); UK actors Brian Murphy (b.1933), Brian Glover (1934–97); UK footballer Brian Clough (b.1935); UK actor Brian Blessed (b.1937); UK rock musician Brian Jones (1942–69); UK actors Brian Protheroe (b.1944), Brian Deacon (b.1949), Brian Regan (b.1957), Brian Bovell (b.1959).

Bridget An English form of *Brighid*, the name of an ancient Celtic fire goddess, itself probably derived from the Celtic word *brigh*, 'strength', 'power' (compare BRIAN). The name has been fairly common in the English-speaking world from the 18th century, especially in Celtic lands such as Ireland and Scotland, although its popularity has declined from the 1950s. It is still generally regarded as an essentially Irish name and was first made famous by the 6th-century patroness of Ireland, St Bridget (or St Bride). In Henry Fielding's novel *Tom Jones* (1749), Bridget Allworthy is the woman who turns out to be Tom's mother, and in Tobias Smollett's novel *Sir Launcelot Greaves* (1762), Bridget Maple is the aunt of the seaman Captain Sam Crowe. Variants of the name have been popularized by various bearers: *Brigitte* by the French actress Brigitte Bardot (b.1933); *Britt* by the Swedish actress Britt Ekland (b.1942); *Brigid* by the UK novelist Brigid Brophy (1929–95). Other variants include German *Birgit* and Scandinavian *Brigitta*, while diminutives *Bride*, *Bridie* and *Gita* exist. The diminutive BIDDY is in independent use.

UK opera manager Dame Bridget D'Oyly Carte (1908–85); UK playwright, screenwriter Bridget Boland (1913–88); UK artist Bridget Riley (b.1931); UK golfer Bridget Jackson (b.1936); UK editor Bridget Rowe (b.1950); US actress Bridget Fonda (b.1964).

Briony see **Bryony**.

Bron see **Auberon**.

Bronwen A Welsh name formed from *bron*, 'breast', and *gwen*, 'white', so meaning 'fair-bosomed'. The name is still primarily Welsh in association but has attracted a wider adoption among English speakers from the late 19th century. Bronwen Morgan is the main female character in Richard Llewellyn's novel *How Green was My Valley* (1939). *Branwen* is sometimes regarded as a variant, but it is really a different Welsh name, meaning 'beautiful raven', from *bran*, 'raven', and *gwen*, 'fair'. *Bronwyn* is a genuine variant, as for the Australian politician Bronwyn Bishop (b.1942), while *Bron* is the usual diminutive.

UK columnist Bronwen Maddox (b.1963).

Brook (m.) From the surname, and in select use, especially among black Americans, from the late 19th century. The alternative spelling *Brooke* exists, as for the UK racehorse trainer and jockey Brooke Sanders (b.1949). The diminutive *Brookie* is sometimes found.

US soul singer Brook Benton (1931–88) (original name Benjamin Franklin Peay).

Brooke (f.) A female adoption of the male name BROOK, in sporadic use in the 20th century. A variant *Brook* exists, while the usual diminutive is *Brookie*.

US actresses Brooke Adams (b.1949), Brooke Shields (b.1965).

Bruce An adoption of the Scottish surname, famous from the 14th-century king of Scotland Robert the Bruce. The name was taken up generally in the English-speaking world from the early 20th century, becoming particularly popular in Australia. The usual diminutive is *Brucie*.

US actor Bruce Bennett (b.1909) (original name Herman Brix); UK detective writer, composer Bruce Montgomery (1921–78); UK TV host Bruce Forsyth (b.1927); New Zealand motor-racing driver Bruce McLaren (1937–70); UK actor Bruce Montague (b.1939); UK writer Bruce Chatwin (1940–89); Australian film director Bruce Beresford (b.1940); Chinese-US actor Bruce Lee (1940–73) (original name Lee Yenn Kam); US rock musician Bruce Springsteen (b.1949);

UK fashion designer Bruce Oldfield (b.1950); US actors Bruce Boxleitner (b.1950), Bruce Willis (b.1955).

Bruno The name comes from an Old German name based on *brun*, 'brown', implying that the bearer has brown hair, eyes or skin, or is, perhaps, bearlike. It has found some favour among English speakers from the late 19th century. In literature it occurs as the name of the fairy boy in Lewis Carroll's children's story *Sylvie and Bruno* (1889), while a more recent literary occurrence is in the name of the central character in Iris Murdoch's novel *Bruno's Dream* (1969).

German-born US conductor Bruno Walter (1876–1962); UK actor Bruno Lawrence (1949–95); US actor Bruno Kirby (b.1949).

Bryan An independently adopted variant of BRIAN, in select but declining use among English speakers from the 1920s. In William Makepeace Thackeray's novel *The History of Henry Esmond* (1852), Bryan Hawkshaw is a school friend of Henry. The diminutive *Bry* occurs.

UK writer, broadcaster Bryan Magee (b.1930); UK actors Bryan Mosley (b.1931), Bryan Pringle (b.1939); UK pop singer Bryan Ferry (b.1945).

Bryony From the flower, a wild climbing plant, the name gained some favour from the 1940s. A variant form is *Briony*, as for the UK actress Briony McRoberts (b.1957).

UK ballerina Bryony Brind (b.1960).

Buck From the nickname, itself from *buck* (a male deer or he-goat), that is often applied to a lively young man. The name is most popular in the US, where it has been in select use from the early 20th century. It was popularized by the cartoon strip spaceman hero Buck Rogers (late 1920s to late 1960s), with a subsequent TV series and movie starring him.

US actor Buck Jones (1889–1942) (original name Charles Gebhardt); US baseball player Buck Leonard (1907–97) (original first names Walter Fenner); US jazzman Buck Clayton (1911–91) (original first names Wilbur Dorsey); US country singer Buck Owens (b.1929) (original first names Alvis Edgar).

Bud From the standard nickname for a friend, itself a short form of *buddy*. The name is still mostly found in the US, where it was taken up from the early 20th century. The diminutive BUDDY is in independent use.

US actors Bud Abbott (1895–1974) (original first name William), Bud Cort (b.1950) (original name Walter Edward Cox).

Buddy From the standard nickname for a friend or as a diminutive of BUD. The name is still mostly in US use, where it has been adopted from the early 20th century.

US actor Buddy Ebsen (b.1908) (original first names Christian Rudolf); US boxer Buddy Baer (1915–86) (original first names Jacob Henry); US bandleader Buddy Rich (1917–87) (original first name Bernard); US actor Buddy Hackett (b.1924) (original name Leonard Hacker); US pop singer Buddy Holly (1936–59) (original name Charles Hardin Holley); US country singer Buddy Alan (b.1948).

Bunny (m.) The name is either an independently adopted diminutive of BERNARD or HENRY, or it arose as a nickname (perhaps for *bunny rabbit* associations of some kind). It has seen some sporadic adoption from the early 20th century.

UK tennis player Bunny Austin (1906–2000) (original first names Henry Wilfred); US bandleader Bunny Berigan (1908–42) (original first names Roland Bernard).

Bunny (f.) The name is either an independently adopted diminutive of BERNICE or an adoption of the child's word for a rabbit, sometimes used as a nickname for a woman or a child. Its use as a first name is mostly modern and irregular. Some of its more recent occurrences may have resulted from the UK film *Bunny Lake is Missing* (1964), about the four-year-old daughter of an American woman in London.

US tennis player Bunny Ryan (1892–1979) (original first names Elizabeth Montague).

Bunty Probably an adoption of the nursery word or the lull-aby about *baby bunting*, but perhaps also popularly associated with BUNNY. The name was in select use among English speakers in the early 20th century and was given a boost by the London comedy *Bunty Pulls the Strings* (1911). More recently, the name has been kept before the public by *Bunty*, a weekly comic for young girls first published in 1958.

UK golfer Bunty Stephens (1924–78) (original first name Frances); UK TV presenter Bunty James (b.1933).

Burt The name is either a variant spelling of BERT or an independently adopted diminutive of BURTON. It has been in select use from the 19th century.

US actor Burt Lancaster (1913–94) (original name Burton Stephen Lancaster); US popular composer Burt Bacharach (b.1929) (father was journalist, writer Bert Bacharach); UK actor Burt Kwouk (b.1930); US actor Burt Reynolds (b.1936).

Burton From the surname and in select use from the mid-19th century, the name may have been initially suggested by the English explorer Sir Richard Burton (1821–90). Theodore Dreiser's novel *An American Tragedy* (1925) has a police officer named Burton Burleigh. US actor Burt Lancaster (1913–94) had the original first name Burton. The normal diminutive is BURT, which is in independent use.

Buster From the nickname for a burly or strong person, and perhaps originally for a fat baby or young boy, one 'busting' out of his clothes. The name is mainly found in the US, where it has been noted from the 19th century.

US actor Buster Keaton (1895–1966) (full first names Joseph Francis); US bandleader Buster Smith (b.1904) (original first name Henry); US swimmer, actor Buster Crabbe (1908–83) (original first name Clarence); US blues singer Buster Brown (1914–76).

Butch From the nickname, usually given to a stocky or tough person (and itself in origin from the word *butcher*), the name is still mainly found in the US, where it has been selectively adopted from the 19th century. It gained wide notoriety from the US outlaw Butch Cassidy (1866–1937) (original name Robert Leroy Parker), who had actually been a butcher. His name was further popularized by the film about him, *Butch Cassidy and the Sundance Kid* (1969).

US country singer Butch Hancock (b.1945) (original first name George); US athlete Butch Reynolds (b.1964) (original first name Harry).

Byron From the surname, famous as that of the poet Lord Byron (1784–1824), and first adopted in the years following his death. The name's resemblance to BRIAN (or BRYAN) may have helped it, and it has won a small increase in popularity from the 1980s. In William Faulkner's novel *The Town* (1957), Byron Snopes is a bank clerk and embezzler.

US film director Byron Haskin (1899–1984); US actor Byron Foulger (1900–70); US golfer Byron Nelson (b.1912); US comedian Byron Allen (b.1961).

C

Cadwalader A Welsh name, formed from *cad*, 'battle', and *gwaladr*, 'disposer', implying someone who deploys troops for battle. The name, which has remained almost exclusively in Welsh use, was originally a royal name, for the sons of kings and princes. St Cadwalader was a 7th-century chieftain who was killed when holding a fort against the invading Saxons. The variant spelling *Cadwallader* exists, as for Cadwallader Crabtree, a deaf elderly man in Tobias Smollett's novel *Peregrine Pickle* (1751).

Caesar An adoption of the Roman imperial family name, which may itself derive from Latin *caesaries*, 'head of hair' (although this would not apply to Julius Caesar, who was bald). The name has been in very select use among English speakers from the 18th century, and has enjoyed some favour among black Americans. Caesar is a black cab-driver in O. Henry's short story 'A Municipal Report' in *Strictly Business* (1910). The variant spelling *Cesar* occurs, as for the US actor Cesar Romero (1907–94).

Caitlín see **Catherine, Kathleen**.

Caleb A biblical name, from Hebrew *Kālēb*, 'dog', perhaps implying devotion to God. The name was taken up by Puritans in the 16th century and has enjoyed selective English-speaking use since then, mainly in the US, although it is now much rarer. In the Bible Caleb is one of the scouts sent by Moses to reconnoitre the Promised Land. The name is that of the central character and narrator in William Godwin's thriller *Caleb Williams* (1794), and Caleb Smith is a miser in Harriet

Beecher Stowe's novel *Oldtown Folks* (1869). In W.H. Hudson's book *A Shepherd's Life* (1910) the central character is the Wiltshire shepherd, Caleb Bawcombe.

Calum This Scottish name is a Gaelic form of the Late Latin name *Columba*, meaning 'dove', and as such it is directly related to MALCOLM. Both this form and its variant, *Callum*, as for the Scottish artist Callum Innes (b.1962), suddenly became very popular in the 1990s.

Calvin From the French surname, made famous by the French Protestant theologian Jean Calvin (1509–1564). The name was taken up by English speakers from the 16th century, especially in the US, and it was adopted as a tribute to the reformer himself. The usual diminutive is *Cal*, as for the US baseball player Cal Ripken (b.1960).

US president Calvin Coolidge (1872–1933); West Indian actor Calvin Lockhart (b.1934); US columnist Calvin Trillin (b.1935); US fashion designer Calvin Klein (b.1942).

Cameron From the Scottish clan name and surname. The name has found selective use, mainly among Scots, from the early 20th century, but has been more widely adopted from the 1990s.

US actor Cameron Mitchell (1894–1994); UK theatrical producer Cameron Mackintosh (b.1946).

Camilla The name represents the feminine form of the Roman clan name *Camillus*, perhaps meaning 'attendant at a sacrifice'. It has been in English-speaking use from the 16th century and is still in modest vogue today. In Virgil's *Aeneid* (30–19BC) Camilla is the virgin queen of the Volscians. In English literature the name is that of the woman loved by Philautus in John Lyly's prose romance *Euphues and his England* (1580). It was bright, attractive Camilla Tyrold, the central character of Fanny Burney's novel *Camilla* (1796), who first made the name popular in recent times. The main variant of the name is the French spelling *Camille*, sometimes used for the heroine of Alexandre Dumas's novel *La Dame aux camélias* (1852) in English translations, as if to reflect the flower name, although in the original she is actually Marguerite. This form of the name was made familiar by the Italian-US feminist Camille Paglia (b.1947). Diminutives include *Cam*, *Cammie*, MILLIE and MILLY, the last two in independent use. The name has acquired an aura of aristocratic sophistication.

Swedish-born US actress Camilla Sparv (b.1943); UK socialite Camilla Parker Bowles (b.1946); UK daughter of Earl of Westmorland, Lady Camilla Hipwood (b.1957).

Candace Despite modern associations with words such as *candid* and *candy*, the origin and meaning of the name remain uncertain. In the Roman era BC the name was borne by various queens of Ethiopia, one of whom is mentioned in the Bible (Acts 8.27). (The name was formerly pronounced in three syllables, 'Can-day-see', but now usually in two, 'Candiss'.) It was selectively adopted in the UK from the early 20th century, but has always gained greater favour in the US. In William Faulkner's novel *The Sound and the Fury* (1929) Candace (Caddy) Compson is the central character. The usual spelling variant is *Candice*, as for the US actress Candice Bergen (b.1946). Diminutives are *Caddy* or CANDY, the latter in independent use.

Candida An adoption of the Latin name *Candida*, the feminine form of *Candidus*, 'white', popular among early Christians for the colour's association with purity. It is found in irregular English-speaking use from medieval times, with a slight increase in popularity in the 20th century. George Bernard Shaw used the name for Candida (Candy) Morell, the central character in his play *Candida* (1894). The best-known variants are *Candie* or CANDY, the latter in independent use.

UK journalist Candida Crewe (b.1964).

Candy The name is either an independent adoption of the diminutive form of CANDACE or CANDIDA or else a direct adoption of the word *candy*, with its connotations of sweetness. The name, which has been chiefly favoured in modern times in the US, was to some extent popularized by the nymphet central character of Terry Southern and Mason Hoffenberg's comic pornographic novel *Candy* (1958). (She was apparently intended to be a female equivalent of Voltaire's hero *Candide*.) The main variant is *Candi*, as for the US soul singer Candi Staton (b.*c*.1950).

US actress Candy Clark (b.1947), Dutch-born US jazz saxophonist Candy Dulfer (b.1970).

Cara The name derives from Latin (or Italian) *cara*, 'dear', or Irish *cara*, 'friend', 'dear one', and it has been in selective English-speaking use from the early 20th century, with a slight increase in popularity in the 1970s. In Evelyn Waugh's novel *Brideshead Revisited* (1945), Cara is the mistress of Lord Marchmain. CARRIE can be a diminutive or an independent name.

US comedienne Cara Williams (b.1925) (original name Bernice Kamiat).

Caradoc The name is a variant spelling of the Welsh name *Caradog*, itself based on the Welsh element *car-*, 'love', and has been in Welsh use from medieval times. A famous historical bearer of the name was the 1st-century British chieftain still sometimes known as *Caractacus* (from the Latin version of the name), who led an unsuccessful rebellion against the Romans.

Welsh writer, journalist Caradoc Evans (*c*.1875–1945).

Carey (m.) An independently adopted variant of CARY, in occasional use among English speakers from the 19th century. From the 1950s the name is more commonly found in female use.

UK composer, children's writer Carey Blyton (b.1932).

Carey (f.) A female adoption of the male name CAREY, presumably influenced by CARRIE or KERRY, and more common than the male name from the 1950s.

UK businesswoman Carey Labovitch (b.1960).

Carl This name is usually a variant spelling of the German name *Karl* (English CHARLES), although it could also be an independently adopted diminutive of CARLTON or its variant CARLETON. It was taken up by English speakers from the mid-19th century and enjoyed a modest vogue in the 1970s and 1980s.

US composer Carl Ruggles (1876–1971); US writer of Swedish parentage Carl Sandburg (1878–1967); US screenwriter, film producer Carl Foreman (1914–84); US actor Carl Reiner (b.1922); US rockabilly musician Carl Perkins (1932–98); US astronomer Carl Sagan (1934–96); US composer, conductor Carl Davis (b.1936); US actor Carl Weathers (b.1948); US athlete Carl Lewis (b.1961) (original first names Frederick Carlton); UK rower Carl Smith (b.1961); UK rugby player Carl Gibson (b.1963); UK table tennis player Carl Prean (b.1967).

Carla A feminine form of CARL, in select English-speaking use in both the UK and US from the 1940s, with an increased vogue in the 1980s. Carla Lemarchant is a murder victim's daughter in Agatha Christie's novel *Five Little Pigs* (1943) (US title *Murder in Retrospect*). The variant spelling *Karla* is sometimes found, as for the US pop singer Karla Bonoff (b.1952). The main diminutive is CARLY, which is in independent use.

Canadian actress Carla Lehmann (1917–90); UK TV screenwriter Carla Lane (b.1935); US jazz musician Carla Bley (b.1938).

Carlene A feminine form of CARL, influenced by a name ending in *-lene* such as ARLENE, CHARLENE or DARLENE. The variant spelling *Carleen* exists, as for the US-born UK soul singer Carleen Anderson (b.1957).

US popular singer, songwriter Carlene Carter (b.1955) (father was Carl).

Carleton An independently adopted variant of CARLTON, taken up by English speakers in the late 19th century and usually the preferred form of the name in the UK. The diminutive CARL exists in its own right for both names.

UK radio actor Carleton Hobbs (1898–1978); US actor Carleton Carpenter (b.1926).

Carlie, **Carley** see **Carly**.

Carlton From the surname, with its aristocratic associations, as for London's Carlton Club, Carlton House and Carlton House Terrace. The name was taken up by English speakers from the end of the 19th century and has since been favoured by black Americans. The variant CARLETON exists in its own right, as does the diminutive CARL.

Carly Either an independently adopted diminutive of CARLA or a feminine form of CARL, found mainly in the US from the 1940s, but coming into fashion in the UK in the 1980s. Variant spellings *Carley* and *Carlie* exist.

US popular singer Carly Simon (b.1945).

Carmel The name was adopted from that of Mount Carmel, Israel, familiar from the Bible as a sacred place (the name itself means 'vineyard') and as the 12th-century founding site of the monastic community on which the order of Carmelite nuns was later based. The name has been chiefly in Roman Catholic English-speaking use from the late 19th century. Diminutives are mostly suffixed forms of the name such as *Carmelina*, *Carmelita* and *Carmencita*.

US fashion writer Carmel Snow (1890–1961); US actress Carmel Myers (1899–1980); UK actress Carmel McSharry (b.c.1920).

Carmen A name that is properly a Spanish form of CARMEL but that is popularly derived from Latin *carmen*, 'song'. It has enjoyed select use among English speakers from the 19th century and was popularized by the heroine of Prosper Mérimée's tale of Spanish gypsy life and love, *Carmen* (1845), and even more by Bizet's opera *Carmen* (1873–4), which was based on this. More recently the name has been made known by the popular musical *Carmen Jones* (1943), in turn based on Bizet's work. Carmen Sylva was the pen name of the writer Elizabeth, Queen of Romania (1843–1916), who chose it to represent her love of singing.

UK art designer Carmen Dillon (1908–2000); Portuguese actress, singer, Carmen Miranda (1909–55) (original name Maria do Carmo Miranda da Cunha); US jazz singer Carmen McRae (1922–94); Canadian actress Carmen Silvera (b.1938); Australian-born UK publisher Carmen Callil (b.1938); Australian politician Carmen Lawrence (b.1948); UK actress Carmen Du Sautoy (b.1952); UK TV presenter Carmen Pryce (b.1961).

Carol (m.) An English form of the Latin name *Carolus* (English CHARLES), in rare English-speaking use from the 19th century, when it declined with the increasing popularity of the female name CAROL. The name may have been regarded as suitable for a boy born at or near Christmas. The spelling variant CARROLL has found some independent adoption, while the Slavic form *Karel* is familiar from the Czech-born UK film director Karel Reisz (b.1926).

UK film director Sir Carol Reed (30 December 1906–76); UK politician Carol Mather (b.3 January 1919).

Carol (f.) The name arose as an independently adopted variant of CAROLINE (or *Carolina*), although it is now often associated with Christmas carols. It became popular from the late 19th century, reaching a popularity peak in the 1950s, since when it has sharply declined. The central character of Sinclair Lewis's novel *Main Street* (1920) is Carol Milford. Variants in independent use include CAROLA, CAROLE, CARROLL and CARYL.

US actresses Carol Dempster (1901–91), Carol Channing (b.1921); US opera producer Carol Fox (1926–81); UK actresses Carol Marsh (b.1926) (original name Norma Simpson), Carol White (1941–91); US actress Carol Lynley (b.1942); UK newsreader Carol Barnes (b.1944); UK actresses Carol Drinkwater (b.1948), Carol Hawkins (b.1949), Carol Royle (b.1954); UK writer Carol Ann Duffy (b.1955).

Carola A feminine equivalent of the male name CAROL, in origin the feminine form of the Latin name *Carolus*. It has enjoyed sporadic adoption among English speakers since at least the 19th century.

UK writer Carola Oman (1897–1978) (father was Charles).

Carole A French form of the female name CAROL, initially adopted to distinguish the male CAROL from this name. Its heyday was in the 1950s and (especially) the 1960s, since when it has waned considerably.

US actress Carole Lombard (1908–42) (original name Jane Peters); UK artist Carole Hodgson (b.1940); US singer Carole King (b.1942); UK radio producer, broadcaster Carole Stone (b.1942).

Caroline The name originated from the Italian feminine form (*Carolina*) of *Carlo* (English CHARLES). It spread from Italy to Germany (as *Karoline*) and was then introduced to England by George II's queen, Caroline of Ansbach (1683–1737). Lady Caroline Lamb (1785–1828) was a novelist and the mistress of the poet Byron. From then on it was generally popular among English speakers, with an increase in vogue in the 1960s and 1970s after many years out of favour. It is now undergoing a gradual decline. In literature Caroline Grandison is the sister of the central character in Samuel Richardson's novel *Sir Charles Grandison* (1753–4) (her name matches his), while Caroline Helstone is a character in Charlotte Brontë's novel *Shirley* (1849), and Lady Caroline Pontefract appears in Oscar Wilde's play *A Woman of No Importance* (1893). A common variant is CAROLYN, which is in independent use. Diminutives adopted independently are CARRIE and LYNN.

UK actress Caroline Blakiston (b.1933); UK writer Caroline Moorehead (b.1944); UK equestrienne Caroline Bradley (1946–83); daughter of US president John F. Kennedy, Caroline Kennedy (b.1957); Princess Caroline of Monaco (b.1957); UK actresses Caroline Langrishe (b.1958), Caroline Goodall (b.1959), Caroline Milmoe (b.1963).

Carolyn An independently adopted spelling of CAROLINE, taken up in the US in the 19th century and then spreading to the UK, where it reached its high point in the 1960s. A variant is *Carolyne*.

US writer Carolyn Wells (1869–1942); US lyricist Carolyn Leigh (1926–83); US actress Carolyn Jones (1929–83); UK actress Carolyn Pickles (b.1952); UK hockey player Carolyn Reid (b.1972).

Caron A Welsh name, probably based on *caru*, 'to love', but now felt to be related to CAROL or KAREN. It has enjoyed general modest adoption among English speakers only from the 1950s.

UK TV presenter Caron Keating (b.1963).

Carrie An independently adopted diminutive of CAROLINE that has been in use among English speakers, especially in the US, from the 19th century, with a surge in American popularity in the 1970s. The name is famous in literature from Carrie Meeber, the central character of Theodore Dreiser's novel *Sister Carrie* (1907). More recently it has been popularized by Carrie White, the adolescent girl with telekinetic powers in Stephen King's horror novel *Carrie* (1974). Variants are *Carri* and *Carry*, the latter familiar from the US temperance reformer Carry Nation (1846–1911). The name often combines with another, such as *Carrie-Ann*.

US suffragist Carrie Catt (1859–1947); UK opera singer Carrie Tubb (1876–1976) (original first name Caroline); US actresses Carrie Nye (b.1937), Carrie Snodgress (b.1945), Carrie Fisher (b.1956); UK magazine editor Carrie McArdle (b.1957); UK actress Carrie Ellis (b.1960) (original first name Carolyn); US actress Carrie Hamilton (b.1963); US tennis player Carrie Cunningham (b.1972).

Carroll (m.) An independently adopted variant of CAROL, its spelling distinguishing it from the female name CAROL. The name has found select English-speaking use, mainly in the US, from the 19th century.

US bandleader Carroll Gibbons (1903–54); Canadian-born UK radio talent spotter Carroll Levis (c.1915–68); US actor Carroll O'Connor (1924–2001).

Carroll (f.) An independently adopted variant form of CAROL, perhaps partly suggested by the male name CARROLL.

US actress Carroll Baker (b.1931).

Carry see **Carrie**.

Cary (m.) From the surname, and in select use from the 19th century, with a slight popularity peak in the 1940s and 1950s. The variant spelling CAREY occurs in independent use.

UK-born US actor Cary Grant (1904–86) (original name Alexander Archibald Leach); US golfer Cary Middlecoff (b.1921); UK actor Cary Elwes (b.1962).

Caryl (f.) An independently adopted variant of CAROL, with its spelling perhaps influenced by a name such as BERYL. It has found some favour from the 19th century.

UK playwrights Caryl Brahms (1901–82), Caryl Churchill (b.1938).

Casey Either from the Irish surname or a direct adoption of the name of the US folk hero, the railroad engineer Casey Jones (1863–1900) (original first names John Luther), who took his name from Cayce, Kentucky, near his place of birth. A variant spelling is *Kasey*.

US baseball player Casey Stengel (1890–1975) (original first names Charles Dillon); US screenwriter Casey Robinson (1903–79); US radio DJ Casey Kasem (b.1933) (original first names Kemal Amin); US actor Casey Siemaszko (b.1961) (original first name Kazimierz).

Caspar The name comes from the Dutch version of JASPER, and it has been in irregular English-speaking use, especially in the US, from the 19th century. It is the traditional name of one of the Magi, the Three Wise Men (although they are not named in the Bible), who brought gifts to the infant Jesus. Variant spellings *Casper*, *Kaspar* and *Kasper* occur, the first of these as for Casper Goodwood, suitor of the central character, Isabel Archer, in Henry James's novel *The Portrait of a Lady* (1881).

UK naval commander Sir Caspar John (1903–84); US statesman Caspar Weinberger (b.1917).

Cass An independently adopted diminutive of CASSANDRA, now generally superseded by CASSIE.

US folk-rock musician Cass Elliot (1943–74).

Cassandra An adoption of the Greek name, itself probably related to ALEXANDER and meaning 'ensnaring men'. It has been in use among English speakers from the 17th century. The Cassandra of Greek mythology is famous as the prophetic daughter of Priam and Hecuba. Shakespeare's *Troilus and Cressida* (1602) has the prophetess under her familiar name, while in more recent literature Cassandra Wilkins is an absurd aesthete in John Dos Passos's novel *Manhattan Transfer* (1925). In the family of the English novelist Jane Austen (1775–1817), Cassandra was the name of her mother, her elder sister, Cassandra Austen (1772–1845), and her novelist cousins, Cassandra Cooke (1744–1826) and Cassandra Hawke (1746–1813). Common diminutive variants in independent use are CASS, CASSIE and SANDRA.

US actress Cassandra Harris (b.1950); US jazz singer Cassandra Wilson (b.1955).

Cassie An independently adopted diminutive of CASSANDRA, since the 1960s generally superseding CASS. A variant spelling is *Cassy*.

UK squash player Cassie Jackman (b.1972).

Cassius From the Roman clan name, of uncertain derivation, but possibly connected with Latin *cassus*, 'empty'. The name, which has been in limited use among English speakers from the 19th century, is historically familiar from the Roman general Cassius who led the conspiracy against Julius Caesar in 44BC, and who appears in Shakespeare's *Julius Caesar* (1599). Usual diminutives are *Cass* and *Cassie*.

US boxer Cassius Clay (b.1942) (from 1964, Muhammad Ali).

Cat Usually from the name of the animal, as a nickname for a spirited person or someone with a fiery temper. Most English-speaking use of the name is not earlier than the 20th century, and in the US it is specially favoured by jazz and popular musicians (who are 'hep-cats').

US jazz trumpeter Cat Anderson (1916–81) (original first name William; nicknamed Cat when he beat up a bully); UK pop musician Cat Stevens (b.1947) (original name Steven Georgiou; from 1978, Yusef Islam).

Catherine The ultimate source of the enduringly popular name is in the Greek name *Aikaterina*, of uncertain meaning. It was at first linked with *aikia*, 'torture', referring to St Catherine of Alexandria, the 4th-century saint (of doubtful authenticity) who was tortured on a spiked wheel (a 'Catherine wheel'), but it was later associated with Greek *katharos*, 'pure'. The spelling of this partly accounts for early versions of the name as KATHARINE, now in independent use. The name has been in English-speaking use from medieval times, and has been borne by many famous people, including three of Henry VIII's six wives (Catherine of Aragon, Catherine Howard and Catherine Parr). In literature the name is famous from Catherine Earnshaw, the central character in Emily Brontë's novel *Wuthering Heights* (1847). There are a large number of variants, mainly alternating the initial *K* with *C*, and the middle vowel *e* with *a*, giving *Catharine*, KATHARINE, KATHERINE, KATHRYN and the like, all now adopted in their own right. Also quite common are the 'continental' variants, such as *Katarina* and *Catarina*, which themselves gave KATRINA and *Catrina*. The Scottish variant CATRIONA is also in independent use, and the Irish form *Caitlín* gave KATHLEEN. The Danish form of the name, KAREN, has found great favour, as have the diminutives KATE, KATIE, KATY, KAY and KITTY. Further diminutives are CATHY and KATHY.

UK romantic novelist Catherine Cookson (1906–98) (mother was Catherine); US actress Catherine Oxenberg (b.1962); UK actress Catherine Zeta-Jones (b.1969).

Cathleen see **Kathleen**.

Cathryn see **Kathryn**.

Cathy An independently adopted diminutive of CATHERINE, in some favour among English speakers from the 1950s, although never as common as its variant spelling, KATHY. The name is familiar from Catherine Earnshaw, the central character of Emily Brontë's novel *Wuthering Heights* (1847), who is referred to as both Catherine and Cathy in the book (the latter chiefly in conversation).

US actress Cathy O'Donnell (1923–70) (original name Ann Steely); UK actress Cathy Tyson (b.1966); UK pop singer Cathy Dennis (b.1969); Australian athlete Cathy Freeman (b.1973).

Catrina see **Catherine**, **Catriona**.

Catriona A Scottish variant of CATHERINE in independent use and usually pronounced 'Catreena'. The name is still favoured mainly by Scots but has also been in general if select use among English speakers from the 19th century. It was made famous by Robert Louis Stevenson's novel *Catriona* (1893), the sequel to *Kidnapped* (1886), in which it is that of the central character, Catriona Drummond, who marries David Balfour. The variant *Catrina* is sometimes found.

UK actress Catriona MacColl (b.1954).

Cecil A name that was originally the English form of the Roman clan name *Caecilius*, from the nickname *Caecus*, 'blind', but that later was adopted from the surname *Cecil*, famous as that of a 16th-century noble English family. The name has been increasingly taken up by English speakers from the mid-19th century, reaching a peak in its popularity at the turn of the 20th century, since when it has sharply declined. Cecil Graham is a character in Oscar Wilde's play *Lady Windermere's Fan* (1892).

UK statesman, founder of Rhodesia, Cecil Rhodes (1853–1902); US film producer, director Cecil B. De Mille (1881–1959); UK actors Cecil Parker (1897–1971), Cecil Trouncer (1898–1953); UK photographer Sir Cecil Beaton (1904–80); Irish-born UK poet Cecil Day-Lewis (1904–72); South African-born viola player Cecil Aronowitz (1916–78).

Cecilia An adoption of the Latin name *Caecilia*, the feminine form of *Caecilius*, which gave CECIL. The name has been in English-speaking use from medieval times but was particularly popular from the late 19th century to the 1920s, when it declined. It was originally associated with the 2nd-century St Cecilia. In literature it is found for Cecilia Beverley, the central character of Fanny Burney's novel *Cecilia* (1782), and for Cecilia Bobster, a character in Charles Dickens's novel *Nicholas Nickleby* (1838–9). Its most familiar variant is CECILY, now in independent use. French *Cecile* also exists, and also the shortened form *Cecil*, as for the US actress Cecil Cunningham (1888–1959) and UK golfer Cecil Leitch (1891–1977). The diminutive CISSIE, sometimes spelled *Cissy* or *Sissy*, is in independent use.

UK actress Cecilia Loftus (1876–1943); Italian opera singer Cecilia Bartoli (b.1966)

Cecily An English variant of the Latin-style CECILIA, adopted from the early 19th century and reaching its (modest) peak of popularity in the 1920s. A well-known literary bearer of the name is Cecily Cardew, Jack Worthing's ward in Oscar Wilde's play *The Importance of Being Earnest* (1895). The most common variant is CICELY, adopted independently. The diminutive CISSIE, sometimes spelled *Cissy* or *Sissy*, is also in independent use.

Cedric A variant of *Cerdic*, the name of the traditional founder of Wessex, as introduced (perhaps as a miscopying) by Walter Scott for the character Cedric of Rotherwood in his novel *Ivanhoe* (1819). The name has been in select English-speaking use from the mid-19th century but is now rare. It is that of the central character, Lord Cedric Errol Fauntleroy, in Frances Hodgson Burnett's novel *Little Lord Fauntleroy* (1886).

UK actor Sir Cedric Hardwicke (1893–1964); UK writer Cedric Belfrage (1904–90); UK composer Cedric Thorpe Davie (1913–83).

Celeste An English female adoption of the French male name *Céleste*, itself from the Latin name *Caelestis*, 'heavenly'. It has won some favour among English speakers in the 20th century.

US actress Celeste Holm (b.1919); US writer Celeste De Blasis (b.1946).

Celia An adoption of the Latin name *Caelia*, the feminine form of the Roman clan name *Caelius*, itself said to derive from *caelum*, 'heaven'. The name was rare among English speakers until the 19th century (although it was borne by the English traveller Celia Fiennes (1662–1741)), when its popularity may have been influenced by CECILIA. It enjoyed a mild boom in the 1950s but is now much less common. Literary characters of the name include Duke Frederick's daughter who marries Oliver in Shakespeare's *As You Like It* (1599); Corvino's wife in Ben Jonson's comedy *Volpone* (1605–6); the captive girl loved by Prince Demetrius and his father Antigonus in Beaumont and Fletcher's comedy *The Humorous Lieutenant* (*c*.1619); and a young girl in William Whitehead's comedy *The School for Lovers* (1762).

UK actress Dame Celia Johnson (1908–82); UK-born Canadian ballerina Celia Franca (b.1921); UK actress Celia Bannerman (b.1944); UK writer Celia Brayfield (b.1945); UK actress Celia Imrie (b.1952).

Ceri This name is either a short form of the Welsh name CERIDWEN or has evolved as a term of affection based on Welsh *caru*, 'to love'. It was originally solely in Welsh use, from the 1940s, but it is now sometimes found more generally among English speakers. In spoken use (pronounced 'Kerry') it can be easily confused with the more familiar KERRY.

Ceridwen A Welsh name, formed from *cerdd*, 'poetry', and *gwen*, 'white', 'fair' (as for GWEN), so meaning 'poetic goddess', or more loosely, 'beautiful enough to be written about in a poem'. It is today found almost exclusively in Wales. In Celtic mythology the name is that of the Celtic goddess of poetical inspiration and the mother of the 6th-century bard (poet) Taliesin. The diminutive, CERI, is an independent name.

Cesar see **Caesar**.

Chad A modern English version of the Old English name *Ceadda*, perhaps based on Celtic *cad*, 'battle' (compare CADWALADER). It enjoyed only modest use among English speakers until the 1970s, when it gained some popularity. Its famous historic bearer was the 7th-century St Chad, Archbishop of York. Recent adoption of the name may have been inhibited (at least in the UK) by the 1940s craze of 'Mr Chad', as a term for a stock graffito of a human head appearing over a wall with the caption 'Wot no ... ?' (for example, 'Wot no beer?'), in reference to shortages of consumer goods after the Second World War.

UK clergyman, founder of Samaritans, Rev. Chad Varah (b.1911); US actor Chad Everett (b.1937) (original name Raymond Cramton).

Chaim The name is a Jewish variant of *Hyam*, itself from the Hebrew word *hayyim*, 'life'. In the English-speaking world it is chiefly found in the US.

Israeli politician Chaim Herzog (1918–97); US novelist Chaim Potok (b.1929); Polish-born UK writer Chaim Bermant (b.1929).

Chantal A French name, from the Old Provençal word *cantal*, 'stone', 'rock', but doubtless associated by English (and even French) speakers with *chant*, 'song', and so equated to CARMEN. It has enjoyed modest English-speaking favour in the 20th century and has been taken up by some black Americans. The original inspiration for the name probably lay with the French saint Jeanne de Chantal (1572–1641), who, with St François de Sales (1567–1622), founded the religious Order of the Visitation.

Charity The name represents the word for the Christian virtue, like the other members of its trio, FAITH and HOPE. It came into vogue after the Reformation in the 17th century, when triplets were sometimes given these three names. In John Bunyan's allegory *The Pilgrim's Progress* (1678, 1684) Charity, Mercy, Piety and Prudence are characters personifying these virtues. In later literature Charity Pecksniff and her sister Mercy are Mr Pecksniff's daughters in Charles Dickens's novel *Martin Chuzzlewit* (1843–4). A fairly common diminutive is CHERRY, which is in independent use.

Charlene A feminine form of CHARLES, taken up by English speakers from the mid-20th century and particularly in vogue in the 1980s. The name has been popularly associated with the character Charlene Mitchell played by Kylie Minogue in the Australian TV soap *Neighbours* (from 1988). Variants and diminutives include *Charleen*, *Charline*, *Charley*, *Charlie* and *Charly*, this last having formerly fashionable 'androgynous' associations.

US actress Charlene Holt (b.1939); US pop singer Charlene (b.c.1955) (original name Charlene Duncan); US actresses Charlene Tilton (b.1958), Charlene McCall (b.c.1958); UK actress Charlene Brooks (b.1981).

Charles A name that ultimately comes from the Old German word *karl*, 'man', implying bravery and freedom of action. It has been in general use among English speakers from medieval times but was especially popular from the 17th century until the early 20th century, when it began a slow decline, only to experience a modest revival from the 1980s. The name's famous historic bearer was the 9th-century Frankish leader and Holy Roman Emperor, Charlemagne (Latin *Carolus Magnus*, Charles the Great). It was widely adopted as a royal name by the kings of many European countries, including England. Britain's Prince Charles (b.1948), if he succeeds to the throne as expected, will be King Charles III. In literature the name is familiar from the central character of Samuel Richardson's novel *Sir Charles Grandison* (1753–4), a 'faultily faultless' English aristocrat. It is also borne by Dr Charles Primrose, the central character of Oliver Goldsmith's novel *The Vicar of Wakefield* (1766) and by Charles Surface, nephew of Sir Oliver Surface in Richard Brinsley Sheridan's play *The School for Scandal* (1777). The stock diminutive in independent use is CHARLIE, with *Chas* also now widely found. The diminutives CHICK and CHUCK have been adopted in their own right in the US.

UK novelist Charles Dickens (1812–70); US aviator Charles Lindbergh (1902–74); UK actors Charles Kay (b.1930), Charles Dance (b.1946).

Charley (f.) see **Charlene**, **Charlotte**.

Charlie (m.) An independently adopted diminutive of CHARLES, in use among English speakers from the 19th century and found mostly among actors, entertainers, sportsmen and the like. A variant spelling is *Charley*, as for the US country musician Charley Pride (b.1938).

UK-born US actor Charlie Chaplin (1889–1977); UK jockey Charlie

Elliott (1904–79); US bandleader Charlie Spivak (1905–82); UK jockey Charlie Smirke (1906–93); UK radio comedian Charlie Chester (1914–97) (original name Cecil Manser); UK comedian Charlie Drake (b.1925); UK boxer Charlie Magri (b.1956); US actor Charlie Korsmo (b.1978).

Charlie (f.) see **Charlene**, **Charlotte**.

Charline see **Charlene**.

Charlotte A French form of the Italian name *Carlotta*, itself a feminine form of *Carlo* (English CHARLES). The name has been in English-speaking use from the 17th century and has enjoyed increasing popularity from the 1970s. An early literary character of the name is Charlotte Montague in Henry Richardson's novel *Clarissa* (1748). The name was notably popularized by George III's queen, Charlotte Sophia (1744–1818), and to a lesser extent by his granddaughter, Princess Charlotte (1796–1817). The many variants include *Charley*, *Charlie*, *Charly*, the independently adopted LOTTA, *Lottie*, *Lotty*, *Tottie* and *Totty*, the fifth of these as for the UK tennis player Lottie Dod (1871–1960).

UK novelists Charlotte Brontë (1816–55), Charlotte M. Yonge (1823–1901); UK writer Charlotte Mew (1869–1928); US actresses Charlotte Greenwood (1890–1978), Charlotte Austin (b.1933); UK actresses Charlotte Rampling (b.1946), Charlotte Coleman (1968–2001); US-French actress Charlotte Gainsbourg (b.1971).

Charlton From the surname, and in select use from the late 19th century.

US actor Charlton Heston (b.1924) (original name John Charlton Carter).

Charly see **Charlene**, **Charlotte**.

Charmaine The name is probably an alteration of CHARMIAN, influenced by the ordinary word *charm* and a name such as LORRAINE. It has found modest favour among English speakers only from the 1950s. Maxwell Anderson's play *What Price Glory?* (1924) has Charmaine as the main female character, a French innkeeper's daughter. The subsequent success and different renderings of the popular song 'Charmaine' (1926) may well have encouraged the adoption of the name. Variant spellings include *Sharmain* and *Sharmaine*. An earlier spelling was often *Charmain*.

Charmian The name ultimately comes from the Greek word *kharma*, 'joy'. Today it is often felt to be a form of CHARMAINE and to relate to English *charm*. The name has been in select English-speaking use since at least the 16th century, and in Shakespeare's *Antony and Cleopatra* (1606–7) Charmian is Cleopatra's favourite attendant. She also appears in John Dryden's tragedy based on this play, *All for Love* (1678).

Australian writer Charmian Clift (1923–69).

Chas see **Charles**.

Chelsea A name that ultimately comes from the fashionable London district. It was taken up by English speakers from the 1950s, at first mainly in Australia, then in the US, and leaped in popularity in the 1990s, thanks to the sudden emergence on the public scene of Chelsea Clinton (see below), who was herself named after the Joni Mitchell song 'Chelsea Morning' (1969). A character of the name was played by Jane Fonda in the US film *On Golden Pond* (1981).

US writer Chelsea Yarbro (b.1942); US actress Chelsea Field (b.1957); daughter of US president Bill Clinton, Chelsea Clinton (b.1980)

Cher The name either derives from French *chère*, 'dear', or represents an independently adopted diminutive of a name such as CHERRY and CHERYL. It has never been widely adopted by English speakers but is found from the 1950s.

US pop singer, actress Cher (b.1946) (original name Cherilyn Sarkisian).

Cherie As it stands, the name is an adoption of the French word *chérie*, 'dear one', and is now usually associated with the family of names related to CHER, such as CHERRY and CHERYL. It has enjoyed some favour among English speakers from the 1950s. Its variants are mainly spellings with *Sh-*, such as *Sheree*, *Sheri*, *Sherie* and SHERRY, this last adopted in its own right. The first of these variants became familiar from the name of the US actress Sheree North (b.1933) (original name Dawn Bethel).

Italo-UK actress Cherie Lunghi (b.1954); wife of UK prime minister Tony Blair, Cherie Blair (b.1954).

Cherry The name originated as an independently adopted diminutive of CHARITY, but is now regarded either as a variant or diminutive of a name such as CHERIE or CHERYL or as a flower name, like MAY or ROSE. It has been in select English-speaking use from the early 20th century but is found in fiction earlier than this. In George Farquhar's play *The Beaux' Stratagem* (1707) Cherry is the daughter of the landlord Boniface; in Charles Dickens's novel *Martin Chuzzlewit* (1843–4) Charity Pecksniff is addressed as 'Cherry'; and in Charlotte M. Yonge's novel *The Daisy Chain* (1856) there is a character named Cherry Elwood.

Cheryl The name appears to be a variant of CHERRY, influenced by a name such as BERYL. It is also associated with CHERIE, especially when this is pronounced with an initial 'Sh-'. The name first made itself known in the English-speaking world in the early 20th century, but was not widely taken up until the 1950s, since when it has tailed off somewhat. The many spelling variants include *Cheryll*, *Cherill*, *Sherill* and SHERYL, the last of which is in independent use. The name has also been linked with LYNN to produce *Cherilyn*, *Cherrylyn*, *Sherilyn* and the like.

US theatrical producer Cheryl Crawford (1902–86); UK actresses Cheryl Kennedy (b.1947), Cheryl Campbell (b.1949); US actress Cheryl Ladd (b.1951); UK pop singer, TV personality Cheryl Baker (b.1954) (original name Rita Crudgington); US basketball player Cheryl Miller (b.1964).

Chesney From the surname, and in very limited English-speaking use from the early 20th century. The diminutive CHET is in independent use and *Ches* is also found.

UK popular singer, comedian Chesney Allen (1894–1982).

Chester From the surname, and taken up fairly widely in the English-speaking world from the late 19th century, especially in the US. In H.G. Wells's novel *Kipps* (1905) Chester Coote is a house agent and social aspirant. The diminutive CHET is in independent use.

US president Chester A. Arthur (1830–86); US actor Chester Conklin (1888–1971) (original name Jules Cowles); US statesman, writer Chester Bowles (1901–86); US actor Chester Morris (1901–70); US novelist Chester Himes (1909–84).

Chet The independently adopted diminutive of CHESNEY or CHESTER, almost exclusively in US adoption from the early 20th century.

US popular musicians Chet Atkins (1924–2001) (original first name Chester), Chet Baker (1929–88) (original first name Chesney).

Chick Either an independently adopted diminutive of CHARLES or a borrowing of the nickname for a young or small person, the name has enjoyed select use from the 19th century, chiefly in the US. In William Faulkner's novel *Intruder in the Dust* (1948) Charles (Chick) Mallison is the nephew of Gavin Stevens.

US golfer Chick Evans (1890–1979); US cartoonist Chick Young (1901–73); US actor Chick Chandler (1905–88); US popular singer Chick Bullock (1908–81); US jazzmen Chick Webb (1909–39) (original first names William Henry), Chick Corea (b.1941) (original first names Armando Anthony).

Chloe A biblical name, from the Greek name and word that means 'young green shoot'. It was taken up rather modestly by 17th-century Puritans but did not become common among English speakers until the 20th century, enjoying a sudden revival in the 1990s. In Greek mythology Chloe is the by-name of Demeter, goddess of agriculture, while in the Bible she is a woman converted by Paul. The name is also familiar from the Greek pastoral romance *Daphnis and Chloe*. In English literature Chloe is a shepherdess in Philip Sidney's prose romance *The Arcadia* (1590), and much later the name appears for Aunt Chloe, wife of the title character in Harriet Beecher Stowe's novel *Uncle Tom's Cabin* (1852). The diminutive is usually *Clo*.

Chris (m.) The independently adopted diminutive of CHRISTOPHER or (less commonly) CHRISTIAN. The name has been regularly adopted among English speakers from the late 19th century. Chris Christopherson is the father of the central character in Eugene O'Neill's play *Anna Christie* (1922). The variant spelling *Kris* is occasionally found, as for the US pop singer and actor Kris Kristofferson (b.1936).

UK athlete Chris Chataway (b.1931); UK mountaineer Chris Bonington (b.1934) (original first name Christian); US TV presenter Chris Kelly (b.1940); US actor Chris Sarandon (b.1942); UK TV presenter Chris Tarrant (b.1946); Irish popular singer Chris De Burgh (b.1948); UK footballer Chris Waddle (b.1960); UK cyclist Chris Boardman (b.1968).

Chris (f.) The independently adopted diminutive of CHRISTINE and other names beginning *Chris-*, in regular English-speaking use from the early 20th century. The usual diminutive is *Chrissie* or *Chrissy*, the former as for the UK actress Chrissie White (1894–1989) and US-born UK pop singer Chrissie Hynde (b.1951).

US popular singer Chris Connor (b.1927); US tennis player Chris Evert (b.1954).

Christabel The name is a compound of *Christ* and Latin *bella*, 'beautiful', intended to mean 'fair follower of Christ'. It was mainly in literary use from the 18th century and is rare today. It was widely popularized by Samuel Taylor Coleridge's poem *Christabel* (Part I, 1797), with the well-known lines: 'The lovely lady, Christabel,/Whom her father loves so well.' The UK writer Christabel Coleridge (1843–1921), granddaughter of the poet, was named for this poem, as was the UK suffragist Christabel Pankhurst (1880–1958). Variants include *Christabella* and *Christobel*, while diminutives have been formed from each half as CHRIS (in independent use), *Christie*, BELLA and BELLE, the last two both in independent use.

Christian The name was originally adopted not from the standard word but from the Latin name *Christianus*, 'follower of Christ'. It has been in fairly modest use among English speakers from the 18th century, with a small but distinct uplift in the 1970s. The name was first popularized in literature by Christian, the central character in John Bunyan's allegory *The Pilgrim's Progress* (1678, 1684). The usual diminutive is CHRIS, which is in independent use.

Danish poet, story writer Hans Christian Andersen (1805–75); US actor Christian Slater (b.1969); UK actor Christian Bale (b.1974).

Christiana An early feminine form of CHRISTIAN, in sporadic vogue among English speakers from the 17th century although rare today, when it has been superseded by CHRISTINE. In John Bunyan's allegory *The Pilgrim's Progress* (1678, 1684), Christiana is the wife of Christian. In Thomas Hardy's novel *Tess of the D'Urbervilles* (1891), Christiana Crick is the wife of Tess's dairy farmer employer. Diminutives are CHRIS and *Christie*, the former in independent use.

Christie see **Christabel, Christiana, Christine, Chrystal.**

Christina This shortened form of CHRISTIANA was in English-speaking adoption from the 18th century but has subsequently given way to CHRISTINE. A literary bearer of the name is Christina Pontifex, the central character in Samuel Butler's novel *The Way of All Flesh* (1903). Diminutives CHRIS, KIRSTY and TINA are in independent use.

UK poet Christina Rossetti (1830–94); Australian novelist Christina Stead (1902–83); UK literary hostess Christina Foyle (1911–99); Greek-born US businesswoman Christina Onassis (1950–88); UK explorer, writer Christina Dodwell (b.1951) (father is Christopher); UK athlete Christina Cahill (b.1957); Australian cricketer Christina Matthews (b.1959); US pop singer Christina Aguilera (b.1980).

Christine This is the French form of the name CHRISTINA, which was adopted by English speakers in the late 19th century. The name achieved a considerable popularity peak in the 1950s, since when it has gradually declined. In literature Christine Mannon is the wife (corresponding to Clytemnestra) who kills herself in Eugene O'Neill's play *Mourning Becomes Electra* (1931), and in A.J. Cronin's novel *The Citadel* (1937) Christine Barlow marries Andrew Manson. The Scandinavian form of the name, KIRSTEN, is used independently, as are the Scottish diminutive, KIRSTY, and the standard diminutive CHRIS. Further diminutives are *Christie* and *Christy*, the latter as for the US country singer Christy Lane (b.1940) (original name Eleanor Johnston).

UK doctor Christine Murrell (1874–1933); US actress Christine Norden (1924–1988) (original name Mary Lydia Thornton); UK tennis player Christine Truman (b.1941); US actress Christine Lahti (b.1950); UK opera singer Christine Teare (b.1956); UK concert singer Christine Cairns (b.1959).

Christmas The name either comes from the surname or is a direct borrowing of the name of the festival (compare NOËL). It enjoyed very select English-speaking use in the 19th century but is now rare. In Richard Llewellyn's novel *How Green* *was My Valley* (1939) Christmas Evans is the father of Iestyn Evans. The expected diminutive would be CHRIS.

UK judge, noted Buddhist, Christmas Humphreys (1901–83).

Christobel see **Christabel**.

Christopher The name is the English version of the Greek name *Khristophoros*, formed from *Khristos*, 'Christ' and *pherein*, 'to bear', so meaning 'bearing Christ' (that is, in the heart), although sometimes popularly interpreted as 'borne by Christ'. The name was taken up in the English-speaking world from late medieval times and became particularly popular from the mid-20th century. Its adoption owes much to St Christopher, traditionally depicted as carrying the Christ-child over a river. In Shakespeare's *The Taming of the Shrew* (*c*.1592) Christopher Sly is a drunken tinker. Historically the name was made famous by the navigator and explorer Christopher Columbus (1451–1506). In England it was also familiar from the dramatist Christopher Marlowe (1564–93). Its regular diminutive is CHRIS, in independent use, although CHRISTY and KIT are also found.

UK playwright Christopher Fry (b.1907); UK writer Christopher Logue (b.1926); UK actors Christopher Benjamin (b.1934), Christopher Timothy (b.1940), Christopher Beeny (b.1941), Christopher Cazenove (b.1945), Christopher Biggins (b.1948), Christopher Blake (b.1949), Christopher Lillicrap (b.1949), Christopher Guard (b.1953); UK opera singer Christopher Robson (b.1953).

Christy (m.) An independently adopted diminutive of CHRISTOPHER, found selectively in English-speaking use but favoured mostly among the Scots and Irish. The variant spelling *Christie* is also found.

US film director Christy Cabanne (1888–1950); Irish golfer Christy O'Connor (b.1924); Irish writer Christy Brown (1932–81); Irish folk musician Christy Moore (b.1945); Irish golfer Christy O'Connor Jr (b.1948).

Christy (f.) see **Christine**, **Chrystal**.

Chrystal An independently adopted variant of CRYSTAL, but with spelling influenced by CHRISTINE or other names beginning *Chris-*. It is found from the 19th century and has diminutives *Christie* or *Christy*. (It was formerly also a male name, used as a diminutive of CHRISTOPHER.)

Scottish feminist, pacifist Chrystal Macmillan (1871–1937); US actress Chrystal Herne (1882–1950); UK TV presenter Chrystal Rose (b.1962).

Chuck Either a borrowing of the standard nickname for a friend, as a term of endearment, or an independently adopted diminutive of CHARLES. The name is mostly favoured in the US, where it has been found from the 19th century. The diminutive *Chuckie* is fairly common. (In the listing below, the original first name of each person was Charles unless otherwise stated.)

US baseball player Chuck Klein (1904–58); US basketball player Chuck Hyatt (1908–78); US actor Chuck Connors (1921–92) (original first name Kevin); US pop singer Chuck Berry (b.1926); US actor Chuck Norris (b.1940) (original first name Carlos); US tennis player Chuck McKinley (1941–86).

Ciaran The Irish name, sometimes anglicized as KIERAN, derives as a diminutive of Irish *ciar*, 'dark', referring to a dark-haired or swarthy person. The proper Irish form of the name is *Ciarán*.

Irish poet Ciaran Carson (b.1948); Northern Ireland actor Ciaran McMenamin (b.1974).

Cicely An independently adopted variant of CECILY, which has been in English-speaking use from the 19th century but is now not common. In literature the name is found for Cicely Gosling, the landlord's daughter in Walter Scott's novel *Kenilworth* (1821), and Cicely Baldwin, attorney George Baldwin's wife in John Dos Passos's novel *Manhattan Transfer* (1925).

UK writer Cicely Hamilton (1872–1952); UK actress Cicely Courtneidge (1893–1980); US actress Cicely Tyson (b.1933).

Cilla An independently adopted diminutive of DRUSILLA and, more often, PRISCILLA, which has been in English-speaking use from the mid-20th century. (The usual diminutive suffix -*y* would produce 'silly'.)

UK singer, TV presenter Cilla Black (b.1943) (original name Priscilla White).

Cindy An independently adopted diminutive of a name such as CYNTHIA or LUCINDA, now sometimes wrongly associated with the heroine of the fairy tale Cinderella (whose name actually represents French *Cendrillon*, 'little cinders'). The name has found a judicious vogue among English speakers from the 1950s. Spelling variants are *Cyndi*, as for the US pop singer Cyndi Lauper (b.1953), and *Sindy*, as for the popular doll. (Its manufacturers wanted to call it 'Cindy', which was the preferred name of four canvassed among little girls, but they were barred from registering an established personal name, so chose the *S*- spelling instead.)

US actress Cindy Williams (b.1948); UK polar explorer, photographer Cindy Buxton (b.1950); US photographic artist Cindy Sherman (b.1954); US water skier Cindy Todd (b.1956); UK actress Cindy Shelley (b.1960); UK photographer Cindy Palmano (b.1963); US model Cindy Crawford (b.1966).

Cissie Either an independently adopted diminutive of CECILIA, CECILY or CICELY, or else the borrowing of *Sissy* as a pet name for a little sister. The name has found some select English-speaking favour from the 19th century, but has been decreasingly common from the 1930s. (The sense of *cissy* to mean 'cowardly', 'effeminate' has probably discouraged use of the name in recent years.) In Rudyard Kipling's short story 'Marklake Witches' in *Rewards and Fairies* (1910) Cissie is a nurse to Philadelphia Bucksteed. Variant spellings *Cissy* and *Sissy* occur, the former as for the US soul singer Cissy Houston (b.1932) (original first name Emily), the latter as for the US actress Sissy Spacek (b.1949) (original first names Mary Elizabeth).

Cissy see **Cecilia**, **Cecily**, **Cissie**.

Claire The name is a French form of the Latin name CLARA, which gave the more directly English CLARE. It was introduced to England by the Normans, but in modern use dates only from the 19th century. It grew steadily in popularity in the 20th century, however, achieving a considerable peak in the second half of the 1970s, since when it has subsided. A variant spelling is *Clair*.

US actresses Claire Windsor (1898–1972) (original name Olga Cronk), Claire Luce (1904–89), Claire Trevor (1909–2000); UK actress Claire Bloom (b.1931); UK 'agony aunt' Claire Rayner (b.1931); UK writer Claire Tomalin (b.1933); UK polo player Claire Tomlinson (b.1944); UK theatre critic Claire Armitstead (b.1958); UK actress Claire King (b.1963); UK jazz singer Claire Martin (b.1968).

Clancy (m.) The name either comes from the (Irish) surname or is an independently adopted diminutive of CLARENCE. It has been in select English-speaking use from the 19th century and is mostly favoured in the US.

US jazzman Clancy Hayes (1908–72) (original first name Clarence); US journalist Clancy Sigal (b.1926).

Clara A re-Latinized form of the English name CLARE, which also happens to represent the Spanish word *clara*, 'clear', 'pure'. The name has been in English-speaking use from the 19th century, although it is now much less common than it was. In Charles Dickens's novel *David Copperfield* (1849–50) Clara Peggotty is David's nurse, while Clara Middleton is the former fiancée of the central character, Sir Willoughby Patterne, in George Meredith's novel *The Egoist* (1879). CLAIRE is a directly related name.

UK singer Clara Novello (1818–1908); US Red Cross nurse Clara Barton (1821–1912) (original first name Clarissa); UK singers Clara Novello-Davies (1861–1943), Dame Clara Butt (1872–1936); US actresses Clara Blandick (1880–1962), Clara Kimball Young (1890–1960), Clara Bow (1905–65).

Clare The name comes from Latin *clara*, the feminine form of *clarus*, 'clear', 'bright', 'famous', which also (though less directly) gave CLARA. It has been current in England from medieval times, gradually gaining in popularity from the 19th century to reach a peak in the second half of the 1970s. It is historically familiar from St Clare, 13th-century founder of the 'Poor Clares', the order of Franciscan nuns. CLAIRE is a directly related name.

US writer and politician Clare Boothe Luce (1903–87); UK writer, yachtswoman Clare Francis (b.1946); UK politician Clare Short (b.1946).

Clarence Modern use of the name was mostly a tribute to Albert Victor, Duke of Clarence (1864–92), the eldest son of Edward VII, whose title dates from the 14th century and ultimately derives from the town of Clare in Suffolk. It was thus in wide vogue among English speakers from the late 19th century, although it is also found before this. It is now much less common. Maria Edgeworth's novel *Helen* (1834) has Clarence Harvey as its central character. The usual diminutive is *Clarrie*, as for the Australian cricketer Clarrie Grimmett (1891–1980), but CLANCY is also found.

US attorney Clarence Darrow (1857–1938); US humorist Clarence Day (1874–1935); US film director Clarence Badger (1880–1964); US writer of westerns Clarence E. Mulford (1883–1956); US actor Clarence Muse (1889–1979); US bluesman Clarence Brown (b.1924); US writer Clarence Major (b.1936); US country musician Clarence White (1944–73).

Claribel The name is probably a blend of CLARA and a name such as ANNABEL or ISABEL, influenced by French *bel*, 'beautiful'. At first it was a 16th-century literary name, but it is still found very occasionally among English speakers today. In literature Claribel is the chosen bride of Phaon in Edmund Spenser's poem *The Faerie Queene* (1590, 1596), with Spenser possibly interpreting the name as a combination of Latin *clarus*, 'bright', and *bellus*, 'fair'.

Clarice An English (and French) form of the Latin name *Claritia*, itself probably based on *clara* (which in turn gave English CLARE). The name has enjoyed select English-speaking use from the late 19th century, although it is now rare. In early French and Italian romances Clarice is the sister of Huon of Bordeaux who marries Rinaldo. The Latinate version of the name, CLARISSA, was adopted independently.

UK popular singer Clarice Mayne (1886–1966).

Clarinda An independently adopted blend of the name CLARE and the *-inda* element of a name such as BELINDA. The name is found in occasional English-speaking use from the 17th century but is rare today. In Edmund Spenser's poem *The Faerie Queene* (1590, 1596) the name is that of the trusted handmaid of Queen Radigund. It occurs subsequently in many other literary works, including those by Philip Massinger, John Fletcher and Thomas Shadwell. In Susannah Centlivre's play *The Beau's Duel* (1702) Clarinda is the central female character. In the late 18th century the Scottish poet Robert Burns addressed his friend Mrs M'Lehose as 'Clarinda' (calling himself 'Sylvander'), and his poems *To Clarinda* were for her.

Clarissa A Latinized form of CLARICE, adopted by English speakers from the 18th century and still in select use today. The name was made famous by Clarissa Harlowe, the central character of Samuel Richardson's novel *Clarissa* (1748). In

Charles Dickens's novel *David Copperfield* (1849–50) Clarissa is one of the elderly maiden sisters of the proctor Mr Spenlow, and Clarissa Dalloway is the central character in Virginia Woolf's novel *Mrs Dalloway* (1925). Diminutives are *Claris* and *Clarry*.

UK daughter of Earl of Plymouth, Lady Clarissa Egleston (b.1931); UK daughter of Earl of Faversham, Lady Clarissa Collin (b.1938).

Clark From the surname, and in select use from the late 19th century, especially in the US. The variant *Clarke* occasionally occurs.

New Zealand billiards player Clark McConachy (1895–1980); US actor Clark Gable (1901–60) (originally middle name, first being William); US jazz trumpeter Clark Terry (b.1920); US ballet dancer, choreographer Clark Tippet (1954–92).

Clarrie see **Clarence**.

Clarry see **Clarissa**.

Claude An adoption of the Roman clan name *Claudius*, itself from the nickname *Claudus*, 'lame'. The name was commonly taken up by English speakers from the 1870s but is now rare. The variant spelling *Claud* is also found.

UK comedian Claude Dampier (1879–1955); UK actors Claude Rains (1889–1967), Claude Hulbert (1900–63); US actor Claude Akins (1918–94).

Claudia A biblical name, in origin the feminine form of the Roman clan name *Claudius*, which gave the male name CLAUDE. The name has been in fairly regular but select use among English speakers from the 16th century, with a discreet increase in popularity in the 1980s. In the Bible Claudia is one of the Christian women of Rome greeted by Eubulus in Paul's letter to Timothy (2 Timothy 4.21). Recent literary occurrences of the name are those of Claudia Naughton, the child-wife and central character in the popular domestic novels by the US writer Rose Franken, beginning with *Claudia: The Story of a Marriage* (1939); Claudia Hardcastle, the murder victim in Agatha Christie's novel *Endless Night* (1967); and Claudia Hampton, the war correspondent who is the central character in Penelope Lively's novel *Moon Tiger* (1987). Variants include the French form *Claude* and the French diminutives *Claudette* and *Claudine*, the former borne by the French actress Claudette Colbert (1905–96), the latter familiar from the series of novels by the French writer Colette and her husband Henri Gauthier-Villars: *Claudine à l'école* (1900), *Claudine à Paris* (1901) and so on.

Italian actress Claudia Cardinale (b.1939); US film director Claudia Weill (b.1947); US swimmer Claudia Kolb (b.1949); US children's writer Claudia Mills (b.1954); German model Claudia Schiffer (b.1971).

Clem see **Clement**, **Clementina**.

Clement From the Latin name *Clemens*, genitive *Clementis*, meaning 'merciful' (modern English 'clement'). The name, which has been in continuous English-speaking use from medieval times, was first familiar from various saints and fourteen popes. In literature it occurs for several religious characters, such as Father Clement in Walter Scott's novel *The Fair Maid of Perth* (1828) and Brother Clement in Charles Reade's novel *The Cloister and the Hearth* (1861). Sir Clement Willoughby is the persistent wooer of the central character in Fanny Burney's novel *Evelina* (1778). The regular diminutive is *Clem*.

UK prime minister Clement Attlee (1883–1967); UK politician, food writer Sir Clement Freud (b.1924).

Clementina A feminine form of CLEMENT, first current among English-speakers from the 17th century but now rare. Literary bearers of the name include Clementina Porretta, romantically involved with the central character in Samuel

Richardson's novel *Sir Charles Grandison* (1753–4); Clementina Clutterbuck, a cadaverous, red-haired poetess in William Make-peace Thackeray's satirical sketches *The Book of Snobs* (1846–7); Clementina, daughter of Lord Pentreath in George Eliot's novel *Daniel Deronda* (1876); and Clementina, Paula Power's French maid in Thomas Hardy's novel *A Laodicean* (1881). The main variant is CLEMENTINE, which is in independent use, as is the common diminutive CLEO. Other diminutives are *Clem*, *Clemmie* and *Clemmy*.

UK trade unionist, suffragist Clementina Black (1853–1922).

Clementine A feminine form of CLEMENT, with the French diminutive suffix *-ine*, in select English-speaking use from the 19th century. The name was popularized by Percy Montrose's song about the 'miner, Forty-niner' and his daughter Clemen-tine (1884). The name's diminutives are as for the directly related CLEMENTINA.

Wife of UK prime minister Winston Churchill, Lady Clementine Spencer-Churchill (1885–1977).

Clemmie, **Clemmy** see **Clementina**.

Cleo An independently adopted diminutive of CLEMENTINA, CLEMENTINE or CLEOPATRA, in select English-speaking vogue from the early 20th century.

US popular singer Cleo Brown (b.1909); UK jazz singer Cleo Laine (b.1927) (original name Clementine Dinah Campbell); US actress Cleo Moore (1928–73); UK TV actress Cleo Rocos (b.c.1955).

Cleopatra An adoption of the Greek name meaning 'father's glory', which, in the English-speaking world, is mostly con-fined to occasional use among black Americans. The name is historically famous as that of several princesses, especially of the beautiful queen of Egypt who was the mistress successively of Julius Caesar and Mark Antony. She appears in such liter-ary works as Shakespeare's *Antony and Cleopatra* (1606–7) and

George Bernard Shaw's play *Caesar and Cleopatra* (1901). The diminutive CLEO is in independent use.

Cliff The independently adopted diminutive of CLIFFORD or (less often) CLIFTON, also associated with the standard word *cliff* or with the name CLIVE. The name, which has been in select English-speaking use from the early 20th century, increased in popularity from the 1960s.

US actor Cliff Clark (1893–1953); US entertainer Cliff Edwards (1895 –1971); US actor Cliff Arquette (1906–74); UK broadcaster Cliff Michelmore (b.1919); US actor Cliff Robertson (b.1925); UK pop singer Cliff Richard (b.1940) (original name Harold Webb); Canadian snooker player Cliff Thorburn (b.1948).

Clifford From the surname, and in fashion from the 19th century, especially in the US, although declining in popularity from the 1930s. Clifford Pyncheon is a character in Nathaniel Hawthorne's novel *The House of the Seven Gables* (1851). The regular diminutive, CLIFF, is in independent use.

UK playwright Clifford Bax (1886–1962); UK lyricist, librettist Clifford Grey (1887–1941); US playwright, actor Clifford Odets (1906–63); UK pianist Clifford Curzon (1907–82); Welsh actor Clifford Evans (1912–85).

Clifton From the surname, and in select use, especially in the US, from the 19th century. The regular diminutive is CLIFF, in independent use.

US actor Clifton Webb (1891–1966) (original name Webb Parmelee Hollenbeck); Australian artist Clifton Pugh (1924–90); US zydeco musician Clifton Chenier (1925–87).

Clint An independently adopted diminutive of the surname *Clinton*, which is well known in the US. The name has been in select use, mainly in the US, from the early 20th century, with as yet little vogue in the UK. The US source of the name was probably the Clinton family, which included two governors of New York: George Clinton (1739–1812) and DeWitt Clinton (1769–1828). It is also now familiar from US president Bill Clinton (b.1946). (He was born William Jefferson Blythe IV three months after his father was killed in a car crash. His present surname, which he legally adopted at the age of fifteen, is thus that of his stepfather, Roger Clinton.)

US actors Clint Walker (b.1927) (original first names Norman Eugene), Clint Eastwood (b.1930); US country singer Clint Black (b.1962).

Clive From the surname, with its suggestion of *cliff*, adopted from the mid-19th century, at first selectively, then increasingly until the 1950s, after which the name's popularity declined. Clive Newcome is the central character in William Makepeace Thackeray's novel *The Newcomes* (1853–5). (His father, Colonel Thomas Newcome, has lived most of his life in India, suggesting that Thackeray may have taken the name from Clive of India, otherwise the UK military leader Robert Clive (1725–74), who strengthened the UK hold in India in the 18th century.)

US actors Clive Brook (1887–1974) (original first name Clifford), Clive Morton (1904–1972), Clive Swift (b.1936); Australian-born UK writer, broadcaster Clive James (b.1939); UK actors Clive Hornby (b.1944), Clive Francis (b.1946).

Clo see **Chloe**, **Clodagh**.

Clodagh From the name of the river in County Tipperary, Ireland, but perhaps felt by some to be associated with CLAUDIA. The name has been in occasional English-speaking use in the 20th century and probably arose as a deliberate creation. A diminutive is *Clo*, normally associated with CHLOE.

Northern Ireland pop singer Clodagh Rogers (b.1947).

Clovis The name is a Latinized form of the French name LOUIS, in rarish English-speaking use from the 19th century. It is historically familiar from Clovis, the 6th-century king of the Franks who ended the Roman domination of Gaul. The name was to some extent popularized by Saki's volume of short stories *The Chronicles of Clovis* (1911), in which it is that of the narrator.

Clyde From the surname, itself from the river in southwest Scotland. The name was taken up by black families in the US from the 19th century, and it is now in select use more generally among English speakers. Clyde Griffiths is the central character in Theodore Dreiser's novel *An American Tragedy* (1925). The name was made familiar by the film *Bonnie and Clyde* (1967), in which the latter is the US bank robber Clyde Barrow (1900–34).

Australian dancer, actor Clyde Cook (1891–1984); US film director Clyde Bruckman (1895–1955); Australian flying doctor pioneer Clyde Fenton (1901–82); US animal trainer, circus owner Clyde Beatty (1903–65); US country singer Clyde Moody (b.1915); US soul singer Clyde McPhatter (1933–72).

Coleen, **Colene** see **Colleen**.

Colin The name is either an independently adopted diminutive of NICHOLAS or (less frequently) the English form of the Scottish name *Cailean*, 'whelp', 'puppy'. An important literary occurrence of the name is for the shepherd Colin Clout, the central character of Edmund Spenser's two great pastoral poems *The Shepheardes Calender* (1579) and its sequel *Colin Clouts come home againe* (1595). The name was popularly adopted by English speakers in the 20th century, winning wide favour in the 1950s and 1960s, but it has since declined in the UK and has never been very common in the US.

Scottish-born US actor Colin Campbell (1883–1966); UK conductor Sir Colin Davis (b.1927); UK sports car designer Colin Chapman (1928–82); UK actor Colin Jeavons (b.1929); UK crime writer Colin Dexter (b.1930); UK cricketer Colin Cowdrey (1932–2000); UK actor Colin Welland (b.1934); US Army chief Colin Powell (b.1937); UK cricketer Colin Milburn (1941–1990); UK actors Colin Baker (b.1943), Colin Firth (b.1960).

Colleen The name derives from the Irish word *cailín*, 'girl', but it is regarded by some as being a feminine form of COLIN. It has enjoyed select adoption among English speakers from the 19th century and has variant forms such as *Coleen* and *Colene*, the former as for the US actress Coleen Gray (b.1922) (original name Doris Jensen).

US actresses Colleen Moore (1900–88) (original name Kathleen Morrison), Colleen Dewhurst (1926–91), Colleen Miller (b.1932); Australian novelist Colleen McCullough (b.1937); Canadian playwright Colleen Curran (b.1954).

Con (m.) see **Conrad**, **Constant**.

Con (f.) see **Constance**.

Connee see **Connie** (f.).

Connie (m.) see **Conrad**, **Constant**, **Cornelius**.

Connie (f.) An independently adopted diminutive of CONSTANCE or *Concetta* (an Italian name, deriving from a title of the Virgin Mary, *Maria Concetta*, Mary of the [Immaculate] Conception). It has been in select English-speaking use from the late 19th century. The US radio series *Our Miss Brooks* (from 1948) had the central character, a schoolteacher, Connie Brooks, which to some extent popularized the name in recent times. The variant spelling *Connee* exists, and the usual diminutive is *Con*.

US actress Connie Gilchrist (1901–85) (original first name Rose); US popular singer Connie (later Connee) Boswell (1907–76); US actresses Connie Marshall (b.1938), Connie Stevens (b.1938) (original first name Concetta); US popular singer Connie Francis (b.1938) (original name Concetta Franconero); UK actress Connie Booth (b.1941); US country singer Connie Eaton (b.1950); US cyclist Connie Carpenter (b.1957).

Connor An Irish name representing an original Irish form *Conchobhar*, perhaps meaning 'hound lover' or possibly 'wolf lover', implying someone fond of hunting. The name is that of an early semi-legendary Irish king. An alternative form of the name is *Conor*, as for the Irish writer and historian Conor Cruise O'Brien (b.1917).

Conrad An English spelling of the German name KONRAD, formed from Old German *kuon*, 'bold', and *rad*, 'counsel', so 'bold counsel'. The name has found select use among English speakers from the mid-19th century, with greater favour in the US than the UK. In Horace Walpole's novel *The Castle of Otranto* (1765) Conrad is the son of Prince Manfred, tyrant of Otranto. Characters of the name appear in Byron's poem *The Corsair* (1814) and Charles Kingsley's poem *The Saint's Tragedy* (1848). Diminutives are usually *Con* or *Connie*.

US hotelier Conrad Hilton (1887–1979); US writer Conrad Aiken (1889–1973); German-born actor Conrad Veidt (1893–1943); Canadian actor Conrad Bain (b.1923); UK actor Conrad Phillips (b.1930); Canadian newspaper publisher Conrad Black (b.1944).

Constance This is an English form of the Late Latin name *Constantia*, 'constancy', 'perseverance', in select English-speaking use from medieval times, but more widely adopted in the 17th century by Puritans as a good 'moral' name. In the 20th century its popularity has gradually declined, so that it is now seldom met. One of William the Conqueror's daughters was named Constance. In Shakespeare's *King John* (*c*.1596), Constance is the devoted mother of King Arthur, while Constance Neville is a character in Oliver Goldsmith's play *She Stoops to Conquer* (1773). The usual diminutives are *Con* or CONNIE, the latter in independent use.

UK translator of Russian fiction Constance Garnett (1861–1946); UK actress Constance Collier (1878–1955) (originally middle name, first being Laura); UK floristy expert Constance Spry (1886–1960); US actress Constance Bennett (1904–65); US-born UK actress Constance Cummings (b.1910); UK opera singer Constance Shacklock (1913–99); UK actress Constance Smith (b.1929).

Constant An English form of the Latin name *Constans*, genitive *Constantis*, 'steadfast', 'constant', which was adopted in the religious sense ('constant in the faith') by Puritans in the 16th century but was not common among English speakers until the 19th century. The name is now in only sporadic use. The diminutive forms *Con* and *Connie* are known.

UK composer, conductor Constant Lambert (1905–51).

Constantine An English form of the Latin name *Constantinus*, itself a derivative of *Constans* (which gave English CONSTANT). The name was taken up selectively in the English-speaking world from the 19th century, although it is now rarely encountered. The name is historically famous from the 4th-century Roman emperor Constantine the Great.

King Constantine of Greece (1868–1923); Irish-US novelist Constantine Fitzgibbon (1919–83); ex-King Constantine of Greece (b.1940).

Cora The name comes from the Greek word *korē*, 'girl', 'daughter', and has been in use among English speakers from the 19th century. It became popular among black Americans in the 1930s but is nowhere common today. In Greek mythology *Kore* was the by-name of the goddess of the underworld, Persephone, because she was the daughter of Zeus. A literary boost for the name was given by Cora Munro, the ill-fated heroine of James Fenimore Cooper's novel *The Last of the Mohicans* (1826). It is possible that Cooper even introduced the name to the English-speaking world. French forms of the name are more popular now, especially CORINNE, which is in independent use, and to a lesser extent *Coralie*.

Anglo-French courtesan Cora Pearl (1842–86) (original name Emma Elizabeth Crouch); Norwegian novelist Cora Sandel (1880–1974); US actresses Cora Witherspoon (1890–1957), Cora Sue Collins (b.1927).

Coral From the ordinary word, borrowed as a jewel name, but doubtless felt by some to be related to CORA. The name has been in steady but modest English-speaking use from the late 19th century. An occasional variant is *Cory*.

Australian-born UK actress Coral Browne (1913–91).

Cordelia The ultimate source of the name is perhaps in the Celtic saint's name *Cordula*, itself associated with Latin *cor*, genitive *cordis*, 'heart'. Although it is rarely found today, the name cannot be said to be entirely obsolete. In literature it was made familiar by Cordelia, the king's youngest daughter in Shakespeare's *King Lear* (1604–5). Diminutives include *Cordy* and DELIA, the latter now an independent name (although usually of a different origin).

Corey From the surname, and increasingly in vogue from the 1960s, especially in the US, with the UK catching on in the 1990s.

US actors Corey Allen (b.1934), Corey Feldman (b.1971); Canadian actor Corey Haim (b.1971).

Corinne This is a French name, ultimately from the same Greek source that gave the name CORA, which has enjoyed judicious English-speaking adoption from the late 19th century. A variant form is *Corinna*, as for the UK water skier Corinna Williams (1975–93).

US actress Corinne Griffith (1898–1979); French-born US actress Corinne Calvet (1925–2001); French actress Corinne Marchand (b.1937).

Cornel see **Cornell**.

Cornelia A feminine form of the Latin (now also English) name CORNELIUS, in English-speaking favour chiefly from the 19th century, although occasionally found earlier. It was first made historically familiar in the 2nd century BC by Cornelia, mother of the Gracchi and famous as an ideal Roman matron.

In literature Cornelia Chickerell is one of the many sisters of the central character, Ethelberta Petherwin, in Thomas Hardy's novel *The Hand of Ethelberta* (1876). Diminutives include *Cornie*, *Corrie* and *Nellie*, although this last is now more often linked with NELL.

US actress Cornelia Otis Skinner (1901–79); Australian actress Cornelia Frances (b.1941).

Cornelius A biblical name, in origin from the Roman clan name *Cornelius*, itself of uncertain origin but perhaps connected with *cornu*, 'horn'. The name has been in select use in the English-speaking world, especially by black Americans, from the 19th century. In the Bible the devout Cornelius is 'a centurion of the band called the Italian band [cohort]' stationed in Caesarea (Acts 10.1). Two characters of the name appear in Shakespeare: a courtier in *Hamlet* (1599–1601) and a physician in *Cymbeline* (1609–10). Another Cornelius is a friend of Faustus in Christopher Marlowe's play *Doctor Faustus* (1604), while in George Bernard Shaw's play *John Bull's Other Island* (1904) Cornelius Doyle is the father of the civil engineer Laurence Doyle. Diminutives *Connie*, *Corney* and *Corny* exist, the first as for the famous US baseball player Connie Mack (1862–1956) (original name Cornelius Alexander McGillicuddy).

US financier Cornelius Vanderbilt (1794–1877).

Cornell From the (American) surname, the name was in select use among English speakers in the US from the 19th century. A variant *Cornel* exists, as for the US actor Cornel Wilde (1915–89).

US mystery writer Cornell Woolrich (1903–68).

Corney, Corny see **Cornelius**.

Cornie, Corrie see **Cornelia**.

Cory see **Coral**.

Cosmo An English adoption of the Italian form of the Greek name *Kosmas*, itself based on *kosmos*, 'order', 'beauty'. The name was brought to Britain in the 18th century by the Scottish dukes of Gordon, who had ties with the ducal house of Tuscany, where the name (in the form *Cosimo*) was traditional. It is rarely found today. Baron Cosmo Bradwardine of Comyne is a character in Walter Scott's novel *Waverley* (1814), and Cosmo Topper is the staid banker who is the central character in Thorne Smith's humorous novel *Topper* (1926).

Scottish-born Archbishop of Canterbury, Cosmo Gordon Lang (1864–1945).

Courtney (m.) From the surname, and taken up selectively by English speakers from the mid-19th century, the name enjoyed a rise in popularity in the 1990s.

US writer Courtney Cooper (1886–1940); UK ice dancer Courtney Jones (b.1933); West Indian cricketer Courteney Walsh (b.1962); UK jazz saxophonist Courtney Pine (b.1964).

Courtney (f.) A female adoption of the male name COURTNEY, with a variant *Courteney,* as for the US actress Courteney Cox (b.1964).

US rock musician Courtney Love (b.1963).

Craig From the surname, itself from a Scottish place-name to which English *crag* relates, this name was taken up in the mid-19th century, first in the US, then in the UK, and it has been fairly popular from the 1970s.

US actor Craig Stevens (1918–2000) (original name Gail Shikles); US food writer Craig Claiborne (1920–2000); Welsh writer Craig Thomas (b.1942); UK poet Craig Raine (b.1944); US actor Craig T. Nelson (b.1946); Canadian actor, female impersonator Craig Russell (1948–90); US actor Craig Wasson (b.1954); Australian actor Craig McLachlan (b.1965); Scottish rugby player Craig Chalmers (b.1968); UK actor Craig McKay (b.1973).

Crispin An English version of the Latin name *Crispinus*, a derivative of the Roman clan name *Crispus*, itself a nickname meaning 'curly-haired'. The name has found selective adoption among English speakers from the 17th century and enjoyed a certain vogue in the mid-20th century. It was first made famous by the 3rd-century martyr St Crispin. An older form of the name is *Crispian*, which is still occasionally met, as for the UK trumpeter Crispian Steele-Perkins (b.1944).

UK diplomat, ambassador Sir Crispin Tickell (b.1930); US actor Crispin Glover (b.1964).

Crystal A borrowing of the standard word for the clear, shiny mineral or for cut glass, in vogue from the 20th century, when it became popular in both the US and the UK, with a special attraction for black Americans. The variant spelling CHRYSTAL occurs independently.

US feminist, pacifist Crystal Eastman (1881–1928); US country singer Crystal Gayle (b.1951) (original name Brenda Gail Webb).

Cuddie see **Cuthbert**.

Curt see **Kurt**.

Curtis An adoption of the surname, current from the 19th century, and especially in favour with black Americans. The wheat speculator Curtis Jadwin is the central character in Frank Norris's novel *The Pit* (1903).

US golfer Curtis Strange (b.1955); UK athlete Curtis Robb (b.1972).

Cuthbert The origin lies in the Old English name *Cuthbeorht*, formed from *cūth*, 'known', and *beorht*, 'bright', 'famous', so 'well known'. The name was in fairly regular use in the English-speaking world until the 1930s, when it declined and has not since revived. It was first made famous by the 7th-century English monk St Cuthbert. In Thomas Hardy's novel *Tess of the D'Urbervilles* (1891) the Rev. Cuthbert Clare is the brother of the central character, Angel Clare. The usual diminutive is BERT, which is in independent use, while *Cuddie* is a Scottish variant.

UK writer Cuthbert Bede (1827–89) (original name Edward Bradley).

Cy An independently adopted diminutive of CYRUS, chiefly in US use from the early 20th century.

US baseball player Cy Young (1867–1955) (original first names Denton True); US film director Cy Endfield (1914–83); US popular musician Cy Coleman (b.1929) (original name Seymour Kaufman); UK actor Cy Chadwick (b.1969).

Cybill see **Sybil**.

Cyndi see **Cindy**.

Cynthia This is an English form of the Greek name *Kynthia*, a by-name of Artemis, goddess of the hunt and moon, who is said to have been born on Mount Kynthos (Cynthus) on the island of Delos. The mountain name itself is of uncertain, pre-Greek origin. The name has been in English-speaking use from the 16th century, at first mainly in literature, then as a personal name in the 19th century in the US, where it was favoured by slave families. The 1st-century BC Roman poet Propertius used the name, for the woman (whose real name was probably Hostia) to whom he addressed love poems. Later, English writers used the name to denote Queen Elizabeth I as a virgin moon goddess. Edmund Spenser dedicated his pastoral poem *Colin Clouts come home againe* (1595) to Walter Raleigh and invited him to come from Ireland to England 'his *Cynthia* to see'. Ben Jonson's allegorical comedy *Cynthia's Revels* (1600) has Elizabeth as the central subject, with a famous song to her (as a goddess) describing her as 'Queen and huntress, chaste and fair'. Cynthia Plyant is one of the main characters in William Congreve's comedy *The Double Dealer* (1693), and Cynthia Gibson is a key character in Elizabeth Gaskell's novel *Wives and Daughters* (1866). The most common diminutive is CINDY, now in independent use.

UK writer Cynthia Asquith (1887–1960); US writers Cynthia Freeman (1915–88) (original name Bea Feinberg), Cynthia Ozick (b.1928); US singer Cynthia Weill (b.1937); US actress Cynthia Daniel (b.1976).

Cyprian The name, from the Latin name *Cyprianus*, 'man of Cyprus', has been in select English-speaking use from medieval times, although it is now not common. It was initially made known by the 3rd-century martyr and bishop of Carthage, St Cyprian.

Nigerian writer Cyprian Ekwensi (b.1921).

Cyril The derivation is in the Greek name *Kyrillos*, itself based on *kurios*, 'lord'. The name was fairly popular in the English-speaking world from the late 19th century to the 1920s, after which it fell from grace and has not been revived. It is historically famous from several saints, including the 9th-century Greek missionary St Cyril who invented the Cyrillic alphabet (named for him) to provide written translations of the gospels for Christians of Slavic lands. In literature Cyril is the friend of Hilarion in Tennyson's poem *The Princess* (1847), and he therefore appears in Gilbert and Sullivan's comic opera based on it, *Princess Ida* (1884). In D.H. Lawrence's novel *The White Peacock* (1911) Cyril Beardsall is the central character and narrator. The catchphrase 'Nice one, Cyril' played on the name's by then risible connotations in the 1970s. A French-style variant, *Cyrille*, is sometimes found, as for the UK footballer Cyrille Regis (b.1958).

UK actor Cyril Smith (1892–1963); UK concert pianist Cyril Smith (1909–74); South African-born Irish actor Cyril Cusack (1910–93); UK comedian Cyril Fletcher (b.1913); UK bandleader Cyril Stapleton (1914–74); UK cricketer Cyril Washbrook (1914–99); UK politician Sir Cyril Smith (b.1928); UK footballer Cyril Knowles (1944–91).

Cyrus A biblical name, from the Greek name *Kyros*, that of several kings of Persia. It is itself of unknown origin but is popularly associated with the Greek word *kurios*, 'lord' (as for CYRIL). The name was adopted by the Puritans in the 17th century, but became nothing like popular until the 19th century, mainly in the US. Cyrus Carve is the brother of Ilam Carve in Arnold Bennett's play *The Great Adventure* (1913). The regular diminutive is CY, in independent use.

US actor Cyrus Q. Kendall (1898–1953); US statesman Cyrus Vance (1917–2002).

D

Daff, **Daffy** see **Daphne**.

Dahlia From the flower, this is a name in very select use among English speakers from the late 19th century. In George Meredith's novel *Rhoda Fleming* (1865), Dahlia Fleming is the sister of the central character. The spelling variant *Dalia* exists.

Dai A Welsh name, originally from Old Celtic *dei*, 'to shine', but now regarded as an independently adopted diminutive of DAVID. The name has almost always been in Welsh use only from the 19th century. Dai Griffiths is a miner in Richard Llewellyn's novel *How Green was My Valley* (1939).

Welsh golfer Dai Rees (1913–83).

Daisy From the flower, this name is conventionally regarded as a pet form of MARGARET, because the French equivalent of this name, MARGUERITE, is the French word for 'daisy'. The English name may thus have been seen as its 'translation'. It was first adopted in the 19th century, but has been decreasingly common from the early 20th century, despite a slight revival in the 1990s. The name is familiar in literature from the central character of Henry James's short story *Daisy Miller* (1879), and also from Daisy Buchanan, married to Tom but worshipped by the central character, Jay Gatsby, in F. Scott Fitzgerald's novel *The Great Gatsby* (1925). The music-hall song 'Daisy Bell' (1892), with its opening line, 'Daisy, Daisy, give me your answer, do!' reflected the current popularity of the name and in turn boosted it.

UK-born Australian social worker Daisy Bates (1861–1951); UK child author Daisy Ashford (1881–1972); US civil rights leader Daisey Bates (1914–99); UK writer Daisy Waugh (b.1967).

Dale (m.) From the surname, and first taken up by English speakers, mainly in the US, in the 19th century, the name achieved a modest rise in popularity in the 1960s and a rather greater one in the first half of the 1980s.

US writer, speaker Dale Carnegie (1888–1955); US actor Dale Robertson (b.1923); UK TV presenter Dale Winton (b.1955).

Dale (f.) A female adoption of the male name DALE, in very select English-speaking use from the 1930s.

US actress Dale Evans (1912–2001) (original name Frances Octavia Smith).

Dalia see **Dahlia**.

Damaris A biblical name, probably of Greek origin and representing *damar*, 'wife', 'spouse', but possibly from *damalis*, 'self', implying an offspring, the name was taken up by English Puritans in the 17th century and is still found in select use today. In the Bible Damaris is an Athenian woman converted to Christianity by Paul at the same time as Dionysius the Areopagite (Acts 17.34). The English scholar Damaris Masham (1658–1708) bore the name.

Damian An English adoption of the Greek name *Damianos*, in turn from *daman*, 'to tame', 'to subdue', so meaning 'tamer'. The name has been in irregular English-speaking use in the 20th century, with a rise in popularity in the second half of the 1970s. It was historically made familiar by the 4th-century martyr St Damian. DAMON is a directly related name, and *Damien* is a variant spelling, as for the UK financial journalist Damien McCrystal (b.1961), and UK artist Damien Hirst (b.1965).

UK business writer, editor Damian Green (b.1956); UK film director Damian Harris (b.1960); UK cricketer Damian D'Oliveira (b.1960);

UK columnist, reviewer Damian Thompson (b.1962); UK rugby player Damian Hopley (b.1970).

Damon An independently adopted variant of DAMIAN, which came into modest vogue only in the mid-20th century. The name has classical associations in the two legendary friends Damon and Pythias. Thomas Hardy's novel *The Return of the Native* (1878) has Damon Wildeve, who is loved by both Eustacia Vye and Thomasin Yeobright.

US humorous short story writer Damon Runyon (1884–1946); US actor Damon Wayans (b.1960); UK motor-racing driver Damon Hill (b.1962); Australian actor Damon Herriman (b.1970).

Dan This is both a biblical name, from Hebrew *Dān*, 'judge'. and an independently adopted diminutive of DANIEL. In the Bible Dan is the son of Jacob and Bilha, Rachel's servant, and is the ancestor of one of the twelve tribes of Israel. In Thomas Hardy's novel *The Hand of Ethelberta* (1876) Dan Chickerell is the brother of the central character, Ethelberta Petherwin, and in Rudyard Kipling's collection of stories *Puck of Pook's Hill* (1906) Dan and Una are the brother and sister who are visited by Puck. The usual diminutive is DANNY, which is in independent use.

US actor Dan Duryea (1907–68); UK tennis player Dan Maskell (1908–92); US actor Dan Dailey (1914–78); South African writer Dan Jacobson (b.1929); Anglo-US TV interviewer Dan Farson (b.1930); US senator Dan Quayle (b.1947) (original first names James Danforth); Canadian comedian Dan Aykroyd (b.1950).

Dana (m.) Either an adoption of the surname or a diminutive of DANIEL, in very select English-speaking use from the 19th century.

US actor Dana Andrews (1909–92) (original first names Carver Daniel).

Dana (f.) Usually an adoption of the male name DANA, but popularly regarded as a variant of DANIELLE or DONNA, and in fairly select English-speaking use from the 19th century.

UK actress Dana Wynter (b.1927) (original first name Dagmar); Irish-born UK popular singer Dana (b.1952) (original name Rosemary Brown); US actress Dana Delany (b.1956).

Dandy A borrowing of the standard word, perhaps also suggesting the word *dainty* or serving as a sort of diminutive of DANIELLE. The name has found occasional use among English speakers from the early 20th century.

UK actress Dandy Nichols (1907–86).

Dane From the surname, itself a variant of DEAN, but perhaps also (in the UK) evoking a 'Viking' connection. The name has found some favour from the 20th century.

US writer of westerns, Dane Coolidge (1873–1940); US actor Dane Clark (1913–98) (original name Bernard Zanville).

Daniel The name is of biblical origin, from Hebrew *Dāni'el*, 'God is my judge', although in some instances it may be an English form of the Irish name *Domhnall*, which gave English DONALD. It has been in use among English speakers from medieval times, with a marked increase in popularity from the second half of the 1970s. It has long been associated with Ireland. In the Bible Daniel is the prophet whose story is told in the book named for him; he is famous for being saved by God from the lions' den into which his enemies had thrown him. (This link may have produced a subconscious association between 'Daniel' and 'den'.) In literature the name is familiar as that of the Jewish central character in George Eliot's novel *Daniel Deronda* (1876). The regular diminutives, both of which are in independent use, are DAN and DANNY.

English novelist Daniel Defoe (1660–1731); US frontiersman Daniel Boone (1734–1820); UK actor Daniel Massey (1933–98); UK rower Daniel Topolski (b.1945); UK actor Daniel Day-Lewis (b.1957).

Dannie see **Danny**.

Danielle A French feminine form of DANIEL, first found in English-speaking use from the 1940s and increasingly popular from the 1980s. Variants include *Daniela*, *Daniella* and *Danniella*, the last as for the UK actress Danniella Westbrook (b.1973), while diminutives are usually *Dan*, *Dani*, *Dannie* and *Danny*, the second of these as for the UK TV presenter Dani Behr (b.1974).

French-born US actress Danielle Darrieux (b.1917); US writer Danielle Steel (b.1947); US actress Danielle Fishel (b.1981).

Danny An independently adopted diminutive of DANIEL, in general use among English speakers from the 1930s, with a long-standing association with Ireland. It was undoubtedly popularized by the song 'Danny Boy' (1913), sung to the melody of the famous Irish folk tune 'The Londonderry Air'. A variant spelling is *Dannie*, as for the UK poet Dannie Abse (b.1923). The usual diminutive is DAN, in independent use.

US jockey Danny Maher (1881–1916); UK film producer Danny Angel (1911–99); US comedian Danny Thomas (1912–91) (original name Amos Jacobs); US actor Danny Kaye (1913–87) (original name David Daniel Kaminsky); Northern Ireland-born UK footballer Danny Blanchflower (1926–93) (original first names Robert Dennis); Irish entertainer Danny La Rue (b.1927) (original name Daniel Patrick Carroll); US actors Danny Aiello (b.1933), Danny de Vito (b.1944), Danny Glover (b.1947); UK columnist Danny Danziger (b.1953); UK athlete Danny Nightingale (b.1954); UK TV presenter Danny Baker (b.1957); UK tennis player Danny Sapsford (b.1969).

Daphne An adoption of the Greek name, famous in classical mythology as that of the nymph who, when chased by Apollo, turned into a laurel tree (Greek *daphnē*). The name has been in English-speaking use from the 18th century, with its peak of popularity from the late 19th century to the 1930s.

After the 1950s it declined sharply and is now rarely found. Diminutives include *Daff*, *Daffy* and *Daph*, with these happening to suggest either *daffodil*, as a flower name, or else *daffy* in the sense of 'daft', 'crazy'. (The latter may have helped the name's demise.)

Australian-born US actress Daphne Pollard (1890–1978); UK novelist Daphne du Maurier (1907–89); UK actress Daphne Anderson (b.1922); UK writer Daphne Wright (b.1951).

Darcey (f.) A female adoption of the male name DARCY, in select use among English speakers in the 20th century, chiefly in the US.

UK ballerina Darcey Bussell (b.1969).

Darcy (m.) From the (Norman) surname, and in selective use among English speakers from at least the 19th century. The name may have owed some of its vogue to the surname of Fitzwilliam Darcy, the central male character of Jane Austen's novel *Pride and Prejudice* (1813). The name has always had an 'aristocratic' ring.

Darlene A name that is apparently based on *darling*, with an ending from a name such as CHARLENE. Its peak of popularity in the US was in the 1950s, although both there and in the UK it has now fallen from favour. Variants *Darleen* and *Darline* occur, the former as for the US actress Darleen Carr (b.1950).

US tennis player Darlene Hard (b.1936); US pop singer Darlene Love (b.1938).

Darrell From the surname, first adopted in the English-speaking world in the late 19th century, the name has been modestly but consistently in favour in the 20th century. DARRYL may not be a related name.

US archer Darrell Pace (b.1956); US athlete Darrell Robinson (b.1963).

Darren The name is apparently an alteration of DARRELL, with its final syllable formed by association with the female names KAREN and SHARON, which were becoming fashionable when it first came into evidence in the 1950s. Its popularity peak was in the 1970s, since when it has gradually declined. It may have owed something of its original vogue to the surnames of the US popular singers James Darren (b.1936) (original surname Ercolani) and/or Bobby Darin (1936–73) (original name Walden Robert Cassotto), and was doubtless boosted by Darrin, husband of the witch Samantha in the US TV series *Bewitched* (1964–71).

US actor Darren McGavin (b.1922); Australian tennis player Darren Cahill (b.1965); UK badminton player Darren Hall (b.1965); UK cricketer Darren Bicknell (b.1967); UK actor Darren Boyd (b.1970); UK footballer Darren Anderton (b.1972).

Darryl Either from the surname or as an independently adopted variant of DARRELL, with a spelling perhaps prompted by a name such as CHERYL. The name has been in modest favour from the 1930s and is still by no means in decline. The variant DARYL is in independent use.

US film executive Darryl F. Zanuck (1902–79); US actor Darryl Hickman (b.1931).

Daryl (m.) An independently adopted variant of DARRYL, in select but regular English-speaking use from the 1940s, especially in the US.

US pop singers Daryl Dragon (b.1942), Daryl Hall (b.1949); UK rugby player Daryl Powell (b.1965).

Daryl (f.) A female adoption of the male name DARYL (or DARRELL), probably influenced by a name such as CHERYL. It has enjoyed modest adoption from the 1950s.

US actress Daryl Hannah (b.1960).

Dave An independently adopted diminutive of DAVID, in regular English-speaking use from the early 20th century, and particularly favoured by sportsmen, entertainers, pop musicians and the like. Its own diminutive is DAVY, which is also in independent use.

US jazz musician Dave Brubeck (b.1920); US bandleader Dave Bartholomew (b.1920); Irish comedian Dave Allen (b.1936); Irish boxer Dave McAuley (b.1961).

Davey see **Davy**.

David A familiar biblical name, from Hebrew *Dāwid*, perhaps meaning 'favourite', the name has been in regular use in the English-speaking world from medieval times and has become especially popular in Wales and Scotland. In the Bible David is the famous 'giant killer' who slew Goliath with a sling-shot and later, after the death of Saul, became king of Judah and eventually all Israel. The 7th-century St David became the patron saint of Wales, while in the 12th century another St David was king of Scotland. In Richard Brinsley Sheridan's play *The Rivals* (1775) David is the servant of Bob Acres, while the name is famously that of the central character of Charles Dickens's novel *David Copperfeld* (1849–50). The diminutives DAVE and DAVY are in independent use.

UK actor David Niven (1910–83); UK actor David Lodge (b.1921); UK naturalists, broadcasters Sir David Attenborough (b.1926), David Bellamy (b.1933); UK writer David Lodge (b.1935); UK TV sports presenter David Vine (b.1936); UK artist David Hockney (b.1937); UK politicians Sir David Steel (b.1938), David Owen, Lord Owen (b.1938); UK TV presenters David Dimbleby (b.1938), Sir David Frost (b.1939); UK actors David Jason (b.1940), David Suchet (b.1946); UK pop singers David Bowie (b.1947), David Essex (b.1947); UK sports commentator David Coleman (b.1949); UK actors David Janson (b.1950), David Yip (b.1951); UK swimmer David Wilkie (b.1954).

Davie see **Davy**.

Davina A Scottish feminine form of DAVID, in very select English-speaking use from the early 20th century, and having aristocratic associations. Variants include *Davida*, *Davena* and *Davinia*.

UK daughter of Earl of Lytton, Lady Davina Woodhouse (1909–95) (original first name Davidema); Scottish daughter of Marquess of Exeter, Lady Davina Barnard (b.1931); UK actress Davina Phillips (b.1941); Northern Ireland daughter of Earl of Erne, Lady Davina Scarr (b.1961); UK TV presenter Davina McCall (b.1967); UK daughter of Duke of Gloucester, Lady Davina Windsor (b.1977).

Davinia see **Davina**, **Divina**.

Davy An independently adopted diminutive of DAVID, in general English-speaking use from the 18th century. Davy Wilson is a character in Walter Scott's novel *The Antiquary* (1816), and Lieutenant David (Davy) Muir is in James Fenimore Cooper's novel *The Pathfinder* (1840). The name also serves as a diminutive of DAVE and has variants *Davey* and *Davie*.

US frontiersman, soldier Davy Crockett (1786–1836).

Dawn A borrowing of the standard word, but perhaps regarded by some as an English translation of the Latin name AURORA. It first came into favour in the 20th century and was used fairly modestly until the second half of the 1960s, when it jumped in popularity. It has since resumed a lower profile and is now much less frequently found.

UK writer Dawn Powell (1897–1965); UK actress Dawn Addams (1930–85); Australian swimmer Dawn Fraser (b.1937); UK politician Dawn Primarolo (b.1954); UK actresses Dawn French (b.1957), Dawn Acton (b.1977).

Dean From the surname, but also having a popular association with the standard word, implying a superior status. The name, which has been in fairly regular use from the late 19th century, was first taken up in the US. In the UK it grew in popularity from the 1960s to peak in the 1980s. DANA and DANE are often regarded as related names.

US statesman Dean Acheson (1893–1971); US actor Dean Jagger (1903–91); US statesman Dean Rusk (1909–94); US actors Dean Martin (1917–95) (original name Dino Crocetti), Dean Jones (b.1931), Dean Stockwell (b.1935); US novelist Dean Koontz (b.1945); US actor Dean Sullivan (b.1955); UK jockey Dean McKeown (b.1960); UK rugby player Dean Richards (b.1963); UK cricketer Dean Hodgson (b.1966).

Deanna A variant of DIANA, influenced by ANNA, in select English-speaking use from the 1930s but never common.

Canadian-born US singer, actress Deanna Durbin (b.1921) (original first names Edna Mae); UK writer Deanna Maclaren (b.1944).

Debbie The name is an independently adopted diminutive of DEBORAH or DEBRA, perhaps to some suggesting *deb* as a colloquial abbreviation of *debutante*. The name has been in fairly regular use from the 1950s, achieving a peak in popularity in the second half of the 1960s. The variant spelling *Debby* exists, as for the US pop singer Debby Boone (b.1956). Diminutives are *Deb* and *Debs*.

US actress Debbie Reynolds (b.1932) (original first names Mary Frances); UK businesswoman Debbie Moore (b.1946); US swimmer Debbie Meyer (b.1952); UK actress Debbie Wheeler (b.1952); UK playwright Debbie Horsfield (b.1955); UK TV presenters Debbie Thrower (b.1957), Debbie Greenwood (b.1959); UK yachtswoman Debbie Jarvis (b.1964); UK croquet player Debbie Cornelius (b.1966); US rock singer Debbie Gibson (b.1970).

Deborah A biblical name, from Hebrew *Debōrāh*, 'bee' (compare MELISSA), adopted in England by the Puritans from the 16th century. The name became suddenly popular in the 1960s, but has since tailed off considerably. In the Bible the name is that of three women: the nurse of Rebecca, the wife of Lapidoth (the prophetess and judge whose story is told in the 'Song of Deborah') and the mother of Ananiel. In later literature it is found for several characters, including Deborah Hornbeck, who is married to a jealous husband in Tobias Smollett's novel *Peregrine Pickle* (1751); Deborah Primrose, the wife of Dr Charles Primrose, the central character in Oliver Goldsmith's novel *The Vicar of Wakefield* (1766); Deborah Jenkyns, in Elizabeth Gaskell's novel *Cranford* (1851–3); and Deborah Beresford, daughter of Tuppence and Tommy Beresford in Agatha Christie's novel *N or M?* (1941). A variant in independent use is DEBRA, while the most common diminutive, also used in its own right, is DEBBIE.

UK actress Deborah Kerr (b.1921); US pop singer Deborah Harry (b.1945); UK actress Deborah Grant (b.1947); UK novelist Deborah Moggach (b.1948); US swimmer Deborah Meyer (b.1952); US actress Deborah Raffin (b.1953); UK ballerina Deborah Bull (b.1963); UK actress Deborah McAndrew (b.1967).

Debra An independently adopted variant of DEBORAH, first found in the 1920s and gaining a rise in popularity in the 1960s, like its source name.

US actresses Debra Paget (b.1933), Debra Winger (b.1955), Debra Blake (b.1961); UK actress Debra Beaumont (b.1967).

Debs see **Debbie**.

Declan This is the English form of the Irish name *Deaglán*, of unknown origin. The name has been mostly in Irish use from the 1940s but began to catch on more generally among English speakers in the 1990s. It was originally associated with the 5th-century St Declan. The UK pop singer Elvis Costello (b.1954) was born Declan MacManus.

UK actor Declan Donnelly (b.1975).

Dee (f.) This name can evolve as a diminutive of any name beginning *D-*, such as DELIA and, especially, DOROTHY. For Scottish bearers, the name could derive from that of the River Dee.

Australian-born UK magazine editor Dee Nolan (b.1953) (original first name Deidre); Scottish actress Dee Hepburn (b.1961).

Deirdre The name comes from the legendary Irish heroine, sometimes known as Deirdre of the Sorrows, and is perhaps related to Irish *deardan*, 'storm', so means something like 'raging one'. To English speakers, however, who adopted it more generally from the 1930s, it suggests *dear*. Various literary works have made the name known, such as the novel *Deirdre* (1903) by 'Fiona Macleod' (William Sharp), W.B. Yeats's drama *Deirdre* (1907) and J.M. Synge play's *Deirdre of the Sorrows* (1910). Variant spellings are *Deidre* and *Diedre*, the former as for the UK 'agony aunt' Deidre Sanders (b.1945), the latter as for Diedre Henderson in Agatha Christie's novel *Mrs McGinty's Dead* (1952) (US title *Blood Will Tell*).

UK magazine editors Deirdre Mcsharry (b.1932), Deirdre Vine (b.1953).

Del see **Derek**.

Delbert The name appears to be a modification of a name such as ALBERT or ROBERT. It has enjoyed selective English-speaking adoption in the 20th century, mainly among black Americans. Some of its vogue in the UK may have resulted from the character, DJ Delbert Wilkins, created by the UK comedian Lenny Henry in his TV series *The Lenny Henry Show* (1987).

US film director Delbert Mann (b.1920); US country musician Delbert McClinton (b.1940).

Delia A classical name, from the Greek island of *Delos*, which in Greek mythology was the home of Artemis and Apollo. The name has enjoyed selective favour among English speakers from the late 16th century, when it was taken up by pastoral poets, as for Samuel Daniel's collection of sonnets *Delia* (1592).

A variant is DELLA, in independent use, and a diminutive is *Dee*.

US writer Delia Bacon (1811–59); UK food writer, broadcaster Delia Smith (b.1941).

Delilah A biblical name, from Hebrew *Delīlāh*, 'delight' (the words are not related), although it has also been traced back to Arabic *dalla*, 'to tease', 'to flirt'. The name was adopted by Puritans in the 17th century, but surprisingly, in view of its attractive sound and sense, it is very rare today. In the Bible Delilah is the woman who took Samson as a lover, then betrayed him to the Philistines. (This prompts some to derive her name from Hebrew *laylah*, 'night', as opposed to Samson's name, which means 'sun'. Compare LEILA.) The name was later familiar from Camille Saint-Saëns's opera *Samson and Delilah* (1877) and to some extent popularized by the song 'Delilah' (1917).

Della An independent adoption of a diminutive of ADELA or a variant of DELIA, in English-speaking use from the late 19th century. Della Williams is a character in John Dos Passos's trilogy *U.S.A.* (1930–36), and Della Street is secretary to the investigative lawyer Perry Mason in the series of crime novels (1933–73) by Erle Stanley Gardner. *Dell* is a frequent diminutive.

US pop singer Della Reese (b.1931) (original name Dellareese Talia-ferro); Welsh opera singer Della Jones (b.*c*.1940).

Delphine A French name, from Latin *Delphina*, 'woman of Delphi', now perhaps associated by English speakers with *delphinium*, as a kind of flower name. It is fairly common among 20th-century American blacks, and may have owed some of its initial fashion to Madame de Staël's novel in letter form, *Delphine* (1802). A frequent variant is *Delphina*, but *Delvene* also exists, as for the Australian actress Delvene Delaney (b.1951).

French actress Delphine Seyrig (1932–90); UK TV costume designer Delphine Roche-Gordon (b.1945).

Demelza A Cornish name in occasional English-speaking use from the 1950s. The name is that of the leading character in the 'Poldark' historical novels by Winston Graham, which are set in 18th-century Cornwall, the second of which was *Demelza* (1946). The name was made familiar by the TV series *Poldark* (1975–7) based on these, in which Demelza was played by Angharad Rees. It is not a genuine Cornish first name, however, but that of a Cornish village adopted by Graham for his heroine. (Perhaps he wanted a female equivalent for the Cornish name DENZIL.)

Den see **Dennis**.

Deneice, Deniece see **Denise**.

Denis An independently adopted variant of DENNIS, in fairly regular 20th-century use among English speakers, but with its prime period in the 1920s.

UK politician Denis Healey, Lord Healey (b.1917); UK cricketer Denis Compton (1918–97); UK pianist Denis Matthews (1919–88); UK broadcaster Denis Norden (b.1922); UK actor Denis Quilley (b.1927); UK footballers Denis Law (b.1940), Denis Smith (b.1947); UK actor Denis Lawson (b.1947).

Denise The name is a French feminine form of DENNIS, found only rarely among English speakers until the 1920s, and with its most popular period of adoption in the 1960s. Variant forms are *Deneice* and *Deniece*, the latter familiar from the US pop singer Deniece Williams (b.1951).

UK romantic novelist Denise Robins (1897–1985) (original first name Naomi; mother was Denise); UK-born US poet Denise Levertov (1923–97); US actress Denise Alexander (b.1945); UK TV actress, presenter Denise Van Outen (b.1974).

Dennis The name has its origin in the medieval spoken form of the Greek name *Dionysios*, originally given someone who revered this classical god of wine. (His own name is probably related to that of *Zeus*.) It was introduced to England by the Normans, and was in select use until the early 20th century. It suddenly became popular in the second half of the 1920s, but it then gradually declined and today is uncommon. It was initially famous from the 3rd-century St Denis, patron of France. In Shakespeare's *As You Like It* (1599) Dennis is a servant to Oliver. The variant spelling DENIS is found independently, although not as widely. Diminutives include *Den* and *Denny*, the latter as for the New Zealand motor-racing driver Denny Hulme (1936–92).

UK actor Dennis Hoey (1893–1960) (original name Samuel David Hyams); UK novelist Dennis Wheatley (1897–1977); UK opera singer Dennis Noble (1899–1966); US actors Dennis O'Keefe (1908–68) (original name Edward 'Bud' Flanagan), Dennis Morgan (1910–94); UK actor Dennis Price (1915–73) (original name Dennistoun Franklyn John Rose-Price); US actor Dennis Weaver (b.1924); UK dramatist Dennis Potter (1935–94); UK actor Dennis Waterman (b.1948); Northern Ireland snooker player Dennis Taylor (b.1949).

Denzil From the (Cornish) surname, and in very select use from the late 19th century. A variant spelling is *Denzel*, as for the US actor Denzel Washington (b.1954).

UK sports writer Denzil Batchelor (1906–69); UK politician Denzil Davies (b.1938).

Derek An English form of the original German name *Theodoric* (which also gave TERRY), itself meaning 'ruler of the people'. The name was taken up in the English-speaking world in the late 19th century, with a popularity peak in the second half of the 1930s, after which it gradually declined. The variant DERRICK is in independent use, and there are a number of other forms of the name, such as *Deryck*, as for the UK actor Deryck Guyler (1914–99). The usual diminutive is *Del*.

UK actors Derek Farr (1912–86), Derek Bond (b.1919), Derek Waring (b.1930), Derek Nimmo (1932–99); UK ballet dancer Derek Rencher (b.1932); UK actors Derek Martin (b.1933), Derek Fowlds (b.1937), Sir Derek Jacobi (b.1938); UK film director Derek Jarman (1942–94).

Dermot This is an English form of the Irish name *Diarmaid*, itself of uncertain origin, but perhaps combining *di*, 'without', and *airmait*, 'envy'. It has remained chiefly in Irish use from the 19th century. Its main claim to fame is as the name of the legendary Irish king of Tara.

UK actor Dermot Walsh (b.1924); Irish actors Dermot Crowley (b.1947), Dermot Morgan (1952–98); Irish writer Dermot Bolger (b.1959); US actor Dermot Mulroney (b.1963).

Derrick This independently adopted variant of DEREK was taken up by some English speakers from the late 19th century and, in the 20th century, was favoured by some black Americans.

UK actor Derrick de Marney (1906–78).

Dervla An Irish name, perhaps meaning 'daughter of a poet', from the prefix *dear-*, 'daughter', and *file*, 'poet', or else 'daughter of Ireland', from *Fál*, a poetic name for Ireland. It remains almost exclusively in Irish use.

Irish travel writer Dervla Murphy (b.1931); Irish actress Dervla Kirwan (b.1971).

Deryck see **Derek**.

Desdemona The name probably represents a Latin form of the Greek word *dusdaimōn*, 'ill-fated', as aptly chosen by Shakespeare for the innocent wife of Othello, tragically murdered by her husband in *Othello* (1602–4). The name is found only rarely in English-speaking use.

Désirée This is an obviously French name that represents the original Latin name *Desiderata*, the feminine form of

Desiderius or *Desideratus*, 'desired'. The name was originally given to a longed-for child, but in its modern form it popularly expresses the wish that the child will grow up to be a desirable woman. It has found select favour among English speakers from the 19th century, mainly among black Americans. The name became familiar from the US film *Désirée* (1957), based on the novel of 1953 so titled by Annemarie Selinko. This was a fictionalized biography of one of Napoleon's early mistresses, in real life Bernardine Eugénie Désirée Clary, who became Queen of Sweden.

Desmond An adoption of the (Irish) surname, with a spelling apparently influenced by ESMOND. The name had been introduced from Ireland to England by the end of the 19th century, when it achieved some popularity until the 1920s, after which it declined, although enjoying something of a revival in the 1960s. In H.A. Vachell's school story *The Hill* (1905), about Harrow, Desmond is a close friend of John Verney. The usual diminutive is *Des*, as for the UK popular singer Des O'Connor (b.1932) and Irish golfer Des Smyth (b.1953).

UK thriller writer Desmond Bagley (1923–83); UK broadcaster Desmond Carrington (b.1926); UK writer Desmond Cory (b.1928); UK popular zoologist, anthropologist Desmond Morris (b.1928); UK TV producer, presenter Desmond Wilcox (1931–2000); UK TV sports presenter Desmond Lynam (b.1942); UK ballet dancer Desmond Kelly (b.1942); UK actor Desmond Barrit (b.1944).

Detta see **Bernadette**.

Devon A name apparently from that of the English county, but found chiefly among black Americans. It has been in evidence only since the 1960s.

Jamaican-born UK cricketer Devon Malcolm (b.1963).

Dexter From the surname, and in select use from the 1930s, mainly in the US, the name may in some cases be popularly associated with English *dexter*, as if meaning 'right-hand person', implying a loyal attendant, although the surname actually means 'dyer'. The usual diminutive is *Dex*.

US jazz saxophonist Dexter Gordon (1923–90); UK actor Dexter Fletcher (b.1966).

Di see **Diana, Dinah**.

Diana The name is that of the Greek goddess of the moon and the hunt, itself probably related to Latin *dea*, 'goddess'. It was first regularly used by English speakers in the 16th century, although its pagan origins ran counter to the many biblical names coming into favour at this time. In the 20th century it achieved its peak of popularity in the 1930s. Literary characters of the name include Diana, a widow's daughter in Shakespeare's *All's Well That Ends Well* (1603–4); Diana Vernon, the heroine of Walter Scott's novel *Rob Roy* (1817); Diana Rivers, sister of St John Rivers, Jane Eyre's cousin in Charlotte Brontë's novel *Jane Eyre* (1847); and Diana Warwick, the central character of George Meredith's novel *Diana of the Crossways* (1885). More recently it was popularized by the Paul Anka hit song 'Diana' (1957). The most popular variant in independent use is DIANE, while the usual diminutive is *Di*.

UK actress Diana Wynyard (1906–64); US ballerina Diana Adams (1926–93); UK actresses Diana Dors (1931–84), Diana Davies (b.1936), Dame Diana Rigg (b.1938); UK rower Diana Ellis (b.1938); US pop singer Diana Ross (b.1944) (original name Diane Earle); UK actress Diana Quick (b.1946); UK aristocrat Lady Diana Spencer, Princess of Wales (1961–97).

Diane A French form of DIANA, in increasingly popular use among English speakers from the 1930s to the 1960s, after which it fairly rapidly fell from favour. It may have been given an early boost by the popular song 'Diane' in the film *What Price Glory* (1926). The variant *Dianne* became quite fashionable, while other variants have been made familiar by their bearers, such as *Dyan*, by the US actress Dyan Cannon (b.1938) (from her middle name Diane), and *Diahann*, by the US singer Diahann Carroll (b.1935) (original name Carol Diahann Johnson).

US photographer Diane Arbus (1923–71); US actress Diane Ladd (b.1932); Australian actress Diane Cilento (b.1933); US actresses Diane Baker (b.1938), Diane Keen (b.1946); UK politician Diane Abbott (b.1953); US actress Diane Lane (b.1963); UK athlete Diane Modahl (b.1966); UK actress Diane Burke (b.1976).

Dick An independently adopted diminutive of RICHARD, in regular English-speaking use from at least the 17th century and borne by the English highwayman Dick Turpin (1706–39). (The substitution of *D-* for *R-* is said to have arisen from the attempts made by the English to pronounce the Norman French trilled *r*.) In Charles Dickens's novel *The Old Curiosity Shop* (1840–41) Dick Swiveller is the disreputable friend of Fred Trent, while Dick Dewy is a central character in Thomas Hardy's novel *Under the Greenwood Tree* (1872). The diminutive DICKIE is in independent use.

UK comedian Dick Emery (1917–83); UK thriller writer Dick Francis (b.1920); US comedian Dick van Dyke (b.1925); US actor Dick Van Patten (b.1928); Irish politician Dick Spring (b.1950).

Dickie An independently adopted diminutive of DICK or its source name RICHARD that has been in fairly regular use from the 19th century. The name is sometimes adopted by people surnamed *Bird*, as for the UK cricket umpire Dickie Bird (b.1933) (original first names Harold Dennis). The alternative spelling *Dicky* also occurs.

UK entertainer Dickie Henderson (1922–85); UK pop singer Dickie Valentine (1929–71); UK TV sports presenter Dickie Davies (b.1933).

Diedre see **Deirdre**.

Diggory The origin of the name is uncertain, but it may derive from the name borne by the central character in the early 14th-century romance *Sir Degaré*, itself perhaps a corruption of French *l'esgaré*, 'the lost one'. The name has enjoyed occasional adoption among English speakers from the 18th century. In Oliver Goldsmith's play *She Stoops to Conquer* (1773) Diggory is a servant; in Charles Dickens's novel *Martin Chuzzlewit* (1843–4) Diggory Chuzzlewit is a family member; and in Thomas Hardy's novel *The Return of the Native* (1878) Diggory Venn, a travelling reddleman (dealer in red ochre), marries Thomasin Yeobright. The variant spelling *Digory* exists, as for Digory Kirke, in C.S. Lewis's 'Narnia' books for children (1950s).

Dil, **Dill** see **Dilys**.

Dilly An independently adopted diminutive of DILYS or some similar sounding name. A variant spelling is *Dillie*, as for the UK entertainer and actress Dillie Keane (b.1952).

UK radio presenter Dilly Barlow (b.1952) (original first name Gillian).

Dilys A Welsh name, from the standard word *dilys* meaning 'genuine', 'sincere'. It has found both Welsh- and English-speaking adoption from the 19th century. Variants are mainly of spelling, such as *Dylis* and *Dyllis*, while diminutives are commonly *Dil*, *Dill* or DILLY, this last variant being in independent use.

UK film critic Dilys Powell (1901–95).

Dinah A biblical name, from Hebrew *Dīnāh*, 'vindicated'. The name is now often associated with DIANA, but that name has a different origin. Dinah was adopted by English Puritans in the 16th century, reaching its greatest popularity in the 19th but in much more modest evidence in the 20th. In the Bible Dinah is the daughter of Jacob and Leah, raped by Shechem and bloodily revenged by her brothers. Literary characters of the name include Dinah, Captain Toby Shandy's wife in Laurence Sterne's novel *Tristram Shandy* (1759–67); Dinah, St Clare's head cook in Harriet Beecher Stowe's novel *Uncle Tom's Cabin* (1852); and Dinah Morris, who marries the title character in George Eliot's novel *Adam Bede* (1859). The popular song 'Dinah' (1925) made the name well known. A not uncommon variant is *Dina*, while *Di* is a frequent diminutive.

US cabaret singer Dinah Shore (1917–94) (original first names Frances Rose); UK actress Dinah Sheridan (b.1920); US singer Dinah Washington (1924–63) (original name Ruth Lee Jones); US actress Dinah Manoff (b.1958).

Dion The name is a shortened form of a Greek name such as *Dionysius* (see DENNIS), which was adopted in very select use among English speakers from the 16th century and from the 19th century was favoured by black Americans. In Shakespeare's *The Winter's Tale* (1610–11) Dion is a Sicilian lord, as he also is in Beaumont and Fletcher's play *Philaster* (*c.*1609).

Irish playwright Dion Boucicault (1820–90) (original name Dionysius Lardner Boursiquot).

Dionne A feminine form of DION, taken up by black people, especially in the US, from the 1930s. Variants include *Dionna* and *Dione*.

US pop singer Dionne Warwick (b.1941).

Dirk A Dutch form of DEREK, popularly associated with the standard word for a Scottish dagger. The name has found occasional adoption among English speakers from the mid-20th century.

UK actor of Dutch descent Dirk Bogarde (1921–99) (original name Derek Gentron Gaspart Ulric van den Bogaerde); US actor Dirk Benedict (b.1945).

Divina The name is probably a variant of DAVINA, influenced by the word *divine*. It has found some favour among English speakers in the 20th century. A variant is *Davinia*, perhaps influenced by LAVINIA.

UK-Polish motor-racing driver, speed skier Divina Galica (b.1944).

Dodie, Dod, Doll see **Dorothy**.

Dolly (m.) see **Adolph, Adolphus**.

Dolly (f.) An independently adopted variant of DOROTHEA or DOROTHY, popularly associated with *doll* or its diminutive *dolly* (a word that probably evolved from that name), the name has been in English-speaking use from the 16th century. It was common in the 18th century, then declined somewhat, but is still found today. In Tobias Smollett's novel *Sir Launcelot Greaves* (1762) Dolly Cowslip is the assumed name of Dorothy Greaves. Later, in Charles Dickens's novel *Barnaby Rudge* (1841) Dolly Varden marries Joe Willet. The name was popularized by the Spanish-American War hit 'Goodbye, Dolly Gray' (1900) and more recently by the musical *Hello, Dolly!* (1964), with the familiar title song of the same name. A variant spelling *Dolley* sometimes occurs, as for the US politician Dolley (also Dolly) Madison (1768–1849). The usual diminutive is *Doll*, as for Doll Tearsheet, Falstaff's, mistress in Shakespeare's *Henry IV, Part 2* (1597).

UK folk musician Dolly Collins (b.1933); US country and western singer Dolly Parton (b.1946).

Dolores The name derives from Spanish *dolores*, 'sorrows', as the last word of a title of the Virgin Mary, *María de los Dolores*, Mary of the Sorrows. It was first adopted on any scale in the 20th century, especially among Spanish speakers, and is today still more common in the US than the UK. Two diminutives that gained independent use are LOLA and LOLITA.

Mexican-born US actress Dolores Del Rio (1905–83); US actress Dolores Costello (1905–79); US singer, dancer Dolores Gray (b.1924); US actresses Dolores Moran (1924–82), Dolores Michaels (b.1930).

Dolph see **Adolph**.

Dominic An English version of the Latin name *Dominicus*, itself based on *dominus*, 'lord'. It has been in use with English speakers from medieval times, especially by Roman Catholics, and it gained a recent popularity peak in the second half of the 1970s. Its famous historic bearer was St Dominic, founder of the Dominican order of monks in the 13th century. In George Eliot's novel *Felix Holt* (1866) Dominic is a valet to Harold Transome. The variant form *Dominick* exists.

Irish writer Dominic Behan (1928–89); UK actor Dominic Guard (b.1954); UK columnist Dominic Lawson (b.1956); UK actor Dominic Jephcott (b.1957).

Dominique A French feminine form of DOMINIC, in select use among English speakers from the 1960s.

UK writer Dominique Moraes (b.1938); French actress Dominique Sanda (b.1948); UK actress Dominique Barnes (b.1966).

Don An independently adopted diminutive of DONALD or DONOVAN that has been in regular if modest use among English speakers from the 19th century. Don Stevens is a character in John Dos Passos's trilogy *U.S.A.* (1930–36). There may be some popular association with the Spanish honorary title *Don*, as for Don Juan or Don Quixote, a misleading link that was perhaps further promoted by the stories by Giovanni Guareschi about the Italian priest Don Camillo, which appeared in English translation in the 1950s. The diminutive DONNY is in independent use.

US writer Don Marquis (1878–1937); US radio and TV announcer Don Wilson (1900–82); US actor Don Ameche (1908–93) (original name Dominic Felix Amici); Australian cricketer Sir Don Bradman (1908–2001); US tennis player Don Budge (1915–2000); UK football manager Don Revie (1927–89); UK actor Don Henderson (b.1932); UK athlete Don Thompson (b.1933); UK religious writer Don Cupitt (b.1934); US country singer Don Williams (b.1939); US pop singer Don McLean (b.1945); US actor Don Johnson (b.1950).

Donald The name is an English form of the Gaelic name *Domhnall*, formed from Celtic *dubno*, 'world', and *val*, 'rule', so having an overall meaning 'powerful worldwide'. (The final *-d* of the name is by association with names such as DUGALD.) The name has long been popular in Scotland, where it is associated with the clan of the same name, and it gained its peak of popularity more generally among English speakers in the 1930s, since when it has declined noticeably, perhaps partly through a trivial link with the Disney cartoon character Donald Duck. It is historically familiar as the name of many early kings of Scotland (to the 11th century). Walter Scott's novels have several characters of the name, such as Donald McDonald, gamekeeper to the Duke of Argyll in *The Heart of Midlothian* (1818). The usual diminutive, DON, is in independent use.

UK actor Donald Crisp (1880–1974); UK popular singer Donald Peers (1908–73); UK actors Donald Tandy (b.1918), Donald Pleasence (1919–95), Donald Sinden (b.1923); UK popular musician, entertainer Donald Swann (1923–94); US actor Donald O'Connor (b.1925); Canadian actor Donald Sutherland (b.1935); Scottish opera singer Donald Maxwell (b.1948).

Donna The name comes from the Italian word for 'lady' (in Italian a title, not a name), and is now popularly (and correctly) associated with MADONNA. It has been in favour with English speakers from the 1920s, especially in the US, and has achieved peaks of popularity twice since: in the 1960s and the 1980s. The name can combine with another, typically as *Donna-Marie*, which links the title of the Virgin Mary with her name.

US actresses Donna Reed (1921–86), Donna Douglas (b.1933) (original name Doris Smith), Donna Anderson (b.1938), Donna Corcoran (b.1943), Donna Mills (b.1947); US soul singer Donna Summer (b.1948) (original name LaDonna Adrian Gaines); US fashion designer Donna Karan (b.1948); US country singer Donna Fargo (b.1949) (original name Yvonne Vaughn); US actress Donna Butterworth (b.1956).

Donny An independently adopted diminutive of DON, DONALD or DONOVAN, in select English-speaking use from the early 20th century.

US popular singers Donny Hathaway (1945–79), Donny Osmond (b.1957) (original first name Donald).

Donovan From the (Irish) surname, itself meaning 'dark brown', referring to the colour of a person's hair, eyes or skin. The name has been in fairly general use among English speakers from the early 20th century. Its usual diminutive is DON, which is in independent use.

Scottish-born folk-rock singer Donovan (b.1946) (original name Donovan Leitch); Canadian athlete Donovan Bailey (b.1967).

Dora The name is an independently adopted short form of a name such as DOROTHEA, EUDORA, ISADORA or THEODORA. It was taken up by English speakers from the 19th century but is now mostly out of favour. It was made familiar by Dora Spenlow, child wife of the central character, in Charles Dickens's novel *David Copperfield* (1849–50). Dora Wordsworth (1804–47), daughter of the poet, was christened Dorothy (for her aunt) but always called herself Dora in adult life. Diminutives are *Dorry* or *Dory*.

UK writer Dora Greenwell (1821–82); Irish poet Dora Sigerson (1866–1918); UK writer Dora Saint (Miss Read) (b.1913); UK actress Dora Bryan (b.1924).

Dorcas The name comes from the Greek word *dorkas*, 'doe', 'gazelle'. It was originally not an actual name and is used in the Bible to explain the name Tabitha: 'A certain disciple named Tabitha, which by interpretation is called Dorcas' (Acts 9.36). The name was adopted by Puritans in the 17th century and has been occasionally found in select use since. Lady Dorcas Clare is one of the main characters in the anonymous romantic comedy *The Merry Devil of Edmonton* (1608), while in Shakespeare's *The Winter's Tale* (1610–11) Dorcas is a shepherdess. Later, Samuel Richardson's novel *Clarissa* (1748) has Dorcas Martindale as Clarissa Harlowe's attendant when she is locked up.

Doreen The name is probably a blend of names such as DORA and DOROTHY and CATHERINE (in its form KATHLEEN) or MAUREEN. It first found favour among English speakers in the late 19th century but, after enjoying a peak of popularity in the second half of the 1930s, has now generally declined. In literature the name is that of the central character in Edna Lyall's novel *Doreen* (1894).

UK jazz singer Doreen Henry (1906–90); UK actress Doreen Sloane (b.1934); UK ballerina Doreen Wells (b.1937); Scottish actress Doreen Cameron (b.1949); UK actress Doreen Ingleton (b.1966).

Dorian This is a name that appears to derive from the Latin name *Dorius*, itself from a Greek name meaning 'Dorian' (for a person from Doris, the ancient region of central Greece). It is sometimes felt to be a male equivalent of DORA or DORIS, with its ending influenced by names such as ADRIAN or JULIAN. It has been very modestly taken up from the early 20th century, and was made familiar by the title character of Oscar Wilde's novel *The Picture of Dorian Gray* (1891).

UK equestrian commentator Dorian Williams (1914–85); US actor Dorian Harewood (b.1951).

Dorinda A name that is a blend of DORA and a name such as BELINDA. It was at first mainly in 17th-century literary use but is now found selectively in general English-speaking adoption. Literary bearers of the name include Dorinda, sister of Miranda in John Dryden and William D'Avenant's version of Shakespeare's *The Tempest* (1667), and, better known, Dorinda, Lady Bountiful's daughter who marries Aimwell in George Farquhar's comedy *The Beaux' Stratagem* (1707).

US writer Dorinda Kamm (b.1952).

Doris An adoption of the Greek name, meaning 'woman from Doris' (a region of central Greece), borne in mythology by the mother of the Nereids. The name was later taken to be a blend of names such as DOROTHY and PHYLLIS. It was taken up among English speakers in the late 19th century but, after enjoying wide popularity in the first quarter of the 20th century, is now entirely out of fashion.

US ballerina, choreographer Doris Humphrey (1895–1958); UK actress Doris Speed (1899–1994); US actress Doris Davenport (1915–80); Southern African novelist Doris Lessing (b.1919); US actress Doris Day (b.1924); US tennis player Doris Hart (b.1925).

Dorothea An earlier form of DOROTHY, from a Latin form of the Greek name that combined *dōron*, 'gift', and *theos*, 'god', so (in Christian terms) 'gift of God'. (The Greek words are reversed in the male name THEODORE.) The name was taken up by English speakers from the 16th century, becoming popular in the 19th, especially in Scotland, but it is now only rarely found. It is historically familiar from the 4th-century virgin martyr St Dorothea. In George Eliot's novel *Middlemarch* (1871–2), Dorothea Brooke marries Edward Casaubon, then Will Ladislaw. The diminutive DORA is in independent use, and other diminutives are mostly as for DOROTHY.

Dorothy The usual English form of DOROTHEA, which has been in use from the 16th century, becoming popular throughout the English-speaking world, although falling from favour for a time in the 18th century. It is now much less common, after a popularity peak in the 1920s. In Tobias Smollett's novel *Sir Launcelot Greaves* (1762) Dorothy Greaves is the illegitimate daughter of the central character's uncle, Jonathan. In Walter Scott's novel *The Fair Maid of Perth* (1828) Dorothy Glover is housekeeper to the father of the central character, Catherine Glover. The many diminutives include DEE (used independently), *Dodo*, *Doll*, DOLLY (also in use in its own right), *Dot*,

Dottie, *Dotty* and *Dodie*. This last, originating from a childish attempt to say the full name, was made familiar by the UK playwright Dodie Smith (1896–1990).

US satirist, humorist Dorothy Parker (1893–1967); UK detective novelist Dorothy L. Sayers (1893–1957); US actress Dorothy Lamour (1914–96); UK popular singer Dorothy Squires (1915–98) (original first names Edna May); Scottish writer Dorothy Dunnett (b.1923); UK actress Dorothy Tutin (1930–2001); US figure skater Dorothy Hamill (b.1956).

Dorry, Dory see **Dora**.

Dosia see **Theodosia**.

Dot, Dottie, Dotty see **Dorothy**.

Doug, Dougie see **Dougal, Douglas**

Dougal An English form of the Gaelic name *Dubhgall*, formed from *dubh*, 'black', and *gall*, 'stranger', said to have been an Irish nickname for the dark-haired Danes who settled in their land, as compared to the blond Norwegians and Icelanders. The name has been mainly in Scottish use, with some general spread among English speakers from the early 20th century. In John Buchan's novel *Huntingtower* (1922), set in Scotland, Dougal is the chief of the 'Gorbals Diehards'. The name was subsequently popularized (or trivialized) by the cult children's TV programme *The Magic Roundabout* (1960s), in which the central character is the long-haired dog, Dougal. Diminutives are *Doug* and *Dougie*.

Douglas From the (Scottish) surname, but now associated with DOUGAL, this name has been in general English-speaking use from the 19th century and was fairly popular to the late 1930s, after which it rather fell from favour. The regular diminutive is *Doug*, as for the UK jockey Doug Smith (1917–89) and US actor Doug McClure (1935–95), with *Dougie*, *Dug* and *Duggie* also found, the first as for the Scottish TV sports presenter Dougie Donnelly (b.1953), the last as for the UK actor Duggie Brown (b.1940).

US Army chief Douglas MacArthur (1880–1964); US actors, father and son, Douglas Fairbanks (1883–1939), Douglas Fairbanks Jr (1909–2000).

Drew An independently adopted diminutive of ANDREW, although sometimes popularly associated with the surname. The name has chiefly been in Scottish use, but from the 1940s it gained a more general, if very modest adoption, in the English-speaking world.

US columnist Drew Pearson (1897–1969) (original first names Andrew Russell); US journalist Drew Middleton (1913–90); Scottish actor Drew Dawson (b.1943); UK food writer Drew Smith (b.1950).

Drusilla A biblical name, in origin a diminutive of the Roman clan name *Drusus*, itself said to be related to Greek *drosos*, 'dew', so meaning 'fruitful'. (On the basis of this doubtful origin, the biblical Drusilla's own name has been fancifully explained as meaning 'dewy-eyed'.) The name has enjoyed judicious adoption among English speakers from the 19th century, although it has never caught on widely. In the Bible Drusilla is the woman who leaves her husband in order to marry Felix, Roman procurator of Judaea. A literary bearer of the name is Drusilla Clack, niece of the late Sir John Verinder in Wilkie Collins's novel *The Moonstone* (1868), in which she is part narrator. In Thomas Hardy's novel *Jude the Obscure* (1894–5) Drusilla Fawley is the great-aunt of the central character, the orphan Jude Fawley. Variants are mainly of spellings, such as *Drucilla* and *Druscilla*, with the diminutive CILLA now an independent name.

UK writer, journalist Drusilla Beyfus (b.1927).

Duane An English version of the Gaelic name *Dubhán*, itself a diminutive form of *dubh*, 'black', so meaning 'little black-haired (or dark-skinned) one'. The name has enjoyed a modest vogue among English speakers from the 1940s, with its greatest popularity peak to date in the latter half of the 1970s. The variant form DWAYNE is in independent use and is the preferred spelling in the US.

US pop guitarist Duane Eddy (b.1938); US country singer Duane Allen (b.1943).

Dudley From the surname, the name has been in select use among English speakers from the mid-19th century. The surname was originally famous from the 16th-century English noble family, as prominently represented in the person of Robert Dudley, Earl of Leicester (*c.*1532–88), who almost married Queen Elizabeth I. The usual diminutive is *Dud*, apparently not influenced by the sense of *dud* to mean 'worthless thing'.

Irish actor Dudley Digges (1879–1947); US screenwriter Dudley Nichols (1895–1960); South African cricketer Dudley Nourse (1910–81); UK naval writer Dudley Pope (b.1925); UK actor Dudley Moore (b.1935).

Dug see **Douglas**, **Dugald**.

Dugald An independently adopted variant of DOUGAL, with the final *-d* by association with a name such as ARNOLD. It has chiefly found favour in Scotland, with some general adoption among English speakers in the 20th century. Dugald Dalgetty is a captain in Montrose's army in Walter Scott's novel *The Legend of Montrose* (1819). The diminutives *Dug* and *Duggie* exist.

Duggie see **Douglas**, **Dugald**.

Duke Either an independently adopted diminutive of MARMADUKE, or from the surname, or from the use of the word as a nickname (as for EARL and KING). The name has been current from the early 20th century, and has been particularly popular in the US. Marmaduke (Duke) Temple is a character in James Fenimore Cooper's novel *The Pioneers* (1823).

US jazz musician Duke Ellington (1899–1974) (original first names Edward Kennedy); US bandleader Duke Pearson (1932–80) (original name Columbus Calvin Jr); UK boxer Duke McKenzie (b.1963).

Dulcie The name ultimately derives from Latin *dulcis*, 'sweet'. It was not common among English speakers until the late 19th century, and came into a certain vogue in the 1920s and 1930s. Today it is rarely met. Agatha Christie's novel *Murder on the Links* (1923) has the twin sisters Dulcie and Bella Duveen, formerly a vaudeville duo performing as 'The Dulcibella Kids'. An occasional diminutive is *Dulce*.

UK actress, novelist Dulcie Gray (b.1920).

Duncan An English form of the Gaelic name *Donnchadh*, formed from Old Celtic *donn*, 'dark', and *cath*, 'battle', so 'dark-haired (or dark-skinned) warrior'. The name has long been in Scottish use, and in the 20th century it gradually gained a wider English-speaking favour until the 1960s, since when it has declined. It is historically famous from the 7th-century Scottish St Duncan and from two 11th-century kings of Scotland, one of whom appears in Shakespeare's *Macbeth* (1606). Major Duncan Heyward is one of the main characters in James Fenimore Cooper's novel *The Last of the Mohicans* (1826). Diminutives *Dunk*, *Dunkie* and *Dunky* occur.

Scottish-born painter Duncan Grant (1885–1978); UK politician Duncan Sandys (1908–87); Scottish actor Duncan Lamont (1918–78); Irish-born UK motor-racing driver Duncan Hamilton (1920–94); UK swimmer Duncan Goodhew (b.1957).

Dunstan From the place-name or the surname, the name has been in general but irregular use among English speakers from medieval times, when it was first made familiar by the 10th-century St Dunstan, Archbishop of Canterbury.

Dustin From the surname, perhaps influenced by names such as AUSTIN or JUSTIN, this name has been in very select use among English speakers in the 20th century.

US actors Dustin Farman (1874–1929); Dustin Hoffman (b.1937).

Dusty The name arose either as an adoption of the standard word (as describing a person's pale hair or complexion) or as a feminine form of DUSTIN. It has found some favour among English speakers from the 1950s.

UK pop singer Dusty Springfield (1939–99) (original name Mary O'Brien).

Dwayne An independently adopted variant of DUANE, in select English-speaking use from the 1940s, and the preferred form of the name in the US.

US actor Dwayne Hickman (b.1934).

Dwight From the surname, and in select use among English speakers, especially in the US, from the late 19th century. It was made famous by the US president Dwight D. Eisenhower (1890–1969), who was himself named for the US clergyman and educator Timothy Dwight (1752–1817) and his brother Theodore Dwight (1764–1846).

US actor Dwight Frye (1899–1943); US writer, critic Dwight Macdonald (1906–82); US athlete Dwight Stones (b.1953); US country singer Dwight Yoakam (b.1956).

Dyan see **Diane**.

Dylan A Welsh name, probably based on a Celtic root word meaning 'sea', to which modern Welsh *dylif*, 'flood' is related. It was at first mainly in Welsh use, but from the 1950s caught on more generally among English speakers. Some of its subsequent popularity may have come from the surname of the US pop singer Bob Dylan (b.1941) (original name Robert Allen Zimmerman).

Welsh poet Dylan Thomas (1914–53).

Dylis, **Dyllis** see **Dilys**.

Dymphna An Irish name, probably a development from the Gaelic name *Damhnait*, which is itself perhaps a feminine diminutive of *damh*, 'stag', or *dámh*, 'poet'. To English speakers the name suggests a blend of DAPHNE and *nymph* (logically enough, for in Greek mythology the former was the latter). Today it is found mainly in Irish use and even then is not common. There was an Irish St Dymphna (Dympna), said to be a pagan king's daughter, but very little is known of her life. The main variant is *Dympna*.

Australian writer Dymphna Cusack (1902–81); Irish travel writer Dymphna Byrne (b.*c*.1940).

E

Eamon An Irish form of EDMUND, still mainly in Irish use (and properly Éamon). A variant spelling is *Eamonn*, as for the Irish-born UK sports commentator and TV host Eamonn Andrews (1922–87).

Irish president Éamon de Valera (1882–1975); UK actor Eamon Boland (b.1947); Irish athlete Éamon Coughlan (b.1952).

Earl Either from the aristocratic title used as a nickname (as for DUKE, KING and PRINCE) or from the surname, the name has been in increasingly popular use among English speakers from the 17th century, especially by black Americans. The variant spelling *Erle* is familiar from the US detective fiction writer Erle Stanley Gardner (1889–1970).

US army officer, Confederate leader Earl Van Dorn (1820–63); US jurist, chief justice of US Supreme Court, Earl Warren (1891–1974); US jockey Earl Sande (1898–1968); US jazzmen Earl Hines (1903–81), Earl Bostic (1913–65); US actor Earl Holliman (b.1928); US country singer Earl Thomas Conley (b.1941).

Eartha An adoption of the standard word *earth*, doubtless understood in the sense 'Mother Earth', as a vital force of nature. (But perhaps some see the name as a 'meaningful' variant of ARETHA, of which it happens to be an anagram.) The name has found some favour in the 20th century.

US pop singer Eartha Kitt (b.1928).

Ebenezer A biblical name (but that of a place, not a person), from Hebrew *eben-ha'ēzer*, 'stone of help'. It was adopted by 17th-century English Puritans (who took it as a personal name) and exported by them to the US, where it was in some vogue until the early 20th century. In the Bible Ebenezer is the stone set up by Samuel to mark his victory over the Philistines. Ebenezer Cruickshanks is a landlord in Walter Scott's novel *Waverley* (1814), and Ebenezer Balfour is the uncle of David Balfour, the central character of Robert Louis Stevenson's novel *Kidnapped* (1886). The best-known literary bearer of the name, however, is the miser and misanthrope Ebenezer Scrooge, the central character of Charles Dickens's story *A Christmas Carol* (1843). The diminutive *Eben* exists.

UK compiler of *Dictionary of Phrase and Fable*, Dr Ebenezer Cobham Brewer (1810–97); UK composer, writer on music Ebenezer Prout (1835–1909); Nigerian bandleader, juju pioneer Ebenezer Obey (b.1942).

Ebony From the standard word for the valuable black wood, taken up popularly by English-speaking black people from the 1970s, especially in the US. The name was popularized by the Paul McCartney and Stevie Wonder hit 'Ebony and Ivory' (1982), in which Wonder was 'Ebony' while McCartney was 'Ivory'. (The words traditionally refer to piano keys, however.) The usual diminutive is *Ebo*.

Ed An independently adopted diminutive of EDGAR, EDMUND, EDWARD or EDWIN, in regular use among English speakers from the early 20th century. Ed Overbrook is a character in Sinclair Lewis's novel *Babbitt* (1922), and Ed Thatcher is the father of Ellen Thatcher, the central character in John Dos Passos's novel *Manhattan Transfer* (1925). The diminutive EDDIE occurs in its own right.

US variety show host Ed Sullivan (1901–74); US crime writer Ed McBain (b.1926) (original name Salvatore A. Lombino); US popular singer Ed Ames (b.1927); US actors Ed Nelson (b.1928), Ed Lauter (b.1940); UK radio, TV presenter Ed Stewart (b.1941); US actor Ed Begley Jr (b.1949).

Eddie An independently adopted diminutive of ED or of a name that gave this diminutive that has been in select

English-speaking use from the late 19th century. The usual variant is *Eddy*, as for the US country singer Eddy Arnold (b.1918).

US actors Eddie Cantor (1892–1964) (original name Edward Israel Itskowitz), Eddie Acuff (1902–56), Eddie Foy Jr (1905–83), Eddie Albert (b.1908), Eddie Bracken (b.1920); US popular singer Eddie Fisher (b.1928); US actor Eddie Murphy (b.1961); Irish motor-racing driver Eddie Irvine (b.1965).

Ede see **Edith**.

Eden Either from the surname, or from the biblical name (the Garden of Eden), from Hebrew '*ēden*, 'delight', 'paradise'. The name has found some favour among English speakers from the 17th century.

UK popular novelist Eden Phillpotts (1862–1960).

Edgar A modern form of the Old English name *Ēadgār*, formed from *ēad*, 'prosperity', 'riches', and *gār*, 'spear', hence 'owning many spears'. The name has been in English-speaking use from medieval times, with its popularity peak in the late 19th century. It is historically famous from the 10th-century English king Edgar, father of Edward the Martyr, and from the 11th-century Anglo-Saxon prince Edgar the Aetheling. Another 11th-century Edgar was a king of Scotland. In Shakespeare's *King Lear* (1604–5) Edgar is Gloucester's son; in Walter Scott's novel *The Bride of Lammermoor* (1819) Edgar is the central character, the Master of Ravenswood; and in Emily Brontë's novel *Wuthering Heights* (1847) Edgar Linton marries the central character, Catherine Earnshaw. Diminutives are ED and EDDIE, both in independent use.

US poet, writer Edgar Allan Poe (1809–49); US novelist Edgar Rice Burroughs (1875–1950); UK thriller writer Edgar Wallace (1875–1932); US jazz musician Edga Winter (b.1946).

Edith A modern form of the Old English name *Eadgyth*, formed from *ēad*, 'riches', and *gȳth*, 'strife', so 'rich in war', 'bringing rich booty'. The name, which has been in English-speaking use from medieval times, became especially popular in the 19th century, although it has tailed off considerably from the early 20th century. It is historically familiar from the 10th-century saint and princess Edith and from Queen Edith (d.1075), wife of William the Conqueror. In Charles Dickens's novel *Dombey and Son* (1847–8) Edith Granger becomes the second wife of Paul Dombey Sr. Diminutives include *Ede* and *Edie*, the latter as for the US comedienne Edie Adams (b.1927) (original name Elizabeth Edith Enke).

US writer Edith Wharton (1862–1937); UK nurse, heroine Edith Cavell (1865–1915); UK poet, critic Dame Edith Sitwell (1887–1964); UK actress Dame Edith Evans (1888–1976); UK politician Dr Edith Summerskill (1901–80); US dress designer Edith Head (1907–81); UK novelist Edith Pargeter (1913–95) (mother was Edith); Scottish actress Edith Macarthur (b.1926).

Edmund A modern form of the Old English name *Ēadmund*, consisting of *ēad*, 'prosperity', 'riches', and *mund*, 'protector', so 'wealth protector'. It has been in general English-speaking use from medieval times and is still selectively found today. It was the name of several early royal and religious figures, notably the 9th-century king of East Anglia who gave the name of Bury St Edmunds, Suffolk. The English poet Edmund Spenser (1552–99) bore the name, while the historic character Edmund Mortimer, Earl of March, appears in Christopher Marlowe's tragedy *Edward II* (1592), and in Shakespeare's *King Lear* (1604–5), Edmund is the bastard son of Gloucester. In Jane Austen's novel *Mansfield Park* (1814) Edmund, the younger son of Sir Thomas Bertram, eventually marries Fanny Price; and in Charles Dickens's novel *Little Dorrit* (1855–7) Edmund Sparkler marries Fanny Dorrit, sister of the central character, Amy Dorrit. Regular diminutives are ED and EDDIE, both in independent use. The variant form *Edmond* also occurs, as for the Anglo-Irish actor Edmond O'Brien (1915–85).

English actor Edmund Kean (1787/90–1833); UK critic, poet Sir Edmund Gosse (1849–1928); UK actor Edmund Gwenn (1875–1959); UK poet Edmund Blunden (1896–1974); New Zealand mountaineer Sir Edmund Hillary (b.1919); UK-born US actor Edmund Purdom (b.1924); US writer Edmund White (b.1940).

Edna The name may perhaps derive from Hebrew ʿ *ēdnāh*, 'rejuvenation', and be related to the biblical name of the Garden of Eden (see EDEN). It has been in English-speaking use from the 18th century, but, after a peak in popularity during the second half of the 1920s, it has fallen from favour. In the Apocrypha, Edna is the wife of Raguel, mother of Sarah. In H.G. Wells's novel *War in the Air* (1908) Edna Bunthorne marries the central character, Bert Smallways. The name became humorously familiar in the 1980s thanks to 'Dame Edna Everage', the outrageous TV interviewer of celebrities, in real life Australian actor Barry Humphries.

UK novelist Edna Lyall (1857–1903) (original name Ada Ellen Bayly); US actress Edna Mae Oliver (1883–1942); US writer Edna Ferber (1887–1968); US actress Edna Purviance (1894–1958); UK-born US actress Edna Best (1900–74); Irish novelist Edna O'Brien (b.1932).

Edward This is the modern form of the Old English name *Ēadweard*, formed from *ēad*, 'prosperity', 'riches', and *weard*, 'guard', hence 'wealth guardian'. It has enjoyed regular and popular use among English speakers from medieval times, with a marked increase in popularity in the second half of the 1920s, since when it has declined somewhat. It is a famous royal name, borne by eight kings (most recently Edward VIII in the 1930s), with its present-day representative Prince Edward (b.1964), the youngest son of Queen Elizabeth II. Edward the Confessor, reigning in the 11th century, was long revered as a model ruler. In literature Edward Knowell is a character in

Ben Jonson's comedy *Every Man in his Humour* (1598), and Edward Franks is a ship's captain in William Makepeace Thackeray's novel *The Virginians* (1857–9). The UK-born US film pioneer Eadweard Muybridge (1830–1904) (original name Edward Muggeridge) adopted the Old English form of the name, taking it from the Coronation Stone (as the name of the 10th-century Saxon king Edward the Martyr) in his native Kingston on Thames, Surrey. Diminutives ED, EDDIE, NED and TED are all in independent use.

UK comic writer Edward Lear (1812–88); UK composer Sir Edward Elgar (1857–1934); US actor Edward G. Robinson (1893–1973) (original name Emanuel Goldenberg); UK artist, illustrator Edward Ardizzone (1900–79); UK prime minister Sir Edward Heath (b.1916); UK actor Edward Woodward (b.1930); US senator Edward M. Kennedy (b.1932); UK actors Edward Clayton (b.1940), Edward Duke (1953–94).

Edweena, Edwena see **Edwina**.

Edwin A modern form of the Old English name *Ēadwine*, composed of *ēad*, 'prosperity'. 'riches', and *wine*, 'friend', so 'friend of riches'. It has enjoyed regular if select use from medieval times but gained popularity among English speakers in the 19th century, since when it has gradually declined. The most famous historical bearer of the name is the 7th-century king Edwin of Northumbria, who was killed in battle and venerated as a martyr. It has not been a noted royal name since. In literature it is familiar from the central character of Charles Dickens's novel *Edwin Drood* (1870). It is also that of the central character, Edwin Clayhanger, in Arnold Bennett's novel *Clayhanger* (1910). The spelling variant *Edwyn* is sometimes found, with diminutives ED and EDDIE in independent use.

UK painter Sir Edwin Landseer (1802–73); US actor Edwin Maxwell (1886–1948); Scottish poets Edwin Muir (1887–1959), Edwin Morgan (b.1920); US astronaut Edwin Eugene ('Buzz') Aldrin (b.1930); UK writer on art Edwin Mullins (b.1933).

Edwina A feminine form of EDWIN, taken up by English speakers when the male name was revived in the 19th century and now mainly in Scottish use. Spelling variants *Edweena* and *Edwena* exist.

UK vicereine of India, Lady Edwina Mountbatten (1901–60); US actress Edwina Booth (1909–91) (original name Josephine Constance Woodruff); UK artist Edwina Leapman (b.1931); UK politician Edwina Currie (b.1946).

Edwyn see **Edwin**.

Effie (m.) see **Ephraim**.

Effie (f.) An independently adopted diminutive of EUPHEMIA, in fairly common use among English speakers in the 19th century but now rare. Effie Deans marries George Staunton in Walter Scott's novel *The Heart of Midlothian* (1818), and Effie Longstaff features in J.B. Priestley's novel *The Good Companions* (1929).

Egbert A modern form of the Old English name *Ecgbeorht*, formed from *ecg*, 'edge' (of a sword), and *beorht*, 'bright', 'famous', so 'famous swordsman'. The name has been in select use from medieval times, with a slight increase in frequency in the 19th century. It is now very rare. It was historically made known by two 8th-century saints and the 9th-century king of Wessex. BERT would be the expected diminutive.

Eglantine From the flower, poetically identified with the honeysuckle. The name has found some slight favour among English speakers from the 19th century, but is now rare. In Chaucer's *The Canterbury Tales* (c.1387) Madame Eglantine is the central character (storyteller) in 'The Prioress's Tale'. In later literature Mrs Eglantine Clall is a cook in David Garnett's novel *The Sailor's Return* (1925). Variants include *Eglantina* and *Eglantyne*, the latter as for the UK children's charity founder Eglantyne Jebb (1876–1928).

Eileen The name is an English form of the Irish name *Eibhlín*, itself probably a form of AVELINE. It is felt by many to be related to ELAINE, but that name has a different origin. It gained sudden popularity among English speakers in the late 19th century, although it fell from favour after a period of considerable popularity in the second half of the 1920s. The name was brought before the public by the US writer Ruth McKenney's humorous account of her family affairs, *My Sister Eileen* (1938), later a play, musical and film. A Scottish form of the name, *Aileen*, also occurs. as for the US actress Aileen Pringle (1895–1989). Rarer spelling variants are *Eilene* and *Ileen*.

Irish furniture designer, architect Eileen Gray (1879–1976); UK historian Eileen Power (1889–1940); UK actress Eileen Beldon (1901–85); Australian-born UK pianist Eileen Joyce (1912–91); UK actresses Eileen Derbyshire (b.1930), Eileen Atkins (b.1934); US actress Eileen Brennan (b.1935); Scottish actress Eileen McCallum (b.1936); UK artist Eileen Cooper (b.1953).

Eirian A Welsh name, adopted direct from the standard word meaning 'bright', 'beautiful', it is almost exclusively in Welsh use and is rarely found before the 1950s.

Welsh opera singer Eirian James (b.1952).

Eirlys A Welsh name, adopted direct from the standard word meaning 'snowdrop'. It remains almost exclusively in Welsh use and is rarely found before the late 19th century.

UK consumer campaigner Eirlys Roberts (b.1911).

Eithne An Irish name, said to derive from *eithne*, 'kernel', presumably in the metaphorical sense 'fruitful'. It is felt by some to be a feminine form of AIDAN, or to be related to EDNA. The usual pronunciation of the name by English speakers is 'Ethny', although in its original Irish it is nearer 'Einya'. The Irish popular singer Enya (b.1962) was originally Eithne Ní Bhraonáin, and chose this spelling of her name to represent the Irish pronunciation. The name is still mainly in Irish use.

Irish poet Eithne Strong (b.1923); UK actress Eithne Browne (b.1954).

Elaine The name, from a French form of HELEN, underwent a gradual increase in popularity among English speakers from the early 20th century to the 1960s, after which it just as gradually declined. In Arthurian legend Elaine is the mother of Sir Galahad, and she appears in subsequent retellings of the tales, such as Tennyson's poem *Idylls of the King*, of which the first four parts, 'Enid', 'Vivien', 'Elaine' and 'Guinevere', appeared in 1859. (In this work she is 'Elaine the fair, Elaine the lovable, Elaine, the lily maid of Astolat', suggesting that Tennyson was consciously equating her with the Fair Helen of classical mythology.) Spelling variants include *Elain* and *Elayne*.

UK politician Elaine Kellett-Bowman (b.1924); US actress Elaine Stritch (b.1926); UK writer Elaine Feinstein (b.1930); US actress Elaine May (b.1932); US feminist literary critic Elaine Showalter (b.1941); Canadian swimmer Elaine Tanner (b.1951); UK singer, actress Elaine Paige (b.1952) (original name Eileen Bickerstaff); UK artist Elaine Shemilt (b.1954); Scottish actress Elaine Smith (b.1962).

Eldred The present name evolved from the Old English name *Ealdred*, formed from *eald*, 'old', and *rǣd*, 'counsel', so giving an overall meaning 'long-standing counsel'. It has undergone modest adoption among English speakers since medieval times, and tends to be found today mainly among the members of religious communities.

Eleanor The name is of problematic origin since it has been recorded in a variety of different forms in entirely unrelated languages. It appears to be either a historic French spelling of a form of HELEN or a name based on Old German *al*, 'all'. It was introduced to England in the 12th century by Eleanor of Aquitaine (1122–1204), wife of Henry II. It is probably better known, however, from Eleanor of Castile (1246–90), wife of Edward I, on whose death 'Eleanor crosses' were set up in towns where her body rested on its journey from Lincoln to London for burial in Westminster Abbey. In the 20th century it has known three peak periods of popularity: the 1900s, the 1960s and, most of all, the 1990s. In Wilkie Collins's novel *The Woman in White* (1860) Eleanor Fairlie marries Count Fosco, while in John Dos Passos's trilogy *U.S.A.* (1930–36) Eleanor Stoddard is an interior decorator. A 'continental' variant of the name occasionally found is *Lenore*, as for the US actress Lenore Ulric (1892–1970). The variant ELINOR is in independent use, as are the diminutives ELLIE and NELL.

UK children's writer Eleanor Farjeon (1881–1965); wife of US president F.D. Roosevelt, Eleanor Roosevelt (1884–1962); US actress Eleanor Boardman (1898–1991); US tap dancer Eleanor Powell (1912–82); US actress Eleanor Parker (b.1922); UK actress Eleanor Bron (b.1934).

Eli A biblical name, from Hebrew *'Ēlī*, 'high', in select use among English speakers from the 17th century, and increasing in popularity in the 19th, but not common after the 1930s. In the Old Testament Eli is the priest and judge who helps to raise the prophet Samuel.

US pharmaceutical chemist Eli Lilly (1885–1977); US actor Eli Wallach (b.1915).

Elias The name, a Greek form of ELIJAH, was adopted by English Puritans in the 17th century, but is now quite rare. The English antiquarian Elias Ashmole (1617–92) founded the Ashmolean Museum, Oxford. In literature Elias Henderson is chaplain to the Lady of Lochleven in Walter Scott's novel *The Abbot* (1820); Dr Elias Bodkin is partner to Dr Finn, father of the central character, in Anthony Trollope's novel *Phineas Finn* (1869); and Elias Spinks appears in Thomas Hardy's novel *Under the Greenwood Tree* (1872).

Elijah A biblical name, from Hebrew *Ēlīyāhū*, 'God is Yah' (that is, Jehovah). It was adopted by 17th-century Puritans but was not widely favoured generally among English speakers until the 19th century. Today it is much less common, although it has found some favour with black Americans (including Muslims). In the Bible Elijah is the Hebrew prophet who was persecuted for denouncing Ahab and Jezebel. The name is also used of John the Baptist in the role of this prophet. Elijah Pogram is a character in Charles Dickens's novel *Martin Chuzzlewit* (1843–4). The Greek variant of the name, ELIAS, gained independent use. The Yiddish diminutive *Elye* occurs.

US Black Muslim leader Elijah Muhammad (1897–1975); UK operatic producer Elijah Moshinsky (b.1946).

Elinor An independently adopted variant of ELEANOR, in select use among English speakers from the 17th century. Shakespeare's *King John* (*c*.1596) has Queen Elinor (now usually referred to as Eleanor of Aquitaine) as the king's mother, and in later literature the name is familiar from Elinor Dashwood, who marries Edward Ferrars in Jane Austen's novel *Sense and Sensibility* (1811). Diminutives are as for ELEANOR.

UK romantic novelist Elinor Glyn (1864–1943); UK painter Elinor Bellingham Smith (1906–88); US actress Elinor Donahue (b.1937).

Eliot, Eliott see **Elliott**.

Eliphalet A biblical name, from Hebrew *Ēlīphelet*, 'God is release', only in rare use among English speakers since its adoption by 17th-century Puritans. In the Bible Eliphalet is a son of King David.

US firearms manufacturer Eliphalet Remington (1793–1861).

Elisabeth, Elise see **Elizabeth**.

Elisha The biblical name derives from Hebrew *Ēlīshā*, 'God is salvation'. It was taken up by English Puritans in the 17th century but has been only selectively favoured since. In the Bible Elisha is the prophet who was the successor to Elijah.

US Arctic explorer Elisha K. Kane (1820–57); Northern Ireland-born UK footballer Elisha Scott (1894–1959); US actor Elisha Cook Jr (1902–95).

Eliza A shortened form of ELIZABETH in independent use, adopted by English speakers from the 18th century but much less common in the 20th century. Literary bearers of the name include Mrs Eliza Pincot in William Makepeace Thackeray's novel *The Virginians* (1857–9); the central character in Barry Pain's novel *Eliza* (1900); and the Cockney flower-seller Eliza Doolittle in George Bernard Shaw's play *Pygmalion* (1913). The related name LIZA is sometimes regarded as a diminutive.

UK writers Eliza Cook (1818–89), Eliza Lynn Linton (1822–98).

Elizabeth A well-known biblical name, from Hebrew *Elīsheba*, 'oath of my God' or 'my God has sworn', in regular English-speaking use since medieval times and still common today. In the Bible the name is that of the mother of John the Baptist. It was popularized in the 13th century by St Elizabeth of Hungary, then later by Queen Elizabeth I of England (1533–1603). Among the many literary bearers of the name are Elizabeth Andrews, mother of the central character in Samuel Richardson's novel *Pamela* (1740–41); Elizabeth Leat, the postmistress in Thomas Hardy's novel *Desperate Remedies* (1871); and Elizabeth Trant, benefactor of the Good Companions in J.B. Priestley's novel *The Good Companions* (1929). More popular than the main name are its many variants, mostly national forms and diminutives. *Elisabeth* is the usual spelling in continental Europe, with the Spanish form, ISABEL, in independent use in English-speaking countries. Chief of the diminutives, all now also in independent use, are BESS, BESSIE, BET, BETH, BETSY, BETTY, ELIZA, LISA, LIZA, ELSIE, LISBETH and LIZ. In Scotland, ELSPETH is also to be found. Continental European diminutives include *Bettina*, ELSA (in independent use), *Elise*, *Ilse*, *Lise* and *Lisette*.

UK writer Elizabeth Taylor (1912–75); UK food writer Elizabeth David (1913–92); UK monarch, Elizabeth II (b.1926); UK actress Elizabeth Spriggs (b.1929); UK-born US actress Elizabeth Taylor (b.1932); UK actress Elizabeth Dawn (b.1939) (original name Sylvia Butterfield); US actress Elizabeth McGovern (b.1961).

Ella The name ultimately derives, through French, from Old German *al*, 'all', as perhaps for ELEANOR, although it is now associated with ELLEN. It was brought to Britain by the Normans but was only rarely adopted until the 19th century. After that it became popular in both the UK and the US. It is now much less common. The usual diminutive, ELLIE, is in independent use, and is itself a diminutive of such names as ISABEL.

US poet Ella Wheeler Wilcox (1850–1919); Scottish-born US singer Ella Logan (1913–69); US singer Ella Fitzgerald (1917–96); US politician Ella Grasso (1919–81); US actress Ella Raines (1921–88).

Ellen An independently adopted form of HELEN, in use among English speakers from the 16th century. The name gradually declined in popularity from 1900 but subsequently revived in the 1950s in the US and in the 1990s in the UK. In James Fenimore Cooper's novel *The Prairie* (1827) Ellen (Nelly) Wade is loved by bee-hunter Paul Hover, while the main character in John Dos Passos's novel *Manhattan Transfer* (1925) is Ellen Thatcher Oglethorpe. The variants ELLIE and NELL are in independent use.

UK actress Ellen Terry (1848–1928); US novelist Ellen Glasgow (1874–1945); UK politician Ellen Wilkinson (1891–1947); US actress Ellen Barkin (b.1954); UK yachtswomen Ellen MacArthur (b.1977).

Ellery An adoption of the surname that is found in occasional use among English speakers in the 20th century.

UK detective writer Ellery Queen, original names Frederick Dannay (1905–82) and Manfred B. Lee (1905–71); UK rugby player Ellery Hanley (b.1961).

Ellie An independently adopted diminutive of ELEANOR, ELLA, ELLEN, HELEN or some other name beginning *El-*, that has been in regular English-speaking use from the 19th century but that now is rather less common. In Erskine Caldwell's novel *Tobacco Road* (1948) Ellie May Lester is the repulsive, hare-lipped daughter of Jeeter Lester. The name was later popularized by Miss Ellie, the female head of the Ewing family in the US TV soap *Dallas* (1978–82), who was played by Barbara Bel Geddes. The spelling variant *Elly* sometimes occurs.

US pop musician Ellie Greenwich (b.1940).

Elliott From the surname, itself more common as *Eliot*, the name has been in restricted use from the 16th century and in recent times has come into vogue from the early 1990s. Spelling variants *Eliot*, *Eliott* and *Elliot* exist, the first of these as for the US photographer Eliot Porter (1901–90) and the third as for the Scottish athlete Elliot Bunney (b.1966).

US film director Elliott Nugent (1899–1980); US writer, businessman Elliott Roosevelt (1910–90) (mother was Eleanor); US actors Elliott Reid (b.1920), Elliott Gould (b.1938) (original name Elliot Goldstein).

Ellis (f.) Either a female adoption of the male name *Ellis* (from the surname) or an anglicized form of the Irish name *Eilis*, itself a derivative of ISABEL, or even a phonetic alteration of ALICE.

UK novelist Ellis Peters (1913–95) (original name Edith Pargeter); Irish writer Ellis Dillon (1920–94); US writer Ellis Ovesen (b.1923); UK fashion designer Ellis Flyte (b.*c*.1955).

Elly see **Ellie**.

Elmer From the surname, and in some vogue among English speakers, especially in the US, from the 19th century. In literature the name is familiar from the title character of Sinclair Lewis's novel *Elmer Gantry* (1927). Diminutives *Elm* and *Elmy* exist.

US film director Elmer Clifton (1890–1949); US writer Elmer Rice (1892–1967); US popular composer Elmer Bernstein (b.1922).

Eloise The name is probably related to the male name LOUIS, through the Latin form of this, ALOYSIUS. It was introduced to England by the Normans, but has enjoyed only limited adoption since. The name became familiar from the love letters written by Eloise (Héloïse) to Abelard in the 12th century and, later, from Pope's version of this, *Eloisa to Abelard* (1717). The most common variant is *Eloisa*.

Elroy A variant form of LEROY, mainly in black American use from the 19th century. In the UK the name came to be associated with the poet James Elroy Flecker (1884–1915), but here it is almost certainly of surname origin.

Elsa An independently adopted short form of the German name *Elisabeth* (English ELIZABETH). It is sometimes regarded as a variant of ELSIE, but that name has a different origin. It has been in select English-speaking use from the 19th century, with some initial encouragement from Wagner's opera *Lohengrin* (1846–8), in which Elsa is Lohengrin's bride. The diminutive ELLIE is in independent use.

US columnist, professional party-giver Elsa Maxwell (1883–1963); UK-born US actress Elsa Lanchester (1902–86) (original name Elizabeth Sullivan).

Elsie The name is an independently adopted form of *Elspie*, itself a diminutive of ELSPETH. It has been in English-speaking use from the 18th century and gained great popularity in Scotland, but fell fast from favour after the 1920s. In literature Elsie is the name of the peasant girl in Henry Wadsworth Longfellow's poem *The Golden Legend* (1851), and of the central character in Oliver Wendell Holmes's novel *Elsie Venner* (1861). Later, Elsie Longstaff marries Herbert Dulver in J.B. Priestley's novel *The Good Companions* (1929). A diminutive is *Else*.

UK children's writer Elsie Oxenham (*c*.1880–1960); US actress Elsie Ferguson (1885–1961); UK radio comedienne Elsie Waters (1895–1990).

Elspeth An independently adopted Scottish diminutive of ELIZABETH, remaining chiefly in Scottish use from the 19th century. In Walter Scott's novel *The Antiquary* (1816) Elspeth Mucklebackit is the old mother of Saunders Mucklebackit. The main diminutive is *Elspie*, which gave the independently adopted ELSIE.

UK actress Elspeth Dudgeon (1871–1955); Kenyan-born UK writer Elspeth Huxley (1907–97); UK actress Elspeth March (1911–99).

Elton From the surname, and enjoying select English-speaking favour in the 20th century.

US country singer Elton Britt (1917–72) (original name James Britt Baker); UK pop musician Elton John (b.1947) (original name Reginald Kenneth Dwight); UK TV sports presenter Elton Welsby (b.1951).

Elvira A Spanish name of uncertain origin but possibly from the Germanic name *Alwara*, itself apparently formed from *al*, 'all', and *wēr*, 'true', so 'true to all'. The name has found some English-speaking use from the 19th century, although it has never been common. It was initially made familiar by characters in well-known operas such as Mozart's *Don Giovanni* (1787), Bellini's *I Puritani* (1835) and Verdi's *Ernani* (1844). In Theodore Dreiser's novel *An American Tragedy* (1925) Elvira Griffiths is the mother of the central character Clyde Griffiths, and in Agatha Christie's novel *At Bertram's Hotel* (1965) Elvira Sedgwick is a young heiress. The name was later popularized by the Swedish romantic film *Elvira Madigan* (1967), which was based on a true story.

Elvis The name is perhaps an alteration of the surname *Elwes*, itself actually from ELOISE. It has become well known (although without being widely adopted) throughout the English-speaking world, but chiefly in the US, where it became famous from the pop singer Elvis Presley (1935–77). Presley was born into a poor white family in the rural South, among the direct descendants of English or Scottish immigrants, and was himself given the name from the middle name of his father, Vernon Elvis Presley.

UK pop singer Elvis Costello (b.1955) (original name Declan Patrick McManus); Canadian ice skater Elvis Stojko (b. 1972).

Elye see **Elijah**.

Em see **Emily**.

Emanuel A biblical name, from Hebrew '*Immānūēl*, 'God with us', in gradually increasing adoption among English speakers from the 17th century, although now much less common. In the Bible Emanuel is the name of the promised Messiah, as prophesied by Isaiah: 'Behold, a virgin shall conceive, and bear a son, and shall call his name Immanuel' (Isaiah 7.14). (Compare Matthew 1.23: 'Behold, a virgin shall be with child, and shall bring forth a son, and they shall call his name Emmanuel, which being interpreted is, God with us.') The variant spelling *Emmanuel* has been fairly common in recent times, while the Spanish variant, MANUEL, is found mainly in the US. The Old Testament version of the name, IMMANUEL, is in independent use. Diminutives are usually *Man* or *Manny*, the latter as for the Dominican swing composer Manny Albam (b.1922) and UK jockey Manny Mercer (1928–59).

UK politician Emanuel Shinwell (1884–1986); UK writer Emanuel Litvinoff (b.1915); UK violinist Emanuel Hurwitz (b.1919).

Emile A French form (properly *Émile*) of the Latin name *Aemilius* (which gave EMILY), in occasional use among English speakers from the mid-19th century. It became familiar from the ideal pupil who is the central character in Rousseau's treatise on education, *Émile* (1762) and later from the French writer Émile Zola (1840–1902). The German form of the name, *Emil*, also occurs, and became known from Erich Kästner's children's novel *Emil and the Detectives* (1929).

UK theatrical producer, impresario Emile Littler (1903–85).

Emilia This is an independently adopted variant of AMELIA, which has been in English-speaking use from medieval times and is chiefly found in literature. It is now much less common. In Shakespeare's *Othello* (1602–4) Emilia is Iago's wife, and in *The Winter's Tale* (1610–11) Emilia is an attendant to Hermione. Emilia is also in John Fletcher and Shakespeare's play *The Two Noble Kinsmen* (1634). In Tobias Smollett's novel *Peregrine Pickle* (1751) Emilia Gauntlet is loved by Peregrine.

Emily The name comes from the Latin name *Aemilia*, the feminine form of the Roman clan name *Aemilius*, which also partly gave AMELIA (and its variant EMILIA) and entirely gave the male name EMILE. The name is not related to EMMA, despite its similarity. It was first current among English speakers in the 18th century and became generally popular in the 19th. It then declined from the early 20th century but regained considerable popularity from the 1970s. Literary bearers of the name include Emily Gervois in Samuel Richardson's novel *Sir Charles Grandison* (1753–4) and Emily Peggotty (Little Em'ly) in Charles Dickens's novel *David Copperfield* (1849–50). Diminutives are usually *Em*, *Emmie* or *Emmy*.

UK novelist Emily Brontë (1818–48); US poet Emily Dickinson (1830–86); US writer on etiquette Emily Post (1873–1960); Australian actress Emily Symons (b.1969); UK actress Emily Lloyd (b.1971).

Emlyn A Welsh name, perhaps from the Latin name *Aemilius* (which gave EMILY). It remains chiefly in Welsh use.

Welsh actor, writer Emlyn Williams (1905–87).

Emma The name has its origin in the Old German word *ermen*, 'entire', found in longer names such as ERMINTRUDE. It has been in English-speaking use since medieval times, becoming popular in the 19th century, then declining, only to revive sharply from the 1960s, with its recent peak in the 1980s. In the 11th century the name was that of the queen of Ethelred the Unready. It was later familiar from Nelson's mistress, Lady Emma Hamilton (1765–1815). Characters in two novels brought the name before the public: Emma Woodhouse in Jane Austen's *Emma* (1816) and Emma Bovary in Gustave Flaubert's *Madame Bovary* (1857). The name's resurgence in the 1960s may be attributed to the character Emma Peel in the TV series *The Avengers*, in which she was played by Diana Rigg. (Her name was devised to mean 'M appeal', that is, 'man appeal'.) Diminutives are *Em*, *Emmie* and *Emmy*, the last of these combining to form compounds, as for the US country singer Emmylou Harris (b.1949).

UK actress Emma Duncan (1875–1966); UK novelist Emma Tennant (b.1937); UK politician Emma Nicholson (b.1941); UK singer Emma Kirkby (b.1949); UK magazine editor Emma Soames (b.1949); UK actress Emma Thompson (b.1959); UK-born US actress Emma Samms (b.1960); UK TV presenter Emma Freud (b.1962); UK actress, singer Emma Wray (b.1965) (original first name Jill); UK actress Emma Davies (b.1970).

Emmanuel see **Emanuel**.

Emmeline The name apparently developed from EMMA (rather than from EMILY). It was in medieval use but then fell from favour until the 18th century, when it revived for selective adoption in the English-speaking world, although today it is rare. In Harriet Beecher Stowe's novel *Uncle Tom's Cabin* (1852) Emmeline is a quadroon sold with Uncle Tom to the plantation owner Simon Legree. The diminutive *Emmie* evolved, as for other names beginning *Em-*.

UK suffragist Emmeline Pankhurst (1858–1928).

Emmie, Emmy see **Emily, Emmeline**.

Emrys A Welsh form of AMBROSE, still mainly in Welsh use.

Welsh-born Scottish politician Emrys Hughes (1894–1969).

Ena An English form of the Irish name EITHNE, in general use from the late 19th century although not common after the 1930s. It was popularized by Queen Victoria's granddaughter, Princess Victoria Eugénie Julia Ena (1887–1969), who became queen of Spain and who was always known as Princess Ena. (Her name is said to be the result of an error: the baptizing minister misread her mother's writing of 'Eva'.) A variant form INA is sometimes found. The name was later familiar from Ena Sharples, the redoubtable old lady (played by Violet Carson) in the highly popular UK TV soap *Coronation Street* (from the 1960s).

Enid The name is of uncertain origin but is perhaps Welsh, from *enaid*, 'soul', 'life'. It was taken up generally by English speakers in the late 19th century and enjoyed a certain vogue in the 1920s, after which it sharply declined. In Tennyson's poems *Idylls of the King* (1859), retelling the Arthurian romances, Enid, daughter of the Earl of Yniol, marries Geraint.

UK novelist Enid Bagnold (1889–1981); UK children's writer Enid Blyton (1897–1968).

Enoch A biblical name, from Hebrew *Hānōk*, perhaps meaning 'dedicated', and in select use among English speakers from the 17th century. In the Bible Enoch is the name of both the son of Cain and the father of Methuselah. The former of these features in Byron's poem *Cain* (1821). In later literature Enoch Bush is a character in James Fenimore Cooper's novel *The Prairie* (1827), and the name is also familiar from that of the central character in Tennyson's poem *Enoch Arden* (1864).

US bandleader Enoch Light (1907–78); UK politician Enoch Powell (1912–98) (originally second name, first being John).

Ephraim A biblical name, from Hebrew *Ephrayim*, 'very fruit-ful', that has been in select use among English speakers from the 18th century, although rare from the 1930s. In the Bible Ephraim is the second son of Joseph: 'And the name of the second called he Ephraim: For God hath caused me to be fruitful in the land of my affliction' (Genesis 41.52). Ephraim Jenkinson is a character in Oliver Goldsmith's novel *The Vicar of Wakefield* (1766), and Ephraim Flintwinch is the twin brother of Jeremiah Flintwinch in Charles Dickens's novel *Little Dorrit* (1855–7). The Jewish diminutive *Effie* occurs.

Eppie see **Euphemia, Hephzibah**.

Erasmus The name represents the Latin form of the Greek name *Erasmos*, itself based on *erān*, 'to love', 'to long for'. It was taken up by English speakers from the 17th century, with some popularity in the 19th century, but is now rare. It was initially made known by the 4th-century bishop and martyr, St Erasmus, and was later famous from the Dutch humanist scholar Desiderius Erasmus (*c.*1466–1536) (original name Gerard Gerards). (He was born out of wedlock as a 'love child': hence his name of Desiderius Erasmus, otherwise 'passion-ately desired longed-for one' in Latin and Greek, with names of synonymous meaning.) The English naturalist and poet Erasmus Darwin (1731–1802) was the grandfather of Charles Darwin. In literature Erasmus Holyday is a learned dominie (teacher) in Walter Scott's novel *Kenilworth* (1821).

Erastus The name, from the Greek name *Erastos*, meaning 'dear one', 'beloved', has enjoyed select use among English speakers from the 18th century. It is historically familiar from the Swiss theologian and physician Thomas Erastus (1524–83), who had graecized his name from Lüber (or Liber, or Liebler). A common variant is *Rastus*.

US financier Erastus Corning (1794–1872).

Eric The modern English name derives from the Old Norse name *Eyrekr*, composed of *ei*, 'ever', 'always', and *rikr*, 'ruler', so 'ever-ruling'. It was first generally adopted by English speakers in the mid-19th century, achieving an impressive period of popularity in the 1920s, but later waning. It is historically familiar from the 10th-century Norse navigator and discoverer of Greenland, Eric the Red, but was not widely taken up until the publication of the famous moralizing school story *Eric, or, Little by Little* (1858) by the UK clergyman F. W. Farrar, the central character being the schoolboy Eric Williams. (Farrar's first name was Frederic, and it is possible that, even if subconsciously, he may have based his young hero's name on his own, as if a diminutive.) In later literature the name is that of the central character in *Eric Brighteyes* (1891), Henry Rider Haggard's re-creation of an Icelandic saga, while Eric Tipstead is a character in J.B. Priestley's novel *The Good Companions* (1929). The variant spelling ERIK and the diminutive RICK are in independent use.

UK actor Eric Blore (1887–1959); UK writer Eric Ambler (1909–98); UK cricketer Eric Bedser (b.1918); UK politician Eric Heffer (1922–91); UK comedians Eric Sykes (b.1923), Eric Morecambe (1926–1984); UK actors Eric Richard (b.1940), Eric Idle (b.1943); UK rock musician Eric Clapton (b.1945); UK actor Eric Deacon (b.1960).

Erica A feminine form of ERIC, now sometimes regarded as a flower name, from *Erica*, the botanical name for the heather genus (compare HEATHER). The name has been in fairly regular English-speaking use from the late 19th century, with a period of popularity in the second half of the 1960s. In literature it became familiar from Erica Raeburn, the central character of Edna Lyall's best-selling novel *We Two* (1884). *Erika* is a Scandinavian variant form, as for the US actress Erika Eleniak (b.1979).

US novelist Erica Jong (b.1942); UK film animator Erica Russell (b.1951).

Erik An independently adopted Swedish variant of ERIC, in English-speaking use from the 19th century, mainly in the US. Erik Valborg is loved by Carol Milford in Sinclair Lewis's novel *Main Street* (1920). The diminutive RICK is in independent use.

Erika see **Erica**.

Erin An Irish name, from the poetic name for Ireland, that has been in select general English-speaking adoption from the late 19th century.

US actress Erin O'Brien-Moore (1902–79); UK social campaigner Erin Pizzey (b.1939); New Zealand athlete Erin Baker (b.1961).

Erle see **Earl**.

Ermintrude This is an Old German name, formed from *ermen*, 'entire' (seen in EMMA), and *traut*, 'beloved', hence 'wholly loved'. It was brought to England by the Normans, but the name was never widely adopted and is now very rare. Historically it is associated with Ermintrude, the 9th-century empress of France. A diminutive in independent use is TRUDY.

Ern see **Ernest**, **Ernie**.

Erna An independently adopted diminutive of *Ernesta* or ERNESTINE, feminine forms of ERNEST, in select use among English speakers from the 19th century.

Jamaican writer Erna Brodber (b.1940).

Ernest The present English name developed from the Old German name *Ernust*, corresponding to the modern German name *Ernst*, meaning 'seriousness', 'earnestness', and implying 'battler to the death'. It was taken up regularly by English speakers from the 18th century but has gradually declined from the early years of the 20th. It is historically familiar as a royal German name: the son of Ernest Augustus (*Ernst August*)

(1629–98) was George I of England, first of the house of Hanover. Much later it was popularized by Oscar Wilde's play *The Importance of Being Earnest* (1895), in which Ernest is the name assumed by man-about-town John (Jack) Worthing when he is staying in London. In Samuel Butler's novel *The Way of All Flesh* (1903) Ernest Pontifex is the central character. (The story was originally called *Ernest Pontifex*.) The diminutive ERNIE is in independent use, and another diminutive is *Ern*.

UK actor Ernest Thesiger (1879–1961); UK statesman, trade unionist Ernest Bevin (1881–1951); US novelist Ernest Hemingway (1898–1961); UK radio pianist Ernest Lush (1908–88); UK boy soprano Ernest Lough (1911–2000); US country singer Ernest Tubb (1914–84); US actor Ernest Borgnine (b.1918) (original name Ermes Effron Borgnino).

Ernesta see **Erna**.

Ernestine A feminine form of ERNEST, mainly in vogue in the late 19th century and early 20th.

US jazz singer Ernestine Anderson (b.1928).

Ernie An independently adopted diminutive of ERNEST, in select English-speaking use from the late 19th century and made familiar by ERNIE, the Premium Bonds genius. The name's own diminutive is usually *Ern*.

US actor Ernie Kovacs (1919–62); US popular singer Ernie Ford (1919–91); UK comedian Ernie Wise (1925–99) (original name Ernest Wiseman).

Errol From the (Scottish) surname but popularly associated with EARL, the name has found some favour among English speakers from the late 19th century and became particularly fashionable among black people. *Erroll* is a variant spelling, as for the US jazz pianist Erroll Garner (1921–77).

Australian-born US actor Errol Flynn (1909–1959); Jamaican-born pop singer Errol Brown (b.1948); US film director Errol Morris (b.1948).

Erskine From the (Scottish) surname, in select English-speaking use from the 19th century.

Irish writer Erskine Childers (1870–1922); US actor Erskine Sanford (1880–1950); US novelist Erskine Caldwell (1903–87); US bandleader Erskine Hawkins (1914–93).

Esau A biblical name, from Hebrew '*Ēsāw*, 'hairy', in select English-speaking use from the 16th century and becoming rather more popular in the 19th, although now rare. In the Bible Esau is the elder twin (the other is Jacob) of Isaac and Rebecca: 'And the first came out red, all over like an hairy garment; and they called his name Esau' (Genesis 25.25).

Esmé (m.) A French name, from Old French *esme* (modern French *aimé* and related to English *esteemed*), meaning 'loved' (compare AMY). The name has enjoyed an irregular vogue among English speakers from the 16th century. It was historically made familiar by the French-Scottish diplomat Esmé Stuart (1542–83), a cousin of James VI of Scotland (James I of England), and he may have actually introduced the name to Scotland and so subsequently to England.

UK actor Esmé Percy (1887–1957); Scottish architect Esmé Gordon (1910–93).

Esmé (f.) A feminine adoption of the male name ESMÉ, perhaps felt by some to be a diminutive of ESMERALDA, but that name has a different origin. It has been in select English-speaking use from the 18th century and became familiar from the character in J.D. Salinger's collection of short stories *For Esme – With Love and Squalor* (1953) (US title *Nine Stories*). The main variant spelling is *Esmée*, as for Esmée Farquhar in Agatha Christie's short story 'The Million Dollar Bond Robbery' in *Poirot Investigates* (1924). The name is also written without an accent.

Esmeralda The name, from the Spanish word *esmeralda*, 'emerald', has been in modest English-speaking use from the 19th century. It was originally made known, and even introduced, by the gypsy girl Esmeralda who is the leading character in Victor Hugo's novel *The Hunchback of Notre Dame* (1831). In this, she is nicknamed 'La Esméralda' for the amulet with an artificial emerald that she wears. ESMÉ is sometimes felt to be a diminutive, but it is really a name of different origin.

Esmond The name is a modern form of the Old English name *Ēstmund*, formed from *ēst*, 'favour', 'grace', and *mund*, 'protection', so 'favoured protector'. It was rare in English-speaking use until the 19th century, when it was selectively adopted, as it still is today. It may have been initially made familiar by William Makepeace Thackeray's novel *The History of Henry Esmond* (1852), in which it is the name (although the surname) of the central character.

Welsh actor Esmond Knight (1906–87).

Essa see **Esther**.

Esta see **Esther, Hester**.

Estelle A French form of STELLA, in English-speaking use from the 19th century and enjoying a mild vogue in the 1970s. The most common variant is *Estella*, which is found in Charles Dickens's novel *Great Expectations* (1860–61) for Miss Havisham's ward, daughter of the escaped convict Abel Magwitch.

UK actress Estelle Winwood (1882–1984); US actresses Estelle Taylor (1899–1958), Estelle Getty (b.1923), Estelle Parsons (b.1927); UK artist Estelle Thompson (b.1960).

Esther A biblical name, perhaps ultimately from a Persian word meaning 'star'. It has been in English-speaking use from the 17th century and increased in popularity until the end of the 19th, when it generally declined. It experienced a brief revival, however, in the early 1980s. In the Bible Esther is the captive concubine who becomes the wife of the Persian king Ahasuerus. She is first referred to (Esther 2.7) by her Hebrew name, *Hadassah*, meaning 'myrtle'. The king then renames her. Literary bearers of the name include Esther Bush in James Fenimore Cooper's romance *The Prairie* (1827), and Esther Summerson ('Dame Burden'), the central character and part-narrator in Charles Dickens's novel *Bleak House* (1852–3). Diminutives include *Essa*, *Esta* and *Etty*, with the variant HESTER in independent use.

US actresses Esther Dale (1885–1961), Esther Ralston (1902–94), Esther Williams (b.1923); US popular singer Esther Phillips (1935–84); UK TV presenter Esther Rantzen (b.1940); UK writer Esther Freud (b.1963).

Eth see **Ethel**.

Ethan A biblical name, from Hebrew *Ēythān*, 'firm', 'strong', in select English-speaking use, mostly in the US, from the 19th century. In the Bible Ethan is an obscure figure, Ethan the Ezrahite, mentioned as being surpassed in wisdom by Solomon. The name was made familiar by the US Revolutionary soldier Ethan Allen (1738–89) and in literature by the central character of Edith Wharton's novelette *Ethan Frome* (1911).

US film director Ethan Coen (b.1958); US actor Ethan Hawke (b.1970).

Ethel The name comes from the first element, meaning 'noble', of an Old German name such as *Ethelburga* ('noble fortress') or *Ethelgive* ('noble gift'). It gained popularity among English speakers from the 19th century, when a few such names were revived by the romantic school. (An example is the central figure in Thomas Hardy's novel *The Hand of Ethelberta* (1876).) Although popular in the early years of the 20th century, the name has now entirely fallen from favour. Examples of literary characters of the name are Ethel Newcome in William Makepeace Thackeray's novel *The Newcomes* (1853–5) and Ethel Henderson, who marries the central character,

George Lewisham, in H.G. Wells's novel *Love and Mr Lewisham* (1900). The usual diminutive is *Eth*.

UK composer Dame Ethel Smyth (1858–1944); UK actress Ethel Griffies (1878–1975); UK romantic novelist Ethel M. Dell (1881–1939); US actress Ethel Barrymore (1879–1959); US popular singer Ethel Waters (1896–1977); UK writer Ethel Mannin (1900–84); US actress Ethel Merman (1909–84).

Ethelbert A modern form of the Old English name *Æthelbeorht*, composed of *æthele*, 'noble', and *beorht*, 'bright', which gave the much more common ALBERT. The name was in only rare use among English speakers until the 19th century, when it became briefly fashionable, mainly in literature. It is now rare again. Ethelbert Stanhope is the son of the Rev. Vesey Stanhope, prebendary of Barchester, in Anthony Trollope's novel *Barchester Towers* (1857).

US popular composer Ethelbert Nevin (1862–1901).

Ethelred The name represents the Old English name *Æthelrǣd*, which is formed from *æthele*, 'noble', and *rǣd*, 'counsel', hence 'noble counsel'. It gained rare English-speaking favour from medieval times and was made familiar from the 10th-century king of England Ethelred the Unready. (His nickname, from Old English *unrǣd*, 'no counsel', referred to his lack of foresight and punned on his real name.)

Etta, **Ettie** see **Henrietta**.

Etty see **Esther**, **Henrietta**.

Eudora A Greek name, composed of *eu*, 'good', and *dōron*, 'gift', so 'good gift'. It acquired a certain vogue among English speakers from the late 19th century but is now very rare. Its main diminutive, DORA, is in independent use (although now usually representing other names).

US writer Eudora Welty (1909–2001).

Eugene The name has its origin in a French form of the Greek name *Eugenios*, itself meaning 'well-born', 'noble'. It was only rarely found in English-speaking use until the 19th century, when it became more popular. It is now only very selectively adopted. The name was historically associated with various early saints and popes, and later was made familiar by the Austrian general Prince Eugene of Savoy (1663–1736), who, with Marlborough, won important victories over the French. In literature Eugene Wrayburn is a young barrister in Charles Dickens's novel *Our Mutual Friend* (1864–5), and Eugene March-banks is a character in George Bernard Shaw's play *Candida* (1894). The diminutive GENE occurs in its own right, chiefly in the US.

US playwright Eugene O'Neill (1888–1953); US actor Eugene Pallette (1889–1954); UK conductor Eugene Goossens (1893–1962); Hungarian-born US conductor Eugene Ormandy (1899–1985) (original name Jenö Ormandy Blau); US ballet dancer, choreographer Eugene Loring (1914–82) (original name LeRoy Kerpestein); US actor Eugene Roche (b.1928).

Eugenie A French feminine form (properly *Eugénie*) of EUGENE, taken up selectively in the English-speaking world from the 19th century but rare today. It became historically familiar from Empress Eugénie (1826–1920), wife of Napoleon III. The variant *Eugenia* was formerly in English-speaking use. Diminutives GENE, which is in independent use, and *Genie* exist.

US actress Eugenie Besserer (1870–1934); UK daughter of Prince Andrew and Duchess of York, Princess Eugenie (b.1990).

Eunice A biblical name, from a Greek name composed of *eu*, 'good', and *nikē*, 'victory', so 'good victory'. It was adopted by English Puritans in the 17th century, but after a certain vogue in the 1920s it is now generally rare. (The name was originally pronounced 'you-*nice*-ee', with the middle syllable stressed, but is now always '*you*-niss', with the stress on the first syllable.) In the Bible Eunice is the mother of Timothy, who introduced him to Christianity. Literary bearers of the name include Eunice Manston, wife of Aeneas Manston in Thomas Hardy's novel *Desperate Remedies* (1871); Eunice Littlefield, who marries Ted Babbitt, son of the central character, in Sinclair Lewis's novel *Babbitt* (1922); and Eunice Gardiner, a schoolgirl member of 'the Brodie set' in Muriel Spark's novel *The Prime of Miss Jean Brodie* (1961). The variant form *Unice* is sometimes found.

US writer Eunice Tietjens (1884–1944); UK actress Eunice Gayson (b.1931).

Euphemia A Greek name, formed from *eu*, 'well', and *phēnai*, 'to speak', thus 'well spoken of'. It enjoyed fairly widespread use among English speakers in the 19th and early 20th centuries but is now rarely found. The most common diminutive is EFFIE, in independent use. *Eppie* also occurs.

Eurydice A Greek name, formed from *eurus*, 'wide', and *dikē*, 'right', 'justice', so having the overall meaning 'wide justice', or effectively 'princess', 'queen'. Although the name is very rare among English speakers, it cannot be said to be entirely obsolete. In classical mythology Eurydice was the dryad married to Orpheus, who sought her in Hades after her death. The name became familiar from Gluck's opera *Orpheus and Eurydice* (1762) as well as from various works of art. Agatha Christie has Eurydice Spragg in her short story 'Motive v. Opportunity' in *The Thirteen Problems* (1932) (US title *The Tuesday Club Murders*).

Eustace The name derives from the French form of the Greek name *Eustakhios*, composed of *eu-*, 'good', 'well', and *stakhus*, 'ear of corn', thus 'fruitful'. It was introduced to England by the Normans but was not common until the 19th century. It is now only in very select use. It was originally made famous by St Eustace, who was said to have been converted to Christianity by seeing a crucifix between the antlers of the deer he was hunting. In literature Eustace Leigh is the son of Amyas Leigh, the central character of Charles Kingsley's novel *Westward Ho!* (1855), while Eustace and Hilda Cherrington are the brother and sister central characters of L.P. Hartley's trilogy *The Shrimp and the Anemone* (1944), *The Sixth Heaven* (1946) and *Eustace and Hilda* (1947). The diminutive STACY gained independent use.

Eustacia A feminine form of EUSTACE, in rare English-speaking use from the 19th century. The name was to some extent made familiar by Eustacia Vye, the central character of Thomas Hardy's novel *The Return of the Native* (1878). The diminutive STACEY, sometimes spelled *Stacy*, is now in independent use.

Eva The Latin and continental European form of EVE, which was taken up by English speakers from the mid-19th century and reached its peak of popularity in the early years of the 20th century. In literature it is found for Little Eva in Harriet Beecher Stowe's novel *Uncle Tom's Cabin* (1852), although in her case the name is a short form of EVANGELINE. The usual diminutive is *Evie*.

UK actress Eva Moore (1870–1955); Canadian-born US popular singer Eva Tanguay (1878–1948); UK opera singer Dame Eva Turner (1892–1990); US actress, dancer Eva Le Gallienne (1899–1991); Hungarian-born actresses Eva Gabor (1921–95), Eva Bartok (1926–98); German-born UK novelist Eva Figes (b.1932); US sculptor Eva Hesse (1936–70); US pop singer Little Eva (b.1945) (original name Eva Narcissus Boyd).

Evadne A Greek name, formed from *eu*, 'well', and another word of uncertain origin. It has enjoyed some favour among English speakers from the 19th century but is now rare. In Beaumont and Fletcher's play *The Maid's Tragedy* (1619), Evadne marries Amintor. In recent times the name became comically associated in the UK with the genteel

TV drag act (from the 1970s) featuring 'Dr Evadne Hinge' and 'Dame Hilda Bracket'.

UK actress Evadne Price (1896–1985).

Evalyn see **Evelyn** (f.).

Evan This is the English form of the Welsh name *Iefan* (corresponding to English JOHN). It became popular in Wales from the 19th century, and was taken up by English speakers generally in the 20th century. The name is that of the central character of George Meredith's novel *Evan Harrington* (1861).

US writer Evan Hunter (b.1926).

Evangeline The name was fancifully formed from the Latin word *evangelium*, 'gospel', itself from Greek *euangelion*, literally 'good news'. It gained a select adoption among English speakers from the mid-19th century but has been favoured more generally by black Americans. It was initially made known by Evangeline Bellefontaine, the central character of Henry Wadsworth Longfellow's narrative poem *Evangeline* (1847). In Harriet Beecher Stowe's novel *Uncle Tom's Cabin* (1852) the planter's daughter Little Eva has the full name Evangeline St Clare. The diminutive EVA is in independent use. *Evie* also occurs.

UK-born US Salvation Army leader, songwriter Evangeline Booth (1865–1950) (author of *Songs of the Evangel* (1927)).

Eve A famous biblical name, from the French form of Latin *Eva*, itself from Hebrew *Havvāh*, 'living', in regular if select use among English speakers from medieval times, and gaining a slight increase in popularity in the last quarter of the 20th century. In the Bible Eve is famous as the first woman, so named by Adam 'because she was the mother of all living' (Genesis 3.20). She appears in many literary works based on the Bible account, such as Milton's epic poem *Paradise Lost* (1667) and Byron's poetic drama *Cain* (1821). The variant EVA exists independently. The Spanish diminutive *Evita* was made famous by the Argentinian political leader Evita (Eva) Perón (1922–52) and the musical (1978) based on her life. The diminutive *Evie* also occurs, as for the Irish painter Evie Hone (1894–1955).

UK agriculturist Lady Eve Balfour (1898–1990) (original first name Evelyn); US actresses Eve Arden (1912–90) (original name Eunice Quedens); US photographers Eve Arnold (b.1913), Eve Brent (b.1930); UK newspaper editor Eve Pollard (b.1945).

Evelina see **Evelyn** (f.).

Evelyn (m.) From the surname, and in fairly select but regular use until the early 20th century, when the name was increasingly adopted for female use. It gained some familiarity from the surname of the English diarist John Evelyn (1620–1706).

UK writer Evelyn Waugh (1903–66).

Evelyn (f.) Either from the surname, itself probably from the French female name AVELINE, or an adoption of the male name EVELYN. In modern times the name is sometimes felt to be a compound of EVE (or EVA) and LYNN. It has been in select English-speaking use from the 19th century, reaching its height of fashion in the 1920s, after which it fell from favour. Agatha Christie's first novel, *The Mysterious Affair at Styles* (1920), has a character Evelyn (Evie) Howard. The variant *Evelina* was popularized by the central character of Fanny Burney's novel *Evelina* (1778), while a later variant is *Evalyn*, as for the US actress Evalyn Knapp (1908–81). The usual diminutive is *Evie*.

UK mystic Evelyn Underhill (1875–1941); US actresses Evelyn Varden (1895–1958), Evelyn Brent (1899–1975) (original name Mary Elizabeth Riggs); UK actress Evelyn Laye (1900–96) (original name Elsie Evelyn Lay); UK oboist Evelyn Rothwell (b.1911); UK actresses Evelyn Ankers (1918–85), Evelyn Keyes (b.1919); UK novelist Evelyn Anthony (b.1928) (original name Eve Stephens); US soul singer Evelyn 'Champagne' King (b.1960); Scottish percussionist Evelyn Glennie (b.1965).

Everard The present name comes from the Old German name *Everart*, formed from *eber*, 'boar', and *hart*, 'brave', 'strong', so 'fierce as a boar'. The name gained some favour among English speakers in the 19th century but was much less common in the 20th century. Sir Everard Waverley is the uncle of the central character, Edward Waverley, in Walter Scott's novel *Waverley* (1814), and Everard Romfrey is the uncle of the central character, Nevil Beauchamp, in George Meredith's novel *Beauchamp's Career* (1876).

Everett From the surname, itself a variant of EVERARD, and in select use among English speakers from the late 19th century. Everett Hills is a character in Eugene O'Neill's play *Mourning Becomes Electra* (1931). The variant spelling *Everitt* occurs,

Evie see **Eva**, **Evangeline**, **Eve**, **Evelyn** (f.)

Evita see **Eve**.

Ewan An English form of the Gaelic name *Eóghan* (which gave English OWEN) but also popularly associated with EVAN. The name is still mainly in Scottish use, although it is also found selectively elsewhere in the English-speaking world. In Willa Cather's novel *My Mortal Enemy* (1928) Ewan Gray is in love with Esther Sinclair. The variant form *Ewen* is sometimes found.

Scottish actor Ewan Roberts (1914–83) (original name Thomas McEwan Hutchinson); Scottish folk musician Ewan McColl (1915–89) (original name James Millar).

Ewart From the surname, and in very select use among English speakers from the late 19th century, doubtless with an initial impetus from the second name of the UK prime minister William Ewart Gladstone (1809–98). This came from the identical surname, itself representing the first name EDWARD, or possibly deriving from a Northumbrian place-name.

Ewen see **Ewan**.

Ezekiel A biblical name, from Hebrew *Yehezqēl*, 'God will strengthen', adopted by the Puritans in the 17th century and in select English-speaking use until the early 20th, with some favour in the US, after which it became much less common. In the Bible Ezekiel is a major prophet, with a book named for him. Ezekiel Edgeworth is a character in Ben Jonson's comedy *Bartholomew Fair* (1614). The usual diminutive is *Zeke*.

Ezra A biblical name, from Hebrew ʿ*Ezrā*, 'help' (that is, that of God). It was adopted by English Puritans in the 17th century and taken by them to the US, where it was regularly but selectively used until the early years of the 20th century. In the Bible Ezra is a prophet and the author of the book named for him. In literature Ezra Jennings is a hypnotist and part-narrator in Wilkie Collins's novel *The Moonstone* (1868), while Ezra Cohen is a pawnbroker in George Eliot's novel *Daniel Deronda* (1876).

US financier, philanthropist Ezra Cornell (1807–74); US poet Ezra Pound (1885–1972); US book illustrator Ezra Jack Keats (1916–83).

F

Fabia The name ultimately derives from the Roman clan name *Fabius*, itself from Latin *faba*, 'bean'. It was taken up by English speakers from the 19th century, although it is now not common.

UK actress Fabia Drake (1904–90).

Fabian The name is an English form of the Latin name *Fabianus*, from the Roman clan name *Fabius*, itself probably deriving from *faba*, 'bean', implying a person known for growing beans. Its adoption by English speakers has been only modest. Fabian is the servant of Olivia in Shakespeare's *Twelfth Night* (1601). The name was to some extent popularized in the UK by the TV series *Fabian of the Yard* (1950s), consisting of semi-fictional re-creations of noted police cases.

US pop singer Fabian (b.1943) (original name Fabian Forte Bonaparte).

Faith The name comes from the ordinary word, denoting the virtue, like its sisters, HOPE and CHARITY. It was adopted by Puritans in the 17th century and is still found in select favour today. A fictional bearer of the name is Faith Julian in Thomas Hardy's novel *The Hand of Ethelberta* (1876). FAY, although sometimes regarded as a diminutive, is actually a name of different origin. A genuine diminutive is *Faithie*.

US romantic novelist Faith Baldwin (1893–1978); UK actress Faith Brook (b.1922); US actress Faith Domergue (b.1925); UK sculptor Faith Tolkien (b.1928); US artist Faith Ringgold (b.1934); UK comedienne, impersonator Faith Brown (b.1944); US businesswoman Faith Popcorn (b.1948).

Fan see **Fannie, Fanny.**

Fancy The name derives from the standard English word, but was probably influenced by FANNY and even *fiancée*. It has enjoyed only selective use from the 19th century. In literature the name is familiar from Fancy Day, the schoolteacher who marries Dick Dewy in Thomas Hardy's novel *Under the Greenwood Tree* (1872).

Fannie An independently adopted variant of FANNY, formerly in regular use among English speakers, but now much less common. The diminutive *Fan* is sometimes found.

US actress Fannie Ward (1865–1952); US popular novelist Fannie Hurst (1889–1968); US TV comedienne Fannie Flagg (b.1941).

Fanny The name is a diminutive of FRANCES, independently adopted. It has been in English-speaking use from the 17th century, but is now mostly avoided because of the vulgar senses of *fanny* (for example, 'buttocks'). It occurs in literature for Fanny Goodwill, the milkmaid sweetheart of the central character in Henry Fielding's novel *Joseph Andrews* (1742); for Fanny Price, the poor cousin brought to live at Mansfield Park in Jane Austen's eponymous novel (1814); and for Fanny Bolton, with whom the title character is temporarily in love in William Makepeace Thackeray's novel *Pendennis* (1848–50). In George Bernard Shaw's play *Fanny's First Play* (1905) the name is that of the central character herself, as it is for Fanny (Vandra) Hooper, the cabinet minister's illegitimate daughter in Michael Sadleir's novel *Fanny by Gaslight* (1940). The US musical play *Fanny* (1954), based on Marcel Pagnol's trilogy, made the name familiar in more recent times. The name also has an undesirable association with 'Fanny Adams' ('Sweet Fanny Adams', or 'S.F.A.', is UK slang for 'nothing at all'). This was the real name of a young girl murdered in the 1860s. The variant FANNIE came into independent use, while a diminutive is *Fan*.

English novelist Fanny Burney (1752–1840); UK actress Fanny Kemble (1809–93); US actress Fanny Brice (1891–1951) (original name Fannie

Borach); UK TV cook Fanny Cradock (1909–94) (original first name
Phyllis); UK actress Fanny Rowe (1913–88); Dutch athlete Fanny
Blankers-Koen (b.1918) (original first name Francina); UK concert
pianist Fanny Waterman (b.1920).

Fatima This is an Arabic name, from *fāṭima*, 'weaning'. As a
Muslim name it was taken up selectively in the English-speaking world in the 20th century. It was historically borne in the
7th century by the favourite daughter of Muhammad, founder
of Islam.

South African anti-apartheid activist Fatima Meer (b.1929); South
African playwright Fatima Dike (b.1948); UK athlete of Cypriot extrac-
tion Fatima Whitbread (b.1961).

Fawn A name presumably referring to the young deer, but
perhaps originally evolving as a blend of names such as FAY
and DAWN. It is not a common name but is occasionally found
among English speakers from the 19th century.

US writer Fawn M. Brodie (1915–81).

Fay The name comes from *fay*, the former English word for
a fairy, although it is popularly associated with FAITH, actually
a name of different origin. It was adopted by English speakers in the 19th century and is still selectively found. Some of
the name's attraction comes from that of Morgan le Fay (Fata
Morgana), the sorceress and sister of King Arthur in modern
retellings of the Arthurian legends, such as those of Tennyson.
The variant spelling FAYE occurs in independent use.

US singer Fay Templeton (1865–1939); US actress Fay Bainter
(1892–1968); UK actresses Fay Holden (1894–1973), Fay Compton
(1894–1978); US actresses Fay Wray (b.1907), Fay Helm (b.1913); New
Zealand-born UK novelist Fay Weldon (b.1931) (original first name
Franklin; father was Frank); UK photographer Fay Godwin (b.1931); UK
writer on restaurants Fay Maschler (b.c.1935); UK textile designer Fay
Morgan (b.1946); UK actress Fay Ripley (b.1966).

Faye An independently adopted variant of FAY, first taken up by English speakers in the early 20th century and steadily increasing in popularity from the 1960s.

US actresses Faye Emerson (1917–83), Faye Dunaway (b.1941); US food writer Faye Levy (b.1951).

Feargus see **Fergus**.

Felicia An independently adopted variant of FELICITY, sometimes regarded as a female equivalent of FELIX. It has found occasional favour from the 18th century, with its most common diminutive *Flick*.

English poet Felicia Hemans (1793–1835); UK novelist Felicia Skene (1821–99); US actress Felicia Farr (b.1932); US opera singer Felicia Weathers (b.1937).

Felicity An adoption of the ordinary word, denoting happiness and good fortune, and taken up by Puritans with other such 'moral' names in the 17th century. The name could also originate as an English version of the Latin saint's name *Felicitas*, itself from Latin *felicitas*, 'fertility', 'good fortune', as for the 3rd-century slave-girl martyr. After a long period of occasional use among English speakers, the name came into greater favour from the 1980s. An independently adopted variant is FELICIA, while the usual diminutive is *Flick*. The fortuitously significant diminutive *Lucky* is also sometimes found.

UK opera singer Felicity Palmer (b.1944); UK actress Felicity Kendal (b.1946); UK opera singer Felicity Lott (b.1947); UK actress Felicity Dean (b.1959).

Felix A biblical name, from the Latin name *Felix*, meaning 'lucky', 'happy', in select English-speaking use from the 19th century and enjoying a revival in the 1990s. In the Bible Felix is a Roman procurator of Judea. The name was borne historically by several saints and four popes. In literature the name is that of the central character in George Eliot's novel *Felix Holt*

(1866), while the Rev. Felix Clare is the brother of Angel Clare, the central character of Thomas Hardy's novel *Tess of the D'Urbervilles* (1891). In recent times the name has been made familiar by Felix the Cat of the 1920s animated cartoons. (His own name was probably influenced by *Felis*, the scientific name of the cat genus.)

UK actor Sir Felix Aylmer (1889–1979); New Zealand-born British artist Felix Kelly (1914–94).

Fenella An English form of the Irish name FIONNUALA, found in English-speaking use from the 19th century. It was made familiar by Walter Scott's novel *Peveril of the Peak* (1823), in which Fenella Christian poses for years as a deaf mute. A variant is *Finella*, while diminutives are *Nella* and NUALA, the latter being in independent use.

UK actress Fenella Fielding (b.1934).

Ferdinand The name is an English form of the Old German name *Fridenand*, formed from *fridu*, 'peace', and *nand*, 'bravery', so 'peace through bravery'. It was introduced to England by the Normans but was never widely adopted by English speakers. The name is historically familiar from various royal families of continental Europe, especially Ferdinand the Great, the 11th-century king of Castile and Leon who fought the Moors. In Shakespeare's *Love's Labour's Lost* (*c*.1595) Ferdinand, king of Navarre, loves the French princess despite himself, and in *The Tempest* (1611) Ferdinand, the son of Alonso, king of Naples, loves Miranda. In recent years the name has been mostly trivially associated with Ferdinand the Bull in *The Story of Ferdinand* (1936), the amusing tale for young children by the US writer Munro Leaf. (The bull was presumably so named for the association between the Spanish name *Fernando*, now adopted by some English speakers, and Spanish bull fights.) Diminutives *Ferd*, *Ferdie* and *Ferdy* exist.

UK-born US actor Ferdinand Gottschalk (1869–1944); UK columnist, editor Ferdinand Mount (b.1939).

Fergus The name is an English form of the Gaelic name *Fearghas*, formed from *fear*, 'man', and *gus*, 'force', so 'man of force'. It is still chiefly found in Scotland, with some spread to English speakers generally. In Walter Scott's novel *Waverley* (1814) Fergus MacIvor is a Highland chieftain. The variant *Feargus* was made familiar by the Irish Chartist leader Feargus O'Connor (1796–1855). The usual diminutives are *Fergie* and *Fergy*.

Irish rugby player Fergus Slattery (b. 1949).

Fern The name comes from the well-known woodland plant with feathery fronds. It has been found in English-speaking use from the 19th century but is hardly common even now. The name may have been popularized to some extent by the surname of the US children's writer Fanny Fern (1811–72) (original name Sara Payson Willis), and in children's literature the name occurs punningly for the farmer's daughter Fern Arable in E.B. White's novel *Charlotte's Web* (1952).

UK TV presenter Fern Britton (b.1957).

Festus The biblical name represents the Latin name *Festus*, meaning 'in holiday mood', 'festal'. It has been in rarish use among English speakers from medieval times, with a slight increase in popularity in the 19th century. It is now rare. In the Bible Festus is the Roman procurator of Judea who succeeded Felix. In Thomas Hardy's novel *The Trumpet Major* (1880) Festus Derriman, the nephew of Benjamin Derriman, owner of Oxwell Hall, marries Matilda Johnson.

UK directory publisher Edward Festus Kelly (1854–1939).

Fidelia The name comes from Latin *fidelis*, 'faithful', and is found in occasional English use from the 17th century, when it was adopted by some Puritans as a 'virtue' name. In William

Wycherly's play *The Plain-Dealer* (1676) the young heiress Fidelia is disguised as a page boy named Fidelio, and so becomes the servant to the central character, Manly. In Edward Moore's comedy *The Foundling* (1748), Fidelia is the title character.

Fidelis A male variant of FIDELIA, now also occasionally found in female use, as for the UK actress and writer Fidelis Morgan (b.1952) (mother is Fidelis).

Fifi The name is used as a diminutive (of French origin) of JOSEPHINE and also occasionally of other names containing the sound *fi* or *if*, such as FIONA or YVONNE. Its French origin also coincidentally suggests *fille*, 'girl', 'daughter'.

Canadian actress Fifi d'Orsay (1904–83) (original name Yvonne Lussier).

Finella see **Fenella**.

Fiona The name derives from Gaelic *fionn*, 'white', 'fair'. It was popularized in the English-speaking world (but not invented) by Fiona Macleod, the pen name of the Scottish author of mystic Celtic tales William Sharp (1855–1905). The name remained in modest vogue in the 20th century, mostly in the UK, but had a popularity boom in the second half of the 1960s. The name has associations of gentility and good breeding, and can imply that its bearer is of aristocratic descent.

UK photographer Fiona Alison (b.1939); UK writer Fiona MacCarthy (b.1940); UK actresses Fiona Lewis (b.1946), Fiona Richmond (b.1947) (original name Julia Harrison), Fiona Spence (b.1949); UK opera singer Fiona Kimm (b.1952); UK poet, travel writer Fiona Pitt-Kethley (b.1954); UK actress Fiona Fullerton (b.1956); UK TV presenter Fiona Armstrong (b.1956); Irish actress Fiona Shaw (b.1958); UK ballerina Fiona Chadwick (b.1960); UK rower Fiona Freckleton (b.1960); UK table tennis player Fiona Elliot (b.1965); UK athlete Fiona May (b.1969); US pop singer Fiona Apple (b.1977).

Fionnuala An Irish name, deriving from Gaelic *fionn*, 'white', 'fair', and *guala*, 'shoulder', so 'having fair shoulders'. The English form of the name is more familiar as FENELLA, while the second part of the name gave the more generally common NUALA.

Irish artist Fionnuala Boyd (b.1944); Irish actress Fionnuala Ellwood (b.1964).

Flavia The name is a feminine form of the Roman clan name *Flavius*, itself from *flavus*, 'yellow', probably referring to the blond hair of its original bearers. It has been in select English-speaking use from at least the 16th century. Flavia is a character in John Lyly's prose romance *Euphues and his England* (1580), while in more recent literature the name occurs for a character in William Dean Howells's novel *A Modern Instance* (1882) and for Princess Flavia in Anthony Hope's novel *The Prisoner of Zenda* (1894). The diminutive *Flave* or *Flavie* is sometimes found.

Fletcher An adoption of the surname, in restricted use among English speakers in the 19th century, but rare in the 20th century. The name became historically familiar from the English ship's mate Fletcher Christian, who, in 1789, led the mutiny against Captain Bligh on the *Bounty*. The event was retold in Charles Nordhoff's novel *Mutiny on the Bounty* (1932).

US publisher Fletcher Harper (1806–77); US writer Fletcher Pratt (1897–1956); Canadian film director Fletcher Markle (1921–91).

Fleur From the standard French word for 'flower', perhaps having an additional suggestion for some of *flirt*. The name is occasionally found as a medieval French name, but it was principally introduced to English speakers by Fleur Forsyte, the daughter of Soames Forsyte in John Galsworthy's *Forsyte* sequence (1906–22), where the name is 'created' from the mother's remark '*ma petite fleur*' when admiring her baby daughter.

US painter, writer Fleur Cowles (b.1910); New Zealand-born UK poet Fleur Adcock (b.1934).

Flick see **Felicia, Felicity**.

Flo see **Floella, Flora, Florence**.

Floella The name appears to have arisen as a blend of FLORA or FLORENCE and ELLA, or with these names and the ending of a name such as ARABELLA. It is found in rarish English-speaking use from the 1950s. A ready diminutive would be *Flo*.

Trinidad-born UK TV presenter Floella Benjamin (b.1955).

Flora The name comes from that of the Roman goddess of flowers and of spring. It has been in use among English speakers from the 18th century, although it is now out of favour. It was popularized by Flora Macdonald (1722–90), the Scottish heroine who helped Bonnie Prince Charlie, the Young Pretender, escape to Skye. In Charles Dickens's novel *Little Dorrit* (1855–7) Flora Finching is the daughter of the landlord Christopher Casby, while Flora Warrington is a character in William Makepeace Thackeray's novel *The Virginians* (1857–9). Like Florence, the name has the diminutives *Flo*, *Florrie*, *Floss* and *Flossie*, the first of these as for the US volleyball player Flo Hyman (1954–86),

UK writer Flora Klickmann (1867–1958); UK actress Flora Finch (1869–1940); UK writer Flora Thompson (1876–1947); UK actress Flora Robson (1902–84); Northern Ireland actress Flora Montgomery (b.1974).

Florence The name is an English form of *Florentia*, the feminine of the Latin name *Florentius*, itself based on *florens*, 'blossoming'. It has enjoyed moderate favour in England (originally also as a male name) from the 17th century, but was more widely adopted in the 19th century. It has now tailed off dramatically from its early 20th-century peak. It was popularized by the English pioneer nurse Florence Nightingale (1820–1910), who was herself so named for her birthplace, Florence in Italy. Charles Dickens has Florence Dombey as the devoted daughter of the central character in his novel *Dombey and Son* (1847–8). Chief diminutives include *Flo*, *Florrie*, *Floss* and *Flossie*.

US actress Florence Roberts (1860–1940); UK popular novelist Florence Barclay (1862–1920); UK actress Florence Arliss (1871–1950); Canadian-US writer Florence Ayscough (1875–1942); US actresses Florence Lawrence (1886–1938), Florence Halop (1923–86), Florence Henderson (b.1934); US athlete Florence Griffith Joyner ('Flo-Jo') (1959–98).

Florian An English form of the Latin name *Florianus*, itself from *Florus*, representing *flos*, genitive *floris*, 'flower'. The name has enjoyed occasional use among English speakers, but it would now be regarded as much too 'flowery'. A historic bearer of the name was the 2nd-century Roman martyr St Florian. In Tennyson's poem *The Princess* (1847), Florian, a friend of Hilarion and brother of Lady Psyche, marries Melissa (a 'flower' marrying a 'bee'). He therefore also appears in Gilbert and Sullivan's comic opera *Princess Ida* (1884), which was based on this work.

Florrie, Floss, Flossie see **Flora, Florence**.

Floyd From the surname, itself a variant of LLOYD, the name has been in mainly black English-speaking use from the 19th century, mostly in the US.

US cinematographer Floyd Crosby (1899–1985); US boxer Floyd Patterson (b.1925); US country pianist Floyd Cramer (b.1933).

Forrest From the surname, and in modest English-speaking use, mainly in the US, from the 19th century. The original inspiration for the name in the US may have been the Confederate army officer Nathan Bedford Forrest (1821–77), head of a famous cavalry raiding force. A variant spelling *Forest* sometimes occurs, as for the US actor Forest Whitaker (b.1961).

Irish writer Forrest Reid (1875–1947); US athlete Forrest Towns (1914–91); US actor Forrest Tucker (1919–86); UK economist Forrest Capie (b.1940).

Fran (f.) An independently adopted diminutive of FRANCES, in use among English speakers from the late 19th century. *Frannie* and *Franny* are diminutives.

US TV personality Fran Allison (1907–89); UK theatrical designer Fran Thompson (b.1955).

Frances A feminine form of FRANCIS, with both spellings formerly found for both sexes. The name has been current among English speakers from the 17th century, gaining wide popularity in the 19th century, but declining gradually in the 20th century. One of the earliest noted bearers of the name was Frances Grey, née Brandon (b.1517), mother of Lady Jane Grey. In literature Frances is a character in John Lyly's prose work *Euphues and his England* (1580), while in James Fenimore Cooper's novel *The Spy* (1821) Frances Wharton is a daughter of the Loyalist Henry Wharton. Continental European variants selectively adopted by English speakers are French *Françoise*, Spanish *Francisca* and Italian *Francesca*, the last as for the UK actress Francesca Annis (b.1944). The most common diminutives in independent use are FANNY and FRAN, while others include *Frankie*, *Frannie* and *Franny*. French *Francine*, a diminutive of *Françoise*, is also in found in English-speaking use.

Anglo-US novelist Frances Hodgson Burnett (1849–1924); US actresses Frances Day (1907–84), Frances Dee (b.1908) (original first name Jean), Frances Rafferty (b.1922); UK actresses Frances White (b.1938), Frances de la Tour (b.1944); UK art historian, biographer Frances Spalding (b.1950); UK actress, singer Frances Ruffelle (b.1966).

Francis The name is an English form of the Late Latin name *Franciscus*, 'Frenchman', which was in regular use from the 17th century, although tailing off rather in the 20th century.

The prime inspirer of the name was St Francis of Assisi (1182–1226), who was actually baptized Giovanni (English JOHN). At the time of his birth, his father was away in France on business, and on his return he renamed the child *Francesco*, 'little Frenchman', intending that his son should follow in his footsteps. He chose God rather than Mammon, however, and founded the Franciscan order of friars. The name was subsequently famous as a royal French name, that of two 16th-century kings Francis (*Françoise*) (Francis II being the husband of Mary, Queen of Scots). The many famous (and aristocratic) bearers of the name include the English navigator Sir Francis Drake (1540/43–1696) and the English philosopher and writer Francis Bacon (1561–1626). The diminutives FRANK and FRANKIE have become names in their own right.

UK poet Francis Thompson (1859–1907); UK yachtsman Sir Francis Chichester (1901–72); UK painter Francis Bacon (1909–92); UK actor Francis Matthews (b.1927).

Frank This was originally a Germanic name relating to the *Franks*, the people who gave the name of France. It is now usually regarded, however, as an independently adopted diminutive of FRANCIS or FRANKLIN. The name has been in popular English-speaking use from the mid-19th to the early 20th century, since when it has gradually fallen from favour. In Walter Scott's novel *Rob Roy* (1817) Frank Osbaldistone is the central character and narrator. The name's best-known diminutive is FRANKIE, in independent use.

US architect Frank Lloyd Wright (1869–1959); Italo-US film director Frank Capra (1897–1991); UK comedian Frank Randle (1901–57) (original name Arthur McEvoy); US popular singer Frank Sinatra (1915–98); UK TV personality Frank Muir (1920–98); UK actor Frank Finlay (b.1926); Northern Ireland comedian Frank Carson (b.1926); UK actor Frank Windsor (b.1927); US rock musician Frank Zappa (1940–93); UK boxer Frank Bruno (b.1961).

Frankie An independently adopted diminutive of FRANCIS (or FRANK), in fairly select English-speaking use from the early 20th century.

UK comedian Frankie Howerd (1921–92); UK popular singer Frankie Vaughan (1928–99); US popular singer, actor Frankie Avalon (b.1939).

Franklin From the surname, and adopted generally in the English-speaking world from the 19th century, being particularly popular in the US. It was given an initial boost by the surname of the famous US statesman and scientist Benjamin Franklin (1706–60), and was subsequently made familiar by the two US presidents Franklin Pierce (1804–69) and Franklin D. Roosevelt (1882–1945). The name occurs in literature for Franklin Blake, the central character and part-narrator of Wilkie Collins's novel *The Moonstone* (1868). The alternative spelling *Franklyn* occurs, as for the West Indian-born UK cricketer Franklyn Stephenson (b.1959). The regular diminutive is FRANK, in independent use.

US actor Franklin Pangborn (1894–1958); UK radio presenter Franklin Engelmann (1908–72); US film director Franklin Schaffner (1920–89).

Frannie, **Franny** see **Fran**, **Frances**.

Fraser From the (Scottish) surname, and in select British use from the 1930s, especially in families with Scottish connections. The variant *Frazer* is fairly common, as for the UK actor Frazer Hines (b.1944).

Fred An independently adopted diminutive of FREDERICK or (less often) ALFRED, in regular use among English speakers from the 19th century, but losing momentum from the early years of the 20th century. In George Moore's novel *Esther Waters* (1894) Fred Parsons is a former rival for the hand of Esther. In the UK the name has now come to be associated with an anonymous dogsbody or menial worker. The name's regular diminutive, FREDDIE, is used in its own right.

UK jockey Fred Archer (1857–86); UK impresario Fred Karno (1866–1941); UK broadcaster on gardening Fred Streeter (1877–1975); US dancer, actor Fred Astaire (1899–1987); UK actor Fred Emney (1900–80); Austrian-born US film director Fred Zinnemann (1907–97); US actor Fred MacMurray (1908–91); UK tennis player Fred Perry (1909–95); UK astronomer, science fiction writer Sir Fred Hoyle (1915–2001); UK jockey, racehorse trainer Fred Winter (b.1926); UK cricketer Fred Trueman (b.1931); US actor Fred Savage (b.1976).

Freda An independently adopted diminutive of a name such as ALFREDA, FREDERICA or WINIFRED, adopted by English speakers in the 19th century, when it was perhaps also felt to be a feminine form of FRED. It enjoyed a brief vogue in the second half of the 1920s, but is now no longer common. Freda Halliday is a character in John Galsworthy's novel *The Apple Tree* (1918), and Freda Clegg is found in Agatha Christie's short story 'The Flock of Geryon' in *The Labours of Hercules* (1947). A variant form of the name, adopted in its own right, is FRIEDA.

UK actress Freda Jackson (1909–90); US jazz singer Freda Payne (b.1945).

Freddie An independently adopted diminutive of FRED (or FREDERICK), in regular use among English speakers from the 19th century. Dr Freddie Hamson is a bogus specialist in A.J. Cronin's novel *The Citadel* (1937). The variant spelling *Freddy* is also found.

UK radio broadcaster Freddie Grisewood (1888–1972); UK cinematographer Freddie Young (1902–98); UK-born US actor Freddie Bartholomew (1924–92); UK actor Freddie Jones (b.1927); Mexican-US pop musician Freddie Fender (b.1937) (original name Baldemar G. Huerta); UK comedians Freddie Davies (b.1937), Freddie Starr (b.1944); Zanzibar-born UK rock singer Freddie Mercury (1946–91) (original name Frederick Bulsara).

Frederica A feminine form of FREDERICK, in English-speaking use from the 19th century, although now much less common. Variants include French *Frédérique* and 'continental' *Frederika* or *Frederike*. Diminutives include *Freddie*, FREDA (in independent use), *Fred*, *Rickie*, *Ricky* and *Rica*.

US opera singer Frederica von Stade (b.1945).

Frederick The name derives from an Old German name that gave modern German *Friedrich*, composed of *fridu*, 'peace', and *ríchi*, 'powerful', 'ruler', so 'peaceful ruler'. It was introduced to England by the Normans, but was only rarely in use until the 18th century, when it was reintroduced by the German royal family. It was very popular until the early years of the 20th century, since when it has declined to a much more modest level. It is historically famous from Frederick the Great (1712–86), king of Prussia (although he was hardly a 'peaceful ruler'). In Shakespeare's *As You Like It* (1599) Frederick is the usurper of the dominions of the duke, his brother. The part-narrator of Wilkie Collins's novel *The Woman in White* (1860) is Frederick Fairlie. Variant spellings include *Frederic*, as for the UK writer Frederic Raphael (b.1931), and *Fredric*, as for the US actor Fredric March (1897–1975). Regular diminutives in independent use are FRED and FREDDIE.

UK actor Frederick Treves (b.1925); UK novelist Frederick Forsyth (b.1938).

Freya The name is that of the Norse goddess of love and fecundity, who gave the name of Friday. The name itself is probably related to modern German *Frau*, 'woman'. It has found some favour among English speakers in the 20th century, especially in Scotland.

UK traveller Dame Freya Stark (1893–1993); US children's writer Freya Littledale (b.*c*.1930); UK actress Freya Copeland (b.1969).

Frieda An independently adopted variant of FREDA, with a spelling influenced by its German equivalent, *Friede*. The name has been favoured by some English speakers from the 19th century.

Scottish-born US actress Frieda Inescourt (1900–76); UK actress Frieda Shand (b.1934).

Fritz This is a diminutive form of the German name *Friedrich* (English FREDERICK), occasionally found in independent use among English speakers in the 20th century.

Austrian-born US violinist Fritz Kreisler (1875–1962); UK actor Fritz Leiber (1883–1949); German-born US film director Fritz Lang (1890–1976); Austrian-born UK broadcaster, columnist Fritz Spiegl (b.1926).

Fulton An adoption of the (Scottish) surname, possibly itself from a place-name, the name has been in sporadic English-speaking use from the late 19th century.

US Roman Catholic prelate Fulton J. Sheen (1895–1979) (original first names Peter John); Scottish actor Fulton Mackay (1922–87).

G

Gabriel A biblical name, from Hebrew *Gabhrī'el*, 'my strength is God', which was in regular but select use among English speakers from the 18th century until the end of the 19th century, after which it was rare, until gaining a modest popular revival in the 1940s. In the Bible Gabriel is the archangel who in the Old Testament appears to Daniel and in the New Testament to Zacharias (to announce the impending birth of John the Baptist) and to the Virgin Mary (to announce that of Jesus). In Milton's poem *Paradise Lost* (1667) Gabriel is the 'chief of the angelic guards'. Walter Scott has a character Gabriel Baillie (also known as Gabriel Faa or 'Hunter Gabbie') in his novel *Guy Mannering* (1815), while Gabriel Parsons is a sugar broker in Charles Dickens's book *Sketches by Boz* (1836) and Gabriel Varden is a locksmith in Dickens's novel *Barnaby Rudge* (1841). Later, Gabriel Betteredge is house steward to Lady Verinder in Wilkie Collins's novel *The Moonstone* (1868), and Thomas Hardy's novel *Far from the Madding Crowd* (1874) has Gabriel Oak as a small farmer. The usual diminutive is *Gabby*, as for the UK TV presenter Gabby Yorath (b.1973).

UK writer Gabriel Fielding (1916–86) (original name Alan Gabriel Barnsley); US actor Gabriel Dell (1920–88); Filipino boxer Gabriel 'Flash' Elorde (1935–85); Irish actor Gabriel Byrne (b.1950).

Gabrielle A French feminine form of GABRIEL, in some favour among English speakers from the late 19th century. Variants include *Gabriela* and *Gabriella*, the latter as for Lady Gabriella Windsor (b.1981), daughter of Prince and Princess Michael of Kent. The usual diminutives are *Gabi* or *Gaby*, the latter as for the UK TV presenter Gaby Roslin (b.1964).

UK actress Gabrielle Ray (1884–1973); Canadian novelist Gabrielle Roy (1909–83); UK actresses Gabrielle Drake (b.1944), Gabrielle Anwar (b.1970).

Gail An independently adopted diminutive of ABIGAIL, first taken up by English speakers in the 1930s and achieving a peak of popularity in the second half of the 1960s. The name was made familiar by Gail Tilsley, a popular character in the UK TV soap *Coronation Street* (played by Helen Worth from 1974). Variant spellings include GALE, in independent use, and *Gayle*, the latter as for the US actress Gayle Hunnicutt (b.1942).

US actresses Gail Patrick (1911–80) (original name Margaret Fitzpatrick), Gail Russell (1924–61), Gail Fisher (b.1935); US country singer Gail Davies (b.1948); UK TV presenter Gail Porter (b.1972).

Gale An independently adopted variant of GAIL, perhaps influenced by the standard word *gale*, and in general winning greater favour in the US than in the UK. The variant spelling *Gayle* occurs.

US actresses Gale Sondergaard (1899–1985) (original first name Edith), Gale Page (1911–83) (original name Sally Rutter), Gale Storm (b.1922) (original name Josephine Cottle), Gale Robbins (1922–80).

Gamaliel A biblical name, from Hebrew *Gamlī'ēl*, 'my reward is God'. It was adopted by 17th-century Puritans but was never taken up generally by English speakers. In the Bible Gamaliel is the teacher of St Paul. Gamaliel is the name of both the father and the younger brother of the title character in Tobias Smollett's novel *Peregrine Pickle* (1751).

US social reformer Gamaliel Bailey (1807–59).

Gareth A Welsh name that is a variant of GERAINT, although it is also popularly associated with GARTH, GARY and even GERARD. It is still mainly in Welsh use, but gained a more general spread among English speakers from the 1930s, achieving its peak of popularity in the 1980s, since when it has tailed off somewhat. In the Arthurian romances Gareth is the nephew of King Arthur. He also appears in Tennyson's poem 'Gareth and Lynette' (1872) in *Idylls of the King*. A diminutive is *Gaz*.

UK flautist Gareth Morris (b.1920); UK actor Gareth Hunt (b.1943); Welsh rugby player Gareth Edwards (b.1947); UK comedian Gareth Hale (b.1953); UK rugby player Gareth Chilcott (b.1956); UK TV presenter Gareth Jones ('Gaz Top') (b.1961); UK canoeist Gareth Marriott (b.1970).

Garey see **Gary**.

Garfield From the surname, and in select English-speaking use, especially among US blacks, from the late 19th century. The name was probably originally adopted as a tribute to the US president James A. Garfield (1831–81). In recent times it has been humorously popularized by the cartoon cat character Garfield, the creation in 1978 of the US artist Jim Davis (who gave the cat his grandfather's middle name). Diminutives GARRY and GARY exist in independent use.

New Zealand-born Rhodesian statesman Sir Garfield Todd (1908–92); UK actor Garfield Morgan (b.1931); Barbadian cricketer Sir Garfield (Gary) Sobers (b.1936).

Garry An independently adopted variant of GARY, or a diminutive of GARFIELD or GARETH. It first became popular among English speakers in the 1950s, and gained its greatest favour in the 1960s, since when it has declined somewhat, giving way to *Gary* itself.

UK actor Garry Marsh (1902–81) (original name Leslie March Geraghty); US TV host Garry Moore (1915–93) (original name Thomas Garrison Morfit); US comedian Garry Shandling (b.1949); UK rock journalist, writer Garry Bushell (b.1955); Russian chess player Garry Kasparov (b.1963); UK rugby player Garry Schofield (b.1965); UK cricketer Garry Parker (b.1965).

Garth From the surname, but often popularly associated with GARETH, the name was taken up selectively by English speakers in the early 20th century, with a modest boost in its popularity in the 1940s. The central character of Florence Barclay's novel *The Rosary* (1909) is Garth Dalmain. Later, the name was made familiar in the UK by the 'superman' character Garth in the *Daily Mirror* science fiction comic strip (from the 1940s).

US illustrator Garth Williams (1912–96); US country singer Garth Brooks (b.1962).

Gary The name has its origin in the surname, but has become popularly associated with GARETH. It enjoyed a growing popularity among English speakers, and especially blacks, from the 1930s to the second half of the 1960s, since when it has declined. It originally gained favour from the popular US actor Gary Cooper (1901–61). He was born Frank Cooper, but took his new first name from his agent's home town, Gary, Indiana. A variant spelling of the name is GARRY, in independent use. *Garey* is also sometimes found, as for the UK actor Garey Bridges (b.1969).

US actor Gary Merrill (1915–90); South African golfer Gary Player (b.1935); US senator, presidential candidate, Gary Hart (b.1936); UK actors Gary Bond (1940–95), Gary Waldhorn (b.1943); US actor Gary Busey (b.1944); US country singer Gary Stewart (b.1944); UK actor Gary Wilmot (b.1954); UK pop singer Gary Numan (b.1958); UK actor Gary Oldman (b.1958); UK footballer Gary Lineker (b.1960); Scottish footballer Gary Gillespie (b.1960); UK footballer Gary Mabbutt (b.1961); UK boxer Gary Mason (b.1962); UK actor Gary Webster (b.1964); Scottish rugby player Gary Armstrong (b.1966); US actor Gary Coleman (b.1968); UK golfer Gary Evans (b.1969); UK pop musician Gary Barlow (b.1971).

Gavin A Scottish form of GAWAIN, originally mainly in Scottish use, but from the early 20th century taken up generally by English speakers, with popularity peaks in the 1970s and the second half of the 1980s. The Rev. Gavin Dishart (with a son also Gavin and a daughter Gavinia) marries Lady Babbie in J.M. Barrie's novel *The Little Minister* (1891). In later literature Gavin Stevens is the lawyer who marries Melisandre Harriss Backus in William Faulkner's Snopes family trilogy (1940–59).

US actors Gavin Gordon (1901–70), Gavin Muir (1907–72); UK writers Gavin Maxwell (1914–69), Gavin Ewart (1916–95), Gavin Young (1928–2001), Gavin Lyall (b.1932); UK film director Gavin Millar (b.1938); UK TV presenters Gavin Campbell (b.1946), Gavin Esler (b.1953); Scottish rugby player Gavin Hastings (b.1962).

Gawain A Welsh name, based on *gwalch*, 'hawk', and in very select use among English speakers from medieval times. In literature, Gawain is famous as the nephew of King Arthur in the Arthurian romances and as the central character of the 14th-century alliterative poem *Sir Gawain and the Green Knight*. GAVIN is an independently adopted popular variant.

Gay The name comes from the ordinary word, or strictly speaking from French *gai*, 'joyful'. It was taken up by English speakers from the 1930s, first in the US, then in the UK. It is now rare, mainly because of the word's use to mean homosexual. Noël Coward's musical play *Gay's the Word* (1951) has Gay Daventry as an ageing operetta star. The name is occasionally found in male use, as for the Irish TV presenter Gay Byrne (b.1934).

US writer Gay Courter (b.1944); UK broadcaster Gay Search (b.c.1947).

Gayle see **Gail**, **Gale**.

Gaylord From the surname, itself a distortion of the French word *gaillard*, 'dandy', 'merry fellow' and influenced by the English *gay lord*. It has found some favour among English speakers from the 19th century, but it is now associated with *gay* meaning homosexual, so is rarely adopted. In the UK it was made humorously familiar by Gaylord, the 'bovver boy' character assumed by Dick Emery in the TV comedy series *The*

Dick Emery Show (from the 1960s). A variant spelling is *Gayelord*, as for the US nutritionist and cookbook writer of the 1950s Gayelord Hauser.

US baseball player Gaylord Perry (b.1938).

Gaynor The name is a medieval form of GUINEVERE, so is related to JENNIFER. It has enjoyed some favour among English speakers from the 1960s, and may have been brought before the public to some extent by the surname of the US actresses Janet Gaynor (1906–84) or Mitzi Gaynor (b.1930).

Gaz see **Gareth**.

Geena see **Gina**.

Gemma The name represents the Italian word for 'gem', 'jewel', and has itself long been established as a name in Italy. Among some English speakers it is perhaps felt to be related to EMMA. It increased fairly rapidly in popularity from the 1960s to the 1980s, since when it has declined somewhat. The variant spelling *Jemma* is also found, as for the UK actress Jemma Redgrave (b.1965) (original first name Jemima).

UK photographer Gemma Levine (b.1939); UK actress Gemma Jones (b.1942); Irish-born UK actress Gemma Craven (b.1950).

Gena see **Gina**.

Gene (m.) This name is an independently adopted diminutive of EUGENE, in select English-speaking use from the early 20th century. It is chiefly found in the US and Canada.

US writer Gene Fowler (1890–1960); Canadian actor Gene Lockhart (1891–1957); UK comedian Gene Gerrard (1892–1971); US boxer Gene Tunney (1898–1978) (original first names James Joseph); US singer Gene Austin (1900–72); US actors Gene Autry (1907–98), Gene Raymond (1908–98) (original name Raymond Guion), Gene Kelly (1912–96),

Gene Nelson (1920–96), Gene Barry (b.1921), Gene Hackman (b.1930), Gene Wilder (b.1934) (original name Jerry Silberman).

Gene (f.) The name is either an independently adopted diminutive of EUGENIE, or a variant spelling of JEAN, or even in some cases a borrowing of the male name GENE. It was taken up in the US from the early 20th century but has won little favour in the UK. The US children's writer Gene Stratton Porter (1863–1924) had the original first name Geneva, itself probably a form of GENEVIEVE. The diminutive *Ginny* usually comes from VIRGINIA.

US actress Gene Tierney (1920–91); UK children's writer Gene Kemp (b.1926).

Genette see **Jeanette**.

Genevieve The name is of French origin and is said to derive ultimately from the Germanic (but ultimately Celtic) words *geno*, 'race', and *wefa*, 'woman', thus having an overall sense 'female'. It has enjoyed a modest English-speaking vogue since the 19th century, when it was introduced from France. The name's best-known historical bearer is the 5th-century nun St Genevieve, patron saint of Paris. Genevieve Crespigny is a Brighton landlady in Clyde Fitch's play *The Truth* (1907). More recently the name came to be popularly associated with the UK film *Genevieve* (1953), in which the 'heroine' is a vintage car returning to London after the annual Veteran Car Run to Brighton. The name is often spelt with an accent, and has a diminutive *Ginny*, more usually associated with VIRGINIA.

French-born US actress Genevieve Tobin (1901–95); French actress Geneviève Page (b.1931); French-Canadian actress Geneviève Bujold (b.1942).

Genie see **Eugenie**.

Geoff An independently adopted diminutive of GEOFFREY, taken up by some English speakers in the 20th century, but never as common as JEFF is for JEFFREY.

UK bandleader Geoff Love (1917–91); UK racing motorcyclist Geoff Duke (b.1923); UK athlete Geoff Capes (b.1949).

Geoffrey The present name represents the Old German name *Gaufrid*, probably formed from *gavja*, 'territory', and *fridu*, 'peace', implying 'peaceful ruler'. Some sources, however, see the name as a variant of GODFREY. It was introduced to England by the Normans and was in fairly general English-speaking use until the 16th century. It then declined until the 19th century but grew in popularity until the 1950s, after which it again gradually fell from favour. A famous early bearer of the name was the poet Geoffrey Chaucer (*c*.1343–1400). In literature, Sir Geoffrey Peveril is the father of Julian Peveril, the central character of Walter Scott's novel *Peveril of the Peak* (1823), and Geoffrey Haredale is the enemy of Sir John Chester in Charles Dickens's novel *Barnaby Rudge* (1841). The variant spelling JEFFREY is in independent use. The regular diminutive is GEOFF.

UK writers Geoffrey Household (1900–88), Geoffrey Trease (1909–98); UK actor Geoffrey Bayldon (b.1924); UK politician Sir Geoffrey Howe, Lord Howe (b.1926); UK actors Geoffrey Palmer (b.1927), Geoffrey Whitehead (b.1939); UK cricketer Geoffrey Boycott (b.1940); UK actors Geoffrey Davies (b.1942), Geoffrey Hughes (b.1944).

George The name is an English version of what is ultimately the Greek name *Georgios*, itself from *geōrgos*, 'farmer' (literally 'earth worker'). It has been in general use among English speakers from the 16th century, enjoying a fairly sustained popularity to the early years of the 20th century, since when it has mostly declined, although with two modest revivals in the 1960s and 1990s. It is primarily famous from St George, the patron saint of England, popularly portrayed slaying a dragon.

It has been equally familiar as a royal name, notably that of six kings of England from the 17th century to the 20th. (George III was given the etymologically tautological nickname 'Farmer George' for his bucolic tastes.) George, Duke of Clarence, brother of Edward IV and the future Richard III, appears as a historical character in Shakespeare's *Richard III* (1591), and George Greengoose is a character in Francis Beaumont's play *The Knight of the Burning Pestle* (1607–8). In later literature Captain George Osborne is one of the main characters in William Makepeace Thackeray's novel *Vanity Fair* (1847–8). Regular diminutives are *Georgie*, *Georgy* and *Geordie*, this last being a Scottish and northern English form and now a general nickname for a Tynesider or person from Newcastle.

UK actors George Cole (b.1925), George Waring (b.1927); US actors George C. Scott (1927–99), George Peppard (1928–94); UK actor George Baker (b.1931); US country musician George Hamilton IV (b.1937); UK pop musician George Harrison (1943–2001); UK actor George Layton (b.1943); UK footballer George Best (b.1946); UK pop singer George Michael (b.1963) (original name Yorgos Panayiotou).

Georgette A French feminine form of GEORGE, in select English-speaking use from the early 20th century. The UK actress Googie Withers (b.1917) was originally Georgette. Diminutives are *Georgie* or simply *George*.

UK historical novelist Georgette Heyer (1902–74) (father was George).

Georgia A Latin-style feminine form of GEORGE, in general English-speaking use from the late 19th century, and gaining some popularity in the 1990s. Diminutives are usually *Georgie* or simply *George*.

US artist Georgia O'Keeffe (1887–1986); US actress Georgia Hale (1903–85); US pop singer Georgia Gibbs (b.1920) (original name Fredda Lipson); UK actress, singer Georgia Brown (1933–92) (original name Lilian Klot); UK actress Georgia Taylor (b.1980).

Georgiana A feminine form of GEORGE, in fairly regular use among English speakers from the 18th century to the late 19th century, after which the name was rarely adopted. Georgiana Podsnap is a character in Charles Dickens's novel *Our Mutual Friend* (1864–5). Diminutives are *Georgie* or *Georgy*.

UK society and court writer Lady Georgiana Bloomfield (1822–1905).

Georgie see **George, Georgia, Georgiana, Georgina**.

Georgina A feminine form of GEORGE, in regular English-speaking use from the 18th century and originally favoured mostly in Scotland. The name has enjoyed periodic spells of popularity in the UK from the early 20th century, but in the US the form GEORGIA is generally preferred. In Thomas Hardy's novel *The Hand of Ethelberta* (1876) Georgina Chickerell is the sister of the central character, the young widow Ethelberta Petherwin. Diminutives are usually *Georgie*, *George* and GINA, this last now in use as an independent name.

UK singer Georgina Weldon (1837–1914); UK biographer Georgina Battiscombe (b.1905); UK actress Georgina Hale (b.1943); UK fashion designer Georgina Godley (b.1955).

Georgy see **George**.

Geraint A Welsh name of uncertain origin, but perhaps influenced by the Greek word *gerōn*, genitive *gerontos*, 'old man'. It is still primarily in Welsh use but was taken up more widely by English speakers from the 1950s. In the Arthurian romances, Geraint is one of the Knights of the Round Table, and as such appears in Tennyson's poem 'Geraint and Enid' (1886) in *Idylls of the King*.

Welsh opera singer Sir Geraint Evans (1922–92).

Gerald The name is an English form of the Old German name *Gerwald*, formed from *gēr*, 'spear', and *waltan*, 'to rule', so 'spear ruler'. It has been popularly associated with GERARD, but that name has a different origin. It has been in fairly popular English-speaking use from the 19th century, although it has generally tailed off since the 1950s. Gerald Arbuthnot is a character in Oscar Wilde's play *A Woman of No Importance* (1893), while Gerald Dawes is engaged to Agnes Pembroke in E.M. Forster's novel *The Longest Journey* (1907). Regular diminutives are GERRY and JERRY, both in independent use.

UK actor-manager Gerald du Maurier (1873–1934); UK pianist Gerald Moore (1899–1987); UK politician Sir Gerald Nabarro (1913–73); UK zoologist, writer Gerald Durrell (1925–95); UK politician Gerald Kaufman (b.1930).

Geraldine A feminine form of GERALD, known in English-speaking use as early as the 16th century, although mainly as a literary name. It was more widely adopted from the 19th century, when Gerald itself became popular. In the 20th century it achieved its greatest popularity in the 1950s. 'The fair Geraldine', the subject of love poems by Henry Howard, Earl of Surrey (1514–47), was actually Lady Elizabeth Fitzgerald, her literary name being created from her surname. She reappears in Samuel Taylor Coleridge's poem 'Christabel' (1816), in which the name rhymes with 'dine', not 'dean'. In Agatha Christie's novel *Lord Edgware Dies* (1933) (US title *Thirteen at Dinner*), Geraldine (Dina) Marsh is the daughter of the central character. The chief diminutives are *Gerrie*, *Gerry*, *Jerrie* and *Jerry*, the last of these familiar from the US model Jerry Hall (b.1956).

US opera singer, actress Geraldine Farrar (1882–1967); Irish actress Geraldine Fitzgerald (b.1912); US actress Geraldine Page (1924–87); UK actress Geraldine McEwan (b.1932); UK writer on art Geraldine Norman (b.1940); UK actresses Geraldine Chaplin (b.1944), Geraldine James (b.1950) (father was Gerald).

Gerard The name is an English form of the Old German name *Gerart*, formed from *gēr*, 'spear', and *hart*, 'strong', 'brave', thus 'brave with the spear'. It has become popularly associated with GERALD, but that name has a different origin. It was in fairly regular use among English speakers until the 17th century, when it sharply declined. It then picked up from the mid-19th century, and has since been in select use, with a modest peak of popularity in the second half of the 1950s. Gerard Eliasson is the central character in Charles Reade's novel *The Cloister and the Hearth* (1861). Diminutives in independent use are GERRY and JERRY.

UK poet Gerard Manley Hopkins (1844–89); UK politician Sir Gerard Vaughan (b.1923); German-born UK musician, cartoonist Gerard Hoffnung (1925–59); UK actor Gerard Bostock (b.1978).

Gerda This name probably derives from Old Norse *garthr*, 'enclosure', 'protected place', but it is now sometimes felt to be a feminine form of GERARD or a variant of GERTRUDE. It has been in select English-speaking use from the 19th century. In Norse mythology, Gerda is the goddess wife of Frey. Literary bearers of the name include the little girl Gerda in Hans Christian Andersen's fairy story *The Snow Queen* (1846); Gerda Grant, wife of Alistair Grant in Agatha Christie's novel *One, Two, Buckle My Shoe* (1940) (US title *The Patriotic Murders*); and Gerda Christow, wife of the murdered Dr John Christow in another Christie novel, *The Hollow* (1946) (US title *Murder After Hours*).

Germaine A French feminine form of the now rare male name *Germain*, itself from the Late Latin *Germanus*, 'brother', with this meaning doubtless originally in a Christian context. The name has been in very select use among English speakers from the early 20th century. The spelling *Jermaine* is usually reserved for males, as for the US pop singer Jermaine Jackson (b.1954), brother of Michael Jackson.

Australian feminist writer Germaine Greer (b.1939).

Gerrie see **Geraldine**.

Gerry (m.) An independently adopted diminutive of GERALD and, less often, GERARD, in select use among English speakers from the early 20th century. JERRY is a spelling in independent use.

US bandleader Gerry Mulligan (1927–96); UK pop musician Gerry Marsden (b.1942); UK circus owner Gerry Cottle (b.1945); Scottish folk-rock musician Gerry Rafferty (b.1947); Northern Ireland politician Gerry Adams (b.1948); UK footballer Gerry Francis (b.1951).

Gerry (f.) see **Geraldine**.

Gershom A biblical name, from Hebrew *Gērshōm*, 'exile', adopted by English Puritans in the 17th century and taken to the US, where it remains in rarish use. In the Bible Gershom is a son of Moses and Zipporah: 'And she bare him a son, and he called his name Gershom: for he said, I have been a stranger in a strange land' (Exodus 2.22).

Gertrude The name derives from an Old German name formed from *gēr*, 'spear', and *traut*, 'strength', and so has the overall meaning 'strong with the spear' or 'strong as a spear'. It was first in English-speaking use in late medieval times, after which it was rare until the mid-19th century, when its popularity increased. It has been in sharp decline, however, from the early years of the 20th century. In Shakespeare's *Hamlet* (1599–1601) Gertrude is Hamlet's mother. Gertrude Grayson is a character in James Fenimore Cooper's novel *The Red Rover* (1827), and Gertrude Chiltern is the wife of Sir Robert Chiltern in Oscar Wilde's play *An Ideal Husband* (1895). Diminutives include *Gert*, *Gertie* and TRUDY, the last of which is in independent use.

US writer Gertrude Atherton (1857–1948); UK travel writer Gertrude Bell (1868–1926); US writer Gertrude Stein (1874–1946); US actress Gertrude Astor (1887–1977); UK actress Gertrude Lawrence (1898–1952) (original name Gertrud Alexandra Dagmar Lawrence Klasen);

US actresses Gertrude Berg (1899–1966), Gertrude Michael (1911–1964); Irish crime novelist Gertrude Moyes (b.1923).

Gervase The name is an English form of the Late Latin name *Gervasius*, which is perhaps in turn based either on Greek *gēras*, 'old age', or is a compound of Old German *gēr*, 'spear', and *vas*, 'servant', 'vassal'. Its greatest favour among English speakers has been with Roman Catholics, who took it up in the 16th century, associating it either with the 4th-century St Gervasius or with one or other (or both) of the 12th-century contemporary English scholars Gervase of Canterbury and Gervase of Tilbury. The variant *Gervaise* exists, while JARVIS is a directly related name.

UK singer Gervase Elwes (1866–1921); UK clarinettist Gervase de Peyer (b.1926).

Ghislaine The name, which comes from an Old French form of GISELLE, has been in select use among English speakers from the 1920s. (The usual pronunciation is 'Gizz-lane', with a hard 'G' as in 'give'.) In the 1950s Ghislaine Alexander was a regular panellist on the UK TV game show *What's My Line?* The diminutive *Gigi* occurs, as for the US actress Gigi Perreau (b.1941) (original name Ghislaine Perreau-Saussine).

Gib see **Gilbert**.

Gideon A biblical name, from Hebrew *Gid'ōn*, 'one who cuts down', that is, a swordsman. The name has found some favour among English speakers since the 17th century, when it was adopted by the Puritans. In the Bible Gideon is a judge called on by God to rescue the Hebrews from the Midianites. Gideon Sharpitlaw is a procurator fiscal in Walter Scott's novel *The Heart of Midlothian* (1818), and Gideon Sarn is the brother of Prudence, the narrator of Mary Webb's novel *Precious Bane* (1924).

Gigi see **Ghislaine**.

Gilbert The name is an English form, derived through French, of an Old German name composed of *gisil*, 'pledge', and *berht*, 'bright', 'famous', so 'famous pledger'. It was brought to England by the Normans but was not in regular use until the 17th century. It is now little used and has fallen from favour since the early 20th century. Some Roman Catholics took up the name in honour of St Gilbert of Sempringham, founder in 1131 of the Gilbertians, the only native religious order in England (subsequently disbanded by Henry VIII). Gilbert Glossin is a 'wily scoundrel' in Walter Scott's novel *Guy Mannering* (1815), while in Henry James's novel *The Portrait of a Lady* (1881) Gilbert Osmond marries Isabel Archer. A common diminutive is *Gib*.

UK writers Gilbert Murray (1866–1957), Gilbert Keith Chesterton (1874–1936); Mexican-born US actor Gilbert Roland (1905–94) (original name Luis de Alonso); UK broadcaster Gilbert Harding (1907–60); UK writer, literary critic Gilbert Phelps (b.1915).

Gilda The name appears to be an Italian diminutive form of the Old German name known to the Anglo-Saxons as *Eormenhild*, with *hild* meaning 'sacrifice'. It has enjoyed only limited popularity among English speakers from the 19th century. Some of its initial adoption may have been prompted by Gilda, Rigoletto's daughter in Verdi's opera *Rigoletto* (1851). Agatha Christie has a murder victim Gilda Glen in her short story 'The Man in the Mist' in *Partners in Crime* (1929). The name was later popularized by the film *Gilda* (1946), with Rita Hayworth in the title role.

Polish-born US dancer Gilda Gray (1901–59) (original name Marianna Michalska); US comedienne Gilda Radner (1946–89).

Giles The name is the English form, through French and much altered, of what was originally the Greek name *Aigidios*, from *aigidion*, 'kid', 'young goat'. The reference is not to youth but to kid leather, which was used for making shields (hence the expression 'under the aegis of'). The name has been in English-speaking use, especially in Scotland, from medieval times but has found little favour in the 20th century, apart from a mild popularity peak in the second half of the 1970s. It was initially made famous by St Giles in the 8th century. Giles Gosling is a landlord in Walter Scott's novel *Kenilworth* (1821), and Sir Giles Wapshot is a character in William Makepeace Thackeray's novel *Vanity Fair* (1847–8). Giles Farnaby (1563–1640) was a noted English composer, and Giles Fletcher (1588–1623) was a famous English poet. 'Farmer Giles' has become a stock rustic figure. The variant spelling *Gyles* is also found, as for the UK MP and TV presenter Gyles Brandreth (b.1948).

UK cartoonist Giles (1916–95) (original name Carl Ronald Giles); UK dramatist Giles Cooper (1918–66); Scottish writer Giles Gordon (b.1940); UK columnist Giles Coren (b.1969).

Gillian The name is either a feminine form of JULIAN, a variant form of JULIANA, or (in popular regard) an extended or 'formal' form of JILL. It was widely adopted until the 1960s, since when it has gradually fallen from favour. A spelling variant is *Jillian*, and diminutives include *Gill*, *Gillie* and *Gilly*, the first as for the UK magazine editor Gill Hudson (b.1955).

UK ballerina, choreographer Gillian Lynne (b.1926); UK opera singer Gillian Knight (b.1934); UK writer, broadcaster Gillian Reynolds (b.1935); UK writer Gillian Tindall (b.1938); UK politician Gillian Shephard (b.1940); New Zealand-born UK organist Gillian Weir (b.1941); UK concert singer Gillian Jason (b.1941); UK children's writer Gillian Cross (b.1945); UK actress Gillian Hills (b.1946); UK badminton player Gillian Gilks (b.1950); UK actress Gillian Taylforth (b.1955); UK concert singer Gillian Fisher (b.1955); UK golfer Gillian Stewart (b.1958); UK badminton players Gillian Clark (b.1961), Gillian Gowers (b.1964); Scottish actress Gillian McNeill (b.1965); UK actress Gillian Kearney (b.1972).

Gina The name is an independently adopted diminutive of GEORGINA or REGINA, in select use among English speakers from the 1920s. The variant spellings *Geena* and *Gena* are also found, as respectively for the US actresses Geena Davis (b.1957) and Gena Rowlands (b.1934) (original first name Virginia).

Irish-German-US actress Gina Malo (1909–63) (original name Janet Flynn); Italian actress Gina Lollabrigida (b.1927) (original first name Luigina); UK actresses Gina McKee (b.1964), Gina Bellman (b.1966).

Ginevra This is an Italian form of GUINEVERE, adopted independently. The name had some vogue among English speakers in the 19th century, and is still occasionally found. Ginevra Fanshawe marries Count de Hamal in Charlotte Brontë's novel *Villette* (1853), while Ginevra Dunbar is a friend of Amy Grey in J.M. Barrie's play *Alice-sit-by-the-fire* (1905). Diminutives *Ginnie* and *Ginny* exist.

Ginger (m.) An adoption of the nickname, usually given to a person with red hair or a fiery temper. The name has found some adoption from the early 20th century and occurs for various characters in popular or children's literature, such as Flight-Lieutenant Ginger Hebblethwaite in W.E. Johns's 'Biggles' books for boys (1930s to 1970s), or Ginger, a close friend of William Brown in Richmal Crompton's 'William' books for boys (1920s to 1970s). In Norman Collins's novel *Children of the Archbishop* (1951) Ginger Woods marries Sweetie Hart. Harry Champion's popular song 'Ginger, You're Barmy'! (1910) at least brought the name before a wide public.

UK fighter pilot Ginger Lacey (1917–89) (original first name James); UK rock drummer Ginger Baker (b.1939) (original first name Peter).

Ginger (f.) The name, either an independently adopted diminutive of VIRGINIA or a nickname for a baby girl with red hair, has found some favour from the 1930s. The usual diminutive, GINNY, is in use in its own right.

US dancer, actress Ginger Rogers (b.1911–95) (original name Virginia McMath).

Ginnie see **Ginevra**.

Ginny An independently adopted diminutive of GINEVRA, GINGER (f.) or VIRGINIA, in occasional use among English speakers in the 20th century. Also, but rarely, a diminutive of GENE (f.) and GENEVIEVE.

US popular singer Ginny Simms (1916–94) (original name Virginia Sims).

Giselle A French name, itself of Germanic origin, with *gisil* meaning 'pledge' (compare modern German *Geisel*, 'hostage'). It has been selectively taken up in the English-speaking world from the mid-19th century but has never been common. (The usual pronunciation is an approximation of the French, with a soft 'G' and the 's' sounding as 'z'. The suggestion of *gazelle* may have assisted its adoption among English speakers.) The ballet *Giselle* (1841) by the French composer Adolphe Adam did much to popularize the name. A variant spelling is *Gisele*, as for the Canadian pop singer Gisele MacKenzie (b.1927).

Gita see **Bridget**.

Gladys The name is an English form of the Welsh name *Gwladys*, itself perhaps a feminine form of *gwledig*, 'ruler', or else a form of CLAUDIA. The name's suggestion of English *glad* is purely fortuitous. The name was adopted fairly widely by English speakers from the late 19th century but has declined dramatically from the early years of the 20th century. In literature the name is often that of a 'lowly' or menial character. Gladys is a servant in J.M. Barrie's play *The Admirable Crichton* (1902), and (with pet name Gladdie) she is a kitchen-maid in Agatha Christie's novel *Murder at the Vicarage* (1930). Another Christie parlourmaid of the name is Gladys Roberts, formerly Evans, referred to in the victim's dying words that form the title of her novel *Why Didn't They Ask Evans?* (1934) (US title *The Boomerang Clue*). Diminutives include *Glad*, *Gladdie* and *Gladdy*, with '*Gladeye*' a humorous nickname based on the latter (or the full name).

UK actress Dame Gladys Cooper (1888–1971); Irish actress Gladys Henson (1897–1983); UK writer Gladys Mitchell (1901–83); UK-Chinese missionary Gladys Aylward (1903–70); UK actress, singer Gladys Ambrose (b.1930); US soul singer Gladys Knight (b.1944).

Glen From the surname, and in irregular use from the 19th century, with a period of popularity in the second half of the 1950s and first half of the 1960s. The variant spelling GLENN is in independent use and is now the regular form of the name.

UK stage director Glen Byam Shaw (1904–86) (original first name Glencairn); US choreographer Glen Tetley (b.1926) (father was Glenford); US country singer Glen Campbell (b.1936); UK artist Glen Baxter (b.1944); Scottish artist Glen Onwin (b.1947).

Glenda A modern Welsh name, formed from *glân*, 'clean', 'pure', and *da*, 'good', but perhaps also half-suggested by the 15th-century Welsh rebel chieftain Owen Glendower (*Owain Glyndŵr*).The name has been in fairly general English-speaking use from the 1930s, although it is now much less common. A common diminutive is *Glen*.

US actress Glenda Farrell (1904–71); UK politician, actress Glenda Jackson (b.1936); UK magazine editor Glenda Bailey (b.1958); UK actress Glenda McKay (b.1971) (named for Jackson).

Glenn (m.) A variant form of GLEN, in use among English speakers from the late 19th century and found fairly regularly from the 1950s.

US actors Glenn Anders (1889–1981), Glenn Hunter (1897–1945); US bandleader Glenn Miller (1904–44); US athlete Glenn Hardin (1910–75); Canadian-born US actor Glenn Ford (b.1916) (original first name Gwyllyn); US actors Glenn Langan (1917–91), Glenn Corbett

(1929–93); Canadian pianist Glenn Gould (1932–82); UK footballers Glenn Hoddle (b.1957); Glenn Cockerill (b.1959).

Glenn (f.) This is either an adoption of the male name GLENN or a diminutive form of GLENDA or GLENYS. The name has found some favour among English speakers from the 1940s.

US actress Glenn Close (b.1947).

Glenys A Welsh name that probably arose as an independent variant of GLYNIS but that could also be a blend of GLADYS and GLENDA. It has been adopted by some English speakers from the 1940s. The usual diminutive is *Glen*.

Welsh politician Glenys Kinnock, wife of former leader of Labour Party (b.1944).

Gloria A name that is a direct borrowing of the Latin word *gloria*, 'glory', doubtless partly prompted by the earlier name *Gloriana*, a poetic epithet for Queen Elizabeth I. It has been in English-speaking use from the early 20th century, enjoying a peak of popularity in the 1930s. In literature the name is found for Gloria Clandon in George Bernard Shaw's play *You Never Can Tell* (1898). An occasional variant is *Glory*.

US actress Gloria Swanson (1899–1983); UK-born US actress Gloria Holden (1908–91); US actresses Gloria Dickson (1916–45) (original name Thais Dickerson), Gloria de Haven (b.1924), Gloria Jean (b.1928); US feminist writer Gloria Steinem (b.1934); Irish TV presenter Gloria Hunniford (b.1940); US popular singer Gloria Gaynor (b.1949); US writer Gloria Naylor (b.1950); Cuban-born US rock singer Gloria Estefan (b.1957).

Glyn A Welsh name, from *glyn*, 'valley', influenced by GLENN and perhaps also by GWYN. It has been in both Welsh and general English-speaking use from the early 20th century, with peaks of popularity in the 1950s and 1960s. The variant spelling *Glynn* exists, as for the UK actor Glynn Edwards (b.1931).

UK archaeologist, broadcaster Glyn Daniel (1914–86); Welsh actor Glyn Houston (b.1926); Welsh TV political reporter Glyn Mathias (b.1945); UK poet Glyn Maxwell (b.1962).

Glynis A Welsh name, perhaps in origin an alteration of GLADYS influenced by the word *glyn*, 'valley'. It has found some general favour among English speakers from the early 20th century, although it has been less popular since the 1950s. The variant form *Glynnis* is sometimes found, as for the US actress Glynnis O'Connor (b.1956). (GLENYS is an independent name.) The usual diminutive is *Glyn*.

Welsh actress Glynis Johns (b.1923); UK tennis player Glynis Coles (b.1954); South African-born actress Glynis Barber (b.1955).

Glynn see **Glyn**.

Glynnis see **Glynis**.

Godfrey The name is an English form of the Old German name *Godafrid*, from *god*, 'god', and *fridu*, 'peace', hence 'peace god'. It has become popularly associated with GEOFFREY, but that is a name of different origin. Godfrey was introduced to England by the Normans and has enjoyed a fairly steady use among English speakers ever since, although it is now much less common than formerly. Godfrey Gauntlet is the brother of Emilia Gauntlet, loved by Peregrine Pickle, the central character in Tobias Smollett's novel *Peregrine Pickle* (1751). In George Eliot's novel *Silas Marner* (1861) Godfrey Cass is the father of Eppie, the child adopted by Silas.

UK actor Sir Godfrey Tearle (1884–1953); UK broadcasters Godfrey Winn (1908–71), Godfrey Talbot (1908–2000); UK cricketer Godfrey Evans (1920–99); US actor Godfrey Cambridge (1929–76).

Godwin This is the modern form of the Old English name *Godwine*, formed from *god*, 'god', and *wine*, 'friend', so 'God (is a) friend' (or 'friend of God'). The name has been in use among English speakers from medieval times and was historically made prominent in the 11th century by Godwin, Earl of Wessex and father of King Harold (who was defeated in the Battle of Hastings). Sir Godwin Lydgate is a character in George Eliot's novel *Middlemarch* (1871–2).

Goldie The name is usually either an adoption of the surname or a borrowing of the nickname for a person with fair hair (compare BLONDIE). It has found select English-speaking adoption from the 19th century.

US country singer Goldie Hill (b.1933); US actress Goldie Hawn (b.1945).

Gordon From the (Scottish) surname and still chiefly in Scottish use, although it is also found widely elsewhere in the English-speaking world, enjoying a peak in popularity in the 1920s and 1930s. Undoubtedly some bearers of the name were so called in tribute to General Charles George Gordon (1833–85), Gordon of Khartoum, who died defending that city. A rarish spelling variant is *Gorden*, as for the UK actor Gorden Kaye (b.1941).

UK actor Gordon Harker (1885–1967); UK jockey Sir Gordon Richards (1904–86); UK film director Gordon Parry (1908–81); Scottish actor Gordon Jackson (1923–90); UK jockey, racehorse trainer Gordon Richards (1930–98); UK athlete Gordon Pirie (1931–91); UK footballer Gordon Banks (b.1937); Northern Ireland TV presenter Gordon Burns (b.1942); UK concert pianist Gordon Fergus-Thompson (b.1952).

Grace An adoption of the ordinary word, denoting the virtue, and not surprisingly taken up by Puritans in the 17th century, like its 'sisters', FAITH, HOPE and CHARITY. The name became generally popular in the English-speaking world from the 19th century, when its religious associations were appreciated, especially in the US. Its appeal was enhanced by the UK folk heroine Grace Darling (1815–42), the lighthouse keeper's daughter who helped to save storm-bound sailors in 1838. In literature Grace Wellborn is a significantly named character in Ben Jonson's comedy *Bartholomew Fair* (1614). Later, the name is found for Grace Poole, Mrs Rochester's housekeeper in Charlotte Brontë's novel *Jane Eyre* (1847). The usual diminutive is *Gracie*, brought before a wide public by the UK singer and comedienne Gracie Fields (1898–1979) (original name Grace Stansfield) as well as by the US comedienne Gracie Allen (1895–1964).

US opera singer Grace Moore (1898–1947); US actress Grace McDonald (b.1921); US novelist Grace Metalious (1924–64); US actress Grace Kelly, later Princess Grace of Monaco (1928–82); US opera singer Grace Bumbry (b.1937); US rock singer Grace Slick (b.1939); West Indian soul singer Grace Jones (b.1952).

Graeme An independently adopted variant of GRAHAM, found in English-speaking use from the early 20th century and particularly favoured in Scotland. Its peak of popularity was in the second half of the 1960s.

Scottish-born actor Graeme Garden (b.1943); South African cricketer Graeme Pollock (b.1944); Scottish footballer Graeme Souness (b.1953); UK cricketer Graeme Hick (b.1966); Australian actor Graeme Squires (b.1980).

Graham From the (Scottish) surname and still primarily a Scottish name, although it is now found much more widely in the English-speaking world, especially in the UK. Its peak period of popularity was the 1950s, since when it has tailed off. A variant spelling GRAEME is in independent use.

UK painter Graham Sutherland (1903–80); UK novelist Graham Greene (1904–91); UK actor Graham Moffatt (1919–1965); UK motor-racing driver Graham Hill (1929–75); UK footballer Graham Turner (b.1947); UK actor Graham Seed (b.1950); UK cricketer Graham Gooch (b.1953).

Grant From the (Scottish) surname, taken up as a first name in the US and Canada in the 19th century and now found in English-speaking use more generally, with a slight rise in popularity in the latter half of the 20th century. Early bearers of the name were often given it as a tribute to the US president and Civil War hero Ulysses S. Grant (1822–85).

Canadian writer Grant Allen (1848–99); US actors Grant Mitchell (1874–1957), Grant Williams (1930–85); Australian actor Grant Dodwell (b.1952); UK actor Grant Thatcher (b.1962).

Granville From the surname, and in select English-speaking use from the 19th century, although never very common. The variant form *Grenville* is also found.

UK composer Granville Bantock (1868–1946) (father's second name); US actor Granville Bates (1882–1940); US critic, writer Granville Hicks (1901–82).

Greer From the (Scottish) surname, itself a form of *Gregor* (English GREGORY), and in very select use among English speakers in the 20th century.

UK-Irish actress Greer Garson (1908–96) (mother's maiden name was Greer).

Greg An independently adopted diminutive of GREGORY, taken up by English speakers from the 1950s.

US actors Greg McClure (b.1918) (original name Dale Easton), Greg Morris (1934–96); Australian cricketer Greg Chappell (b.1948); US writer Greg Bear (b.1951); Australian actor Greg Benson (b.1967); UK rower Greg Searle (b.1972).

Gregory The name is an English form of the Greek name *Gregōrios*, itself from *gregōrein*, 'to watch', so 'watchful', 'vigilant'. It has found fairly select use among English speakers from medieval times, with a slight increase in popularity from the 1950s. The name was borne by many well-known early Christians, who adopted it with reference to the biblical ordinance 'be vigilant' (1 Peter 5.8). It was then made familiar by several popes. In Shakespeare's *Romeo and Juliet* (1595) Gregory is a servant to Capulet, while Gregory Vigil (perhaps with deliberately significant surname) is the guardian of Hellen Bellew in John Galsworthy's novel *The Country House* (1907). The usual diminutive is GREG, in independent use (also *Gregg* and *Greig* in Scotland).

US film director Gregory La Cava (1892–1952); US actor Gregory Peck (b.1916); UK conductor Gregory Rose (b.1948).

Grenville see **Granville**.

Greta An independently adopted diminutive of *Margareta*, the Swedish form of MARGARET, which has been in select English-speaking use from the 1920s, although it is now much less common. In literature the name is found for Greta Miller, a character in Theodore Dreiser's novel *An American Tragedy* (1925), and later for Greta Anderson, a Swedish au pair in Agatha Christie's novel *Endless Night* (1967).

Swedish actress Greta Garbo (1905–90); Italian-born UK actress Greta Scacchi (b.1958).

Gretchen The name is a German diminutive form of *Margarete* (English MARGARET), with the *-chen* denoting 'little' (compare MÄDCHEN). It has found some favour among English speakers from the 19th century, and was originally made known to the public at large by the simple country girl seduced by Faust in Goethe's *Faust* (1808), as a result of which it has come to be a stock name for a typical German girl.

UK actress Gretchen Franklin (b.1911); US actress Gretchen Corbett (b.1947).

Greville From the surname, and in very select English-speaking use from the 17th century. The surname that originally gave the first name was that of the earls of Warwick (from 1759).

UK politician Greville Janner (b.1928); UK jockey Greville Starkey (b.1939).

Griffith The name is the English form of the Welsh name *Gruffudd*, the second part of which means 'lord', 'chief'. It has been mainly in Welsh use from the 16th century. *Henry VIII* (1613) by Shakespeare and Fletcher has Griffith as a gentleman usher to Queen Catherine. The usual diminutive is *Griff*, as for the Welsh comedian and actor Griff Rhys Jones (b.1953).

UK actor Griffith Jones (b.1910).

Griselda The name is probably of Germanic origin, formed from *gris*, 'grey', and *hild*, 'battle'. It has been associated with modern English *grizzle*, but this word's origin is unknown. The name has enjoyed a rather limited English-speaking use from medieval times but is now rarely found. It was originally made familiar by the story of the long-suffering wife 'patient Griselda', retold by Chaucer after Boccaccio as 'The Clerk's Tale' in *The Canterbury Tales* (*c*.1387). More recent literary adoption of the name includes Griselda Oldbuck, sister of Jonathan Oldbuck, Laird of Oldbarns, in Walter Scott's novel *The Antiquary* (1816); Griselda Grantly, daughter of the Bishop of Barchester, in Anthony Trollope's novel *The Warden* (1855); and Griselda Clement, wife of the murdered Leonard Clement, in Agatha Christie's novel *Murder at the Vicarage* (1930). A diminutive is ZELDA, which is in independent use.

UK art historian Griselda Pollock (b.1949).

Gudrun This is a Germanic name, with elements corresponding to Old English *gūth*, 'battle', and *rūn*, 'secret' (modern English *rune*), so having the overall meaning 'wily in battle'. It is found occasionally among English-speakers from the 19th century. In literature Gudrun Brangwen is an art student in D.H. Lawrence's novels *The Rainbow* (1915) and *Women in Love* (1921).

Scottish actress Gudrun Ure (b.1926).

Guinevere The name is a French form of the Old Welsh name *Gwenhwyfar*, composed of *gwen*, 'white', 'fair', and *hwyfar*, 'smooth', 'soft', so perhaps overall meaning 'with soft fair hair' or 'with smooth fair skin' (or even with both). It has now been almost entirely superseded among English speakers by its Cornish equivalent, JENNIFER, presumably as this name looks more 'English', with its suggestion of JENNY. Guinevere was famous in early Arthurian legend as the beautiful wife of King Arthur, and she occurs in later works based on the tales, such as Tennyson's poem 'Guinevere' (1859) in *Idylls of the King*. GAYNOR is a form of the name.

Gus (m.) An independently adopted diminutive of ANGUS, AUGUSTUS or GUSTAV, in select use among English speakers from the 19th century.

UK music-hall artiste Gus Elen (1862–1940); US actor Gus McNaughton (1884–1969); US lyricist, author Gus Kahn (1886–1941); US bandleader Gus Arnheim (1897–1955); Welsh rugby player Gus Risman (b.1911); UK artist Gus Cummins (b.1943).

Gus (f.), **Gussie** (f.) see **Augusta**.

Gustav A Scandinavian name, originally *Gotstaf*, and perhaps formed from *got*, 'god', and *stafr*, 'staff', so meaning 'staff of the gods'. The name has found some favour among English speakers from the late 19th century and was familiar as a royal Swedish name, especially that of King Gustav VI (1882–1973), who married Princess Margaret of Great Britain. The usual diminutive is GUS, which is in independent use.

UK composer Gustav Holst (1874–1934).

Guy The name is an English form (through French) of an Old German name, perhaps itself derived from *wīt*, 'wide', or *witu*, 'wood'. It was introduced by the Normans to England but was in only select use until the 19th century, when it became popular generally in the English-speaking world, first in the US, then in the UK. It gained historic notoriety (or even fame) from the English conspirator Guy Fawkes (1570–1606), who took part in the plot to blow up King James I and Parliament in 1605. Early literature has the 14th-century popular verse romance *Guy of Warwick*. Later, the name occurs for the title character of Walter Scott's novel *Guy Mannering* (1815); for Sir Guy Morville, the central character of Charlotte M. Yonge's novel *The Heir of Redclyffe* (1853); and for the lawyer Guy Pollock in Sinclair Lewis's novel *Main Street* (1920). In modern times it has been associated with the standard word *guy* (that is, male), which itself came from the name of Guy Fawkes.

US actor Guy Kibbee (1882–1956); US playwright Guy Bolton (1884–1979); UK actor Guy Middleton (1906–73); UK film directors Guy Green (b.1913), Guy Hamilton (1922–86); US actors Guy Madison (1922–96) (original name Robert Moseley), Guy Williams (1924–89) (original name Armand Catalano), Guy Siner (b.1947); UK footballer Guy Butters (b.1969).

Gwen A Welsh name, either an independently adopted diminutive of GWENDOLEN or GWYNETH, or direct from the word *gwen*, the feminine form of *gwyn*, 'white', 'fair'. The name is still mainly in Welsh use, but it is also found more generally among English speakers in the 20th century, although rarely after the 1960s. (The popularity of *Gwen*- and *Gwyn*-names among English speakers may have resulted from their suggestion of *queen*, a word actually from Old English *cwēn*, 'woman'.)

Welsh painter Gwen John (1876–1939); UK artist, writer Gwen Raverat (1885–1957); UK actress Gwen Ffrangcon-Davies (1891–1992); US writer Gwen Bristow (1903–80); Australian poet Gwen Harwood (b.1920); UK writer Gwen Moffat (b.1924); US actress, dancer, singer Gwen Verdon (1925–2000) (original first name Gwyneth); UK actresses Gwen Watford (1927–94), Gwen Taylor (b.1939); Scottish artist Gwen Hardie (b.1962).

Gwenda A Welsh name, formed from *gwen*, 'white', 'fair', and *da*, 'good', which has been in general but very select English-speaking use from the early 20th century. Gwenda Reed is a young New Zealand woman in Agatha Christie's novel *Sleeping Murder* (1976).

Gwendolen A Welsh name that derives from *gwen*, 'white', 'fair', and apparently *dolen*, 'ring', 'bow'. The name has been taken up more generally in the English-speaking world from the mid-19th century, attaining a peak of popularity in the latter half of the 1920s. In Welsh legend Gwendolen is the wife of the mythical king Locrine (or Logrin). Gwendolen Harleth is a central character in George Eliot's novel *Daniel Deronda* (1876); and Gwendolen Fairfax is Lady Bracknell's daughter in Oscar Wilde's play *The Importance of Being Earnest* (1895). The variant spellings *Gwendoline* and *Gwendolyn* are also found, the latter as for the US poet Gwendolyn Brooks (1917–2000) and Canadian poet Gwendolyn MacEwen (1941–87), and were, respectively, influenced by names such as CAROLINE and MARILYN. Gwendoline Chickerell is the sister of the central character Ethelberta Petherwin in Thomas Hardy's novel *The Hand of Ethelberta* (1876).

Gwyn (m.) A Welsh name, and originally a nickname, from *gwyn*, 'white', 'fair', 'blessed' (compare GWENDOLEN). The name is still mainly in Welsh use, but it has also sometimes gained wider use in the English-speaking world from the early 20th century.

Welsh writer Gwyn Thomas (b.1936).

Gwyneth A Welsh name, from *gwynaeth*, 'luck', 'happiness'. The name was taken up from the 19th century, first in Wales, then more generally among English speakers. Variant spellings include *Gwynneth*, *Gwenyth*, *Gweneth* and *Gwenneth*, with the diminutive GWEN in independent use.

Welsh poet Gwyneth Vaughan (original name Annie Harriet Hughes) (1852–1910); UK politician Gwyneth Dunwoody (b.1930); Scottish actress Gwyneth Guthrie (b.1936); Welsh opera singer Gwyneth Jones (b.1936); Welsh writer Gwyneth Jones (b.1952); UK actress Gwyneth Strong (b.1959).

Gyles see **Giles.**

Gypsy An adoption of the ordinary word, with its associations of romance, magic and 'the open road'. The name has found some favour among English speakers from the 19th century, and has been taken up by fairground fortune tellers, palmists and the like. It is familiar in children's literature from the twelve-year-old central character of *Gypsy Breynton* (1866) and other stories by the US writer Elizabeth Stuart Phelps. A variant spelling is *Gipsy*.

US actress Gypsy Rose Lee (1913–70) (original name Rose Louise Hovick).

H

Habakkuk A biblical name, from Hebrew *Habaqqūq*, 'embrace', which was taken up by 17th-century Puritans but never widely adopted among English speakers generally. In the Bible Habakkuk is a minor prophet, said to have written the book named for him. In Walter Scott's novel *Old Mortality* (1816), Habakkuk Mucklewrath is an insane preacher.

Hagar A biblical name, from Hebrew *Hāghār*, 'forsaken', in select use among English speakers in the 19th century but rare after the 1920s. In the Bible Hagar is an Egyptian maid of Sarah, who bore Ishmael to Sarah's husband, Abraham. (Sarah allowed this because she was herself barren, but subsequently, at her request, Abraham sent Hagar and her baby son away, so that she was 'forsaken'.)

US screenwriter Hagar Wilde (1904–71).

Haidee The name perhaps derives from the Greek word *aidoios*, 'modest', although it is now popularly thought of as a variant of HEIDI. It has been in select English-speaking use from the 19th century and in literature occurs for the beautiful Greek girl Haidee in Byron's poem *Don Juan* (1819–24).

Hal An independently adopted diminutive of HARRY or HENRY, in occasional use among English speakers from the early 20th century. In Shakespeare's *Henry IV* (1597) Hal is the king's son, the future Henry V.

US film producer Hal Roach (1892–1992); UK actor Hal Gordon (1894–1946); US film producer Hal B. Wallis (1898–1986); Australian writer Hal Porter (1911–84); US actor Hal Holbrook (b.1925).

Hamilton From the (Scottish) surname, and in select English-speaking use, especially in the US, from the early 19th century. American use of the name was doubtless prompted by the US Secretary of State Hamilton Fish (1808–93). Hamilton Veneering is a character in Charles Dickens's novel *Our Mutual Friend* (1864–5).

Irish composer Hamilton Harty (1879–1941) (originally second name, first being Herbert); US film director Hamilton McFadden (1901–77).

Hamish The name is an English form of the Gaelic name *Sheumais*, the vocative form of *Seumas* (English JAMES). It is chiefly found in Scotland and only very selectively in the English-speaking world at large.

UK publisher Hamish Hamilton (1900–88); Scottish mountain rescue expert Hamish MacInnes (b.1930).

Hamlet This name is the English form (through a French diminutive) of the Old German name *Heimo*, from *heim*, 'house', 'home' (so etymologically equated with modern English *hamlet*). It has enjoyed some adoption among English speakers from the 16th century and was made famous by the semi-legendary prince of Denmark who is the central character of Shakespeare's *Hamlet* (1599–1601). (Shakespeare used a variant of the name, *Hamnet*, for his own son.) The related name HAMMOND is in independent use.

Hammond From the surname, itself from the Old German name that gave HAMLET. The name has found some favour among English speakers from the 19th century.

UK novelist Hammond Innes (1913–98) (original name Ralph Hammond Innes; Hammond was father's surname and Innes mother's maiden name).

Hank The name originated as a form of *Hankin*, a diminutive of *Han* (a form of JOHN), but is now generally regarded as an independently adopted diminutive of HENRY. It has been in select use from the 19th century, mainly in the US.

US actors Hank Mann (1887–1971) (original name David Liebermann), Hank Worden (1901–92) (original first names Norton Earl); Canadian country musician Hank Snow (1914–99) (original first names Clarence Eugene); US country singer Hank Williams (1923–53) (original first names Hiram King); US baseball player Hank Aaron (b.1934) (original first names Henry Louis); US soul singer Hank Ballard (b.1936); UK pop guitarist Hank Marvin (b.1941) (original name Brian Rankin); US country musician Hank Williams Jr (b.1949) (son of Hank Williams; original first names Randall Hank).

Hannah A biblical name, from Hebrew *Hannāh*, 'favour', 'grace', which also gave ANN. The name was increasingly popular in English-speaking use from the 17th century to the end of the 19th century, when it declined. It revived, however, from the 1970s, reaching a new peak of popularity in the 1990s. The Bible has the name for three people: the mother of Samuel, the wife of Tobit and the prophetess daughter of Phanuel. In later literature Hannah Burton is the maid to the central character, Clarissa Harlowe, in Samuel Richardson's novel *Clarissa* (1748), and in William Makepeace Thackeray's novel *The Newcomes* (1853–5) Hannah Hicks is, likewise, a maid to Martha Honeyman. Diminutives include *Hannie* and *Hanny*, while NANCY is an independently adopted variant.

German-born US political theorist Hannah Arendt (1906–75); Scottish actress Hannah Gordon (b.1941) (mother is Hannah); UK artist, photographer Hannah Collins (b.1956).

Hannibal The present form of the name is the Latin one, itself from a Phoenician name composed of *hann*, 'grace' (indirectly related to HANNAH), and *Baal* (the name of a god), so overall meaning 'grace of Baal'. The name, which has found some favour among English speakers from the 19th century, is historically famous from the Carthaginian general of the 3rd century BC who led an army from Spain to Italy across the Alps to attack the Romans. Hannibal Chollop is a character in

Charles Dickens's novel *Martin Chuzzlewit* (1843–4). The name was done no favours by Hannibal 'The Cannibal' Lecter, the serial killer and psychiatrist in Thomas Harris's novel *The Silence of the Lambs* (1988), popularized by the film of the same name (1990), in which he is played by Anthony Hopkins.

US vice-president Hannibal Hamlin (1809–91).

Hannie, **Hanny** see **Hannah**.

Hans A German form of JOHN, in select use among English speakers from the 19th century and most familiar from the Irish scientist and traveller Sir Hans Sloane (1660–1753) and the Danish writer Hans Christian Andersen (1805–75).

UK psychologist Hans Eysenck (1916–97); US actor Hans Conried (1917–82).

Hardy From the surname, perhaps with an influence from the standard word *hardy*, the historic form of which is actually represented in names such as BERNARD and RICHARD. The name has been in select English-speaking use from the early 20th century.

UK fashion designer Hardy Amies (b.1909) (originally second name, first being Edwin); German actor Hardy Kruger (b.1928).

Harlan From the surname, and in select English-speaking use, mainly in the US, from the 19th century. The name was perhaps initially made familiar by the surname of the US judge and civil rights supporter, John Marshall Harlan (1833–1911).

US popular musicians Harlan Leonard (1905–83), Harlan Lattimore (b.1908), Harlan Howard (b.1929).

Harley From the surname, and finding modest favour among English speakers from the 19th century. The name is familiar from London's Harley Street, the home of leading medical consultants. Harley Bagot is a character in Theodore Dreiser's novel *An American Tragedy* (1925).

Harold A modern form of the Old English name *Hereweald*, formed from *here*, 'army', and *wealdan*, 'to rule', so 'army ruler', with a spelling influenced by that of the Scandinavian equivalent name *Haraldr*. The name was in only rare use among English speakers until the 19th century, when it became very popular. It tailed off from the early 20th century, however, and is now much less common. It is historically familiar from King Harold, whose defeat at the Battle of Hastings (1066) was the direct cause of its long-lasting unpopularity. In literature the name is found for Harold Skimpole, a sponger in Charles Dickens's novel *Bleak House* (1852–3), and for Harold Smith, a former politician in Anthony Trollope's novel *Framley Parsonage* (1861). The name HARRY is sometimes regarded as a diminutive, but it really derives from HENRY. A related name is WALTER.

US comedian Harold Lloyd (1893–1971); UK prime minister Harold Macmillan, Earl of Stockton (1894–1986); UK composer, pianist Harold Truscott (1914–92); UK prime minister Harold Wilson, Baron Wilson of Rievaulx (1916–95); US writer Harold Robbins (1916–97); US theatrical producer, director Harold Prince (b.1928); UK playwright Harold Pinter (b.1930); UK actor Harold Innocent (b.1936).

Harriet A feminine form of HARRY, increasingly popular among English speakers from the 17th century to the early 20th century. It then declined only to revive sharply in the 1990s. In Samuel Richardson's novel *Sir Charles Grandison* (1753–4) Harriet Byron is the central character and main letter writer. In Anthony Trollope's novel *Framley Parsonage* (1861) Harriet Sowerby is the sister of Nathaniel Sowerby, the friend of the central character, the Rev. Mark Robarts. Spelling variants include *Harriett*, *Harrietta* and *Harriette*, the first as for the UK fashion editor Harriett Jagger (b.1959). Common diminutives are *Harrie* and *Harry*, with HATTIE in independent use.

US novelist Harriet Beecher Stowe (1811–96); UK pianist Harriet Cohen (1895–1967); US film producer Harriet Parsons (1906–83); UK politician Harriet Harman (b.1950); UK actress Harriet Walter (b.1950).

Harrison From the surname, and in select use among English speakers from the 19th century, mainly in the US. Some of the name's original popularity could have resulted from the surnames of the two US presidents William H. Harrison (1773–1841) and Benjamin Harrison (1833–1901). The name itself also suggests a form of HARRY, although this name is really of a different origin.

US actor Harrison Ford (1892–1957); US writer on Russia, Harrison Salisbury (1908–93); UK composer Sir Harrison Birtwistle (b.1934); US actor Harrison Ford (b.1942).

Harry An independently adopted diminutive of HENRY, in regular English-speaking use from medieval times. The name was highly popular in the 19th century but fell from favour after the 1920s. Shakespeare uses the name for the king in *Henry V* (1599); 'Cry God for Harry! England and Saint George.' Harry Clinton is the central character in Henry Brooke's novel *The Fool of Quality* (1765–70), and the name is also that of the central character in George Meredith's novel *The Adventures of Harry Richmond* (1871). The diminutive HAL is in independent use.

Irish singer Harry Plunket Greene (1865–1936); Scottish music-hall singer Sir Harry Lauder (1870–1950); US president Harry S. Truman (1884–1972); South African-born UK popular musician Harry Rabinowitz (b.1916); UK comedian Harry Worth (1920–89); UK actor, singer Sir Harry Secombe (1921–2001); UK TV sports commentator Harry Carpenter (b.1925); UK actors Harry H. Corbett (1925–82), Harry Fowler (b.1926); US singer, actor Harry Belafonte (b.1927); UK comedian Harry Enfield (b.1961); UK son of Prince and Princess of Wales, Prince Harry (b.1984) (formally Henry).

Hartley From the surname, and in some favour among English speakers, especially in the UK, from the 19th century, although it is now much less common.

UK lawyer Sir Hartley Shawcross (b.1902).

Harvey From the surname, and selectively adopted by English speakers from the 19th century. Harvey Birch is the central character in James Fenimore Cooper's novel *The Spy* (1821), and Harvey Cheyne (with his father having the same name) is the main character in Rudyard Kipling's novel *Captains Courageous* (1897).

US actors Harvey Lembeck (1925–82), Harvey Korman (b.1927); UK showjumper Harvey Smith (b.1938) (originally second name, first being Robert); US actor Harvey Keitel (b.1939); US bluesman Harvey Mandel (b.1945); US playwright, actor Harvey Fierstein (b.1954).

Hattie An independently adopted diminutive of HARRIET that has been in select English-speaking use from the late 19th century. The variant spelling *Hatty* occurs, and a diminutive is *Hat*.

US political leader Hattie Caraway (1878–1950); US actress Hattie McDaniel (1895–1952); UK actress Hattie Jacques (1924–80).

Havelock From the surname, and gaining some adoption among English speakers in the 19th century.

UK sex psychologist, Havelock Ellis (1859–1939) (originally second name, first being Henry).

Haydn (m.) The name apparently derives from the surname of the Austrian composer Joseph Haydn (1732–1809). It has been in select English-speaking use from the 19th century, mainly among the music-loving Welsh (who perhaps also regard it as a variant of the Celtic name AIDAN).

UK composer, songwriter Haydn Wood (1882–1959).

Haydn (f.) An adoption of the male name HAYDN, probably influenced by HEIDI. The name has found some sporadic adoption in the 20th century, mainly among the Welsh.

UK actress Haydn Gwynne (b.*c*.1955).

Hayley From the surname, and enjoying widespread adoption among English speakers from the 1960s, with a peak in the second half of the 1980s. The name appears to owe its popularity entirely to the UK actress Hayley Mills (b.1946), daughter of the actor Sir John Mills. She was herself named for her mother, the playwright Mary Hayley Bell, and leapt to fame after her performance as the main character in the film *Tiger Bay* (1959).

Hazel The name comes from the bush but was later popularly associated with the eye colour. It was first adopted in the English-speaking world, like other plant names, in the late 19th century, but after a peak of popularity in the second half of the 1930s it has gradually fallen from favour. In literature Hazel is the name of the rabbit hero in Richard Adams's cult novel *Watership Down* (1972). In the *US Saturday Evening Post* Hazel was a bossy housemaid in cartoons by Ted Key from 1943 to 1969. A common diminutive is *Haze*.

US tennis player Hazel Wightman (1886–1974); US popular pianist, singer Hazel Scott (1920–81); US actress Hazel Brooks (b.1924); UK actress Hazel Court (b.1926); US theatrical producer Hazel Bryant (1939–83); UK popular singer, actress Hazel O'Connor (b.1955).

Heather The name comes from the plant (see also ERICA), and has been in English-speaking use from the late 19th century, with a period of greatest popularity in the 1950s and 1960s, after which it underwent something of a decline. In literature, the name is found for Heather Badcock, wife of Arthur Badcock in Agatha Christie's novel *The Mirror Crack'd from Side to Side* (1962).

UK actresses Heather Thatcher (1897–1987), Heather Angel (1909–1986); UK opera singer Heather Harper (b.1930); UK actress Heather Sears (1935–94); UK wildlife photographer Heather Angel (b.1941); UK astronomer Heather Couper (b.1949); UK art critic, photographer Heather Waddell (b.1950); UK actress Heather Peace (b.1975).

Hebe A Greek name, representing the feminine form of *hēbos*, 'young', which was in modest adoption among English speakers from the 19th century, but now rare. In Greek mythology, Hebe is the minor goddess of youth.

US writer on world affairs Hebe Spaull (b.1893).

Hector This is an adoption of the Greek name *Hektōr*, itself probably based on *ekhein*, 'to hold', 'to resist'. The name was taken up by English speakers in the 19th century, but it is now rarely found. In classical legend Hector was famous as the hero of Troy who was killed by Achilles. He appears in Shakespeare's *Troilus and Cressida* (1602), and the name occurs in later literary use for Lieutenant-Colonel Hector McTavish in William Makepeace Thackeray's novel *Vanity Fair* (1847–8). The Scottish diminutive *Heckie* exists.

US actor Hector Elizondo (b.1936).

Hedda An independently adopted diminutive of the Scandinavian name *Hedvig*, itself formed from Germanic words meaning (more or less synonymously) 'battle' and 'war'. The name has found some use among English speakers from the 19th century, and it was initially made familiar by the central character of Henrik Ibsen's play *Hedda Gabler* (1890).

US actress Hedda Hopper (1890–1966) (original name Elda Furry).

Heidi The name comes from the diminutive form of the German name *Adelheid*, which equates to English ADELAIDE. It has been in vogue among English speakers from the 1960s and seems to have been initially picked up from English translations of the Swiss writer Johanna Spyri's children's classic *Heidi* (1881). Two entirely English sequels to the book, *Heidi Grows Up* and *Heidi's Children*, by Charles Tritten, appeared in 1958 and may explain the particular period of adoption.

US actress Heidi Bohay (b.1959).

Helen The long popular name is an English form of the Greek name *Hēlēnē*, perhaps related to *hēlios*, 'sun', and having a general meaning 'shining one'. The name's prime inspiration was the mythological Helen of Troy, who was famed for her beauty. In the 20th century the name increased in popularity up to the late 1960s, since when it has fallen back somewhat. It is found widely in literature. Shakespeare's *Troilus and Cressida* (1602), set around the siege of Troy, recasts Helen in her role as the wife of Menelaus, while in *Cymbeline* (1609–10) Helen is the attendant to Imogen. Maria Edgeworth's last novel was *Helen, A Tale* (1834). In Charles Jackson's novel *The Lost Weekend* (1944) Helen is the friend of the central character, alcoholic Don Birnam. The name has many variants, several of which are now in independent use, including HELENA, ELLA, ELLEN and NELL.

US blind and deaf author, lecturer Helen Keller (1880–1968); US actress Helen Hayes (1900–93); UK opera singer Helen Watts (b.1927); US opera singer Helen Donath (b.1940); Australian pop singer Helen Reddy (b.1941); UK pop singer Helen Shapiro (b.1946); UK actresses Helen Mirren (b.1946), Helen Worth (b.1951), Helen Lederer (b.1954); UK TV sports presenter Helen Rollason (1956–99); UK astronaut Helen Sharman (b.1963); UK badminton player Helen Troke (b.1964); US actress Helen Hunt (b.1963); UK actress Helen Baxendale (b.1971).

Helena The name, a Latinized form of HELEN, has been in regular English-speaking use for as long as its source name, but on a much more modest level. It is historically familiar from the 4th-century St Helena, mother of Constantine the Great. Shakespeare has Helena in love with Demetrius in *A Midsummer Night's Dream* (1595–6) and as a gentlewoman in *All's Well That Ends Well* (1603–4). Helena Landless is a character in Charles Dickens's novel *Edwin Drood* (1870). Variants and diminutives are mostly as for the source name, with LENA in independent use.

UK actress Helena Faucit (1817–98); Polish-born US beautician Helena Rubinstein (1871–1965); US actress Helena Carter (1923–2000) (original name Helen Rickerts); UK actress Helena Bonham Carter (b.1966) (mother is Elena).

Henrietta This is an English form of the French name *Henriette*, itself a feminine diminutive form of *Henri* (English HENRY). The name has been in English-speaking use from the 17th century, achieving general popularity in the late 19th century and being sporadically in vogue in the 20th century. It was introduced to England from France by Henriette-Marie (1609–69), known to the English as Henrietta Maria, the daughter of Henri IV and wife of Charles I of England. In literature Henrietta Boffin is a character in Charles Dickens's novel *Our Mutual Friend* (1864–5), while Mrs Henrietta Noble is the sister of Mrs Farebrother in George Eliot's novel *Middlemarch* (1871–2). The name has aristocratic associations. It also has a large number of diminutives, including *Etta*, *Ettie*, *Etty*, *Hennie*, *Henny*, *Hettie*, HETTY, NETTIE and *Netty*.

US actress Henrietta Crosman (1861–1944); US writer Henrietta Buckmaster (1909–83); UK bohemian Henrietta Moraes (1931–99).

Henry The name is an English form of the Old German name *Heimerich*, formed from *heim*, 'house', 'home', and *rīchi*, 'ruler', 'owner', hence 'home ruler', 'house owner' and, as it were, 'lord of the manor'. It has been in generally popular English-speaking use from medieval times, although it has generally fallen from favour from the early 20th century, despite a modest revival in the 1990s. It has been familiar as a royal name from the 11th century, with eight English kings named Henry, many of them appearing in plays by Shakespeare. In later literature the name is that of the central character in William Makepeace Thackeray's novel *The History of Henry Esmond* (1852). In George Bernard Shaw's play *Pygmalion* (1913) Professor Henry Higgins is speech therapist to the Cockney flower-seller Eliza Doolittle. Regular diminutives, HAL, HANK and HARRY, are in independent use, and BUNNY is sometimes also found.

US poet Henry Wadsworth Longfellow (1807–82); US-born UK novelist Henry James (1843–1916); UK conductor Sir Henry Wood

(1869–1944); UK bandleader Henry Hall (1898–1989); US actor Henry Fonda (1905–82); US boxer Henry Armstrong (1912–88); US diplomat Henry Kissinger (b.1923); UK actor Henry McGee (b.1929); UK boxer Henry Cooper (b.1934); UK son of Prince Charles and Princess of Wales, Prince Henry (b.1984) (informally Harry).

Hephzibah A biblical name, from Hebrew *Hephtsībāh*, 'in her is my delight' (that is, in a newborn daughter). The name was taken up by Puritans in the 17th century but was adopted only sporadically by English speakers from then until the 20th century, when it virtually died out except in Jewish families. In the Bible Hephzibah is the wife of Hezekiah, king of Judah. It is also a prophetic name for the new Jerusalem: 'Thou shalt be called Hephzibah... : for the Lord delighteth in thee' (Isaiah 6.4). Hephzibah Pyncheon is an aged shopkeeper in Nathaniel Hawthorne's novel *The House of the Seven Gables* (1851), while in Mary Webb's novel *Precious Bane* (1924) Hephzibah Beguildy is the mother of Jancis Beguildy. The variant spelling *Hepzibah* exists. The usual diminutive is *Hepsie*, but in George Eliot's novel *Silas Marner* (1861), Silas's adopted daughter, Hephzibah Cass, is known as *Eppie*.

US-born pianist Hephzibah Menuhin (1920–81).

Herb An independently adopted diminutive of HERBERT, mostly in US use from the early 20th century. The diminutive HERBIE also occurs independently.

US actor Herb Edelmann (1930–96); US popular musician Herb Alpert (b.1935); Australian athlete Herb Elliott (b.1938).

Herbert The present name evolved from the Old English name *Herebeorht*, composed of *here*, 'army', and *beorht*, 'bright', 'famous', giving an overall meaning of 'famous army', with this in turn being a variant of an Old German name of identical meaning. The name has been in use among English speakers from medieval times. It increased in popularity in the 19th and early 20th centuries, after which it declined. In some cases the name has been adopted from the surname of the earls of Pembroke in the 16th and 17th centuries. In literature the name is found for Herbert Dulver, married to Elsie Longstaff in J.B. Priestley's novel *The Good Companions* (1929). Diminutives HERB and HERBIE are in independent use.

US president Herbert C. Hoover (1874–1964); UK film director Herbert Wilcox (1890–1977); UK cricketer Herbert Sutcliffe (1894–1978); Czech-born UK actor Herbert Lom (b.1917).

Herbie An independently adopted diminutive of HERBERT or HERB, in select use among English speakers from the early 20th century, mostly in the US.

South African cricketer Herbie Taylor (1889–1973); US jazz musicians Herbie Mann (b.1930), Herbie Hancock (b.1940); UK photographer Herbie Knott (b.1949).

Hercules The famous name is a Latin form of the Greek name *Hēraklēs*, traditionally derived from *Hēra* (queen of the Olympian gods) and *kleos*, 'glory', thus meaning 'glory of Hera'. It has found occasional favour among English speakers from the 19th century. In Greek legend Hercules was the 'strong man' hero who carried out the twelve labours. Agatha Christie used the French form of the name for her detective Hercule Poirot.

Herman The name is an English form of the Old German name *Hariman*, formed from *hari*, 'army', and *man*, 'man', so 'army man', 'warrior'. It enjoyed modest adoption among English speakers from the mid-19th to the early 20th century, especially in the US, but it has never been widely popular. The variant spelling *Hermann* also exists.

US novelist Herman Melville (1819–91); US screenwriter Herman Mankiewicz (1897–1953); US novelist Herman Wouk (b.1915); US film producer Herman Cohen (1928–85).

Hermia This name is a contracted (but not diminutive) form of HERMIONE, in very select English-speaking use from late medieval times. Shakespeare has Hermia in love with Lysander in *A Midsummer Night's Dream* (1595–6), in which her name may have been chosen to contrast with that of Helena. (Hermia is a brunette, and Helena a blonde.) Agatha Christie has a character Hermia Redcliffe in her novel *The Pale Horse* (1961).

Hermione The name is the Greek feminine form of *Hermes*, found selectively in English-speaking use from medieval times. In classical mythology Hermione is the daughter of Menelaus and Helen who becomes the wife of Neoptolemus, then of her cousin Orestes. In literature the name occurs for the queen of Leontes in Shakespeare's *The Winter's Tale* (1610–11) and for Lady Hermione in Walter Scott's novel *The Fortunes of Nigel* (1822). HERMIA, although sometimes regarded as a diminutive, is really a distinct name.

UK actresses Hermione Gingold (1897–1987); Hermione Baddeley (1906–86); UK writer, conservationist Hermione Hobhouse (b.1934); UK literary critic Hermione Lee (b.1948).

Hertha The name, ultimately meaning 'strong', 'bold', is that of the German goddess of fertility and growth who is also known as *Nertha* (with *N* at some stage apparently misread as *H*). It has found very occasional adoption among English speakers from the 19th century.

UK physicist, suffragist Hertha Ayrton (1854–1923) (original first name Sarah).

Hesba The name appears to be a form of *hespera*, the Greek word for 'western', as in the name of *Hesperus*, the evening star, otherwise the planet Venus. It is found in occasional use among English speakers from the 19th century, although it is hardly common.

UK popular religious writer Hesba Stretton (1832–1911) (original name Sarah Smith); Australian children's writer Hesba Brinsmead (b.1922)

Hester The name is an independently adopted variant of
ESTHER, in select English-speaking use from the 17th century
but now mostly rare. It was borne by three noted 18th-
century women: the US silversmith Hester Bateman (1709–90),
the English writer Hester Thrale (1741–1821), and the English
eccentric and traveller Lady Hester Stanhope (1776–1839). In
Nathaniel Hawthorne's novel *The Scarlet Letter* (1850) Hester
Prynne is the 'scarlet woman'. Later literary bearers of the
name include Hester Worsley in Oscar Wilde's play *A Woman
of No Importance* (1893), and Hester (Esta) Griffiths is the sister
of the central character, Clyde Griffiths, in Theodore Dreiser's
novel *An American Tragedy* (1925). Diminutives include *Esta*,
Hettie and HETTY, the last in independent use.

Hettie see **Henrietta, Hester.**

Hetty An independently adopted diminutive of HENRIETTA
or HESTER, which has been in fairly common use among English speakers from the 19th century to the 1930s but is now
relatively rare. Aunt Hetty is a character in a short story of the
same name in Martin Armstrong's collection *Sir Pompey and
Madame Juno* (1927). A variant form *Hettie* exists.

US financier Hetty Green (1834–1916).

Hezekiah A biblical name, from Hebrew *Hizqīyāh*, 'my
strength is Yah' (that is, Jehovah or God). The name found
sporadic adoption among English speakers in the 19th century, although it has never been widely taken up. In the Bible
Hezekiah is a king of Judah. Thomas Hardy's novel *Two on a
Tower* (1882) has a character Hezekiah Biles.

Hilary (m.) The name is an English form of the Latin name
Hilarius, itself from *hilaris*, 'cheerful' (hence English *hilarious*).
It has found selective use among English speakers from
medieval times until the present, although it is now less frequently given. It is historically associated with St Hilarius of

Poitiers, the 4th-century theologian. In John Galsworthy's *Forsyte* series (1906–22) the Rev. Hilary Charwell is the son of the Right Rev. Cuthbert Charwell, bishop of Porthminster, and in J.B. Priestley's novel *The Good Companions* (1929) Hilary Trant is the nephew of Elizabeth Trant and a benefactor of the 'Good Companions'. A variant spelling is *Hillary*.

UK literary agent, writer Hilary Rubinstein (b.1926).

Hilary (f.) A female adoption of the male name HILARY, occurring in medieval times, when the name was in use for both sexes, but thereafter mostly in abeyance until the 19th century, when it was taken up again. Hilary Craven is a suicidal woman in Agatha Christie's novel *Destination Unknown* (1954) (US title *So Many Steps to Death*). A variant spelling is *Hillary*, as for the US actress Hillary Brooke (1914–1999) (original name Beatrice Peterson) and wife of US president Bill Clinton, Hillary Clinton (b.1947), while diminutives are usually *Hil* or *Hilly*.

UK literary reviewer, writer Hilary Spurling (b.1940); UK journalist Hilary Bonner (b.1949); UK novelist Hilary Mantel (b.1952); UK restaurateur Hilary Brown (b.1952); US actress Hilary Swank (b.1975).

Hilda The name is an adoption of the first part of a German name beginning *Hild-*, such as HILDEGARD, with the element itself meaning 'battle'. It was in English-speaking use in medieval times, then declined before enjoying a revival in the 19th century. It has decreased dramatically in popularity since the 1920s, however. The name is historically famous from St Hilda, the 6th-century abbess of Whitby. In Nathaniel Hawthorne's novel *The Marble Faun* (1860) Hilda is a New England art student, and in Arnold Bennett's *Clayhanger* series (1910–18) Hilda Lessways is the central character. Hilda Adams (Miss Pinkerton) is a nurse doubling as a private detective in the crime novels and stories of the 1930s by the US writer Mary Roberts Rinehart, and in the UK the name has been popularly associated with Hilda Ogden, the tough, nosy wife with a lazy husband (Stan) in the TV soap *Coronation Street* (from 1960), played by Jean Alexander. The most common variant is *Hylda*, as for the UK comedienne Hylda Baker (1909–86).

US writer Hilda Doolittle ('H.D.') (1886–1961); US artist, writer Hilda Katz (b.1909); UK actress Hilda Braid (b.1934).

Hildegard This is an Old German name, formed from *hild*, 'battle', and *gard*, 'enclosure', 'protected area', hence with the effective overall meaning of 'comrade in arms'. It is occasionally found in English-speaking use, especially among US women of German descent. The variant spelling *Hildegarde* is fairly common, as for the South African actress Hildegarde Neil (b.1939), while the diminutive HILDA is in independent use.

German-born actress Hildegard Neff (b.1925).

Hillary see **Hilary** (m.) and (f.).

Hilly see **Hilary** (f.).

Hiram A biblical name, from Hebrew *Hīrām*, perhaps a short-ened form of *Ahīrām*, 'my brother is exalted'. It was adopted by Puritans in the 17th century and favoured by English speak-ers generally in the 19th. It is now rare, except in the US, where it is still fairly widely found. In the Bible Hiram is the king of Tyre who sent Solomon wood and workmen to construct tem-ples of worship. Hiram Doolittle is a character in James Feni-more Cooper's novel *The Pioneers* (1823), and Hiram B. Otis is an American ambassador in Oscar Wilde's short story *The Can-terville Ghost* (1887). *Hyram* is a variant spelling.

US senator Hiram R. Revels (1822–1901).

Holly The name comes from the tree, with its colourful berries and Christmas associations. It has been in English-speaking use from the late 19th century but was first popular only in the 1980s and 1990s. In John Galsworthy's *Forsyte* sequence (1906–22) Holly is the daughter of Jolyon Forsyte (with Jolly as her brother). Holly Golightly, in Truman Capote's novel *Breakfast at Tiffany's* (1958), has the full first name Holiday. (Both names symbolize her colourful life as a call girl.) The film of 1961 based on the novel, with Audrey Hepburn as Holly, may have boosted the name. A variant spelling is *Hollie*.

US pop singer, actress Holly Near (b.1949); US actress Holly Hunter (b.1958); UK actress Holly Aird (b.1969).

Homer The name comes either from the Greek name *Homēros*, perhaps meaning 'hostage', or from the surname. It has been in fairly regular use in the US from the 19th century but is now much less common elsewhere in the English-speaking world. It was initially made famous by the great Greek epic poet. The name occurs in children's literature for the small boy who is the main character of Robert McCloskey's novel *Homer Price* (1943).

US soldier, writer Homer Lea (1876–1912).

Honor The name is either an English form of the Latin name *Honoria*, the feminine of *Honorius*, 'man of honour', or a direct adoption of the ordinary word *honour*. It was taken up by Puritans as a 'virtue' name in the 17th century and has been in select English-speaking use since, although less frequently in the US. Literary characters of the name include Honor Blake in John Millington Synge's play *The Playboy of the Western World* (1907) and Honor Klein in Iris Murdoch's novel *A Severed Head* (1961). The best-known variant is *Honoria* itself, as for the UK glass engraver Honoria Marsh (b.1923). Its diminutive, NORA, has gained independent use. Honoria Dedlock is a character in Charles Dickens's novel *Bleak House* (1852–3).

UK writers Honor Wyatt (b.1910), Honor Tracy (1913–1989); UK actress Honor Blackman (b.1926).

Hope The name was adopted from the word for the virtue, matching its 'sisters' FAITH and CHARITY. It has been in

English-speaking use from the 16th century, when it was adopted by the Puritans. It is now generally more common in the US than in the UK, although British use of the name showed an upturn in the 1990s.

US actresses Hope Emerson (1897–1960), Hope Hampton (1899–1982), Hope Lange (b.1931).

Horace This is an English form of the Roman clan name *Horatius*, perhaps itself related to Latin *hora*, 'time', 'hour'. The name was selectively taken up by English speakers in the 18th and 19th centuries but has since fallen almost entirely out of favour. In literature Sir Horace Fogle is a character in William Makepeace Thackeray's novel *The Newcomes* (1853–5), and Colonel Horace de Craye is in George Meredith's novel *The Egoist* (1879). HORATIO is a directly related name. The original first name of English writer Sir Horace Walpole (1717–1797) was Horatio.

US educationist Horace Mann (1796–1859); US editor Horace Greeley (1811–72); US actor Horace MacMahon (1907–71).

Horatio An independently adopted variant of HORACE, influenced by the Latin form *Horatius* and the Italian form *Orazio*. It has been in select use among English speakers from the 16th century. Shakespeare's *Hamlet* (1599–1601) has Horatio as a friend of Hamlet. Horatio Fizkin is a character in Charles Dickens's novel *Pickwick Papers* (1836–7).

US army commander Horatio Gates (1728–1806); English admiral, naval hero Horatio Nelson (1758–1805) (named for godfather, Horace Walpole, himself baptized Horatio); UK soldier Horatio Herbert Kitchener (Kitchener of Khartoum) (1850–1916) (father was Henry Horatio); UK politician, fraudster Horatio Bottomley (1860–1933).

Hortense The name is a French form of *Hortensia*, the Latin feminine equivalent of *Hortensius*, a Roman clan name probably based on Latin *hortus*, 'garden'. The name has been in English-speaking use from the 19th century but is now rarely found. In Charlotte Brontë's novel *Shirley* (1849) Hortense Moore is the sister of the half-English, half-Belgian mill-owner Robert Gérard Moore, one of the main characters, while Charles Dickens's novel *Bleak House* (1852–3) has Hortense as a maid to Lady Dedlock. In Theodore Dreiser's novel *An American Tragedy* (1925) Hortense Briggs is the girlfriend of the central character, Clyde Griffiths. The variant *Hortensia* is also found.

US writer Hortense Calisher (b.1911).

Howard From the surname, and in select but regular use among English speakers from the early 19th century, with a subsequent popularity peak in the 1960s. The surname is familiar as that of the dukes of Norfolk (from the 15th century). Dr Howard Littlefield is a character in Sinclair Lewis's novel *Babbitt* (1922). *Howie* is sometimes a diminutive.

UK novelist Howard Spring (1889–1965); US film director Howard Hawks (1896–1977); US businessman Howard Hughes (1905–76); UK actor Howard Marion-Crawford (1914–69); US actors Howard Keel (b.1917) (original first name Harold), Howard Duff (1917–90); UK literary reviewer Howard Jacobson (b.1942); UK concert pianist Howard Shelley (b.1950).

Howell The name, in select English-speaking use from the mid-19th century, is either an adoption of the surname or an English form of the Welsh name HYWEL. The spelling *Hywel* is traditionally used for early Welsh rulers, such as Hywel Dda (Hywel the Good) in the 10th century.

Howie see **Howard**.

Hubert The name is an English form of the Old German name *Hugibert*, formed from *hug*, 'heart', 'mind' (as for HUGH), and *beraht*, 'bright', 'shining', so 'bright spirit'. It was introduced to England by the Normans and has been in select use ever since, although falling fast from favour in the 20th century. It initially gained fame from St Hubert in the 8th century. Hubert de Burgh, a 13th-century justice of England, is a historical character in Shakespeare's *King John* (*c*.1596). Hubert Ratcliffe is the benefactor of Sir Edward Mauley in Walter Scott's novel *The Black Dwarf* (1816).

UK writer, broadcaster Hubert Phillips (1891–1964); US vice-president Hubert Humphrey (1911–78); UK songwriter, actor Hubert Gregg (b.1914).

Hugh The name is an English form of a Germanic name based on *hug*, 'heart', 'mind' (as for HUBERT). It was brought to England by the Normans and was popular generally among English speakers until the 17th century, when it declined. It was taken up again in the 19th century and has remained in modest favour since. It is historically familiar from St Hugh of Lincoln, noted in the 12th century for his charity and piety, and also (though not to be confused with him) from Hugh of Lincoln (1246–55), an English boy put to death by Jews at Lincoln. The latter appears in 'The Prioress's Tale' in Chaucer's *The Canterbury Tales* (*c*.1387). Hugh le Despenser is a character in Christopher Marlowe's tragedy *Edward II* (1592), and Sir Hugh Evans is a Welsh parson in Shakespeare's *The Merry Wives of Windsor* (1597). In later literature Hugh Strap is a school friend of Roderick in Tobias Smollett's novel *Roderick Random* (1748). The diminutive HUGHIE is in independent use, as are the name's Latin revival HUGO and the Welsh form HUW.

UK novelist Sir Hugh Walpole (1884–1941); UK children's writer Hugh Lofting (1886–1947); UK actors Hugh Wakefield (1888–1971), Hugh Williams (1904–69) (original first name Brian); UK architect Sir Hugh Casson (1910–99); Welsh actor Hugh Griffith (1912–80); US publisher, founder of *Playboy*, Hugh Hefner (b.1926); UK actor Hugh Grant (b.1961).

Hughie An independently adopted diminutive of HUGH, in select English-speaking use from the 19th century. Hughie Dun is the body-servant of the Archbishop of St Andrews in Walter Scott's novel *The Fair Maid of Perth* (1828).

Scottish footballer Hughie Gallacher (1903–57); Canadian-UK TV host Hughie Green (1920–97); Irish-born UK artist Hughie O'Donoghue (b.1953).

Hugo The name is an English adoption of the Latin form of HUGH, in select English-speaking use from the mid-19th century.

UK columnist Hugo Young (b.1938); UK writer Hugo Williams (b.1942) (father was actor Hugh Williams); UK journalist Hugo Davenport (b.1953); UK actor Hugo Keith-Johnston (b.1954).

Humbert This is an English form of an Old German (later Old English) name composed of *hun*, 'Hun', and *beraht*, 'bright', 'famous', so 'famous Hun'. It was introduced to England by the Normans and has been in very select use since. In literature it was made familiar by Humbert Humbert, the sex-obsessed narrator and stepfather of Lolita in Vladimir Nabokov's novel *Lolita* (1955). A diminutive *Hum* exists.

Humphrey The name is an English form of the Old German (later Old English) name *Hunfred*, formed from *hun*, 'Hun', and *fridu*, 'peace', so 'peaceful Hun'. It was brought to England by the Normans and has enjoyed select adoption since. The name was made famous by Duke Humphrey, the 15th-century Duke of Gloucester and youngest son of Henry IV, who appears as a historical character in Shakespeare's *Henry IV* (1597). Humphrey Wasp is a character in Ben Jonson's comedy *Bartholomew Fair* (1614), and a variant spelling of the name is that of the central character of Tobias Smollett's novel *Humphry Clinker* (1771). This same spelling still occurs, as for the UK writer and broadcaster Humphry Berkeley (b.1926). A frequent diminutive is *Humph*.

US actor Humphrey Bogart (1899–1957); UK composer Humphrey Searle (1915–82); UK jazz musician Humphrey Lyttelton (b.1921); UK writer, broadcaster Humphrey Carpenter (b.1946); UK artist Humphrey Ocean (b.1951).

Huw A Welsh form of HUGH, in mainly Welsh use from the early 20th century.

Welsh TV director, presenter Sir Huw Wheldon (1916–86); UK actor Huw Higginson (b.1964).

Hyacinth A borrowing of the flower name but also serving as a feminine adoption of the identical male name. It has been in select English-speaking use, like most other flower names, from the late 19th century, although it is rare today. The UK revue artiste Hy Hazell (1920–70) had the original full name Hyacinth Hazel O'Higgins.

Hylda see **Hilda**.

Hypatia A Greek name, from *hupatos*, 'highest', in rare English-speaking use from the late 19th century. The name was historically made famous by the 5th-century philosopher and mathematician Hypatia, who was killed by Christian fanatics and who in literature is the subject of Charles Kingsley's novel *Hypatia* (1853). George Bernard Shaw's play *Misalliance* (1910) has a character Hypatia (Patsy) Tarleton. A diminutive would be PATSY, in independent use.

UK writer Hypatia Bradlaugh Bonner (1858–1935).

Hyram see **Hiram**.

Hywel A Welsh name, meaning 'eminent', 'prominent' (and giving the English surname, later first name, HOWELL). It is still found mainly in Welsh use, although it has known some selective adoption more generally in the English-speaking world from the 1950s.

UK actor Hywel Bennett (b.1944).

I

Iain The name is a Gaelic form of IAN, in mainly Scottish use from the late 19th century and achieving a modest boom among English speakers generally in the 1970s and 1980s.

Scottish actor Iain Cuthbertson (b.1930); Scottish novelist Iain Banks (b.1954); UK Conservative Party leader Iain Duncan Smith (b.1954); UK ballet dancer Iain Webb (b.1959); Scottish actor Iain Glen (b.1961).

Ian The name is a Scottish version of JOHN, in popular English-speaking use, both in Scotland and generally, from the 19th century, with a peak period of adoption in the second half of the 1960s. The Gaelic variant IAIN is in independent use.

Australian-born UK actor Ian Fleming (1888–1969); UK writer Ian Fleming (1906–64); UK politician Ian Mikardo (1908–93); UK light opera singer Ian Wallace (b.1919); UK actor Ian Carmichael (b.1920); Northern Ireland politician Rev. Ian Paisley (b.1926); UK actors Ian Bannen (1928–99), Ian Holm (b.1931), Ian Richardson (b.1934), Sir Ian McKellen (b.1935), Ian McShane (b.1942), Ian Ogilvy (b.1943); UK novelist Ian McEwan (b.1948); UK cricketer Ian Botham (b.1955); UK footballer Ian Rush (b.1961).

Ianthe A Greek name, from *ion*, 'violet', and *anthos*, 'flower'. The name was given some prominence in 19th-century English literature, but has been only rarely adopted for first-name use. Byron dedicated Canto I of *Childe Harold's Pilgrimage* (1812) to 'Ianthe' (the twelve-year-old Lady Charlotte Mary Harley), and there is a character of the name in Percy Bysshe Shelley's poem *Queen Mab* (1813). Shelley also gave his daughter (1813–76) this name.

Ibby see **Isabel**.

Ichabod A biblical name, from Hebrew *Ī-khābhōdh*, 'where is the glory?' (popularly interpreted as 'without glory'), which has been in rare English-speaking use from the 17th century, when it was adopted by the Puritans. In the Bible Ichabod is the son of Phinehas and grandson of Eli, born on the day the Ark of the Covenant is captured by the Philistines: 'And she named the child Ichabod, saying, The glory is departed from Israel: because the ark of God was taken' (1 Samuel 4.21). In literature the name was made familiar by Ichabod Crane, the schoolteacher in Washington Irving's short story 'The Legend of Sleepy Hollow', which was included in *The Sketch Book* (1820), subsequently re-presented as Douglas Moore's operetta *The Headless Horseman* (1936) and further popularized by the Disney cartoon film *Ichabod and Mr Toad* (1949), combining Irving's story with Kenneth Grahame's children's classic *The Wind in the Willows* (1908).

Ida The name either derives from an element found in some Old German names, *īd*, 'work', or is a shortening of *Iduna*, the name of the Norse goddess of youth and the spring. It is also associated with Mount Ida, Crete, which has classical connections. The name became popular in the last quarter of the 19th century, but it has tailed off considerably from the 1920s. In William Makepeace Thackeray's novel *The Luck of Barry Lyndon* (1844) Countess Ida is a German heiress whom Lyndon wants to marry. In Tennyson's poem *The Princess* (1847) Princess Ida is the central character. This work is loosely the subject of Gilbert and Sullivan's opera *Princess Ida* (1884).

US actress Ida Moore (1883–1964); US jazz singer Ida Cox (1889–1967); UK-born US actress, film director Ida Lupino (1918–95); Polish-born UK violinist Ida Haendel (b.1924).

Idris A Welsh name, composed of *iud*, 'lord', and *rīs*, 'ardent', so 'impulsive ruler'. It has been in regular use among the Welsh from medieval times, with a slight increase in popularity in the 19th century. It is now occasionally found elsewhere in the English-speaking world. In Welsh legend Idris is a magician and astronomer who is said to have given the name of the mountain Cader Idris ('throne of Idris'). In Richard Llewellyn's novel *How Green was My Valley* (1939) Idris Atkinson is the murderer of Dilys Pritchard.

Ifor A Welsh name, of uncertain origin but traditionally derived from *iôr*, 'lord'. It is now popularly associated with IVOR, but that name has a different origin. It is found in mainly Welsh use from the early 20th century and became familiar from various personages in Welsh history, especially Ifor Hael (Ifor the Generous), a 14th-century patron of Welsh literature.

Ignatius This is a borrowing of a Late Latin name, itself from the Roman clan name *Egnatius*, of uncertain origin, but altered by association with Latin *ignis*, 'fire'. The name has found some English-speaking favour from the 16th century, especially among Roman Catholics, who use it to honour one of the early saints Ignatius or, more commonly, the Spanish founder of the Jesuits, St Ignatius Loyola (1491–1556). In James Joyce's short story 'A Little Cloud' in *Dubliners* (1914) Ignatius Gallaher is a London journalist.

US writer, politician Ignatius Donnelly (1831–1901).

Igor A well-known Russian name, from the Scandinavian name *Ingvarr*, composed of *Ing*, 'Ing' (a Norse fertility god), and *varr*, 'careful', 'attentive', giving an overall meaning of 'cared for by Ing'. The name has attracted some English-speaking adoption from the 19th century. It was made familiar by Borodin's opera *Prince Igor* (first performed 1890).

Russian-born US composer Igor Stravinsky (1882–1971); Russian violinist Igor Oistrakh (b.1931).

Ike see **Isaac**.

Ileen see **Eileen**.

Illtyd A Welsh name, formed from *il*, 'multitude', and *tud*, 'land', hence 'land of the people'. The name has chiefly been in Welsh use from the 19th century. The famous 6th-century St Illtyd gave the name of the Welsh town Llantwit Major (the first word meaning 'church of Illtyd'). A variant spelling *Illtud* exists.

UK politician Illtyd Harrington (b.1931).

Ilona This name is a Hungarian form of HELEN, occasionally used by English speakers.

Hungarian-born US actress Ilona Massey (1912–74).

Ilse see **Elizabeth**.

Imelda A name of Spanish or Italian origin, which appears to be formed from the Old German words *irm* or *erm*, 'whole' (as in ERMINTRUDE), and *hild*, 'battle', thus giving an overall meaning 'entire in battle', 'all-conquering'. It has been occasionally adopted by English speakers in the 20th century. The name is favoured by Roman Catholics to honour the 14th-century saint Imelda Lambertini, Virgin of Bologna. The diminutive *Mel* exists, as for the UK politician Mel Read (b.1939).

Filipino politician, socialite Imelda Marcos (b.1930); UK actress Imelda Staunton (b.1958).

Immanuel An independently adopted variant of EMANUEL, in select English-speaking use from the 17th century, mainly among Jewish families. The spelling is the Old Testament form of the name. It was made generally familiar by the German philosopher Immanuel Kant (1724–1804). A regular diminutive is *Manny*.

Imogen The name arose by way of a mistake, as a misreading of *Innogen*, this in turn deriving either from Latin *innocens*, 'innocent', or, more likely, from a Celtic word related to Irish *inghean*, 'daughter', 'girl'. The suggestion of English *image* or *imagine* may attract modern givers or adopters of the name, which has enjoyed a modest vogue among English speakers generally from the late 19th century, with a slight increase in favour from the 1990s. The error in the name occurred in the first printing of Shakespeare's *Cymbeline* (1609–10), the source of which had the name of Cymbeline's daughter with *nn* not *m*. A variant form is *Imogene*, as for the US comedienne Imogene Coca (1908–2001). A diminutive is *Immy*.

US photographer Imogen Cunningham (1883–1976); UK composer Imogen Holst (1907–84) (mother was Isobel); UK concert pianist Imogen Cooper (b.1949); UK actress Imogen Stubbs (b.1961).

Ina The name is an independent adoption of the final element of a name such as EDWINA, GEORGINA or MARTINA, or else in some cases a variant spelling of ENA. English speakers took up the name in the 19th century, but it is rarely found today.

US actress Ina Claire (1892–1985); US all-girl bandleader Ina Ray Hutton (1916–84) (original name Odessa Cowan); US actress Ina Balin (1937–90).

India An adoption of the name of the country, in select English-speaking use from the late 19th century, when India was important in the British Empire. The name was made familiar by India Wilkes, sister of the central character, Ashley Wilkes, in Margaret Mitchell's novel *Gone with the Wind* (1936).

US journalist, political activist India M. Edwards (1895–1990); UK bridesmaid to Lady Diana Spencer at her marriage (1981) to Prince Charles, India Hicks (b.1961) (grandfather was Lord Mountbatten of Burma, last viceroy of India and first governor general).

Indiana This is either an adoption of the US state name or an elaboration of INDIA. The name has found some general favour among English speakers in the 20th century. In Edith Wharton's novel *The Custom of the Country* (1913) Indiana Frusk marries James Rolliver. But Indiana Jones in the cult movies *Raiders of the Lost Ark* (1981), *Indiana Jones and the Temple of Doom* (1984) and *Indiana Jones and the Last Crusade* (1989) is a male US archaeologist! *Indy* is a diminutive.

Ingrid A Scandinavian name, from a combination of the name of *Ing*, the Norse fertility god (compare IGOR), and either *fríthr*, 'fair', or *rída*, 'to ride'. The name has been in English-speaking use from the mid-19th century, but has now fallen from favour. Diminutives include *Inga* and *Inge*.

Swedish-born US actress Ingrid Bergman (1915–82); Polish-born UK actress Ingrid Pitt (b.1944).

Inigo A name that is the English form of the Spanish name *Oñigo* (English IGNATIUS). It has occurred in occasional English-speaking use from the 19th century and was first made familiar by the English architect Inigo Jones (1573–1652), whose father bore the same name. In literature it is found for Inigo Jollifant, the ex-schoolmaster and pianist who marries Susie Dean in J.B. Priestley's novel *The Good Companions* (1929).

Iolanthe This name is probably a modern coinage, from Greek *iolē*, 'violet', and *anthos*, 'flower', perhaps influenced by a name such as VIOLETTA. It has also been linked with the name YOLANDE. It has been found in occasional use among English speakers from the 19th century and was to some extent pop-ularized by Gilbert and Sullivan's comic opera *Iolanthe* (1882), in which the title character is a fairy.

Iolo A Welsh name, evolving as an independently adopted diminutive of IORWERTH, although popularly associated with JULIUS. It has been in mainly Welsh use from the 19th century and was brought before the Welsh public by Iolo Morgannwg

(1747–1826) (original name Edward Williams), the poet and scholar who created the modern eisteddfod and gorsedd ritual.

Iona A name that usually comes from the Scottish island, where St Columba founded a monastery in the 6th century. The name has been in mainly Scottish use from the 19th century. A variant is *Ione*, as for the UK actress Ione Skye (b.1970) (original name Ione Skye Leitch).

UK folklorist of Scottish descent Iona Opie (b.1923); Scottish writer of historical fiction for children Iona McGregor (b.1929).

Iorwerth A Welsh name, composed from *iôr*, 'lord', and *berth*, 'beautiful', hence 'handsome lord'. The name has been almost exclusively in Welsh use from the 19th century.

Welsh politician Iorwerth Thomas (1895–1966).

Ira A biblical name, from Hebrew *'Īrā*, 'watchful', in select use among English speakers from the 19th century, mostly in the US. The name is sometimes wrongly assumed to be female, perhaps through an association with IDA or IRMA (or both). In the Bible Ira is one of the chief officers of King David. Ira Mackel is a character in Eugene O'Neill's play *Mourning Becomes Electra* (1931).

US lyricist Ira Gershwin (1896–1983); US writer Ira Levin (b.1929).

Irene An English adoption of the Greek name *Eirene*, meaning 'peace', which was taken up by English speakers from the mid-19th century but is now rarish after a high but brief period of popularity in the second half of the 1920s. The name was formerly pronounced 'I-re-ne', in three syllables, but is now almost always in two, as in the popular song 'Good Night, Irene' (1950). It gained literary fame from Irene Forsyte, the divorced wife of Soames Forsyte in John Galsworthy's *Forsyte* sequence (1906–22). A variant is *Rene*, pronounced 'Ree-nee', which should not be confused with RENÉE, a name of different origin.

UK actresses Irene Vanbrugh (1872–1949), Irene Browne (1891–1965);

US dancer Irene Castle (1893–1969); UK actress Irene Handl (1901–87); US actresses Irene Dunne (1901–90), Irene Ryan (1903–73), Irene Worth (b.1916); UK actresses Irene Manning (b.1917) (original name Inez Harvuot), Irene Cara (b.1957).

Iris The name is probably partly an adoption of the name of the Greek goddess of the rainbow, partly a borrowing of the flower name. It came into favour among English speakers in the late 19th century, when other plant names were in vogue, but fell from favour after the 1930s.

US actress Iris Adrian (1913–94); UK novelist Iris Murdoch (1919–99) (mother was Irene Alice); US pop singer Iris DeMent (b.1961).

Irma The name comes from the first element of German names such as *Irmgard* (compare ERMINTRUDE), in which it means 'whole'. It was taken up by English speakers from the late 19th century, gaining special favour in the US, but it is today much less frequently found. It became familiar from the two US movies: *My Friend Irma* (1949), with Marie Wilson in the title role of the dumb blonde Irma, and *Irma la Douce* (1963), in which Shirley Maclaine plays the prostitute Irma.

US 'agony aunt' Irma Kurtz (b.c.1945).

Irving From the (Scottish) surname and in select English-speaking use, mainly in the US, from the 19th century.

US writer Irving Bacheller (1859–1950); Russian-born US songwriter Irving Berlin (1888–1989) (original name Israel Baline); US actor Irving Bacon (1892–1965); US biographical novelist Irving Stone (1903–89); Polish-US film producer Irving Allen (1905–87); US writer Irving Wallace (1916–90).

Irwin From the surname, although sometimes associated with IRVING. The name enjoyed select adoption among English speakers from the mid-19th to the mid-20th century, when it declined.

US novelist Irwin Shaw (b.1913); US film producer Irwin Allen (1916–91).

Isaac A biblical name, from Hebrew *Yitschāq*, 'he will laugh', adopted by English Puritans in the 17th century and increasingly popular until the early years of the 20th century, especially among Jews, after which it fell from favour. In the Bible Isaac is the son of the elderly couple Abraham and Sarah: 'And Sarah said, God hath made me to laugh, so that all that hear will laugh with me' (Genesis 21.6). In Walter Scott's novel *Ivanhoe* (1819) Isaac of York is the father of Rebecca. Isaac Pierston is married to Ann Avice Caro in Thomas Hardy's novel *The Well Beloved* (1897), and Isaac (Ike) Snopes is a member of the Snopes family in William Faulkner's trilogy *The Hamlet* (1931), *The Town* (1957) and *The Mansion* (1959). The name is famous from the English scientist and mathematician Sir Isaac Newton (1642–1727). The variant spelling *Izaak* was made known by Izaak Walton (1593–1683), author of *The Compleat Angler* (1653). The former Israeli president Yitzhak Shamir (b.1915) and Israeli violinist Itzhak Perlman (b.1945) have the Hebrew form of the name. Diminutives are *Ike* and *Zak*.

US jockey Isaac Murphy (1861–96); Polish-born US Yiddish writer Isaac Bashevis Singer (1904–91); Russian-born US science fiction writer Isaac Asimov (1920–92); Russian-born US violinist Isaac Stern (1920–2001); US musician Isaac Hayes (b.1942).

Isabel This is a Spanish form of ELIZABETH, long used as an independent name. It became particularly popular among English speakers in the 19th century, after which it fell out of fashion for some time, although it picked up in the 1990s. Isabel Burton (1831–96) was the wife of the English explorer Sir Richard Burton. In literature Lady Isabel Vane is the central character of Mrs Henry Wood's novel *East Lynne* (1861), while Isabel Winterbourne is the mother of the central character, George Winterbourne, in Richard Aldington's novel *Death of a Hero* (1929). The Italian form of the name, ISABELLA, is in independent use, as is the variant spelling ISOBEL. Diminutives include BELLA and ELLA, now also adopted in their own right, as well as *Ibby*, *Isa*, *Nib*, *Sib* and similar short forms. The second of these was the name of the Scottish feminist and poet Isa Craig (1831–1903).

UK traveller Isabel Burton (1831–96); UK actress Isabel Jeans (1891–1985); US actress Isabel Jewell (1913–72); UK actress Isabel Dean (1918–97); UK novelist Isabel Colegate (b.1931).

Isabella An Italian form of ELIZABETH, adopted by English speakers in the second half of the 19th century but becoming much less popular in the 20th century. The name remains more common in Scotland than in England, but it has never really caught on in the US. It is familiar historically from various European queens, some of whom found their way into English literature, such as Queen Isabella in Christopher Marlowe's play *Edward II* (1594). In Shakespeare's *Measure for Measure* (1604) Isabella is the sister of Claudio, while Isabella Wardour marries the central character, 'Mr Lovel' (Lord William Geraldin), in Walter Scott's novel *The Antiquary* (1816). Isabella Mayson was the maiden name of the famous UK cookery writer Mrs Beeton (1837–65). The name mostly has the same variants and diminutives as the closely related ISABEL. The French equivalent *Isabelle* is also found, as for the French film actress Isabelle Huppert (b.1955).

UK writer, traveller Isabella Bishop (1832–1904); Italian-born US actress Isabella Rossellini (b.1952).

Isadora The name is a feminine form of ISIDORE, in select English-speaking use from the 19th century. In recent literature it occurs for Isadora Wing, the liberated central character of Erica Jong's best-seller *Fear of Flying* (1973) and its sequel *How To Save Your Own Life* (1977). The most common variant of the name is *Isidora*, while diminutives include DORA, *Issy* and *Izzy*.

US dancer Isadora Duncan (1878–1927).

Isaiah A famous biblical name, from Hebrew *Yĕsha'yāh*, 'salvation of Yah' (that is, Jehovah or God), adopted by English Puritans in the 17th century and taken to the US, where it remained in regular if select use until the early 20th century, after which it declined. It is now chiefly a Jewish name. In the Bible Isaiah is the chief of the major prophets, with an Old Testament book named for him.

Russian-born UK philosopher Sir Isaiah Berlin (1909–97); US conductor Isaiah Jackson (b.1945).

Ishmael A biblical name, from Hebrew *Yishmā'ēl*, 'God will hearken', in rarish use among English speakers from the 19th century. In the Bible Ishmael is the first son of Abraham by Hagar, servant to his barren wife Sarah: 'And the angel of the Lord said unto her. Behold, thou art with child, and shalt bear a son, and shalt call his name Ishmael; because the Lord hath heard thy affliction' (Genesis 16.11). Ishmael Bush is one of the main characters in James Fenimore Cooper's novel *The Prairie* (1827), and the outcast youth Ishmael is the narrator, the sole survivor of the *Pequod*, in Herman Melville's novel *Moby-Dick* (1851).

US writer Ishmael Reed (b.1938).

Isidora see **Isadora**.

Isidore This is an English form of the Greek name *Isidōros*, formed from *Isis* (the Egyptian goddess) and *dōron*, 'gift', so overall meaning 'gift of Isis', and originally regarded as a Christian version of the Jewish name ISAIAH. It has been in select use among English speakers from the 19th century. An early famous bearer of the name in the 6th century was the Spanish archbishop and scholar St Isidore of Seville. A diminutive is *Izzy*.

Isla A Scottish name that is more likely to have been adopted from the name of the island of Islay than to be a variant of ISABELLA. It has found some favour generally among English speakers from the 1930s.

UK actress Isla Blair (b.1944); Scottish folk-singer, TV presenter Isla St Clair (b.1952); UK actress Isla Fisher (b.1977).

Isobel An independently adopted variant of ISABEL, in regular English-speaking use, especially among the Scots, from the late 19th century, and enjoying a modest peak period of popularity in the 1920s and 1930s. Diminutives are mostly the same as for ISABEL.

UK actress Isobel Elsom (1893–1981); Scottish-born opera singer Isobel Baillie (1895–1983) (mother was Isabella); US screenwriter Isobel Lennart (1915–71); UK TV panellist Lady Isobel Barnett (1918–80); UK writer Isobel English (1920–94) (original name June Jolliffe); Scottish actress Isobel Black (b.1943).

Isolde The name comes from the Old French name *Iseult* (*Yseult*), itself from a Celtic root meaning 'fair'. (The Welsh equivalent is *Esyllt*.) It has long been in select English-speaking use. In the later Arthurian romances Isolde is the Irish princess who is married to Mark, king of Cornwall, but who is in love with his knight, Tristram. (In another account she is the daughter of the king of Brittany, married to Tristram.) Hence the coupling of their names in, for example, Wagner's opera *Tristan and Isolde* (1865), which itself popularized the name. A variant spelling is *Isolda*.

Israel A biblical name, from Hebrew *Yisrā'ēl*, formed from *sārāh*, 'to struggle', and *ēl*, 'God', so 'he who struggles with God', 'rival against God'. The name was adopted by 17th-century Puritans and taken by them to the US, where it continues to find some favour, mostly among Jews. In the Bible Israel is a by-name of Jacob, later applied to his descendants, the Children of Israel, and now the name of the modern state of Israel. The name was given to Jacob after he had wrestled with an angel: 'And he said, Thy name shall be called no more Jacob, but Israel: for as a prince hast thou power with God and with men, and hast prevailed' (Genesis 32.28). In literature the name is familiar from the central character of Herman Melville's novel *Israel Potter* (1855). Diminutives include *Issy* and *Izzy*, the former as for the UK radio comedian Issy Bonn (1903–77) (original name Benjamin Levin).

US Revolutionary commander Israel Putnam (1718–1790); UK writer on Jewish themes Israel Zangwill (1864–1926).

Issy see **Isadora, Israel**.

Ivan Perhaps the best-known Russian name, a form of JOHN, this has been in select but fairly regular use in the English-speaking world from the late 19th century, but tailing off after the 1930s. The name may have owed some of its original popularity to the Russian novelist Ivan Turgenev (1818–83), who was read widely in English translation. It may also have been suggested (erroneously) by Walter Scott's popular novel *Ivanhoe* (1819), although that is the title of the central character, Wilfred, Knight of Ivanhoe. (Scott took the title from the village of Ivinghoe in Buckinghamshire.) VAN is a diminutive in independent use.

Scottish actor Ivan Simpson (1875–1951); US painter Ivan Albright (1897–1983); Irish-born business columnist, editor Ivan Fallon (b.1944); UK canoeist Ivan Lawler (b.1966).

Ivor The name is an English form of the Scandinavian name *Ivarr*, composed of *ýr*, 'yew', and *herr*, 'warrior', hence 'bowman' (bows were made of yew). It is now popularly associated with IFOR, although that name has a different origin. It has found some favour among English speakers from the 19th century, but became unfashionable after the 1930s.

UK actor Ivor Barnard (1887–1953); UK writer Ivor Brown (1891–1974); UK pianist Ivor Newton (1892–1981); Welsh actor, songwriter Ivor

Novello (1893–1951) (original name David Ivor Davies); UK film producer, director Ivor Montagu (1904–84); Welsh churchman, writer Ivor Bulmer-Thomas (1905–93); UK popular guitarist Ivor Mairants (b.1908); US actor Ivor Francis (*c.*1911–86); UK dance historian Ivor Guest (b.1920); Scottish radio broadcaster, poet Ivor Cutler (b.1924); UK actors Ivor Roberts (b.1925), Ivor Danvers (b.1932); UK artist Ivor Abrahams (b.1935).

Ivy A borrowing of the plant name, taken up in the late 19th century, but now out of favour after a period of considerable popularity in the 1920s. Ivy Barton is the central character in John Galsworthy's novel *Fraternity* (1909).

UK novelist Ivy Compton-Burnett (1884–1969); UK all-girl bandleader Ivy Benson (1918–93).

Izaak see **Isaac**.

Izzy see **Isadora**, **Isidore**, **Israel**.

J

Jabez A biblical name, from Hebrew *Ya'bēts*, 'he causes sorrow', in very select use among English speakers from the 18th century but now only rarely found. In the Bible Jabez is a descendant of Judah: 'And his mother called his name Jabez, saying, Because I bare him with sorrow' (1 Chronicles 4.9). In Rudyard Kipling's short story 'Friendly Brook' in *A Diversity of Creatures* (1917) Jabez is a woodman.

Jacalyn see **Jacqueline**.

Jack The name is an independently adopted diminutive of JOHN, through Middle English *Jankin* (later, *Jackin*), where *-kin* is a diminutive suffix (as in *manikin*). It was in gradually increasing popularity among English speakers from the mid-19th century until the 1920s, after which it declined, only to revive again in the 1990s. In literature it is the name of the central character in Daniel Defoe's romantic adventure story *Colonel Jack* (1722). Jack Morris is a friend of Lord March in William Makepeace Thackeray's novel *The Virginians* (1857–9). The name was popularized by the 18th-century fairy story *Jack and the Beanstalk*, and it has acquired a generic use to denote a person whose real name is unknown, as in the nursery rhyme about 'Jack and Jill' (where the names mean little more than 'boy and girl'), or the unknown Victorian murderer of prostitutes, Jack the Ripper. The name is particularly favoured by sportsmen, entertainers and other popular celebrities. The variant JAKE and the diminutive JACKIE are in independent use.

US boxer Jack Johnson (1878–1946); UK cricketer Jack Hobbs (1882–1963); UK actor Jack Buchanan (1891–1957); US comedian Jack

Benny (1894–1974) (original name Benjamin Kubelsky); US boxer
Jack Dempsey (1895–1983) (original first names William Harrison);
Canadian actor Jack Carson (1910–63); UK actor Jack Hawkins
(1910–73); UK broadcaster Jack de Manio (1914–88); US actors Jack
Palance (b.1920) (originally second name, first being Walter), Jack
Lemmon (1925–2001); Australian motor-racing driver Jack Brabham
(b.1926); UK footballer Jack Charlton (b.1935); US actor Jack Nicholson
(b.1937); US golfer Jack Nicklaus (b.1940); UK actor Jack Shepherd
(b.1940); UK politician Jack Straw (b.1946).

Jackey, Jacki see **Jackie** (f.).

Jackie (m.) An independently adopted diminutive of JACK
or its source name JOHN, in some vogue among English speakers from the late 19th century. A spelling variant is *Jacky*.

US boxer Jackie Fields (1908–87) (original name Jacob Finkelstein);
US actor Jackie Coogan (1914–84); US comedian Jackie Gleason
(1916–87); US baseball player Jackie Robinson (1919–72); US actor
Jackie Cooper (b.1921); UK footballer Jackie Millburn (1924–88); US
actor Jackie Moran (1925–90); Northern Ireland-born UK rugby player
Jackie Kyle (b.1926); US R&B singer Jackie Wilson (1934–84); Scottish
motor-racing driver Jackie Stewart (b.1939); Hong Kong actor Jackie
Chan (b.1954) (original name Chan Kwong Sang).

Jackie (f.) The name is usually an independently adopted
diminutive of JACQUELINE, but it can also be a female borrowing of the male name JACKIE. It has found some favour from
the 1930s, and some of the name's recent popularity may have
resulted from *Jackie*, a weekly magazine for teenage girls published from 1964 to 1993. Among the many variant spellings
of the name are *Jackey*, *Jacki*, *Jacky*, *Jacqui* and *Jakki*, three of
these respectively as for the UK writer and broadcaster Jacky
Gillott (*c*.1939–80), UK actress Jacki Piper (b.1948) and UK
radio presenter Jakki Brambles (b.1967).

US popular novelist Jackie Collins (b.1937); US pop singer Jackie
DeShannon (b.1944); UK magazine editor Jackie Highe (b.1947); UK TV

political presenter Jackie Ashley (b.1954); UK actress Jackie Lye (b.1959); US athlete Jackie Joyner-Kersee (b.1962); Northern Ireland hockey player Jackie McWilliams (b.1964).

Jackson From the surname, and in select but regular use among English speakers from the 19th century. In the US the name was doubtless originally adopted as a compliment to president Andrew Jackson (1767–1845) or the Confederate general Thomas 'Stonewall' Jackson (1824–63). Diminutives are mostly as for JACK.

US artist Jackson Pollock (1912–56).

Jacky see **Jackie** (m.) and (f.).

Jaclyn see **Jacqueline**.

Jacob A biblical name, from Hebrew *Ya'akub'ēl*, 'May God protect', but traditionally derived from Hebrew *āqēb*, 'heel', or the closely related word *āqāb*, 'to usurp', these together implying a person who follows on the heels of another and supplants him. The name was in regular use among English speakers during the 18th and 19th centuries but was mostly out of favour in the 20th century until a revival in the 1990s. In the Bible Jacob is the younger twin son (the elder was Esau) of Isaac and Rebecca and the father of twelve sons who gave the names of the twelve tribes of Israel: 'And after that [the birth of Esau] came his brother out, and his hand took hold on Esau's heel; and his name was called Jacob' (Genesis 25.26). Jacob subsequently persuaded Esau to part with his right to his inheritance in exchange for 'a mess of pottage' and tricked Isaac into blessing him in place of Esau: 'And he [Esau] said, Is not he rightly named Jacob? for he hath supplanted me these two times: he took away my birthright; and, behold, now he hath taken away my blessing' (Genesis 27.36). Sir Jacob Swinford is a character in Samuel Richardson's novel *Pamela* (1740–41), and in Walter Scott's novel *The Antiquary* (1816)

Jacob Caxon is a barber. Jacob Flanders is the central character of Virginia Woolf's novel *Jacob's Room* (1922). JAKE, in independent use, is sometimes regarded as a diminutive.

US-born (of Russo-Polish parents) UK sculptor Sir Jacob Epstein (1880–1959).

Jacqueline The name, a French feminine diminutive of *Jacques* (English JAMES), has been in English-speaking use from medieval times, but it reached its greatest popularity only in the mid-20th century. There are many variant forms, including *Jacalyn*, *Jaclyn*, *Jaqueline* and *Jacquelyn*, the second of these as for the US actress Jaclyn Smith (b.1947). The diminutive JACKIE is in independent use, and a related name is JACQUETTA.

US aviator Jacqueline Cochran (1910–80); US novelist Jacqueline Susann (1921–74); US socialite, former First Lady, Jacqueline (Jackie) Kennedy Onassis (1929–94) (father, John, was known as 'Black Jack'; mother was Janet Lee); UK actresses Jacqueline Clarke (b.1942); Jacqueline Bisset (b.1944); UK cellist Jacqueline du Pré (1945–87); Irish actress Jacqueline Reddin (b.1956); UK actress Jacqueline Dankworth (b.1963).

Jacquetta Like JACQUELINE this is a French feminine diminutive of *Jacques* (English JAMES). It has been current among English speakers from medieval times but became most popular in the 20th century. The now rare variant *Jaquenetta* is the name of 'a country wench' in Shakespeare's *Love's Labour's Lost* (*c*.1595). Diminutives are mostly as for JACQUELINE itself.

UK writer, archaeologist Jacquetta Hawkes (1910–96).

Jacqui see **Jackie** (f.).

Jade A borrowing of the word for the semiprecious stone, in selective English-speaking use from the late 19th century, but increasing in favour from the 1970s.

UK artist Jade Jagger (b.1971); Australian actress Jade Amenta (b.*c*.1975).

Jaime see **Jamie** (f.).

Jake A variant of JACK in independent use, also sometimes regarded as a diminutive of JACOB. It has been current among English speakers from the early 20th century, with a surge in popularity in the 1990s. In literature it occurs for Jake Barnes, the central character of Ernest Hemingway's novel *The Sun Also Rises* (1926).

UK popular singer Jake Thackray (b.1938); Scottish sculptors Jake Kempsall (b.1940); Jake Harvey (b.1948); UK artist Jake Tilson (b.1958).

Jakki see **Jackie** (f.).

James A biblical name, from the Late Latin name *Jacomus*, a variant of *Jacobus* (English JACOB), in English-speaking use from medieval times and in widespread adoption from the 16th century. In the 20th century the name fell from favour somewhat in the 1950s and 1960s but then recovered its former popularity. In the Bible the name is that of two disciples: James the son of Zebedee and James the son of Alphaeus. The name has long been in royal use, and it is particularly associated with the Scottish house of Stewart (Stuart), where its bearers range from James I of Scotland in the 15th century to James VI (James I of England) and his grandson James II (James VII of Scotland) in the 17th century. In literature James Harlowe is the father of the central character, Clarissa Harlowe, in Samuel Richardson's novel *Clarissa* (1748). James Ratcliff is a thief turned turnkey in Walter Scott's novel *The Heart of Midlothian* (1818), and James Carker is the office manager of the central character, Paul Dombey, in Charles Dickens's novel *Dombey and Son* (1847–8). In recent times the name has been popularly associated with James Bond, the spy who is the central character of Ian Fleming's novels and their subsequent film versions (from the 1960s). The regular diminutives JIM and JAMIE are in independent use.

Irish writer James Joyce (1882–1941); US actors James Cagney (1899–1986), James Stewart (1908–97); UK actor James Mason

(1909–84); Australian actor James Condon (b.1923); US actors James Garner (b.1928), James Dean (1931–55), James Darren (b.1936); UK actors James Bolam (b.1938), James Warwick (b.1947); UK motor-racing driver James Hunt (1947–93); Scottish broadcaster James Naughtie (b.1951).

Jami see **Jamie** (f.).

Jamie (m.) An independently adopted diminutive of JAMES, chiefly in Scottish use from the 18th century. Jamie Stinson is a character in Walter Scott's novel *Waverley* (1814).

South African film director Jamie Uys (1921–96); UK TV presenter Jamie Theakston (b.1970); UK TV cook Jamie Oliver (b.1975).

Jamie (f.) A, female adoption of the male name JAMIE, used as a feminine equivalent for JAMES. The name has enjoyed increasing popularity among English speakers from the early 1970s, with an impressive surge in the 1990s. The variant forms *Jaime* and *Jami* exist, the latter as for the US actress Jami Gertz (b.1965).

US actress Jamie Lee Curtis (b.1958).

Jan (m.) The name is either a modern revival of a medieval form of JOHN or else a borrowing of this name's equivalent from some continental European language, such as Dutch or Danish *Jan*. It has found sporadic adoption among English speakers since the early 20th century.

US opera singer Jan Peerce (1904–84) (original name Jacob Pincus Perlemuth); UK children's writer Jan Needle (b.1943).

Jan (f.) This name is either an independently adopted diminutive of JANET or JANICE, or a female borrowing of the male name JAN, or simply an alternative to JANE, JEAN or JOAN. It has enjoyed modest but fairly consistent favour among English speakers from the early 20th century.

UK poet Jan Struther (1901–53) (original name Joyce Anstruther; pen name derives from 'J. Anstruther'); US actress Jan Sterling (b.1923) (original name Jane Sterling Adriance); Scottish writer Jan Webster (b.1924); UK journalist, travel writer Jan Morris (b.1926) (original first name James; changed sex 1973); UK TV newsreader Jan Leeming (b.1942); UK writer Jan Mark (b.1943); UK actresses Jan Harvey (b.1947), Jan Francis (b.1951), Jan Ravens (b.1958).

Jancis This rarish name, enjoying some favour among English speakers from the 1920s, is apparently a blend of JANE and either FRANCES or CICELY. It occurs in literature for Jancis Beguildy, a character in Mary Webb's novel *Precious Bane* (1924), and this is possibly its first occurrence.

UK wine writer, broadcaster Jancis Robinson (b.1950) (named for Mary Webb character).

Jane The name is an English form of the Latin name *Johanna*, itself a feminine form of *Johannes* (English JOHN). It has been in regular English-speaking use from the 16th century and has increasingly replaced the related names JOAN and JEAN. It had two peaks of popularity in the 20th century – in the 1920s and 1960s. The name's most famous literary bearer is the central character of Charlotte Brontë's novel *Jane Eyre* (1847), while Jane Sheepshanks marries Pitt Crawley in William Makepeace Thackeray's novel *Vanity Fair* (1847–8). 'Calamity Jane', the US frontierswoman, was the nickname of Martha Jane Cannary (1852–1903). Well-known royal bearers of the name include Jane Seymour (1509–37), third wife of Henry VIII, and the tragic 'nine-day queen' Lady Jane Grey (1537–54). Later, the name was famously connected with the English novelist Jane Austen (1775–1817). In recent times the name has been popularized in the UK by Jane, the glamorous heroine of the *Daily Mirror* strip cartoon (1932–59) ('strip' being the operative word). JANET, JANICE, JENNIE and JENNY are directly related names. The variant spelling JAYNE is in independent use. Diminutives include *Janie* and *Janey*. The name is often added to another to form a compound, such as *Mary Jane* or *Sarah Jane* (sometimes with a hyphen).

US actresses Jane Wyatt (b.1911), Jane Wyman (b.1914) (original name Sarah Jane Faulks), Jane Russell (b.1921); UK writer Jane Gardam (b.1928); UK actresses Jane Lapotaire (b.1944), Jane Asher (b.1946), Jane Seymour (b.1951) (original name Joyce Frankenberg), Jane Cunliffe (b.1962), Jane Horrocks (b.1964), Jane Hazlegrove (b.1968).

Janet The name, an independently adopted diminutive of JANE, was taken up as a Scottish name in the 19th century and was in growing favour in the English-speaking world generally until the 1960s, when it began to lose popularity, so that today it is only rarely given. In Charles Dickens's novel *David Copperfield* (1849–50) Janet is a maid to Betsey Trotwood. Possibly the name by then had already acquired its 'menial' association, which occurs again in A.J. Cronin's novel *Beyond This Place* (1953), where Janet is a housekeeper to Dr Cameron and Dr Finlay. This novel was later televised as the popular series *Dr Finlay's Casebook* (1959–66), in which Barbara Mullen played Janet, so bringing the name again before the public. In Scotland bearers of the name have long been called *Jess* or *Jessie*. A French-style variant is *Janette*, as for the UK actress Janette Scott (b.1938). The diminutives JENNIE, JENNY and NETTA are in independent use, and *Jinty* sometimes occurs.

UK actress Janet Achurch (1864–1916); US actresses Janet Gaynor (1906–84) (original name Laura Gainor), Janet Blair (b.1921) (original name Martha Lafferty); New Zealand writer Janet Frame (b.1924); US actress Janet Leigh (b.1927) (original name Jeanette Morrison); UK comedienne Janet Brown (b.1927); UK opera singer Dame Janet Baker (b.1933); UK fashion designer Janet Reger (b.1937); South African actress Janet Suzman (b.1939); US actress Janet Margolin (1943–93); US writer Janet Dailey (b.1944); UK actress Janet Key (b.1945); UK TV presenter Janet Street-Porter (b.1946); UK actress Janet McTeer (b.1961); US pop singer Janet Jackson (b.1966).

Janey see **Jane**.

Janice An independently adopted diminutive of JANE, with the *-ice* from a name such as BERNICE or CANDICE. The name has been taken up on a selective basis by English speakers from the early 20th century, but after a boom in the 1950s it is now much less common. An early literary occurrence of the name is that of the central character in Paul Leicester Ford's novel *Janice Meredith* (1899). A variant is JANIS, which is in independent use.

US actress Janice Rule (b.1931); UK novelist Janice Elliott (b.1931); UK radio DJ Janice Long (b.1955).

Janie see **Jane**.

Janine This is an alteration of the French name *Jeannine*, a feminine form of *Jean* (English JOHN), which has been in fairly modest favour among English speakers from the 1930s, with a peak period of popularity in the late 1960s and early 1970s. A variant spelling is *Jannine*, and the usual diminutive, JAN, is in independent use.

UK actress Janine Wood (b.1963).

Janis An independently adopted variant of JANICE, influenced by other names ending *-is* or *-ys*, such as MAVIS or GLADYS as well as by JANET. The name has been in select but fairly regular use among English speakers from the early 20th century.

US actresses Janis Carter (1917–94), Janis Paige (b.1922) (original name Donna Mae Jaden); US rock singers Janis Joplin (1943–70), Janis Ian (b.1951).

Jannine see **Janine**.

Japheth A biblical name, from Hebrew *Yepheth*, 'enlargement', 'expansion', in rather rare English-speaking use from the 17th century, when it was adopted by the Puritans. In the Bible Japheth is the eldest son of Noah: 'God shall enlarge Japheth' (Genesis 9.27). He is traditionally one of the ancestors of postdiluvian mankind, with his descendants peopling Asia Minor, the islands of the Mediterranean and the Palestinian coast.

Jaqueline see **Jacqueline**.

Jared A biblical name, from Hebrew *Yeredh*, 'descended', enjoying some favour among English speakers from the 17th century, when it was taken up by the Puritans. In the Bible Jared is a descendant of Adam and the father of Enoch.

Jarvis From the surname, itself a form of GERVASE, and in select but regular use among English speakers from the 19th century. Jarvis Lorry is a confidential bank clerk in Charles Dickens's novel *A Tale of Two Cities* (1859). The variant *Jervis* occasionally occurs.

Jasmine A borrowing of the flower name, now usually spelled *jasmin*. The name was taken up by English speakers, with other flower names, at the end of the 19th century, but it is now in only occasional use, although by no means obsolete. In Carson McCullers's novel *The Member of the Wedding* (1946) the central character is twelve-year-old F. Jasmine Addams. (Her brother is named Jarvis, and Jarvis's bride is Janice.) Variant spellings are *Jasmin* and YASMIN, the latter now in independent use.

UK TV announcer Jasmine Bligh (1913–91); Welsh-born US novelist Jasmine Cresswell (b.1941).

Jason This name is an English form of the Greek name *Iasōn*, itself probably based on Greek *iasthai*, 'to heal'. It is also a biblical name, probably arising as a classical form of JOSHUA. The name was in only moderate use among English speakers from the 17th century until the 1970s, when it suddenly took off and became hugely popular. It is now more selectively adopted. In Greek legend Jason is the famous leader of the Argonauts who went in search of the Golden Fleece. The biblical Jason is an early Christian who gave hospitality to St Paul. Jason Newcome is a character in James Fenimore Cooper's novel *The Chainbearer* (1845). In later literature Jason is a name in four generations of the Compson family in William Faulkner's fiction, notably in the novel *The Sound and the Fury* (1929). The name was popularized in modern times by the film *Jason and the Argonauts* (1963) and by various characters in TV fiction, such as Jason King, in the UK thriller series *Department S* (1970) and *Jason King* (1971), and Jason Colby, in the US soap *The Colbys* (1985–87).

US actors, father and son, Jason Robards (1893–1963, 1922–2000); US actor Jason Evers (b.1922) (original first name Herbert); US playwright, actor Jason Miller (b.1939); US actor Jason Alexander (b.1959) (original name Jay Greenspan); UK actor Jason Connery (b.1963); US actor Jason Patric (b.1966); Australian actor, pop singer Jason Donovan (b.1968); UK rugby player Jason Leonard (b.1968); US actor Jason Bateman (b.1969); UK cricketer Jason Ratcliffe (b.1969); UK jazz pianist Jason Rebello (b.1969); UK actor Jason Hope (b.1970); UK rock singers Jason Orange (b.1970).

Jasper The name perhaps ultimately comes from a Persian word meaning 'treasurer', although it is now popularly associated with the word for the gemstone. It has found occasional use among English speakers from the 17th century, with a slight increase in popularity in the 20th. In Francis Beaumont's play *The Knight of the Burning Pestle* (1607–8) Jasper is a merchant's apprentice. Later literary characters of the name include Jasper Dryfesdale, a steward of Lochleven Castle in Walter Scott's novel *The Abbot* (1820); Sir Jasper Cranbourne, an old cavalier in the same author's *Peveril of the Peak* (1823); Jasper Western, married to Mabel Dunham in James Fenimore Cooper's novel *The Pathfinder* (1840); Sir Jasper Rogers, the chief justice in William Makepeace Thackeray's novel *Pendennis* (1848–50); and Jasper Cliff, married to the title character of Thomas Hardy's short story 'Netty Sargent's Copyhold' in *Life's Little Ironies* (1894). In modern times the name has gained the general (or in some cases derogatory) sense of 'person', especially when applied to someone whose real name is unknown. The Dutch variant CASPAR is in independent use.

UK historian Jasper Ridley (b.1920); US artist Jasper Johns (b.1930); UK comedian Jasper Carrott (b.1945) (original name Robert Davies); UK dress designer Jasper Conran (b.1959).

Jay (m.) The name is either an adoption of the surname or the diminutive form of a name beginning *J-*, such as JAMES. It is not from the name of the bird, which itself probably evolved from the Latin name *Gaius* (compare ROBIN). The name has been in select English-speaking use from the 19th century, with a greater popularity in the US and Canada than in the UK.

US actor Jay Adler (1899–1978); US American football player Jay Berwanger (b.1914) (original first names John Jacob); US writer Jay Anson (1924–80); US actors Jay Robinson (b.1930), Jay North (b.1952); US novelist Jay McInerney (b.1955); UK pop singer Jay Kay (b.1971) (original first name Jason).

Jay (f.) Either a borrowing of the male name JAY or an independently adopted diminutive of a name beginning *J-*, such as JANE or JAYNE. The name has found some favour among English speakers from the early 20th century. The link with the bird may have helped, although this is not the origin.

Jayne An independently adopted variant spelling of JANE, in fairly popular English-speaking use from the 1950s, but later tailing off somewhat. A common diminutive is *Jaynie*.

US actresses Jayne Meadows (b.1920), Jayne Mansfield (1933–67) (original name Vera Jayne Palmer); UK bowls player Jayne Roylance (b.1947); UK TV presenter Jayne Irving (b.1956); UK ice dancer Jayne Torvill (b.1957); UK royal photographer Jayne Fincher (b.1958).

Jean The name has its origin in an Old French form (*Jehane*) of the Latin name *Johanna*, the feminine of *Johannes* (English JOHN). It has long been popular in Scotland, but was more generally taken up by English speakers only in the late 19th century. After a peak period of popularity in the 1930s, the name has now mostly been superseded by JANE and JAN. In literature two central characters of the name are Jean Paget in Nevil Shute's novel *A Town Like Alice* (1950) and the Scottish schoolteacher Jean Brodie in Muriel Spark's novel *The Prime of Miss Jean Brodie* (1961). Diminutives include JEANETTE (in independent use), *Jeanie* and *Jeannie*. The second of these is familiar from Stephen Foster's song 'Jeanie with the Light Brown Hair' (1854), the last from the UK actress and entertainer Jeannie Carson (b.1928) and the Scottish actress Jeannie Fisher (b.1947). Jeanie Deans is a character in Walter Scott's novel *The Heart of Midlothian* (1818).

UK novelist Jean Rhys (1894–1979) (original name Ella Gwendolen Rees Williams); US actress Jean Arthur (1900–91) (original name Gladys Greene); Scottish actress Jean Anderson (1908–2001); UK actresses Jean Heywood (b.1921), Jean Alexander (b.1926), Jean Simmons (b.1929); UK fashion editor Jean Rook (1931–91); US-born actress Jean Seberg (1938–79); UK actress Jean Marsh (b.1935).

Jeanette The name, an independently adopted French diminutive of *Jeanne* (English JEAN), has long been in Scottish use, but in the 20th century it was taken up more generally in the English-speaking world, with a peak period in the 1960s. A variant spelling is *Jeannette*, as for the UK ice skater Jeannette Altwegg (b.1930). *Genette* is also found, but much less frequently.

US pacifist, feminist Jeanette Rankin (1880–1973); US actresses Jeanette MacDonald (1901–65), Jeanette Nolan (1911–98); UK novelist Jeanette Winterson (b.1959).

Jeanie see **Jean**.

Jeannette see **Jeanette**.

Jeannie see **Jean**.

Jed An independently adopted diminutive of JEDIDIAH or JACOB, in select use among English speakers, mainly in the US, from the 19th century.

US actor Jed Prouty (1879–1956); US theatrical impresario Jed Harris (1906–79).

Jedidiah A biblical name, from Hebrew *Jedīd'yāh*, 'friend of Yah' (that is, Jehovah), otherwise 'befriended by God', in rarish use among English speakers from the 17th century, when it was taken up by English Puritans. In the Bible Jedidiah is a by-name of Solomon: 'And she [Bathsheba] bare a son, and he [David] called his name Solomon: and the Lord loved him. And he sent by the hand of Nathan the prophet; and he called his name Jedidiah, because of the Lord' (2 Samuel 12.25–6). The regular diminutive is JED, which is in independent use.

Jeff An independently adopted diminutive of JEFFREY or (less often) JEFFERSON, which has been in regular use among English speakers, especially in the US, from the early 20th century. Jeff Merivale is a character in John Dos Passos's novel *Manhattan Transfer* (1925).

US actors Jeff Morrow (1913–93), Jeff Chandler (1918–61) (original name Ira Grossel); UK fashion designer Jeff Banks (b.1943); UK rock guitarist Jeff Beck (b.1944); US actor Jeff Bridges (b.1949); UK actor Jeff Rawle (b.1951); Scottish actor Jeff Stewart (b.1955); US actor Jeff Fahey (b.1956).

Jefferson From the surname, and in select English-speaking use, mostly in the US, from the 19th century. The original impetus for the name came both from the US president Thomas Jefferson (1743–1826), famous for the text of the Declaration of Independence, and from the president of the Confederate States of America during the Civil War, Jefferson Davis (1808–89). Jefferson Brick is a war correspondent in Charles Dickens's novel *Martin Chuzzlewit* (1843–4), and Jefferson

Almond is a character in Henry James's novel *Washington Square* (1881). The regular diminutive, JEFF, is in independent use.

Jeffrey An independently adopted variant of GEOFFREY, originating as a medieval spelling of the name. The name caught on in the US from the 19th century, where it was perhaps helped by JEFFERSON, which as a surname actually evolved from this form. It is found fairly generally in the English-speaking world, with a peak period in the 1950s and 1960s. The regular diminutive is JEFF, in independent use.

West Indian cricketer Jeffrey Stollmeyer (1921–89); UK columnist Jeffrey Bernard (1932–97); US biographer, literary critic Jeffrey Meyers (b.1939); UK politician, writer Jeffrey Archer, Lord Archer (b.1940); UK conductor Jeffrey Tate (b.1943); UK actor Jeffrey Holland (b.1946); US actor Jeffrey Jones (b.1947); US soul singer Jeffrey Osborne (b.1951).

Jem (m.) This name was originally a diminutive form of JAMES, but is now regarded as an independently adopted diminutive of JEREMY. It enjoyed select English-speaking use in the 19th century, but is now rare. Elizabeth Gaskell's novel *Mary Barton* (1848) has Jem Wilson as Mary's husband. A diminutive *Jemmy* exists.

English jockey Jem Robinson (1793–1865).

Jemima A biblical name, from Hebrew *Yĕmīmah*, 'wild dove', which was adopted by English-speaking Puritans in the 17th century but is not often found today. In the Bible Jemima is the eldest of Job's three beautiful daughters. Later literature has Jemima Pinkerton as the sister of Miss Barbara Pinkerton, head of Pinkerton's Seminary for Young Ladies in William Makepeace Thackeray's novel *Vanity Fair* (1847–8). In the popular children's stories by Beatrix Potter the name is familiar from *The Tale of Jemima Puddle-Duck* (1908). More recently the name has been to some extent made known by Jemima Shore, the glamorous crime reporter in the UK TV series *Jemimah*

Shore Investigates (1983), based on a literary series by Antonia Fraser, with Patricia Hodge in the title role. The main diminutives are *Jem*, *Jemmy* and *Mima*.

Jemma see **Gemma**.

Jemmy see **Jem**, **Jemima**.

Jeni see **Jennie**, **Jenny**.

Jenifer see **Jennifer**.

Jenna A Latin-style form of JENNY, adopted by some English speakers from the 1970s. The name was popularized by the character Jenna Wade in the US TV soap *Dallas* (1978–82), in which she is played by Priscilla Presley.

Jenni see **Jennie**, **Jenny**.

Jennie An independently adopted variant of JENNY or diminutive of JENNIFER, long in Scottish use but now found more widely among English speakers. The mother of the UK prime minister Sir Winston Churchill was American-born Jennie Jerome (d.1921), and the name was brought before the public by the praised UK TV series on her life, *Jennie, Lady Randolph Churchill* (1975). The variants *Jenni* and *Jeni* also occur, as for the UK radio presenter Jenni Murray (b.1950) (original first name Jennifer) and the UK TV presenter Jeni Barnett (b.1949).

UK politician Jennie Lee (1904–88); UK actress Jennie Linden (b.1939).

Jennifer This name, a Cornish form of GUINEVERE, has been in English-speaking use from the 18th century and is still widely current today, with a spectacular 'high' for the name in the 1950s, when it suddenly became popular. In literature it occurs for Jennifer Dubedat, a character in George Bernard Shaw's play *The Doctor's Dilemma* (1906), and for Jennifer Brent, the first wife of George Brent in Noël Coward's play *The Young*

Idea (1923). A spelling variant occasionally found is *Jenifer*, while the diminutives JENNIE and JENNY are both in independent use.

US actress Jennifer Jones (b.1919) (original name Phyllis Isley); UK opera singer Jennifer Vyvyan (1925–74); Irish writer Jennifer Johnston (b.1930); UK actress Jennifer Jayne (b.1932); US actress Jennifer Warren (b.1941); UK organist Jennifer Bate (b.1944); UK businesswoman Jennifer d'Abo (b.1945); Canadian-born UK ballerina Jennifer Penney (b.1946); UK comedienne Jennifer Saunders (b.1958); US actresses Jennifer Grey (b.1960), Jennifer Jason Leigh (b.1962), Jennifer Beals (b.1963); Canadian actress Jennifer Calvert (b.1963); US actress, singer Jennifer Lopez (b.1970); UK actress Jennifer Ehle (b.c.1970); US tennis player Jennifer Capriati (b.1976).

Jenny This name, an independently adopted diminutive of JANE, JANET or JENNIFER, was taken up by English speakers from the 18th century and has long been specially favoured in Scotland. Jenny Jones (Mrs Waters) is the supposed mother of the central character in Henry Fielding's novel *Tom Jones* (1749). In Walter Scott's novel *The Antiquary* (1816) Jenny Caxon is the daughter of the barber Jacob Caxon, and in the same author's *Old Mortality* (1816) Jenny Blane is the daughter of the town piper Niel Blane, while Jenny Dennison is a maid to Edith Bellenden. The name occurs elsewhere for literary maids, such as Jenny, maid to the Misses Jenkyns in Elizabeth Gaskell's novel *Cranford* (1851–3). The name has been popularized by Jenny Wren, either as a nickname for the bird or as used for a person. In Charles Dickens's novel *Our Mutual Friend* (1864–5) the dolls' dressmaker Fanny Cleaver is nicknamed thus. In more recent literature Kingsley Amis's novel *Take A Girl Like You* (1960) has Jenny Bunn as a sexually innocent schoolmistress, and in Muriel Spark's novel *The Prime of Miss Jean Brodie* (1961) Jenny Gray is a (Scottish) schoolgirl member of 'the Brodie Set'. The most common variant is JENNIE, in independent use, and both *Jenni* and *Jeni* exist.

Swedish opera singer Jenny Lind (1820–87) (original first name Johanna); UK actress Jenny Laird (b.1917); UK writer Jenny Joseph (b.1932); South African-born UK actress Jenny Runacre (b.1943); UK broadcasting executive Jenny Abramsky (b.1946); UK racehorse trainer Jenny Pitman (b.1946); UK writer Jenny Diski (b.1947); UK actresses Jenny Hanley (b.1947), Jenny Agutter (b.1952), Jenny Seagrove (b.1957); UK TV presenter Jenny Powell (b.1968).

Jephthah A biblical name, from Hebrew *Yiphtah*, 'he [that is, God] opens', in some favour among English speakers in the 19th century, although now rare. In the Bible Jephthah is the judge of Israel who sacrifices his only daughter to God. The variant spellings *Jephtha* and *Jeptha* sometimes occur.

Jeremiah A biblical name, from Hebrew *Yirmĕyāh*, 'exalted by Yah' (that is, Jehovah), that was taken up by Puritans in 17th century. Although now largely superseded by JEREMY, it is still found selectively in the English-speaking world, especially in Ireland. In the Bible Jeremiah is a famous prophet whose story is recorded in the book named for him. Jeremiah Flintwich is a character in Charles Dickens's novel *Little Dorrit* (1855–7), and Jeremiah Cruncher (with son Jerry) is in the same author's *A Tale of Two Cities* (1859). The name is familiar from Jeremiah Clarke (*c*.1674–1707), the composer of the well-known *Trumpet Voluntary*. The regular diminutive, JERRY, is in use in its own right.

Jeremy The name is an English form of the biblical name JEREMIAH, in increasingly popular use among English speakers from the early years of the 20th century to the 1950s and 1960s, after which it fell from favour. The name is sometimes popularly associated with JEROME, but that has a different origin. In William Congreve's comedy *Love for Love* (1695) Jeremy is a servant to Valentine, the central character, and Jeremy (Jerry) Melford is a character in Tobias Smollett's novel *Humphry Clinker* (1771). In recent literature the name became familiar from Jeremy Cole, the small boy central character in Hugh Walpole's novels *Jeremy* (1919), *Jeremy and Hamlet* (1923) (Hamlet is Jeremy's dog) and *Jeremy at Crale* (1927). At the same time the name was popularized by Jeremy Fisher, the frog in Beatrix Potter's children's books of the early 20th century. The diminutive JERRY is in independent use.

English philosopher Jeremy Bentham (1748–1832); UK politician Jeremy Thorpe (b.1929); UK actors Jeremy Brett (1935–95), Jeremy Kemp (b.1935) (original name Edmund Jeremy James Walker), Jeremy Spenser (b.1937), Jeremy Child (b.1944), Jeremy Bulloch (b.1945); UK TV presenter Jeremy Beadle (b.1947); UK actors Jeremy Irons (b.1948), Jeremy Sinden (1950–96), Jeremy Gittins (b.1956); UK tennis player Jeremy Bates (b.1962).

Jermaine (m.) A male variant of the female name GERMAINE, popular among black Americans from the 1970s.

Jermaine (f.) see **Germaine**.

Jerome An English form of the Greek name *Hieronymos*, composed of *hieros*, 'holy', and *onoma*, 'name', thus 'one who bears a holy name'. The name is popularly associated with JEREMY, but that has a different origin. It was in irregular use among English speakers until the 19th century, when it became rather more popular. The famous original bearer of the name was St Jerome, the 4th-century monk and scholar who translated the Bible into Latin. In Horace Walpole's novel *The Castle of Otranto* (1765) Father Jerome is legally Count of Falconara. The usual diminutive is JERRY, which is in independent use.

UK writer Jerome K. Jerome (1859–1927) (father was Jerome C. Jerome); US songwriter Jerome Kern (1885–1945); US actor Jerome Cowan (1897–1972); US ballet dancer, choreographer Jerome Robbins (1918–98); US actor Jerome Courtland (b.1926); US writer Jerome Charyn (b.1937); UK actor Jerome Flynn (b.1963).

Jerrie see **Geraldine**.

Jerry (m.) This name is either an independently adopted diminutive of JEREMY, JEREMIAH or JEROME, or a spelling variant of GERRY. It was selectively taken up by English speakers from the 18th century. Jeremy (Jerry) Melford is a character in Tobias Smollett's novel *Humphry Clinker* (1771), and Jerry Cruncher is the son of Jeremiah Cruncher in Charles Dickens's novel *A Tale of Two Cities* (1859). Sean O'Casey's play *Juno and the Paycock* (1925) has Jerry Devine as the leader of the local labour movement. In modern times the name has been popularized by the cartoon cat and mouse Tom and Jerry (from the late 1930s), but their two names come from the roistering man-about-town characters in Pierce Egan's comic tale *Life in London; or, The Day and Night Scenes of Jerry Hawthorn, Esq. and His Elegant Friend Corinthian Tom* (1821).

UK actor Jerry Verno (1895–1975); US actors Jerry Colonna (1903–86), Jerry Paris (1925–86), Jerry Lewis (b.1926) (original name Joseph Levitch), Jerry Orbach (b.1935); US country musicians Jerry Lee Lewis (b.1935), Jerry Reed (b.1937); UK-born US chat show host Jerry Springer (b.1944); US comedian Jerry Seinfeld (b.1954).

Jerry (f.) see **Geraldine**.

Jervis see **Jarvis**.

Jess (m.) An independently adopted diminutive of JESSE, in select use among English speakers, black and white, from the 19th century.

UK TV personality Jess Yates (1919–93); US opera singer Jess Thomas (1927–93); UK pop singer, actor Jess Conrad (b.1940).

Jess (f.) see **Janet**.

Jesse A biblical name, from Hebrew *Yīshay*, meaning either 'Jehovah exists' or 'gift of Jehovah'. (The pronunciation is normally as the female JESSIE, but sometimes as JESS.) The name has been in select English-speaking use from the 18th century, with greater favour in the US. In the Bible Jesse is the father of King David. Jesse Bush is a character in James Fenimore Cooper's novel *The Prairie* (1827), and in Rudyard Kipling's short story 'Friendly Brook' in *A Diversity of Creatures* (1917) Jesse is a woodman. Later, Jesse Blackless is a 'red' artist in Upton Sinclair's novel *Dragon's Teeth* (1942), set in the 1930s. The usual diminutive is JESS, in independent use.

US outlaw Jesse James (1847–82); US singer Jesse Fuller (1896–1976); US R&B musician Jesse Stone (1901–99); US athlete Jesse Owens (1913–80) (from initials of original first names, James Cleveland); US actor Jesse White (1918–97); UK actor Jesse Birdsall (b.1963).

Jessica This name was apparently introduced by Shakespeare as a form of the biblical name *Iscah*, itself Hebrew in origin and meaning 'God beholds'. It is now sometimes regarded as a feminine form of JESSE. It was modestly popular from the 19th century to the 1990s when it suddenly became fashionable. In Shakespeare's *The Merchant of Venice* (1596–8) Jessica is the daughter of Shylock, and for this reason the name was at first associated with Jews. In H.G. Wells's novel *The War in the Air* (1908) Jessica Smallways is the wife of the central character, Bert Smallways. The usual diminutive is JESSIE, in independent use, although *Jess* also exists, as for the UK photographer Jess Koppel (b.1963).

UK-born US actress Jessica Tandy (1909–94); UK writers Jessica Mitford (1917–96), Jessica Mann (b.1937); US actress Jessica Walter (b.1944); US TV news reporter Jessica Savitch (1947–83); US actresses Jessica Harper (b.1948), Jessica Lange (b.1949); UK actress Jessica Martin (b.1962).

Jessie A name that is either a Scottish diminutive of JEAN or JANET, or an independently adopted diminutive of Jessica. It has been taken up by English speakers from the 19th century, especially in Scotland, though has been rather less common since the 1920s. Variant spellings include *Jessi*, as for the US country singer Jessi Colter (b.1947) (original first name Miriam) and *Jessye*, as for the US concert singer Jessye Norman (b.1945). The main diminutive is *Jess*.

UK novelist Jessie Fothergill (1851–91); US actresses Jessie Ralph (1864–1944), Jessie Royce Landis (1904–72); UK dancer, singer Jessie Matthews (1907–81).

Jethro A biblical name, from Hebrew *Yitrŏ*, 'excellence', and in select English-speaking use from the 16th century until the late 19th, after which it mainly fell from favour. In the Bible Jethro is the father of Zipporah, the wife of Moses. The name is famous in history from the English agricultural reformer and seed-drill inventor Jethro Tull (1674–1741).

US country musician, comedian Jethro Burns (1920–89) (original first name Kenneth).

Jill The name is a modern spelling of *Gill*, itself a diminutive of GILLIAN. It has been in English-speaking use from at least the 17th century, but only became anything like popular in the 1930s. Since the 1970s it has again been only modestly adopted. The pairing of 'Jack and Jill' to mean 'lad and lass' (or 'boy and girl') goes back to at least the 15th century. The diminutive JILLY is in independent use.

UK actresses Jill Esmond (1908–90), Jill Summers (1910–97), Jill Balcon (b.1925); UK politician Dame Jill Knight (b.1927); UK actresses Jill Bennett (1931–90), Jill Adams (b.1931), Jill Day (1932–90), Jill Ireland (1936–90), Jill Gascoine (b.1937); UK children's writer Jill Paton Walsh (b.1937) (original first name Gillian); US actresses Jill St John (b.1940), Jill Clayburgh (b.1945), Jill Eikenberry (b.1947); UK TV presenter Jill Dando (1961–99); UK athlete Jill Hunter (b.1966).

Jillian see **Gillian**.

Jilly An independently adopted diminutive of JILL or GILLIAN, in favour from the 1950s. An alternative form of the name is *Jillie*.

UK writer Jilly Cooper (b.1937); UK skier Jilly Curry (b.1961); UK radio, TV presenter Jilly Parton (b.1964) (original first names Isabel Elizabeth Gillian; mother is Gillian).

Jim An independently adopted diminutive of JAMES, in regular English-speaking use from the mid-19th century. The name is famous in literature from Jim Hawkins, the narrator and central character of Robert Louis Stevenson's novel *Treasure Island* (1883). In Mark Twain's novel *Huckleberry Finn* (1884) Jim is a runaway slave. The diminutive is JIMMY, in independent use, and now more frequent than its source name.

UK rugby player Jim Sullivan (1903–77); UK athlete Jim Peters (1918–99); Scottish motor-racing driver Jim Clark (1936–68); Scottish footballer Jim McLean (b.1937); UK comedian, TV presenter Jim Bowen (b.1937); UK TV sports presenter Jim Rosenthal (b.1947); UK comedian Jim Davidson (b.1953); UK rock singer Jim Kerr (b.1959).

Jimmy An independently adopted diminutive of JAMES and its own diminutive Jim, which it has now largely superseded. It has been current among English speakers from the late 19th century, and in the 20th is chiefly found for sports personalities, TV celebrities and the like. Jimmy Herf is a cub reporter in John Dos Passos's novel *Manhattan Transfer* (1925), and Jimmy Porter is the central character in John Osborne's play *Look Back in Anger* (1957). The spelling variants *Jimmie* and *Jimi* exist, the latter, as for the US rock musician Jimi Hendrix (1942–70) (original first name James).

US comedian Jimmy Durante (1893–1980); UK comedian Jimmy Jewel (1912–95); UK actors Jimmy Hanley (1918–70), Jimmy Edwards (1920–88); UK pop musician, investigative radio presenter Jimmy Young (b.1923) (original first names Leslie Ronald); US president Jimmy Carter (b.1924); UK TV presenter Jimmy Savile (b.1926); US country singer Jimmy Dean (b.1928); UK footballers, TV sports presenters Jimmy Hill (b.1928), Jimmy Greaves (b.1940); UK comedians Jimmy Tarbuck (b.1940), Jimmy Cricket (b.1945) (original name James Mulgrew); US tennis player Jimmy Connors (b.1952); UK actor Jimmy Nail (b.1954) (original name James Bradford).

Jinty see **Janet**.

Jo (m.) An independently adopted diminutive of JOHN, JONATHAN or JOSEPH or a variant spelling of JOE, in rarish use among English speakers from the 19th century. In Charles Dickens's novel *Bleak House* (1852–3) Jo is a crossing sweeper.

US jazz drummer Jo Jones (1911–85) (original first name Jonathan); UK politician Jo Grimond (1913–93) (original first name Joseph).

Jo (f.) An independently adopted diminutive of JOAN, JOANNA, JOANNE, JOSEPHINE or some similar name, now sometimes regarded as a feminine equivalent of JOE. The name has been in English-speaking use from the 19th century, with a period of popularity from the 1940s to the 1960s, but it is now less common. One of the first literary characters to make it familiar was Jo March (with full first name Josephine) in Louisa M. Alcott's children's novel *Little Women* (1868–9). Jo, with her male-sounding name, is significantly the tomboy of the four sisters (the others are Meg, Beth and Amy). A later book in the series with the same characters was *Jo's Boys* (1886). In recent fiction the name is found for Jo, the teenage central character of Shelagh Delaney's play *A Taste of Honey* (1958), and Jo Armitage, the central character of Penelope Mortimer's novel *The Pumpkin Eaters* (1960). The name sometimes combines with others to form a compound, as for the US actress Jobeth Williams (b.1953).

US writer Jo Sinclair (b.1913) (original name Ruth Seid); US actress Jo Van Fleet (1919–96); US pop singer Jo Stafford (b.1920); UK politician Jo Richardson (1923–94) (original first name Josephine); US actress Jo Morrow (b.1940); UK actress Jo Kendall (b.1943); UK tennis player Jo Durie (b.1960) (original first name Joanna; father was John); UK radio, TV presenter Jo Whiley (b.1965).

Joab A biblical name, from Hebrew *Yō'ābh*, 'Jehovah is father', in rarish use among English speakers from the 17th century. In the Bible, Joab is King David's general.

Joachim A biblical name, from Hebrew *Yehoyaqim*, 'Jehovah will establish', it was in select English-speaking use from the 17th century but became rare in the 20th. In the Bible Joachim is a king of Judah. Traditionally, the name is also regarded as that of the father of the Virgin Mary, although he is not named in the Bible.

Joan This is an English form of the Latin name *Johanna*, a feminine form of *Johannes* (English JOHN). It has been in English-speaking use from medieval times but was not all that common from the 17th to the 19th century, after which it staged a striking but short-lived comeback in the 1920s and 1930s. It has since tailed off to a very modest level. One of the name's most famous bearers is the 15th-century French heroine Joan of Arc. (She was canonized in 1920, which may at least partly explain the sudden interest in the name then.) Literary characters of the name include Joan Trash in Ben Jonson's play *Bartholomew Fair* (1614), Joan Elliott in Walter Scott's novel *The Black Dwarf* (1816) and Joan Debenham, the central character in H.G. Wells's novel *Joan and Peter* (1918). Related forms of the name in independent use are JOANNA and JOANNE. See also JO.

US actress Joan Crawford (1904–77) (original name Lucille le Sueur); UK actresses Joan Hickson (1906–98), Joan Kemp-Welch (b.1906); US actresses Joan Blondell (1909–79), Joan Bennett (1910–90); New Zealand opera singer Dame Joan Hammond (b.1912); UK actress Joan Sanderson (1912–92); US actresses Joan Chandler (1923–79), Joan Leslie (b.1925); Australian opera singer Dame Joan Sutherland (b.1926); UK actress Joan Sims (1930–2001); UK politician Joan Lestor (b.1931); UK actress Joan Collins (b.1933); US comedienne Joan Rivers (b.1933); UK TV presenter Joan Bakewell (b.1933); US actress Joan Hackett (1934–83); US folk-rock singer Joan Baez (b.1941); West Indian pop singer Joan Armatrading (b.1950); UK opera singer Joan Rodgers (b.1954); US actress Joan Cusack (b.1962).

Joanna This originated as a biblical name, as a Latin form of the Greek name *Iōanna*, a feminine form of *Iōannes* (English JOHN), but it later came to be regarded as an independently adopted variant of JOAN. It has been in English-speaking use from the 18th century and essentially took over when Joan fell from favour, from the 1930s. In the Bible Joanna is the wife of Herod's steward and a friend of Jesus. In later literature the name is found for Joanna (Johnsy), an artist in O. Henry's short story 'The Last Leaf' in *The Trimmed Lamp* (1907), and Joanna Burden, the lover of Joe Christmas (who murders her) in William Faulkner's novel *Light in August* (1932). JOANNE is now regarded as a directly related name.

US actress Joanna Miles (b.1940); UK writer Joanna Trollope (b.1943); US actress Joanna Cassidy (b.1944); UK actresses Joanna Lumley (b.1946), Joanna David (b.1947); UK writer Joanna Bogle (b.1952); UK concert pianist Joanna MacGregor (b.1959).

Joanne An English adoption of the Old French feminine form of *Joanne* (English JOHN), so essentially the equivalent of JOAN. The name is now more readily associated with JOANNA, however, although that name has a different origin. Its popularity increased among English speakers to reach a peak in the 1970s, since when it has declined somewhat. The name is sometimes 'split' into *Jo Anne* (with or without a hyphen), as if it represented a combination of JO and ANNE, and it is regularly pronounced in two syllables.

US actresses Joanne Dru (1923–96), Joanne Woodward (b.1930); US popular musician Joanne Brackeen (b.1938); UK actresses Joanne Campbell (b.1964), Joanne Whalley (b.1964); UK hockey player Joanne Reddy (b.1969); UK actress Joanne Ridley (b.1970).

Job A biblical name, from Hebrew *Iyyōbh*, 'persecuted'. The name was adopted by the Puritans in the 17th century and continued in modest favour until the 19th century, after which it was much less common. In the Bible Job is a man who suffers much but who remains faithful to God, and the book named for him tells of his endurance and patience in many trials. In Charles Dickens's novel *Pickwick Papers* (1836–7) Job Trotter is a servant of Jingle; in George Eliot's novel *Felix Holt* (1866) Job Tudge is a protégé of Felix; and in Robert Louis Stevenson's novel *Treasure Island* (1883) Job Anderson is a member of the crew of the *Hispaniola*.

Jocasta This is a Greek name of uncertain origin. It is derived by some from the name of the mythological character *Io*, whom some stories associate with the moon, and *kaustikos*, 'burning' (English *caustic*) so that the overall sense may be 'shining moon'. It has enjoyed only very select English-speaking use in the 20th century. Most early literary references are to the mythological Jocasta, the tragic queen of Thebes who unwittingly married her son Oedipus, then killed herself. An example is George Gascoigne's blank verse tragedy *Jocasta* (1575), translated from an Italian adaption of Euripides's tragedy *Phoenissae*. The usual diminutive is JO.

UK cookbook writer Jocasta Innes (b.1938).

Jocelyn (m.) From the surname, itself from the personal name *Joscelin* introduced to England by the Normans, in turn ultimately deriving from the name of the *Gauts*, a Germanic tribe. The name was in fairly regular use among English speakers from medieval times to the early 20th century, when it declined as a male name and was adopted for female use. Jocelyn Pierston is a sculptor in Thomas Hardy's novel *The Well Beloved* (1897). The many spelling variants include *Jocelin*, *Josceline* and *Josslyn*. The diminutive JOSS is in independent use.

UK writer Jocelyn Brooke (1908–66); UK feature writer, newspaper editor Jocelyn Targett (b.1965).

Jocelyn (f.) A female adoption of the male name JOCELYN, now usually felt to be a blend of JOYCE and LYNN. It was taken up among English speakers in the early 20th century but has never been common. There are several variant spellings, including *Jocelin*, *Joceline*, *Joscelin*, *Josceline* and *Joselyn*, the fourth of these as for the UK food writer Josceline Dimbleby (b.1943) (her father's first names were Thomas Josceline). The usual diminutive is JOSS.

UK theatrical designer Jocelyn Herbert (b.1917); US actress Jocelyn Brando (b.1919); Irish astronomer Jocelyn Bell-Burnell (b.1943).

Jock A Scottish variant of JACK or its source name JOHN, frequently used by the English as a typical name of a Scotsman. The name is not usually favoured by the Scots themselves, but it is sometimes accepted as a nickname for a popular Scot. A diminutive is *Jocky*, as for the Scottish darts player Jocky Wilson (b.1950) (original first name John).

US actor Jock Mahoney (1919–89) (original name Jacques O'Mahoney); Scottish footballer Jock Stein (1922–85); Scottish oarsman, yachtsman Jock Wishart (b.1953).

Jody (m.) This appears to be an independently adopted diminutive of a name such as GEORGE or JUDE, or an elaborated form of JOE. It has found some favour among English speakers from the 19th century. Jody Varner is a character in William Faulkner's novel *The Hamlet* (1940). A spelling variant is *Jodi*, as for the South African motor-racing driver Jodi Scheckter (b.1950).

US country musician, comedian Cousin Jody (1914–76) (original name James Summey).

Jody (f.) This is either a diminutive form of a name such as JO, JOSEPHINE, JOSIE or JUDITH, or a blend of these, or simply an adoption of the male name JODY. It has been in English-speaking use from the 1950s, with its greatest popularity in the US and Canada. Variant spellings *Jodi* and *Jodie* exist, the latter as for the US actress Jodie Foster (b.1962) (original first names Alicia Christian).

US actress Jody Lawrance (1930–86) (original name Josephine Lawrence Goddard); US pop singers Jody Miller (b.1941), Jody Watley (b.1959).

Joe An independently adopted diminutive of JOSEPH or (less often) JOHN or JOSHUA, widely popular in the English-speaking world from the 19th century. A well-known literary bearer of the name is Joe the Fat Boy in Charles Dickens's novel *Pickwick Papers* (1836–7), while Joe Gargery is the blacksmith in the same author's *Great Expectations* (1860–61). The central character of John Braine's novel *Room at the Top* (1957) is the provincial 'angry young man' Joe Lampton. 'Joe Bloggs' has become a generic name for an ordinary person, especially one doing routine work, while 'Joe Public' and 'Joe Soap' are used in a similar way and tend to have derogatory overtones. Diminutives in independent use are JO and JOEY. (In the listing below, the original name of the person was *Joseph* unless otherwise indicated.)

US boxer Joe Gans (1874–1910); UK snooker player Joe Davis (1901–78); UK bandleader Joe Loss (1909–90) (original first name Joshua); US boxer Joe Louis (1914–81); UK footballer Joe Mercer (1914–90); US popular musician Joe Albany (1924–88); UK political writer Joe Haines (b.1928); UK jockey Joe Mercer (b.1934); UK pop singer Joe Cocker (b.1944) (original first name John); US boxer Joe Frazier (b.1944); UK mountaineer Joe Simpson (b.1960).

Joel A biblical name, from Hebrew *Yō'ēl*, 'Yah is god' (that is, Jehovah is the only true god). The name was taken up by English Puritans in the 16th century, and from the 19th century it has been fairly popular in the US, with its vogue in the UK beginning only slowly from the 1970s. In the Bible Joel is a minor prophet with a book named for him, in which the prophecy is spoken partly in his name, partly in that of Jehovah. In George Eliot's novel *Daniel Deronda* (1876) Joel Dagge is a blacksmith's son.

US children's writer Joel Chandler Harris (1848–1908); US actors Joel McCrea (1905–90), Joel Fluellen (1908–90); US singer, entertainer Joel

Grey (b.1932); US actor Joel Schumacher (b.1939); West Indian cricketer Joel Garner (b.1952); US film director Joel Coen (b.1955).

Joey An independently adopted diminutive of JOSEPH, JOSHUA or JOE, in select use among English speakers, especially black Americans, from the 19th century. Joey Chickerell is the brother of the central character Ethelberta Petherwin in Thomas Hardy's novel *The Hand of Ethelberta* (1876), and Joseph (Joey) Pontifex is a younger brother of Ernest Pontifex, the central character in Samuel Butler's novel *The Way of All Flesh* (1903).

Northern Ireland racing motorcyclist Joey Dunlop (1952–2000) (original first names William Joseph).

John A biblical name, from Hebrew *Yōhānān*, 'Yah [that is, Jehovah] has been gracious', brought to England by the Normans in the 11th century and from the 16th in regular and widespread use throughout the English-speaking world. In the 20th century, however, it has shown a slow but sure decline from the 1950s. In the Bible the name is that of several important characters, including John the Baptist (the precursor of Christ), John the Apostle (one of the twelve disciples and the brother of James), and John the Evangelist (the author of the fourth gospel, traditionally identified with the apostle John). The first of these makes the name eminently appropriate as a baptismal Christian name. The name was also borne by many saints, popes (down to John XXIII in the 20th century) and royal persons. In Shakespeare's *Henry IV* (1597) and *The Merry Wives of Windsor* (1597) the name is that of the fat, drink-loving wit Sir John Falstaff. John Bull is a personification of England and the English. The spelling variant JON is a name in its own right. Regular diminutives in independent use include JACK, JOHNNY and HANK. Non-English forms of the name in independent English-speaking use include HANS, IAN, IVAN, JUAN and SEAN.

UK actor Sir John Gielgud (1904–2000); UK poet Sir John Betjeman

(1906–84); US president John F. Kennedy (1917–63); UK writer John Wain (1925–94); UK motor-racing driver John Surtees (b.1934); UK actor John Bird (b.1936); UK politician John Smith (1938–94); UK actors John Cleese (b.1939), John Alderton (b.1940); UK pop musician John Lennon (1940–1980); UK prime minister John Major (b.1943).

Johnathan see **Jonathan**.

Johnny An independently adopted diminutive of JOHN or JONATHAN, in fairly regular use among English speakers from the 19th century. Johnny, of the *Hispaniola*, is a character in Robert Louis Stevenson's novel *Treasure Island* (1883), and Johnny-the-Priest is in Eugene O'Neill's play *Anna Christie* (1921). The spelling *Johnnie* is also found, as for the US popular singer Johnnie Ray (1927–90) and UK radio DJ Johnnie Walker (b.1945), and the variant form *Jonny* sometimes occurs, as for the UK rower Jonny Searle (b.1969).

US athlete, actor Johnny Weissmuller (1904–84); US songwriter Johnny Mercer (1909–76); US country singer, actor Johnny Bond (1915–78) (original first name Cyrus); UK broadcaster Johnny Morris (1916–99); US comedian, chat show host Johnny Carson (b.1925); US pop musician Johnny Ace (1929–54) (original name John Marshall Alexander Jr); US country musician Johnny Cash (b.1932); UK actors Johnny Shannon (b.1932); Johnny Briggs (b.1935), Johnny Caesar (b.1936); UK TV presenter Johnny Ball (b.1938); US country singer Johnny Carver (b.1940); US actor Johnny Depp (b.1963).

Jolene The name appears to be a blend of JO and a name such as MARLENE. Some English speakers, mostly in the US, took it up from the 1940s. Dolly Parton's hit song 'Jolene' (1974) may have helped to increase public awareness of the name.

Jolyon An independently adopted northern English form of JULIAN, in select use among English speakers from the early 20th century, when it was made familiar in literature by the family head Jolyon Forsyth in John Galsworthy's *Forsyte* sequence (1906–22). A diminutive *Jolly* exists.

Jon This name is either an independently adopted diminutive of JONATHAN or a spelling variant of JOHN. It came into vogue among English speakers in the 1920s and has enjoyed modest but fairly regular use since.

US actor Jon Hall (1913–79) (original name Charles Locher); Australian novelist Jon Cleary (b.1917); UK actor Jon Pertwee (1919–96); Canadian singer Jon Vickers (b.1926); UK poet Jon Silkin (b.1930); US actor Jon Voight (b.1938); UK actors Jon Finch (b.1941), Jon Whiteley (b.1945); UK TV news presenter Jon Snow (b.1947); UK actors Jon Strickland (b.1952), Jon Iles (b.1954); US actor Jon Lovitz (b.1957); UK hockey player Jon Potter (b.1963); UK athlete Jon Ridgeon (b.1967).

Jonah A biblical name, from Hebrew *Yōnāh*, 'dove', in select English-speaking use from the 17th century. In the Bible Jonah is a prophet who is swallowed by a whale, with the story told in the book named for him. Jonah Featherstone is the poor brother of Peter Featherstone, a rich, miserly widower, in George Eliot's novel *Middlemarch* (1871–2). The variant JONAS is in independent use.

Irish historian Jonah Barrington (c.1760–1834); US jazz musician Jonah Jones (1908–2000); UK squash player Jonah Barrington (b.1940).

Jonas An English form of the Greek name *Iōnas* (English JONAH), in select English-speaking use since at least the 19th century. Jonas Chuzzlewit is the son of Anthony Chuzzlewit in Charles Dickens's novel *Martin Chuzzlewit* (1843–4). A diminutive *Joney* exists.

Jonathan A biblical name, from Hebrew *Yāhōnāthān*, 'Yah [that is, Jehovah] has given' (compare NATHAN and NATHANIEL). The name, in select use among English speakers from the 17th century, is popularly associated with JOHN, but that name has a different origin. In the Bible Jonathan is the son of King Saul and devoted friend of young David. A well-known literary bearer of the name is the rogue central character of Henry Fielding's novel *Jonathan Wild* (1743), and a famous real literary author of the name was the Irish satirist Jonathan Swift (1667–1745). In Walter Scott's novel *The Antiquary* (1816) Jonathan Oldbuck is the laird of Monkbarns, and in George Eliot's novel *Adam Bede* (1859) Jonathan Burge is Adam's employer. The spelling variant *Jonathon* occurs, as less frequently (by association with JOHN) does *Johnathan*. The usual diminutive is JON, in independent use. *Jonty* also occurs, as for the UK rugby player Jonty Parkin (1897–1972).

UK crime writer Jonathan Ross (b.1916) (original name John Rossiter); UK medical man, TV presenter Jonathan Miller (b.1934); UK writer Jonathan Raban (b.1942); UK broadcaster Jonathan Dimbleby (b.1944); UK actor Jonathan Pryce (b.1947); UK TV presenter Jonathan Ross (b.1960).

Joni The name is probably an independently adopted respelling of *Joanie*, a diminutive of JOAN. It came into vogue among English speakers from the 1950s, mainly in the US and Canada. A diminutive JO exists.

US popular singer Joni James (b.1930) (original name Joan Carmello Babbo); Canadian popular singer, guitarist Joni Mitchell (b.1943) (original name Roberta Joan Anderson).

Jonny see **Johnny**.

Jonty see **Jonathan**.

Jools see **Jules**.

Jordan An adoption of the name of the River Jordan, at first used among English speakers in medieval times when Crusaders brought back water from this holy river to baptize their children. In modern times the name has been in select use from the 19th century.

US pop singer Jordan Knight (b.1970).

Joscelin, **Josceline** see **Jocelyn** (m.) and (f.).

Joselyn see **Jocelyn** (f.).

Joseph A biblical name, from Hebrew *Yōsēph*, '[God] may add [another son]', in increasingly popular use among English speakers to the early 20th century, when it began a slow decline, only to pick up sharply again in the 1990s. In the Bible Joseph is the name of three important characters: Joseph, son of Jacob, sold in slavery, Joseph, husband of the Virgin Mary, and Joseph of Arimathea, who took the body of Jesus from the Cross to be buried in a tomb. In literature the name is that of the central character of Henry Fielding's novel *Joseph Andrews* (1742), while Joseph Surface is the nephew of Sir Oliver Surface in Richard Brinsley Sheridan's play *The School for Scandal* (1777) and Major Joseph Bagstock is a character in Charles Dickens's novel *Dombey and Son* (1847–8). The usual diminutives are JOE and JOEY, both in independent use.

Polish-born UK novelist Joseph Conrad (1857–1924) (original name Josef Konrad Korzeniowski); US actor Joseph Cotten (1905–94); US-born UK film director Joseph Losey (1909–84).

Josephine The name is a French diminutive of *Josèphe*, the feminine form of *Joseph* (English JOSEPH), in English-speaking use from the 19th century, and gaining a modest increase in popularity in the 1930s and 1960s. It is historically familiar from Napoleon's wife, Joséphine Beauharnais (1763–1814), whose original first names were Marie-Josèphe-Rose. In literature the name is that of Josephine Sleary, a circus owner's daughter in Charles Dickens's novel *Hard Times* (1854). Agatha Christie has Josephine (Josie) Turner as a character in her novel *The Body in the Library* (1942). The name came to be associated with the catch-phrase 'Not tonight, Josephine', which probably arose in the Victorian music-hall. A regular diminutive is JOSIE, in independent use, with FIFI and JO also current.

UK socialist reformer Josephine Butler (1828–1906); US doctor Josephine Baker (1873–1945); US actress Josephine Hull (1884–1957);

Scottish playwright, crime novelist Josephine Tey (1896–1952) (original name Elizabeth MacKintosh); US-born French dancer, singer Josephine Baker (1906–75); UK opera singers Josephine Veasey (b.1930), Josephine Barstow (b.1940); UK actress Josephine Tewson (b.1941); US writer Josephine Humphreys (b.1945); UK ballerina Josephine Jewkes (b.1964).

Josh An independently adopted diminutive of JOSHUA or JOSIAH, adopted occasionally by English speakers from the 19th century. The name was made famous in literature by the US humorist Josh Billings (1818–85) (original name Henry Wheeler Shaw), who used it for his first book, *Josh Billings, His Sayings* (1865).

US baseball player Josh Gibson (1912–47); US blues singer Josh White (1915–69); UK jockey Josh Gifford (b.1941); US actor Josh Hartnet (b.1977).

Joshua A biblical name, from Hebrew *Yĕhōshū'a*, 'Yah [that is, Jehovah] saves', in regular use among English speakers, especially Jews, from the 18th to the mid-19th century, after which it declined in the UK while undergoing a revival in the US in the 1950s. In the UK it then enjoyed a spectacular comeback in the 1990s. In the Bible Joshua led the Children of Israel to the Promised Land after the death of Moses. In George Eliot's novel *Adam Bede* (1859) Joshua Rann is a shoemaker and parish clerk. Diminutives include JOE and JOSH, both in independent use.

US stage director Joshua Logan (1908–88); Zimbabwean politician Joshua Nkomo (1917–99); US conductor, pianist Joshua Rifkin (b.1944); US-born UK violinist Joshua Bell (b.1967).

Josiah A biblical name, from Hebrew *Yōshīyāh*, 'Yah supports' (Yah being Jehovah). The name has been in irregular English-speaking use from the 17th century, although it is now mostly rare. It was borne by two English potters, Josiah Wedgwood (1730–95) and Josiah Spode (1754–1827). In the Bible Josiah is a king of Judah. The Rev. Josiah Crawley is the incumbent of Hogglestock in Anthony Trollope's novel *Framley Parsonage*

(1861), and Josiah Borden is a character in Eugene O'Neill's tragedy *Mourning Becomes Electra* (1931). The US humorist Marietta Holley (1836–1926) used the pen name 'Josiah Allen's Wife' for her many books, the last of which was *Josiah Allen on the Woman Question* (1914). The diminutive JOSH is used in its own right.

Josie An independent adoption of a diminutive of JOSEPHINE, taken up by English speakers in the early 20th century. Josie Brooke is one of the children of John and Meg Brooke (formerly Meg March) in the sequels to Louisa M. Alcott's children's novel *Little Women* (1868). The name's own usual diminutive is JO.

UK actress Josie Lawrence (b.1959).

Joss (m.) An independently adopted diminutive of JOCELYN, in select English-speaking use from the late 19th century.

UK actors Joss Ambler (1900–59), Joss Ackland (b.1928) (original first names Sidney Edmond Jocelyn).

Joss (f.) see **Jocelyn** (f.).

Josslyn see **Jocelyn** (m).

Jotham A biblical name, from Hebrew *Yōthām*, 'Yah [that is, Jehovah] is perfect', in rare English-speaking use from the 17th century. In the Bible Jotham is the youngest surviving son of Gideon after the massacre of his brothers by Abimelech. Jotham Riddle is a character in James Fenimore Cooper's novel *The Pioneers* (1823).

Joy An adoption of the ordinary word. The name has been in English-speaking use since medieval times but was seized on in the 17th century by Puritans, who aimed to be 'joyful in the Lord'. From then on it enjoyed modest favour, with a slight increase in popularity to the 1950s, after which it declined.

Austrian-born wildlife expert, working in Kenya, Joy Adamson (1910–80); UK film animator Joy Batchelor (1914–91); UK actress Joy Shelton (1922–2000).

Joyce The name is either an adoption of the surname or an English form of the Norman male name *Josce*, itself ultimately of Celtic origin and meaning 'lord'. The popular association is with JOY or the ordinary words *joy* or *rejoice*. The name was taken up generally by English speakers from the 19th century, but after booming in the 1920s it is now much less common. In literary use Joyce Hallijohn is a servant to Lady Isabel Carlyle in Mrs Henry Wood's novel *East Lynne* (1861), while in Edna Lyall's novel *In the Golden Days* (1885) the central character is named Joyce (although the story itself is set in the 17th century). A frequent diminutive is JOY, which is in independent use.

UK actress Joyce Carey (1898–1993); UK golfer Joyce Wethered (1901–97); UK comedienne Joyce Grenfell (1910–79); UK crime novelist Joyce Porter (1924–90); US actress Joyce Van Patten (b.1934); US novelist Joyce Carol Oates (b.1938); Scottish artist Joyce Cairns (b.1947).

Juan The usual Spanish form of English JOHN, enjoying some favour among English speakers, mostly in the US. The name is famous as that of the proverbial ruthless seducer Don Juan, who appears in many works of the 17th to 19th centuries, such as Mozart's opera *Don Juan* (*Don Giovanni*, 1787) and Byron's epic satire *Don Juan* (1819–24). In George Eliot's poem *The Spanish Gypsy* (1868) Juan is the poet and minstrel in love with Fedalma.

Juanita An English adoption of the Spanish diminutive of the male name *Juan* (English JOHN), in select English-speaking use from the 19th century, mainly in the US where it was introduced by Spanish settlers. A diminutive *Nita* exists.

US actress Juanita Hansen (1895–1961); US actress, singer Juanita Hall

(1901–68); US actress Juanita Moore (b.1922); US fantasy writer Juanita Coulson (b.1933).

Jubal A biblical name, from Hebrew *Jōbel*, 'horn', 'trumpet' (giving English *jubilee*), found in isolated adoption by English speakers from the 17th century. In the Bible Jubal is the son of Lamech, regarded as the 'father of all such as handle the harp and organ' (Genesis 4.21). He appears in biblical guise in George Eliot's poem *The Legend of Jubal* (1874).

US military leader Jubal A. Early (1816–94).

Judah A biblical name, from Hebrew *Yĕhūdhāh*, 'he who is praised', in rarish use among English speakers from the 17th century. In the Bible Judah is the fourth son of Jacob and Leah and the ancestor of one of the twelve tribes of Egypt: 'And she conceived again, and bare a son: and she said, Now will I praise the Lord: therefore she called his name Judah' (Genesis 29.35). Judah Eddison is a character in Theodore Dreiser's novel *The Titan* (1914). JUDAS and JUDE are directly related names.

Judas A biblical name, the Greek form of JUDAH, in only very select English-speaking use. The name occurs in the Bible for various people, but is notoriously associated with Judas Iscariot, the apostle who betrayed Christ. (There is another apostle named Judas, referred to as Judas son of James in St Matthew and Jude son of James in Acts.) Also in the Bible is Judas Maccabaeus, who liberated Judea from the Syrians. In English literature Judas is a corporal and cowardly knave in John Fletcher's play *Bonduca* (1614). The name has never become popular as a result of its generic sense of 'traitor'. JUDAH and JUDE are directly related names.

Jude A biblical name, the English shortened form of JUDAS, taken up by some English speakers from the 17th century. In the Bible Jude is an alternative name for the apostle Judas, son of James (Judas Thaddaeus), to whom the Epistle of Jude is ascribed. (The spelling was doubtless adopted to distinguish this Judas from the notorious Judas Iscariot.) In literature the name is famous as that of the fated Jude Fawley, the central character of Thomas Hardy's novel *Jude the Obscure* (1894–5).

Judi An independently adopted variant (or diminutive) of JUDITH or a respelling of JUDY, in general favour among English speakers from the 1950s. (Those listed below were all originally Judith.)

UK actress Dame Judi Dench (b.1934); UK TV presenter Judi Spiers (b.1953); UK actress Judi Bowker (b.1954).

Judith A biblical name, from Hebrew *Yēhūdhīth*, 'woman of Judea', 'Jewess'. The name was not common in English-speaking use until the 19th century, since when it has remained fairly popular, especially as a Jewish name, enjoying a peak of popularity in the 1950s and 1960s. In the Bible Judith is one of the wives of Esau, while in the Apocrypha (in the book named for her) she is a beautiful young widow who saves her native town by using trickery to kill its besieger, the Persian general Holofernes. Other literary bearers of the name include Judith Hutter, daughter of Tom Flutter in James Fenimore Cooper's novel *The Deerslayer* (1841); Judith Anderson, wife of the Rev. Anthony Anderson in George Bernard Shaw's play *The Devil's Disciple* (1897); and the central character of Hugh Walpole's novel *Judith Paris* (1931) and of the Irish writer Brian Moore's novel *Judith Hearne* (1955, later retitled *The Lonely Passion of Judith Hearne*). The diminutives JODY, JUDI and JUDY are now in independent use.

Australian actress Dame Judith Anderson (1898–1992); UK actress Judith Furse (1912–74); US novelists Judith Krantz (b.1928), Judith Rossner (b.1935); UK TV presenter Judith Chalmers (b.1935); US opera singer Judith Nelson (b.1939); US ballerina Judith Jamison (b.1943); UK actress Judith Paris (b.1944); US actress Judith Ivey (b.1951); UK athlete Judith Oakes (b.1958).

Judy This name is a diminutive form of JUDITH in independent use. It has been in English-speaking use from the 18th century, with a revival in the 1920s after a fall from favour from the 1850s, doubtless through its association with *judy* as a colloquial word for a woman of low morals. The name is well known from the popular *Punch and Judy* puppet show, although Punch's wife was originally named Joan. Charles Dickens's novel *Bleak House* (1852–3) has Judy Smallweed as the granddaughter of the blackmailer Joshua Smallweed, while in George Bernard Shaw's play *John Bull's Other Island* (1904) Judy Doyle is the aunt of Laurence Doyle. The variant spelling JUDI is in independent use.

UK actress Judy Campbell (b.1916); US comedian Judy Canova (1916–83) (original first name Juliette); US actress Judy Garland (1922–69) (original name Frances Gumm); UK actress Judy Parfitt (b.c.1930); US children's writer Judy Blume (b.1938); US folksinger Judy Collins (b.1939) (original first name Judith); UK swimmer Judy Grinham (b.1939) (original first name Judith); UK actresses Judy Carne (b.1939) (original name Joyce Botterill), Judy Cornwell (b.1940), Judy Loe (b.1947); Australian actress Judy McBurney (b.1948); UK actress Judy Geeson (b.1948); UK TV presenter Judy Finnigan (b.1948); New Zealand-born Scottish ballerina Judy Mohekey (b.1954); UK hang glider Judy Leden (b.1959); UK actress Judy Brooke (b.1970).

Jules (m.) A name that is either a French form of JULIUS or an independently adopted diminutive of JULIAN. It has been in select use among English speakers from the late 19th century. In Rudyard Kipling's short story 'The Horse Marines' in *A Diversity of Creatures* (1917) Jules is a French sailor. The spelling variant *Jools* exists, as for the UK pop keyboardist Jools Holland (b.1958) (original first name Julian).

US show business entrepreneur Jules Stein (1896–1981); US actor Jules Munshin (1915–70); US cartoonist, writer Jules Feiffer (b.1929).

Jules (f.) see **Julia, Julie, Juliet.**

Julia An adoption of the Latin name, itself the feminine form of JULIUS, and in English-speaking use, at first selectively, from the 16th century, with a recent popularity peak in the second half of the 1960s. Shakespeare's *Two Gentlemen of Verona* (1592–3) has Julia as a lady of Verona, her name representing an English form of the Italian name *Giulia*. In Tobias Smollett's novel *Peregrine Pickle* (1751) Julia Pickle is Peregrine's sister, while Julia Melville is a friend of Lydia Languish in Richard Brinsley Sheridan's play *The Rivals* (1775). The French form of the name, JULIE, is in independent use. A diminutive *Jules* is sometimes found.

US author of 'The Battle Hymn of the Republic' Julia Ward Howe (1819–1910); UK actresses Julia Foster (b.1941), Julia Lockwood (b.1941); UK singer, comedienne Julia Mackenzie (b.1942); UK rabbi, writer, broadcaster Julia Neuberger (b.1950); UK singer Julia Fordham (b.1962); US actress Julia Roberts (b.1967) (original first name Julie); UK actress Julia Sawalha (b.1968).

Julian An English form of the Late Latin name *Julianus*, itself a derivative of JULIUS. The name has been in fairly regular if select English-speaking use from the 18th century, with a recent popularity peak in the 1960s. It is familiar historically from various early figures, such as (the probably mythical) St Julian the Hospitaller, patron of travellers, and the 4th-century Roman emperor Julian the Apostate, who attempted to revive paganism. At one time the name was in female use as a fore-runner of the modern GILLIAN, hence the famous 14th-century mystic, Julian of Norwich. Count Julian is a charac-ter in Robert Southey's poem *Roderick* (1814), and the central character of Walter Scott's novel *Peveril of the Peak* (1823) is Julian Peveril. JOLYON is a variant form of the name, while JULES is a regular diminutive in independent use. The spelling *Julyan* also occurs.

UK artist Julian Trevelyan (1910–88); UK crime writer Julian Symons (1912–94); UK film producer Julian Wintle (1913–80); UK actor Julian

Orchard (1930–79); UK composer of musicals Julian Slade (b.1930); UK guitarist Julian Bream (b.1933); UK actor Julian Glover (b.1935); UK TV presenter Julian Pettifer (b.1935); UK playwright Julian Mitchell (b.1935); UK actor Julian Holloway (b.1944); UK writer Julian Barnes (b.1946); UK cellist Julian Lloyd Webber (b.1951); UK actor Julian Sands (b.1957); UK TV entertainer Julian Clary (b.1959).

Juliana A feminine form of the Latin name *Julianus* (English JULIAN), in select English-speaking use from the 16th century, but rare today. The name is found in literature for Juliana, the wife of Virolet in Philip Massinger's play *The Double Marriage* (*c*.1621). Variant forms *Julianna* and *Julianne* occur, as well as the derivative compound *Julie Ann*.

UK children's writer Juliana Ewing (1841–85); US singer Juliana Hatfield (b.1967).

Julie A French form of JULIA, in English-speaking use from the late 19th century and, for almost the whole of the 20th century, much more popular than JULIA itself. A diminutive *Jules* exists.

US actresses Julie Harris (b.1925), Julie Adams (b.1926) (earlier Julia; original first names Betty May); US popular singer Julie London (1926–2000); UK singer, actress Julie Andrews (b.1934) (original name Julia Elizabeth Wells); UK actresses Julie Christie (b.1941), Julie Goodyear (b.1943), Julie Walters (b.1950); US actress Julie Hagerty (b.1955); UK actress Julie Dawn Cole (b.1957); UK writer, journalist Julie Burchill (b.1960); US jockey Julie Krone (b.1963); UK actresses Julie Foy (b.1970), Julie Buckfield (b.1976).

Juliet The name is an English form of the Italian name *Giulietta*, itself a diminutive of *Giulia* (English JULIA). It has been in regular use among English speakers from the 16th century, and enjoyed a special vogue for a time in the 1960s. The name gained lasting fame from the heroine of Shakespeare's *Romeo and Juliet* (1595). He used the name only once again, for the beloved of Claudio in *Measure for Measure* (1604). In Agatha Christie's novel *They Do It with Mirrors* (1952) (US title *Murder* *with Mirrors*) Juliet ('Jolly') Bellever is Carrie Louise Serrocold's elderly nurse. The French spelling JULIETTE is in independent use. The usual diminutive is either JULIE, now also used independently, or *Jules*.

UK royal portrait painter Juliet Pannett (b.1911); UK actress Juliet Prowse (1936–96); New Zealand-born UK feminist Juliet Mitchell (b.1940); UK actresses Juliet Mills (b.1941), Juliet Stevenson (b.1956), Juliet Aubrey (b.1967).

Juliette The French form of JULIET, in occasional independent use among English speakers from the early 20th century.

French popular singer Juliette Gréco (b.1927); UK actress Juliette Kaplan (b.1939); US actress Juliette Lewis (b.1973).

Julius An English adoption of the Roman clan name, itself of uncertain origin. Bearers of the name claimed descent from *Iulus*, the son of Aeneas. The name found some favour among English speakers from the 19th century to the early 20th, after which it declined. It was made world famous by the 2nd-century BC Roman general and statesman Gaius Julius Caesar and was also the name of three popes (down to the 16th century). Julius Caesar himself appears in various literary works, notably Shakespeare's tragedy *Julius Caesar* (1599). JULES is a directly related name.

US flautist Julius Baker (b.1915); Tanzanian statesman Julius Nyerere (1922–99).

Julyan see **Julian**.

June An adoption of the name of the month, when spring passes into summer, in increasing favour among English speakers from the early years of the 20th century to the late 1930s, but then suffering a gradual decline. The name is suitable for a girl born in this month. It occurs in literature for the daughter of 'Young' Jolyon in John Galsworthy's *Forsyte* sequence (1906–22).

US screenwriter June Mathis (1892–1927); US actresses June Collyer (1907–68) (original name Dorothy Heermance), June Lang (b.1915), June Havoc (b.1916) (original name Ellen Evangeline Hovick); US dancer, actress June Allyson (b.1917) (original name Ella Geisman); US actresses June Vincent (b.1919), June Preisser (1921–84); US popular singer June Christy (1925–90) (original name Shirley Luster); UK actress June Whitfield (b.1925); US actresses June Lockhart (b.1925), June Haver (b.1926); US country singer June Carter (b.23 June 1929); UK writer, broadcaster June Knox-Mawer (b.1930); UK crime writer June Thomson (b.24 June 1930); UK actresses June Thorburn (1931–67), June Ritchie (b.1939); UK fashion editor June Marsh (b.1948); US opera singer June Anderson (b.1950); Scottish artist June Redfern (b.16 June 1951).

Junior From the nickname for a young person, or the US family designation 'Jr' for a younger namesake. Perhaps in some cases the name has been felt to be a form of JULIAN, or some similar name. It is found in occasional favour from the early 20th century, mainly in the US.

US actors Junior Durkin (1915–35) (original first name Trent), Junior Coghlan (b.1916) (original first name Frank); US comedian Junior Samples (1927–83) (original first name Alvin); US jazzman Junior Mance (b.1928) (original name Julian Clifford Mance Jr); US bluesman Junior Wells (1934–98) (original name Amos Blakemore); US bandleader Junior Walker (1942–25) (original name Autry DeWalt).

Justie see **Justin, Justine**.

Justin A name that is an English form of the Latin name *Justinus*, a derivative of JUSTUS. It has long been favoured in Ireland and was in some vogue generally among English speakers in the 1970s. The name is familiar as that of various early saints, notably the 2nd-century Greek theologian Justin Martyr. Diminutives *Justie* and *Justy* occur.

Irish writer, politician Justin M'Carthy (1830–1912); US industrialist Justin Dart (1907–84); UK restaurateur Justin de Blank (b.1927); UK opera singer Justin Lavender (b.1951); US actor Justin Henry (b.1971).

Justine A French feminine form of JUSTIN, in modish English-speaking use from the 19th century, with a more popular adoption for a while in the 1970s. The name became familiar in literature from the wife of Nessim Hosnani in Lawrence Durrell's novel *Justine* (1957), the first of the *Alexandria Quartet*. The variant *Justina* was the former regular form, and occurs in Anthony Trollope's novel *Framley Parsonage* (1861) as the name of Lady Meredith's daughter. It is still found occasionally today. The diminutives *Justie* and *Justy* are sometimes used.

US actress Justine Bateman (b.1966); UK pop singer Justine Frischmann (b.1969); UK actress Justine Kerrigan (b.1971).

Justus A Latin name, meaning 'fair', 'just', in rarish English-speaking use from the late 19th century. It is known from various saints, including the (probably mythical) 3rd-century boy martyr Justus of Beauvais. One such saint gave the name of the Cornish town St Just.

Justy see **Justin**, **Justine**.

K

Kane This is an English form of the Gaelic name *Cathán*, itself a diminutive of Irish *cath*, 'battle'. It has been in select English-speaking use from the 1950s, enjoying greatest favour in Australia.

US actor Kane Richmond (1906–73) (original name Frederick W. Bowditch).

Karel see **Carol** (m.).

Karen This once highly popular name is an independent adoption of a Danish diminutive of the equivalent of English CATHERINE. It was first taken up by English speakers in the 1920s, when it was introduced to the US by Scandinavian settlers. Its peak period of adoption was in the 1960s, since when it has dropped to a much more modest level. The name may also have been popularly helped by the writings of the Danish author Karen Blixen (1885–1962), notably her *Out of Africa* (1937), the account of her experiences in British East Africa (now Kenya), published simultaneously in Danish and English. Fictional bearers of the name include Karen Blum, wife of the sculptor Walther Blum, the central character of Oliver Onions's short story *The Smile of Karen* (1935), and Karen Stone, the wealthy widowed actress who is the central character of Tennessee Williams's novelette *The Roman Spring of Mrs Stone* (1950). Variant spellings are KARIN, in independent use, and *Karyn*, the latter as for US R&B singer Karyn White (b.1965).

German-born US psychoanalyst Karen Horney (1885–1952); US actress Karen Morley (b.1905) (original name Mildred Linton); German actress Karen Verne (1915–67) (original name Ingabor Katrine Klinckerfuss); US actress Karen Black (b.1942); UK religious writer, broadcaster Karen

Armstrong (b.1944); US actress Karen Valentine (b.1948); UK popular singer Karen Kay (b.1948) (original name Adrienne Pringle); US pop singer Karen Carpenter (1950–83); Canadian ballerina Karen Kain (b.1951); South African swimmer Karen Muir (b.1952); UK actress Karen Dotrice (b.1955); UK judoist Karen Briggs (b.1963); Scottish athlete Karen Hargrave (b.1965); UK actress Karen Murden (b.1970); UK swimmer Karen Pickering (b.1971).

Karin An independently adopted variant of KAREN, in select use among English speakers from the 1920s.

US actresses Karin Booth (1919–92), Karin MacCarthy (b.1942).

Karl see **Carl**.

Karyn see **Karen**.

Kasey see **Casey**.

Kaspar, **Kasper** see **Caspar**.

Katarina see **Catherine**.

Kate An independently adopted diminutive of CATHARINE, CATHERINE, KATHARINE, KATHERINE, KATHLEEN, KATHRYN, KATRINA or a variant form of any of these, in English-speaking use from medieval times, and popular from the late 19th century, though with something of a 'slump' from the 1930s to the 1960s. Shakespeare has the name for two leading characters. In *Henry V* (1599) the king woos (and wins) Katharine, daughter of the king of France, and from addressing her formally at first soon moves to the more intimate diminutive. It is in *The Taming of the Shrew* (*c.*1592) that Petruchio makes great play with the name on first meeting Katharina (the 'shrew' of the title) as her potential suitor:

Petruchio: Good morrow, Kate; for that's your name, I hear.

Katharina: Well you have heard, but something hard of hearing: They call me Katharine that do talk of me.

Petruchio: You lie, in faith; for you are call'd plain Kate,
And bonny Kate, and sometimes Kate the curst;
But, Kate, the prettiest Kate in Christendom;
Kate of Kate-Hall, my super-dainty Kate,
For dainties are all cates [delicacies]: and therefore, Kate,
Take this of me, Kate of my consolation.

(This play also has 'Kiss me, Kate', adopted as the title of the Broadway musical based on it.) Later characters of the name include Kate Hardcastle in Oliver Goldsmith's play *She Stoops to Conquer* (1773), and Kate Nickleby, sister of the central character in Charles Dickens's novel *Nicholas Nickleby* (1838–9). The variant spelling *Cate* was popularized by the Australian actress Cate Blanchett (b.1970), while regular diminutives are KATIE and KATY.

UK music-hall entertainer Kate Carney (1869–1950); Irish writer Kate O'Brien (1897–1974); Polish-born US travel writer Kate Simon (1912–90) (original first name Kaila); UK-born Canadian actress Kate Reid (1930–93); US actress Kate Manx (1930–64); US feminist Kate Millett (b.1934) (original first name Katherine); UK actress Kate O'Mara (b.1939); US country singer Kate Wolf (1942–86) (original name Kathryn Louise Allen); UK TV reporter Kate Adie (b.1945) (original first name Kathryn); UK politician Kate Hoey (b.1946) (original first name Catharine); UK actress Kate Dove (b.1947); Canadian-born UK actress Kate Nelligan (b.1951); UK pop singer Kate Bush (b.1958) (original first name Catherine); UK actress Kate Beckinsale (b.1974); Australian actress Kate Ritchie (b.1980).

Katharine An independent form of CATHERINE, taken up mainly in the US but also slowly gaining in popularity in the UK from the 1960s. Common diminutives are KATHY, KATIE and KATY, all in independent use. *Kath* is also found.

Australian writer Katharine Prichard (1883–1969); US actresses Katharine Hepburn (b.1907), Katharine Ross (b.1942), Katharine Houghton (b.1945), Katharine Rogers (b.1960).

Katherine An independent variant form of CATHERINE, increasingly popular in English-speaking use from the 1960s.

Common diminutives are KATHY, KATIE and KATY, all in independent use. *Kath* is also found.

New Zealand-UK writer Katherine Mansfield (1888–1923) (original first name Kathleen); US writer Katherine Anne Porter (1890–1980); US actress Katherine Alexander (1901–81); Welsh crime writer Katherine John (b.1948) (original name Karen Jones); UK fashion designer Katherine Hamnett (b.1952).

Kathleen An English form of the Irish name *Caitlín*, itself ultimately a form of CATHERINE. The name was highly popular in the UK in the 1920s, but has since mostly declined in favour, although there was a revival of interest in the 1950s. In the US its vogue followed rather later. Julia Crawford's memorable 'Kathleen Mavourneen' (where *Mavourneen* represents the Irish for 'my dear one') dates from 1835, and the popular American song 'I'll take you home again Kathleen' was first heard in the 1870s. The variant spellings *Cathleen* and *Kathlyn* (influenced by KATHRYN) are occasionally found, as for the UK actress Cathleen Nesbitt (1888–1982) and US actress Kathlyn Williams (1888–1960). Common diminutives are KATHY, KATIE and KATY, all in independent use. *Kath* also exists.

UK actress Kathleen Harrison (1898–1995); UK writer Kathleen Nott (b.c.1909); UK singer Kathleen Ferrier (1912–53); Irish actress Kathleen Ryan (1922–85); UK actress Kathleen Byron (b.1922); UK journalist, writer Kathleen Tynan (b.1937–95); US actress Kathleen Widdoes (b.1939); US actresses Kathleen Turner (b.1954), Kathleen Beller (b.1955).

Kathryn An independently adopted variant of CATHERINE, taken up among English speakers, especially in the US, from the early 20th century, and remaining in steady favour since. The variant spelling *Cathryn* is fairly common, as for the US actress Cathryn Damon (1931–87). Diminutives *Kath*, *Kathie* and KATHY exist, the last in independent use.

US actresses Kathryn Givney (1897–1978), Kathryn Grayson (b.1922) (original name Zelma Hedrick), Kathryn Grant (b.1933) (original name

Olive Grandstaff), Kathryn Harrold (b.1950); UK opera singer Kathryn Harries (b.1951); US film director Kathryn Bigelow (b.1951); UK athlete Kathryn Cook (b.1960).

Kathy An independently adopted diminutive of CATHERINE, KATHERINE, KATHLEEN, KATHRYN, or any directly related variants of these, in modest favour among English speakers from the 1950s. A less common spelling is CATHY.

UK jazz musician Kathy Stobart (b.1925); UK actress Kathy Staff (b.1928); US golfer Kathy Whitworth (b.1939) (original first name Kathrynne); UK pop singer Kathy Kirby (b.1940); US writer Kathy Acker (1944–97); US actress Kathy Bates (b.1948); US tennis player Kathy Jordan (b.1959); US country singer Kathy Mattea (b.1959); UK actress Kathy Burke (b.1964); UK hockey player Kathy Johnson (b.1967); UK swimmer Kathy Read (b.1969).

Kati see **Katy**.

Katie An independently adopted diminutive of KATE or one of its source names, in select but regular English-speaking use from the mid-19th century. The variant spelling KATY is also found in its own right.

UK actress Katie Johnson (1878–1957); Italian-born UK broadcaster, writer Katie Boyle (b.1926) (original first name Caterina); UK rower Katie Brownlow (b.1964) (original first name Katharine).

Katina This is a modern Greek diminutive form of CATHERINE, in some favour among English speakers from the early 20th century.

Greek actress Katina Paxinou (1900–73); UK actress Katina Noble (b.1950).

Katrina A continental European form of CATHERINE, taken up by English speakers from the early 20th century and steadily increasing in popularity from the 1960s.

UK TV actress Katrina Buchanan (b.1963).

Katy An independently adopted diminutive of KATE, in select English-speaking adoption from the mid-19th century and increasing in popularity from the 1970s. In fiction it is famous from the schoolgirl Katy Carr, the central character of Susan Coolidge's stories, beginning with the perennially popular *What Katy Did* (1872), which probably did much to boost the name. The music-hall song 'K-K-K-Katy' (1918) also brought the name before the public. The variant spelling KATIE exists in its own right, and *Kati* occasionally occurs, as for the UK radio presenter Kati Whitaker (b.1957) (original first name Catherine).

UK mountaineer Katy Richardson (1864–1927) (original first name Kathleen); Mexican-born US actress Katy Jurado (b.1927) (original name Maria Jurado Garcia).

Kay (m.) The name is probably an English form of the Latin name *Gaius*, itself of uncertain origin. It is occasionally found among English speakers, and is familiar from Sir Kay, the steward to King Arthur in Arthurian legend. His churlish nature makes him unattractive for purposes of first-name adoption, however, and this may partly explain the rarity of the name. Where it is found, it may be simply a short form of a name that begins with *K-*.

US bandleader Kay Kyser (1906–85) (original first names James King Kern).

Kay (f.) This is the independently adopted diminutive of a name beginning with *K* or a hard *C*, especially KATHERINE and CATHERINE, and their directly related variants. It was taken up by English speakers from the late 19th century, and increased in popularity to the 1960s, after which it gradually declined. A variant spelling is *Kaye*, as for the UK children's writer and publisher Kaye Webb (1914–96).

US actress Kay Francis (1899–1968) (original first name Katherine); US writer Kay Boyle (1902–92) (original first name Katherine); US actress Kay Johnson (1904–75) (original name Catherine Townsend); UK actresses Kay Hammond (1909–80) (original name Dorothy Standing), Kay Walsh (b.1914); US actress Kay Medford (1914–80); US pop singer Kay Starr (b.1922) (original name Katherine Starks); US actress Kay Ballard (b.1926) (original name Catherine Balotta); UK actress Kay Kendall (1927–59) (original name Justine McCarthy); US country singer Kay T. Oslin (b.1942); UK magazine editor Kay Goddard (b.1954).

Kayleigh A name that may be a development from KELLY or KYLIE, influenced by LEIGH. It has enjoyed increasing popularity among English speakers from the 1970s and may owe some of its favour to the Marillion pop hit 'Kayleigh' (1985). Variant spellings *Kayley* and *Kayly* exist, among others.

Keir From the (Scottish) surname, and in select, mainly Scottish use from the 19th century. The name's original adoption may have been a popular tribute to the Scottish-born politician and Labour Party leader, Keir Hardie (1856–1915). (His original first names were James Keir, with Keir his mother's maiden name.)

US actor Keir Dullea (b.1936).

Keith From the (Scottish) surname, itself from the town southeast of Elgin. The name was taken up more generally among English speakers in the 19th century, increasing in popularity to reach a 'high' in the second half of the 1950s, since when it has declined.

New Zealand prime minister Sir Keith Holyoake (1904–83); UK politician Sir Keith Joseph (1918–94); Australian-born UK actor Keith Michell (b.1926); UK radio DJ Keith Fordyce (b.1928); UK journalist, novelist Keith Waterhouse (b.1929); UK actor Keith Barron (b.1934); UK rock musician Keith Richards (b.1943); UK TV chef Keith Floyd (b.1943); UK politician Keith Vaz (b.1956); UK TV presenter Keith Chegwin (b.1957); US R&B singer Keith Sweat (b.1961).

Kellie see **Kelly** (f.).

Kelly (m.) An adoption of the (Irish) surname, from the 1960s becoming increasingly popular as a female name in the English-speaking world.

US country singer Kelly Harrell (1899–1942); US aircraft designer Kelly Johnson (1910–90) (original first name Clarence); US civil rights leader Kelly Alexander (1915–85); New Zealand tennis player Kelly Evernden (b.1961); US tennis player Kelly Jones (b.1964).

Kelly (f.) A female adoption of the male name KELLY, popularly associated with names such as KERRY, KYLE and KYLIE, especially in Australia. Its popularity among English speakers increased rapidly from the 1960s to the 1980s, since when it has tailed off considerably. An initial boost to the name may have been given by the US actress Grace Kelly (1928–82), first on screen in the 1950s. A variant spelling is *Kellie*.

US actresses Kelly McGillis (b.1957), Kelly Lynch (b.1959), Kelly Le Brock (b.1960), Kelly Preston (b.1962); UK actresses Kelly Lawrence (b.1966), Kelly Clark (b.1970), Kelly Greenwood (b.1982).

Kelvin A name taken up by English speakers from the 1920s, and perhaps evolving from a blend of names such as CALVIN and MELVIN, influenced by the title of the UK scientist William Thomson, Baron Kelvin of Largs (1824–1907). His own title derives from the Scottish river Kelvin.

UK speedway rider Kelvin Tatum (b.1964).

Ken An independently adopted diminutive of KENNETH or of some other name beginning *Ken-*. The name came into regular use among English speakers in the 20th century. The diminutive KENNY is in independent use.

US actors Ken Maynard (1895–1973), Ken Curtis (1916–91) (original name Curtis Gates); UK film director Ken Russell (b.1927); UK jazzman Ken Colyer (1928–88); UK actors Ken Jones (b.1930), Ken Parry (b.1930); UK comedian Ken Dodd (b.1931); Australian tennis player Ken Rosewall (b.1934); US writer Ken Kesey (1935–2001); UK film director Ken Loach (b.1936); US actor Ken Kercheval (b.1936); UK politician Ken Livingstone (b.1945); UK writer Ken Follett (b.1949); Scottish radio presenter Ken Bruce (b.1951).

Kendal From the surname, and a name in occasional favour among English speakers from the mid-19th century, perhaps originally as a compliment to the UK actor-manager William Kendal (1843–1917) (whose original surname was actually Grimston). The variant spelling *Kendall* is also found.

Kendrick From the (Welsh or Scottish) surname, and in select English-speaking use from the mid-19th century. The surname may have been adopted simply because of its suggestion of KENNETH or some other name beginning *Ken-*. The variant form *Kenrick* exists.

Kenelm This represents the Old English name *Cenelm*, formed from *cēne*, 'bold', 'keen', and *helm*, 'helmet', 'protection', so 'bold defender'. One of the earliest bearers of the name was the English writer, naval commander and diplomat Sir Kenelm Digby (1603–1665), and it is also found in occasional English-speaking use from the 19th century. It is familiar historically from St Kenelm, who lived in the 9th century.

Irish writer Kenelm Digby (1800–80).

Kennedy An adoption of the Irish surname, in select use among English speakers from the mid-20th century. In the US, the name was almost certainly given in many cases as a tribute to a member of the famous Kennedy family, such as President John F. Kennedy (1917–63) or his brother, Senator Robert F. Kennedy (1925–68).

Kenneth The name is an English form of two Gaelic names: *Cinead*, perhaps meaning 'born of fire', and *Cainneach*, meaning 'handsome'. It was originally a Scottish name, but was taken up more generally by English speakers from the late 19th century, reaching a peak of popularity in the 1920s in the UK and in the 1950s in the US. It is historically famous from two kings of Scotland, Kenneth I, Kenneth MacAlpin (d.*c*.858), who subdued the Picts and is regarded as the founder of the Scottish kingdom, and Kenneth II, who warred with the English in the 10th century. Sir Kenneth is the central character of Walter Scott's novel *The Talisman* (1825), set in the time of the Crusades. In Sinclair Lewis's novel *Babbitt* (1922) Kenneth Escott marries Verona Babbitt. Variant spellings are *Kennith* and *Kenith*, and the usual diminutives, both in independent use, are KEN and KENNY.

Scottish-born writer Kenneth Grahame (1859–1932); US adventure novelist Kenneth Roberts (1885–1957); UK TV art critic Kenneth Clark, Lord Clark (1903–83); UK actors Kenneth More (1914–82), Kenneth Connor (1918–93); Zambian president Kenneth Kaunda (b.1924); UK actor Kenneth Williams (1926–88); UK choreographer Sir Kenneth MacMillan (1929–92); UK TV newsreader Kenneth Kendall (b.1924); UK politicians Kenneth Baker (b.1934); Kenneth Clarke (b.1940); UK actor Kenneth Cranham (b.1944); Northern Ireland-born UK actor Kenneth Branagh (b.1960).

Kenny The name is an independently adopted diminutive of KEN or its source name KENNETH, in regular but modest English-speaking use from the early 20th century.

US radio personality Kenny Delmar (1911–84); US popular singer Kenny Baker (1912–85); US-born Danish jazz pianist Kenny Drew (1928–93); UK bandleader, jazz trumpeter Kenny Ball (b.1930); US country singer Kenny Rogers (b.1938); UK entertainer Kenny Everett (1944–95) (original name Maurice Cole); Scottish footballer Kenny Dalglish (b.1951); Northern Ireland rugby player Kenny Hooks (b.1960).

Kenrick see **Kendrick**.

Kent From the surname, rather than the English county, and in select English-speaking use from the 20th century, mainly in the US.

US actors Kent Smith (1907–85) (originally second name, first being Frank), Kent Taylor (1907–87) (original name Louis Weiss), Kent Douglass (1908–66) (original name Robert Douglas Montgomery), Kent McCord (b.1942).

Kerenhappuch A biblical name, from a Hebrew word meaning 'horn of eyelash paint'. The name was adopted by English Puritans in the 17th century but has been in only very occasional favour since, perhaps partly because of its length. In the Bible Kerenhappuch is the youngest of Job's three beautiful daughters. Correspondence in the London *Times* (1986) expressing doubts about the name's active use prompted reports of its survival, one of which was the following letter to the editor (in its entirety); 'Sir, Yours faithfully, Caroline Sophia Kerenhappuch Parkes (aged 7).' The usual diminutive is *Keren*, which more regularly represents KAREN.

Keri see **Kerry** (f.).

Kermit The name, an English form of the Gaelic surname *Mac Dhiarmaid* (which itself gave DERMOT), has found occasional favour in the English-speaking world from the 19th century. It is historically familiar from the US soldier, explorer and businessman Kermit Roosevelt (1889–1943), son of president Theodore Roosevelt and brother of Theodore Roosevelt Jr. In recent times the name has been humorously popularized by the puppet character Kermit the Frog in the US TV series *Sesame Street* (from 1969) and the similar UK series *The Muppet Show* (1976–80).

US actor Kermit Maynard (1898–1971).

Kerrie see **Kerry** (f.).

Kerry (m.) An adoption of the surname, in select English-speaking use, mostly in Australia, from the early 20th century. The variant spelling *Kerrie* also occurs.

US composer Kerry Mills (1869–1948) (original first names Frederick Allen); UK art historian Kerry Downes (b.1930); Australian businessman Kerry Packer (b.1937).

Kerry (f.) The name is of Australian origin and is probably either an alteration of KELLY or simply an adoption of the male name KERRY. It has been in general English-speaking use from the 1960s, increasing in popularity until the 1980s, after which it began a gradual decline. Variants are *Kerrie* and *Keri*, as respectively for the New Zealand fashion designer Kerrie Hughes (b.1959) and New Zealand writer Keri Hulme (b.1947).

Australian athlete Kerry Saxby (b.1961); New Zealand actress Kerry Fox (b.1966).

Kevin This is an English form of the Gaelic name *Caoimhín*, itself based on Irish *caomh*, 'gentle', 'fair', 'friend'. The name was originally solely in Irish use, but from the 1920s it was taken up by English speakers generally, reaching its peak of popularity in the 1960s, since when it has fallen from favour. Historically it is familiar from St Kevin, a patron saint of Dublin in the 7th century. A literary bearer of the name is Kevin Donnelly, a Sinn Feiner in Howard Spring's novel *My Son, My Son* (1938) (US title *O Absalom!*). *Kevan* is an occasional variant spelling, as for the UK cricketer Kevan James (b.1961), while the usual diminutive is *Kev*.

US actor Kevin McCarthy (b.1914); UK politician Kevin McNamara (b.1934); UK writer Kevin Crossley-Holland (b.1941); US actor Kevin Kline (b.1947); UK actors Kevin Lloyd (1949–98), Kevin Whately (b.1951); UK footballer Kevin Keegan (b.1951); US actor Kevin Costner (b.1955); UK actor Kevin McNally (b.1956); US actors Kevin Bacon (b.1958), Kevin Spacey (b.1959) UK actor Kevin Kennedy (b.1961); Welsh rugby player Kevin Ellis (b.1965); UK actor Kevin Carson (b.1974).

Keziah A biblical name, from Hebrew *Qĕtsī'āh*, 'cassia' (the tree yielding cinnamon), adopted by Puritans in the 17th century and in very selective use among English speakers since.

In the Bible, Keziah is the second of Job's three beautiful daughters (the eldest is Jemima, the youngest Kerenhappuch). Keziah Wesley was the sister of the 18th-century English religious leader John Wesley, and she may well have taken the name to the US. In literature Keziah Badger is a character in Harriet Beecher Stowe's novel *Oldtown Folks* (1869). A variant spelling is *Kezia*, while a diminutive is *Kizzie*.

Kid An adoption of the nickname for a young or young-looking person, which has been in select English-speaking adoption only in the 20th century. The Canadian-born UK radio and TV personality David Jensen (b.1950) began his career as a DJ at the age of sixteen, and was nicknamed 'Kid' for his youth and youthful appearance. He retained the name as his first name until about 1980.

US bandleader Kid Ory (1886–1973) (original first name Edward).

Kieran This name is an English form of the Gaelic name CIARAN (*Ciarán*), itself a diminutive of the Irish word *ciar*, 'black', so that the sense is 'little black-haired (or dark-skinned) one'. The name is still chiefly in Irish use but was adopted more generally in the English-speaking world from the 1950s, with an increase in popularity from the 1970s. Historically the name is that of two Irish saints, respectively of the 5th and 6th centuries. The variant form *Kieron* exists, as for the Irish actor Kieron Moore (b.1925).

Irish playwright, theatre critic Kieran Tunney (b.1922); Irish film director Kieran Hickey (1936–93); UK TV reporter Kieran Prendiville (b.1947).

Kim(m.) An independently adopted diminutive of KIMBERLEY, which found some favour among English speakers from the late 19th century, after which it was increasingly adopted as a female name. It is famous in literature from the central character of Rudyard Kipling's novel *Kim* (1901), although the young boy who bore it, the orphaned son of an Irish sergeant in India, had the original full name Kimball O'Hara. (*Kimball* is a surname adopted as a first name.)

UK double agent Kim Philby (1912–88) (original first names Harold Adrian Russell); US pop musician Kim Fowley (b.1939); Welsh politician Kim Howells (b.1946); UK opera singer Kim Begley (b.1952); UK racehorse trainer Kim Bailey (b.1953); UK cricketer Kim Barnett (b.1960).

Kim (f.) This name originally arose as an independently adopted diminutive of the male name KIMBERLEY, and like it was also at first used for males (see KIM). Later, it was regarded as a diminutive of the female KIMBERLEY. As the latter, it was taken up by English speakers from the 1920s, especially in the US, and increased in popularity to the 1960s, after which it mostly declined, apart from a revival in the second half of the 1980s. In literature the name is found as that of the actress Kim Ravenal in Edna Ferber's novel *Show Boat* (1926). A varient is *Kym* as for the UK actress Kym Valentine (b.1977).

US actresses Kim Hunter (b.1922) (original name Janet Cole), Kim Stanley (1925–2001) (original name Patricia Kimberly Reid), Kim Novak (b.1933) (original first name Marilyn); US singer, songwriter Kim Carnes (b.1945); Canadian prime minister Kim Campbell (b.1947) (original first names Avril Phaedra); US actresses Kim Darby (b.1947) (original name Deborah Zerby), Kim Basinger (b.1954) (original first name Kimila); UK actresses Kim Hartman (b.1955), Kim Cattrall (b.1956); US model Kim Alexis (b.1960); UK pop singer Kim Wilde (b.1960); Australian actress Kim Lewis (b.1963); US actress Kim Fields (b.1969); US singer Lil' Kim (b.1975) (original name Kimberley Jones).

Kimberley (m.) The name was adopted from that of the South African town, and was an expression of British patriotism resulting from the UK relief (1900) of Kimberley in the Boer War as an important diamond-mining centre. It is now virtually obsolescent as a male name, and has been in declining use throughout the 20th century. The variant spelling *Kimberly* also occurs.

Kimberley (f.) The name is a female adoption of the male name KIMBERLEY, which first gained general favour among English speakers from the 1940s, becoming particularly popular in the 1980s and 1990s. The variant spelling KIMBERLY is also found, and is the preferred US form of the name. The usual diminutive is KIM, in independent use.

Daughter of UK rock singer Rod Stewart, Kimberley Stewart (b.1979).

Kimberly (f.) The preferred US form of KIMBERLEY, found also in the UK from the 1950s. The regular diminutive is KIM.

King An adoption of the royal title, like that of DUKE or EARL. (Compare also LEROY.) The name has been in English-speaking use, especially latterly among black Americans, from the 19th century.

US safety-razor inventor King Camp Gillette (1855–1932); US actor King Baggott (1874–1948); US jazzman King Oliver (1885–1938) (original first name Joseph); US film director King Vidor (1894–1982); US actor King Donovan (1919–87); US saxophonist King Curtis (1934–71) (original name Curtis Ousley).

Kingsley From the surname, and in select English-speaking use from the mid-19th century. The name may have originally come into favour as a compliment to the popular UK novelist Charles Kingsley (1819–75).

UK editor Kingsley Martin (1897–1969) (originally second name, first being Basil); UK novelist Kingsley Amis (1922–95); UK footballer Kingsley Black (b.1968).

Kirk From the (Scottish) surname, and in general English-speaking use from the mid-19th century, with a slight peak of popularity in the second half of the 1980s. The latter may owe something to the character Captain James Kirk of the starship *Enterprise* in the cult US TV series *Star Trek* (1966–9). The spelling *Kirke* is sometimes found.

US actors Kirk Douglas (b.1916) (original name Issur Danielovitch Demsky), Kirk Cameron (b.1970).

Kirsten This name is a Danish or Norwegian form of CHRISTINE. It was first taken up in Scotland in the 19th century but was adopted more generally by English speakers from the 1950s, with a peak period of popularity in the 1970s. Variant forms are *Kirsteen* and *Kirstin*. A diminutive, KIRSTY, is in independent use but properly has a different origin.

Norwegian opera singer Kirsten Flagstad (1895–1962); UK hockey player Kirsten Spencer (b.1969).

Kirstie An independently adopted variant of KIRSTY, in popular English-speaking use from the 1960s. In Robert Louis Stevenson's novel *Weir of Hermiston* (1896) Christina Elliott, housekeeper to Lord Weir, is frequently referred to as Kirstie, as is her identically named niece.

US actress Kirstie Alley (b.1955).

Kirstin see **Kirsten**.

Kirsty An independently adopted Scottish diminutive of CHRISTINE, increasingly popular among English speakers generally from the 1970s. Kirsty Gilmour is the central character in the novel *Pink Sugar* (1924) by the Scottish writer 'O. Douglas' (Anna Buchan). The variant spelling KIRSTIE is in independent use.

Scottish TV presenter Kirsty Wark (b.1955); Scottish-US pop singer Kirsty MacColl (1959–2000); Scottish TV presenter Kirsty Young (b.1968).

Kit An independently adopted diminutive of CHRISTOPHER, in some favour among English speakers from the 19th century. Christopher (Kit) Nubbles is a shopboy in Charles Dickens's novel *The Old Curiosity Shop* (1840–41).

US trapper, scout Kit Carson (1809–68); UK artist Kit Williams (b.1946); UK theatrical designer Kit Surrey (b.1946).

Kitty An independently adopted diminutive of *Catharine*, CATHERINE, KATHARINE, KATHERINE, KATHLEEN or some similar directly related name. The name came into general use among English speakers in the 18th century, but is now much less common. The name has always been more popular in the US than the UK, as for the character Miss Kitty in the long-running US TV family western *Gunsmoke* (1955–75), regularly played by Amanda Blake. A variant spelling is *Kittie*, while the usual diminutive is *Kit*.

English actress Kitty Clive (1711–1785); UK tennis player Kitty Godfree (1896–1992); US opera singer Kitty Carlisle (b.1915) (original name Catherine Holzman); US country singer Kitty Wells (b.1919) (original name Muriel Ellen Deason); US biographer Kitty Kelley (b.1942); UK actress Kitty Aldridge (b.1961).

Kizzie see **Keziah**.

Kris see **Chris** (m.).

Kurt An independently adopted diminutive of the German name *Konrad* (English CONRAD), in select use among English speakers from the 1950s and gaining in popularity from the 1980s. The variant spelling *Curt* exists.

German-born US composer Kurt Weill (1900–55); US writer Kurt Vonnegut (b.1922); US rock musician Kurt Cobain (1965–94).

Kyle (m.) From the (Scottish) surname, and taken up among English speakers from the 1940s, at first in the US.

US actor Kyle MacLachlan (b.1959).

Kyle (f.) The name is a female adoption of the male name KYLE, although popularly regarded as a diminutive of KYLIE. It has gained increasing popularity among English speakers from the 1960s, with Australia leading the way.

UK publisher Kyle Cathie (b.1948).

Kylie This name is popularly derived from an Aborigine word meaning 'boomerang'. But this seems unlikely, and the name is probably a development of KYLE or even KELLY. It is first and foremost an Australian name but came into more general favour among English speakers from the late 1970s. A frequent diminutive is KYLE itself, although this usually has another origin.

Australian novelist Kylie Tennant (1912–88) (original first name Kathleen); Australian actress, pop singer Kylie Minogue (b.1968); Australian actress Kylie Watson (b.1978).

Kym see **Kim**.

L

Laban A biblical name, from Hebrew *Lābhān*, 'white', the name has found some favour among English speakers from the 17th century, when it was adopted by the Puritans, with a slight increase in popularity in the 19th century. In the Bible Laban is the father of Leah and Rebecca, Jacob's wives. In Thomas Hardy's novel *Far from the Madding Crowd* (1874) Laban Tall is a farmhand.

Lachlan This is an English form of the Scottish name *Lachlann*, earlier *Lochlann*, said to refer to an immigrant from Norway, a 'land of lochs'. The name is still mainly in Scottish use or is at least given to a person with Scottish connections. It was made famous by the Scottish-born UK soldier and colonial administrator Lachlan Macquarie (1761–1824), governor of New South Wales, Australia, who gave the name of the rivers Lachlan and Macquarie in that state. The Scottish diminutive *Lachie* exists, but the form *Lockie* is preferred in Canada.

Laetitia see **Letitia**.

Laila see **Leila**.

Lalage A Greek name, from *lalagein*, 'to prattle', 'to babble', with the usual pronunciation in three syllables (like 'allergy') but with either a hard or a soft 'g'. The name is only in occasional English-speaking use and that mainly in the US or literary. An early example of the name in classical literature is that of Lalage, the woman to whom the 1st-century BC Roman poet Horace addressed his Odes. It is more recently found for the central character in E. Arnot Robertson's novel *Ordinary Families* (1933), and for a young girl in John Fowles's novel

The French Lieutenant's Woman (1969). Diminutives include *Lalla*, *Lallie* and *Lally*, the first of these as for the UK actress Lalla Ward (b.1951).

UK educationalist Lalage Bown (b.1927).

Lambert The present English name has its origins in an Old German name, formed from *lant*, 'land', 'territory', and *beraht*, 'bright', 'famous', so 'famous landowner'. It has been in English-speaking use from the 16th century but gradually declined in popularity so that it is rarely found today. A famous historical bearer of the name was the 7th-century St Lambert, venerated in Flanders. In later history, the name became familiar from the English impostor Lambert Simnel (1475–1535), who personated the Duke of Clarence's son, Edward, and claimed to be Edward VI. More recently the name was borne by the US cabinet-maker Lambert Hitchcock (1795–1852). The American editor Lambert Strether is a central character in Henry James's novel *The Ambassadors* (1903). A diminutive is BERT, although that usually represents some other source name.

Lana The name is either a form of the rarish name *Alana*, itself a feminine equivalent of ALAN, or simply a euphonious invention. The name was taken up in the US in the 1920s, but has found little favour in the UK.

US actress Lana Turner (1920–95) (original first name Julia); UK actress Lana Morris (1930–98); Australian singer, actress Lana Cantrell (b.1943).

Lance This name is either an independently adopted diminutive of LANCELOT, or perhaps comes from an Old German name based on *lant*, 'land' (as for LAMBERT), or is even an adoption of the French word *lance*, 'lance' (the weapon), giving a meaning 'warrior'. It has been in select use among, English speakers from the late 19th century. Lance Outram is a park-keeper in Walter Scott's novel *Peveril of the Peak* (1823).

UK film director Lance Comfort (1908–66); UK tennis correspondent

Lance Tingay (1915–90); UK actor Lance Percival (b.1933); UK writer Lance Secretan (b.1939); US cyclist Lance Armstrong (b.1971).

Lancelot The name is of doubtful origin, but is almost certainly *not* connected with *lance*, despite its knightly connotations. It; may have evolved under the influence of Old French *l'ancelle* from Latin *ancillus*, 'servant', or (more likely) from some earlier Celtic source. It has been in select use among English speakers from the early 19th century but is now rare. It was made famous by Sir Lancelot, the brave and valiant knight of the Arthurian romances who was loved by Queen Guinevere. The variant spelling *Launcelot* is found fairly widely in literature, as is the diminutive *Launce*. In Shakespeare's *Two Gentlemen of Verona* (1592–3) Launce is a servant to Proteus, and in *The Merchant of Venice* (1596–8) Launcelot Gobbo is a clown. Launcelot Crab is a surgeon in Tobias Smollett's novel *Roderick Random* (1748), and the name is also that of the central character in the same author's *The Life and Adventures of Sir Launcelot Greaves* (1762). More recently the name occurs for the scientific detective Dr Lancelot Priestley in the crime novels (1920–60s) by the UK writer John Rhode (pen name of Cecil John Charles Street), while Sir Lancelot Spratt (with a punning name) is a leading figure in the series of humorous novels by Richard Gordon beginning with *Doctor in the House* (1952). The regular diminutive, LANCE, remains in active use.

UK scientist, educator Lancelot Hogben (1895–75).

Lara An independently adopted diminutive of the Russian name *Larissa*, itself linked with the identically named ancient Greek city. In recent times the name became popularly associated with the tragic character Lara in Boris Pasternak's novel *Doctor Zhivago* (1957) or, more precisely, with the film of 1965 based on it, with the haunting 'Lara's Theme' as a musical refrain. The name has found select favour among English speakers from the 1970s.

US actress Lara Flynn Boyle (b.1970).

Laraine The name, chiefly in US use, is probably a variant form of LORRAINE, in some cases influenced by French *la reine*, 'the queen'.

US actress Laraine Day (b.1917); UK model Laraine Ashton (b.1946).

Larry An independently adopted diminutive of LAURENCE or LAWRENCE, in regular use among English speakers from the early 20th century, and mostly favoured in the US. Laurence (Larry) Doyle is a civil engineer in George Bernard Shaw's play *John Bull's Other Island* (1904), and Larry is also a character in Eugene O'Neill's play *Anna Christie* (1922). The diminutive *Laz* sometimes occurs.

US harmonica player Larry Adler (1914–2001) (original first name Lawrence); US actor Larry Parks (1914–75) (original first name Lawrence); UK entertainer, TV host Larry Grayson (1923–95) (original name William White); UK newspaper editor Sir Larry Lamb (1929–2000); US actor Larry Hagman (b.1930); US screenwriter Larry Kramer (b.1935); US writer Larry McMurtry (b.1936); UK actor Larry Dann (b.1941); Irish rock musician Larry Mullen Jr (b.1961) (father is Larry).

Launce, **Launcelot** see **Lancelot**.

Laura The name is a feminine form of Latin *laurus*, 'laurel', 'bay', so figuratively implies 'victory', 'triumph'. It has been in regular English-speaking use from the 16th century. It rose to a peak of popularity in the 19th century but then suffered a gradual decline to the 1960s, after which its favour again increased steadily to the present time. The name was first made famous by the Laura to whom the 14th-century Italian poet Petrarch addressed many love lyrics. She was a real person: the Frenchwoman Laure de Noves (1308–48). Literary characters of the name range from the 'rose-cheekt Lawra' of Thomas Campion's poem in *Observations in the Art of English*

Poesie (1602) to Laura Howard, Donald Howard's wife in C.P. Snow's novel *The Affair* (1960). Variants and diminutives in independent use include LAUREN, LAURETTA and LAURIE, while *Lolly* and *Lori* are also sometimes found.

UK artist Dame Laura Knight (1877–1970); US poet, novelist Laura Riding (1901–91); UK fashion designer Laura Ashley (1925–85); US popular singers Laura Nyro (1947–97), Laura Branigan (b.1957); US actress Laura San Giacomo (b.1962); UK golfer Laura Davies (b.1963); UK artist Laura Godfrey-Isaacs (b.1964); US actress Laura Dern (b.1967).

Lauren The name is probably an independent variant of LAURA, influenced by the male name LAURENCE. Taken up by some English speakers from the 1960s, it suddenly became popular in the 1990s.

US actresses Lauren Bacall (b.1924) (original name Betty Joan Perske), Lauren Hutton (b.1943) (original first name Mary).

Laurence This name is an English form (through French) of the Latin name *Laurentius*, 'man from Laurentum' (a town in Latium whose own name is associated with Latin *laurus*, 'laurel', with the implied sense 'triumph', 'victory'). It was introduced to England by the Normans and gradually declined in frequency until the 19th century, when it was taken up generally in the English-speaking world, especially in the US. It is now only moderately popular. It was first associated with the 3rd-century martyr St Laurence and, later, in England with St Laurence of Canterbury in the 6th century. The Hon. Laurence Fitzgibbon is a character in Anthony Trollope's novel *Phineas Finn* (1869), and the civil engineer Laurence (Larry) Doyle is a central character in George Bernard Shaw's play *John Bull's Other Island* (1904). The variant spelling LAWRENCE is in independent use, as are the diminutives LARRY and LAURIE.

UK actor, director Sir Laurence Olivier (1907–89); Lithuanian-born US actor Laurence Harvey (1928–73) (original name Larushka Mischa Skikne).

Lauretta An independently adopted diminutive of LAURA, in select use among English speakers from the mid-19th century. An early literary occurrence of the name is that of Lauretta Credulous in Richard Brinsley Sheridan's play *St Patrick's Day* (1775). The variant spelling LORETTA has been adopted in its own right.

Laurie (m.) An independently adopted diminutive of LAWRENCE or LAURENCE, in moderate vogue among English speakers from the early 20th century.

UK writer Laurie Lee (1914–97); UK sociologist, broadcaster Laurie Taylor (b.1936); UK photographer Laurie Evans (b.1955); Australian-born UK cricketer Laurie Potter (b.1963).

Laurie (f.) An independently adopted variant of LAURA or LAURETTA, in occasional favour among English speakers from the 19th century.

UK magazine editor Laurie Purden (b.1928) (original first names Roma Laurette); UK radio newsreader Laurie Macmillan (b.1947); US performance artist Laurie Anderson (b.1950); US actress Laurie Metcalf (b.1956).

Lavinia A feminine form of the Latin place-name *Lavinium*, an ancient town south of Rome. The name has been in steady but mostly very select English-speaking use from the 18th century. As a classical name, Lavinia is the daughter of Latinus in Virgil's *Aeneid* (30–19BC). Later literary bearers of the name include Lavinia, Titus's daughter in Shakespeare's *Titus Andronicus* (1590–94); Lavinia Spenlow in Charles Dickens's novel *David Copperfield* (1849–50); Lavinia Penniman, Dr Sloper's housekeeper in Henry James's novel *Washington Square* (1880); and Lavinia (Lavvie) Skinner, sister of the central character, Emily Skinner, in Agatha Christie's short story 'The Case of the Perfect Maid' in *Three Blind Mice and Other Stories* (1950) (US title *The Mousetrap and Other Stories*). Diminutives are *Vinnie* or *Vinny*, but hardly now *Lavvie*, except privately or facetiously.

(Though it could, of course, sound like 'Lovey'.) The name has an aristocratic cachet.

UK wife of Duke of Norfolk, Lavinia, Duchess of Norfolk (1916–95); Irish daughter of Earl of Meath, Lady Lavinia Jobson (b.1945).

Lawrence This is an English form of the French-style spelling LAURENCE. The spelling of the name with -w- for -u- was increasingly common from the 16th century, and now predominates in the US and Canada. Lawrence Boythorn is a friend of Mr Jarndyce in Charles Dickens's novel *Bleak House* (1852–3). The usual diminutive is LARRY, in independent use, with *Lawrie* also found, as for the UK yachtsman Lawrie Smith (b.1956).

Dutch-UK painter Sir Lawrence Alma-Tadema (1836–1912); UK writer Lawrence Durrell (1912–90).

Layton see **Leighton**.

Laz see **Larry**.

Lazarus A biblical name, from the Latinized version of Hebrew *El'āzār*, 'God has helped' (the same name as the biblical *Eleazar*). The name has enjoyed only slight favour among English speakers from the 18th century and is now rare. In the Bible Lazarus is the name of two people: the brother of Mary and Martha of Bethany, whom Jesus raised from the dead, and the beggar in the parable of Dives and Lazarus. The latter was 'full of sores', so that *lazar* came to be a word for a person with an unpleasant infectious disease. Lazarus is a sponging housekeeper in William Makepeace Thackeray's novel *The Newcomes* (1853–5).

Lea see **Lee** (m.).

Lea (f.) An independently adopted variant of LEAH or LEE, in modest use from the early 20th century, with a slight popularity peak in the 1960s.

UK actress Lea Rochelle (b.1961); US actress Lea Thompson (b.1962); Filipino actress, singer Lea Salonga (b.1971).

Leah A biblical name, from Hebrew *Le'ah*, 'gazelle', 'antelope', adopted by Puritans in the 17th century and enjoying moderate favour ever since, mainly among Jewish families. From the 1970s the name has found increasing popularity overall. In the Bible Leah is the eldest daughter of Laban, the sister of Rachel, and the first wife of Jacob. The variant LEE is fairly commonly found in independent use, as also is LEA.

UK actress Leah Bracknell (b.1964).

Leander This is a Latin form of the Greek name *Leandros*, formed from *leōn*, 'lion', and *anēr*, genitive *andros*, 'man', so 'lion man', 'strong and brave man'. The name came into general English-speaking use in the 20th century, finding special favour among black Americans. In Greek mythology the name is famous as that of the youth who swam the Hellespont nightly to visit his beloved Hero but who was finally drowned in a storm. It is historically familiar from St Leander who became archbishop of Seville in the 6th century. The name appears (in its French form of *Léandre*) for various characters in the plays of Molière, such as the rival of Lélie in *L'Étourdi* (1655), the lover of Lucinde in *Le Médecin malgré lui* (1666), and the son of Géronte in *Les Fourberies de Scapin* (1671).

Leanne A variant form in independent use of LIANNE, regarded as a blend of LEE and ANNE. The name came into favour generally only in the 1960s. A variant is *LeAnn*, as for the US country singer LeAnn Rimes (b.1982)

Australian ballerina Leanne Benjamin (b.1964).

Leda A Greek name, itself perhaps representing a Lycian word meaning simply 'woman'. It is surprisingly rare in the English-speaking world, in view of the popularity of similar names such as LENA and LINDA. In Greek mythology Leda is the mother of Clytemnestra, of Helen of Troy, and of Castor and Pollux. In Dashiell Hammett's novel *The Thin Man* (1934) Leda Edge is the wife of Halsey Edge.

Lee (m.) From the surname, and in fairly regular English-speaking use from the 19th century, especially in the US, where it was adopted by many in honour of the Confederate general Robert E. Lee (1807–70). In literature Lee Goodwin is a character in William Faulkner's novel *Sanctuary* (1931). Variant spellings *Lea* and *Leigh* also exist, the latter as for the US actor Leigh Whipper (1877–1975) and UK actor Leigh Lawson (b.1943).

US inventor, 'father of radio', Lee De Forest (1873–1961); US actors Lee Tracy (1898–1968), Lee Bowman (1910–79), Lee J. Cobb (1911–76) (original name Leo Jacoby), Lee Marvin (1924–87); US R&B singer Lee Dorsey (1924–86); UK actor Lee Montague (b.1927); US actor Lee Kinsolving (1938–74); US golfer Lee Trevino (b.1939); UK poet Lee Harwood (b.1939) (original surname Lee-Harwood); US actor Lee Majors (b.1940) (original name Harvey Lee Yeary II); US country musician Lee Greenwood (b.1942); UK rock musician Lee Brilleaux (1953–94); UK rugby player Lee Crooks (b.1963); UK footballer Lee Sharpe (b.1971).

Lee (f.) This name is either a female adoption of the male name LEE, or a diminutive of LEAH in independent use. It was taken up by English speakers in the early 20th century and grew steadily in popularity to the early 1980s, since when it has somewhat fallen from favour. A variant spelling in independent use is LEA. *Leigh* is also found, as for the US actress Leigh Taylor-Young (b.1944).

US actress Lee Patrick (1906–82); UK photographer Lee Miller (1907–77); US painter Lee Krasner (1908–84) (original name Lenore Krassner); US jazz singer Lee Wiley (1915–75); US actresses Lee Grant (b.1929) (original name Lyova Rosenthal), Lee Meriwether (b.1935), Lee Remick (1935–91).

Leigh see **Lee** (m.) and (f.).

Leighton An adoption of the surname, in select use among English speakers from the late 19th century. Variant forms *Layton* and *Leyton* exist.

Leila This is an Arabic name, meaning 'night', so has the meaning 'dark-haired', 'dark-skinned' or 'dark-eyed', as of an ideal oriental, sultry beauty. It was taken up generally at a fairly modest level by English speakers from the 19th century. In Byron's poem *The Giaour* (1813) Leila is a beautiful slave girl, and in his *Don Juan* (1824) she is a young Turkish child. Lord Lytton's novel *Leila* (1838) has the name for its central character, and in Gilbert and Sullivan's comic opera *Iolanthe* (1882) Leila is a fairy. A variant form is *Laila*.

US actress Leila Hyams (1905–77); UK children's writer Leila Berg (b.1917).

Lemmy An independently adopted diminutive of LEMUEL, in select English-speaking use from the 1930s. It was made familiar in recent literature by Lemmy Caution, the 'G-man' central character and narrator in the pseudo-American thrillers (1936–46) by the UK writer Peter Cheyney. The same character appears in the science fiction film *Alphaville* (1965), in which he is played by Eddie Constantine.

Lemuel A biblical name, from Hebrew *Lĕmū'ēl*, 'devoted to God', in occasional use among English speakers from the mid-19th century to the 1930s, after which it became rare. In the Bible Lemuel is the king who is the writer of 'the prophecy that his mother taught him' (Proverbs 31). The name is famous in literature from that of Lemuel Gulliver, the central character of Jonathan Swift's novel *Gulliver's Travels* (1725). The diminutive LEMMY is in independent use.

Len An independently adopted diminutive of LEONARD, in select use among English speakers from the 1920s. Its own diminutive form LENNIE is in independent use.

UK cricketer Len Hutton (1916–90); UK trade union leader Len Murray (b.1922) (original name Lionel); UK spy fiction writer Len Deighton (b.1929); UK artist Len Tabner (b.1946).

Lena The name arose as an independently adopted diminutive of a name such as HELENA. It has been in general English-speaking use from the mid-19th century, retaining a modest popularity ever since. LENI is a diminutive in independent use.

UK politician Lena Jeger (b.1915); UK novelist Lena Kennedy (1916–86); US singer, actress Lena Horne (b.1917); Scottish popular singer Lena Zavaroni (1963–99).

Leni An independently adopted diminutive of LENA, enjoying a certain vogue among English speakers from the early 20th century.

German film director Leni Riefenstahl (1902–93) (original first name Helene); US popular singer Leni Lynn (b.1925); Scottish actress Leni Harper (b.1954).

Lennard see **Leonard**.

Lennie An independently adopted diminutive of LEONARD or LEN, in select use among English speakers from the 1920s. In John Steinbeck's novella *Of Mice and Men* (1937) Lennie Small is the 'dumb as hell' fellow farmworker of George Milton. The variant spelling LENNY is in independent use.

UK popular composer Lennie Hayton (1908–71); US jazz musician Lennie Niehaus (b.1929); UK comedian Lennie Bennett (b.1938).

Lennox From the (Scottish) surname and earldom, in mainly Scottish use from the 19th century. The spelling *Lenox* sometimes occurs.

UK actor Lennox Pawle (1872–1936); UK composer Sir Lennox Berkeley (1903–89); UK boxer Lennox Lewis (b.1965).

Lenny An independently adopted variant of LENNIE, in some favour among English speakers from the 1930s.

US comedian Lenny Bruce (1926–66); UK footballer Lenny Lawrence (b.1947); UK comedian Lenny Henry (b.1958).

Lenore see **Eleanor**.

Lenox see **Lennox**.

Leo An English adoption of the Late Latin name, meaning 'lion', in select use among English speakers from medieval times. Its greatest period of popularity was from the 1870s to the 1920s, after which it declined. The name was borne by many early saints and popes. The young boy Leo Colston, the central character of L.P. Hartley's novel *The Go-Between* (1953), has the original first name Lionel. LEON is a directly related name.

US actor Leo G. Carroll (1892–1972); US lyricist Leo Robin (1899–1985); UK actor Leo Genn (1905–78); US writer Leo Rosten (1905–97); UK politician Leo Abse (b.1917); Australian-born UK actor Leo McKern (b.1920) (original first name Reginald); UK pop singer Leo Sayer (b.1948) (original first names Gerard Hugh).

Leon The ultimate source of the name is in Greek *leōn* or Latin *leo*, genitive *leonis*, 'lion'. It has been in fairly general English-speaking use, especially among Jews, from the 19th century. The Jewish favour for the name stems from Jacob's dying words to his sons in the Old Testament: 'Judah is a lion's whelp: from the prey, my son, thou art gone up: he stooped down, he couched as a lion, and as an old lion; who shall rouse him up?' (Genesis 49.9).

Australian-born US actor Leon Errol (1881–1951); UK oboist Leon Goossens (1897–1988); US actor Leon Ames (1903–93); US country musician Leon McAuliffe (1917–88); UK children's writer Leon Garfield

(1921–96); US writer Leon Uris (b.1924); UK actors Leon Sinden (b.1927), Leon Eagles (b.1932); UK politician Sir Leon Brittan (b.1939).

Leona see **Leonie**.

Leonard The name comes from the French form of an Old German name formed from *lewo*, 'lion', and *hart*, 'strong', 'hard', so having the overall meaning of 'strong as a lion'. It was in fairly steady but modest English-speaking use from the 18th century until the early 20th. Its popularity then suddenly increased to the 1930s, after which it gradually declined. St Leonard, living in the 5th century, helped to make the name initially familiar. Leonard Charteris is a character in George Bernard Shaw's play *The Philanderer* (1893). The spelling *Lennard* sometimes occurs, and the regular diminutives in independent use are LEN and LENNIE.

UK actor Leonard Sachs (1909–90); US composer Leonard Bernstein (1918–90) (original first name Louis); US sculptor Leonard Baskin (1922–2000); UK actor Leonard Rossiter (1926–84); UK TV newsreader Leonard Parkin (1929–93) (father was Leonard); US actor Leonard Nimoy (b.1931); UK actor Leonard Whiting (b.1950).

Leonie The name represents the French feminine form (properly *Léonie*) of *Léon* (English LEON). It was taken up by English speakers, frequently Jews, from the late 19th century, and remained at a fairly modest level until the 1990s when its popularity suddenly increased. The variant form *Leona* is often found in the US, as for the US country musician Leona Williams (b.1943).

Australian literary critic Dame Leonie Kramer (b.1924); German-born UK actress Leonie Mellinger (b.1959).

Leonora This name is a short form of *Eleonora*, itself a variant of ELEANOR. It was taken up by English speakers in the 19th century, when it was brought before the public by at least three operatic Leonoras: the central character in Beethoven's

Fidelio (1806, 1814), the King of Castile's mistress in Donizetti's *La Favorite* (1840), and the tragic heroine of Verdi's *Il Trovatore* (1853). In literature Leonora is a character in John Dryden's tragi-comedy *The Spanish Fryar* (1681), and another character of the name is in Henry Fielding's novel *Joseph Andrews* (1742). The diminutive NORA is in independent use.

UK actresses Leonora Braham (1853–1931), Leonora Corbett (1907–60).

Leontine This is a French form (properly *Léontine*) of the Italian name *Leontina*, itself a feminine form of the Latin name *Leontius*, in turn a derivative of LEO. The name is sometimes popularly regarded as a blend of LEONORA and a name ending in -*tine* such as CLEMENTINE. It has found some favour among English speakers from the 19th century. In Michael Sadleir's novel *Fanny by Gaslight* (1940) Leontine Bonnet is the niece of the pensionnaire Madame Bonnet. The spelling *Leontyne* also exists, as for the US opera singer Leontyne Price (b.1927) (original first names Mary Leontine).

Austrian-born South African film director Leontine Sagan (1899–1974); US United Methodist bishop Leontine T.C. Kelly (b.1920).

Leopold A name that is the English form of the Old German name *Liutpold*, formed from *liut*, 'people', 'race', and *bald*, 'bold', 'brave', so 'of a brave people'. It was in modest favour among English speakers from the mid-19th century to the early 20th, after which it declined. The name was made historically familiar by various royal European personages, especially King Leopold of the Belgians (1790–1865), uncle of Queen Victoria. She named her third son Prince Leopold (1853–84) after him. In literature the name is famous from Leopold Bloom, the central character of James Joyce's novel *Ulysses* (1922).

UK-born US conductor Leopold Stokowski (1882–1977).

Leroy The name has its origin in Old French *le roy*, 'the king', and was at first simply a nickname (compare KING). It was increasingly adopted by English speakers from the 19th century, first in the US, then (from the 1960s) in the UK. It is now regarded as a typical black name, which in the UK means among the West Indian community. The variant forms *LeRoy* and *LeRoi* are also found.

US bluesman Leroy Carr (1905–35); US baseball player Leroy Paige (*c.*1906–82); US composer, conductor Leroy Anderson (1908–75); US country musician Leroy Van Dyke (b.1929).

Les An independently adopted diminutive of LESLIE or LESTER, in select English-speaking use in the 20th century.

US bandleader Les Brown (b.1912) (original first name Lester); US actor Les Tremayne (b.1913); UK comedian Les Dawson (1933–93); Australian poet Les Murray (b.1938); UK comedian Les Dennis (b.1954).

Lesbia A Greek name, meaning 'woman of Lesbos' (largest of the Greek islands). It has gained some currency among English speakers from the 19th century, although it is now mostly avoided because of its association with lesbians (so named because the 7th-century BC Greek poetess Sappho, who wrote love lyrics to other women, came from Lesbos). In classical literature Lesbia was the name used by the Roman poet Catullus in the 1st century BC to address the woman he loved, her real name probably being Clodia. The Irish poet Thomas Moore has a poem with an opening line 'Lesbia hath a beaming eye' in his *Irish Melodies* (1807), and Algernon Charles Swinburne used the name for the central character of his posthumously published novel *Lesbia Brandon* (1952). Lesbia Grantham is a character in George Bernard Shaw's play *Getting Married* (1908). Some of the characters in the schoolgirl novels by the UK writer Angela Brazil have the name, such as Lesbia Carrington in *For the School Colours* (1918) and Lesbia Farrars in *Loyal to the School* (1920).

Australian poet, novelist Lesbia Harford (1891–1927).

Lesley Either from the (Scottish) surname, which also gave the male name LESLIE, or directly as a female equivalent of the latter. The name has been in English-speaking use from the 18th century and enjoyed a period of popularity in the 1950s and 1960s. It seems to have been given initial impetus by the 18th-century Scots poet Robert Burns, who wrote the poem *Bonnie Lesley* ('O saw ye bonnie Lesley/As she gaed o'er the border?'). The spelling LESLIE (identical with the male name) is in independent use.

UK actress Lesley Brook (b.1916); UK politician, writer Lesley Abdela (b.1945); US actress Lesley Ann Warren (b.1946); UK TV presenter Lesley Judd (b.1946); US pop singer Lesley Gore (b.1946); UK actresses Lesley-Anne Down (b.1954), Lesley Dunlop (b.1956), Lesley Fitz-Simons (b.1961), Lesley-Anne Sharpe (b.1964).

Leslie (m.) From the (Scottish) surname, itself from a place-name (not necessarily the town in Fife). The name has been in regular English-speaking use from the late 19th century, with a period of high popularity in the second half of the 1920s, since when it has gradually fallen from favour. It has never been as popular in the US as in the UK. In D.H. Lawrence's novel *The White Peacock* (1911) Leslie Tempest marries Lettice Beardsall. The diminutive, LES, is in independent use.

UK popular composer Leslie Stuart (1864–1928) (original name Thomas Augustine Barrett); UK judge, politician Leslie Scott (1869–1950); UK actors Leslie Howard (1890–1943), Leslie Banks (1890–1952), Leslie Henson (1891–1957); UK singer, entertainer Leslie Sarony (1897–1985); UK film director Leslie Arliss (1901–87); UK TV announcer Leslie Mitchell (1905–85); Chinese-UK crime novelist Leslie Charteris (1907–93); UK film producer, director Leslie Norman (1911–93); UK actor Leslie Phillips (b.1924); UK writer Leslie Thomas (b.1931); UK TV host Leslie Crowther (1933–96); UK actor Leslie Grantham (b.1947).

Leslie (f.) A female adoption of the male name LESLIE, in select use among English speakers from the 1950s, mainly in the US.

US actress Leslie Brooks (b.1922); French-born US and UK actress Leslie Caron (b.1931); US revue actress Leslie Uggams (b.1943); UK actress Leslie Ash (b.1960).

Lester From the surname, and in select English-speaking use from the mid-19th century.

Canadian prime minister Lester B. Pearson (1897–1972); UK actor Lester Matthews (1900–75); US screenwriter Lester Cole (1904–85); US jazzman Lester Young (1909–59); US country singer, guitarist Lester Flatt (1914–79); UK jockey Lester Piggott (b.1935); US jazzman Lester Bowie (1941–99); US rock critic Lester Banks (1948–82).

Letitia The name, from the Latin word *laetitia*, 'joy', 'gladness', has enjoyed select English-speaking use from medieval times. A literary bearer of the name is Letitia Hardy in Hannah Cowley's play *The Belle's Stratagem* (1780). A variant spelling is *Laetitia*, as for the wife of the banker Fondlewife in William Congreve's play *The Old Bachelor* (1693), and governess Miss Laetitia Prism in Oscar Wilde's play *The Importance of Being Earnest* (1895). A variant spelling *Leticia* exists, as for the US actress Leticia Roman (b.1939), and the English form of the name, LETTICE, was adopted in its own right. Diminutives include LETTY, also in independent use, as well as *Tish*, *Tisha* and *Titia* (pronounced 'Teesha').

UK poet Letitia Landon (1803–38); UK actress Letitia Dean (b.1967).

Lettice This name is a purely English form of the Latin-derived name LETITIA. It was in general if modest English-speaking use from medieval times to the early 20th century. It then fell from favour, perhaps partly through a frivolous association with *lettuce*. One of the ladies-in-waiting to Queen Elizabeth I was Lettice Knollys. In literature the name occurs for Lettice Beardsall, sister of the central character in D.H. Lawrence's novel *The White Peacock* (1911). The diminutive LETTY gained independent adoption.

UK novelist Lettice Cooper (1897–1994).

Letty An independently adopted diminutive of ALETHEA, LETITIA or LETTICE, in some favour among English speakers from the mid-19th century to the 1930s, since when it has declined. It is not obsolete, however, and remains in active adoption among US blacks. Letty Garth is the daughter of the land agent Caleb Garth in George Eliot's novel *Middlemarch* (1871–2), and Letty Corner is a character in H.G. Wells's novel *Mr Britling Sees It Through* (1916). The variant spelling *Lettie* also occurs.

Levi A biblical name, from Hebrew *Lēwī*, 'associated', 'attached', in rarish English-speaking use from the 17th century, mainly among Jews. In the Bible Levi is the third son of Jacob and Leah from whom the priestly tribe of Levites were descended: 'And she conceived again, and bare a son; and said, Now this time will my husband be joined unto me, because I have born him three sons: therefore was his name called Levi' (Genesis 29.34). (Leah was concerned that Jacob loved his other wife, Rachel, more than her.) In Thomas Hardy's novel *Far from the Madding Crowd* (1874) Levi Everdene is the father of Bathsheba Everdene, the central character. The name has become commercially familiar from 'Levi's' jeans, first sold by the US manufacturer Levi Strauss (1829–1902). The spelling *Levy* also occurs.

Lew An independently adopted diminutive of LEWIS, in use among English speakers from the 19th century.

US actors Lew Cody (1888–1934), Lew Ayres (1908–96); Australian tennis player Lew Hoad (1934–94).

Lewis An English form of the French name LOUIS, in fairly regular English-speaking use from medieval times, and suddenly becoming popular in the 1990s. The usual diminutive, LEW, is in independent use.

UK children's writer Lewis Carroll (1832–98) (original name Charles Lutwidge Dodgson); US actor Lewis Stone (1879–1953); US film producer Lewis M. Allen (b.1922); UK actor Lewis Collins (b.1946).

Lex An independently adopted diminutive of ALEXANDER, perhaps modelled on REX, in rare use among English speakers from the 19th century (Latin *lex*, 'law', is hardly relevant). The diminutive *Lexy* occurs. See also ALEX.

US actor Lex Barker (1919–73).

Lexie see **Alex**.

Leyton see **Leighton**.

Lia A name that is the Italian equivalent of LEAH, but that could equally be taken to represent the final element of an English name such as AMELIA or DELIA. It has enjoyed select favour among English speakers from the 1950s.

UK actress Lia Williams (b.1963).

Liam This name is an independently adopted (Irish) diminutive of WILLIAM. It is still chiefly in Irish use but has also been found more generally among English speakers from the 1930s, with a sharp rise in popularity in the 1990s.

Irish novelist Liam O'Flaherty (1897–1984); Irish actor Liam Redmond (1913–89); Irish prime minister Liam Cosgrave (b.1920); UK writer on psychology Liam Hudson (b.1933); Northern Ireland actor Liam Neeson (b.1952); Irish footballer Liam Brady (b.1956).

Lianne The name probably arose as a short form of the French name *Julianne*, itself evolving as a feminine form of the male Latin name *Julianus* (English JULIAN). However, the name is now usually regarded as a blend of LEE and ANNE. It was taken up by English speakers in the 1940s, but apart from a period of popularity in the first half of the 1980s, has not widely caught on. A variant form is LEANNE.

Libby A name that is one of the many independently adopted diminutives of ELIZABETH, in this case based on a child's attempt to say the full name. It has been in regular use among

English speakers from the early 20th century. A diminutive *Lib* exists.

US actress, singer Libby Holman (1906–71); UK columnist Libby Purves (b.1950); UK TV reporter Libby Wiener (b.*c*.1955).

Lilian This name is probably an independently adopted variant of ELIZABETH, influenced by the Italian name *Liliana* and subsequently by English LILY, as if a blend of the latter name and ANNE. It has been in English-speaking use from the late 19th century but tailed off rapidly from the 1920s after a period of considerable popularity. The variant spelling LILLIAN exists independently. A frequent diminutive is *Lil*.

UK actress Dame Lilian Braithwaite (1873–1948); UK theatre manager Lilian Baylis (1874–1937); UK actress Lilian Bond (1910–91); UK radio broadcaster Lilian Duff (1915–94).

Lillian An independently adopted variant of LILIAN, in general use among English speakers, especially in the US, from the late 19th century, although it is now much less common. The usual diminutive is *Lil*, as for the US jazz musician Lil Armstrong (1898–1971).

US singer, entertainer Lillian Russell (1861–1922) (original name Helen Louise Leonard); US actress Lillian Gish (1893–1993); mother of US president Jimmy Carter, Lillian Carter (1898–1983); US playwright Lillian Hellman (1905–84); US actresses Lillian Roth (1910–80), Lillian Bond (1910–91); South African-born UK athlete Lillian Board (1948–70).

Lily From the name of the flower, but also sometimes felt to be a diminutive of ELIZABETH. The name was fairly popular among English speakers from the mid-19th century to the early years of the 20th century, when it began a sharp decline. The flower has long been a symbol of purity, and the many literary comparisons between the lily and a beautiful woman doubtless popularized the name, such as Tennyson's 'lily maid of Astolat' (Elaine), or the poetic use of 'lily', 'lily-white', 'fair as the lily' and the like to describe a woman's brow, breast, hand or foot. The music-hall song 'Lily of Laguna' (1898) also made the name widely known. Variants include *Lillie* and *Lilly*, with *Lil* a frequent diminutive. The Jersey-born actress Lillie Langtry (1853–1929), nicknamed 'the Jersey Lily' for her beauty, had the original first names Emilie Charlotte.

UK croquet player Lily Gower (1877–1959) (original first name Lilias); French-born US opera singer Lily Pons (1898–1976) (original first names Alice Joséphine); US actress Lily Tomlin (b.1939).

Lina An independent adoption of the diminutive of one of the names ending -*lina*, such as ADELINA, ANGELINA or SELINA, although it is popularly thought of as a variant spelling of LENA. The name has found some favour among English speakers from the mid-19th century.

US actress Lina Basquette (1907–94).

Linda The popular name probably arose as the shortening of a name such as BELINDA, although Spanish *linda* happens to mean 'pretty' and Italian *linda* is 'neat', 'tidy'. The name has been in English-speaking use from the 19th century, and it was very much in fashion in the 1950s and (although rather less so) the 1960s, since when it has faded somewhat. In literature the name is that of the central character of Joseph Hergesheimer's novel *Linda Condon* (1919). (She is a beauty, and the author may well have named her with the Spanish word in mind.) An early bearer of the name was the UK writer Linda Villari (1836–1915), who was probably so called after her mother's maiden name, Lind. The variant spelling LYNDA is in independent use, as is the diminutive LYNN. Another diminutive is *Lindy*, as for the UK film and TV costume designer Lindy Hemming (b.1948). This often forms compounds such as *Lindybeth* or *Lindylou*.

US actresses Linda Arvidson (1884–1949), Linda Darnell (1921–65) (original first names Monetta Eloise); Mexican-born US actress Linda

Christian (b.1923) (original name Blanca Rosa Welter); Argentinian-born US actress Linda Cristal (b.1934) (original name Victoria Maya); US-born UK photographer Linda McCartney (1941–98); US actresses Linda Gray (b.1942), Linda Evans (b.1943), Linda Harrison (b.1945); US pop singer Linda Ronstadt (b.1946); UK actress Linda Robson (b.1958); US actress Linda Blair (b.1959); UK opera singer Linda Kitchen (b.1960); UK model, actress Linda Lusardi (b.1960); Canadian-born US model Linda Evangelista (b.1965).

Lindsay (m.) From the (Scottish) surname, and in some favour among English speakers from the 19th century, but from the 1930s declining on the increasing adoption of the name for female use. A spelling variant is *Lindsey*.

Australian cricketer Lindsay Hassett (1913–93); UK film director Lindsay Anderson (1923–94).

Lindsay (f.) A female adoption of the male name LINDSAY, in increasingly popular English-speaking use from the 1940s, especially in the US. The many variant spellings include *Lindsey*, *Linsey*, *Linzi* and *Lynsey*, as respectively for the UK writer Lindsey Davis (b.1949); US-born UK actress Linsey Beauchamp (b.1960) (original first name Linda); UK actress Linzi Hateley (b.1970) and UK pop singer and writer Lynsey de Paul (b.1951). Diminutives *Lin* and *Lyn* exist.

US actresses Lindsay Crouse (b.1948), Lindsay Wagner (b.1949); Scottish actress Lindsay Duncan (b.1950); UK financial journalist Lindsay Cook (b.1951).

Lindy see **Linda**.

Linnet, **Linnette** see **Lynette**.

Linus A biblical name, from the Greek name *Linos*, itself perhaps from *lineos*, 'flaxen', so 'flaxen-haired', 'blond'. The name occasionally appears in English-speaking use, mainly in the US. In the Bible, Linus is a Christian of Rome greeted by St Paul (2 Timothy 4.21). The Linus of Greek mythology is a musician who gives lessons to Hercules. (An early pope of the name may have been the biblical Linus.) In modern times the name has been humorously popularized by the small boy Linus in Charles Schulz's comic strip series *Peanuts* (from 1950).

US chemist Linus Pauling (1901–94); UK actor Linus Roache (b.1964).

Linzi see **Lindsay** (f.).

Lionel The English name is a straight adoption of the French name *Lionel*, a diminutive of LEON. It has been in select English-speaking use from medieval times, but gained only modest favour in the 20th century, and after the 1930s largely faded from the scene. In the Arthurian romances, Sir Lionel is one of the Knights of the Round Table, and it was for him that Edward III named his second son, Lionel of Antwerp, Duke of Clarence (d.1368). Isaac Bickerstaffe's play *Lionel and Clarissa* (1768) has Lionel in love with Clarissa Flowerdale, while the name is also that of the central character in James Fenimore Cooper's novel *Lionel Lincoln* (1825), in which he marries Cecil Dynever. LEO is a related name.

UK composer Lionel Monckton (1861–1924); UK actor Lionel Belmore (1867–1953); UK viola player Lionel Tertis (1876–1975); US actor Lionel Barrymore (1878–1954); UK-born US actor Lionel Atwill (1885–1946); UK broadcaster Lionel Gamlin (1903–67); US jazzman Lionel Hampton (b.1909); UK actor Lionel Jeffries (b.1926); UK composer Lionel Bart (1930–99); UK rabbi, writer Lionel Blue (b.1930); UK dancer, actor Lionel Blair (b.1934); US soul singer Lionel Richie (b.1949).

Lisa An independently adopted diminutive of ELIZABETH, using the European or 'continental' spelling. The name was increasingly popular among English speakers from the 1960s to the 1980s, since when it has mostly fallen from favour. The variant spelling LIZA is in independent use, and diminutives *Lisette* and *Lysette* exists, the latter as for the UK-born Polish actress Lysette Anthony (b.1963).

UK-French actress Lisa Daniely (b.1930); US novelist Lisa Alther (b.1944); Anglo-US writer Lisa St Aubin de Terán (b.1953); UK actress, TV presenter Lisa Maxwell (b.1963); US actress Lisa Kudrow (b.1963); UK soul singer Lisa Stansfield (b.1966); UK hockey player Lisa Bayliss (b.1966); UK actress Lisa Riley (b.1976).

Lisbeth The name is a shortened form of ELIZABETH, in independent use. It was taken up by English speakers in the 19th century and is now chiefly found in the US and Scotland. Lisbeth Bede is the mother of the central character in George Elliot's novel *Adam Bede* (1859). The spelling *Lizbeth* is also found.

Lise see **Elizabeth**.

Lisette see **Elizabeth**, **Lisa**.

Livia The name is either a shortened form of OLIVIA or a feminine form of the Roman clan name *Livius*, itself perhaps related to *lividus*, 'leaden-coloured'. It is found chiefly in literary use among English speakers from at least the 16th century. Livia is a character in John Fletcher's play *The Woman's Prize* (1604–17), and in Thomas Middleton's posthumously published play *Women Beware Women* (1657) Livia betrays Bianca. In Shakespeare's *Romeo and Juliet* (1595) Livia is the name of one of the guests invited to the Capulets' party.

Liz An independently adopted diminutive of ELIZABETH or LIZA, in English-speaking use from about the 1930s. The name's own diminutive is LIZZIE, now given or adopted in its own right.

US fashion designer Liz Claiborne (b.1929); US country singer Liz Anderson (b.1930); UK actress Liz Fraser (b.1933); Scottish poet, playwright Liz Lochhead (b.1947); UK ballerina, choreographer Liz Aggiss (b.1953); UK radio presenter Liz Kershaw (b.1958); Scottish athlete Liz McColgan (b.1964); UK actress Liz Carling (b.1967).

Liza A diminutive of ELIZABETH in independent use. The name was taken up generally among English speakers in the 19th century, but it has never been as popular as its variant form, LISA. A literary bearer of the name is the central character in Somerset Maugham's novel *Liza of Lambeth* (1897). The usual diminutives are LIZ and LIZZIE, now given in their own right.

US actress, singer Liza Minnelli (b.1946); UK actress Liza Goddard (b.1950).

Lizbeth see **Lisbeth**.

Lizzie An independently adopted diminutive of ELIZABETH or LIZA, in regular English-speaking use from the mid-19th century. Lizzie Hexam is a character in Charles Dickens's novel *Our Mutual Friend* (1864–5). The well-known rhyme about Lizzie Borden (who 'took an axe/And gave her mother forty whacks') arose after the murder trial of this American woman in 1893. LIZ is a directly related name.

Australian politician Lizzie Ahern (1877–1969) (original first name Elizabeth); UK TV fitness presenter Lizzie Webb (b.1948); US film director Lizzie Borden (b.1954).

Llewellyn A well-known Welsh name, originally *Llywelyn*, and popularly derived from *llyw*, 'leader', and *eilun*, 'likeness', with the modern form influenced by *llew*, 'lion', but actually going back to an Old Celtic name of uncertain meaning. It is still almost exclusively in Welsh use. The name is historically famous from two 13th-century princes of Gwynedd, Llywelyn ap Iorwerth and his grandson Llywelyn ap Gruffudd. The regular diminutive is LYNN, in independent use. *Llew* is also common.

Lloyd From the (Welsh) surname, and taken up generally in the English-speaking world, especially in the US, from the early 20th century, with a slight but steady increase in popularity to the 1990s. The name was long historically associated with the UK prime minister David Lloyd George (1863–1945), where it represented his mother's maiden name.

US film director Lloyd Bacon (1890–1955); US actors Lloyd Hughes (1896–1958), Lloyd Nolan (1902–85), Lloyd Bridges (1913–98); Australian-born UK actor Lloyd Lamble (b.1914); UK boxer Lloyd Honeyghan (b.1960); Northern Ireland actor Lloyd Hutchinson (b.1967).

Lo see **Lois, Lola, Lolita**.

Lockie see **Lachlan**.

Logan From the (Scottish) surname, and still a name chiefly in Scottish use. It originated from the place of the same name in Ayrshire.

US-born UK writer on literary subjects Logan Pearsall Smith (1865–1949).

Lois A biblical name, explained as from Greek *lōiōn*, 'more desirable', 'better', but now popularly associated with LOUISA and LOUISE. It has enjoyed select adoption among English speakers from the 17th century, and in the 20th century it was more common in the US than the UK. In the Bible Lois is Timothy's grandmother. Lois Badger is a character in Harriet Beecher Stowe's novel *Oldtown Folks* (1869). An occasional diminutive is *Lo*.

US film director, actress Lois Weber (1882–1939); US actresses Lois Moran (1909–90), Lois Collier (b.1919) (original name Madelyn Jones), Lois Andrews (1924–68); Canadian-born UK actress Lois Maxwell (b.1927); US actresses Lois Nettleton (b.1930), Lois Chiles (b.1950).

Lola The name, an independently adopted diminutive of DOLORES, has been in select English-speaking use from the 19th century. It was made famous by the Irish-born American dancer Lola Montez (1818–61) (original name Marie Dolores Eliza Rosanna Gilbert). Agatha Christie's short story 'Yellow Iris' in *The Regatta Mystery* (1939) has a Peruvian dancer Lola

Valdez, with a name perhaps punningly based on this ('valley' as opposed to 'mountain'). The usual diminutive is *Lo*.

US actress Lola Albright (b.1925); US entertainer Lola Falana (b.1943).

Lolita An independently adopted diminutive of DOLORES, in English-speaking use, mostly in the US, from the 19th century. In the 20th century the name was made familiar by the nymphet central character of Vladimir Nabokov's novel *Lolita* (1955); 'She was Lo, plain Lo, in the morning: … She was Lola in slacks. She was Dolly at school. She was Dolores on the dotted line. But in my arms she was always Lolita.' As a result of this, the name came to be used for any under-age sex kitten. Common diminutives are *Lo* and LOLA, the latter now used independently.

Canadian actress Lolita Davidovich (b.1961); UK actress Lolita Chakrabarti (b.1969).

Lolly see **Laura**.

Lonnie The name is either an independently adopted diminutive of ALONSO or a variant of LENNIE, influenced by names such as DON or RON. It has found some favour among English speakers in the 20th century, mostly in the US. The variant spelling *Lonny* exists, while the diminutive is usually *Lon*, as for the US actor Lon Chaney (1883–1930) (original first name Alonzo). His son, Lon Chaney Jr (1906–73) (original first name Creighton), adopted his name.

US bluesman Lonnie Johnson (1899–1970) (original first name Alonzo); Scottish pop singer, guitarist Lonnie Donegan (b.1931) (original first name Anthony); US bluesman Lonnie Mack (b.1941).

Loraine see **Lorraine**.

Lorenzo The name, the Italian equivalent of LAURENCE, was taken up in the English-speaking world from the 19th century, mainly in the US. It is familiar from Shakespeare's *The Merchant of Venice* (1596–8), in which Lorenzo is loved by

Shylock's daughter, Jessica, who elopes with him. Another Lorenzo appears in Thomas Kyd's play *The Spanish Tragedy* (1592). In James Shirley's tragedy *The Traitor* (1631) Lorenzo is the central character. (The play is based on a historic event: the assassination of the Florentine duke Alessandro de' Medici by his kinsman Lorenzo.)

US actor Lorenzo Lamas (b.1958).

Loretta The name is a respelled form of LAURETTA, itself a diminutive of LAURA. It has been in English-speaking use since the 19th century, mostly in the US. A diminutive is *Lorrie*, as for the US country singer Lorrie Morgan (b.1960).

US actress Loretta Young (1913–2000) (original first name Gretchen); US country singer Loretta Lynn (b.1935); US actress Loretta Swit (b.1937).

Lori see **Laura**.

Lorna This name was apparently invented by the UK novelist R.D. Blackmore for the central character of his novel *Lorna Doone* (1869). He claims he based it on the Scottish place-name *Lorn* (an area of Argyll in the west of the country), but he may also have had the word *forlorn* in mind, especially as the tale begins with the kidnapping of the child Lorna by the Doones. The name has been in English-speaking use, mainly in the US, from the late 19th century, and has been in and out of fashion ever since. A variant form of the name is *Lorne*, as for the UK equestrian sculptor Lorne McKean (b.1939).

UK actress Lorna Wilde (b.1943); UK literary critic Lorna Sage (1943–2001); UK TV producer Lorna Dickinson (b.1958).

Lorraine The name is an adoption of the (Scottish) surname, but it is now felt to be a variant of LAURA (rather than a borrowing of the name of the historic French province). It was taken up by English speakers in the 19th century, and was increasingly popular from the early 1950s to the late 1960s, since when it has faded from fashion. Variant spellings include LARAINE, in independent use, and *Loraine*, as for the character Loraine Wade in Agatha Christie's novel *The Seven Dials Mystery* (1929).

US playwright Lorraine Hansberry (1930–65); US actress Lorraine Gary (b.1937); Australian swimmer Lorraine Crapp (b.1938); UK actress Lorraine Chase (b.1951); US actress Lorraine Bracco (b.1955); UK rock singer Lorraine McIntosh (b.1964)

Lorrie see **Loretta**.

Lotta An independently adopted diminutive of CHARLOTTE, in rarish English-speaking use from the 19th century. Lotta Gascoigne is the daughter of the Rev. Henry Gascoigne in George Eliot's novel *Daniel Deronda* (1876). *Lottie* is a frequent diminutive.

Lottie, **Lotty** see **Charlotte**.

Lou An independently adopted diminutive of LOUIS, in select English-speaking use, mainly in the US, from the late 19th century.

German-born US circus performer Lou Jacobs (1903–92) (original name Jacob Ludwig); US comedian Lou Costello (1906–59) (original name Louis Cristillo); US actor Lou Diamond Phillips (b.1962).

Louella The name is a blend of *Lou* (as a diminutive of LOUISA) and ELLA, in general adoption among English speakers from the 19th century, mostly in the US.

US gossip columnist Louella Parsons (1893–1972).

Louis This name originated as a French form of the Old German name *Hlutwig* (modern *Ludwig*), formed from *hlūt*, 'famous', and *wig*, 'battle', so 'famous in battle'. It was taken up in its present form by English speakers in the mid-19th century, gaining in popularity until the 1920s, when it declined.

It revived sharply, however, in the 1990s. The name normally retains its French pronunciation (with the final -s not sounded). It is historically famous from many French kings, especially the long-reigning 'Sun King' Louis XIV (1638–1715) and the ill-fated Louis XVI (guillotined 1793). In Charlotte Brontë's novel *Shirley* (1849) Louis Moore marries the central character, Shirley Keeldar. Directly related names are CLOVIS, LEWIS (the English form) and LUDOVIC. A regular diminutive is LOU, in independent use.

Russian-born US film producer Louis B. Mayer (1885–1957) (original first name Eliezer); US jazz trumpeter Louis Armstrong (1901–71); Irish poet Louis MacNeice (1907–63); South African-born US actor Louis Hayward (1909–85) (original name Seafield Grant).

Louisa The feminine form of LOUIS, common among English speakers from the 18th century, but from the early 20th century largely superseded by LOUISE. In literature Louisa is the daughter of Don Jerome in Richard Brinsley Sheridan's play *The Duenna* (1775), and Louisa Grant is a rector's daughter in James Fenimore Cooper's novel *The Pioneers* (1823). The chief diminutives are *Lou* and LOUIE.

US children's writer Louisa M. Alcott (1832–88); UK actress Louisa Rix (b.1955); UK writer and broadcaster on art Louisa Buck (b.1960).

Louise The French form of LOUISA, which it began to supersede among English speakers from the 1950s. It grew rapidly in popularity to a peak in the 1980s, since when it has rather fallen out of fashion. In literature the name occurs for the central character of Viola Meynell's story *Louise* (1954). Diminutives include *Lou* and *Louie*, with LULU now often in independent use.

US actresses Louise Carver (1898–1956), Louise Brooks (1906–85), Louise Fletcher (b.1936), Louise Lasser (b.1939), Louise Sorel (b.1944); UK actresses Louise Jameson (b.1951), Louise English (b.1962), Louise Lombard (b.1970).

Lucas The name is either an English adoption of the Latin name *Lucas* (English LUKE) or comes from the surname. It has found modest favour among English speakers from the 1930s. Lucas Holderness is an author and swindler in H.G. Wells's novel *Love and Mr Lewisham* (1900), and in William Faulkner's novel *Intruder in the Dust* (1948) Lucas Beauchamp is an ageing black farmer.

Lucetta An independently adopted diminutive of LUCIA or LUCY, in rarish use among English speakers from the 16th century. In Shakespeare's *Two Gentlemen of Verona* (1592) Lucetta is a servant to Julia. The French spelling *Lucette* is occasionally found, as for the Australian ballerina Lucette Aldous (b.1938).

Lucia This is a feminine form of the Roman clan name LUCIUS, which has been in modest favour among English speakers from the early 20th century, when it has sometimes been preferred to LUCY. It is historically familiar from the 4th-century martyr St Lucia. More recently it has been made known by Donizetti's opera *Lucia di Lammermoor* (1835), with the modern Italian form of the name. This was based on Walter Scott's novel *The Bride of Lammermoor* (1819), in which the original character was Lucy Ashton.

US ballerina Lucia Chase (1897–1986).

Lucian An English form of the French name *Lucien* or Italian name *Luciano*, themselves coming from the Latin name *Lucianus*, a derivative of LUCIUS. The name has occurred surprisingly rarely in English-speaking use from the 19th century, considering the popularity of ADRIAN, JULIAN and similar names. Historically it was made famous by the 2nd-century Greek satirist and humorist Lucian of Samosata and, to a lesser extent, by the 3rd-century martyr St Lucian.

German-born UK painter Lucian Freud (b.1922).

Lucie A French form of LUCY, in select but increasing popularity among English speakers from the 1980s. The name is familiar in literature as that of Lucie Manette, who marries Charles Darnay in Charles Dickens's novel *A Tale of Two Cities* (1859).

German-born US actress Lucie Mannheim (1895–1976).

Lucilla The name, a Latin diminutive of LUCIA, has been in occasional English-speaking use from the 16th century. Lucilla is one of the main characters in John Lyly's prose romance *Euphues, The Anatomy of Wit* (1578). The variant spelling LUCILLE is now much more common.

Lucille A French form of the Latin name LUCILLA, in use among English speakers from the 19th century, mostly in the US. A variant spelling is *Lucile*, as for Lucile McKelvey in Sinclair Lewis's novel *Babbitt* (1922) and for the Canadian actress Lucile Watson (1879–1962). The usual diminutive is LUCY, although this is a full name in its own right.

US actress Lucille Gleason (1886–1947); US racehorse owner Lucille Markey (1896–1982); US comedienne Lucille Ball (1911–89); US dancer Lucille Bremer (1922–96); South African-born UK fashion designer Lucille Lewin (b.1948).

Lucinda The name is an independently adopted variant of LUCIA or LUCY, with the *-inda* element seen also in BELINDA. It was first in literary use from the 17th century, and was then adopted generally by English speakers from the 19th century. Lucinda Roanoke is a character in Anthony Trollope's novel *The Eustace Diamonds* (1873). The name is now usually regarded as 'superior' and often implies an aristocratic background. CINDY is a diminutive now in use in its own right.

Scottish daughter of Earl of Inchcape, Lady Lucinda Mackay (b.1941); UK TV presenter Lucinda Lambton (b.1943); UK equestrienne Lucinda Green (b.1953); US country singer Lucinda Williams (b.1953).

Lucius A biblical name, identical in Latin, and probably from *lux*, genitive *lucis*, 'light'. It has been occasionally taken up by English speakers from the 19th century. In the Bible Lucius is the name of three people: a Roman consul, one of the 'prophets and teachers' of the church at Antioch, and a Jewish Christian compatriot of St Paul. The name is also found several times in Shakespeare, including the son of Titus, and his son in turn, in *Titus Andronicus* (1590–94), a boy servant of Brutus in Julius Caesar (1599), a lord in *Timon of Athens* (*c*.1607), and a Roman general in *Cymbeline* (1609–10). (Shakespeare seems to have had a fascination for *Luc*- names: *Timon of Athens* has two characters Lucius as well as Lucilius and Lucullus. Perhaps significantly, material for the play is drawn from Lucian's *Timon*.) In Richard Brinsley Sheridan's play *The Rivals* (1775) Sir Lucius O'Trigger is a fierce-tempered Irishman. (His punning name suggests he is 'loose on the trigger'.) The diminutive LUCKY is sometimes found in independent use.

Lucky (m.) This is either a borrowing of the nickname, with its obvious meaning, or the independent adoption of a diminutive of LUCIUS or LUKE. It has found some favour among English speakers in the 20th century, mainly in the US.

US bandleader Lucky Millinder (1900–66) (original first name Lucius); US jazzman Lucky Thompson (b.1924) (original first name Eli).

Lucky (f.) see **Felicity**, **Lucy**.

Lucretia A feminine form of the Roman clan name *Lucretius*, itself of uncertain origin (but possibly related to LUCIUS). The name has enjoyed some sophisticated adoption among English speakers from the 19th century. In Roman history, Lucretia, the wife of Tarquinius Collatinus, was raped by Sextus, the son of Tarquinius Superbus, and took her own life after telling her husband of this. The story is the subject of Shakespeare's poem *The Rape of Lucrece* (1594) (in which he uses the French form of the name). In later literature Princess Lucretia is a character in Benjamin Disraeli's novel *Coningsby* (1844), and the central character also has the name in Lord Lytton's novel *Lucretia, or the Children of the Night* (1846).

US reformer, feminist Lucretia Coffin (1793–1880); US First Lady, wife of president James A. Garfield, Lucretia R. Garfield (1832–1918).

Lucy The name, an English form of the Latin name LUCIA, has been in English-speaking use since medieval times, with popularity peaks in the late 19th and (even more) late 20th centuries. Thomas Tickell wrote the sentimental ballad *Lucy and Colin* (1725), and Lucy Lockit is the jailer's daughter in John Gay's comic opera *The Beggar's Opera* (1728). In Richard Brinsley Sheridan's play *The Rivals* (1775), Lucy is a maid of Lydia Languish, and in Walter Scott's novel *The Bride of Lammermoor* (1819) Lucy Ashton is the central character. Another main character of the name is Lucy Snowe in Charlotte Brontë's novel *Villette* (1853). In recent times the name has been popularized by the character Lucy Ricardo in the US TV series *I Love Lucy* (1951–7), played by Lucille Ball, who herself later starred in *The Lucy Show* (1962–74). The French form of the name, LUCIE, is in independent use, as also occasionally is the diminutive LULU. A diminutive *Lucky* sometimes occurs.

US suffragist Lucy Stone (1818–93); UK children's writer Lucy Boston (1892–1990); UK writer, critic Lucy Hughes-Hallett (b.1951); UK artist Lucy Jones (b.1955); UK actress Lucy Gutteridge (b.1956); UK castaway Lucy Irvine (b.1956); UK writer Lucy Ellmann (b.1956); UK actresses Lucy Briers (b.1967), Lucy Benjamin (b.1970).

Ludovic This name is either an English form of the Latin name *Ludovicus*, representing an Old German name *Hlutwig* (English LOUIS), or an English form of the Gaelic name *Maol Dòmhnaich*, 'devotee of the Lord'. It has enjoyed select adoption among English speakers from the 19th century, but is more particularly favoured in Scotland. Ludovic Lesly is a member of the Scottish guard of the French king Louis XI in Walter Scott's novel *Quentin Durward* (1823). The variant form *Ludovick* is sometimes found, while the usual diminutive is *Ludo*.

Scottish writer, broadcaster Sir Ludovic Kennedy (b.1919) (grandfather was Ludovic).

Luke A biblical name, from Greek *Loukas*, 'man from Lucania' (a region on the west coast of southern Italy). The name was brought to England by the Normans and has been in regular use among English speakers ever since, with a general gain in popularity from the 1970s, increasing sharply in the 1990s. In the Bible Luke is one of the four evangelists, a doctor and a friend of St Paul. Luke Moggs is a miller in George Eliot's novel *The Mill on the Floss* (1860), and Sir Luke Street is a famous doctor in Henry James's novel *The Wings of the Dove* (1902). More recently the name was popularized by the earnest, innocent character Luke Skywalker in the film *Star Wars* (1977), with a name perhaps deliberately reflecting that of the film's creator, George Lucas. LUCAS is a directly related name, and the diminutive LUCKY sometimes occurs in independent use.

US actors Luke Halpin (b.c.1950); Luke Perry (b.1964).

Lulu The name is either an independently adopted diminutive of LOUISE or LUCY, or it represents a colloquial word *lulu* used of an attractive person or thing ('a real lulu'). It has found a certain fashion among English speakers in the 20th century. In Sinclair Lewis's novel *Elmer Gantry* (1927) Lulu Bains is Gantry's mistress. The diminutive *Lu* exists.

US popular singer Lulu Belle (b.1913) (original name Myrtle Eleanor Cooper); Scottish popular singer Lulu (b.1948) (original name Marie Lawrie); UK fashion designer Lulu Guinness (b.1960) (original first name Lucinda).

Luther From the (German) surname, and in select English-speaking use from the 19th century, but specially honoured by black Americans from the 1970s. The name owes its adoption to two men: the German religious reformer Martin Luther (1483–1546) and the assassinated US Baptist pastor and civil rights leader Martin Luther King (1929–68). (The latter was named for the former, as his identically named father had been before him.)

US actor Luther Adler (1903–84) (original first name Lutha); US blues singer Luther Allison (1939–97); US soul singer Luther Vandross (b.1951).

Lydia A biblical name of Greek origin meaning 'woman of Lydia' (a region of Asia Minor). The name has been in English-speaking use from the 17th century, although it is now generally much less common, despite a renewed vogue for it in the 1990s. In the Bible Lydia is a Christian convert who gave hospitality to St Paul, who had converted her. In Tobias Smollett's novel *Humphry Clinker* (1771) Lydia Melford is the romantic sister of Jeremy Melford, and in Richard Brinsley Sheridan's comedy *The Rivals* (1775) Lydia Languish is the central character. In Jane Austen's novel *Pride and Prejudice* (1813), Lydia, the youngest of the five daughters of Mr and Mrs Bennet, marries George Wickham.

US children's writer, editor Lydia Child (1802–80); UK suffragist Lydia Becker (1827–90); Russian ballerina Lydia Lopokova (1891–1981); US 'Tex-Mex' singer Lydia Mendoza (b.1916); UK painter Lydia De Burgh (b.1923); US actress Lydia Cornell (b.1957); US performer, poet Lydia Lunch (b.1959).

Lyn see **Lindsay** (f.).

Lynda An independently adopted spelling variant of LINDA, coming suddenly into fashion among English speakers in the 1950s, although since tailing off to a much more modest level. The diminutive LYNN is in independent use.

UK actress Lynda Baron (b.1942); US actress Lynda Day George (b.1944); Canadian actress Lynda Bellingham (b.1948); US actress

Lynda Carter (b.1951); UK opera singer Lynda Russell (b.1952); US cartoonist Lynda Barry (b.1956).

Lyndon From the surname, and winning some favour among English speakers from the mid-19th century, with a slight gain in popularity in the 1960s.

US president Lyndon B. Johnson (1908–73).

Lynette The name is an independently adopted diminutive of LYNN, formed by adding the French feminine diminutive ending -*ette*. It has found some favour among English speakers from the 19th century and was to some extent popularized by Tennyson's poem 'Gareth and Lynette' (1872) in *The Idylls of the King*. Here, however, it is a form of an earlier Celtic name variously spelled *Linet*, *Lunet* or *Lunete*, popularly associated with the moon (French *lune*) but actually based on a word meaning 'image' (modern Welsh *llun*). An alternative form of the name is *Lynnette*, as for the Welsh actress Lynnette Davies (1950–94). The variant spellings *Linnet* and *Linnette* came to be associated with the linnet (the songbird). Agatha Christie's novel *Death on the Nile* (1937) has Linnet Doyle as a murder victim.

US basketball player Lynette Woodard (b.1959).

Lynn (m.) The name, an independently adopted diminutive of LLEWELYN or LYNDON, has been in select, mainly Welsh, use from the 19th century. The variant spellings *Lyn* and *Lynne* also exist, as respectively for the UK actor Lyn Harding (1867–1952) (original second name Llewellyn) and the US actor Lynne Overman (1887–1943).

US popular composer Lynn Udall (1870–1963) (original name John Henry Keating); UK sculptor Lynn Chadwick (b.1914).

Lynn (f.) The name is either a diminutive form of LINDA, LINDSEY or LYNDA used in its own right, or evolved from the final -*line* of a name such as CAROLINE (or its variant CAROLYN).

It has been in English-speaking use from the 19th century, with its greatest period of popularity in the 1950s and 1960s. The variant spelling LYNNE is in independent use. The forms *Lyn* or *Lin* also occur, as respectively for the UK ice sports-woman Lyn Guest de Swarte (b.1941) (original first name Lindsey) and UK writer Lin Summerfield (b.1952).

US actresses Lynn Fontanne (1887–1983) (original first names Lillie Louise), Lynn Bari (1915–89) (original name Marjorie Fisher or Bitzer); Canadian ballerina Lynn Seymour (b.1939); UK actress Lynn Redgrave (b.1943); UK journalist Lynn Barber (b.1944); US country singer Lynn Anderson (b.1947).

Lynne (f.) An independently adopted variant spelling of LYNN, in popular English-speaking use in the 1950s, but since falling from favour.

US actresses Lynne Carver (1909–55) (original name Virginia Reid Sampson), Lynne Roberts (1919–78) (original name Mary Hart); UK writer Lynne Reid Banks (b.1929); UK actresses Lynne Perrie (b.1931) (original name Jean Dudley), Lynne Frederick (1954–94).

Lynnette see **Lynette.**

Lynsey see **Lindsay** (f.).

Lysette see **Lisa.**

M

Mabel This name is properly a shortened variant of AMABEL, adopted in its own right, but it is also interpreted as a form of French *ma belle*, 'my lovely'. It was in popular use among English speakers from the mid-19th to the early 20th century, when it fell from favour, never (as yet) to recover. In literature Mabel Dunham is a character in James Fenimore Cooper's novel *The Pathfinder* (1840), and Mabel Sweetwinter is a miller's daughter in George Meredith's novel The *Adventures of Harry Richmond* (1871). The usual diminutives are *Mab* or *Mabs*.

UK children's writer, illustrator Mabel Lucie Attwell (1879–1964); UK radio artiste Mabel Constanduros (1880–1957); New Zealand politician Mabel Howard (1893–1972); US actress Mabel Normand (1894–1930); UK-born US cabaret singer Mabel Mercer (1900–84); US actress Mabel Albertson (1901–82); UK actress Mabel Poulton (1905–94); UK woodcarver Mabel Pakenham-Walsh (b.1937).

Mädchen An English untranslated adoption of the German word for 'girl', coming into some favour among English speakers from the 1960s. Compare MADDY and MAIDIE.

US actress Mädchen Amick (b.1970).

Maddy An independently adopted diminutive of MADELEINE or MADONNA, in select English-speaking use from the 1950s. The name suggests a modern revival of the formerly fashionable MAIDIE. Compare MÄDCHEN.

UK folksinger Maddy Prior (b.1947).

Madeleine The name is a French form of MAGDALENE, sometimes popularly associated with *maid*. (Compare MÄDCHEN.) It was taken up by English speakers in the mid-19th century, and has been in modest favour ever since, with a slight up-turn in the 1980s and 1990s. An early literary bearer of the name is Madeleine Trevor in Benjamin Disraeli's novel *Vivian Grey* (1826). The English form of the name, MADELINE, has been adopted in its own right, as has the diminutive, MADDY.

UK actress Madeleine Carroll (1906–87) (original name Marie Madeleine Bernadette O'Carroll); French actress Madeleine Robinson (b.1916); Canadian actress Madeleine Sherwood (b.1926); US diplomat Madeleine Albright (b.1937); UK actress Madeleine Howard (b.1951); US actress Madeleine Stowe (b.1958).

Madeline An English form of the French name MADELEINE, in English-speaking use from the 19th century, but later losing out to its French source name. Keats used the name in his poem *The Eve of St Agnes* (1820), in which it rhymes with 'line'. In Charles Dickens's novel *Nicholas Nickleby* (1838–9) Madeline Bray marries Nicholas. The diminutive MADDY is in independent use.

US pop singer Madeline Bell (b.1942); US actress Madeline Kahn (1942–99); US athlete Madeline Manning (b.1948); UK actress Madeline Smith (b.1949).

Madge An independently adopted diminutive of MARGARET, with pronunciation influenced by MARGERY, in English-speaking use from the early 20th century, although it is now mostly out of fashion.

UK figure skater Madge Syers (1882–1917) (original first names Florence Madeline); Australian-born UK fashion editor Madge Garland (1898–1990); US actresses Madge Blake (1900–69), Madge Bellamy (1902–90), Madge Evans (1909–81); Australian actress Madge Ryan (1919–94); UK actress Madge Hindle (b.1938).

Madonna A name that is a straight adoption of the (Italian) title of the Virgin Mary, literally meaning 'my lady'. The name came into vogue among English speakers from the 1980s, mostly in the US, when it was brought before a wide public by the US pop singer Madonna (b.1958) (original name Madonna Louise Veronica Ciccone), who was herself named for her mother. Diminutives are DONNA (properly a name of different origin) and MADDY, both in independent use.

Mae A variant of MAY or diminutive of MARY in independent use, more common in the US than the UK, and taken up by some English speakers in the late 19th or early 20th century.

US actresses Mae Murray (1889–1965) (original name Marie Adrienne Koenig), Mae West (1892–1980), Mae Marsh (1895–1968) (original first names Mary Warne); Australian-born US actress Mae Busch (1897–1946); US actress Mae Clarke (1907–92) (original name Mary Klotz); US astronaut Mae Jemison (b.1956).

Maeve This name is an English form of the Irish name *Meadhbh*, said to derive from Irish *meadhbhán*, 'intoxication', so meaning 'she who inebriates'. (The English word *mead* is related.) The name is still chiefly in Irish use. In Irish folklore Maeve is the legendary queen of Connacht. Shakespeare's Queen Mab, 'the fairy's midwife', in *Romeo and Juliet* (1595) may derive her name from her. A variant spelling is *Maev*, as for the Scottish actress Maev Alexander (b.1948), while a form closer to the original Irish is *Medbh*, as for the Northern Ireland poet Medbh McGuckian (b.1950).

Irish writer Maeve Binchy (b.1940); UK writer Maeve Haran (b.1950).

Magdalene A biblical name, from that of Mary *Magdalene*, Mary of Magdala, one of the women who accompanies Jesus and the first to see him risen. The name is now felt to be more German than English and is associated by Germans with the word *Magd*, 'maid'. (Compare MÄDCHEN.) It has been in select use among English speakers from medieval times. Agatha Christie's novel *Hercule Poirot's Christmas* (1938) (US title *Murder for Christmas*) has a character Magdalene Lee. A spelling variant is *Magdalen*, and diminutives are *Magdala* and *Magda*. The former of these is found for Magdala (Maggie) Buckley in Agatha Christie's novel *Peril at End House* (1932). The French form of the name, MADELEINE, has always been more popular, however.

Maggie An independently adopted diminutive of MARGARET, in regular English-speaking use from the 19th century, but following the fashion of its source name. Literary characters of the name include Maggie Tulliver, the young daughter of the miller Edward Tulliver in George Eliot's novel *The Mill on the Floss* (1860), and Maggie Johnson, the central character of Stephen Crane's first novel, *Maggie: A Girl of the Street*s (1893). The name was to some degree popularized by the song 'Maggie May' (a hit as sung by Rod Stewart in 1971) and by the early musical (1964) of this title. The variant spelling *Maggi* is sometimes found, as for the UK artist Maggi Hambling (b.1945).

US popular singer Maggie Cline (1857–1934); US actress Maggie McNamara (1928–78); UK actress Dame Maggie Smith (b.1934) (mother was Margaret); US romantic novelist Maggie Osborne (b.1941); Scottish popular singer Maggie Bell (b.1945); UK novelist Maggie Gee (b.1948); US-born UK harpsichordist Maggie Cole (b.1952); UK popular singer Maggie Moone (b.1953); UK magazine editor Maggie Alderson (b.1959); UK actress Maggie O'Neill (b.1964).

Magnus This is an English adoption of the identical Latin by-name, meaning 'great', in select English-speaking use in the 20th century, first in Scotland, then more generally in the UK from the 1960s. The name's actual origin is in the second half of the Latin name, *Carolus Magnus* (Charles the Great), of the famous 9th-century Holy Roman Emperor *Charlemagne*. The name was taken up by various medieval kings of Norway and also became familiar from the 12th-century Scandinavian St Magnus, to whom Kirkwall cathedral, in the Orkneys, is dedicated.

UK food scientist, TV personality Magnus Pyke (1908–92); Icelandic-

Scottish TV presenter, quizmaster Magnus Magnusson (b.1929); Scottish columnist Magnus Linklater (b.1942).

Mahalia A name that may be an adaptation of the biblical name *Mahalath*, that of a wife of Esau (Genesis 28.9) and of a wife of King Rehoboam (2 Chronicles 11.18). This name is itself said to derive from a Hebrew musical term. The name has found very occasional adoption by English speakers from the 19th century.

US gospel singer Mahalia Jackson (1911–72).

Mai see **May**.

Maidie A name that probably derives direct from the word *maid* but that was influenced by MAISIE. It also served as one of the many diminutives of MARY, perhaps through an association with the Virgin Mary (as Maid Mary or Maiden Mary, with *maid* and *maiden* both originally meaning 'virgin') or with the legendary Maid Marian. The name was in select English-speaking use from the 19th century to the 1930s, when maids lost their innocence and it fell from favour. *Maidy* sometimes occurs as a variant form. (Compare MÄDCHEN.)

Maisie An independently adopted variant of the Scottish name *Mairead*, itself a Gaelic form of MARGARET. The name was fairly popular among English speakers in the 1920s and 1930s, since when it has largely gone out of fashion, although there were signs of a modest revival in the 1990s. In literature Maisie is the chief female character in Rudyard Kipling's novel *The Light That Failed* (1890), and the name was also made familiar by the small girl title character of Henry James's novel *What Maisie Knew* (1897).

UK writer Maisie Mosco (b.*c*.1920).

Mal An independently adopted diminutive of MALCOLM or MALDWYN, in select English-speaking use in the 20th century.

The name is found chiefly among popular musicians, entertainers and sportsmen: the UK football manager Malcolm Allison (b.1927) was regularly nicknamed 'Big Mal'.

UK jazzman Mal Waldron (b.1926); UK architect Mal Parker (b.1946); UK athlete Mal Edwards (b.1958); Australian rugby player Mal Meninga (b.1960).

Malachi A biblical name, from Hebrew *Malākhī* 'my messenger', in rare use among English speakers from the 17th century, when it was adopted by the Puritans. In the Bible Malachi is the last (in the Old Testament) of the minor prophets, foretelling the coming of Christ: 'Behold, I will send my messenger ... saith the Lord of hosts' (Malachi 3.1). In Captain Frederick Marryat's novel *Settlers in Canada* (1844) Malachi Bone is a Canadian guide, while in Anthony Trollope's novel *Phineas Finn* (1869) Malachi Finn is Phineas's father, and in James Joyce's novel *Ulysses* (1922) Malachi Mulligan is a medical student. Walter Scott adopted the pseudonym Malachi Malagrowther from the character Mungo Malagrowther in his own novel *The Fortunes of Nigel* (1822).

US actor Malachi Throne (b.1927).

Malandra A classical-style name that appears to be a blend of names such as MELANIE and ALEXANDRA. It found a certain modest vogue in the latter half of the 20th century and was doubtless helped by the UK actress Malandra Burrows (b.1965). Her own name, however, is a blend of those of her parents, *Mal*colm and *Sandra*.

Malcolm The name, long popular in Scotland, is an English form of the Gaelic name *Mael Coluim*, 'devotee of (St) Columba'. It was taken up generally in the English-speaking world from the 1930s, but declined following a 'peak' in the 1950s. Devotion to the 6th-century St Columba (whose own name means 'dove') arose through his conversion of the Scots to Christianity. The name was subsequently favoured by Scottish royalty, down to Malcolm IV in the 12th century. It is the 11th-century Malcolm III, son of Duncan I, who appears in Shakespeare's *Macbeth* (1606). Sir Malcolm Fleming is the lover of Margaret Hautlieu in Walter Scott's novel *Castle Dangerous* (1831). Diminutives MAL and *Malc* exist, the former in its own right. See also CALUM.

UK motor-racing driver Sir Malcolm Campbell (1885–1948); UK conductor Sir Malcolm Sargent (1895–1967); UK children's writer Malcolm Saville (1901–82); UK writer, broadcaster Malcolm Muggeridge (1903–90); US actor Malcolm Atterbury (1907–92); UK composer Malcolm Arnold (b.1921); US Black Muslim leader Malcolm X (1925–65) (original name Malcolm Little); Australian prime minister Malcolm Fraser (b.1930); Australian-born UK composer Malcolm Williamson (b.1931); UK novelist Malcolm Bradbury (1932–2001); UK actor Malcolm McDowell (b.1943).

Maldwyn This name is the Welsh equivalent of English BALDWIN. It is also the Welsh name of the former county of *Montgomery*. (The county took its English and Welsh names from different Norman lords, respectively Roger de Montgomery and Baldwyn de Boller.) The name is rare outside Wales but is common for Welshmen surnamed Davies. The regular diminutive in independent use is MAL.

Welsh opera singer Maldwyn Davies (b.1950).

Malinda see **Melinda**.

Malvina This is apparently an invented name, derived by the 18th-century Scottish poet James Macpherson from the Gaelic words *mala mhìn*, 'smooth brow'. It has found some favour among English speakers from the 19th century. Macpherson used the name for a character in poems that he claimed were translations from the ancient bard Ossian.

US sculptor Malvina Hoffman (1887–1966); US songwriter, singer Malvina Reynolds (1900–78).

Malvolia This name presumably arose as a sort of female counterpart of Shakespeare's *Malvolio* (meaning 'ill-will'). It occasionally occurs in English-speaking use from the 19th century. Malvolia (Mally) Brown is the sister of the central character, Velvet Brown, in Enid Bagnold's novel *National Velvet* (1935).

Mamie An independently adopted diminutive of MARGARET, MARY or (in extended form) MAY, in mainly US use from the 19th century, but now much less common. (The second *m* may have appeared under the influence of *ma'am* or *mam*, 'madam', or of *mama* or *mammy*, 'mother'.) A literary bearer of the name is Mamie Pocock in Henry James's novel *The Ambassadors* (1903). The variant form *Mame* was popularized by the US musical of 1966 and its title song.

US blues singer Mamie Smith (1883–1946); wife of US president Dwight D. Eisenhower, Mamie Eisenhower (1896–1979); US actress Mamie Van Doren (b.1933) (original name Joan Lucille Olander).

Man see **Emanuel**.

Manasseh A biblical name, from Hebrew *Měnasseh*, 'causing to forget', in rare English-speaking use from the 17th century to the 19th century, when it became virtually obsolete. In the Bible Manasseh is the name of several characters, two of the most important being the elder son of Joseph, adopted together with his brother Ephraim by Jacob, and a king of Judah. In William Makepeace Thackeray's novel *Vanity Fair* (1847–8), Manasseh is the chief creditor of Rawdon Crawley. The variant form *Manasses* exists.

Mandy An independently adopted diminutive of AMANDA or, less often, MIRANDA, popular among English speakers, especially in the UK, in the 1960s and 1970s, although familiar well before this and falling from favour since. The name was brought before the public by various shows and songs, such as the song 'Mandy Lee' (1899), Irving Berlin's hit 'Mandy' from the Ziegfeld Follies (1919), the song 'Mandy Make Up Your Mind' from *Dixie to Broadway* (1924) and Barry Manilow's chart-topper 'Mandy' (1975). In literature Mandy is a waitress in Ernest Hemingway's novel *The Torrents of Spring* (1926). The UK semi-documentary film *Mandy* (1952) about a little deaf girl, played by her real-life namesake, Mandy Miller (b.1944), further boosted the name. It is also familiar from the schoolgirl comic *Mandy* (later *Mandy/Judy*), first issued in 1967. The variant forms *Mandi* and *Mandie* are sometimes found, the latter as for the UK TV and film director Mandie Fletcher (b.1954).

UK models Mandy Rice-Davies (b.1944) (original first name Marilyn), Mandy Smith (b.1960); UK hockey players Mandy Davies (b.1966), Mandy Nicholls (b.1968).

Manfred The name comes from an Old German name formed from *man*, 'man', or *magin*, 'strength', and *fridu*, 'peace', so with the meaning 'man of peace' or 'strong man'. It has been occasionally taken up by English speakers from the 18th century. Prince Manfred, the tyrant of Otranto, is the central character in Horace Walpole's novel *The Castle of Otranto* (1765), and it was probably he who inspired the name of the subject of Byron's poetic drama *Manfred* (1817), in which Count Manfred sells himself to the Prince of Darkness.

US mystery writer Manfred B. Lee (1905–71) (original name Manford Lepofsky); South African-born UK pop musician Manfred Mann (b.1940) (original name Michael Lubowitz).

Manley From the surname, suggesting *manly*, and in select use among English speakers in the 19th century, though rare in the 20th. A variant is *Manly,* as for the central character, an honest but misanthropic sea-captain, in William Wycherley's comedy *The Plain-Dealer* (1676). (The dramatist was nicknamed 'Manly' Wycherley because of him.)

Manny see **Emanuel, Immanuel**.

Manon see **Marie**.

Manuel This is the Spanish form of EMANUEL, in select English-speaking use from the 19th century, mainly in the US. Manuel Chaver is Kit Carson's wealthy rival in Willa Cather's novel *Death Comes for the Archbishop* (1927).

UK-born US popular composer Manuel Klein (1876–1919).

Mara A biblical name, traditionally said to mean 'bitter', and popularly regarded as a variant of MARY. It has occurred from time to time in English-speaking use from the 19th century. In the Bible, the name is one that Naomi (the mother-in-law of Ruth) gives herself on her return from Moab: 'Call me not Naomi [that is, 'sweetness'], call me Mara: for the Almighty hath dealt very bitterly with me' (Ruth 1.20).

US actress Mara Corday (b.1932) (original name Marilyn Watts).

Marc An independently adopted diminutive of MARCUS or a (French) spelling variant of MARK, in fashion among English speakers from the 1950s, though tailing off somewhat in the 1980s and 1990s.

US playwright Marc Connelly (1890–1980) (original first name Marcus); US actor Marc Lawrence (b.1910) (original name Max Goldsmith); UK cartoonist Marc (1931–88) (original name Mark Boxer); UK artist Marc Vaux (b.1932); UK pop singer Marc Bolan (1947–77) (original name Mark Feld); US actor Marc Singer (b.1948); UK actor Marc Sinden (b.1954); UK pop singer Marc Almond (b.1957).

Marcel A familiar French name, from the Latin name *Marcellus*, a diminutive of MARCUS. It was taken up by English speakers from the late 19th century, with a special vogue among black Americans. The name became popularly associated with a professional hairdresser, mainly through the fashionable 'marcel wave' of the 1920s, itself named for the French coiffeur who invented it, Marcel Grateau.

French writer Marcel Proust (1871–1922); French mime artist Marcel Marceau (b.1923).

Marcella The name is a feminine form of MARCEL, used to some extent in the English-speaking world, especially in Ireland.

UK playwright Marcella Evaristi (b.1953); US rock singer Marcella Detroit (b.1956).

Marcia This name is a feminine form of the Latin name *Marcius*, related to MARCUS and so to MARK. It has been in mainly US use from the late 19th century, although is now much less common. Marcia Gaylord is one of the main characters in William D. Howells's novel *A Modern Instance* (1882), while Marcia Bencombe is an elderly widow who eventually marries Jocelyn Pierston, the central character of Thomas Hardy's novel *The Well-Beloved* (1897). The name has been largely superseded by its respelled form MARSHA.

US actresses Marcia Mae Jones (b.1924), Marcia Henderson (1930–87); UK secretary to prime minister Harold Wilson, Marcia Falkender (b.1932); UK actress Marcia Ashton (b.1932).

Marcus This name is a straight English adoption of the Latin name *Marcus*, which also gave MARK, traditionally (but probably mistakenly) associated with Mars, the Roman god of war. It enjoyed increasing favour among English speakers, especially black Americans, from the mid-19th century to the 1970s, since when its popularity has generally fallen. As a classical name, it appears for Marcus Andronicus, brother of the central character in Shakespeare's *Titus Andronicus* (1590–94). In modern times the name was made familiar by Marcus Welby, the doctor in the US TV film *Marcus Welby MD* (1968) and subsequent series (1969–76), with Welby played by Robert Young. The diminutive MARC is in independent use.

UK-born Australian writer Marcus Clarke (1846–1881); US Black Consciousness leader Marcus Garvey (1887–1940); UK politician Marcus

Lipton (1900–78); UK magazine editor, publisher Marcus Morris (1915–89); UK historian Marcus Cunliffe (1922–90); UK politician Sir Marcus Fox (b.1927); UK architectural writer Marcus Binney (b.1944).

Margaret The familiar name derives from the Latin name *Margarita*, itself from Greek *margaron*, 'pearl'. The English form of the name was first in Scottish use from the 11th century, then more generally among English speakers from the 17th century, with a gradual increase in popularity in the 20th century to the 1930s, after which it began a gradual decline. It was initially made famous by the 3rd-century martyr St Margaret, who was widely venerated in medieval times. Many royal families bore the name from then on, such as St Margaret of Scotland (1046–93), queen of Malcolm III of Scotland, Margaret (1240–75), queen of Alexander III of Scotland, Margaret (?1282–1318), queen of Edward I of England, Margaret (1283–90), queen of Scotland, the 'Maid of Norway', Margaret of Anjou (1430–1482), queen of Henry VI of England, and Margaret Tudor (1489–1541), queen of James IV of Scotland. It is still royally represented today by Princess Margaret (b.1930), younger sister of Queen Elizabeth II. In literature the name occurs for Margaret, a gentlewoman in Shakespeare's *Much Ado About Nothing* (1598–9); for Margaret Ramsey, who marries Nigel in Walter Scott's novel *The Fortunes of Nigel* (1822); and for Margaret Windermere, the central character in Oscar Wilde's play *Lady Windermere's Fan* (1892). The many diminutives in independent use include MADGE, MAGGIE, MAY, MEG and PEGGY. *Marge*, *Margi*, *Margie* and *Marji* also exist, the second of these as for the UK actress Margi Clarke (b.1954). Related names are MARJORY, the Welsh MEGAN, and various continental European equivalents such as *Margarete*, *Margarita* (giving the independent RITA), French MARGUERITE and MARGOT, and an English version of the latter, MARGO.

UK actresses Margaret Rutherford (1892–1972), Margaret Rawlings (1906–96), Margaret Lockwood (1916–90), Margaret Leighton

(1922–76), Margaret Courtenay (1923–96); UK prime minister Margaret Thatcher, Lady Thatcher (b.1925); UK actress Margaret Tyzack (b.1933); UK radio presenter Margaret Howard (b.1938); UK novelist Margaret Drabble (b.1939); Canadian novelist Margaret Atwood (b.1939); Australian tennis player Margaret Court (b.1942); UK politician Margaret Beckett (b.1943).

Margaux see **Margot**.

Marge see **Margaret**, **Marjorie**.

Margery A variant of MARJORIE formerly favoured by English speakers, and enjoying a peak period in the 1920s.

UK penal reformer Margery Fry (1874–1958); UK-born US children's writer Margery Bianco (1881–1944); UK detective fiction writer Margery Allingham (1904–66).

Margi, **Margie** see **Margaret**, **Marguerite**.

Margo An independently adopted English spelling of the French name MARGOT, mainly in Scottish use, but also found in the US and Australia. Margo Dowling is a film star in John Dos Passos's trilogy *U.S.A.* (1930–36), and Margo Channing is a glamorous but ageing actress in the film *All About Eve* (1950), in which she is played by Bette Davis.

Mexican actress, dancer Margo (1918–85) (original name Maria Marguerita Guedelupe Boldao Castilla y O'Donnell); US country singer Margo Smith (b.1942) (original first names Betty Lou); Scottish politician Margo MacDonald (b.1944).

Margot This name is a French diminutive form of MARGUERITE, but as an English name it is usually regarded as a diminutive of the corresponding MARGARET. It was taken up by English speakers generally in the 19th century, and has found occasional favour since. Agatha Christie's novel *The Mirror Crack'd from Side to Side* (1962) has Margot Bence as a professional photographer. The main variant is the independent spelling MARGO, but *Margaux* was adopted by the US model and actress Margaux Hemingway (1955–96), granddaughter of Ernest Hemingway. (She was originally *Margot*, but changed the spelling to commemorate the wine, from the French village of Margaux, that was drunk by her parents on the night she was conceived.)

UK political hostess Margot Asquith (1864–1945); UK actresses Margot Bryant (1897–1988), Margot Grahame (1911–82); UK ballerina Dame Margot Fonteyn (1919–91); Canadian actress Margot Kidder (b.1948).

Marguerite The name is an English adoption of the French equivalent of MARGARET, now also associated with the garden flower. (Compare DAISY.) The name has been selectively adopted by English speakers from the mid-19th century. The diminutive MARGOT is in independent use. Others are *Margie* or *Margy*.

US actress Marguerite Clark (1883–1940); UK novelist Marguerite Steen (1894–1975); US actresses Marguerite de la Motte (1903–50), Marguerite Churchill (1910–2000).

Mari see **Marie**.

Maria A name that is not only the Latin but the modern Spanish and Italian form of MARY. It has been in use among English speakers since at least the 16th century, and underwent a sudden rise in popularity in the 1960s, since when it has kept a generally lower profile. The many literary bearers of the name include Maria, an attendant of the princess of France in Shakespeare's *Much Ado About Nothing* (1598–9); Maria, an attendant of Olivia in his *Twelfth Night* (1601); the mad woman Maria in Laurence Sterne's novels *Tristram Shandy* (1759–67) and *A Sentimental journey* (1768); Maria, ward of Sir Peter Teazle in Richard Brinsley Sheridan's play *The School for Scandal* (1777); and Maria, Robert Jordan's mistress in Ernest Hemingway's novel *For Whom the Bell Tolls* (1940). A variant spelling *Mariah* is sometimes found, as for the US soul singer

Mariah Carey (b.1970). The French name MARIE and its diminutives are directly related, as are the Italian diminutives MARIELLA and MARIETTA.

US actress Maria Montez (1919–51); Greek-born US opera singer Maria Callas (1923–77); Austrian actress Maria Schell (b.1926); UK actresses Maria Charles (b.1929), Maria Aitken (b.1945); US opera singer Maria Ewing (b.1950); German actress Maria Schneider (b.1952); US rock singer Maria McKee (b.1964); UK cyclist Maria Blower (b.1964).

Marian The name is an English form of the French name MARION, itself a diminutive of MARIE, although it is now often regarded as a blend of MARY and ANN. It has been in English-speaking use from medieval times and was popularized by Maid Marian, companion to Robin Hood. In literature the name occurs for Marian Halcombe, half-sister to Laura in Wilkie Collins's novel *The Woman in White* (1860), and for Marian, a dairymaid in Thomas Hardy's novel *Tess of the D'Urbervilles* (1891). Variant forms of the name in independent use are MARIANA and MARIANNE.

US opera singer Marian Anderson (1897–1993); US actresses Marian Nixon (1904–83), Marian Marsh (b.1913) (original name Violet Krauth); UK popular musician Marian McPartland (b.1920); UK ballerina Marian St Claire (b.1946).

Mariana This name is a Latinized form of MARIAN, in modern times felt by some to be a blend of MARIA and ANNA. It has been adopted by English speakers from at least the 16th century. Literary characters of the name include Mariana ('at the moated grange'), betrothed to Angelo in Shakespeare's *Measure for Measure* (1604); Mariana, Diana's friend in his *All's Well That Ends Well* (1603–4); and the Mariana who was the subject of Tennyson's poems *Mariana* (1830) and *Mariana in the South* (1832). (This last Mariana was suggested by the one in *Measure for Measure*.) The variant form MARIANNA is in independent use.

Marianna Like MARIANA, this name is a Latinized form of MARIAN or MARIANNE, although it was later felt to be a blend of MARIA and ANNA. It has been in English-speaking use since the 18th century. In literature Marianna Selby is the wife of George Selby in Samuel Richardson's novel *Sir Charles Grandison* (1753–4).

Marianne An independently adopted variant of MARIAN, with a spelling as if to suggest a blend of MARIE (or MARY) and ANNE. It has been in use among English speakers from the 18th century. In Jane Austen's novel *Sense and Sensibility* (1811), Marianne Dashwood represents the 'sensibility' of the title. Directly related names are MARIANA and MARIANNA, both in independent use.

US poet, critic Marianne Moore (1887–1972); UK actress Marianne Stone (b.1923); US actress Marianne McAndrew (b.1938); UK pop singer Marianne Faithfull (b.1947).

Marie A name that is the standard French counterpart of MARY, in English-speaking use from the 19th century, at first mostly in the US, then in the UK, where it was fashionable in the 1960s and 1970s. Agatha Christie's short story 'The Arcadian Deer' in *The Labours of Hercules* (1947) has the bad-tempered lady's maid Marie Hellin. A French diminutive of the name, *Manon*, is very occasionally found, perhaps through the heroine of Massenet's opera *Manon* (1884), based on L'Abbé Prévost's novel *Manon Lescaut* (1731). There is also a spelling variant *Mari*, as for the US writers Mari Sandoz (1896–1966) and Mari Evans (b.1923).

UK actress, singer Marie Tempest (1864–1942); French physicist Marie Curie (1867–1934); UK actress Marie Ault (1870–1951) (original name Mary Cragg); UK music-hall artiste Marie Lloyd (1870–1922) (original name Matilda Alice Victoria Wood); UK birth control campaigner Marie Stopes (1880–1958); Australian actress Marie Lohr (1890–1975); US actresses Marie Blake (1896–1978) (original name Blossom

MacDonald), Marie Wilson (1916–72) (original name Katherine Elizabeth White), Marie Windsor (1919–2000) (original name Emily Marie Bertelson); US model, actress Marie McDonald (1923–65); US-Japanese model, TV presenter Marie Helvin (b.1952); US country singer Marie Osmond (b.1959).

Mariel This name, occasionally taken up by English speakers in the 20th century, seems to be either a short form of the Italian name MARIELLA or else an altered spelling of MERIEL or MURIEL. The form *Marielle* sometimes occurs.

US actress Mariel Hemingway (b.1961).

Mariella The name, an Italian diminutive of MARIA, found some favour among English speakers in the 20th century.

UK TV presenter of Norwegian-Scottish ancestry, Mariella Frostrup (b.1962).

Marietta This is an English adoption of the Italian diminutive of MARIA, in some favour among English speakers from the 19th century. Marietta Cignolesi is a servant of Peter Marchdale in Henry Harland's novel *The Cardinal's Snuffbox* (1900), and the name was brought before the public by the popular US operetta *Naughty Marietta* (1910), with a theme song of this title. The French form of the name, *Mariette*, is also sometimes found, as for the US actress Mariette Hartley (b.1940).

US humorous writer Marietta Holley (1836–1926); US actress Marietta Canty (1906–86); UK actress Marietta Meade (b.1961).

Marigold A borrowing of the flower name, in select English-speaking use from the late 19th century, although now seldom found. (The flower name itself derives from that of the Virgin Mary, which gives the first name a special association.) A diminutive GOLDIE is in independent use, but is usually of different origin.

Marilyn The name is a blend of MARY and the final -*line* found in names such as CAROLINE (or its variant CAROLYN), although it is now usually regarded as a combination of MARY and LYNN. It was taken up in the English-speaking world in the early 20th century, and became especially popular in the US. In the UK it leaped into favour in the 1950s, but has since been much more modestly adopted. Marilyn Monroe (see below) did much to make the name famous, and its peak of popularity coincides with her best-known movies.

US actresses Marilyn Miller (1898–1936) (original name Mary Ellen Reynolds), Marilyn Maxwell (1921–72) (original first name Marvel), Marilyn Monroe (1926–62) (original name Norma Jean Mortensen); US children's writer Marilyn Sachs (b.1927); US writer Marolyn French (b.1929); US songwriter Marilyn Bergman (b.1929); UK model Marilyn Jackson (b.1945); US actress Marilyn Hassett (b.1947); UK opera singer Marilyn Hill Smith (b.1952).

Marina This name is a feminine form of the Roman clan name *Marinus*, itself a diminutive of MARIUS but early associated with the Latin word *mare*, 'sea', and in modern times with variants of MARY. It has been in select use among English speakers from the 1930s, with its most popular adoption in the UK. Marina in Shakespeare's *Pericles* (1606–8) has a name alluding to her birth at sea. Later, Agatha Christie's novel *The Mirror Crack'd from Side to Side* (1962) has a film actress Marina Gregg.

Wife of Prince George (fifth son of George V), Princess Marina of Greece (1906–68); French actress Marina Vlady (b.1938); US art critic Marina Vaizey (b.1938); UK writer Marina Warner (b.1946); UK daughter of Princess Alexandra, Marina Mowatt (b.1966); Canadian actress Marina Orsini (b.*c*.1968).

Marion (m.) The name, an English form of the Latin name *Marianus*, itself a derivative of MARIUS, has found occasional adoption among English speakers from the 19th century, mainly in the US. The famous US actor John Wayne (1907–79) had the original name Marion Michael Morrison.

US jazzman Marion Brown (b.1935).

Marion (f.) This name, a French diminutive of MARIE, has been in English-speaking use from medieval times, vying with MARIAN for popularity from the 19th century, and now mostly favoured in Scotland. In James Joyce's novel *Ulysses* (1922) the maiden name of Molly Bloom is Marion Tweedy.

US actresses Marion Lorne (1886–1968), Marion Davies (1897–1961), Marion Martin (1916–85); US singer Marion Hutton (1920–87); UK writer, publisher Marion Boyars (b.1929); US science fiction writer Marion Bradley (b.1930); Trinidadian writer Marion Patrick Jones (b.1934); UK fashion designer Marion Foale (b.1939); UK equestrienne Marion Mould (b.1947); US athlete Marion Jones (b.1975).

Marisa A variant form of MARIA or MARINA, influenced by LISA, in vogue among English speakers from the 1950s.

French actress Marisa Mell (1929–92) (original name Marlies Moitzi); Italian actress Marisa Pavan (b.1932); US model, actress Marisa Berenson (b.1946); US film director Marisa Silver (b.1960); US actress Marisa Tomei (b.1964).

Marius This is a Latin name, itself a Roman clan name, perhaps derived either from *Mars*, the Roman god of war, or from *mas*, genitive *maris*, 'male', 'manly' (with which the name of Mars has in turn been associated). The name has found some slight favour among English speakers from the 19th century.

UK actor Marius Goring (1912–98).

Marje see **Marjorie**.

Marji see **Margaret**.

Marjorie A name that is an independent adoption of an English vernacular form of MARGARET. It has been in English-speaking use from medieval times but gained wider favour only in the 19th century, especially in the US. It was very much in vogue in the UK in the 1920s, but has since been much more modestly adopted. In John Galsworthy's novel *The Silver Spoon* (1926), and elsewhere in his *Forsyte* series, Marjorie Ferrar is a rival of Fleur Forsyte. The appearance of margarine ('marge') on the culinary scene may have blunted enthusiasm for the name in recent times. A frequent variant spelling is *Marjory*, while the earlier form of the name was usually MARGERY, as in the nursery rhyme, 'See saw, Margery Daw'. Common diminutives are *Marge* or *Marje*, the former as for the US feminist writer Marge Piercy (b.1936).

UK writer Marjorie Bowen (1888–1952) (original name Gabrielle Margaret Vere Long); UK actress Marjorie Fielding (1892–1956); US opera singer Marjorie Lawrence (1907–79); UK 'agony aunt' Marjorie Proops (1911–96); UK actress Marjorie Yates (b.1941); UK radio and TV presenter Marjorie Lofthouse (b.1943).

Mark A biblical name, in origin the English form of the Latin name MARCUS. The name enjoyed only modest favour in the English-speaking world from the 17th century to the 1960s, when it suddenly took off. It remained extremely popular throughout the 1970s but has now settled to a more modest level. In the Bible Mark is one of the four evangelists, to whom the second gospel is ascribed. The Arthurian romances have Mark as the king of Cornwall and husband of Isolde (Yseult) of Ireland (or Brittany), who was brought to him as a bride by Tristram (Tristan). He appears in many subsequent stories based on Arthurian legend, such as Thomas Malory's cycle *Le Morte d'Arthur* (1470) or Tennyson's poem 'The Last Tournament' (1859) in *Idylls of the King*. As a historic figure, the 1st-century Roman general Mark Antony appears in Shakespeare's *Julius Caesar* (1599) and *Antony and Cleopatra* (1606–7). Later, Mark Gilbert is a hosier's apprentice in Charles Dickens's novel *Barnaby Rudge* (1841). The diminutive *Markie* or *Marky* is sometimes found.

US writer Mark Twain (1835–1910) (original name Samuel Langhorne Clemens); US athlete, actor Mark Forest (b.1933) (original name Lou

Degni); UK rock musician Mark Knopfler (b.1949); US swimmer Mark
Spitz (b.1950); US actor Mark Hamill (b.1951); UK actor Mark Tandy
(b.1957); UK TV presenter Mark Curry (b.1961); UK actor Mark Farmer
(b.1962).

Marlene This name is a contracted form of the German name
Maria Magdalene (English Mary Magdalene, see MAGDALENE),
but became subsequently associated with MARILYN. It enjoyed
some favour among English speakers in the 1930s and 1940s
but then declined. Its vogue was largely due to the German-
born US actress Marlene Dietrich (1901–92) (original name
Maria Magdalene von Losch) and to the song 'Lili Marlene',
which she regularly sang during the Second World War. Agatha
Christie has Marlene Tucker as a murder victim in her novel
Dead Man's Folly (1956). The diminutive *Marla* sometimes
occurs.

Marlin The name appears to be an alteration (perhaps
through French) of MERLIN or else a variant of MARLON. It
is occasionally found in English-speaking use in the 20th
century.

US TV zoo presenter Marlin Perkins (1905–86); US popular composer
Marlin Skiles (b.1906); US diplomat Marlin Fitzwater (b.1942).

Marlon This name may have originated as a derivative of
the French name MARC, with the *-lon* a French diminutive
suffix, or else as an alteration of MARION or MERLIN, or even a
blend of these. It is occasionally encountered among English
speakers from the 1950s, and probably owed its original vogue
to the US actor Marlon Brando (b.1924), whose father had the
same name.

Marmaduke This distinctive name is of uncertain origin,
although some authorities trace it back to a Celtic name *Mael
Maedóc*, 'devotee of Maedóc', the latter being the name of various Irish saints. Its use among English speakers has been

modest since its initial adoption in the 16th century. Judge Marmaduke (Duke) Temple, a retired Quaker merchant, is the central character in James Fenimore Cooper's novel *The Pioneers* (1823), and Sir Marmaduke Morecombe is a politician in Anthony Trollope's novel *Phineas Finn* (1869). In Virginia Woolf's novel *Orlando* (1928) the central character, a man who becomes a woman, marries Marmaduke Bonthrop Shelmerdine. The name now has aristocratic but also faintly comical overtones, perhaps through the incongruous association of a word such as *marmalade* with *duke*. The usual diminutive actually is DUKE, although this is normally a 'title' name in its own right.

UK broadcasting executive Marmaduke Hussey (b.1923).

Marsha A variant spelling of MARCIA, reflecting the name's actual pronunciation. It was taken up in the US in the 1920s and rather later, but more modestly, in the UK.

US actresses Marsha Hunt (b.1917) (original first name Marcia), Marsha Mason (b.1942); UK actress Marsha Fitzalan (b.*c*.1950).

Marshall (m.) From the surname, with its suggestion of *marshal*, and a name in select use among English speakers from the 19th century.

Canadian writer Marshall McLuhan (1911–80) (originally second name, first being Herbert); US actor Marshall Thompson (1925–92) (originally second name, first being James).

Marshall (f.) A female adoption of the male name MARSHALL, influenced by MARSHA. The name is found in occasional use from the 1940s.

US country singer Marshall Chapman (b.1949).

Martha A biblical name, from Aramaic *Mārthā*, 'lady', in use among English speakers from the 16th century, and especially popular in the US from the 19th century. The biblical Martha, the sister of Lazarus and Mary of Bethany, was 'cumbered with much serving', so that her name came to be associated with housewives and domestic toil. In later literature Martha Buskbody is a maker of mantuas (gowns) in Walter Scott's novel *Old Mortality* (1816). The vogue for the name in the US owes much to Martha Washington (1732–1802), wife of president George Washington and the first First Lady. Diminutives include MARTI, *Martie* and *Marty*, while MATTIE is sometimes found in independent use.

US dancer, choreographer Martha Graham (1894–1991); US writer Martha Gellhorn (1908–98); US actress Martha Scott (b.1914); US comedienne Martha Raye (1916–94) (original name Margaret Reed); US country singer Martha Carson (b.1921) (original first name Irene); US actress Martha Hyer (b.1924); US businesswomen Martha Stewart (b.1941); US film director Martha Coolidge (b.1946).

Marti An independently adopted diminutive of MARTINA, or a variant spelling of *Marty* as a female name, in select use among English speakers in the second half of the 20th century.

UK popular singer Marti Webb (b.c.1930); UK comedienne, TV presenter Marti Caine (1945–95) (original name Lynne Shepherd).

Martie see **Martha**.

Martin The name is an English form of the Latin name *Martinus*, itself probably from *Mars*, genitive *Martis*, the Roman god of war. The name has come to be popularly associated by some with that of the bird, as for JAY and ROBIN. It has been in regular English-speaking use from medieval times, with a period of popularity in the 1960s and 1970s. The name was initially made known by the 4th-century ecclesiastic St Martin of Tours, famed in popular legend for dividing his cloak in two and giving half to a beggar. Literary bearers of the name include the central characters of two novels: Charles Dickens's *Martin Chuzzlewit* (1843–4) and Jack London's *Martin Eden* (1909). The name has also come to be associated with that of the German founder of Protestantism, Martin Luther (1483–1546), familiar in modern times from the black US civil rights leader named for him, Martin Luther King (1929–68). The variant spelling *Martyn* its sometimes found, as for the UK TV newsreader Martyn Lewis (b.1945), while the diminutive MARTY is in independent use.

US president Martin van Buren (1782–1862); US actor Martin Gabel (1912–86); UK astronomer Sir Martin Ryle (1918–84); UK actors Martin Jarvis (b.1941), Martin Shaw (b.1945); UK novelist Martin Amis (b.1949); UK TV entertainer Martin Daniels (b.1963).

Martina A feminine form of MARTIN, in English-speaking use from the mid-19th century. A spelling variant is the French form *Martine*, as for the UK actresses Martine Beswick (b.1941) and Martine McCutcheon (b.1976). A diminutive in independent use is MARTI.

US opera singer Martina Arroyo (b.1936); Czech-born tennis players Martina Navratilova (b.1956), Martina Hingis (b.1980).

Martita An independently adopted diminutive of the Spanish name *Marta* (English MARTHA), found among some English speakers in the 20th century, chiefly in the US but also occasionally in the UK.

UK actress Martita Hunt (1900–69).

Marty (m.) An independently adopted diminutive of MARTIN, in select English-speaking use from the mid-20th century. In literature the name is that of the butcher who is the title character of Paddy Chayefsky's play *Marty* (1955).

US country singer Marty Robbins (1925–82); UK comedian Marty Feldman (1933–83); US actor Marty Ingels (b.1936); UK pop singer Marty Wilde (b.1939) (original name Reginald Smith); US country singer Marty Stuart (b.1958).

Marty (f.) see **Martha, Marti.**

Marvin From the surname, itself a form of MERVYN. The name caught on in the US in the 19th century, rising to a popularity peak in the 1920s, especially among blacks, after which it gradually declined. It has never been common in the UK. The usual diminutive is *Marv*, as for the US soul singer Marv Johnson (1938–93).

US actors Marvin Miller (1913–85), Marvin Kaplan (b.1924); American Indian country singer Marvin Rainwater (b.1925); US film director Marvin Chomsky (b.1929); US fantasy writer Marvin Kaye (b.1938); US soul singer Marvin Gaye (1939–84); US popular composer Marvin Hamlisch (b.1944); US boxer Marvin Hagler (b.1952).

Mary The long-familiar name evolved as an English form of the French name MARIE, from Latin MARIA, itself from the Greek name *Mariam* which is a form of the Hebrew name *Miryām*, from which modern MIRIAM more directly derives. The precise origin of the name is uncertain, but it may be ultimately based on a root element -*mrh*- meaning 'to swell', referring to pregnancy (implying fertility) or to 'fullness' in the sense of completeness or perfection. The same element may link with the word for 'mother' in many languages, such as Latin and Greek *mater*, French *mère*, Spanish *madre* and English *mother* itself. If so, the Virgin Mary, the mother of Jesus, is the embodiment of all senses: her pregnancy produced a perfect person. The name has been in constant English-speaking use from medieval times, and only from the 1920s did it show any signs of falling from favour. There are six Marys in the Bible: the Virgin Mary herself, Mary Magdalene, Mary the sister of Martha and Lazarus, Mary the mother of James and Joseph, Mary the mother of Mark, and the Mary who was a Christian woman active in Rome. The name was popularized by its royal bearers, as in the English-speaking world by Mary I (1516–58) and Mary II (1662–94), queens of England, Mary Stuart (1542–87), queen of Scotland (Mary, Queen of Scots), and Mary of Teck (1867–1953), queen of George V and mother of George VI, Britain's Queen Mother before Queen Elizabeth. Literary bearers of the name include, among others, the central character of Elizabeth Gaskell's novel *Mary Barton* (1848), and Mary, maid to Mrs Brandon in William Makepeace Thackeray's novel *The Adventures of Philip* (1861–2). The name's many variants and diminutives, of which several have been independently adopted, include MAMIE, MAY and MOLLY. The name also frequently combines with another to form a double name, typically *Mary Ann*, as for the UK journalist Mary Ann Sieghart (b.1961). (See also MARIAN.)

US founder of Christian Science movement Mary Baker Eddy (1821–1910); Canadian actress Mary Pickford (1893–1976) (original name Gladys Mary Smith); UK media campaigner Mary Whitehouse (1910–2001); US writer Mary McCarthy (1912–89); US actress, singer Mary Martin (1913–90); UK fashion designer Mary Quant (b.1934); US soul singer Mary Wells (1943–92); UK actress Mary Tamm (b.1950).

Mathias see **Matthias**.

Matilda The English name has its origin in the Old German name *Mahthilda*, formed from *macht*, 'might', and *hiltja*, 'battle', giving an overall meaning of 'mighty in battle'. It was introduced to England by Matilda (d.1083), wife of William the Conqueror, but was little favoured generally by English speakers until the 18th century, when it enjoyed a period of reasonable popularity until the early years of the 20th century, after which it declined. In Horace Walpole's novel *The Castle of Otranto* (1765) Matilda is the daughter of the tyrant prince Manfred. Later, Matilda ('Tilda) Price is a character in Charles Dickens's novel *Nicholas Nickleby* (1838–9). The popular Australian song 'Waltzing Matilda' refers not to a person but to a 'matilda' (knapsack) that 'waltzes' (sways) on the back of a 'swagman' (itinerant labourer) as he trudges along. Diminutives include the independently adopted MATTIE and TILLY. *Tilda* also exists, as for the UK actress Tilda Swinton (b.1961). MAUD is a directly related name.

UK actress Matilda Ziegler (b.1964).

Matt An independently adopted diminutive of MATTHEW, in select use among English speakers in the 20th century. The variant spelling *Mat* also occurs, as for the Australian actor Mat Stevenson (b.1969), and a frequent diminutive is *Mattie*.

UK footballer Matt Busby (1909–94); UK cabaret singer Matt Monro (1930–85) (original name Terry Parsons); US actor Matt Dillon (b.1964); US swimmer Matt Biondi (b.1965); US actor Matt LeBlanc (b.1967).

Matthew A biblical name, from Hebrew *Mattathiāh*, 'gift of God'. The name was in only modest use among English speakers until the 1960s, when it suddenly became popular. Since then it has gone from strength to strength, entering the 1990s as one of the top names of the century. In the Bible Matthew is one of the four evangelists, to whom the first gospel is ascribed. Matthew is a 'town gull' in Ben Jonson's comedy *Every Man in his Humour* (1598). In later literature Matthew Bramble is the father of the central character in Tobias Smollett's novel *Humphry Clinker* (1771), while Matthew Moon is a farmhand in Thomas Hardy's novel *Far from the Madding Crowd* (1874). The diminutive MATT is in independent use. MATTHIAS is a directly related name.

UK poet Matthew Arnold (1822–88); US Army general Matthew B. Ridgway (1895–1993); UK TV entertainer Matthew Corbett (b.1948); UK TV presenter Matthew Kelly (b.1950); US actor Matthew Broderick (b.1962); UK actor Matthew Vaughan (b.1964).

Matthias A biblical name, representing an Aramaic variant of the Hebrew original that gave MATTHEW. The name has found some favour among English speakers from the 17th century. In the Bible Matthias is the apostle chosen to replace Judas Iscariot, with the form of his name (at least in English Bible translations) distinguishing him from the evangelist Matthew. The variant spelling *Mathias* exists, as for Mathias Bede, father of Adam in George Eliot's novel *Adam Bede* (1859).

Mattie (m.) see **Matt**.

Mattie (f.) An independently adopted diminutive of MATILDA and, less often, MARTHA, taken up by English speakers from 18th century but falling from favour in the 19th century, only to revive in the mid-20th, when it again declined. In Walter Scott's novel *Rob Roy* (1817) Mattie is Nicol Jarvie's servant. The main variant is *Matty*, familiar in literature from Miss Matty (Matilda Jenkyns), the central character in Elizabeth Gaskell's novel *Cranford* (1851–3).

Maud This name is a French contracted form of MATILDA, in English-speaking use from medieval times, when it was introduced to England by the Normans. It was popularized by Tennyson's poem *Maud* (1855) and by the musical version of it that was staged the following year, with its familiar line, 'Come into the garden, Maud'. (Tennyson seems to have chosen the name for its suggestion of *maudlin*, *morbid*, *mood* or even *mad*: the narrator tells of his father's death, his killing of Maud's brother and his subsequent descent into insanity.) In Jack London's novel *The Sea Wolf* (1904) Maud Brewster is a writer who marries Humphrey van Weyden. The name has royal associations, as for Maud (1869–1938), daughter of Edward VII and Queen Alexandra, who married Prince Charles of Denmark and became queen of Haakon VII of Norway. The usual diminutive is *Maudie*.

Irish political activist Maud Gonne (1865–1953); US children's writer, illustrator Maud Petersham (1889–1971); Swedish-born US actress Maud Adams (b.1945).

Maureen The name is an English form of the Irish name *Máirín*, a diminutive of *Máire* (English MARY). It came into fashion among English speakers in the late 19th century, but after reaching a peak of popularity in the 1930s and 1940s gradually fell from favour. Spelling variants *Maurene*, *Maurine* and *Moreen* are sometimes found. A diminutive in popular use is *Mo*.

Irish-born US actresses Maureen O'Sullivan (1911–98), Maureen O'Hara (b.1920); Irish writer Maureen Daly (b.1921); US actress Maureen Stapleton (b.1925); UK novelist Maureen Duffy (b.1933); US tennis player Maureen Connolly ('Little Mo') (1934–69); UK actress Maureen Lipman (b.1946) (father was Maurice).

Maurice The name is an English version (influenced by French) of the Late Latin name *Mauricius*, a derivative of *Maurus*, itself meaning 'Moor', that is, 'dark-skinned'. It was introduced to England by the Normans, but remained in only modest favour until the mid-19th century, when it gradually rose in popularity until the 1920s and 1930s, after which it declined. Maurice Christian Bycliffe is a character in George Eliot's novel *Felix Holt* (1866), and a later literary bearer of the name is Maurice Hall, the central character of E.M. Forster's novel *Maurice* (written 1913, published 1971). The diminutives *Mo* and *Moss* are sometimes found, the latter as for the Irish rugby player Moss Keane (b.1948).

French singer, actor Maurice Chevalier (1888–1972); UK actors Maurice Evans (1901–89), Maurice Denham (b.1909).

Maurine see **Maureen**.

Mavis The name has its origin in the poetic word for a song thrush: 'The mavis mild wi' many a note,/Sings drowsy day to rest' (Robert Burns, *A Lament for Mary, Queen of Scots*, 1791). (Compare MERLE.) It was taken up by English speakers in the late 19th century, but after a boom in the 1930s went quite quickly out of fashion. There is a character called Mavis in Marie Corelli's novel *The Sorrows of Satan* (1895), and this may have helped popularize the name. A diminutive *Mave* occasionally occurs.

UK bowls player Mavis Steele (b.1928); UK broadcaster, TV presenter Mavis Nicholson (b.1930).

Max The name is an independently adopted diminutive of MAXIMILIAN or MAXWELL, adopted by English speakers from the late 19th century, mostly in the UK, but not widely fashionable until the 1990s. Diminutives *Maxey* and *Maxie* exist.

UK critic, wit Sir Max Beerbohm (1872–1956) (original first names Henry Maximilian); Austrian theatrical producer Max Reinhardt (1873–1943); Canadian newspaper proprietor Max Aitken, 1st Baron Beaverbrook (1879–1964) (original first names William Maxwell); French-born US comedian Max Linder (1883–1925) (original name Gabriel Leuvielle); UK comedian May Miller (1895–1963) (original name Harold Sargent); Irish actor Max Adrian (1902–73); UK comedian Max Wall (1908–90) (original name Maxwell George Lorimer); UK popular musician Max Jaffa (1911–91); UK comedian Max Bygraves (b.1922) (original first names Walter William); UK newspaper editor Max Hastings (b.1945) (based on father's first name, Macdonald, as if 'Mac's'); UK athlete Max Robertson (b.1963).

Maxene, **Maxie** see **Maxine**.

Maximilian The name, an English version of the Latin name *Maximilianus*, a diminutive of *Maximus*, 'greatest', has found occasional favour among English speakers from the 19th century. It was historically made familiar by the royal house of Bavaria (in the 16th to 19th centuries) and became well known from the ill-fated archduke of Austria and emperor of Mexico, Maximilian (1832–67). The diminutive MAX is in independent use.

Austrian actor Maximilian Schell (b.1930).

Maxine A feminine form of MAX, with the *-ine* from a name such as CAROLINE. Its popularity among English speakers increased from the 1930s to the 1960s, since when it has gradually declined. The variant spelling *Maxene* exists, as for Maxene Andrews (1916–95) of the Andrews Sisters, the US close harmony trio. Diminutives *Maxie*, *Micki* and *Mickie* exist, the second of these as for the US diver Micki King (b.1944).

US actress Maxine Elliott (1868–1940) (original name Jessie Dermot); US jazz singer Maxine Sullivan (1911–87) (original name Marietta Williams); UK actress Maxine Audley (1923–92); Chinese-born US writer Maxine Hong Kingston (b.1940); Australian actress Maxine Klibingaitis (b.1964).

Maxwell From the (Scottish) surname, and a name long favoured in Scotland, but taken up generally by English speakers from the 19th century, with a small rise in popularity in the 1990s. The name became familiar as that regularly used in the Aitken family: the family bore the title Beaverbrook from 1916 as a result of the peerage awarded that year to the Canadian newspaper owner William Maxwell Aitken (1879–1964). The diminutive, MAX, is in independent use.

US playwright Maxwell Anderson (1888–1959); UK architect Maxwell Fry (1899–1987); US film director Maxwell Shane (1905–83); UK film producer Maxwell Setton (b.1909); UK businessman Maxwell Joseph (1910–82); Irish actor Maxwell Reed (1920–74); UK actors Maxwell Shaw (1929–85), Maxwell Caulfield (b.1959).

May The name originated as a diminutive of MARGARET or MARY, but came to be thought of subsequently as a flower name or that of the month. It was adopted by English speakers in the 19th century, but after a period of popularity in the early years of the 20th century fell quite rapidly from favour. May Fielding is a character in Charles Dickens's novel *The Cricket on the Hearth* (1846). Variants include MAE, in independent use, and *Mai*, as for the Swedish actress Mai Zetterling (1925–94).

Australian actress May Robson (1858–1942) (original name Mary Robison); UK novelist May Sinclair (1863–1946); UK actress Dame May Whitty (1865–1948); UK-born US tennis player May Sutton (1886–1975); US actress May McAvoy (1901–87); US artist May Stevens (b.1924).

Maya This name is a Latin-style form of May, influenced by the name of the Roman goddess *Maia* (who may have given the name of the month). It was taken up by English speakers in the first half of the 20th century, mainly in the US. It became familiar from the US writer Maya Angelou (b.1928) (original name Marguerite Annie Johnson), although for her the name is said to have originated as a nickname, from the way her younger brother referred to her as 'maya sista'.

Russian-born US film director Maya Deren (1908–61).

Medbh see **Maeve**.

Meg An independently adopted diminutive of MARGARET, mainly in Scottish use from the 19th century. One of the best-known literary bearers of the name is Meg Merrilies, the gypsy queen in Walter Scott's novel *Guy Mannering* (1815). Its own most common diminutive is *Meggie*, with *Megs* familiar from the UK actress Megs Jenkins (1917–98).

US journalist Meg Greenfield (b.1930); US actresses Meg Foster (b.1948), Meg Tilly (b.1960), Meg Ryan (b.1962) (original name Margaret Hyra).

Megan This name is a Welsh form of MEG, itself a diminutive of MARGARET. It is still mainly in Welsh use, but in the 1990s caught on more generally among English speakers. The public was initially made aware of it by Lady Megan Lloyd George (1902–66), daughter of the UK prime minister David Lloyd George. She was Welsh-born, like her father, and was named for her mother, Margaret. In Agatha Christie's novel *The A.B.C. Murders* (1935), Megan Barnard is the sister of the second murder victim, Betty Barnard.

US playwright Megan Terry (b.1932).

Meggie, Megs see **Meg**.

Mel (m.) An independently adopted diminutive of MELVILLE, MELVIN or MELVYN, in use among English speakers from the early 20th century.

US actor Mel Ferrer (b.1917) (original first name Melchior); US popular singer Mel Tormé (1925–99) (original first name Melvin); US film director Mel Brooks (b.1926) (original name Melvin Kaminsky); US jazzman Mel Lewis (1929–90) (original name Melvin Sokoloff); US country singer Mel Tillis (b.1932) (original first names Lonnie Melvin); Welsh racehorse owner Mel Davies (b.1948) (original first name Melvyn); UK actor Mel Smith (b.1952) (original first name Melvyn); Australian actor Mel Gibson (b.1956); UK footballer Mel Sage (b.1964) (original first name Melvyn).

Mel (f.) see **Imelda, Melanie**.

Melanie A name that is a French form of the Latin name *Melania*, itself from Greek *melas*, 'black', in the sense of a person having dark hair, eyes or skin. The name is found in English-speaking use as early as the 17th century, but only became widely popular in the 1960s and 1970s, since when it has been adopted more modestly. It was given something of a boost by Melanie Hamilton, who marries Ashley Wilkes in Margaret Mitchell's novel *Gone with the Wind* (1936). A diminutive *Mel* occurs.

Austrian-born UK child psychoanalyst Melanie Klein (1882–1960); US popular singer Melanie (b.1947) (original name Melanie Safka); US actresses Melanie Mayron (b.1952), Melanie Griffith (b.1957).

Melba The name was probably adopted from that of the Australian operatic singer Dame Nellie Melba (1861–1931) (original name Helen Mitchell), who based her stage name on that of her native city of Melbourne. The name has found some favour among English speakers from the early 20th century. The US novelist James Purdy has a popular singer named Melba in his novel *Malcolm* (1959).

US country singer Melba Montgomery (b.1938).

Melina This name is probably a shortened form of a name such as EMMELINE, influenced by other *Mel-* names such as MELINDA or MELISSA. It has been taken up by some English speakers from the 19th century.

Greek-born actress Melina Mercouri (1925–94).

Melinda This is a name that seems to be a form of BELINDA, with or without conscious reference to Latin *mel*, 'honey'. It has found modest favour among English speakers from the 18th century. In Tobias Smollett's novel *Roderick Random* (1748) Melinda Goosetrap is courted by Roderick. More recently Melinda Pink is a detective in the crime novels (1970s–1980s) by the UK writer Gwen Moffat. A spelling variant is *Malinda*.

US actress Melinda Dillon (b.1939); UK TV presenter Melinda Messenger (b.1971).

Melissa A Greek name, from the word *melissa*, 'bee', itself from *meli*, 'honey'. (Compare DEBORAH.) The name has been known to English speakers since at least the 16th century, although it was not generally adopted until the 20th century, chiefly in the US. Its popularity in the UK has been steadily growing since the 1970s. An early literary character of the name is Melissa, the beneficent witch in Ariosto's poem *Orlando Furioso* (1532). Later characters include Melissa in Edmund Spenser's poem *The Faerie Queene* (1590–96); Melissa Wackles in Charles Dickens's novel *The Old Curiosity Shop* (1840–41); Melissa, the daughter of Lady Blanche, in Tennyson's poem *The Princess* (1847); Melissa the bee in Rudyard Kipling's short story 'The Mother Hive' in *Actions and Reactions* (1909); and Melissa Artemis, a Greek dancer and prostitute in Lawrence Durrell's *Alexandria Quartet* (1957–60). The diminutive *Missie* or *Missy* exists, as for the US R&B singer Missy Elliott (b.1917).

Irish daughter of Earl of Dunraven, Lady Melissa Brook (b.1935); UK daughter of Earl of Darnley, Lady Melissa Levey (b.1945); US screenwriter Melissa Mathison (b.1949); US popular singer Melissa Manchester (b.1951); UK artist Melissa Scott-Miller (b.1959); US rock singer Melissa Etheridge (b.1961); US actresses Melissa Sue Anderson (b.1962), Melissa Gilbert (b.1964); UK daughter of Earl of Kinnoull, Lady Melissa Hay (b.1964); US actress Melissa Hart (b.1976).

Melody A borrowing of the standard word, doubtless partly prompted by the equation expressed in the Irving Berlin song 'A pretty girl is like a melody' (1919) and partly by association with names such as MELANIE and MELISSA. The UK actress Susan George (b.1950) has Melody as her second name. The name has been in English-speaking use from the 19th century, slightly gaining in popularity from the 1950s.

US historian, authority on Alaska Melody Webb (b.1946).

Melville From the (Scottish) surname, and still mainly in Scottish use, with some spread generally to other English speakers in the 20th century. The usual diminutive, MEL, is in independent use.

UK actor Melville Cooper (1896–1973); US screenwriter Melville Shavelson (b.1917).

Melvin From the (Scottish) surname, and in select use among English speakers from the late 19th century, with something of a rise in favour in the 1950s. Melvin Twemlow is a character in Charles Dickens's novel *Our Mutual Friend* (1864–5). The variant spelling MELVYN is used in its own right, as is the usual diminutive, MEL.

US scriptwriter, film producer Melvin Frank (1917–88); US film producer Melvin Simon (b.1925); US film director Melvin Van Peebles (b.1932).

Melvyn An independently adopted variant of MELVIN, taken up by some English speakers from the early 20th century. The diminutive MEL exists in its own right.

US actor Melvyn Douglas (1901–81); UK actor Melvyn Hayes (b.1935); UK novelist, TV arts presenter Melvyn Bragg (b.1939).

Mercedes A name based on the Spanish word *merced*, 'mercy', as specifically occurring in a title of the Virgin Mary, *María de las Mercedes* (Mary of the Mercies). The name has been in select use among English speakers, mainly among Roman Catholics in the US, from the 19th century. Diminutives include MERCY and SADIE, both in independent use (although the first of these normally has a different origin).

US actresses Mercedes McCambridge (b.1918), Mercedes Ruehl (b.1954).

Mercy An adoption of the word for the virtue, taken up by Puritans in the 17th century for its Christian significance, but now rare. Mercy is one of the characters with allegorical names in John Bunyan's *A Pilgrim's Progress* (1678, 1684). The name later occurs for one of Mr Pecksniff's two daughters (the other is CHARITY) in Charles Dickens's novel *Martin Chuzzlewit* (1843–4). The diminutive MERRY is in independent use.

UK racehorse trainer Mercy Rimell (b.1919).

Meredith (m.) This is the English form of the Welsh name *Maredudd*, later *Mereddudd*, perhaps a blend of *mawredd*, 'greatness', and *iudd*, 'chief', so giving an overall sense of 'great chief'. Although the name is still mainly in Welsh use, it has realized a more general adoption among English speakers in the 20th century. A diminutive MERRY is sometimes found.

US composer, flautist Meredith Willson (1902–84); Welsh actor Meredith Edwards (1917–99); UK conductor Meredith Davies (b.1922) (originally middle name, first being Albert).

Meredith (f.) A late 19th- or early 20th-century adoption for female use of the male name MEREDITH, mainly for its association with MERRY. The name occurs in fiction for Meredith (Merry) Brown, sister of the central character Velvet Brown in Enid Bagnold's novel *National Velvet* (1935).

US musician, dancer Meredith Monk (b.1942); US actress Meredith Baxter Birney (b.1947); US tennis player Meredith McGrath (b.1971).

Meriel An independently adopted variant of MURIEL, in select adoption among English speakers from the early 20th century.

UK actress Meriel Forbes (1913–2000); UK opera singer Meriel Dickinson (b.1940).

Merle (m.) The name may be an adoption of the surname Merrill, or even (unusually) a male appropriation of the female name MERLE. It has found some favour among English speakers, mainly in the US, from the early 20th century.

US country singer Merle Travis (1917–83); US writer Merle Miller (1919–86); US country singers Merle Kilgore (b.1934), Merle Haggard (b.1937).

Merle (f.) The name seems to have originated as the variant of a name such as MERYL or MURIEL, but it soon became associated with French *merle*, 'blackbird' or with the identical English poetic name for this bird: 'The merle, in his noontide bow'r,/Makes woodland echoes ring' (Robert Burns, *A Lament for Mary, Queen of Scots*, 1791). (Compare MAVIS.) It has been in select English-speaking use from the late 19th or early 20th century.

US actress Merle Oberon (1911–79) (original name Estelle Merle O'Brien Thompson).

Merlin This is an English form of the Welsh name *Myrddin*, probably composed of Old Celtic words meaning respectively 'sea' (modern Welsh *môr*) and 'fort' (modern Welsh *dinas*), so 'holder of the sea fort'. It has found selective favour in mainly Welsh use from the early 20th century. Merlin is famously the name of the magician in the Arthurian romances, who according to some accounts is said to have derived his name from the town of Carmarthen, the Welsh form of which is *Caerfyrddin*, 'Myrddin's fort'. The variant spelling *Merlyn* exists, as for the Welsh politician Merlyn Rees (b.1920).

US American football player Merlin Olsen (b.1940).

Merry The name is either an independently adopted diminutive of MERCY or MEREDITH (m. and f.), or a borrowing of the standard word. (It is subconsciously associated in the US with MARY, since the two names are pronounced alike by Americans.) The name has been in English-speaking use, mostly in the US, from the 19th century. Charles Dickens has the name in his novel *Martin Chuzzlewit* (1843–4) as the nickname for Mercy Pecksniff, one of Mr Pecksniff's two daughters. (The other is CHARITY, similarly nicknamed CHERRY.)

US actress Merry Anders (b.1932).

Mervyn This is an English form of the Welsh name *Merfyn*, probably formed from Old Celtic words meaning respectively 'sea' (modern Welsh *môr*) and 'great' (as in modern Welsh *mynydd*, 'mountain'), so effectively 'sea ruler'. The name is popularly associated, however, with MARVIN. It has been mostly in Welsh use from the late 19th century but is found more generally for English speakers from the 1930s. Mervyn Ellis is the son of Dai ('The Stable') Ellis in Richard Llewellyn's novel *How Green was My Valley* (1939). The usual diminutive is *Merv*, as for the US TV personality Merv Griffin (b.1925) or the Australian cricketer Merv Hughes (b.1961).

Welsh actor Mervyn Johns (1899–1992); US actor, film director Mervyn LeRoy (1900–87); Irish writer Mervyn Wall (b.1908); UK writer, illustrator Mervyn Peake (1911–68); UK novelist Mervyn Jones (b.1922).

Meryl An independently adopted variant of MURIEL, in select English-speaking use from the early 20th century onwards.

US actress Meryl Streep (b.1951) (original first names Mary Louise); UK actress Meryl Hampton (b.1952).

Mia This name is properly a Scandinavian diminutive of MARIA, although it also suggests 'my' (implying 'my own one'), as in Spanish or Italian *mia*. It has found some favour among English speakers from the early 20th century.

US actresses Mia Farrow (b.1946) (original first name Maria), Mia Dillon (b.1955); US soccer player Mia Hamm (b.1972).

Micah A biblical name, from Hebrew *Mikhāh*, 'who is like Yah?' (that is, Jehovah), so the equivalent of MICHAEL. It has enjoyed only very selective adoption among English speakers from the 17th century, when it was originally taken up by English Puritans. In the Bible Micah is a prophet, with a book named for him. In literature the name is familiar from the central character of Arthur Conan Doyle's historical novel *Micah Clarke* (1889).

Michael A name of biblical origin, from Hebrew *Mīkha'ēl*, 'who is like God?'. (Compare MICAH.) It was in fairly regular English-speaking use until the 19th century. It then went into something of a decline until the 1930s, when it suddenly came into favour. Its popularity increased until the 1950s, after which it settled to a more modest level. It is still firmly fashionable, however. It has long been regarded as a typical Irish name. In the Bible, Michael is the archangel who led the other angels in a victorious war against Satan. St Michael thus symbolizes the 'Church Militant' and is the patron of soldiers. William Wordsworth's pastoral poem *Michael* (1800) concerns an old shepherd of the name. Later, Michael Brady is the uncle of the central character in William Makepeace Thackeray's novel *The Luck of Barry Lyndon* (1844), while Michael Mail is a villager in Thomas Hardy's novel *Under the Greenwood Tree* (1872). Michael Mont, an heir to a barony, marries Fleur Forsyte in John Galsworthy's *Forsyte* cycle (1906–22). The name has been favoured by European royalty, and in modern times is familiar from Prince Michael of

Kent (b.1942), grandson of George V. Diminutives MICK, MICKY and MIKE are in independent use.

UK actors Sir Michael Redgrave (1908–85), Sir Michael Hordern (1911–95), Michael Denison (1915–98); UK comedian Michael Bentine (1922–96); UK actor Michael Caine (b.1933) (original name Maurice Micklewhite); UK TV presenter Michael Aspel (b.1933); UK actors Michael Williams (1935–2001), Michael Gambon (b.1940), Michael Crawford (b.1942), Michael York (b.1942), Michael Palin (b.1943), Michael Redfern (b.1943), Michael Elphick (b.1946); UK entertainer Michael Barrymore (b.1952); US pop singer Michael Jackson (b.1958).

Michaela A feminine form of MICHAEL, usually pronounced 'Mi*kay*la'. The name was first taken up by English speakers in the 1930s. A rare variant is *Michael*, identical to the male name, as for the US actress Michael Learned (b.1939).

UK broadcaster on wildlife Michaela Denis (b.1915); UK TV presenter Michaela Strachan (b.1966).

Michèle A French feminine form of *Michel* (English MICHAEL), adopted by English speakers from the 1940s, initially in the US. The name later lost out to MICHELLE, but is still in evidence. Many bearers of the name drop the accent (see below).

French actress Michèle Morgan (b.1920) (original name Simone Roussel); US actress Michele Lee (b.1942); UK actress Michele Dotrice (b.1947); UK writer Michèle Roberts (b.1949); UK theatrical director Michele Frankel (b.1954); US actress Michele Greene (b.1962); UK barefoot water skier Michele Nutt (b.1964).

Michelle A variant spelling of MICHÈLE, taken up by English speakers from the 1950s and much in vogue in the 1970s, after which it rather fell from favour. Diminutives *Shell* and *Shelley* exist, although the latter could equally be the independent name SHELLEY, of different origin.

Australian writer, entertainer Michelle Magorian (b.1947); US actress Michelle Pfeiffer (b.1957); UK actresses Michelle Collins (b.1963),

Michelle Holmes (b.1967), Michelle Byatt (b.1970); Irish athlete Michelle Smith (b.1970); UK actress Michelle Gayle (b.1971).

Mick An independently adopted diminutive of MICHAEL, in select English-speaking use from the 19th century. In Benjamin Disraeli's novel *Sybil* (1845) Mick Dandy is a trade union leader. MICKEY is a directly related name.

UK rock musician Mick Jagger (b.1943); UK rugby player Mick Skinner (b.1958); UK rock musician Mick Hucknall (b.1960).

Mickey An independently adopted diminutive of MICHAEL, MIKE or MICK, in fairly popular 20th-century use among English speakers, mostly in the US. Adoption of the name does not appear to have been affected one way or the other by the appearance in the 1920s of the popular Walt Disney cartoon character Mickey Mouse. Variant spellings include *Mickie*, as for the UK pop producer Mickie Most (b.1938) (original name Michael Hayes), and *Micky*.

US boxer Mickey Walker (1901–81) (original first names Edward Patrick); US crime writer Mickey Spillane (b.1918) (original first names Frank Morrison); US actor Mickey Rooney (b.1920) (original name Joe Yule Jr); US baseball player Mickey Mantle (1931–95); US politician Mickey Leland (1944–89) (original first names George Thomas); US actor, pop singer Mickey Dolenz (b.1945); US actor Mickey Rourke (b.1950).

Micki, Mickie see **Maxine**.

Midge This name is probably an alteration of MADGE or a diminutive of a name such as MICHELLE. Perhaps by some it is felt to be a feminine equivalent of MICK. It has enjoyed modest favour among English speakers in the 20th century. Agatha Christie has Midge Hardcastle as a young cousin of Lady Lucy Angkatell in her novel *The Hollow* (1946) (US title *Murder After Hours*).

Mignon This name comes from the French word (not name) meaning 'cute', 'darling', and is also associated with the *mignonette* as a kind of flower name. It has been taken up in some parts of the English-speaking world from the 19th century. In literature the name is that of the leading character, a young Italian sideshow dancer, in Goethe's novel *Wilhelm Meisters Lehrjahre* (*Wilhelm Meister's Apprenticeship*, 1795–6), on which Charles Thomas's popular opera *Mignon* (1866) was loosely based. The diminutive *Mignonette* exists.

US mystery novel writer Mignon Eberhart (1899–96).

Mike An independently adopted diminutive of MICHAEL, in fairly common English-speaking use from the 1940s, and specially favoured in the US. It is widely found among sportsmen, entertainers and the like. MICK and MICKEY are directly related names in their own right. A diminutive *Mikey* exists.

US actors Mike Todd (1907–58) (original name Avrom Goldenbogen), Mike Mazurki (1909–90) (original name Mikhail Mazurwski), Mike Connors (b.1925) (original name Kreker Ohanian); UK motor-racing driver Mike Hawthorn (1929–58); German-born US entertainer Mike Nichols (b.1931) (original name Michael Igor Peschkowsky); UK comedian Mike Reid (b.1940); UK TV host, impressionist Mike Yarwood (b.1941); US actor Mike Farrell (b.1942); UK cricketer Mike Brearley (b.1942); UK playwright Mike Leigh (b.1943); UK pop musician Mike Oldfield (b.1953); UK TV presenter Mike Smith (b.1955); US athlete Mike Tully (b.1956); UK cricketer Mike Gatting (b.1957); US athlete Mike Conley (b.1962); US boxer Mike Tyson (b.1966).

Mildred The present name represents an Old English name *Mildthryth*, formed from *milde*, 'mild', and *thrȳth*, 'strength', thus 'gentle strength'. It has been in English-speaking use from the 17th century onwards and became popular in the US in the 19th century. It never really caught on in the UK, however, and after some modest favour in the early years of the 20th century is now rarely found. (Its suggestion of the word *mildew* may have something to do with it.) The name became historically familiar from the 7th-century abbess St Mildred. In literature it is that of the central character, a hard-working American mother betrayed by her daughter, in James M. Cain's novel *Mildred Pierce* (1941). The usual diminutives, MILLIE and MILLY, are both in independent use.

UK missionary, traveller Mildred Cable (1878–1952); US actresses Mildred Harris (1901–44), Mildred Dunnock (1904–91); US jazz, blues singer Mildred Bailey (1907–51).

Miles This name is perhaps an English form of the Latin name MILO, itself possibly connected with the Slavonic root word *mil*, 'dear', but popularly associated with Latin *miles*, 'soldier', and hence with MICHAEL (a similar name with a similar 'military' sense). It has been in English-speaking use from the 18th century but has been subject to vagaries of fashion. It enjoyed a mild boom in the 1960s, for example, then declined only to revive in the 1990s. The name is traditionally favoured in Ireland, and it is historically familiar from the first translator of the Bible into English, Miles Coverdale (1488–1568). His complete name was adopted by Nathaniel Hawthorn for a fictional self-portrait in his novel *The Blithedale Romance* (1852). In later literature Miles is one of the two young children (the other is Flora) in Henry James's tale *The Turn of the Screw* (1898), and Miles Bjornstam is a Swedish vagabond in Sinclair Lewis's novel *Main Street* (1920). The Irish connection is mainly due to *Milesius*, the fictitious king of Spain whose sons, the Milesians, were said to have conquered Ireland in prehistoric times. The variant spelling *Myles* exists, as for Myles Standish (1584–1656), the English colonist and military leader of the Pilgrim Fathers, who is the subject of Henry Wadsworth Longfellow's poem *The Courtship of Miles Standish* (1858).

UK playwright, actor Miles Malleson (1888–1969); UK actor Miles Mander (1888–1946) (original first name Lionel); US jazz trumpeter Miles Davis (1926–91); UK humorist Miles Kington (b.1941); US actor Miles O'Keeffe (b.1954).

Millicent This name is an English variant of the French name *Mélisande*, itself from an Old German name *Amalswint*, formed from *amal*, 'industry', 'hard work', and *swind*, 'strong', so 'hard worker'. It was introduced to England by the Normans but was only selectively adopted by English speakers before the 17th century. The diminutives MILLIE and MILLY are in independent use.

UK suffragist Millicent Fawcett (1847–1929); UK harpsichordist Millicent Silver (b.c.1920); UK singer, dancer Millicent Martin (b.1934).

Millie An independently adopted diminutive of CAMILLA, MILDRED or MILLICENT, in English-speaking use since at least the mid-19th century. The film *Thoroughly Modern Millie* (1967) made the general public aware of the name, but the variant spelling MILLY is also quite well known.

US actress Millie Perkins (b.1939); US soul singer Millie Jackson (b.1944); Jamaican pop singer Millie (b.1948) (original name Millicent Small).

Milly An independently adopted diminutive of CAMILLA, MILDRED or MILLICENT, in English-speaking use since at least the mid-19th century. Milly Richards is a character in Thomas Hardy's novel *Life's Little Ironies* (1894), and Milly Theale is a rich American girl in Henry James's novel *The Wings of the Dove* (1902). The UK children's writer Joyce Lancaster Brisley created (1928) the popular little girl character Milly-Molly-Mandy, her full first names being Millicent Margaret Amanda. The variant form of the name is MILLIE, in use in its own right.

Italian actress Milly Vitale (b.1928).

Milo This name is an English adoption of the Latin name that perhaps gave MILES. It has enjoyed selective favour among English speakers but is chiefly associated with Ireland.

Irish actor Milo O'Shea (b.1925).

Milton From the surname, famously that of the English poet John Milton (1608–74). The name has been in select English-speaking use from the early 19th century and has always been more popular in the US than the UK. In fiction Milton K. Rogers is a partner of the central character in William D. Howells's novel *The Rise of Silas Lapham* (1885). The usual diminutive is *Milt*, as for the US jazz musician Milt Buckner (1915–77).

UK actor Milton Rosmer (1881–1971) (original name Arthur Milton Lunt); US actor Milton Sills (1882–1930); US popular composer Milton Ager (1893–1979); US comedian Milton Berle (b.1908) (original name Mendel Berlinger); US actor Milton Frome (1911–80); US economist Milton Friedman (b.1912); Canadian-born UK theatre critic Milton Shulman (b.1913); Ugandan prime minister Milton Obote (b.1934); UK actor Milton Johns (b.1938) (original name John Robert Milton).

Mima see **Jemima**.

Mina An independently adopted diminutive of a name such as WILHELMINA, in select English-speaking use from the 19th century. Mina Beaufoy is the wife of Philip Beaufoy, of the Playgoers' Club, in James Joyce's novel *Ulysses* (1922). The variant spelling MINNA is in independent use.

Mindy The name is (or was) mostly in US use and became familiar from the US TV comedy series *Mork and Mindy* (1978–81), in which Robin Williams played the space alien Mork and Pam Dawber the girl who befriends him, Mindy. The name seems to be an alteration of MANDY influenced by a name such as CINDY.

US actresses Mindy Carson (b.1926), Mindy Cohn (b.1966).

Minerva A name that is famous as that of the Roman goddess of wisdom, itself usually linked to the Latin root *men-*, 'mind'. It has occasionally found favour with English speakers from the 19th century. Minerva Pott is a character in

Charles Dickens's novel *Pickwick Papers* (1836–7). The usual diminutive, MINNIE, is in independent use, although it is usually associated with other names.

US actress Minerva Urecal (1896–1966); US radio comedienne Minerva Pious (1909–79).

Minna An independently adopted variant of MINA, itself from a name such as WILHELMINA, adopted very selectively by English speakers from the 19th century. Minna and Brenda are daughters of Magnus Troil in Walter Scott's novel *The Pirate* (1821).

German feminist Minna Cauer (1841–1922) (original first name Wilhelmine); US actress Minna Gombell (1900–73).

Minnie This is a diminutive of a name such as WILHELMINA, adopted for independent use and taken up by English speakers from the mid-19th century. Minnie Meagles is a character in Charles Dickens's novel *Little Dorrit* (1855–7), and there is a Minnie in Eugene O'Neill's play *Mourning Becomes Electra* (1931). The name has been humorously popularized by the cartoon character Minnie Mouse, 'wife' of Mickey Mouse in Disney cartoons from the 1930s. In the UK TV soap *Coronation Street* (from the 1960s) the name came to be affectionately associated with the character Minnie Caldwell, played by Margot Bryant. MINA and MINNA are directly related names in independent use.

US singer Minnie Hank (1851–1929) (original first names Amalia Mignon); US actresses Minnie Maddern Fiske (1865–1932) (original first names Marie Augusta), Minnie Dupree (1873–1947); US country singer, comedienne Minnie Pearl (1912–96) (original name Sarah Ophelia Colley); US popular singer Minnie Riperton (1947–79).

Minta see **Araminta**.

Mira see **Myra**.

Mirabel A name adopted from the Latin word *mirabilis*, 'wonderful', but associated with French *belle*, 'beautiful'. It has been in English-speaking use from medieval times, but was originally a male name. Edmund Spenser has a (female) character Mirabella in his poem *The Faerie Queene* (1590, 1596).

UK racecourse owner Mirabel Topham (*c*.1900–80).

Miranda This name, meaning 'fit to be admired', from Latin *mirari*, 'to wonder at', was devised by Shakespeare for the main character (Prospero's daughter) in his play *The Tempest* (1611). (For a similar name, compare AMANDA.) It has been in select use among English speakers from the 17th century, and now has aristocratic overtones. In Noël Coward's play *Relative Values* (1951), Miranda Frayle is a film star, while Agatha Christie's novel *Hallowe'en Party* (1969) has Miranda Butler as the twelve-year-old daughter of Judith Butler. (When the detective Hercule Poirot says that the name suits her, she replies, 'Are you thinking of Shakespeare?') The diminutives MANDY and RANDY are in independent use.

English doctor working in Canada, Miranda Stuart (1795–1865); Scottish daughter of Earl of Kilmuir, Lady Miranda Cormack (b.1938); UK actress Miranda Connell (b.1938); UK novelist Miranda Seymour (b.1948); UK actress Miranda Richardson (b.1958); Scottish daughter of Earl Beatty, Lady Miranda Stewart (b.1963).

Miriam A biblical name, from Hebrew *Miryām*, which also gave MARY, and perhaps meaning 'full' in the sense 'good', 'complete'. It was taken up by English speakers from the 18th century, and in the 20th gained favour with Jewish families. In the Bible Miriam is the prophetess sister of Aaron and Moses. In Charles Kingsley's novel *Hypatia* (1853) Miriam is an old Jewess, while in H.G. Wells's novel *The History of Mr Polly* (1910) Miriam Larkins marries her cousin, the central character Alfred Polly.

US actresses Miriam Cooper (1892–1976), Miriam Hopkins (1902–72);

UK scientific writer Miriam Rothschild (b.1908); UK actress Miriam Karlin (b.1925); South African singer Miriam Makeba (b.1932); UK TV medical presenter Miriam Stoppard (b.1937); UK literary editor Miriam Gross (b.1939); UK actress Miriam Margolyes (b.1941); UK rower Miriam Batten (b.1964).

Misha The name is the standard Russian diminutive of *Mikhail* (English MICHAEL), occasionally found in use among English speakers from the 19th century. The Germanic variant spelling *Mischa* also exists, as for the Russian actor Mischa Auer (1905–67).

Russian-born UK architect, industrial designer Misha Black (1910–77).

Missie see **Melissa**.

Misty An adoption of the standard word, evoking a hazy island, a summer morning or some other romantic or poetic image: 'For I have seyn, of a ful misty morwe,/Folwen ful ofte a mery someres day' (Chaucer, *Troilus and Criseyde*, *c*.1385). It has been in select English-speaking use from the 1970s and may have owed some of its original vogue to the film *Play Misty For Me* (1971), in which 'Misty' is the name of a recorded song (originally written in 1954) played by a radio DJ.

US country singer Misty Morgan (b.1945) (original first name Mary); UK soul singer Misty Oldland (b.*c*.1970) (original first name Michelle).

Mitchell From the surname, itself a form of MICHAEL, and in select use among English speakers from the mid-19th century, mainly in the US. The usual diminutive is *Mitch*, as for the US popular music arranger Mitch Miller (b.1911).

US film director Mitchell Leisen (1898–1972); US bandleader Mitchell Ayres (1910–69); US writer Mitchell Goodman (b.1923); US actor Mitchell Ryan (b.1928); UK writer Mitchell Symons (b.1957).

Mitzi This is a German diminutive of MARIA, in rare English-speaking use from the 1930s.

US actress Mitzi Green (1920–69) (original name Elizabeth Keno); Hungarian-born US actress Mitzi Gaynor (b.1930) (original name Francesca Mitzi von Gerber).

Mo see **Maureen, Maurice, Moses.**

Moreen see **Maureen.**

Modesty An adoption of the ordinary word, regarded as a 'virtue', in select English-speaking use in the 20th century. In modern times the name came to be associated with the UK cartoon character Modesty Blaise, first appearing in the 1960s as a kind of female James Bond.

Moira This is an English form of the Irish name *Máire* (English MARY), with a spelling to reflect the pronunciation. The name was taken up by English speakers generally in the 19th century, gaining most of its favour in Scotland. A character of the name appears in William Makepeace Thackeray's novel *The Adventures of Philip* (1861–2). A variant spelling *Moyra* exists, as for the Australian comedienne Moyra Fraser (b.1923).

South African-born UK actress Moira Lister (b.1923); Scottish-born ballerina Moira Shearer (b.1926); Scottish popular singer Moira Anderson (b.1940); UK newsreader Moira Stuart (b.c.1950); UK actress Moira Foot (b.1953); US actress Moira Kelly (b.1969).

Mollie An independent variant of MOLLY, in some favour among English speakers in the first quarter of the 20th century, but now much less common.

US fashion designer Mollie Parnis (c.1900–92); UK actress Mollie Maureen (1904–87) (original name Elizabeth Mary Campfield); Scottish children's writer Mollie Hunter (b.1922); UK actress Mollie Sugden (b.1924).

Molly The name, in English-speaking use from at least the 18th century, is an independently adopted diminutive of MARY, with -*r*- becoming -*ll*- as in the alteration of SARAH to SALLY.

Molly Seagrim is a gamekeeper's daughter in Henry Fielding's novel *Tom Jones* (1749), and the name is used for other 'lowly' characters elsewhere in literature, as for a servant in William Makepeace Thackeray's novel *The Virginians* (1857–9); a house-maid in George Eliot's novel *Adam Bede* (1859); a housekeeper in Charles Dickens's novel *Great Expectations* (1960–61); and a servant in Thomas Hardy's novel *The Trumpet Major* (1880). The name has Irish associations through Molly Malone, the central character in the popular song 'Cockles and Mussels', as well as through the secret society of the 1840s known as the Molly Maguires. The diminutive *Moll* is familiar from the central character of Daniel Defoe's novel *Moll Flanders* (1722). The variant spelling MOLLIE is in independent use.

US actress, singer Molly Picon (1898–1992); Irish novelist Molly Keane (1904–96); US country singer Molly O'Day (1923–87) (original name LaVerne Lois Williamson); US writer Molly Parkin (b.1932); US actress Molly Ringwald (b.1968).

Mona The name is an English form of the Irish name *Muadhnait*, a diminutive of *muadh*, 'noble'. It has been in fairly general, if modest, use among English speakers from the late 19th century, and may owe something of its attraction to an association with Leonardo da Vinci's famous painting *Mona Lisa* (1503–6).

UK writer Mona Caird (1858–1932); UK-Argentinian actress Mona Maris (1903–91) (original name Maria Capdevielle); UK actress Mona Washbourne (1903–88); US actresses Mona Barrie (1909–64), Mona Freeman (b.1926) (original first name Monica); Lebanese-born UK artist Mona Hatoum (b.1952).

Monica Although well known in English-speaking use from the 19th century, this name remains of uncertain origin. It has been associated with Greek *monos*, 'alone', or with Latin *monere*, 'to warn', 'to advise'. Its peak period of popularity was in the 1930s, since when it has been more out of favour than in. It is historically familiar from the 4th-century St Monica, mother of St Augustine. In literature the name occurs for Monica Thorne in Anthony Trollope's novel *Doctor Thorne* (1858). For some reason the name came to be regarded as that of a typical pigtailed, sports-loving schoolgirl, perhaps through an association with *monitor* as a term for a prefect in girls' schools. Monica Douglas is a schoolgirl member of 'the Brodie set' in Muriel Spark's novel *The Prime of Miss Jean Brodie* (1961). The French equivalent MONIQUE is sometimes found in English-speaking use, while the usual diminutive is *Monny*.

UK writer Monica Dickens (1915–92); UK geographer Monica Cole (1922–94); Canadian children's writer Monica Hughes (b.1925); UK religious writer Monica Furlong (b.1930); Italian actress Monica Vitti (b.1931); UK TV hostess Monica Rose (1948–94); UK violinist Monica Huggett (b.1953) (mother is Monica); Yugoslavian tennis player Monica Seles (b.1973); US pop singer Monica (b.1980) (original name Monica Arnold).

Monique The French form of MONICA, in occasional use among English speakers from the 1950s, and perhaps influenced by similar names such as *Angelique* (see ANGELICA) and DOMINIQUE.

US tennis player Monique Javer (b.1967).

Monny see **Monica**.

Montague From the surname, and in select English-speaking use from the early 19th century. In Charles Dickens's novel *Martin Chuzzlewit* (1843–4) Montague Tigg is a swindler friend of Chevy Slyme. The name has been commercially promoted by the Montague Burton menswear stores. These were founded in the 1920s by Montague Maurice Burton (1885–1952), a Lithuanian immigrant to England whose original name was Meshe David Osinsky. (He adopted his new name in 1904, perhaps from a pub called the Lord Montague.) The aristocratic associations of the surname have to some extent passed to the first name. The usual diminutive is MONTY, which is in use in its own right.

Montgomery From the surname, and in very select English-speaking use in the 20th century. Montgomery Ward Snopes is a pornographer in William Faulkner's trilogy about the Snopes family, *The Hamlet* (1940), *The Town* (1957) and *The Mansion* (1959). The name became famously associated with the Second World War hero, Viscount Bernard Montgomery (1887–1976), regularly nicknamed 'Monty'. The name shares the aristocratic associations of MONTAGUE and also its regular diminutive, MONTY.

US film director Montgomery Tully (1904–88); US actor Montgomery Clift (1920–66).

Monty An independently adopted diminutive of MONTAGUE or MONTGOMERY, in select English-speaking use from the 1920s. During the Second World War the name was familiar as the nickname of the UK military leader Field Marshal Bernard Montgomery (1887–1976).

Italian-born UK actor, film director Monty Banks (1897–1950) (original name Mario Bianchi); US baseball player Monty Stratton (1912–82); UK radio broadcaster Monty Modlyn (1922–94); Jamaican-born US jazz pianist Monty Alexander (b.6 June 1944) (original first names Bernard Montgomery; he was born on D-Day, when Field Marshal Bernard Montgomery led the Allied invasion of Normandy).

Morag The name is an English form of the Scottish name *Mórag*, a diminutive of *mór*, 'great', found chiefly in Scottish use in the 20th century.

UK opera singer Morag Noble (1931–93); Scottish actress Morag Hood (b.1942).

Mordecai This is a biblical name that is probably of Persian origin meaning 'devotee of Marduk' (the chief Babylonian god). It was in fairly regular English-speaking use from the 17th century until the 19th century, but it is now rare. In the Bible Mordecai is the foster father of Esther. In George Eliot's novel

Daniel Deronda (1876) Mordecai is a Jew with a mission to reunite the Jewish people. The diminutives *Mordy* and *Morty* exist.

Canadian novelist Mordecai Richler (b.1931).

Morgan (m.) The name is an English form of the Welsh name *Morcant*, itself of uncertain origin but popularly derived from *môr*, 'sea', and *cant*, 'circle', 'edge', as if for a person born by or defending land on the edge of the sea. The name has long been in regular if select use among the Welsh, and it is now found more widely among English speakers. It is historically associated with the 7th-century Welsh prince who gave the name of Glamorgan in South Wales.

US actor Morgan Conway (1900–81); US radio journalist Morgan Beatty (1902–75); US actor Morgan Freeman (b.1937).

Morgan (f.) This Welsh name has been current since medieval times and was originally adopted from that of Morgan le Fay (see FAY), the sister of King Arthur and queen of Avalon in Arthurian legend. (Hence *fata Morgana* as the name of a type of mirage seen in the Strait of Messina.) It was later taken up more generally by English speakers and came to be associated with the male name MORGAN (which see for the possible origin). A variant form *Morgana* exists, as for the US pop singer Morgana King (b.1930).

US-born Irish writer Morgan Llywelyn (b.1937); US actresses Morgan Fairchild (b.1950) (original name Patsy McClenny), Morgan Brittany (b.1953) (original name Suzanne Caputo).

Morris An independently adopted variant of MAURICE, in select and increasingly rare use among English speakers from the 19th century. Morris Townsend is a cousin of Arthur Townsend in Henry James's novel *Washington Square* (1881). A diminutive *Morrie* or *Morry* exists.

US actor Morris Carnovsky (1897–1992); Australian writer Morris West (1916–99).

Mort An independently adopted diminutive of MORTIMER or MORTON, in select English-speaking use, mainly in the US, from the early 20th century. A diminutive *Morty* sometimes occurs.

US political comedian Mort Sahl (b.1926).

Mortimer From the surname, and in select English-speaking use from the 19th century, but fading in the 20th. In Anthony Trollope's novel *Doctor Thorne* (1858) Mortimer Gazebee marries Lady Amelia de Courcy, while in Charles Dickens's novel *Our Mutual Friend* (1864–5) Mortimer Lightwood is the barrister friend of Eugene Wrayburn. The regular diminutive MORT is in independent use.

Scottish-born archaeologist, broadcaster Sir Mortimer Wheeler (1890–1976).

Morton From the surname, and in select English-speaking use from the mid-19th century, mostly among Jewish families. Morton Mitcham is a member of the 'Good Companions' concert party in J.B. Priestley's novel *The Good Companions* (1929). The diminutive, MORT, is in independent use.

US writer, sociologist Morton Hunt (b.1920).

Morty see **Mordecai**, **Mort**.

Moses A familiar biblical name, from Hebrew *Mōshel*, perhaps from Egyptian *mes*, 'child', 'son' (as in the middle element of the royal name *Rameses*, 'child of Ra'). The name has long been favoured by Jews in the English-speaking world, but it was also taken up by Puritans from the 17th century. It is now much less common, with many Jews Anglicizing the name as MORTIMER, MORTON or the like. In the Bible Moses, the brother of Aaron and Miriam, is the patriarch who led the Israelites out of Egypt and who gave them divinely revealed laws (the Ten Commandments). Authorship of the first five books of the Old Testament (the Pentateuch) is also attributed to Moses. In Oliver Goldsmith's novel *The Vicar of Wakefield* (1766) Moses Primrose is one of the sons of the central character, Dr Charles Primrose, while in Richard Brinsley Sheridan's comedy *The School for Scandal* (1777) Moses is a Jewish moneylender. Diminutives include *Mo*, *Mose* and *Moy*. (The first of these gave the derogatory nickname *Ikey Mo* for a Jew, *Ikey* being ISAAC.) The Israeli soldier and statesman Moshe Dayan (1915–81) had the Jewish (Yiddish) form of the name.

US actor Moses Gunn (1929–93); US basketball player Moses Malone (b.1955).

Moss see **Maurice**.

Moy see **Moses**.

Moyra see **Moira**.

Muhammad A famous Arabic name, from *muḥammad*, 'praiseworthy', itself from *ḥamida*, 'to praise'. (Compare AHMED.) The name is borne by many Muslims in the English-speaking world, and its adoption honours the founder of Islam himself, with full name Muhammad ibn-ʿAbd-Allāh ibn-ʿAbd-al-Muttalib (570–632). The traditional English spelling of the name was long *Mahomet* or *Mohammed*.

US boxing champion Muhammad Ali (b.1942) (original name Cassius Marcellus Clay).

Mungo This is a Scottish name, perhaps from a Celtic root word related to modern Welsh *mwyn*, 'kind', 'gentle', 'dear'. It is found today almost exclusively in Scottish use. It was taken up by way of a tribute to the 6th-century ecclesiastic St Kentigern, first bishop of Glasgow, whose by-name it was. The embittered courtier Sir Mungo Malagrowther is a character in Walter Scott's novel *The Fortunes of Nigel* (1822).

Scottish explorer of Africa, Mungo Park (1771–1806).

Murgatroyd From the surname, and gaining select favour among English speakers from the 19th century. Murgatroyd Arkroyd is a character in William de Morgan's novel *It Can Never Happen Again* (1909).

Muriel This name is probably an English variant of the Irish name *Muirgheal*, formed from *muir*, 'sea', and *geal*, 'bright', thus 'sea-bright'. It has been in English-speaking use from the mid-19th century, mostly in Scotland, but after a period of popularity in the 1920s and (to a lesser extent) 1930s, has now largely fallen from favour. It is found in literature for Muriel Halifax, the blind daughter of the central character in Mrs Craik's novel *John Halifax, Gentleman* (1856). MERIEL is an independently adopted variant.

UK actresses Muriel George (1883–1965), Muriel Aked (1887–1955); US actress Muriel Kirkland (1903–71); UK writer, film director Muriel Box (1905–91); Scottish-born novelist Muriel Spark (b.1918); UK actress Muriel Pavlow (b.1921); UK TV presenter Muriel Young (1928–2001); Scottish TV presenter Muriel Gray (b.1958).

Murray From the (Scottish) surname, and in select but regular use among English speakers, especially those with Scottish connections, from the 19th century. The spelling *Murry* is sometimes found.

US actors Murray Alper (1904–84), Murray Hamilton (1923–86); US literary critic Murray Krieger (b.1923); US science fiction writer Murray Matheson (b.1926); UK actor Murray Melvin (b.1932); New Zealand athlete Murray Halberg (b.1933); UK swimmer Murray Rose (b.1939); UK actor, pop singer Murray Head (b.1946); US pianist Murray Perahia (b.1947); New Zealand rugby player Murray Mexted (b.1953).

Myfanwy A Welsh name, composed of the prefix *my-* denoting affection and the word *manwy*, 'fine', 'rare', so 'dear fine one', 'precious darling'. The name is pronounced approximately 'Mu*van*wy'. It is still primarily in Welsh use, and in literature was made familiar by the dressmaker Myfanwy Price in Dylan Thomas's play *Under Milk Wood* (1954). The diminutive variant *Myf* (pronounced 'Muv') is sometimes found.

Welsh art editor, opera librettist Myfanwy Piper (1911–97).

Myles see **Miles**.

Myra This name was apparently invented by the English poet Fulke Greville (1554–1628), who perhaps based it on Greek *muron*, 'myrrh', or Latin *mirari*, 'to wonder at' (compare MIRANDA), or who even devised it as an anagram of MARY. It was later associated with MOIRA. It has been in general English-speaking use from the 19th century, and has been a favourite with the Scots. In Sinclair Lewis's novel *Babbitt* (1922) Myra Babbitt is the wife of the central character, and in Theodore Dreiser's novel *An American Tragedy* (1925) Myra Griffiths is the daughter of the main character Clyde Griffiths. Later, the transsexual central character of Gore Vidal's novel *Myra Breckinridge* (1968) made the name well known, as did the film of 1970 based on it. The variant spelling *Mira* is sometimes found.

US lawyer Myra Bradwell (1831–94); UK concert pianist Dame Myra Hess (1890–1965).

Myrna This is an English form of the Irish name *Muirne*, from *muirne*, 'tenderness', 'affection'. It has enjoyed a certain favour among English speakers from the 19th century. Myrna Harris is a waitress in Agatha Christie's novel *A Murder Is Announced* (1950).

US actress Myrna Loy (1905–93); US magazine editor Myrna Blyth (b.1939).

Myron A straight adoption of the Greek name, meaning 'myrrh', in select English-speaking use in the 20th century, mostly among black Americans. The name is historically famous from the Greek sculptor Myron who created the well-known *Discobolus* ('Discus Thrower') in the 5th century BC. Christians took up the name for its favourable associations with *myrrh*, which was not only one of the gifts made by the Magi to the infant Jesus but was used as an embalming spice, implying the preservation of life after death.

US film producer Myron Zelznick (1898–1944); US actors Myron McCormick (1908–62), Myron Healey (b.1922).

Myrtle An adoption of the name of the plant, with its pink or white flowers and aromatic berries. The name came into fashion among English speakers in the mid-19th century, but became rare after the 1950s. In Thomas Hardy's novel *The Hand of Ethelberta* (1876) Myrtle Chickerell is a sister of the central character, Ethelberta Petherwin. Theodore Dreiser's novel *The Genius* (1915) has Myrtle Witla as the sister of the central character, Eugene Witla, and in P.G. Wodehouse's novel *Meet Mr Mulliner* (1927) Myrtle Banks marries William Mulliner.

US writer Myrtle Reed (1874–1911); UK cricketer Myrtle Maclagan (1911–93); UK athlete Myrtle Augee (b.1965).

N

Nadia This is a diminutive of the Russian name *Nadezhda* (English HOPE), which came into fashion among English speakers in the 20th century. The spelling variant *Nadya* (closer to the Russian form) is sometimes found, as for Queen Nadya in Noël Coward's play *The Queen Was In The Parlour* (1926).

French music teacher, conductor Nadia Boulanger (1887–1979); Russian-Romanian actress Nadia Gray (1923–94); South African ballerina Nadia Nerina (b.1927) (original name Nadine Judd); Romanian gymnast Nadia Comaneci (b.1961).

Nadine A French elaboration of NADIA, in select English-speaking use from the late 19th century. The original name of the South African ballerina Nadia Nerina (b.1927) was Nadine Judd.

US opera singer Nadine Conner (b.1913); South African novelist Nadine Gordimer (b.1923); US opera singer Nadine Secunde (b.1951).

Nadya see **Nadia**.

Nahum A biblical name, from Hebrew *Nahūm*, 'comforter', in very select use among English speakers from the 17th century, when it was adopted by the Puritans. The Irish-born playwright Nahum Tate (1652–1715) rewrote *King Lear* to give it a happy ending. In the Bible Nahum is the prophet who foretold the destruction of Nineveh.

Nan The name is an independently adopted diminutive of ANN, and subsequently also of NANCY. It came into fashion among English speakers in the 18th century, but in the 20th century fell from favour, partly through the use of 'Nan' as a child's name for a grandmother. There is a character of the name in Samuel Richardson's novel *Pamela* (1740–41). NANA is a directly related name.

US actress Nan Grey (1918–93) (original name Eschal Miller); Scottish opera singer Nan Christie (b.1948).

Nana An independently adopted diminutive of ANN, subsequently felt to be a variant of NAN. It was taken up by some English speakers in the late 19th century, although by the 1950s was completely out of favour, partly through the use of 'Nana' as a child's name for a nurse (nanny). The name may have been given initial impetus by the central character of Emile Zola's novel *Nana* (1880), despite its seedy subject.

US actress Nana Bryant (1888–1955); Greek popular singer Nana Mouskouri (b.1936).

Nancy This name is an independently adopted diminutive of ANN or some similar but now abandoned medieval name. (Compare NAN.) It was generally adopted by English speakers in the late 18th century and remained more or less consistently popular until the 1930s, when it declined. It later underwent a more modest revival in the 1970s and 1980s, but has now once again faded. It has always been more popular in the US than the UK. In literature Nancy Williams is a character in Tobias Smollett's novel *Roderick Random* (1748), and in Charles Dickens's novel *Oliver Twist* (1837–8) Nancy is the mistress of Bill Sikes. The more recent vogue for the name in the US may have owed something to the fictional teenage detective Nancy Drew (from the 1930s on). The variant spelling *Nanci* sometimes occurs, as for the US country singer Nanci Griffith (b.1953). The usual diminutive is *Nance*, as for Nance Mockridge in Thomas Hardy's novel *The Mayor of Casterbridge* (1886) and, in real life, the US actress Nance O'Neil (1875–1965).

Anglo-US politician Lady Nancy Astor (1879–1964); UK actress Nancy Price (1880–1970); US political activist Nancy Cunard (1896–1965); US actress Nancy Carroll (1905–65) (original name Ann La Hiff); UK writers Nancy Mitford (1907–73), Nancy Spain (1917–64); wife of US president Ronald Reagan, Nancy Reagan (b.1921) (original first names Anne Frances); US actresses Nancy Kelly (1921–95), Nancy Walker (1922–92) (original name Anna Myrtle Swoyer), Nancy Marchand (1928–2000), Nancy Sinatra (b.1940), Nancy Allen (b.1950), Nancy Travis (b.1962); US ice dancer Nancy Kerrigan (b.1969).

Nanette An independently adopted diminutive of NAN, in select English-speaking use from the early 20th century. The name was doubtless popularized by the musical *No, No, Nanette* (1924). The variant spelling *Nannette* is sometimes found.

US actress, singer Nanette Fabray (b.1920); UK actress Nanette Newman (b.1939).

Naomi A biblical name, from Hebrew *Nā'omī*, 'my delight', in regular use among English speakers from the 18th century, and gradually increasing in popularity from the 1970s. The name is now usually stressed on the *o* rather than the *a*, as formerly. In the Bible Naomi is the mother-in-law of Ruth.

UK popular novelists Naomi Royde-Smith (1875–1964), Naomi Jacob (1884–1964); Scottish-born writer Naomi Mitchison (1897–1999); US poet Naomi Madgett (b.1923); UK actress Naomi Chance (b.1930); UK yachtswoman Dame Naomi James (b.1949); US feminist writer Naomi Wolf (b.1963); UK-born US actress Naomi Watts (b.1968); UK model Naomi Campbell (b.1970); UK actress Naomi Lewis (b.1971).

Napoleon This is the English form of the Italian name *Napoleone*, perhaps originally of Germanic origin, but popularly associated with the name of Naples (Italian *Napoli*, from Greek *nea polis*, 'new city') and Italian *leone*, 'lion'. The name has found some favour among English speakers from the 19th century, mainly among black Americans. The source of the name was exclusively the French emperor Napoleon Bonaparte (1769–1821), born in Corsica of a family of Italian origin.

US baseball player Napoleon Lajoie (1874–1959).

Narcissus An English (originally Latin) form of the Greek name *Narkissos*, itself almost certainly of pre-Greek origin, but popularly associated with Greek *narkē*, 'numbness'. It has occasionally been adopted by English speakers from the 19th century. It is familiar in Greek mythology as the name of the beautiful youth who fell in love with his own reflection in a pool and remained benumbed until he turned into the flower that is now named for him. (However, the English name of the flower, although deriving from *narkē*, 'numbness', probably refers to the property that some of the species have to benumb.) The name was that of various early holy men, including one mentioned in the Bible: 'Greet them that be of the house of Narcissus' (Romans 16.11). Early instances of its use include English-born Irish archbishop Narcissus Marsh (1638–1713) and English diarist Narcissus Luttrell (1657–1732).

Nat An independently adopted diminutive of NATHAN or NATHANIEL, in select English-speaking use in the 20th century.

US actor Nat Pendleton (1895–1967); US jazz pianist Nat 'King' Cole (1917–65) (original name Nathaniel Adams Coles); US country singer Nat Stuckey (1933–88).

Natalie This name is a French form of the Russian name *Natalya*, itself from Latin *dies natalis*, 'birthday', specifically *dies natalis Domini*, 'birthday of the Lord', that is, Christmas (compare NOEL). It joined the stock of English first names in the late 19th century, and although in only modest evidence for several years rose considerably in popularity from the 1970s. Natalia was a 4th-century saint (but not a martyr), and the actual spelling *Natalia* is sometimes found. It was made known by the Russian-born US ballerina Natalia Makarova (b.1940).

US actresses Natalie Talmadge (1899–1969), Natalie Schafer (1912–91), Natalie Wood (1938–81) (original name Natasha Gurdin), Natalie Trundy (b.1940); US pop singer Natalie Cole (b.1950); Scottish actress

Natalie Robb (b.1974); Australian-born UK pop singer Natalie Imbruglia (b.1975); UK actresses Natalie Casey (b.1980), Natalie Cassidy (b.1983).

Natasha This is the standard Russian diminutive of *Natalya* (English NATALIE), which has been in favour among English speakers from the early 20th century, with a steady rise in popularity from the 1970s. The name was made famous in literature by Natasha Rostova, the central character in Tolstoy's novel *War and Peace* (1863–9), and its adoption was undoubtedly helped by the popular TV versions of this in the UK, especially the first, in 1963. Variant spellings include *Natashia* and *Natashya*, and a common diminutive is *Tasha*.

UK actresses Natasha Parry (b.1930), Natasha Pyne (b.1946), Natasha Richardson (b.1963); US actress Natasha Wagner (b.1970) (mother was Natasha); UK actress Natasha Little (b.1971).

Nathan A biblical name, from Hebrew *Nāthān*, 'he [that is, God] has given'. The name is now often regarded as a short form of NATHANIEL, however. It has gradually grown in favour from the 1970s, although it has been in general use among English speakers from the 18th century. In the Bible Nathan is the prophet who rebuked King David for sending Uriah the Hittite to his death so that he could take his wife Bathsheba. In William Makepeace Thackeray's novel *The Virginians* (1857–9) Nathan is a majordomo at Castlewood House. The regular diminutive is NAT, in independent use.

US military leader Nathan B. Forrest (1821–77); US Air Force officer Nathan Twining (1897–1982); Polish-born US novelist Nathan Asch (1902–64); US country musician Nathan Abshire (1913–81); US civil rights campaigner Nathan Perlmutter (1923–87); US historian Nathan I. Huggins (1927–89).

Nathaniel A biblical name, from Hebrew *Nĕthan'el*, 'God has given' (compare NATHAN), in select English-speaking use from the 17th century. In the Bible Nathaniel is one of the disciples, subsequently identified by biblical scholars with

Bartholomew. In Shakespeare's *Love's Labour's Lost* (*c*.1595) Sir Nathaniel is a curate, and in Charles Dickens's novel *Pickwick Papers* (1836–7) Nathaniel Winkle is the Pickwick Club member who marries Arabella Allen. A variant spelling *Nathanael* occurs, as for the US writer Nathanael West (1903–40) (original name Nathan Wallenstein Weinstein). The regular diminutive is NAT, in independent use. *Natty* is also found, as for Natty Bumppo, the deer-slayer central character of James Fenimore Cooper's *Leather-Stocking Tales* (1823–46).

US writers Nathaniel Hawthorne (1804–64), Nathaniel Benchley (1915–81).

Neal see **Neil**.

Ned An independently adopted diminutive of EDWARD or (less often) EDMUND, in use among English speakers from medieval times, and still subject to periodic revival. Ned Winwife is a character in Ben Jonson's comedy *Bartholomew Fair* (1614), and the name is also that of the central character in James Fenimore Cooper's fictional biography *Ned Myers* (1843). TED is a directly related name, and *Neddy* is a frequent diminutive.

US actor Ned Glass (1905–84); UK film, TV producer, director Ned Sherrin (b.1931); US actor Ned Beatty (b.1937).

Nehemiah A biblical name, from Hebrew *Nĕhemyāh*, 'consoled by Yah' (that is, by Jehovah), in select English-speaking use from the 17th century, when it was adopted by the Puritans, until the early 20th century, after which it was increasingly rare. In the Bible Nehemiah is the official at the court of King Artaxerxes who plays a leading part in the rebuilding of Jerusalem after the Babylonian captivity. His deeds are recorded in the book named for him. In Walter Scott's novel *Woodstock* (1826) Nehemiah Holdenough is a Presbyterian minister.

Israeli-born US actor Nehemiah Persoff (b.1920).

Neil The name is an English form of the Gaelic name *Niall*, from *niadh*, 'champion'. It was taken up by English speakers generally in the 19th century, at first chiefly as a Scottish name, and subsequently became increasingly popular until the 1960s, after which it gradually sank to a much more modest level. Neil Duncan is a character in Robert Louis Stevenson's novel *Catriona* (1893). Variant spellings include *Neal*, *Neill* and *Niall* itself, the last as for the Irish footballer Niall Quinn (b.1966). NIGEL is a directly related name.

US actor Neil Hamilton (1899–1984); US playwright Neil Simon (b.1927); US astronaut Neil Armstrong (b.1930); US pop singers, songwriters Neil Sedaka (b.1939), Neil Diamond (b.1941); UK politician Neil Kinnock (b.1942); Canadian pop musician Neil Young (b.1945); UK TV presenter Neil Buchanan (b.1961); UK actor Neil Morrissey (b.1962); UK footballer Neil Ruddock (b.1968); UK gymnast Neil Thomas (b.1968).

Nell An independently adopted diminutive of ELEANOR, ELLEN or HELEN, in use among English speakers from at least the 17th century. It became famous through the mistress of Charles II, Nell Gwyn (1650–87), whose original name was Elinor (or Eleanor) Gwyn (or Gwynne). The full name of Little Nell, the central character of Charles Dickens's novel *The Old Curiosity Shop* (1840–41), was Elinor Trent. The diminutive NELLIE is in independent use.

UK writer Nell Dunn (b.1936); US actress Nell Carter (b.1948).

Nella see **Fenella**.

Nellie An independently adopted diminutive of NELL, in general English-speaking use from the mid-19th century, although much less common from the 1930s. In James Fenimore Cooper's novel *The Prairie* (1827) Ellen Wade is known as Nellie, and in Charles Dickens's novel *The Old Curiosity Shop* (1840–41) the child Little Nell is more formally referred to as Nellie Trent. (She was christened Elinor.) The popular song 'Nellie Dean'

(1906) may have boosted the name, and it was also brought before the public by the Australian opera singer Dame Nellie Melba (1861–1931) (original name Helen Mitchell). The variant spelling *Nelly* is fairly common, as for 'Nelly Bly', the pseudonym adopted (from a Stephen Foster song) by the US journalist Elizabeth Cochrane Seaman (1867–1922).

UK music-hall artiste Nellie Wallace (1870–1948).

Nelson From the surname, famously that of the English admiral Horatio Nelson (1758–1805), victor of the Battle of Trafalgar. The name was taken up by English speakers, at first largely in tribute to him, from the mid-19th century, and gained special favour in the US. Its popularity has since sunk to a much lower level.

US popular singer Nelson Eddy (1901–67); US governor of New York Nelson Rockefeller (1908–79); US novelist Nelson Algren (1909–81); South African politician, civil rights leader Nelson Mandela (b.1918); US popular composer Nelson Riddle (1921–85); Brazilian motor-racing driver Nelson Piquet (b.1952).

Nerissa This name, in select English-speaking use since at least the 19th century, is probably based on Greek *nērēis*, 'nymph'. It was made famous by Nerissa, Portia's waiting maid in Shakespeare's *The Merchant of Venice* (1596–8).

Nerys A Welsh name, perhaps intended as a feminine form of *nêr*, 'lord', but by English speakers associated with NERISSA. It has spread little beyond Welsh use from the time of its adoption in the 20th century.

Welsh actress Nerys Hughes (b.1940).

Nessa see **Vanessa**.

Nessie An independently adopted diminutive of AGNES or VANESSA, in mainly Scottish use from the early 20th century. In literature Nessie Brodie is the daughter of James Brodie in A.J.

Cronin's novel *Hatter's Castle* (1931). The name is more popularly familiar, however, as a humorous nickname (since at
least the 1940s) for the Loch Ness Monster.

Nesta This name is a Welsh diminutive of AGNES, adopted
independently. It has been in general English-speaking
use from the 19th century, but was an established Welsh
name long before this. The grandmother of the 12th-century
chronicler Giraldus Cambrensis (Gerald the Welshman) was
named Nesta. The usual diminutive, in Welsh and English, is
Nest.

UK writer, radio producer Nesta Pain (b.c.1910).

Netta This name seems to have arisen either as a form of
NETTIE or as the independent adoption of the ending *-netta* or
-nette from a name such as ANNETTE. It has been in select use
among English speakers since the 19th century. Netta Gryse-
worth is a character in Maria S. Cummins's popular moralis-
tic romance *The Lamplighter* (1854).

Nettie An independently adopted diminutive of a name
ending *-nette*, such as ANNETTE or HENRIETTA, in select English-
speaking use from the 1880s to about the 1920s. H.G. Wells's
novel *In the Days of the Comet* (1906) has Nettie Stuart as its
central character. The main spelling variant is *Netty*, as for
the central character of Thomas Hardy's short story 'Netty
Sargent's Copyhold' in *Life's Little Ironies* (1894).

UK equestrienne Nettie Miller (b.1964) (original first name Annette).

Neville From the surname, and increasingly popular among
English speakers, albeit on a modest scale, from the mid-19th
century to the 1960s, after which it lost momentum. In Charles
Dickens's novel *Edwin Drood* (1870) brother and sister Neville
and Helena Landless are wards of Luke Honeythunder. Vari-
ant spellings *Nevil*, *Nevile* and *Nevill* exist, the first of these as for
the UK novelist Nevil Shute (1899–1960).

UK prime minister Neville Chamberlain (1869–1940) (originally middle name, first being Arthur); UK writer, critic Neville Cardus (1889–1975); US soldier, actor Neville Brand (1921–92).

Niall see **Neil**.

Niamh The Irish name (usually pronounced 'Neeve' in English) is that of a goddess in Celtic mythology and is the standard Irish word meaning 'brightness', 'radiance'.

Irish actress Niamh Cusack (b.1959); Irish pop singer Niamh Kavanagh (b.1968).

Nicholas The name is an English form of the Greek name *Nikolaos*, formed from *nikē*, 'victory', and *laos*, 'people', so 'victorious among the people'. It has been in use among English speakers from medieval times, and although it declined in popularity in the 18th century and the second half of the 19th century, it revived steadily from the 1950s, reaching its peak of popularity in the 1970s. It then faded somewhat, only to pick up again in the 1990s. The name was initially made famous by the 4th-century bishop of Myra, Asia Minor, St Nicholas, who generated many legends and who became the patron saint of Greece, Russia and children, among others, undergoing a popular reincarnation for his young charges in the person of Santa Claus (an alteration of his Dutch name, *Sinterklaas*). Chaucer has a clerk Nicholas in 'The Miller's Tale' in *The Canterbury Tales* (*c*.1387), and a famous literary bearer of the name is the central character of Charles Dickens's novel *Nicholas Nickleby* (1838–9). The English bishop Nicholas Ridley (1500–55) was burnt at the stake for refusing to renounce his Protestant beliefs. *Nickolas* is an occasional variant spelling, as for the UK actor Nickolas Grace (b.1949), but *Nicolas* is more common, as for the UK illustrator Nicolas Bentley (1907–78). The regular diminutive is NICK, in independent use.

UK TV presenter Nicholas Parsons (b.1928); US secretary of US Treasury

Nicholas Brady (b.1930); UK TV reporter Nicholas Witchell (b.1953); UK actors Nicholas Lyndhurst (b.1961), Nicholas Cochrane (b.1973).

Nick An independently adopted diminutive of NICHOLAS, in popular English-speaking use from the late 19th century. Nick Bottom is a weaver in Shakespeare's *A Midsummer Night's Dream* (1595–6). Nick Carter is a popular detective in stories from the 1880s by various authors, several of whom assumed the name as a pseudonym, while Nick Carraway is the narrator in F. Scott Fitzgerald's novel *The Great Gatsby* (1925). The name is frequently found for entertainers, sportsmen and the like. The variant spelling *Nik* also occurs, as for the UK pop singer Nik Kershaw (b.1940) and UK TV news presenter Nik Gowing (b.1951). The usual diminutive is *Nicky*, as for the UK actor Nicky Henson (b.1945) and UK TV presenter Nickey Campbell (b.1961).

US actor Nick Nolte (b.1940); UK TV presenters Nick Owen (b.1947), Nick Ross (b.1947); UK radio presenter Nick Clarke (b.1948); UK athlete Nick Rose (b.1951); UK golfer Nick Faldo (b.1957); UK actor Nick Orchard (b.1957); South African golfer Nick Price (b.1957); UK tennis player Nick Brown (b.1961); UK fashion designer Nick Coleman (b.1961); UK actors Nick Conway (b.1962), Nick Reding (b.1962).

Nickie see **Nicola**.

Nickolas see **Nicholas**.

Nicky see **Nick**, **Nicola**.

Nicola A feminine form of NICHOLAS, in popular English-speaking use from the 1940s. Variant spellings include *Nichola* and the French NICOLE, the latter in independent use. The many diminutives include *Nick*, *Nicki*, *Nickie*, *Nicky*, and NIKKI, the last of these in independent use.

UK actress Nicola Pagett (b.1945); UK composer Nicola Lefanu (b.1947); UK artist Nicola Hicks (b.1960); UK actresses Nicola Cowper (b.1967), Nicola Stephenson (b.1971).

Nicolas see **Nicholas**.

Nicole A French feminine form of *Nicolas* (English NICHOLAS), in gradually increasing popularity among English speakers from the 1930s. A diminutive *Nicolette* exists.

Australian actress Nicole Kidman (b.1967).

Nigel This name is an English form of the medieval Latin name *Nigellus*, itself a sort of diminutive (based on *niger*, 'black') of *Niel* (English NEIL). The name has been in increasingly popular use among English speakers, almost entirely in the UK, from the late 19th century to the 1960s, after which it gradually faded from the limelight. In literature the name was made familiar by Nigel Olifaunt, the central character of Walter Scott's novel *The Fortunes of Nigel* (1822). A diminutive is *Nige*.

UK actor-manager Sir Nigel Playfair (1874–1934); UK actors Nigel de Brulier (1878–1948), Nigel Bruce (1895–1953); UK politician Nigel Birch (1906–81); UK writers Nigel Balchin (1908–70), Nigel Dennis (1912–89); UK actors Nigel Patrick (1913–81), Nigel Stock (1919–86), Nigel Davenport (b.1928), Nigel Hawthorne (1929–2001), Nigel Havers (b.1952), Nigel Planer (b.1953); UK motor-racing driver Nigel Mansell (b.1953); UK violinist Nigel Kennedy (b.1956).

Nik see **Nick**, **Nikki**.

Nikki An independently adopted variant spelling of *Nicky* as a diminutive of NICOLA, taken up by English speakers from the 1960s and becoming fairly popular in the 1980s. Its own diminutive *Nik* is sometimes found, as for the UK judoist Nik Fairbrother (b.1970) (original first names Nicola Kim).

US poet Nikki Giovanni (b.1943) (original first names Yolande Cornelia); UK actress Nikki Brooks (b.1968) (original name Nicola Ashton).

Nina The standard Russian diminutive of *Antonina* (English ANTONIA), adopted in the English-speaking world from the 19th century. Anthony Trollope's novel *Phineas Finn* (1869) has Nina Fawn as one of the six sisters of Lord Frederic Fawn, while in Evelyn Waugh's novel *Vile Bodies* (1930) Nina Blount is the fiancée of Adam Fenwick-Symes.

Russian-born US writer Nina Berberova (1901–93); US actress Nina Mae McKinney (1909–67); Russian-born UK concert pianist Nina Milkina (b.1919); Dutch-born US actress Nina Foch (b.1924); UK novelist Nina Bawden (b.1925); Danish actress Nina Van Pallandt (b.1932); US jazz singer Nina Simone (b.1933) (original name Eunice Kathleen Wayman); West Indian actress Nina Baden-Semper (b.1945); UK interior decorator Nina Campbell (b.1945); UK political leader Nina Temple (b.1956).

Nita see **Anita**, **Juanita**.

Noah A familiar biblical name, from Hebrew *Nōah*, traditionally said to mean 'rest', in regular but select use among English speakers from the 17th century, when it was adopted by the Puritans. It is rarely found today, however. In the Bible Noah, the grandson of Methuselah, son of Lamech, and father of Shem, Ham and Japhet, is famous for building an ark to save his family and all animals from the flood ordained by God: 'And he [that is, Lamech] called his name Noah, saying, This same shall comfort us concerning our work and toil of our hands, because of the ground which the Lord hath cursed' (Genesis 5.29). Noah Claypole is a charity boy and thief working for Fagin in Charles Dickens's novel *Oliver Twist* (1837–8).

US lexicographer Noah Webster (1758–1843); US actors, father and son, Noah Beery (1884–1946), Noah Beery Jr (1913–94); US conductor Noah Greenberg (1919–66).

Noel (m.) A French name, meaning 'Christmas', ultimately from Latin *natalis dies* (*Domini*), 'birthday (of the Lord)', in variable favour among English speakers since medieval times. The name is appropriate for a child born at or around Christmas, with *Nowell* in carols a reminder of this meaning. (Birthdates are exceptionally given below for original bearers of the name to illustrate this.) The name is sometimes spelled with its French diaeresis, that is, as *Noël*.

UK popular composer Noel Gay (1898–1954) (original name Reginald

Moxon Armitage); US actor Noel Madison (1898–1975) (original name Nathaniel Moscovitch); UK actor, writer, composer Noël Coward (16 December 1899–1973); South African writer Noel Langley (25 December 1911–80); UK columnist Noel Whitcomb (25 December 1919–93); UK music and dance critic Noël Goodwin (b.25 December 1927); UK TV host Noel Edmonds (b.22 December 1948).

Noel (f.) A French name, from *Noël*, 'Christmas', in English-speaking use for both sexes from medieval times (see male NOEL), but coming to the fore in female favour from the early 20th century. The name is appropriate for a child born at or around Christmas. (Birthdates are exceptionally given for name-bearers below to illustrate this.) Variant spellings are *Noele* or *Noelle*, as respectively for the UK actress Noele Gordon (25 December 1923–85) and UK magazine editor Noelle Walsh (b.26 December 1954). All versions of the name can be spelt with a diaeresis, that is, as *Noël*.

UK children's writer Noel Streatfeild (24 December 1895–1986); UK actress Noel Dyson (b.23 December 1916).

Noll see **Oliver**.

Nora This is an independently adopted diminutive of a name such as *Eleonora* (a form of ELEANOR), *Honora* (a form of HONOR) or LEONORA. It has been in English-speaking use from the 19th century, and is traditionally associated with Ireland. It fell from favour after the 1930s and has not as yet seen any revival. Nora Helmer is the central character in Henrik Ibsen's play *A Doll's House* (1879). In English literature the name is found for Nora Reilly, an Irish character in Bernard Shaw's play *John Bull's Other Island* (1904), and for Nora Clitheroe, Irish wife of the bricklayer Jack Clitheroe in Sean O'Casey's play *The Plough and the Stars* (1926). The variant spelling NORAH exists in its own right.

US popular singer Nora Bayes (1880–1928) (original name Dora Goldberg); UK actresses Nora Nicholson (1892–1973), Nora Swinburne

(1902–2000) (original name Elinore Johnson); UK writer Nora Beloff (1919–97); US screenwriter Nora Ephron (b.1941).

Norah A pseudo-biblical variant of NORA, fairly frequently found among English speakers down to the 1930s.

UK writer of historical romances Norah Lofts (1904–83); UK social campaigner Baroness Norah Phillips (1910–92).

Norbert The English name derives from an Old German name that is composed of *nord*, 'north', and *beraht*, 'bright', 'famous', thus giving an overall meaning of 'famous north-man' or 'famous man in the north'. It has enjoyed only modest adoption among English speakers from the late 19th century, chiefly in the US. St Norbert was a famous early bearer of the name in the 11th century. The expected diminutive would be BERT, although this is usually associated with other names.

US cinematographer Norbert Brodine (1893–1970); Austrian-born UK violinist Norbert Brainin (b.1923).

Noreen This is an English form of the Irish name *Nóirín*, a diminutive of *Nóra* (English NORA). It was taken up on a modest scale by English speakers generally in the early 20th century, and has perhaps come to be thought of by some as a variant form of DOREEN.

UK actress Noreen Kershaw (b.1950).

Norm see **Norman**.

Norma This name is probably an adoption of the standard Latin (or Italian) word *norma*, 'norm', 'rule', 'standard', but it is now popularly regarded as the female counterpart of NORMAN. (Norma Major, wife of the UK prime minister John Major, was named after her father, Norman Johnson.) The name was taken up by English speakers in the 19th century, and in the 20th century was in increasing favour until the 1930s, after which it gradually declined. Its original adoption may have been prompted by Bellini's popular opera *Norma* (1831). (This was itself based on a contemporary tragedy by the French writer Alexandre Louis Soumet, in which Norma is a Druid priestess.)

US actress Norma Talmadge (1893–1957); Canadian-born US actress Norma Shearer (1900–83); US actress, singer Norma Terris (1904–89) (named for Bellini opera); UK opera singer Norma Procter (b.1928); US children's writer Norma Klein (1938–89); US country singer Norma Jean (b.1938) (original name Norma Jean Beasler); Northern Ireland opera singer Norma Burrowes (b.1946).

Norman The present name represents the Old English name *Northmann*, 'Norseman'. It was current both before and after the Norman Conquest of 1066 but was then almost exclusively in Scottish use until the mid-19th century, after which it became increasingly popular until the 1920s, when it began a gradual decline. The usual diminutive is *Norm*, though *Norrie* is also found in Scottish use.

UK dress designer Norman Hartnell (1901–79); UK comedian Norman Wisdom (b.1918); UK actor Norman Birch (b.1919); UK conductor Norman Del Mar (1919–94); US critical writer Norman Mailer (b.1923); UK actor Norman Rossington (1928–99); UK politicians Norman St John-Stevas, Lord Stevas of Fawsley (b.1929), Norman Tebbit, Lord Tebbit (b.1931), Sir Norman Fowler (b.1938), Norman Lamont (b.1942); UK actor Norman Eshley (b.1945); UK comedian Norman Pace (b.1953).

Nuala An independently adopted diminutive of the Irish name FIONNUALA, occasionally found in general use among English speakers. See also FENELLA.

Irish poet, playwright Nuala Ní Dhomhnaill (b.1952).

Nyree This name is an English spelling of the Maori name *Ngaire*, of uncertain meaning. It has enjoyed some modest adoption among English speakers from the 1970s, mostly in the UK, where it was brought before the public by the New Zealand actress Nyree Dawn Porter (1940–2001).

O

Obadiah A biblical name, from Hebrew *'Ōbadhyah*, 'servant of Yah' (that is, of Jehovah), in select use among English speakers from the 17th century, when it was adopted by the Puritans. In the Bible Obadiah is the name of a dozen people, two of the most important being the master of the palace of King Ahab of Israel, famous for saving the lives of a hundred prophets in a cave from persecution by Queen Jezebel, and a minor prophet with a book named for him (the shortest in the Old Testament). In literature the name is familiar as that of Obadiah, the servant of Walter Shandy in Laurence Sterne's novel *Tristram Shandy* (1759–67), and of the Rev. Obadiah Slope, chaplain to Bishop Proudie in Anthony Trollope's novel *Barchester Towers* (1857).

Ocky see **Oscar**.

Octavia This is a feminine form of the Latin name OCTAVIUS ('eighth'), taken up by English speakers in the 19th century, although it is now much less common. It was originally familiar from members of the Roman imperial family, such as the Octavia who in the 1st century BC was the sister of Octavian (the emperor Augustus) and the second wife of Mark Antony, or the Octavia who in the 1st century AD was the teenage wife of Nero (and murdered on his order). The first of these is represented in Shakespeare's *Antony and Cleopatra* (1606–7). The UK housing reformer Octavia Hill (1838–1912) actually was an eighth daughter.

UK actress Octavia Verdin (b.1964).

Octavius An English adoption of the Roman clan name, itself from Latin *octavus*, 'eighth'. The name was in select use among English speakers from the mid-19th century until the early 20th century, when it became rare. A famous historic bearer of the name was the Roman emperor Augustus of the 1st century BC. He was originally named Caius Octavius, and in early life was known as *Octavianus* (English *Octavian*). He was the son of Octavius and Atia, the niece of Julius Caesar, who adopted him as his son and heir. He appears as a historical character (under the name Octavius Caesar) in Shakespeare's *Julius Caesar* (1599) and *Antony and Cleopatra* (1606–7). Octavius Guy is a character in Wilkie Collins's novel *The Moonstone* (1868), and Octavius Robinson is in Bernard Shaw's play *Man and Superman* (1903). The name was often used in large Victorian families to name an eighth child. The derivative name *Octavian* is in occasional use.

Odette This is an independently adopted feminine diminutive of the Old French name *Oda*, itself related to OTTO, in select English-speaking use from the 1930s. The name became widely known in the Second World War from the French Resistance heroine Odette Brailly (1912–95), captured and tortured by the Germans. She wrote of her experiences in various books and her story was retold in the film *Odette* (1950). A variant of the name is *Odetta*, as for the US folksinger Odetta (b.1930) (original name Odetta Holmes).

French-born US actress Odette Myrtil (1898–1978).

Ogden From the surname, and in only occasional English-speaking use from the 19th century.

US humorous versifier Ogden Nash (1902–71).

Olaf This Scandinavian name, formed from *anu*, 'ancestor', and *leifr*, 'heir', hence 'family descendant', has been popularly (and possibly correctly) associated with OLIVER. It was introduced to England before the Norman Conquest, but was in only rare use until the 19th century, when it was taken up by Scandinavian immigrants to the US. It is historically famous from various kings of Norway, from the 11th-century St Olaf to the recent Olaf V (1903–91). The variant *Olave* is familiar to English speakers from church dedications, such as St Olave's in London.

UK writer Olaf Stapledon (1886–1950); Scottish actor Olaf Hytten (1888–1955).

Olave see **Olive**.

Olga A familiar Russian name, in origin a feminine form of *Oleg* and the equivalent of the Scandinavian name *Helga*, 'holy'. It has found certain favour among English speakers from the 19th century, and was given something of a boost in recent times by the popular Russian gymnast Olga Korbut (b.1955), champion at the 1972 Olympics.

UK-born US actress Olga Petrova (1886–1977) (original name Muriel Harding); UK Red Cross nurse Olga Franklin (1895–1987); Anglo-Norwegian actress Olga Lindo (1898–1968); Russian actress Olga Baclanova (1899–1974); UK writer Olga Franklin (b.1912); Australian writer Olga Master (1919–86); US dancer, comedienne Olga San Juan (b.1927); UK politician Lady Olga Maitland (b.1944).

Olive An adoption of the plant name, which itself implies peace (the familiar 'olive branch'). The name has been in the English-speaking world from the mid-19th century. It became very popular in the 1920s, then declined (largely being superseded by OLIVIA) only to return to favour in the 1990s. A variant form of the name is *Olave*, as for Lady Olave Baden-Powell (1889–1977), founder of the Girl Guides. A diminutive *Olivette* also exists (or existed).

South African-born writer, pacifist Olive Schreiner (1855–1920); Welsh opera singer Olive Gilbert (1898–1981); US actress Olive Borden (1907–47) (original name Sybil Tinkle).

Oliver This is an English form of the French name *Olivier*, popularly derived from Latin *olivarius*, 'olive tree', but more likely to be of Germanic origin, and akin to OLAF. The name has been in English-speaking use since medieval times and has become increasingly popular from the 1970s. In legend Oliver is famous as the paladin (retainer) of Charlemagne and, as a result of the inconclusive duel between them, a close companion of Roland. In England famous bearers of the name were English soldier and politician Oliver Cromwell (1599–1658) and the novelist and playwright Oliver Goldsmith (1728–74). In literature Sir Oliver Surface is a character in Richard Brinsley Sheridan's comedy *The School for Scandal* (1777), and the name is well known from the central character of Charles Dickens's novel *Oliver Twist* (1837–8). The musical *Oliver!* (1960), based on the latter, further popularized the name. Diminutives include *Noll*, *Ollie* and *Olly*, the first of these mostly in historical contexts, the second as for the US American football player Ollie Matson (b.1930).

US writer Oliver Wendell Holmes (1809–94); US comedian Oliver Hardy (1892–1957); South African anti-apartheid leader Oliver Tambo (1917–93); UK actor Oliver Reed (1938–99); US Marine officer Oliver North (b.1943); UK actor Oliver Cotton (b.1944); US film director Oliver Stone (b.1946).

Olivette see **Olive**.

Olivia The name derives from Latin or (later) Italian *oliva*, 'olive', and is now sometimes regarded as a feminine equivalent of OLIVER. It was taken up generally by English speakers in the 18th century and is now more common in the US than the UK. (Romantics point out that if said rapidly the name suggests 'I love you'.) After a lengthy period of only modest favour, the name began an upturn in popularity from the 1970s.

Shakespeare has Olivia as the central character (a rich heiress wooed by a duke) in *Twelfth Night* (1601). William Wycherly then has Olivia as Manly's mistress in his comedy *The Plain-Dealer* (1677). In Oliver Goldsmith's novel *The Vicar of Wakefield* (1766) Olivia is one of the six children of the central character, Dr Charles Primrose, and the same author's comedy *The Good-Natured Man* (1768) also has a character Olivia. (The name echoes Goldsmith's own.)

UK novelist Olivia Manning (1908–80); British-born US actress Olivia de Havilland (b.1916); US actress Olivia Cole (b.1942); English-born Australian pop singer Olivia Newton-John (b.1948); UK actress Olivia Hussey (b.1951).

Ollie, **Olly** see **Oliver**.

Olwen A Welsh name, from *ôl*, 'footprint', 'track', and *gwen*, 'white', 'fair', so 'white footprints', in mainly Welsh use from the 19th century. Olwen of Welsh legend caused white flowers to spring up wherever she walked. The name was popularized by the haunting theme tune 'Dream of Olwen' in the film *While I Live* (1947).

UK magazine editor Olwen Rice (b.1960).

Omar This is either a biblical name, from a Hebrew word meaning 'eloquent', or an English form of the Arabic name *'Umar*, representing *'āmir*, 'flourishing' (related to English *emir*). The name has found occasional favour among English speakers from the 19th century, and was more readily taken up in the 20th century by black Americans. In the Bible Omar is the second son of Eliphaz, listed in a lengthy genealogy (Genesis 36). The name is famous from the 12th-century Persian poet Omar Khayyám, whose *Rubáiyát* ('quatrains') were freely rendered in a popular English version (1859) by Edward Fitzgerald.

US Army general Omar N. Bradley (1893–1981); Egyptian-born actor Omar Sharif (b.1932) (original name Michael Shalhoub).

Ona A name that is either an alteration of OONA or an independent adoption of the final letters of a name such as FIONA. It has found some favour among English speakers in the 20th century.

US actress Ona Munson (1906–55).

Oona An English form of the Irish name UNA, in select English-speaking use from the 1950s. The variant spelling *Oonagh* also exists.

Daughter of US playwright Eugene O'Neill, wife of UK actor Charlie Chaplin, Oona Chaplin (1925–91).

Opal A name, from the precious stone, occasionally adopted by English speakers from the late 19th century. Opal Felis is a character in Theodore Dreiser's novel *An American Tragedy* (1925).

Ophelia This name is apparently a feminine form of the Greek name *Ōphelos*, meaning 'profit', 'help', perhaps intended in the sense 'helpmate', 'wife'. It has been in irregular favour among English speakers from the 19th century, with its widest adoption among black Americans. The name was made famous by Ophelia, the beautiful daughter of Polonius in Shakespeare's *Hamlet* (1599–1601). In Harriet Beecher Stowe's novel *Uncle Tom's Cabin* (1852) Ophelia Vermont (Miss Ophelia) is the unmarried cousin of St Clare (the purchaser of Uncle Tom).

Oprah A variant of the biblical name *Orpah*, itself said to mean 'she who turns her back', in very occasional English-speaking use from the 1980s.

US actress, chat-show host Oprah Winfrey (b.1954) (her intended name, Orpah, was misspelled on her birth certificate).

Oriana The name may have its origin in Latin *oriri*, 'to rise', so meaning 'dawn', 'sunrise' (compare DAWN), or else was based on a word that gave French *or*, 'gold'. It has found some favour among English speakers since the 16th century. In medieval tales Oriana was the beloved of the knight Amadis of Gaul. The name was used in later literature to refer to Queen Elizabeth I, and there is a character Oriana in at least three comedies: Sir Francis Beaumont's *The Woman Hater* (1607), John Fletcher's *The Wilde Goose Chase* (1621) and George Farquhar's *The Inconstant* (1702). In the latter two she is the principal character and virtually identical. An early Tennyson poem, *The Ballad of Oriana* (1830), mentions the name forty-four times in a total of eleven verses. Stanley Weyman's novel *Sophia* (1900) has an actress Oriana Clark (original name Sarah Grocott) as the mistress of the adventurer Hawkesworth (alias Count Plomer).

Orinthia The origin of this name may lie in the Greek word *orinein*, 'to excite', 'to stir the mind'. Occasional adoptions of it have occurred among English speakers in the 20th century. The name was used by Bernard Shaw for the woman loved by King Magnus in his play *The Apple Cart* (1929), in which all characters have classical names. The play includes the following dialogue:

> *Orinthia*: The name you pretended to invent specially for me, the only woman in the world for you. Picked up out of the rubbish basket in a secondhand bookseller's! And I thought you were a poet!
>
> *Magnus*: Well, one poet may consecrate a name for another. Orinthia is a name full of magic for me. It could not be that if I had invented it myself. I heard it at a concert of ancient music when I was a child, and I have treasured it ever since.

Orlando The name is an Italian form of ROLAND, in occasional English-speaking use from the mid-19th century. In the stories about Roland, the paladin who attended Charlemagne, it has an important literary appearance in Boiardo's poem *Orlando Innamorato* (*Roland in Love*, 1487), continued in

Ariosto's poem *Orlando Furioso* (*Roland Mad*, 1532). In Shakespeare's *As You Like It* (1599) Orlando, who marries Rosalind, is the youngest son of Sir Rowland de Bois, so that his name echoes that of his father. Virginia Woolf's novel *Orlando* (1928) concerns a character of the name who is first a man, then a woman.

West African actor Orlando Martins (1899–1985).

Orpah see **Oprah**.

Orson A name that was either adopted from the surname or devised as an English form of the French name *Ourson*, 'bear cub'. (Compare URSULA.) It has known sporadic adoption by English speakers from medieval times.

US actor, film director Orson Welles (1915–85) (originally middle name, first being George); US comedian, chat-show host Orson Bean (b.1928) (original name Dallas Burrows).

Orville This name is apparently an adoption of the mock aristocratic surname invented by Fanny Burney for Lord Orville, the central character of her novel *Evelina* (1778). It is found in occasional English-speaking use from the 19th century. In later literature Orville W. Mason is a district attorney in Theodore Dreiser's novel *An American Tragedy* (1925).

US Unitarian theologian Orville Dewey (1794–1882); US aviation pioneer Orville Wright (1871–1948) (named for Dewey); US writer, authority on China Orville Schell (b.1920).

Osbert The modern name represents the Old English name *Osbeorht*, formed from *ōs*, 'god', and *beorht*, 'bright', 'famous', so 'famous as a god'. It has found some favour among English speakers from the 19th century. Diminutives *Ozzie* and *Ozzy* exist.

UK writer Sir Osbert Sitwell (1892–1969); UK cartoonist Osbert Lancaster (1908–86).

Osborn The name is either an adoption of the surname or else represents the Old English name *Osbern*, itself from the Scandinavian name *Asbiorn*, composed of *áss* (Old English *ōs*) 'god', and *bjorn* (Old English *beorn*) 'bear', hence 'godlike warrior'. It enjoyed a certain fashion among English speakers in the 19th century and may have been suggested to some by Osborne House, Isle of Wight, the mansion at which Queen Victoria frequently stayed. Diminutives *Ozzie* and *Ozzy* are known.

Oscar The name either evolved from the Old English name *Ansgar*, formed from *ōs*, 'god', and *gar*, 'spear', so 'godlike spearsman', or derives from a Gaelic name composed of *os*, 'deer', and *cara*, 'friend', so 'gentle friend'. It has been in select English-speaking use from the 19th century. A Gaelic source for the name is supported by Oscar, son of the poet Ossian in the Irish Fenian sagas. These were retold by the 18th-century antiquarian and poet James Macpherson, who claimed to have translated them from the Gaelic writings of Ossian (although against a Scottish background). One early 'Ossianic' fragment of his was 'The Death of Oscar' (1759). Macpherson's works were admired by Napoleon, who gave the name to his godson Oscar Bernadotte, later king of Sweden, Oscar I (1799–1859). The name is now thus current in Sweden. In the English-speaking world, one of the name's most famous bearers is the Irish writer Oscar Wilde (1854–1900), who was himself named for King Oscar II of Sweden, treated by Wilde's eye-surgeon father. In modern times the name has been (quite literally) brought before the public by the 'Oscar', the gold-plated statuette awarded annually since 1928 for outstanding achievement in films by the American Academy of Motion Picture Arts and Sciences. (The award is said to have been named in 1931 by a former Academy secretary because of its fanciful resemblance to her uncle, Oscar Pierce.) Diminutives include *Ocky*, *Ozzie* and *Ozzy*.

US actor Oscar Apfel (1874–1938); US lyricist Oscar Hammerstein II (1895–1960); Austrian-born US actor Oscar Homolka (1899–1978); US pianist, actor Oscar Levant (1906–72); US jazzman Oscar Peterson (b.1925); UK film journalist Oscar Moore (b.1960).

Osmond The name was either adopted from the surname or else represents the Old English name *Osmund*, formed from *ōs*, 'god', and *mund*, 'protector', thus 'protected by gods' or 'godlike protector'. It has enjoyed sporadic favour among English speakers from the mid-19th century. An early historic bearer of the name was St Osmund, appointed bishop of Salisbury by William the Conqueror in the 11th century. The spelling *Osmund* also occurs.

Oswald The name either comes from the surname or represents the Old English name *Osweald*, formed from *ōs*, 'god', and *weald*, 'rule', so 'godlike ruler'. It has found some favour among English speakers from the 19th century. Two saints of the name gained fame: the 7th-century Christian martyr, king Oswald of Northumbria, and the 10th-century bishop Oswald of Worcester, archbishop of York. (The first of these is said to have given the name of Oswestry in Shropshire, but any historic link is doubtful.) In Shakespeare's *King Lear* (1604–5) Oswald is a steward to Goneril. In later literature Oswald Millbank is an industrialist's son in Benjamin Disraeli's novel *Coningsby* (1844), while Oswald Sydenham is an ex-midshipman naval hero in love with his cousin Dolly Stubland in H.G. Wells's novel *Joan and Peter* (1918). A notorious real-life bearer of the name was the UK founder of the British Union of Fascists, Sir Oswald Mosley (1896–1980). (His name was that of his father and grandfather.) Diminutives *Oz*, *Ozzie* and *Ozzy* exist.

Otis From the surname, itself related to OTTO, and in select English-speaking use from the 19th century, mostly among black Americans. In many cases the name will have been originally adopted as a tribute to the US Revolutionary hero James Otis (1725–83).

US actor Otis Skinner (1858–1942); US pop musician Otis Blackwell (b.1931); US actor Otis Young (b.1932); US soul singer Otis Redding (1941–67).

Otto A German name, formed as the diminutive of a name containing *ot*, 'prosperity' (corresponding to Old English *ēad* in names such as EDWARD and EDWIN). Some English speakers took up the name in the 19th century, but it has been rare in the UK from the early 20th, although maintained in the US until the 1940s by German immigrants. The name became historically familiar from Roman emperors and from various German and Austrian royal families. A further public aware- ness of the name was due to the Prussian statesman Otto von Bismarck (1815–98), Germany's 'Iron Chancellor'.

US actor Otto Kruger (1885–1974); Austrian-US film director Otto Preminger (1906–86).

Ottoline This name is an independently adopted diminu- tive of the French (or German) name *Ottilie*, itself from the medieval name *Odila*, a feminine form of OTTO. It has found some favour among English speakers from the 19th century.

UK literary and artistic hostess Lady Ottoline Morrell (1873–1938).

Owen A Welsh name, said to represent the Latin name *Eugenius* (English EUGENE). It was first taken up by English speakers in the 17th century, and has enjoyed modest but fairly consis- tent favour since then. The name's famous historic bearer was the 15th-century Welsh chieftain Owen Glendower (*Owain Glyndŵr*), who led a revolt against the English. He appears in Shakespeare's play *Henry IV* (1597). In later literature Owen Graye is the son of the architect Amos Graye in Thomas Hardy's novel *Desperate Remedies* (1871). 'Owen Meredith' was the pseudonym adopted by the UK writer Edward Robert

Bulwer Lytton (1831–91), 1st Earl of Lytton and son of the better-known novelist and dramatist 1st Baron Lytton (Lord Lytton) (1803–73). *Owain*, as the Welsh form of the name, is found almost exclusively in Wales, as for the Welsh conductor Owain Arwel Hughes (b.1942).

US writer Owen Wister (1860–1938); UK actor Owen Nares (1888–1943); UK opera singer Owen Brannigan (1908–73); US popular musician, record producer Owen Bradley (1915–98); UK actor Owen Teale (b.1961).

Oz see **Oswald**.

Ozzie, **Ozzy** see **Osbert**, **Oscar**, **Oswald**.

P

Paddy (m.) An independently adopted diminutive of PATRICK, in irregular use among English speakers from the 19th century and long a name associated with Ireland, as is its source name. (The name is now derogative generically.)

US playwright Paddy Chayefsky (1923–81) (original first name Sidney); UK politician Paddy Ashdown (b.1941) (original first name Jeremy); UK rock musician Paddy McAloon (b.1957); Irish film director Paddy Breathnach (b.1964); Irish rugby player Paddy Johns (b.1968).

Paddy (f.) An independently adopted diminutive of PATRICIA, in occasional use from the 19th century.

UK fashion designer Paddy Campbell (b.1940).

Pam An independently adopted diminutive of PAMELA, popularly taken up by English speakers in the 20th century.

UK playwright Pam Gems (b.1925); UK actress Pam St Clement (b.1942); UK writer, entertainer Pam Ayres (b.1947); US actresses Pam Grier (b.1949), Pam Dawber (b.1951); US country singer Pam Tillis (b.1957); US tennis player Pam Shriver (b.1962).

Pamela The name was invented by the poet Sir Philip Sidney for his prose romance *The Arcadia* (1590), presumably intending it to mean 'all sweetness', from Greek *pan*, 'all', and *meli*, 'honey'. He stressed the name on the second syllable, 'Pamela'. It was first generally adopted by English speakers in the 19th century, then grew fairly rapidly in popularity from the turn of the 20th century to the 1950s, after which it gradually faded. The name was first widely famous in literature from Pamela Andrews, the central character of Samuel Richardson's novel *Pamela* (1740–41). The same name reappeared in Henry

Fielding's novel *Joseph Andrews* (1742), which begins as a parody of *Pamela* (Joseph Andrews being Pamela's brother). (The previous year Fielding had pseudonymously published *Shamela Andrews* as a travesty of Richardson's book.) The spelling *Pamella* sometimes occurs. The regular diminutive is PAM, adopted in its own right.

UK writers Pamela Frankau (1908–67), Pamela Hansford Johnson (1912–81); US actress Pamela Britton (1923–74); UK actress Pamela Franklin (b.1949); UK TV presenter Pamela Armstrong (b.1951); New Zealand actress, comedienne Pamela Stephenson (b.1951); US actress Pamela Sue Martin (b.1954); Canadian actress Pamela Anderson (b.1967).

Pandora A Greek name, from *pan*, 'all', and *dōron*, 'gift', so 'many gifted'. The name was selectively taken up by English speakers in the 20th century. In Greek mythology, Pandora was the first woman, made out of the earth as the gods' revenge on man for obtaining fire from Prometheus. Given the box ('Pandora's box') that she was told not to open, she nevertheless did so out of curiosity and released all ills that beset mankind, leaving only hope in the box. Her name was thus ironic.

Pansy From the flower name, itself associated with thought (French *pensée*), and taken up by English speakers in the late 19th century, when other flower names came into fashion. It has now fallen from favour, perhaps partly through the use of *pansy* to denote an effeminate man. Pansy Osmond is the daughter of Gilbert Osmond who marries the central character, Isabel Archer, in Henry James's novel *The Portrait of a Lady* (1881). In real life 'Pansy' was the pen name adopted (from her childhood nickname) by the US writer of sentimental religious children's fiction Isabella Macdonald Alden (1841–1930).

Parker From the surname, sometimes adopted by English speakers for first-name use from the 19th century, mostly in the US. Dr Parker Peps attends Mrs Dombey in Charles Dickens's novel *Dombey and Son* (1847–8).

US film critic Parker Tyler (1904–74).

Parthenia A Greek name, from *parthenos*, 'virgin', in very occasional use among English speakers from the late 19th century. The Parthenon, in Athens, was the temple of the goddess Athena Parthenos, Athena the Maid. In Sir Philip Sidney's prose romance *The Arcadia* (1590) Parthenia is the wife of Argalus.

Parthenope A Greek name, from *parthenos*, 'virgin' (as for PARTHENIA) and *ōps*, 'face', so 'maiden-faced'. The name found a few English speakers to adopt it in the 19th century. In Greek mythology, Parthenope was the siren who drowned herself in frustration when avoided by Odysseus. Her body was later washed ashore at Naples in Italy. The famous UK hospital reformer Florence Nightingale had an elder sister Frances Parthenope (d.1890), so named as she had been born at Naples. (Florence was herself named in similar fashion.)

Pascal A name of French origin, meaning 'of Easter' (English *paschal*), suitable for a child conceived or born at this time. English speakers have used the name from the 1950s.

Pascale The female equivalent of the French male name PASCAL, appropriate for a child conceived or born at Easter. English speakers have taken up the name from the 1960s.

UK fashion designer Pascale Smets (b.1964).

Pat (m.) An independently adopted diminutive of PATRICK, first in use among English speakers in the 19th century. The name later came to be favoured chiefly by entertainers, sportsmen and the like. PATSY is a diminutive in independent use.

UK escape officer, writer Major Pat Reid (1910–90); US actor Pat Hingle (b.1923); US popular singer Pat Boone (b.1934) (original first names Charles Eugene); US tennis player Pat Dupre (b.1953); Scottish boxer Pat Clinton (b.1964); Australian tennis player Pat Cash (b.1965).

Pat (f.) An independently adopted diminutive of PATRICIA, in English-speaking use from the early 20th century. The usual diminutives are PATTI, PATTY and PATSY, all in independent use.

UK actresses Pat Paterson (1911–78), Pat Kirkwood (b.1921), Pat Phoenix (1923–86); UK equestrienne Pat Smythe (1928–96); UK actress Pat Coombs (b.1930); UK political activist, writer Pat Arrowsmith (b.1930); UK magazine editor Pat Roberts-Cairns (b.1947); US pop singer Pat Benatar (b.1953).

Patience The name, from the virtue, was taken up by 16th-century Puritans and was increasingly popular among English speakers until the 20th century, when it gradually declined. In Shakespeare's *Henry VIII* (1613) Patience is a servant to the king. Patience Oriel is the sister of the Rev. Caleb Oriel in Anthony Trollope's novel *Doctor Thorne* (1858). The name was popularized by the Gilbert and Sullivan opera *Patience* (1881), in which the title character is a dairymaid loved by the idyllic poet Archibald Grosvenor.

UK inspirational poet Patience Strong (1905–90) (original name Winifred May); UK actress Patience Collier (1910–87).

Patricia In origin the name is a feminine form of the Latin name *Patricius*, 'noble man', but it later came to be regarded as a female equivalent of PATRICK. It was relatively rare in English-speaking usage until the early 20th century, when it suddenly became very popular. It then began a gradual decline, which steepened from the 1960s. The fashion for the name was undoubtedly helped by the granddaughter of Queen Victoria, Princess Patricia (1886–1974), who married Sir Alexander Ramsay in 1919. In H.G. Wells's novel *War in the Air* (1908) Miss Patricia Giddy discovers gold ore in Anglesea. The usual diminutive is PAT, in independent use, as are such other diminutives as PADDY, PATSY, PATTI and PATTY. *Tricia, Trish* and *Trisha* are also quite common, as, respectively, for the UK actress Tricia Penrose (b.1970), US actress Trish Van Devere (b.1943) and US country singer Trisha Yearwood (b.1964).

Irish-US actress Patricia Collinge (1892–1974); UK actress Patricia Hayes (1910–98); wife of US president Richard Nixon, Patricia Nixon (1912–93) (original first names Thelma Catherine); UK actress Patricia Roc (b.1915) (original name Felicia Riese); US writer Patricia Highsmith (1921–95); UK poet Patricia Beer (b.1924); UK actress Patricia Lawrence (b.1926); US actress Patricia Neal (b.1926); UK actresses Patricia Routledge (b.1929), Patricia Garwood (b.1941), Patricia Shakesby (b.1942), Patricia Hodge (b.1946); US actress Patricia Arquette (b.1968).

Patrick The name is an English form of the Latin name *Patricius*, 'patrician' (that is, belonging to the Roman nobility). It has long been in Irish use, but was adopted more widely in the English-speaking world from the 18th century, and throughout the 20th century has never really been out of fashion. The Irish association of the name derives from its most famous bearer, the 5th-century British missionary St Patrick, patron of Ireland. (It is likely, however, that his own name was of Celtic origin, not Latin.) Patrick Earnscliff marries Isabel Vere in Walter Scott's novel *The Black Dwarf* (1816). The variant spelling *Patric* sometimes occurs. The most common diminutive is PAT, in independent use. Other diminutives adopted in their own right include PADDY and PATSY.

Irish poet Patrick Kavanagh (1905–67); UK actors Patrick Troughton (1920–87), Patrick Macnee (b.1922); UK astronomer Patrick Moore (b.1923); UK actors Patrick Magee (1924–82), Patrick Malahide (b.1945); US actors Patrick Duffy (b.1949), Patrick Swayze (b.1952).

Patsy (m.) An independently adopted diminutive of PATRICK, taken up by some English speakers from the 19th century. Patsy Farrell is an Irish character in Bernard Shaw's play *John*

Bull's Other Island (1904). The name is now generally avoided in the US, where *patsy* is a term for a dupe. In the UK, also, the name is now generally thought of as female, not male. PAT is a directly related name.

Patsy (f.) An independently adopted diminutive of PATRICIA or, less often, of HYPATIA, or a female adoption of the male name PATSY, that has been in vogue among English speakers from the early 20th century, although less common in the US and Australia, since *patsy* is a term for a dupe in the former country and for a homosexual in the latter.

US actresses Patsy Ruth Miller (1905–95), Patsy Kelly (1910–81) (original first names Bridget Veronica); US country singers Patsy Montana (1914–96) (original name Rubye Blevins), Patsy Cline (1932–63) (original name Virginia Patterson Hensley); UK actresses Patsy Byrne (b.1933), Patsy Rowlands (b.1934), Patsy Kensit (b.1968).

Patti An independently adopted spelling of PATTY, in select but increasing English-speaking favour from the 1950s. The spelling *Pattie* is also sometimes found.

US soul singer Patti Page (b.1927) (original name Clara Fowler); US pop singer Patti LaBelle (b.1944); US soul singer Patti Austin (b.1948); Nigerian-born UK actress, singer Patti Boulaye (b.1954).

Patty This name began as an independently adopted diminutive of a name such as MARTHA or MATILDA (via *Matty*), but later regularly came from PATRICIA. It was taken up by English speakers in the mid-19th century but is now much less common. The name is found in literature for Patty Sampson, sister of the chaplain to Lord Castlewood in William Makepeace Thackeray's novel *The Virginians* (1857–9), as well as for Patty, maid to Miss Throssel in J.M. Barrie's play *Quality Street* (1902). The variant spelling PATTI is in independent use, and *Pattie* also exists, as for the UK TV presenter Pattie Coldwell (b.1952).

US golfer Patty Berg (b.1918); US actresses Patty McCormack (b.1945),

Patty Duke (b.1946), Patty D'Arbanville (b.1951); US golfer Patty Sheehan (b.1956); US country musician Patty Loveless (b.1957); US tennis player Patty Fendick (b.1965).

Paul A familiar biblical name, deriving from the Latin family name *Paulus*, meaning 'small', and originally a nickname. It was taken up generally by English speakers in the 18th century, reaching its peak period of popularity in the US by the end of the 19th century and in the UK in the 1960s, since when it has gradually gone out of fashion. In the Bible St Paul is famous as the co-founder (with St Peter) of the Christian church, and as the author of many of the epistles in the New Testament. In James Fenimore Cooper's novel *The Prairie* (1827) Paul Hover is a beekeeper in love with Ellen Wade. Unusually, the name appears to have no regular variant spelling or regular diminutive.

US singer Paul Robeson (1898–1976); US actor Paul Douglas (1907–59); Canadian actor Paul Carpenter (1921–64); UK actors Paul Scofield (b.1922), Paul Daneman (b.1925); US actor Paul Newman (b.1925); UK nightclub owner Paul Raymond (b.1925); UK actor Paul Eddington (1927–95); UK magician Paul Daniels (b.1938); UK actor Paul Shane (b.1940); Canadian popular singer Paul Anka (b.1941); UK pop singer Paul McCartney (b.1942); UK pop musician, actor Paul Jones (b.1942); UK actors Paul Freeman (b.1943), Paul Young (b.1944), Paul Nicholas (b.1945), Paul Bown (b.1957); Scottish TV presenter Paul Coia (b.1957); UK footballer Paul Gascoigne ('Gazza') (b.1967).

Paula A feminine form of PAUL, in general English-speaking use from the early 20th century. The name gradually grew in popularity to a peak period in the 1960s, since when it has tailed off, particularly from the 1980s. It is not a modern name in itself, however, and was borne by various early Christian martyrs. A literary bearer of the name is Paula Power, who marries George Somerset in Thomas Hardy's novel *A Laodicean* (1881). In Sir Arthur Wing Pinero's play *The Second Mrs Tanqueray* (1893) Paula Tanqueray is the title character.

US novelist Paula Fox (b.1923); US actresses Paula Raymond (b.1923), Paula Corday (1924–92), Paula Kelly (b.1939), Paula Prentiss (b.1939); UK actress Paula Wilcox (b.1949); UK TV presenter Paula Yates (1959–2000); US singer, dancer Paula Abdul (b.1963); UK athlete Paula Dunn (b.1964); UK actress Paula Frances (b.1969).

Pauleen, **Paulene** see **Pauline**.

Paulette An independently adopted French feminine diminutive of PAUL, coming into fashion among English speakers in the 1920s, with a modest peak in the second half of the 1960s.

US actress Paulette Goddard (1911–90) (original name Pauline Marion Goddard Levy).

Paulina A feminine form of the Latin name *Paulinus*, itself a diminutive of *Paulus* (English PAUL). It came into vogue among English speakers in the 19th century, but has since been more or less ousted by the much more popular PAULINE. In Shakespeare's *The Winter's Tale* (1610–11) Paulina is the wife of Antigonus.

Pauline A French form of PAULINA, taken up by English speakers in the 19th century, and at first more popular in the US than the UK, where it reached its peak in the 1950s. In Walter Scott's novel *The Fortunes of Nigel* (1822) Mademoiselle Pauline (or Monna Paula) is an attendant of Lady Hermione, and in William Makepeace Thackeray's novel *Vanity Fair* (1847–8) Pauline is the cook at Joseph Sedley's lodgings in Brussels. The popular film serial *The Perils of Pauline* (1914) may have boosted the name, as may Compton Mackenzie's novel *Guy and Pauline* (1915). The spellings *Paulene* and *Pauleen* also occur.

US actresses Pauline Frederick (1883–1938), Pauline Lord (1890–1950); US film critic Pauline Kael (1919–2001); UK book illustrator Pauline Baynes (b.1922); UK opera singer Pauline Tinsley (b.1928); UK actresses Pauline Collins (b.1940), Pauline Peart (b.1951), Pauline Daniels (b.1955), Pauline Quirke (b.1959).

Pearl A borrowing of the gem name, in English-speaking use from the mid-19th century, but gradually declining in popularity from the 1920s and now very rare. In Nathaniel Hawthorne's novel *The Scarlet Letter* (1850) Pearl is the illegitimate daughter of the central character, Hester Prynne, who so names her because she is 'her mother's only treasure'. The diminutive *Pearlie* is sometimes found.

US novelist Pearl Buck (1892–1973); US actress Pearl White (1889–1938) (original first names Victoria Evans); US singer, entertainer Pearl Bailey (1918–90); West African dancer Pearl Primus (1919–94).

Peggy This name is an independently adopted variant of MAGGIE, itself a diminutive of MARGARET. (The *M-* changed to *P-* as it did with POLLY from MOLLY.) The name was first taken up by English speakers in the 18th century, but it gained wide popularity only in the 1920s, after which it fairly rapidly fell from favour. In William Makepeace Thackeray's novel *Vanity Fair* (1847–8) Margaretta O'Dowd, the wife of Major O'Dowd, is popularly known as Peggy. The usual diminutive is *Peg*. (In Charles Dickens's novel *David Copperfield* (1849–50) the name of Peggotty, David's nurse, is not a form of Peggy but her surname. She is always so addressed because her first name, Clara, is the same as that of David's mother, her mistress.)

US actress Peggy Wood (1894–1978); US art collector Peggy Guggenheim (1898–1979); UK actresses Dame Peggy Ashcroft (1907–91), Peggy Mount (1916–2001); US comedienne Peggy Ryan (b.1924); US children's writer Peggy Parish (1927–88); US figure skater Peggy Fleming (b.1948).

Penelope This well-known Greek name is perhaps based on *pēne*, 'thread', so that the overall sense is 'seamstress'. However, this does not account for the second part of the name. Some authorities have related the name as a whole to the Greek word *pēnelops*, a kind of duck, but the sense seems unlikely. The name has been in select English-speaking use from the 16th century. It became quite fashionable in the 1950s and 1960s, but has now lost its former attraction. According to classical mythology, in a story that seems to support the 'seamstress' origin, Penelope remained faithful to her husband Odysseus during his long absence, telling would-be suitors that she would not remarry until she had finished weaving a shroud for her father-in-law, Laertes. But she delayed completion of the tapestry by unravelling at night what she wove by day. In English literature Penelope is a character in James Shirley's comedy *The Gamester* (1633). Later, Lady Penelope Penfeather is the chief patroness of the well mentioned in the title of Walter Scott's novel *St Ronan's Well* (1823), and Penelope Betteredge is the daughter of Gabriel Betteredge, house steward to Lady Verinder, in Wilkie Collins's novel *The Moonstone* (1868). The name's usual diminutive is PENNY, in independent use.

UK writers Penelope Fitzgerald (1916–2000), Penelope Mortimer (1918–99), Penelope Gilliatt (1932–93), Penelope Lively (b.1933); UK child psychologist Penelope Leach (b.1937); UK actresses Penelope Keith (b.1939), Penelope Wilton (b.1946); UK writer Penelope Shuttle (b.1947); US actress Penelope Ann Miller (b.1964).

Penny A name that is an independently adopted diminutive of PENELOPE but that also evokes the familiar coin, with its associations of homeliness, honesty and thrift. The name has been in general use among English speakers from the 1930s, first in the US, then in the UK, where it achieved a modest boom in the 1970s. The further diminutive *Pen* is sometimes found.

US actresses Penny Singleton (b.1908) (original name Mariana McNulty), Penny Edwards (1919–98); UK writer Penny Vincenzi (b.1939); UK columnist Penny Perrick (b.1941); US actress Penny Marshall (b.1942); UK theatrical director Penny Cherns (b.1948); UK TV presenter Penny Junor (b.1949); UK racing driver Penny Mallory (b.1966).

Perce see **Percy**.

Percival This name is an English form of the French name *Perceval*, popularly interpreted as composed of *perce*, 'pierce', and *val*, 'valley', giving an overall meaning of 'one who penetrates the valley'. It is likely, however, to be a form of the Celtic name *Peredur*, perhaps meaning 'hard steel'. The name was probably influenced by PERCY, but this is a different and unrelated name. It has been in English-speaking use from medieval times, gradually rising to a popularity peak in the late 19th century. It is now rare in the UK but is still in favour among black Americans. It is famous in legend from Sir Percival, the pure and innocent knight of the Arthurian romances, one of the three, with Sir Galahad and Sir Bors, who succeed in their quest for the Holy Grail. He features in many later versions of the tales, down to Tennyson's poem 'The Holy Grail' (1859) in *Idylls of the King*. Sir Percival Glyde is a character in Wilkie Collins's novel *The Woman in White* (1860). The UK writer P.C. Wren (1885–1941), author of the romantic adventure *Beau Geste* (1924), had first names Percival Christopher.

Percy The name is a borrowing of the surname, but is popularly regarded as a diminutive of PERCIVAL, even though that name has a quite different origin. It became increasingly popular among English speakers from the early 19th century, reaching its peak in the 1900s. It is now rare in the UK, although still found among black Americans. One of its most famous bearers was the poet Percy Bysshe Shelley (1792–1822), who was distantly related to the aristocratic Percy family. Percy Sibwright is a character in William Makepeace Thackeray's novel *The Newcomes* (1853–5), while Percy Bresnahan is in Sinclair Lewis's novel *Main Street* (1920). The diminutive *Perce* exists.

UK musicologist Percy Scholes (1877–1958); Australian-born US composer Percy Grainger (1882–1961) (originally second name, first being George); UK TV gardener Percy Thrower (1913–88).

Perdita The name, from Latin *perdita*, 'lost', was devised by Shakespeare for the character in *The Winter's Tale* (1610–11). Its use among English speakers has been rare. (In the play Perdita, the daughter of Leontes and Hermione, is abandoned on a beach and was so named by her mother as she was 'counted lost for ever'. She duly reappears some years later.) The daughter of the US writer 'H.D.' (Hilda Doolittle) was named Perdita (b.1919) as her mother nearly died when in labour.

Peregrine The name is the English form of the Latin name *Peregrinus*, 'foreigner', 'stranger' (compare related English *pilgrim*). It was first generally taken up by English speakers in the 18th century but has enjoyed only modest adoption from the 19th century. The name was borne by various early saints, but it is perhaps best known from the central character of Tobias Smollett's novel *Peregrine Pickle* (1751). Later, Sir Peregrine Blandy is a governor of Coventry Island and successor to Rawdon Crawley in William Makepeace Thackeray's novel *The Newcomes* (1853–5). The usual diminutive, in independent use, is PERRY.

UK newspaper editor Peregrine Worsthorne (b.1923).

Perry If not a borrowing of the surname, this name is an independently adopted diminutive of PEREGRINE. It has been in select English-speaking use from the 19th century and began a gradual increase in favour from the 1980s. It was popularized by Perry Mason, the detective-lawyer who is the chief character in the stories (from the 1930s) by the US writer Earle Stanley Gardner, subsequently featuring in the familiar TV series *Perry Mason* (1957–65) and its sequel *Perry Mason Returns* (1985).

US popular composer Perry Bradford (1893–1970); Italian-born US crooner Perry Como (1913–2001) (original first name Pierino); US actor Perry King (b.1948); UK violinist Perry Montague-Mason (b.1956).

Persephone A Greek name, formed from *pherein*, 'to bring', and *phonē*, 'death', thus with the meaning of 'bringing death', and (not surprisingly) in rare use among English speakers. In Greek mythology Persephone is abducted by Hades (Pluto) and made his wife and the queen of the underworld. She is thus a sort of goddess of the dead and may even have evolved as such.

Persis A biblical name, from the Greek meaning 'Persian woman', adopted by some Puritans in the 17th century but never generally catching on among English speakers. In the Bible Persis is mentioned by St Paul as a woman 'which laboured much in the Lord' (Romans 16.12). In William D. Howells's novel *The Rise of Silas Lapham* (1885) Persis Lapham is the wife of the central character.

Peta A feminine equivalent of PETER, taken up by some English speakers from the 1930s.

Pete An independently adopted diminutive of PETER, in select use among English speakers in the 20th century, when it is found mainly among entertainers, sportsmen and the like.

US folksinger Pete Seeger (b.1919); UK radio presenter Pete Murray (b.1928); US baseball player Pete Rose (b.1941); UK rock musician Pete Townshend (b.1945); US tennis player Pete Sampras (b.1971).

Peter A famous biblical name, and the English form of the Latin name *Petrus*, itself from Greek *petros*, 'rock'. The name has been in regular use among English speakers from medieval times, becoming very popular in the early years of the 20th century and remaining so until the 1960s, when it subsided to a more modest level. In the Bible Peter is the best known of the apostles, and co-founder (with St Paul) of the Christian church. His original name was Simon, and he was given the by-name Peter, translating Aramaic *Cephas*, so as to be distinguished from his namesake, the disciple Simon Zelotes: 'And when Jesus beheld him, he said, Thou art Simon the son of Jona; thou shalt be called Cephas, which is by interpretation, A stone' (John 1.42). (Matthew 16.18 spells out the symbolic sense of the name: 'And I say unto thee, That thou art Peter, and upon this rock I will build my church.') Sir Peter Teazle is a character in Richard Brinsley Sheridan's play *The School for Scandal* (1777), and Peter Featherstone is a rich, miserly widower in George Eliot's novel *Middlemarch* (1871–2). The name was doubtless popularized by the central character of J.M. Barrie's play *Peter Pan* (1904), the motherless, half-magical 'boy who wouldn't grow up'. The regular diminutive is PETE, in independent use, although *Peterkin* has enjoyed favour in the past, as for Peterkin Gay, one of the shipwrecked boys (with Ralph Rover and Jack Martin) in R.M. Ballantyne's novel *The Coral Island* (1857).

Hungarian-born US actor Peter Lorre (1904–64) (original name Laszlo Loewenstein); UK actors Peter Cushing (1913–94), Peter Finch (1916–77), Sir Peter Ustinov (b.1921), Peter Jones (1920–2000), Peter Sellers (1925–80); US actor Peter Falk (b.1927); UK actors Peter Barkworth (b.1929), Peter Jeffrey (1929–99), Peter O'Toole (b.1932), Peter Bowles (b.1936); UK entertainer Peter Cook (1937–95); US film director Peter Bogdanovich (b.1939); UK TV newsreader Peter Sissons (b.1942); UK actor, TV presenter Peter Duncan (b.1954).

Petra A Latinized feminine equivalent of PETER, in select English-speaking use from the 1940s.

German environmentalist Petra Kelly (1947–92).

Petronella This is an English form of the Latin name *Petronilla*, a feminine diminutive of the Roman clan name *Petronius*, long associated with PETER. The name has been adopted in some English-speaking circles from the 1940s. A variant form *Petronilla* exists.

Dutch-born UK children's writer Petronella Breinburg (b.1927); UK actress Petronella Ford (b.1946); UK writer Petronella Pulsford (b.1946).

Petula The original source of this name may have been in Latin *petere*, 'to seek', 'to beg', as if 'one sought for', or in Latin *petulans*, 'bold', but it is now usually felt to be a feminine form of PETER. It also suggests *petal* or even *pet*. It found some favour among English speakers in the 20th century.

UK actress, singer Petula Clark (b.1932) (original name Sally Owen).

Phil An independently adopted diminutive of PHILIP, in select but increasingly popular use among English speakers from the mid-19th century. Phil Barker is a character in Charles Dickens's novel *Oliver Twist* (1837–8). A diminutive *Philly* exists, as for the US jazz drummer Philly Joe Jones (1923–85) (original first names Joseph Rudolph).

UK cartoonist Phil May (1864–1903); Russian-born US film director Phil Rosen (1888–1951); US all-girl bandleader Phil Spitalny (1890–1970); US comedian Phil Silvers (1912–85); UK naturalist Phil Drabble (b.1914); US motor-racing driver Phil Hill (b.1929); US folksinger Phil Ochs (1940–76); US hockey player Phil Esposito (b.1942); US diver Phil Boggs (1949–90); UK rock musicians Phil Collins (b.1951), Phil Collen (b.1957); UK actor Phil Daniels (b.1958).

Philemon A biblical name, from the Greek name *Philēmōn*, from *philēma*, 'kiss', in rarish English-speaking adoption, mainly in the US, from the 19th century. In the Bible Philemon is the 'dearly beloved fellow-labourer' of Paul, to whom the latter addresses the epistle named for him. In classical mythology the name is familiar from the story of the modest elderly couple, Philemon and Baucis, who give hospitality to the gods Zeus and Hermes, disguised as travellers, without realizing their true identity.

Philip A biblical name, from the Greek name *Philippos*, formed from *philein*, 'to love', and *hippos*, 'horse', so 'horse lover', 'horseman'. The name was fairly common in English-speaking use from the 16th century to the 19th, when it declined. It revived strongly from the 1920s to reach a peak of high popularity in the 1960s, since when it has once more gradually faded. In classical times the name gained fame as that of the father of Alexander the Great (4th century BC), among others. In the Bible the name is that of several people, including Philip the apostle, the first-named of the second group of four to be chosen, and Philip the evangelist, one of seven deacons appointed after the death of Christ. (Some commentators equate the two, however.) It was the name of six kings of France, one of whom, Philip II, appears as a historical character in Shakespeare's *King John* (*c*.1596). Philip Firmin is the central character in William Makepeace Thackeray's novel *The Adventures of Philip* (1861–2), and the orphan Philip Pirrip (Pip) is the main character in Charles Dickens's novel *Great Expectations* (1860–61). The variant spelling *Phillip* is sometimes found, as for the UK TV presenter Phillip Schofield (b.1962), while the regular diminutive, PHIL, is in independent use. The diminutive PIP also sometimes occurs in its own right.

Greek-born UK husband of Queen Elizabeth II, Prince Philip (b.1921); UK poet Philip Larkin (1922–85); UK actors Philip Locke (b.1928), Philip Madoc (b.1934); UK newsreader Philip Hayton (b.1947).

Philippa A feminine equivalent of PHILIP, in English-speaking use from the 19th century, and in and out of fashion since. An early bearer of the name was Philippa (1314–69), queen of Edward III of England. The regular diminutive, PIPPA, has become adopted in its own right.

UK novelist Philippa Carr (*c*.1910–93) (original name Eleanor Burford); UK children's writer Philippa Pearce (b.1920); UK waterskier Philippa Roberts (b.1960); UK TV presenter Philippa Forrester (b.1969).

Phillip see **Philip**.

Phillis, **Phillys** see **Phyllis**.

Philly see **Phil**.

Philo An English version of the Late Greek name *Philōn*, 'loved', based on the element *phil-* found more familiarly in PHILIP. The name has found occasional favour among English speakers from the 18th century, mainly in the US. It was popularized by Philo Vance, the dandy detective in the crime novels (1926–39) by the US writer 'S.S. Van Dine' (Willard Huntington Wright).

US sewing-machine and typewriter manufacturer Philo Remington (1816–89).

Philomela A Greek name, formed from *philos*, 'dear', 'sweet', and *melos*, 'song', giving the meaning of 'sweet singer' or, alternatively, 'nightingale' (from *philomela*, combining the two elements). The name has found some favour among English speakers from the 16th century. In classical mythology Philomela is the Athenian king Pandion's daughter who was metamorphosed into a nightingale. In English literature the name is that of the central character of Robert Greene's romance *Philomela* (1592), addressed to Lady Fitzwalter. The variant spelling *Philomel* is also found.

Philomena A Greek name, formed from *philein*, 'to love', and *menos*, 'strength', so 'strength-loving' or 'strongly loved', in occasional English-speaking use from the 19th century. The obscure St Philomena lived in Italy in the 3rd century.

UK sculptor Philomena Davidson Davis (b.1949).

Phineas A biblical name, said to represent the Hebrew name *Pīnĕhās*, 'serpent's mouth' (that is, oracle), but more likely to be an Egyptian by-name originally meaning 'the black' (that is, Nubian). The name was taken up by Puritans in the 17th century, and has since found occasional favour among English speakers. In the Bible (with the spelling *Phinehas*) Phineas is the name of a high priest of Israel, the son of Eleazar and grandson of Aaron, and of a priest at the sanctuary of Shiloh, the son of Eli and brother of Ophni. In literature the name is famous as that of the Irish barrister who is the central character of Anthony Trollope's novels *Phineas Finn* (1869) and *Phineas Redux* (1874).

US showman Phineas T. Barnum (1810–91); UK cartoonist Phineas May (b.1906); US jazz pianist Phineas Newborn Jr (b.1931).

Phoebe A biblical name, from Greek *phoibē*, 'bright', taken up by English speakers in the 16th century and rising to a peak of popularity in the late 19th century. It then fell from favour, but showed signs of a revival in the 1990s. In classical mythology Phoebe is the by-name of Artemis, goddess of the moon and of hunting. In the Bible Phoebe is 'a deaconess of the church at Cenchreae' (Romans 16.1). The English poet John Byrom wrote a popular pastoral *Colin and Phoebe* (1714), while Phoebe Bush is a character in James Fenimore Cooper's novel *The Prairie* (1827).

UK writer Phoebe Hesketh (b.1909); US pop singer Phoebe Snow (b.1952); UK actress Phoebe Nicholls (b.1958); US actress Phoebe Cates (b.1963).

Phyllis A Greek name, from *phullis*, 'foliage', 'green branch', in general use among English speakers from the 18th century, and in recent times enjoying a sudden boom in the second half of the 1920s, after which it faded fast. In Greek mythology Phyllis was turned into an almond tree. English 17th-century pastoral poetry often uses the name (because of its literal meaning) for a typical country girl. The tradition is drawn on for Gilbert and Sullivan's comic opera *Iolanthe* (1882), in which Phyllis marries the shepherd Strephon. Phyllis Grove is a character in Thomas Hardy's short story 'The Melancholy Hussar' in *Life's Little Ironies* (1894). The variant spellings *Phillis*, *Phillys* and *Phylis* are sometimes found, the last as for the UK athlete Phylis Smith (b.1965).

UK novelist Phyllis Bottome (1882–1963); UK actresses Phyllis Dare (1890–1975), Phyllis Neilson-Terry (1892–1977); UK writer Phyllis

Bentley (1894–1977); US actress Phyllis Haver (1899–1960); UK artist Phyllis Pearsall (1906–96); UK composer Phyllis Tate (1911–87); UK pianist Phyllis Sellick (b.1911); UK actress Phyllis Calvert (b.1915); US comedienne Phyllis Diller (b.1917); US actress Phyllis Thaxter (b.1921); US anti-feminist campaigner Phyllis Schafly (b.1924); US children's writer Phyllis Krasilovsky (b.1926); US jazz singer Phyllis Hyman (1950–95); Scottish actress Phyllis Logan (b.1954).

Pia The name probably represents Latin or Italian *pia*, 'pious', 'obedient' (that is, to one's parents). It became mildly fashionable among English speakers from the 1970s.

Swedish actress Pia Degermark (b.1949); US actress Pia Zadora (b.1956).

Piers This name is a medieval form of PETER, influenced by French *Pierre*. It enjoyed only occasional patronage from medieval times until the 1930s, when it was taken up rather more widely in the English-speaking world, if still at a modest level. It is famous in literature from William Langland's long and complex allegorical poem *Piers Plowman* (1367–86).

UK-born US science fiction writer Piers Anthony (b.1934) (original name Anthony Dillingham Jacob); UK film director Piers Haggard (b.1939); UK writer Piers Paul Read (b.1941); UK architect Piers Gough (b.1946); UK radio music presenter Piers Burton-Page (b.1947); Australian concert pianist Piers Lane (b.1958); UK artist Piers Wardle (b.1960).

Piety An adoption of the word for the virtue, in very select English-speaking use from the 17th century. Piety, Prudence and Charity are the personifications of the named virtues encountered by Christian in the Palace Beautiful in John Bunyan's allegory *The Pilgrim's Progress* (1678, 1684).

Pip An independently adopted diminutive of PHILIP, in fairly select English-speaking use from the 19th century. In literature, the name is familiar from Philip Pirrip (Pip), the orphan central character of Charles Dickens's novel *Great Expectations*

(1860–61). It is also that of the RAF recruit Pip Thompson in Arnold Wesker's play *Chips With Everything* (1962).

Pippa This name, an independently adopted diminutive of PHILIPPA, has been in fairly regular if select English-speaking use from the 19th century. It was popularized by Robert Browning's poem *Pippa Passes* (1841), where the named character is an Italian child silk worker (although the name itself is not Italian). The diminutive *Pip* is current.

US actress Pippa Scott (b.1935); UK actress Pippa Guard (b.1952); UK TV executive Pippa Cross (b.1956).

Plaxy This is a Cornish name, in origin said to be a form of the Greek name *Praxedes*, 'active', from *praxis*, 'action', 'doing'. It has been occasionally taken up by English speakers in the 20th century. It is found in fiction for Plaxy Trelone, the central character in Olaf Stapledon's science fiction novel *Sirius* (1944).

Pleasant An adoption of the ordinary word, in rare English-speaking use from the 19th century. Pleasant Riderhood is a character in Charles Dickens's novel *Our Mutual Friend* (1864–5).

Polly The name is an independently adopted variant of MOLLY, itself a diminutive of MARY, in fairly regular English-speaking use from the 18th century, but rather less common in the 20th century. In John Gay's opera *The Beggar's Opera* (1728) Polly is Peachum's daughter, seduced by Macheath. In literature, Polly Toodle (with her comic name) is a character in Charles Dickens's novel *Dombey and Son* (1847–8), and Aunt Polly is Tom's aunt in Mark Twain's children's novel *The Adventures of Tom Sawyer* (1876). A common diminutive is *Poll*, and POLLYANNA is a directly related name.

US comedienne Polly Moran (1884–1952); UK actress Polly Ward (b.1908) (original name Byno Poluski); UK TV presenter Polly Elwes

(1928–87); US actress Polly Bergen (b.1929) (original name Nellie Burgin); UK actress Polly James (b.1941) (original name Pauline Devaney); UK journalist, TV reporter Polly Toynbee (b.1946).

Pollyanna The name probably arose as a combination of POLLY and ANNA. It has found some favour among English speakers in the 20th century, mostly in the US. It was popularized by Pollyanna Whittier, the eleven-year-old central character of Eleanor H. Porter's children's novel *Pollyanna* (1913). The story tells how the little girl was named for her mother's two sisters, Aunt Polly and Aunt Anna. Pollyanna was constantly 'glad', as a result of which the name became generic for an unduly optimistic person.

Poppy An adoption of the flower name, taken up by English speakers from the late 19th century, and still in modest favour today, unlike many other flower names. (This may be partly due to the name's suggestion of *poppet*, as a term of endearment.) Poppy Carlyle is a character in Compton Mackenzie's novel *Sinister Street* (1913–14), while Poppy Sellars is in J.B. Priestley's novel *Angel Pavement* (1930).

Portia The name is an English form of the Latin name *Porcia*, a feminine form of the Roman clan name *Porcius*, itself of uncertain origin but perhaps derived from *porcus*, 'pig'. The name has enjoyed some favour among English speakers from the 17th century. Shakespeare has two characters of the name: Portia the beloved (later wife) of Bassanio in *The Merchant of Venice* (1596–8), and Portia the wife of Brutus in *Julius Caesar* (1599). The latter was a historical character, but it was the former Portia who popularized the name. In later literature Portia Copeland is the daughter of the black doctor Benedict Copeland in Carson McCullers's novel *The Heart is a Lonely Hunter* (1940).

Australian actress Portia De Rossi (b.1973) (original name Amanda Rogers).

Posy The name originally arose as an independent adoption of a diminutive of JOSEPHINE, but it is now usually associated with the standard word for a bunch or bouquet of flowers. It has found some favour among English speakers in the 20th century.

UK cartoonist, illustrator Posy Simmonds (b.1945).

Preston From the surname, and in select use among English speakers from the 19th century. The name appears to honour no particular Preston but was perhaps taken up for its (etymologically justifiable) suggestion of *priest*.

US screenwriter, director Preston Sturges (1898–1959) (original name Edmund Preston Biden); US actor Preston Foster (1901–70); US film production designer Preston Ames (1905–83); US playwright Preston Jones (1936–79).

Primrose From the flower name, in occasional English-speaking use from the late 19th century. Primrose Chalmers is a child character in the novel *The Widow's Cruise* (1959) by Nicholas Blake (Cecil Day-Lewis).

Prince An adoption of the royal title (compare DUKE, EARL and KING). The name came into vogue mainly among black Americans from the 19th century, and was originally a slave name. In Charles Dickens's novel *Bleak House* (1852–3) Prince Turveydrop marries Caddy Jellyby.

UK theatre proprietor, impresario Prince Littler (1901–73); US soul singer Prince (b.1958) (original name Prince Rogers Nelson).

Priscilla This is a biblical name, a feminine diminutive of the Roman clan name *Priscus*, itself meaning 'previous', 'ancient'. It was adopted by Puritans in the 17th century and was in fairly regular use among English speakers until the 1960s, when it declined, perhaps through an association with *prissy* in the sense 'fussily prim', 'prudish'. In the Bible Priscilla is the

Jewish woman, newly converted to Christianity, with whom St Paul stays in Corinth. Priscilla is also a character in Edmund Spenser's *The Faerie Queene* (1590, 1596). In later literature the name is found for Priscilla Beyard in James Fenimore Cooper's novel *The Chainbearer* (1845); Priscilla, a maid of Mrs Jellyby in Charles Dickens's novel *Bleak House* (1852–3); Priscilla Mullens, a maid wooed by John Alden in Henry Wadsworth Longfellow's poem *The Courtship of Miles Standish* (1858); and Priscilla Hamble, a childhood sweetheart of the central character, George Winterbourne, in Richard Aldington's novel *Death of a Hero* (1929). Diminutives of the name include CILLA, in independent use, and *Prissy*, as for Prissy Jakin, a character in George Eliot's novel *The Mill on the Floss* (1860).

US-born UK architectural historian Priscilla Metcalf (1915–89); US actress Priscilla Presley (b.1945).

Proserpine This is the Roman name for the Greek PERSEPHONE, related by some to Latin *proserpere*, 'to creep forth', as of flowers in the spring. The name has found some favour among English speakers from the 19th century. Bernard Shaw's play *Candida* (1894) has a typist Proserpine (Prossy) Garnett. Diminutives *Pross* and *Prossy* are known.

Prudence An adoption of the word for the virtue, taken up by Puritans from the 16th century and in occasional use since among English speakers, although now much less common than formerly. In John Bunyan's allegory *The Pilgrim's Progress* (1674, 1684), Prudence, Piety and Charity are the personified virtues encountered by Christian in the Palace Beautiful. Diminutives are *Pru* or *Prue*, the latter as for the clumsy country girl Miss Prue in William Congreve's comedy *Love for Love* (1695).

South African-UK cookery writer Prudence (Prue) Leith (b.1940).

Prunella An adoption of the plant name, botanically that of self heal (*Prunella vulgaris*), influenced by Late Latin *prunella*, 'little plum'. The name has been in modest English-speaking favour from the mid-19th century. The usual diminutives are *Pru* or *Prue*, as for PRUDENCE.

UK actresses Prunella Scales (b.1932), Prunella Ransome (b.1943), Prunella Gee (b.1950).

Psyche A Greek name, from *psukhē*, 'soul', in rare English-speaking adoption from the 19th century. In classical mythology, Psyche is a beautiful girl who personifies the human soul. Her love for Eros (Cupid) inspired various literary, artistic and musical works. Lady Psyche is professor of the humanities and sister of Florian in Tennyson's poem *The Princess* (1847), and thus also in Gilbert and Sullivan's comic opera based on this, *Princess Ida* (1884).

Q

Queenie This name is an independently adopted diminutive of the nickname *Queen*, taken up among English speakers from the late 19th century. It enjoyed some popularity in the 1920s but has since fallen from favour. The wife of the UK literary critic F.D. Leavis was Queenie Dorothy Leavis (1906–81) (although she normally preferred to use her initials). In literature, Queenie Bell is a character in G.B. Stern's novel *A Deputy was King* (1926).

UK blues singer Queenie Watts (b.1926).

Quentin An independently adopted variant of QUINTIN, in select use among English speakers, especially in Scotland, from the 19th century. The name is familiar in literature from the central character of Walter Scott's novel *Quentin Durward* (1823), and it is also found for Quentin Compson, the Harvard student incestuously in love with his vanished sister Candace (Caddy) Compson in William Faulkner's novel *The Sound and the Fury* (1929).

UK writer, raconteur Quentin Crisp (1910–99) (original name Denis Pratt); UK art writer Quentin Bell (1910–96); UK food writer Quentin Crewe (1926–98); UK illustrator Quentin Blake (b.1932); UK businessman Quentin Bell (b.1944); Australian film director Quentin Masters (b.1946); UK book designer Quentin Newark (b.1961); UK columnist Quentin Letts (b.1963).

Quincy From the surname, and in select use among English speakers, mostly black Americans, from the 19th century. The name initially paid tribute to the US president John Quincy Adams (1767–1848), himself named for his maternal great-grandfather, John Quincy (1689–1767). (The future president was born in Braintree, Massachusetts, renamed Quincy in honour of this ancestor.)

US newscaster Quincy Howe (1900–77); US jazzman, composer Quincy Jones (b.1933).

Quintin The name is an English form of the Latin name *Quintinus*, a derivative of *Quintus*, 'fifth'. It is thus a suitable name for the fifth male child in a family, and has found some currency among English speakers from the 19th century. QUENTIN is a variant form of the name.

UK politician Quintin Hogg, Lord Hailsham (1907–2001) (father was Quintin); UK actor Quintin Lawson (b.1959).

R

Rabbie see **Robbie, Robert.**

Rachel A biblical name, from Hebrew *Rāhēl*, 'ewe', adopted by English Puritans in the 16th century. The name gained suddenly in favour in the late 1960s and has remained consistently popular since then. In the Bible Rachel is the daughter of Laban, the wife of Jacob, and the mother of Joseph and Benjamin. Rachel Warrington, née Esmond, is the wife of Henry Esmond then of George Warrington in William Makepeace Thackeray's novels *The History of Henry Esmond* (1852) and *The Virginians* (1857–9), and Rachel Verinder is the English girl to whom the moonstone is given in Wilkie Collins's novel *The Moonstone* (1868). Variant spellings include *Rachael* and *Racheal*, the former, presumably influenced by MICHAEL, as for the UK cricketer Rachael Heyhoe Flint (b.1939) and UK actress Rachael Lindsay (b.1972). The Spanish form RAQUEL is in independent use. Diminutives *Rachie*, *Rae* and *Ray* also occur, the last as for the UK feminist Ray Strachey (1887–1940).

US playwright Rachel Crothers (1878–1958); US novelist Rachel Field (1894–1942); US conservationist Rachel Carson (1907–64); UK actress Rachel Kempson (b.1910); Welsh actress Rachel Roberts (1927–80); UK writer Rachel Billington (b.1942); UK actress Rachel Ward (b.1957); UK artist Rachel Budd (b.1960); UK canoeist Rachel Crosbee (b.1969).

Ralph This name is an English form of the Scandinavian name *Rathulfr*, with its Old English equivalent *Rǣdulf*, formed from *rǣd*, 'counsel', and *wulf*, 'wolf', so 'wise and strong'. The modern spelling with -*ph* came much later through (Greek) classical associations (compare RANDOLPH). The name is usually pronounced to rhyme with 'Alf', but some bearers of the name prefer 'Rafe'. The name gained increasing popularity among English speakers from the early 19th century until the 1920s, after which it tailed off. It has since remained at a very modest level of adoption. A famous literary bearer of the name is the braggart lover who is the central character of Nicholas Udall's comedy *Ralph Roister Doister* (1566). Later, Ralph Mouldy is one of Falstaff's recruits in Shakespeare's *Henry IV* (1597), and the name frequently occurs in other plays of the period, such as Ralph, the citizen's apprentice in Sir Francis Beaumont's comedy *The Knight of the Burning Pestle* (1607–8). A more recent character is Ralph Rover, the boy captured by pirates in R.M. Ballantyne's novel *The Coral Island* (1857). His name is mirrored by Ralph, one of the three main boy island castaways in William Golding's novel *Lord of the Flies* (1954).

US poet, essayist Ralph Waldo Emerson (1803–82); UK poet Ralph Hodgson (1871–1962); UK composer Ralph Vaughan Williams (1872–1958); US song composer Ralph Rainger (1901–42); UK actor Sir Ralph Richardson (1902–83); US actor Ralph Bellamy (1904–91); US harpsichordist Ralph Kirkpatrick (1911–84); UK writer Ralph Hammond Innes (1913–98); US actor Ralph Waite (b.1929); UK actor Ralph Fiennes (b.1962).

Ramona The name is a feminine form of the Spanish name *Ramón* (English RAYMOND), in occasional English-speaking use, mainly in the US, from the late 19th century. It was popularized by Ramona Ortegna, the half-Indian, half-Scots central character of Helen Hunt Jackson's novel *Ramona* (1884). In modern times the name was further brought before the public by the popular song 'Ramona' (1927).

Randal From the surname, itself a form of RANDOLPH, in regular if select English-speaking use from the 19th century. Randal Olifaunt is the father of Nigel Olifaunt, Lord Glenvarloch, the central character of Walter Scott's novel *The Fortunes of Nigel* (1822). Of the many variant spellings,

RANDALL is the most common in independent use. The regular diminutive, also used in its own right, is RANDY.

Randall An independent adoption of a variant spelling of RANDAL, in fairly steady, if modest, favour among English speakers from the 19th century. Randall Utterword is a character in Bernard Shaw's play *Heartbreak House* (1919). The usual diminutive, RANDY, is in independent use.

Randolph An adoption of the surname, itself an English form of the Scandinavian name *Rannulfr*, with its Old English equivalent *Randulf*, formed from *rand*, 'edge' (that is, of a shield), and *wulf*, 'wolf', so with an overall meaning of 'strong defender'. As with RALPH, the final -*ph* appeared much later through classical associations. In the UK the name has long regularly alternated with WINSTON in the Churchill family: the father of Sir Winston Churchill was the politician Lord Randolph Churchill (1849–95), while his son was the author Randolph Churchill (1911–68). A spelling variant is *Randolf*. The usual diminutive is RANDY, in independent use.

UK artist, illustrator Randolph Caldecott (1846–66); US actor Randolph Scott (1898–1987); US publisher Randolph Hearst (1915–2000).

Randy (m.) A name that is an independently adopted diminutive of RANDAL or RANDOLPH and that has been in select English-speaking use, mainly in the US, from the 19th century. The sense of the word to mean 'lustful', 'lecherous' appears to have had no adverse effect on the name's continued use, at any rate in the US.

US jazz pianist Randy Weston (b.1926); US folksinger Randy Sparks (b.1933); Canadian rock musician Randy Bachman (b.1943); US singer, songwriter Randy Newman (b.1943); US athlete Randy Matson (b.1945) (original first names James Randel); US country singer Randy Meisner (b.1946); US journalist Randy Shilts (1951–94); US actor Randy Quaid (b.1953); US country singer Randy Travis (b.1959).

Randy (f.) The name is either a female borrowing of the male name RANDY or an independently adopted diminutive of MIRANDA or some similar name. It has been in select English-speaking use from the early 20th century, mainly in the US.

US soul singer Randy Crawford (b.1952) (original first name Veronica; *Randy* presumably comes from *Ronny*, that name's diminutive).

Ranulph This name is an English form of the Scandinavian name *Reginulfr*, formed from *regin*, 'advice', and *úlfr*, 'wulf', so with the overall meaning of 'well-counselled and strong'. The final -*ph* appeared later, as with RALPH and RANDOLPH. The name has found some favour among English speakers from medieval times, chiefly in Scotland. The spelling *Ranulf* also occurs.

UK polar explorer Sir Ranulph Fiennes (b.1944).

Raphael A biblical name, from Hebrew *Rĕphā'ēl*, 'God has healed', in regular English-speaking use in the 16th and 17th centuries, after which it underwent a decline. It revived for a while in the late 19th century, however, only to fall once more from favour soon after. It is now rare. In the Apocrypha Raphael is the archangel who restores the sight of the aged Tobit and heals his daughter-in-law Sarah when she is possessed by the evil spirit Asmodeus.

German-born UK postcard publisher Raphael Tuck (1821–1900); Russian-born US artist Raphael Soyer (1899–1987).

Raquel A Spanish form of RACHEL, in some favour among English speakers in the 20th century, mainly in the US.

US actresses Raquel Torres (1908–87) (original name Paula Marie Osterman), Raquel Welch (b.1940).

Rastus see **Erastus**.

Ray (m.) The name originated as an independently adopted diminutive of RAYMOND but is now popularly associated with the surname *Ray*. It first came into select use among English speakers in the mid-19th century.

US writer Ray Stannard Baker (1870–1946); US athlete Ray Ewry (1873–1937); US actor, singer Ray Bolger (1904–87); Welsh-born US actor Ray Milland (1905–86) (original name Reginald Truscott-Jones); US popular musician Ray Conniff (b.1916); US actor Ray Walston (1917–2001); US science fiction writer Ray Bradbury (b.1920); Irish actor Ray McAnally (1926–89); US country singer Ray Price (b.1926); US soul musician Ray Charles (b.1930); UK TV presenter Ray Alan (b.1930); UK cricketer Ray Illingworth (b.1932); UK footballer Ray Wilson (b.1934) (original first name Ramon); UK actors Ray Smith (b.1936), Ray Brooks (b.1939), Ray Lonnen (b.1940); UK radio announcer, DJ Ray Moore (1942–89); US actor Ray Liotta (b.1955); UK actor Ray Burdis (b.1958); UK judoist Ray Stevens (b.1963).

Ray (f.) see **Rachel**.

Raymond This is an English form of the French name *Raimont*, itself from an Old German name composed of *ragin*, 'counsel', and *mund*, 'protector', so 'well-advised protector'. The name was first taken up on any scale by English speakers in the mid-19th century. It then enjoyed a fairly lengthy period of popularity from the 1920s to the 1950s, after which it sank to a more modest level. Raymond Gray is a barrister in William Makepeace Thackeray's satirical sketches *The Book of Snobs* (1846–7). The regular diminutive, RAY, is in independent use.

US crime novelist Raymond Chandler (1888–1959); Canadian actor Raymond Massey (1896–1983); US actor Raymond Bailey (1904–80); US composer, bandleader Raymond Scott (1908–94) (original name Harry Warnow); UK actor Raymond Francis (1911–87); Canadian actor Raymond Burr (1917–93); UK broadcaster Raymond Baxter (b.1922); UK conductor Raymond Leppard (b.1927).

Rebecca A biblical name, from Hebrew *Ribqah*, perhaps a form of *Biqrah*, 'cow' (compare LEAH), that was adopted by English Puritans in the 16th century and has been in regular use since then among English speakers, with a rise in popularity from the 1960s that continued unchecked until the 1990s. In the Bible Rebecca is the sister of Laban, the wife of Isaac, and the mother of Esau and Jacob. The many literary characters of the name include Rebecca, the beautiful daughter of Isaac of York in Walter Scott's novel *Ivanhoe* (1819); Rebecca (Becky) Sharp, the central character of William Makepeace Thackeray's novel *Vanity Fair* (1847–8); Rebecca West, in love with Johannes Rosmer and committing suicide with him in Henrik Ibsen's play *Rosmersholm* (1886); Rebecca Randall, the central character of Kate D. Wiggin's children's novel *Rebecca of Sunnybrook Farm* (1903); and Rebecca, wife of Max De Winter in Daphne du Maurier's novel *Rebecca* (1938). This last boosted the popularity of the name considerably, as did the film (1940) based on it. The UK novelist Dame Rebecca West (1892–1983), born Cicily Fairfield, took her pen name from that of the Ibsen character. The biblical form of the name is *Rebekah*, and this is sometimes found in modern times, as for the US dance patron Rebekah Harkness (1915–82). The usual diminutive is BECKY, in independent use.

US actress Rebecca DeMornay (b.1962); UK actresses Rebecca Callard (b.1975), Rebecca Cartwright (b.1981), Rebecca Ritters (b.1984).

Red An adoption of the nickname, often given to a red-haired person or serving as a diminutive of a name containing *r* or *d*, such as RICHARD or EDWARD. In some cases the person adopting the name is a member of an organization with 'Red' in its title, such as the US baseball player Red Ruffing (1904–86) (original first names Charles Herbert), who began his career with the Boston Red Sox, or the Canadian ice hockey player Red Kelly (b.1927) (original first names Leonard Patrick), who first played with the Detroit Red Wings. The name caught on chiefly among English speakers in the US from the early 20th century. Many of the name's bearers are jazz musicians. The variant spelling *Redd* also sometimes occurs, as for US actor Redd Foxx (1922–91) (original name John Elroy Sanford).

US baseball player Red Faber (1888–1976) (original first names Urban Charles); US American football player Red Grange (1903–91) (original first names Harold Edward); US sports writer Red Smith (1905–82) (original first names Walter Wellesley); US bandleader Red Norvo (1908–99) (original name Kenneth Norville); US country musician Red Foley (1910–68) (original first names Clyde Julian); US actor Red Skelton (1910–97) (original first name Richard); US jazzman Red Callender (b.1916) (original first name George); US actor Red Buttons (b.1918) (original name Aaron Chwatt); US jazzmen Red Garland (1923–84) (original first name William), Red Rodney (1927–94) (original name Robert Roland Chudnik), Red Mitchell (b.1927).

Rees see **Rhys**.

Reg An independently adopted diminutive of REGINALD, in select English-speaking use from the early 20th century. The diminutive, *Reggie*, also occurs, as for US baseball player Reggie Jackson (b.1946).

UK cyclist Reg Harris (1920–92); UK comedian Reg Varney (b.1922); UK politician Reg Prentice (b.1923); UK TV sports commentator Reg Gutteridge (b.1924).

Regina The name, a straight adoption of Latin *regina*, 'queen', has been in select English-speaking use from the 18th century, mainly in the US. St Regina was a 3rd-century virgin martyr. Modern Roman Catholics mostly derive the name not from her, however, but from *Regina Coeli* (Queen of Heaven), one of the titles of the Virgin Mary. Regina Gordon is a character in Elmer Rice's play *Counsellor-at-Law* (1931); Regina Giddens is the central character in Lillian Hellman's play *The Little Foxes* (1939); and Regina Durham is the husband of Rex Durham (and mistress of Philip Warren) in Gore Vidal's novel *The Judgment of Paris* (1952). The diminutive GINA is an independent name. The French form of the name was made familiar by the French nightclub owner Régine (b.1929) (original name Rachel Zylberberg).

Irish novelist Regina Maria Roche (1764–1845); US opera singer Regina Resnik (b.1922); US soul singer Regina Belle (b.c.1957).

Reginald This name is an English form of the Latin name *Reginaldus*, itself a form of the name that gave REYNOLD. It was first taken up by English speakers in the early 19th century, but after enjoying a brief period of great popularity in the 1920s has now long been low in public favour. The name has always been more popular in the UK than in the US. Sir Reginald Front-de-Boeuf is a Norman knight in Walter Scott's novel *Ivanhoe* (1819), and Reginald Wilfer is the father of the central character, Bella Wilfer, in Charles Dickens's novel *Our Mutual Friend* (1964–5). Later, the name appears as that of the central figure in the short stories by 'Saki' (H.H. Munro), *Reginald* (1904) and *Reginald in Russia* (1910). The usual diminutive is REG, in independent use. *Reggie* also occurs.

UK actors Reginald Owen (1887–1972), Reginald Denny (1891–1967), Reginald Denham (1894–1983); UK conductor Sir Reginald Goodall (1901–90); UK actor Reginald Gardiner (1903–90); UK cinema organist Reginald Dixon (1905–85); UK actor Reginald Beckwith (1908–65); UK politician Reginald Maudling (1917–79); UK actor Reginald Marsh (b.1926); UK TV newsreader Reginald Bosanquet (1932–84).

Remus An adoption of the Latin name, derived by some (obscurely) from *remus*, 'oar', but which like the name of *Romulus*, legendary brother of Remus and cofounder with him of Rome, may be linked with *Rome* itself. The name occurs in rarish English-speaking use from the 19th century. Its famous literary bearer in modern times is the Negro ex-slave Remus who is the narrator of Joel Chandler Harris's *Uncle Remus* stories (1880–1910).

Renata This name is a direct English adoption of the Latin name that, through French, gave the more common RENÉE. It is still in sporadic use.

US writer Renata Adler (b.1938).

René A French name, from the Latin name *Renatus*, 'reborn'. The traditional pronunciation is mostly as 'Rennie', but now increasingly (especially in the US) as 'Ren*ay*'. The name was adopted by English Puritans in the 17th century, and has enjoyed very moderate favour among English speakers since. Early Christians adopted the Latin name for its sense of 'spiritual rebirth'. One of its most famous bearers was the French philosopher René Descartes (1596–1650). The name is now often spelt without its accent, as for the UK actor Rene Zagger (b.1973).

UK journalist, broadcaster René Cutforth (1909–84); US actor René Auberjonois (b.1940).

Renée This name, the French feminine equivalent of RENÉ, evolved from the Latin name RENATA. It has been in select use among English speakers from the late 19th century, mostly in the UK. The spelling variant *René* is also found, as for the UK actress René Ray (1912–93) (original name Irene Creese). The English pronunciation of the name as 'Renny' has led to further variant spellings such as *Rennie*, *Renny* and the like.

French actress Renée Adorée (1898–1933) (original name Jeanne de la Fonte); UK actress Renée Houston (1902–80) (original name Katherina Houston Gribbin); German-born UK sculptor Renée Mendel (b.1908); UK politician Renee Short (b.1919); UK actress Renée Asherson (b.1920); US opera singer Renée Fleming (b.1959).

Reuben A biblical name, from Hebrew *Rĕ'ūbēn*, 'behold, a son', in steady if very moderate favour among English speakers from the 18th century until the early 20th century, after which it suffered a more or less permanent decline. In the Bible Reuben is the eldest of the sons of Jacob and the first child of Leah, and thus an ancestor of one of twelve tribes of Israel: 'And Leah conceived, and bare a son, and she called his name Reuben; for she said, Surely the Lord hath looked upon my affliction; now therefore my husband will love me'

(Genesis 29.32). (Her 'affliction' was that Jacob loved his other wife, barren Rachel, more than her.) In Walter Scott's novel *The Heart of Midlothian* (1818) Reuben Butler is the Presbyterian minister who marries Jeanie Deans, while Reuben Dewy is the father of Dick Dewy, the central character of Thomas Hardy's novel *Under the Greenwood Tree* (1872). The regular diminutive is *Rube*, especially in the US. *Reub* and *Ruby* are also found, the latter as for the US jazzman Ruby Branff (b.1927).

Rex A name that ostensibly derives from the Latin word for 'king' (compare KING), but that has always been linked closely to REGINALD (or its diminutive REG), perhaps aided by an association with *regal*. It was in select but fairly regular use among English speakers from the late 19th to the mid-20th century, when it fell from favour. Rex Gascoigne is one of the sons of the Rev. Henry Gascoigne, rector of Pennicote, in George Eliot's novel *Daniel Deronda* (1876).

US detective story writer Rex Stout (1886–1975); Irish-born US actor Rex Ingram (1892–1950) (original name Reginald Hitchcock); US actor Rex Ingram (1895–1969); UK radio cricket commentator Rex Alston (1901–94) (originally second name, first being Arthur); UK artist Rex Whistler (1905–44) (original first names Reginald John); US actor Rex Bell (1905–62) (original name George F. Beldam); US jazz cornetist Rex Stewart (1907–67); UK actor Rex Harrison (1908–90) (original first names Reginald Carey); UK sports writer Rex Bellamy (b.1928); US TV interviewer, gossip columnist Rex Reed (b.1938).

Reynold From the surname, itself from an Old German name formed from *ragin*, 'counsel', and *wald*, 'ruler', so 'well-counselled ruler'. (In some cases the adoption may have been made from the surname *Reynolds*.) The name has found some favour among English speakers from the 19th century, mainly among black Americans. REGINALD and RONALD are directly related names.

Rhett A name of uncertain origin. It may perhaps be an alter-ation of BRETT or a formation based on the Greek word *rhētōr*, 'speaker', 'orator'. It has been found in very occasional Eng-lish-speaking use from the 1940s. It seems to have stemmed entirely from the fictional character for whom it was appar-ently originally invented: Rhett Butler, the blockader who mar-ries (as her third husband) the central character, Scarlett O'Hara, in Margaret Mitchell's popular novel *Gone with the Wind* (1936).

Rhoda A biblical name, itself from Greek, either from *rhodon*, 'rose', or meaning 'woman of Rhodes'. It has been in general use among English speakers from the 18th century, with a rise in popularity in the late 19th century, followed by a gradual falling off. In the Bible Rhoda is a servant in the house of Mary, mother of John. Rhoda Swartz is a wealthy mulatto in William Makepeace Thackeray's novel *Vanity Fair* (1847–8), and Rhoda Whitefield is a character in Bernard Shaw's play *Man and Superman* (1903). The name was made widely known by the US TV comedy series *Rhoda* (1974–8), with Valerie Harper in the title role.

UK novelist Rhoda Broughton (1840-1920).

Rhona A Scottish name, perhaps from the island of *Rona*, with a spelling alteration influenced by RHODA. The name has been in mostly Scottish favour since the late 19th century. The variant spelling RONA is in independent use.

Rhonda A name that is apparently a blend of RHODA and RHONA, in select adoption from the 1940s, mostly in the US.

US actress Rhonda Fleming (b.1922) (original name Marilyn Louis).

Rhys A Welsh name, meaning 'ardour', 'impetus', long estab-lished in Welsh use but only rarely found more widely among English speakers. It is famous from various historical rulers, such as the 12th-century Rhys ap Gruffydd in south Wales. (The name is now also a surname, and itself produced the surname *Price*, 'son of Rhys'.) The English version of the name is *Rees*.

Welsh-born US actor Rhys Williams (1892–1969).

Rica see **Frederica**.

Richard The modern English name has evolved from an Old German name composed of *rīchi*, 'power' (modern German *Reich*, modern English *rich*), and *hart*, 'strong', 'hardy', so giving an overall meaning of 'powerful ruler'. The name was introduced to England by the Normans and was in regular use among English speakers until the 19th century. It then went into something of a decline, only to revive sharply in the early years of the 20th century. After a further slight fall from favour, it reached a new level of popularity in the 1950s and an even more impressive 'high' in the 1960s and 1970s, since when it has subsided somewhat. It is familiar as a royal name, especially from Richard I Coeur-de-Lion (Lion-Heart) (1157–99), leader of the Third Crusade, who features as a historical character in Walter Scott's novel *Ivanhoe* (1819). Richard III similarly appears as the central character in Shakespeare's play (1591) that bears his name. This same Richard also figures in Robert Louis Stevenson's novel *The Black Arrow* (1888), as well as other historical fiction devoted to the Wars of the Roses. Richard (Dick) Dudgeon is the reprobate central character of Bernard Shaw's play *The Devil's Disciple* (1897), set in America at the time of the Revolution. The regular diminutives DICK and RICK are in independent use, as also is the rather less common RICHIE.

UK actor, broadcaster Richard Murdoch (1907–90); US president Richard Nixon (1913–94); US actors Richard Widmark (b.1914), Richard Basehart (1914–84); UK actors Richard Todd (b.1919), Sir Richard Attenborough (b.1923); Welsh actor Richard Burton (1925–84); UK

TV presenter Richard Baker (b.1925); UK actors Richard Vernon (1925–97), Richard Pasco (b.1926); US actor Richard Mulligan (1932–2000); UK actors Richard Thorp (b.1932), Richard Briers (b.1934); US actor Richard Chamberlain (b.1935); UK actors Richard Wilson (b.1936), Richard O'Brien (b.1942); UK TV presenter Richard Stilgoe (b.1943); UK actor Richard O'Sullivan (b.1944); US actor Richard Gere (b.1949); UK artist Richard Wilson (b.1953); UK actor Richard Gibson (b.1954); UK TV presenter Richard Madeley (b.1956); UK actor Richard Keyes (b.1957).

Richenda A rarish feminine form of RICHARD, apparently influenced by a name such as BRENDA, GLENDA or GWENDA.

UK writer Richenda Francis (b.1939).

Richie An independently adopted diminutive of RICHARD, found selectively among English speakers from the early 20th century.

Australian cricketer Richie Benaud (b.1930); West Indies cricketer Richie Richardson (b.1952).

Rick An independently adopted diminutive of RICHARD or (less often) of DEREK, ERIC or FREDERICK, in fairly regular if modest English-speaking favour from the 1950s. The variant spelling *Rik* occurs, as for the UK actor Rik Mayall (b.1958), while the diminutive RICKY is in independent use.

US actor Rick Jason (1929–2000); US country singer Rick Nelson (1940–85) (original first name Eric); US pop musician Rick Derringer (b.1947); UK pop musician Rick Parfitt (b.1948); Australian-born US pop singer, actor Rick Springfield (b.1949); UK popular musician Rick Wakeman (b.1949); US soul singer Rick James (b.1955) (original name James Johnson); UK rock musician Rick Savage (b.1960); UK pop singer Rick Astley (b.1966).

Rickie see **Frederica**.

Ricky (m.) A name that is an independently adopted diminutive of RICK or its source name RICHARD or (less often) of DEREK, ERIC or FREDERICK, taken up by English speakers in the 1940s and gaining in popularity from the 1980s. The variant spelling *Rickie* exists, as for Rickie Elliott (originally Frederick), the sensitive, lame teacher in E.M. Forster's novel *The Longest Journey* (1907).

US country singer Ricky Skaggs (b.1954); UK rock singer Ricky Ross (b.1957); US actor Ricky Schroder (b.1970).

Ricky (f.) see **Frederica**.

Rik see **Rick**.

Rita This name is an independently adopted diminutive of the Spanish name *Margarita*, the Italian name *Margherita* (both the equivalent of English MARGARET), or a similar name ending *-rita*. It has been in general English-speaking use from the early 20th century.

US actresses Rita Johnson (1912–65), Rita Hayworth (1918–87) (original name Margarita Carmen Cansino), Rita Gam (b.1928); Puerto Rican actress, dancer Rita Moreno (b.1931) (original name Rosita Dolores Alverio); UK opera singer Rita Hunter (1933–2001); UK actress Rita Tushingham (b.1942); US pop singer Rita Coolidge (b.1945); UK actress Rita Wolf (b.1960).

Roald A Norwegian name, combining *hróthr*, 'fame', and *valdr*, 'ruler', hence 'famous ruler'. The name has been associated by some with RONALD, to which it is, in fact, partly related. It has found very occasional adoption by English speakers in the 20th century.

Norwegian polar explorer Roald Amundsen (1872–1928); Norwegian-born UK writer Roald Dahl (1916–90).

Rob An independently adopted diminutive of ROBERT, in use among English speakers, especially in Scotland, from at least the 17th century. The name is famous (or infamous) from the Scottish outlaw Rob Roy (1671–1734), the hero of Walter Scott's novel *Rob Roy* (1817). (See also ROY.) A variant spelling is *Robb*, as for the UK comedian Robb Wilton (1881–1957), while the diminutive ROBBIE is in independent use.

UK actors Rob Spendlove (b.1953), Rob Heyland (b.1954); UK rock musician Rob Manzoli (b.1954); US actor Rob Lowe (b.1964).

Robbie An independently adopted diminutive of ROB or its source name ROBERT, in general use among English speakers from the 1920s, but found much earlier in Scotland, where it has always been well favoured. A variant spelling is *Robby*, as for the US actor Robby Segal (b.1956), or *Rabbie* in Scotland.

Scottish actor Robbie Coltrane (b.1950) (original name Anthony Robert McMillan).

Robert The English name represents the Old German name *Hrodebert*, which had the Old English equivalent *Hrodbeorht*, formed from *hrōd*, 'fame', and *beraht*, 'bright', 'famous', so (tautologically) 'famed famous one'. The name has been in regular English-speaking use, especially in Scotland, from medieval times and has been consistently popular throughout the 20th century, with 'peaks' in the early 1950s and late 1960s. It is historically famous as a royal name, notably for the 11th-century Robert the Devil, father of William the Conqueror, and 14th-century Robert the Bruce, king of Scotland. Robert Faulconbridge appears as a historical character in Shakespeare's *King John* (c.1596), while a central character of Samuel Richardson's novel *Clarissa* (1748) is the dashing rake Robert Lovelace, who is in love with Clarissa Harlowe. In Charlotte Brontë's novel *Shirley* (1849) Robert Gérard Moore proposes to Shirley Keeldar but marries Caroline Helstone. ROBIN is a related name. The most familiar diminutive is BOB, in independent use. ROB and ROBBIE also exist in their own right. In Scotland these last two often have their equivalent in *Rab* and *Rabbie*.

US general Robert E. Lee (1807–70); Scottish writer Robert Louis Stevenson (1850–94); UK actors Robert Newton (1905–56), Robert Donat

(1905–58), Robert Morley (1908–92); Canadian actor Robert Beatty (1909–92); US actors Robert Ryan (1909–73), Robert Taylor (1911–69) (original name Spangler Arlington Brugh), Robert Mitchum (1917–97); UK actor Robert Hardy (b.1925); US actors Robert Wagner (b.1930), Robert Redford (b.1936); UK actors Robert Powell (b.1944), Robert Lindsay (b.1949).

Roberta A feminine form of ROBERT, taken up by English speakers from the 1870s, and always more popular in the US than the UK until the 1950s, when the name fell generally from favour. Roberta Alden is a girl murdered by the central character, Clyde Griffiths, in Theodore Dreiser's novel *An American Tragedy* (1925). Jerome Kern's musical *Roberta* (1933) kept the name before the public, especially in the US. The diminutive *Berta* is sometimes found, as for the UK popular novelist Berta Ruck (1878–1978).

US soul singer Roberta Flack (b.1939); US opera singer Roberta Alexander (b.1949).

Robin (m.) This name is an independently adopted historic diminutive of ROBERT, formed from ROB with the French diminutive suffix -*in*. It has been actively current among English speakers from medieval times, but has gradually fallen from favour since the 1950s, perhaps as a result of its adoption for female use. The name is famously that of the legendary (or semi-legendary) outlaw Robin Hood, whose own name is mirrored in that of Robin Goodfellow, otherwise Puck, the mischievous sprite in Shakespeare's *A Midsummer Night's Dream* (1595–6). Robin Adair is the subject of an 18th-century Irish folksong, subsequently popular in Scotland. In Daniel Defoe's novel *Moll Flanders* (1722), Robin is the name of Moll's first husband, while Robin Toodle is a stoker in Charles Dickens's novel *Dombey and Son* (1847–8). In recent times the name has been made popularly familiar by Robin the Boy Wonder, sidekick to Batman in comic-book (later film) adventures that date from 1939.

US wrestler Robin Reed (1899–1978); UK writer Robin Maugham (1916–81) (original first name Robert); UK actor Robin Bailey (1919–99); UK TV interviewer Sir Robin Day (1923–2000); UK diplomat Robin Byatt (b.1930) (original first name Ronald); UK writer Robin Cook (1931–94) (original first name Robert); UK yachtsman Robin Knox-Johnston (b.1939) (original first names William Robert Patrick); UK actor Robin Phillips (b.1941); UK politician Robin Cook (b.1946) (original first name Robert); UK actor Robin Askwith (b.1950); US actor Robin Williams (b.1952); UK boxer Robin Reid (b.1971).

Robin (f.) A female adoption of the male name ROBIN, perhaps influenced by the name of the bird. The name has been in select English-speaking use from the 1940s, mainly in the US. The variant spelling *Robyn* is also found, as for the UK actress Robyn Moore (b.1963).

New Zealand novelist Robin Hyde (1906–39) (original name Iris Wilkinson); Australian film producer Robin Dalton (b.1920) (father was Robert); US feminist Robin Morgan (b.1941); US children's artist Robin James (b.1953); US actresses Robin Givens (b.1964), Robin Wright (b.1966).

Rod An independently adopted diminutive of RODERICK or RODNEY, in select English-speaking use in the 20th century. Diminutives *Roddie* and *Roddy* exist, as for the UK actor Roddy McDowall (1928–98) (original first name Roderick) and the Irish novelist Roddy Doyle (b.1958).

Canadian actor Rod Cameron (1910–83) (original name Nathan Cox); US actor Rod Steiger (b.1925) (original first name Rodney); Australian-born US actor Rod Taylor (b.1929) (original first name Rodney); UK entertainer Rod Hull (1935–99) (original first name Rodney); Australian tennis player Rod Laver (b.1938) (original first name Rodney); UK pop singer Rod Stewart (b.1945) (original first name Roderick).

Roderick This name is an English form of the Old German name *Hrodrich*, formed from *hrōd*, 'fame', and *rīchi*, 'power', hence 'famously powerful'. It has found predominantly

Scottish favour from the 19th century, although since then it has been adopted more generally in the English-speaking world. The name's frequent occurrences in literature include the central character of Tobias Smollett's novel *Roderick Random* (1748); the highland chief Roderick Dhu (Roderick the Black) in Walter Scott's poem *The Lady of the Lake* (1810); the central character, last king of the Visigoths, in Scott's poem *Roderick, Vision of a Don* (1811) (where the name is a form of Spanish *Rodrigo*); the central character (identical with the last-mentioned) in Robert Southey's poem *Roderick, The Last of the Goths* (1814); the central character of Henry James's novel *Roderick Hudson* (1876); and the detective Roderick Alleyn in the crime novels (1930s to 1980s) by the New Zealand writer Ngaio Marsh. A variant spelling is *Roderic*, and the regular diminutive is ROD, which is in independent use.

Rodger see **Roger**.

Rodney An adoption of the surname, in select English-speaking use from the mid-19th to the mid-20th century, after which the name declined. It owed much of its initial favour to the English admiral Lord Rodney (1719–92), who defeated the Spanish at Cape St Vincent in 1780 and the French off Dominica in 1782. In literature the name is familiar from the central character of Conan Doyle's novel *Rodney Stone* (1896). The usual diminutive, ROD, has been adopted in its own right.

US actor Rodney Dangerfield (b.1921) (original name Jacob Cohen); UK composer Richard Rodney Bennett (b.1936); UK actor Rodney Bewes (b.1937); UK yachtsman Rodney Pattisson (b.1943).

Roger This name is an English form, through French, of the Old German name *Hrodgar*, composed of *hrōd*, 'fame', and *gēr*, 'spear', so 'famous warrior'. (The Old English equivalent name was *Hrothgar*.) The name has been in English-speaking use since medieval times, but it gradually declined in popularity until the early 19th century. It then revived from the 1840s and slowly gained in popularity until the 1950s, when it suddenly rose to a record 'high'. It subsequently settled to a more modest level until the 1970s, when it faded generally. The name was made historically famous by the 12th-century bishop, Roger of Salisbury, chancellor of England and next in power to the king, Henry I. A few years later it was also associated with the English philosopher Roger Bacon (1214–94). Roger Formal is a character in Ben Jonson's comedy *Every Man in his Humour* (1598). It was then popularized by Sir Roger de Coverley, a character in Sir Richard Steele's essays in *The Spectator* (1711), for whom the well-known country dance came to be named. The 'Jolly Roger', a nickname for the pirate flag, has also made the public at large aware of the name. The spelling variant *Rodger* is sometimes found, while a fairly common diminutive is *Rog*, pronounced 'Rodge'.

UK actors Roger Livesey (1906–76), Roger Moore (b.1927); UK athlete Roger Bannister (b.1929); UK cartoonist Roger Hargreaves (1935–88); UK poet Roger McGough (b.1937); UK actors Roger Lloyd Pack (b.1944), Roger Rees (b.1944); UK rock musician Roger Daltry (b.1944).

Roland This is an English form, through French, of the Old German name *Hrōdland*, formed from *hrōd*, 'fame', and *lant*, 'land', 'territory', hence 'famous landowner'. The name has been in select use among English speakers from medieval times, achieving a modest period of popularity in the 1920s, after which it has mostly remained at a much lower level of adoption. Its famous early bearer was the legendary hero Roland, the most illustrious of the paladins (knights) of Charlemagne, whose exploits (especially his duel and friendship with Oliver) are described in the 12th-century French epic poem known as the *Chanson de Roland*. Roland Graeme is a character in Walter Scott's novel *The Abbot* (1820). The spelling ROWLAND is in independent use.

UK actors Roland Young (1887–1953), Roland Culver (1900–84); UK film director Roland Joffé (b.1945); UK ballet dancer Roland Price (b.1961).

Rolf This is an English contraction of the original Old German name that gave RUDOLPH, in occasional English-speaking favour from the mid-19th century. The spelling *Rolph* also exists.

UK-born Australian writer Rolf Boldrewood (1826–1915) (original name Thomas Alexander Brown); Australian entertainer, cartoonist Rolf Harris (b.1930).

Romaine The French feminine form of *Romain* (English ROMAN), found in select use among English speakers from the 19th century onwards. A variant spelling is *Romayne*.

US painter Romaine Brooks (1874–1970) (born in Rome).

Roman An English adoption of the Late Latin name *Romanus*, 'Roman', 'man from Rome', in occasional favour among English speakers from the 19th century.

US actor Roman Bohnen (1894–1949); Polish-born US film director Roman Polanski (b.1933).

Romayne see **Romaine**.

Romeo A famous Italian name, meaning 'one who has made a pilgrimage to Rome', in very occasional favour among English speakers from the 19th century, mostly in the US. The name is inseparable from the tragic hero of Shakespeare's *Romeo and Juliet* (1595). (Shakespeare did not invent the name, but took it from his source material for the story.)

Romy see **Rosemary**.

Ron An independently adopted diminutive of RONALD, in select use among English speakers in the 20th century. The diminutive RONNIE is in independent use.

UK comedian Ron Moody (b.1924); UK TV sports commentator Ron Pickering (1930–91); US actors Ron Carey (b.1935), Ron Leibman (b.1937).

Rona A Scottish name, adopted either as an independent variant of RHONA, or from the Scottish island of *Rona*. The name has also come to be regarded as a feminine form of RONALD. It has been in select English-speaking use from the 1870s and is still chiefly associated with Scotland.

UK actress, theatre critic Rona Laurie (b.1916); Scottish actress Rona Anderson (b.1926); US writer Rona Jaffe (b.1932); US movie gossip columnist Rona Barrett (b.1934).

Ronald This name is an English form of the Old Norse name *Rögnvaldr*, equivalent in meaning to the Old German name REYNOLD (which itself gave REGINALD). It has been in select English-speaking use, at first chiefly in Scotland, from the late 19th century. It was at its most popular level in the UK in the 1920s, with the US following in the 1940s. It soon declined after its UK peak but is still fairly common in the US. Its regular diminutives, RON and RONNIE, are now adopted in their own right.

UK actors Ronald Squire (1886–1958), Ronald Colman (1891–1958); UK comedian Ronald Frankau (1894–1951); US president, former actor Ronald Reagan (b.1911); UK cartoonist Ronald Searle (b.1920); UK actors Ronald Magill (b.1920), Ronald Fraser (1930–97); UK theatrical director, writer Ronald Hayman (b.1932); UK actor, writer Ronald Harwood (b.1934); UK actor Ronald Pickup (b.1940).

Ronan An Irish name, familiar from various early saints, one a 5th-century missionary, which derives from the diminutive of Irish *rón*, 'seal', presumably for some special attribute this animal was believed to have. In literature the name is familiar from Walter Scott's novel *St Ronan's Well* (1823).

Irish-born pianist Ronan O'Hora (b.1964); Irish pop singer Ronan Keating (b.1977).

Ronnie (m.) An independently adopted diminutive of RON or its source name RONALD, in select use among English speakers from the 1910s.

UK actor Ronnie Stevens (b.1925); UK popular singer Ronnie Hilton (b.1926); UK jazz club owner Ronnie Scott (1927–96); UK comedians Ronnie Barker (b.1929), Ronnie Corbett (b.1930).

Ronnie (f.) see **Veronica**.

Roo see **Rue, Ruth**.

Rory The name is an English form of the Gaelic name *Ruaidhrí*, formed from Old Celtic words corresponding to modern Irish *rua*, 'red', and *rí*, 'king', so overall meaning 'great king', 'famous ruler'. It is still mainly in Scottish use, but since the 1940s has been found more generally in the English-speaking world, with a sudden rise in popularity in the 1990s. The name is historically famous from Rory O'Connor, the last high king of Ireland in the 12th century. Modern variants of the name are sometimes adopted from the original Gaelic, as for the UK rugby player Ruari Maclean (b.1961).

US actor Rory Calhoun (1922–99) (original name Francis Timothy Durgin); Irish blues guitarist Rory Gallagher (1948–95); UK actor, singer Rory Campbell (b.1961); UK actor, impersonator Rory Bremner (b.1961); UK rugby player Rory Underwood (b.1963).

Ros An independently adopted diminutive of a name beginning *Ros-*, such as ROSALIND or ROSAMUND, in fairly common English-speaking use from the early 20th century. The variant spelling *Roz* also exists.

UK writer Ros Drinkwater (b.1944).

Rosa This name is a straight adoption of the Latin or Italian name *Rosa*, corresponding to English ROSE. It has enjoyed modest popularity among English speakers from the 19th century. In Charles Dickens's novel *David Copperfield* (1849–50),

Rosa Dartle is a companion to Mrs Steerforth. The name, or the Latin *rosa* that gave it, lies behind many independently adopted derivatives, such as ROSALBA, ROSALIE, ROSALIND, ROSALINE, ROSAMUND, ROSANNA, ROSEMARY, ROSINA and ROSITA.

UK hotelier Rosa Lewis (1867–1952); US opera singer Rosa Ponselle (1897–1981); UK artist Rosa Lee (b.1957); UK opera singer Rosa Mannion (b.1962).

Rosalba The name is apparently a compound of Latin *rosa*, 'rose', and *alba*, 'white', so meaning 'white rose'. It has been in select use among English speakers from the late 19th century. In William Makepeace Thackeray's novel *The Rose and the Ring* (1855), Rosalba is the rightful queen of Crim Tartary who marries Prince Giglio. Diminutives are mostly as for ROSE.

Rosalie This is a French form of the Latin or Italian name *Rosalia*, itself based on *rosa*, 'rose' (English ROSA or ROSE). It has been in fairly regular English-speaking use from the mid-19th century, although it has now somewhat fallen from favour. In literature Rosalie Murray marries Sir Thomas Ashby in Anne Brontë's novel *Agnes Grey* (1847), and Rosalie is a maid in Oscar Wilde's play *Lady Windermere's Fan* (1892). Diminutives are mostly as for ROSE.

UK actress Rosalie Crutchley (1921–97); US country singer, yodeller Rosalie Allen (b.1924) (original name Julie Marlene Bedra).

Rosalind The name probably came from Late Latin *rosa linda*, 'pretty rose', although it has been derived by some from Old German *hros*, 'steed', 'horse', and *linta*, 'lime', 'shield made of lime wood', so with an overall meaning 'horse shield'. It has been in general English-speaking use from the mid-19th century, although it is now rather unfashionable after a modest 'high' in the 1950s. In Shakespeare's *As You Like It* (1599) Rosalind, daughter of the banished duke, is loved by Orlando. A variant form of the name in independent use is ROSALINE, while diminutives are mostly as for ROSE.

US actresses Rosalind Ivan (1884–1959), Rosalind Russell (1908–76), Rosalind Cash (1938–95); UK writer Rosalind Brackenbury (b.1942); UK actress Rosalind Ayres (b.1944); UK opera singer Rosalind Plowright (b.1949); UK actress Rosalind Bennett (b.1966).

Rosaline An independently adopted variant of ROSALIND, in general English-speaking use from the mid-19th century. In Shakespeare's *Love's Labour's Lost* (*c*.1595) Rosaline is an attendant of the French princess. The variant spelling ROSALYN is in independent use. Diminutives are mostly as for ROSE.

Rosalyn An independently adopted variant of ROSALINE that, from the 1920s, was more common among English speakers than its source name.

US harpsichordist Rosalyn Tureck (b.1914); US writer Rosalyn Drexler (b.1926); South African-born US tennis player Rosalyn Fairbank Nideffer (b.1960).

Rosamund This name probably derives from Late Latin *rosa munda*, 'pure rose' or *rosa mundi*, 'rose of the world', but some authorities trace it back to Old German *hros*, 'steed', 'horse', and *munt*, 'protection', so that it would mean 'horse protection'. It has been in general use among English speakers from the early 19th century, with the alternative spelling *Rosamond* equally common. The name is famously that of 'Fair Rosamond', a 12th-century woman said to have been the mistress of Henry II. Her story has been retold several times, for example in Joseph Addison's opera *Rosamund* (1707) and Algernon Charles Swinburne's play *Rosamund* (1861). For many the name is further associated with Schubert's music for the play *Rosamunde* (1823). (The play failed from the first, but the music is perennially popular.) Rosamund Vincy marries Tertius Lydgate in George Eliot's novel *Middlemarch* (1871–2). The alternative spelling of the name was that given to UK novelist Rosamond Lehmann (1901–90).

Irish novelist Rosamund Langbridge (1880–1964); UK actress Rosamund John (1913–98) (original name Nora Rosamund Jones).

Rosanna A name that is probably a compound of ROSE and ANNA but that is perhaps regarded by some as an alteration of ROXANA. It was taken up by English speakers in the 18th century and is now in select use. In Wilkie Collins's novel *The Moonstone* (1868) Rosanna Spearman is second housemaid to Lady Verinder. The variant forms *Rosanne* and *Roseanne* are fairly common, as respectively for the US country singer Rosanne Cash (b.1955) and US comedienne Roseanne Barr (b.1953).

Italian actress Rosanna Schiaffino (b.1939); US actress Rosanna Arquette (b.1959).

Rose This name has long been connected with that of the flower, but it has been traced back by some to the Old German word *hros*, 'steed', 'horse', or *hrōd*, 'fame'. It has been in English-speaking use from medieval times, reaching its peak of popularity at the end of the 19th century. It has since remained more or less out of favour, although it showed signs of an upturn in the 1990s. In William Makepeace Thackeray's novel *Vanity Fair* (1847–8) Rose Dawson becomes the second wife of Sir Pitt Crawley, and Rose Jocelyn marries the central character in George Meredith's novel *Evan Harrington* (1861). Since the rose is the emblem of England, the name has also found royal favour, currently from the second name of Queen Elizabeth II's sister Princess Margaret (b.1930) and the Duke of Gloucester's daughter Lady Rose Windsor (b.1980). The main variant is ROSA, which was formerly the standard written form of the name. Diminutives are ROSIE, now in independent use, and its variant forms *Rosey* and *Rosy*.

UK writer Rose Macaulay (1881–1958); US personality Rose Kennedy (1890–1995); US popular singer Rose Murphy (1913–89); UK actress Rose Hill (b.1914); US country singer Rose Maddox (b.1925) (original name Rosea Brogdon); UK writer Rose Tremain (b.1943).

Rosemary Originally an adoption of the plant name, but now also taken as a compound of ROSE and MARY. The name has been in general use among English speakers from the late 19th century. It enjoyed a moderate rise in popularity from the 1920s until the 1960s, since when it has rather lost favour. The most common variant is *Rosemarie* (sometimes as two words), which was popularized by the romantic musical *Rose Marie* (1924) and its title song. A frequent diminutive is *Romy*, as for the Austrian actress Romy Schneider (1938–82) (original first name Rosemarie).

UK children's writer Rosemary Sutcliff (1920–92); UK writers Rosemary Timperley (b.1920), Rosemary Anne Sisson (b.1923); UK children's writer Rosemary Harris (b.1923); US actress Rosemary Murphy (b.1925); US popular singer Rosemary Clooney (b.1928); UK actress Rosemary Harris (b.1930); UK writer Rosemary Tonks (b.1932); UK actress Rosemary Leach (b.1935); US actress Rosemary Forsyth (b.1944); US tennis player Rosemary Casals (b.1948); UK writer, broadcaster Rosemary Hartill (b.1949).

Rosetta This is an independently adopted Italian diminutive of *Rosa* (English ROSE). At first the name was mainly in 18th-century literary use, but was then taken up more generally in the English-speaking world, although it is hardly common today. Characters of the name appear in Edward Moore's play *The Foundling* (1748) and Isaac Bickerstaffe's comic opera *Love in a Village* (1763). In modern times the name has come to be associated by some with the famous Rosetta Stone in Egypt, discovered in 1799 and providing a key to Egyptian hieroglyphics. The French variant *Rosette* is still occasionally found.

US popular composer, actress Rosetta Duncan (1900–59); US gospel and blues singer Sister Rosetta Tharpe (1915–73).

Rosie An independently adopted diminutive of ROSE, ROSA, ROSEMARY or some similar name, in English-speaking use from the mid-19th century. Rosie Redmond is a character in Sean

O'Casey's play *The Plough and the Stars* (1926). The spellings *Rosey* and *Rosy* also exist.

UK politician Rosie Barnes (b.1946) (original first names Rosemary Susan); UK romantic novelist Rosie Thomas (b.1947) (original name Janey King); UK writer, editor Rosie Boycott (b.1951) (original first names Rosel Marie).

Rosina An Italian-style diminutive of ROSA (English ROSE), taken up by English speakers from the early 19th century. The name was brought before the music-loving public by Rosina, a character in Rossini's opera *The Barber of Seville* (1816) (based on Beaumarchais's play of 1775, in which she is *Rosine*), and it is found in later literature for Rosina de Courcy, daughter of the Countess de Courcy in Anthony Trollope's novel *Doctor Thorne* (1858), as well as for Rosina, the central character in Austin Dobson's poem *The Story of Rosina* (1895). Diminutives are mainly as for ROSE.

UK novelist Rosina Bulwer-Lytton (1802–82); UK actress, singer Rosina Brandram (1846–1907).

Rosita The name is an English adoption of a Spanish diminutive of ROSA (English ROSE), in select use among English speakers from the 19th century. Initial public interest in the name may have come from the popular operetta *Rosita* (1864). Diminutives are chiefly as for ROSE.

UK travel writer Rosita Forbes (1890–1967).

Ross An adoption of the (Scottish) surname, in select use among English speakers from the mid-19th century, and gradually increasing in popularity from the 1970s. The name has long been familiar in Scottish history, and as such is represented by Ross, one of the 'noblemen of Scotland' in Shakespeare's *Macbeth* (1606).

US actor Ross Alexander (1907–37); US mystery writer Ross Macdonald (1915–83) (original name Kenneth Millar); Polish-US actor Ross Martin

(1920–81) (original name Martin Rosenblatt); US film producer Ross Hunter (1921–96) (original name Martin Fuss); UK journalist Ross Benson (b.1948); Scottish actor Ross Davidson (b.1949).

Rowan (m.) From the (Irish) surname, and in select English-speaking use from the 1950s.

UK comedian Rowan Atkinson (b.1955).

Rowan (f.) Either a female adoption of the male name ROWAN, or from the name of the tree, with its bright red berries. A variant form *Rowanne* exists, perhaps influenced by a name such as JOANNE, as for the UK radio presenter Rowanne Pasco (b.1938).

Rowena This name is either a form of the Welsh name *Rhonwen*, said to be composed of *rhon*, 'pike', 'lance', and *gwen*, 'white', 'fair', so having the overall meaning 'slender and fair', or else a modern version of an (unrecorded) Old English name based on Old German *hrōd*, 'fame' and *wynn*, 'joy'. It was taken up by English speakers in the 19th century, and has remained in modest but consistent favour since then. In literature the name became familiar from Walter Scott's novel *Ivanhoe* (1819), in which Lady Rowena, a descendant of King Alfred, marries the central character, Wilfred, Knight of Ivanhoe. The name generally has aristocratic associations.

Rowland This is either a borrowing of the surname or an independently adopted variant of ROLAND (which gave that surname). The name has been in select use among English speakers from medieval times and enjoyed a modest rise in popularity in the 1980s. In literature Rowland Lacy is the nephew of Sir Hugh Lacy, earl of Lincoln, in Thomas Dekker's play *The Shoemaker's Holiday* (1599), while Sir Rowland Meredith is the matchmaking Welsh uncle of Mr Fowler, one of Harriet Byron's suitors, in Samuel Richardson's novel *Sir Charles Grandison* (1753–4).

English postal reformer Sir Rowland Hill (1795–1879); US film directors Rowland V. Lee (1891–1975), Rowland Brown (1901–63); UK painter Rowland Hilder (1905–93).

Roxana A name representing the Persian name *Roschana* (the equivalent of English DAWN), in select use among English speakers, mainly in the US, from the 17th century. A famous historical Roxana (d.310BC) was the Persian wife of Alexander the Great. The name became familiar in literature from the central character of Daniel Defoe's novel *Roxana* (1724). The heroine gains her name as a nickname for her dancing, for which the historical Roxana was noted. Variant forms *Roxane* and *Roxanne* exist, with diminutives including *Roxie* and *Roxy*.

Roy This name arose as an English form of the Gaelic name *Ruadh*, 'red', that is, 'red-haired', implying 'outstanding', 'famous', but it is now popularly associated with the Old French word *roy* (modern French *roi*), 'king' (compare KING and LEROY, also RUFUS). It has been in select English-speaking use from the late 19th century, and was given prominence by the central character of Walter Scott's novel *Rob Roy* (1817). In this, Rob Roy MacGregor is a historical character, the outlaw and freebooter Robert (or Robin) M'Gregor (1671–1734), nicknamed 'Roy' for his red hair.

Canadian-born Scottish newspaper proprietor Roy Thomson (Lord Thomson of Fleet) (1894–1976); US bandleader Roy Acuff (1903–92); UK film producer Roy Rich (1909–70); US actor Roy Rogers (1912–98) (original name Leonard Slye); UK radio interviewer Roy Plomley (1914–85); UK entertainer Roy Castle (1932–94); UK politician Roy Hattersley (b.1932); UK actors Roy Kinnear (1934–88), Roy Barraclough (b.1935), Roy Hudd (b.1936); US country musician Roy Orbison (1936–88); UK comedian Roy Walker (b.1940); UK actor Roy Marsden (b.1941).

Royce An adoption of the surname, in select use among English speakers from the late 19th century, and in the 20th associated with the prestigious Rolls-Royce car.

UK playwright Royce Ryton (b.1924).

Roz see **Ros**.

Rube, **Ruby** see **Reuben**.

Ruby (f.) A borrowing of the word for the gem, in regular use among English speakers from the 1870s, but after the 1920s declining to a much more modest level. Ruby Kenny is a character in Theodore Dreiser's novel *The Genius* (1915). The variant spelling *Rubie* is sometimes found.

UK popular novelist Ruby M. Ayres (1883–1955); UK actress Ruby Miller (1889–1976); Canadian-born US actress, dancer Ruby Keeler (1909–93) (original first name Ethel); US actress Ruby Dee (b.1923); US actress, chat show host Ruby Wax (b.1953).

Rudolph The modern form of the name evolved from the Old German name *Hrōdulf*, formed from *hrōd*, 'fame', and *wulf*, 'wolf', so 'famous warrior' (exactly as for ROLF), with the *-ph* appearing much later through classical associations. The name has enjoyed irregular favour among English speakers from the 19th century. The spelling *Rudolf* also exists.

Italo-US actor Rudolph Valentino (1895–1926) (original first name Rodolfo).

Rue This name was either borrowed from that of the plant, itself a strongly scented shrub that is (punningly) symbolic of repentance or compassion, or was otherwise adopted as an independent diminutive of RUTH. It has found some favour among English speakers in the 20th century. The spelling *Roo* is sometimes found.

US actress Rue McClanahan (b.1936).

Rufus A biblical name, from the identical Latin name meaning 'red', 'red-haired', so 'prominent' (compare ROY). The name was moderately fashionable among English speakers from the early 19th century to the early 20th century, when it declined, although it is still actively adopted by black Americans. In the Bible Rufus is the son of Simon the Cyrenian, the man made to carry Jesus's cross to Golgotha. The name is historically familiar from the 11th-century king of England William Rufus (William II), son of William the Conqueror. (His by-name was not for his red hair, however, but for his ruddy complexion.) In fiction the Rev. Rufus Lyon is the supposed father of Esther Lyon, actually Esther Bycliffe, the heiress who marries the central character in George Eliot's novel *Felix Holt* (1866).

Rupert This English name evolved as a form of the German name *Ruprecht*, itself from Old German *Hrodebert*, the name that gave ROBERT. The name was increasingly popular among English speakers from the 18th to the late 19th century, since when it has remained at a much lower level of favour. It became historically famous in England from the dashing cavalry leader Prince Rupert of the Rhine (1619–92), who came to the aid of his uncle, Charles I, in the Civil War. In literature it was made popular by the swashbuckling villain, Rupert of Hentzau, in the novel of this name by Anthony Hope (1898), itself a sequel to *The Prisoner of Zenda* (1894), in which he also appears. In recent times the name has come to be more mundanely associated with the children's comic-strip character Rupert Bear, appearing in the *Daily Express* from 1920 and regularly in annuals.

UK poet Rupert Brooke (1887–1915); UK writer Rupert Croft-Cooke (1903–79); UK actor Rupert Davies (1916–76); US actor Rupert Crosse (1927–73); Australian-born US newspaper owner Rupert Murdoch (b.1931); UK actors Rupert Everett (b.1961), Rupert Graves (b.1963).

Russ An independently adopted diminutive of RUSSELL, in select use among English speakers from the 19th century.

US bandleaders Russ Morgan (1904–69), Russ Columbo (1908–34) (original name Ruggerio de Rudolpho Columbo); UK popular pianist Russ Conway (1925–2000) (original name Trevor H. Stanford); UK comedian Russ Abbot (b.1947) (original name Russell Allan Roberts).

Russell An adoption of the surname, itself that of the earls of Bedford from the 16th century, giving an aristocratic association. (Compare PERCY and SIDNEY.) The name has been in fairly regular if modest use among English speakers from the late 19th century, with its greatest favour in the US. The regular diminutive, RUSS, is in use in its own right.

US actors Russell Collins (1897–1965), Russell Gleason (1908–45), Russell Hayden (1912–81) (original name Pate Lucid); Scottish actor Russell Hunter (b.1926); UK TV host, interviewer Russell Harty (1934–88); UK astrologer Russell Grant (b.1952).

Rusty The name, used for either sex, usually arises as a nickname for someone with *rusty*-coloured (reddish-brown) hair, although for males it is sometimes a diminutive form of RUSSELL.

US country musician Rusty Young (b.1946); US actor Rusty Hamer (1947–90) (original first name Russell).

Ruth A biblical name, perhaps from Hebrew *Rĕ'uth*, 'friend', 'companion', but (at first) popularly associated with the English word *ruth* meaning 'compassion' (the source of modern *ruthless*). The name was taken up by 17th-century Puritans and has been in regular English-speaking use since, enjoying its greatest popularity in the US. In the Bible Ruth (in the story told in the book named for her) is a Moabite woman who leaves her own people to live with her mother-in-law Naomi and who later marries her relative Boaz. In English literature the name is that of Ruth Hilton, the central character of Elizabeth Gaskell's novel *Ruth* (1853); of Ruth Morse, engaged to the central character of Jack London's novel *Martin Eden* (1909); and of Ruth Prynne, an actress in John Dos Passos's novel *Manhattan Transfer* (1925). Diminutives *Roo* and *Ruthie* exist, as, respectively, for the US poet Roo Borson (b.1952) and UK theatrical performer Ruthie Henshall (b.1967).

UK poet, children's writer Ruth Manning-Sanders (1888–1988); US variety artiste Ruth Draper (1889–1956); US actresses Ruth Roland (1893–1937), Ruth Chatterton (1893–1961), Ruth Gordon (1896-1985); UK artist, poet Ruth Pitter (1897–1992); UK actress Ruth Dunning (1911–83); US actresses Ruth Hussey (b.1914), Ruth Roman (1923–99); South African anti-apartheid campaigner Ruth First (1925–82); UK crime novelist Ruth Rendell (b.1930); US writer Ruth Fainlight (b.1931); Welsh actress Ruth Madoc (b.1934).

Rutland From the surname, and in modest English-speaking use from the 19th century.

UK actor, singer Rutland Barrington (1853–1922) (originally middle name, first being George); UK composer Rutland Boughton (1878–1960) (father's middle name).

Ryan From the (Irish) surname, and in select use among English speakers from the 1930s, but with a considerable increase in popularity from the 1980s.

US actor Ryan O'Neal (b.1941).

S

Sabina This name, an adoption of the Latin name *Sabina*, 'Sabine woman', was first taken up by English speakers in the 17th century and has been in very select use since. St Sabina was a 2nd-century Christian martyr, and Poppaea Sabina was Nero's mistress in the 1st century AD. A character in Thornton Wilder's play *The Skin of Our Teeth* (1942) is the maid Lily Sabina. The name is sometimes associated with SABRINA, but that name has a different origin. Diminutives include *Sabbie*, *Sabby* and *Bina*.

UK actress Sabina Franklyn (b.*c*.1950).

Sabrina The name has been in English-speaking use from the 19th century but was generally rare in the 20th century before picking up somewhat from the early 1980s. Welsh legend tells how the maiden Sabrina, the illegitimate daughter of king Locrine, was drowned in the Severn on order of the king's widow Gwendolen. As a result, the river was named after her. She later appears in various literary works, such as Michael Drayton's poem *Poly-Olbion* (1598–1622), John Fletcher's tragi-comedy *The Faithful Shepherdess* (1610) and John Milton's poem *Comus* (1637). Samuel Taylor's play *Sabrina Fair* (1954) takes its title from Milton's poem ('Sabrina fair,/Listen where thou art sitting/Under the glassy, cool, translucent wave'), and the film *Sabrina* (1954) was based on it. The US TV series *Charlie's Angels* (1976) had a character Sabrina (played by Kate Jackson) as the leader of the four 'angels' (girl detectives). The name is thus not related to SABINA, which has a different origin. Diminutives *Sabbie* and *Sabby* exist.

UK actress Sabrina (b.1931) (original name Norma Sykes); UK socialite Sabrina Guinness (b.1954).

Sacha see **Sasha** (f.).

Sadie An independently adopted diminutive of SARAH, in modest favour among English speakers from the late 19th century, with a moderate increase in popularity from the 1970s. In literature, Sadie Thompson is a prostitute in Somerset Maugham's short story 'Rain' in *The Trembling of a Leaf* (1921), with various films based on it, including *Sadie Thompson* (1928), *Rain* (1932) and *Miss Sadie Thompson* (1953). In Robert Penn Warren's novel *All the King's Men* (1946) Sadie Burke is Willie Stark's mistress.

Sally The name arose as an independently adopted diminutive of SARAH, the *r* becoming *ll* as for MOLLY from MARY. The name has been in regular use among English speakers from at least the 18th century, with its two recent peaks of popularity in, respectively, the US in the 1920s and the UK in the 1960s, since when it has mostly been superseded by SARAH itself. Sally Godfrey is a character in Samuel Richardson's novel *Pamela* (1740–41), and Sally Brass is the sister of Sampson Brass, Quilp's lawyer, in Charles Dickens's novel *The Old Curiosity Shop* (1840–41). The name was popularized by Henry Carey's song *Sally in our Alley* (1729): 'Of all the girls that are so smart/ There's none like pretty Sally,/ She is the darling of my heart,/ And she lives in our alley.' This resurfaced in modern guise in the film *Sally in Our Alley* (1931), with Gracie Fields's popular theme song 'Sally' ('Sally, Sally,/ Down in our alley'). Later literature has the cabaret artiste Sally Bowles in Christopher Isherwood's novella *Sally Bowles* (1937), incorporated into the novel *Goodbye to Berlin* (1939). This became the play and film *I am a Camera* (respectively 1951, 1955, with Sally played by Julie Harris in the latter), then the stage musical and musical film *Cabaret* (respectively 1961, 1972, with Liza Minnelli as

Sally in the film). The name is often coupled with others to form a compound, especially *Sally Ann* or *Sally Jane* (often hyphenated), the former as for the UK actresses Sally Ann Howes (b.1930) and Sally Ann Matthews (b.1970). The usual diminutive is *Sal*.

US short story writer Sally Benson (1900–72); US fan dancer Sally Rand (1904–79) (original name Helen Gould Beck); US actress Sally Forrest (b.1928) (original name Katharine Scully Feeney); UK politician Sally Oppenheim (b.1930); US actress Sally Field (b.1946); US astronaut Sally Ride (b.1951); UK ballerina, choreographer Sally Owen (b.1952); UK actress Sally Whittaker (b.1963); UK athlete Sally Gunnell (b.1966).

Salome A biblical name, from Hebrew *shālōm*, 'peace', taken up by English speakers from the 19th century, but never very common. In the Bible Salome was one of the women at Christ's tomb at the time of his resurrection (Mark 15.40). The name is more familiar, however, as that of King Herod's stepdaughter, the daughter of Queen Herodias. She danced so well on Herod's birthday that he granted her any wish. Prompted by her mother, she asked for, and got, the head of John the Baptist. Salome is not named in this Bible story (Mark 6.17–28). She is the central character of Oscar Wilde's play *Salome* (1893) on which Richard Strauss based his opera of the same name (1905).

US actress Salome Jens (b.1935).

Sam An independently adopted diminutive of SAMUEL or (less often) SAMSON, in select use among English speakers from the mid-19th century, with a modest but distinct gain in popularity from the 1980s. The name is familiar in literature from Sam Weller, the friend and servant of Mr Pickwick (who has the same name) in Charles Dickens's novel *Pickwick Papers* (1836–7). Later, Sam Clark is a character in Sinclair Lewis's novel *Main Street* (1920). In the US the name is popularly associated with 'Uncle Sam' as a personification of the United

States (the initials of which probably prompted his name). The usual diminutive, SAMMY, is in independent use.

US actor Sam Levene (1905–80); UK popular singer, radio presenter Sam Costa (1910–81); US entertainer Sam Levenson (1911–80); US film directors Sam Wanamaker (1919–93), Sam Peckinpah (1926–85); US actor Sam Shepard (b.1943); UK actors Sam Kelly (b.1943), Sam Miller (b.1962); UK film director Sam Mendes (b.1965).

Samantha The popular name probably arose as a feminine form of SAMUEL, perhaps influenced by a name such as ANTHEA. It has been in English-speaking use, initially in the American South, from the 18th century, but achieved its real height of fashion only in the late 1960s, since when it has continued to enjoy wide favour. In literary use it first famously occurs for Samantha, Josiah Allen's wife in the humorous books that appeared from 1873 to 1914 by the US writer Marietta Holley. In Philip Barry's play *The Philadelphia Story* (1939) Tracy Lord is a young heiress. A film of the same title followed (1940), with Katharine Hepburn as Tracy Lord, and was then reworked as *High Society* (1956), in which the heiress is renamed Tracy Samantha Lord, played by Grace Kelly. (The film had the popular song 'I love you, Samantha'.) This helped to popularize the name, and a further boost came from the US TV fantasy comedy *Bewitched* (1964–71) (screened in the UK in the 1980s), with the central character, the attractive young witch Samantha Stephens, played by Elizabeth Montgomery. The usual diminutives are *Sam* and *Sammy*.

UK actress Samantha Eggar (b.1939); UK model Samantha Fox (b.1966); UK actresses Samantha Beckinsale (b.1968), Samantha Janus (b.1972).

Sammy An independently adopted diminutive of SAM or SAMUEL, in select English-speaking use from the mid-19th century. In Thomas Hardy's novel *Two on a Tower* (1882) Sammy Blore is a farmhand.

US popular composer Sammy Fain (1902–87); US bandleader Sammy

Kaye (1913–87); US lyricist Sammy Cahn (1913–93); US diver Sammy Lee (b.1920); US singer, entertainer Sammy Davis Jr (1925–90).

Sampson This name is either a borrowing of the surname or an independently adopted variant of SAMSON. It has found select favour among English speakers from the 19th century. In Charles Dickens's novel *The Old Curiosity Shop* (1840–41), Sampson Brass is Daniel Quilp's lawyer. The usual diminutive is SAM, which is in independent use.

Samson A biblical name, from Hebrew *Shimshōn*, a diminutive of *shemesh*, 'sun', which has been in irregular use among English speakers from medieval times but is still occasionally found. In the Bible Samson is the last of the twelve judges of Israel, famed for his prodigious strength. He was betrayed to the Philistine oppressors by his mistress Delilah, but brought the temple of the Philistines crashing down in a final heroic but suicidal feat. (The meaning of his name may relate to his 'sunlocks', which were cut off on the orders of Delilah.) He is the central character of John Milton's tragedy *Samson Agonistes* (1671). The name has been taken up by circus 'strong men' and the like, and 'Samsonite' is a US tradename for a make of tough suitcase. SAMPSON is a spelling variant in independent use. The usual diminutive is SAM, also adopted in its own right. US playwright Samson Raphaelson (1896–1983).

Samuel A biblical name, from Hebrew *Shēmū'ēl*, 'name of God' (literally 'his name is El'). (The interpretation 'asked for' in 1 Samuel 1.20 is more suited to Saul.) The name has enjoyed several regular periods of popularity from the 17th century, when it was first adopted by English speakers. Two of the most recent are those of the late 19th and late 20th centuries. In the Bible Samuel is a famous prophet and judge of Israel, with two Old Testament books named for him. (In the Roman Catholic and Orthodox versions of the Bible, 1 and 2 Samuel are 1 and 2 Kings, and in the Anglican, or Protestant Bible, 1 and 2 Kings are 3 and 4.) Well-known bearers of the name include English diarist Samuel Pepys (1633–1703), English lexicographer Dr Samuel Johnson (1709–84) and US revolutionary leader Samuel Adams (1722–1803). The name is famous in literature from Samuel Pickwick, the central character of Charles Dickens's novel *Pickwick Papers* (1836–7). (His close friend, Sam Weller, has the same name.) The regular diminutive is SAM, which is in independent use.

English poet Samuel Taylor Coleridge (1772–1834); US film producer Samuel Goldwyn (1879–1974) (original name Schmuel Gelbfisz); Irish dramatist, novelist Samuel Beckett (1906–89).

Sandie A variant spelling of SANDY, as an independently adopted diminutive of SANDRA, more common in the UK than the US.

UK popular singer Sandie Shaw (b.1947) (original name Sandra Goodrich); UK hockey player Sandie Lister (b.1961).

Sandra An independently adopted diminutive of the Italian name *Alessandra* (English ALEXANDRA), first finding favour in the English-speaking world in the 1930s and achieving a peak of popularity in the 1950s, since when it has gradually declined. It attracted attention in literature from its use for Emilia Sandra Belloni, the Italian central character of George Meredith's novel *Emilia in England* (1864), retitled *Sandra Belloni* for the edition that appeared in 1886. Later, Mrs Sandra Wentworth-Williams appears in Virginia Woolf's novel *Jacob's Room* (1922), and Sandra Finchley is a character ('Miss X' at the trial of the central character, Clyde Griffiths) in Theodore Dreiser's novel *An American Tragedy* (1925). The occasional variants *Saundra* and *Sondra* occur in the US, the latter as for the actress Sondra Locke (b.1947). A variant form ZANDRA is in independent use, as is SANDY, the usual diminutive.

US actress Sandra Dorne (1925–92); US judge Sandra Day O'Connor (b.1930); US actresses Sandra Dee (b.1942) (original name Alexandra Zuck), Sandra Church (b.1943); UK ballerina Sandra Conley (b.1943); UK actress Sandra Bryant (b.1945); UK magazine editor Sandra Harris (b.1946); US children's writer Sandra Boynton (b.1953); UK milliner Sandra Phillipps (b.1962); US actress Sandra Bullock (b.1966).

Sandy (m.) An independently adopted diminutive of ALEXANDER, possibly influenced by the word *sandy*, as this is the typical hair colour of many Scots. The name has found selective use among English speakers from the mid-19th century, chiefly in Scotland, where its source name is largely favoured. In William Makepeace Thackeray's novel *The Newcomes* (1853–5), Sandy M'Collop is a Scottish fellow art student of the central character, Clive Newcome. Another fictional Scottish art student of the name is Sandy McAllister, who marries Mrs Bagot in George du Maurier's novel *Trilby* (1894).

UK music-hall comedian Sandy Powell (1898–1982) (original first name Albert); UK lyricist Sandy Wilson (b.1924); UK TV newsreader, reporter Sandy Gall (b.1927); US baseball player Sandy Koufax (b.1935) (original first name Sanford); Scottish golfer Sandy Lyle (b.1958).

Sandy (f.) This name is an independently adopted diminutive of ALEXANDRA or SANDRA, in English-speaking use from the mid-20th century. It may have been given something of an initial popular boost by the baby girl central character in the US series of films *East Side of Heaven* (1939), *Unexpected Father* (1939) (UK title *Sandy Takes a Bow*), *Little Accident* (1939), *Sandy Gets Her Man* (1940), *Sandy is a Lady* (1940) and *Sandy Steps Out* (1941), in each of which the baby was played by 'Baby Sandy', otherwise Sandra Henville (b.1938). The variant spelling SANDIE is in independent use.

US actress Sandy Dennis (1937–92); UK folk-rock singer Sandy Denny (1941–78); US actress Sandy Duncan (b.1946); UK popular singer Sandy Denny (b.1947); UK actress Sandy Ratcliff (b.1950); UK film costume designer Sandy Powell (b.1960).

Sara An independently adopted spelling variant of SARAH, taken up by English speakers in the 19th century and enjoying a modest vogue in the 1970s and 1980s, but now rather less popular.

UK writer Sara Coleridge (1802–52); Irish actress Sara Allgood (1883–1950); US poet Sara Teasdale (1884–1933); US actress Sara Haden (1897–1981); UK-born Canadian mystery writer Sara Woods (1922–85); UK actress Sara Kestelman (b.1944); UK environmental campaigner Sara Parkin (b.1946); US crime writer Sara Paretsky (b.1947); UK actress Sara Sugarman (b.1962); UK tennis player Sara Gomer (b.1964); UK badminton player Sara Sankey (b.1967).

Sarah A biblical name, from Hebrew *Sārāh*, 'princess', which has been in English-speaking use from the 16th century. The name was popular at the turn of the 20th century, then declined somewhat, only to rise to new heights in the 1960s and (especially) the 1970s, since when it has subsided to a more moderate level. In the Bible Sarah is the wife of Abraham and mother of Isaac. (According to Genesis 17.15, her name was originally *Sarai*, perhaps meaning 'contentious'.) Literary occurrences of the name include, among others, Sarah Gamp, the drunken midwife in Charles Dickens's novel *Martin Chuzzlewit* (1843–4); Sarah Stone, a character in George Eliot's novel *Adam Bede* (1859); Sarah Hartright, sister of the part-narrator, Walter Hartright, in Wilkie Collins's novel *The Woman in White* (1860); and Sarah, maid to the Pooters in George Grossmith's novel *The Diary of a Nobody* (1892). Both *Sarah* and its independent variant SARA frequently form a compound with another name, especially *Sarah Jane*, whether separately or combined, as for the UK art critic Sarah Jane Checkland (b.1954) and UK fashion editor Sara-Jane Hoare (b.1955). Diminutives in independent use are SADIE and SALLY. *Sassie* is also found among the black community.

English tragedienne Sarah Siddons (1755–1831); French actress Sarah Bernhardt (1844–1923); UK actress Sarah Churchill (1914–82); US jazz singer Sarah Vaughan (1924–90); UK actresses Sarah Miles (b.1941), Sarah Badel (b.1943); UK radio presenter Sarah Kennedy (b.1950); UK actresses Sarah Woodward (b.1963), Sarah Lancashire (b.1964); UK swimmer Sarah Hardcastle (b.1969); Welsh tennis player Sarah Loosemore (b.1971).

Sasha (m.) This name, an adoption of the Russian diminutive of ALEXANDER, has been in select use among English speakers from the mid-20th century. The French variant of the name, *Sacha*, is also found, and was made popular by the French singer Sacha Distel (b.1933). A diminutive *Sy* exists, as for the US screenwriter Sy Bartlett (1900–78) (original first name Sacha).

Russian-born US actor Sasha Mitchell (b.1967).

Sasha (f.) This is an adoption of the Russian diminutive of ALEXANDRA, in select English-speaking use from the early 20th century. Virginia Woolf's novel *Orlando* (1928) has Sasha as the Russian princess loved by Orlando. The French variant spelling *Sacha* is sometimes found.

Saskia This name, of Dutch origin, has found favour with some English speakers from the 1950s. Its source is uncertain, but it has been linked by some with a Germanic word for 'Saxon'. The name was that of the wife of the 17th-century Dutch artist Rembrandt, and as such became familiar from the titles of some of his paintings, such as *Portrait of Saskia as Flora* (1634).

UK actresses Saskia Reeves (b.1962), Saskia Wickham (b.1967).

Sassie see **Sarah**.

Saul A biblical name, from Hebrew *Shā'ū l*, 'asked for', 'desired' (that is, of God). (See also SAMUEL.) The name has been in English-speaking use from the 19th century and has been mainly favoured by Jews. In the Bible Saul is one of the first kings of Israel. The name was also that of St Paul before his conversion. Saul is a character in John Dryden's poem *Absalom and Achitophel* (1681), and the name was to some extent popularized by Handel's oratorio *Saul* (1739), with its famous funeral march (the 'Dead March in *Saul*').

US composer, pianist Saul Chaplin (1912–97); Canadian-born US novelist of Russian descent Saul Bellow (b.1915).

Saundra see **Sandra**.

Scarlett A name that arose as a borrowing of the surname, but that also suggests the bright colour *scarlet*. It has made the occasional appearance among English speakers from the 1940s, and was made famous by Scarlett O'Hara, the central character of Margaret Mitchell's novel *Gone with the Wind* (1936) and of the classic film of 1939 based on it. The novel gives the character's full name as Katie Scarlett O'Hara, her middle name being her grandmother's maiden name. No doubt adoption of the name has been inhibited by its associations with the biblical 'scarlet woman' of Revelation 17, together with the popular sense of this phrase to mean 'prostitute'.

Scott From the (Scottish) surname, taken up by English speakers generally in the late 19th century and increasingly popular from the 1970s. Possibly the original vogue for the name may have stemmed from the US novelist F. Scott Fitzgerald (1896–1940), himself named for Francis Scott Key, author of 'The Star-Spangled Banner', the US national anthem. A variant spelling is *Scot*, as for the Scottish footballer Scot Gemmill (b.1971). The usual diminutives are *Scottie* or *Scotty*.

US ragtime pianist Scott Joplin (1868–1917); US writer Scott O'Dell (1898–1989); US actors Scott Brady (1924–85) (original name Gerald Tierney), Scott Glenn (b.1942), Scott Wilson (b.1942); US popular singer Scott Walker (b.1944); US writer Scott Turow (b.1949); UK actor Scott Antony (b.1950) (original name Anthony Scott); US actor Scott Baio (b.1961); US tennis player Scott Davis (b.1962); Scottish footballer Scott Nisbet (b.1968).

Seamus This is the English form of the Irish name *Séamas* (English JAMES), pronounced '*Shay*mus'. It is still chiefly in Irish use but has been taken up selectively elsewhere in the English-speaking world from the mid-20th century. Variant spellings are *Seamas* or *Seumas*.

Northern Ireland politician Seamus Mallon (b.1936); Irish poet Seamus Heaney (b.1939).

Sean This name is the English form of the Irish name *Seán* (English JOHN), pronounced 'Shawn'. It is still largely in Irish use, but has been increasingly found elsewhere among English speakers from the 1920s, with something of a 'boom' in the 1990s. SHANE is a related name, and the variant spelling SHAUN is even more popular.

Irish playwright Sean O'Casey (1880–1964); Irish prime minister Sean Lemass (1899–1971); Irish writer Sean O'Faolain (1900–91); Irish statesman Sean McBride (1904–88); Scottish actor Sean Connery (b.1929) (original first name Thomas); US actors Sean Garrison (b.1937); Sean Flynn (1941–70); UK artist Sean Scully (b.1945); UK actor Sean Bean (b.1958); US actor Sean Penn (b.1960); New Zealand rugby player Sean Lineen (b.1961); UK actor Sean Wilson (b.1965); US actor Sean Astin (b.1971); Irish-born UK actor Sean Maguire (b.1976).

Sebastian The name is an English form of the Greek name *Sebastianos*, 'man from Sebasta' (a city in Asia Minor), but has also been linked with Greek *sebastos*, 'reverenced', 'august' (compare AUGUSTUS). It has enjoyed modest favour among English speakers from the early 20th century, with a rise in popularity in the 1990s. The name is famously that of the 3rd-century martyr St Sebastian, who was, as depicted in numerous paintings, shot to death by arrows. It occurs for characters in two Shakespeare plays: the twin brother of Viola in *Twelfth Night* (1601) and the brother of Alonso, king of Naples, in *The Tempest* (1611). The name has somewhat 'upper class' overtones, as exemplified in modern literature by Sebastian Flyte, the handsome, whimsical younger son of Lord

Marchmain in Evelyn Waugh's novel *Brideshead Revisited* (1945). The usual diminutive is *Seb*, but *Baz* and *Bazza* also exist.

UK actor Sebastian Shaw (1905–94); UK-born Canadian actor Sebastian Cabot (1918–77); UK composer Sebastian Forbes (b.1941); UK feature writer, editor Sebastian Faulks (b.1953); UK athlete Sebastian Coe (b.1956).

Selena see **Selina**.

Selima This name, popularly seen as a variant of SELINA, but perhaps a variant of the Arabic name *Selim*, 'peace' (compare SALOME), has been in rare English-speaking use from the 18th century. It occurs as the name of Horace Walpole's cat in Thomas Gray's poem 'Ode on the Death of a Favourite Cat' (1748), where it is pronounced 'Selima', stressed on the first syllable: 'Demurest of the tabby kind,/The pensive Selima, reclined.' (Gray queried the name with Walpole before writing the poem, asking whether the cat was Selima or Fatima.)

UK poet Selima Hill (b.1940).

Selina This is an English form of the Greek name *Sēlēnē*, that of the goddess of the moon, from *sēlēnē*, 'moon'. It came into favour among English speakers in the 19th century and remains in regular if modest use, with a slight increase in popularity in the late 1980s. It is familiar in history as the name of Selina Hastings, Countess of Huntingdon (1707–91), the religious leader who founded the Calvinist Methodist sect. In literature Selina Halborough is the second wife of the master millwright Joshua Halborough Sr in Thomas Hardy's short story 'A Tragedy of Two Ambitions' in *Life's Little Ironies* (1894). The variant *Selena* sometimes occurs, as for the US actress Selena Royle (1904–83). The name generally has aristocratic associations.

Irish children's writer Selina Bunbury (1802–82); UK playwright, songwriter Helen Selina Sheridan, Countess of Dufferin (1807–67); UK writer Lady Selina Hastings (b.1945); UK daughter of Countess of Loudon, Lady Selina Newman (b.1946); UK TV presenter Selina Scott (b.1951).

Selma The name is probably a contraction of SELIMA, possibly influenced by THELMA. It has enjoyed occasional use among English speakers from the 19th century.

US actress, TV writer Selma Diamond (1920–85).

Selwyn From the surname, and in very modest English-speaking use from the late 19th century. The variant spelling *Selwin* occasionally occurs.

UK politicians Selwyn Lloyd (1904–78) (in full John Selwyn Brooke Lloyd), John Selwyn Gummer (b.1939) (father's first name).

Septimus This is an English adoption of the identical Late Latin name meaning 'seventh'. It has been in select use among English speakers from the 19th century, when Victorian families sometimes gave it to a seventh child, if male. In literature the Rev. Septimus Harding is the central character in Anthony Trollope's novel *The Warden* (1855); Septimus Luker is an antique dealer in Wilkie Collins's novel *The Moonstone* (1868); and the Rev. Septimus Crisparkle is a minor canon in Charles Dickens's novel *Edwin Drood* (1870). Septimus often has ecclesiastical associations: the central character of the 'Saki' (H.H. Munro) short story 'The Secret Sin of Septimus Brope' in *The Chronicles of Clovis* (1911) is an expert on church liturgy and church architecture.

US popular composer Septimus Winner (1827–1902).

Serena This is the feminine form of the Latin word *serenus*, 'calm', 'serene', adopted selectively as a name by English speakers in the 18th century. In literature it occurs earlier, as for the character Serena in Edmund Spenser's work *The Faerie Queene* (1590, 1596). The name has aristocratic associations.

UK daughter of Earl of Scarbrough, Lady Serena James (1901–2000);

UK wine writer Serena Sutcliffe (b.1945); UK actress Serena Scott Thomas (b.1962); UK aristocrat Hon. Serena Stanhope, Viscountess Linley (b.1970); US tennis player Scerena Williams (b.1981).

Seth A biblical name, from Hebrew *Shēth*, 'appointed', 'set', in select use among English speakers from the 18th century to the late 19th century, when it declined. In the Bible Seth is the third son of Adam and Eve: 'And Adam knew his wife again; and she bare a son, and called his name Seth: For God, said she, hath appointed me another seed instead of Abel, whom Cain slew' (Genesis 4.25). Seth Pecksniff is an architect and arch-hypocrite in Charles Dickens's novel *Martin Chuzzlewit* (1843–4), and Seth Bede is the brother of the central character in George Eliot's novel *Adam Bede* (1859). Later, Seth Starkadder is the son of the central characters Judith and Amos Starkadder in Stella Gibbons's novel *Cold Comfort Farm* (1932).

UK film director Seth Holt (1923–71); US screenwriter Seth Freeman (b.1945); US writer Seth Morgan (b.1949).

Seumas see **Seamus**.

Seymour From the surname, and in select but declining use among English speakers from the 19th century. In George Meredith's novel *Evan Harrington* (1861) Seymour Jocelyn is one of the sons of Sir Franks and Lady Jocelyn. In later literature Seymour Glass is the eldest brother of Franny and Zooey Glass in J.D. Salinger's stories in *Franny and Zooey* (1961) and in the subsequent stories in *Raise High the Roof-Beam, Carpenters* and *Seymour: An Introduction* (both 1963).

UK theatre manager, writer Sir Seymour Hicks (1871–1949) (originally middle name, first being Edward); US actor Seymour Cassel (b.1935).

Shane (m.) This is either a borrowing of the (Irish) surname or an English form of the Irish name SEAN. The name originated in Irish use in the 19th century, but was taken up increasingly in the English-speaking world from the 1940s, since when it has remained in moderately but consistently popular use, especially in Australia. It was perhaps given general impetus by the US film *Shane* (1953), although here it was actually the surname of the central character, a mysterious stranger who helps homesteaders. Variant forms of the name are mostly as for SEAN.

Australian actor Shane Porteous (b.1942); UK actor Shane Briant (b.1946); Irish actor, screenwriter Shane Connaughton (b.1951); Australian actor Shane Withington (b.1958); UK actor Shane Richie (b.1964).

Shane (f.) A female adoption of the male name, perhaps regarded by some as a variant of SIÂN, in select adoption by English speakers from the 1950s and, like its male counterpart, favoured mostly in Australia.

Australian swimmer Shane Gould (b.1956).

Shannon (f.) The name appears to be a blend of SHANE and SHARON. It has enjoyed modest popularity, mainly in the US, since the 1950s. A variant is *Shannen*, as for the US actress Shannen Doherty (b.1971).

US gymnast Shannon Miller (b.1977).

Sharmain, **Sharmaine** see **Charmaine**.

Sharon This is a biblical name, but that of a place (a valley in Palestine) not of a person, and itself from Hebrew *Sarōn*, probably from *sar*, 'to sing', 'singer'. The name has been in use among English speakers from the 1930s, building fairly rapidly to a peak of popularity in the 1960s and 1970s, then gradually declining to a much more modest level, so that by the 1990s it was virtually out of favour. The biblical verse that gave the name runs: 'I am the rose of Sharon, and the lily of the valleys' (Song of Solomon 2.1). (The same words gave 'rose of Sharon' as a plant name.) In literature Sharon Falconer is an evangelist in Sinclair Lewis's novel *Elmer Gantry* (1927), and Rose of Sharon ('Rosaharn') Joad is a character in John

Steinbeck's novel *The Grapes of Wrath* (1939). The variant spelling *Sharron* became mildly popular in the 1960s, as for the UK swimmer Sharron Davies (b.1962). *Sharyn* is also found, as for the US actress Sharyn Moffett (b.1936) and the Australian actress Sharyn Hodgson (b.1968). A diminutive is *Shari*, as for the Canadian ventriloquist (with 'Lamb Chop') Shari Lewis (1930–98). The name has found occasional male use in the past, as for the UK historian Sharon Turner (1768–1847).

US actress Sharon Lynn (1910–63); Canadian playwright, actress Sharon Pollock (b.1936); Canadian actress Sharon Acker (b.1936); US poet Sharon Olds (b.1942); US actresses Sharon Tate (1943–69), Sharon Gless (b.1943), Sharon Farrell (b.1946); UK actresses Sharon Duce (b.1948), Sharon Maughan (b.1951); US actress Sharon Stone (b.1957); UK judoist Sharon Rendle (b.1966).

Shaun The name is an English form of the Irish name SEAN, taken up by English speakers from the 1920s and remaining fairly popular since. The preferred spelling of the name in the US is *Shawn*.

UK writer, TV producer Shaun Sutton (b.1919); UK film critic Shaun Usher (b.1937); UK writer Shaun Hutson (b.1958); US actor, singer Shaun Cassidy (b.1958); UK racing cyclist Shaun Wallace (b.1961); UK rugby player Shaun Edwards (b.1966); UK canoeist Shaun Pearce (b.1969); UK cricketer Shaun Udal (b.1969).

Sheba The name is an independently adopted diminutive of BATHSHEBA, in select use among English speakers from the mid-20th century. As a name of (ultimately) biblical origin, it became associated with the Queen of Sheba (Queen of the South), who came to Jerusalem to consult Solomon, bring him gifts and trade with him. (Sheba is actually a male personal name in the Bible.) The name's adoption for female use was boosted by the film *Come Back Little Sheba* (1952), based on the play of the same name (1950) by the US playwright William Inge. A variant is *Shebah*, as for the UK actress Shebah Ronay (b.1972).

Sheelagh see **Shelagh**.

Sheena This name, an English form of the Scottish name *Sine* (English JANE), has been in select English-speaking use from the 1930s, mainly among Scots. It was given a popular boost by Sheena, the jungle girl heroine in the US comic-books (from 1938), with a subsequent TV series *Sheena, Queen of the Jungle* (1955–6) and a film *Sheena* (1984). The variant spelling *Shena* is sometimes found, as for the UK writer Shena Mackay (b.1944). The variant form *Sheenagh* was presumably influenced by SHELAGH.

South African social reformer Sheena Duncan (b.1932); Scottish TV presenter Sheena McDonald (b.1954); Scottish pop singer Sheena Easton (b.1959).

Sheila This is the English form of the Irish name *Síle* (English CELIA), in use among English speakers from the late 19th century, mainly in the UK and Canada. It was very popular in the UK in the 1930s, but since then has declined to a much more modest level. The variant spelling SHELAGH came to be adopted in its own right.

UK novelist Sheila Kaye-Smith (1887–1956); UK actress Sheila Mercier (b.1919); Scottish actress Sheila Keith (b.1920); UK actress Sheila Sim (b.1922); UK aviator Sheila Scott (1927–88); UK actress Sheila Hancock (b.1933); South African actress Sheila Steafel (b.1935); US pop singer Sheila E (b.1957); Scottish actress Sheila Grier (b.1959).

Shelagh An independently adopted variant spelling of SHEILA, taken up by English speakers from the early 20th century. A variant spelling *Sheelagh* also exists.

UK writer Shelagh Macdonald (b.1937); Irish playwright Shelagh Delaney (b.1939); Canadian actress Shelagh McLeod (b.1960).

Sheldon From the surname, and in select use among UK speakers from the early 20th century, first in the US, then in the UK. The central character in Frank Norris's novel *The Pit* (1903) is the artist Sheldon Corthell, in love with Laura Dearborn.

US actors Sheldon Lewis (1868–1958), Sheldon Leonard (1907–97); US radio and TV writer Sheldon Reynolds (b.1923).

Shell see **Michelle**.

Shelley (f.) This name is an altered form of SHIRLEY, influenced by the surname *Shelley* (as for the poet). It has been in English-speaking use since the mid-19th century, and achieved its peak period of favour in the 1970s and 1980s, since when it has declined to a much lower level. In Eudora Welty's novel *Delta Wedding* (1946) Shelley Fairchild is the sister of the central character, the bride Dabney Fairchild, who marries Troy Flavin. (See also MICHELLE.)

US actress Shelley Winters (b.1922) (original name Shirley Shrift); US cabaret monologuist Shelley Berman (b.1926); US actresses Shelley Fabares (b.1944), Shelley Hack (b.1948), Shelley Duvall (b.1949), Shelley Long (b.1949); US country singer Shelley West (b.1958).

Shem A biblical name, from a Hebrew word meaning 'name' (compare SAMUEL). It has never been in common use among English speakers but is still occasionally found. In the Bible Shem is the eldest of the three sons of Noah, and ancestor of both the postdiluvian human race and the eponymous Semites (the people, especially Arabs and Jews, who speak a Semitic language).

Shena see **Sheena**.

Sheree, **Sheri** see **Cherie**.

Sheridan From the (Irish) surname, and in select use among English speakers from the mid-19th century, at first in Ireland, but now rather more generally. Initial interest in the name may have been sparked by the famous Irish playwright Richard Brinsley Sheridan (1751–1816). The Irish novelist Sheridan Le Fanu (1814–73) was born of a family related to him. (It was originally his second name, his first being Joseph). A frequent diminutive is *Sherry*.

US screenwriter Sheridan Gibney (1903–88); UK stage and screen biographer, critic Sheridan Morley (b.1941) (named for the playwright).

Sherie see **Cherie**.

Sherill see **Cheryl**.

Sherley see **Shirley**.

Sherry (f.) This name is either an anglicized form of the French name CHERIE or an independently adopted diminutive of SHIRLEY, with perhaps also an influence from *sherry* (the wine). The name has been in modest English-speaking use from the mid-20th century. A variant is *Sherrie*, as for the UK actress Sherrie Hewson (b.1950).

US film executive Sherry Lansing (b.1944).

Sheryl An independent variant form of CHERYL, in modest favour among English speakers from the 1950s.

US popular singer Sheryl Crow (b.1963); US actress Sheryl Lee (b.1966).

Shirley (f.) A borrowing of the surname, taken up by English speakers from the 1860s. The name became hugely popular in the second half of the 1930s, thanks to the child actress Shirley Temple (see below), and enjoyed a more modest period of favour in the 1950s, since when it has gradually declined. Initial interest in the name was probably generated by Shirley Keeldar, the central character of Charlotte Brontë's novel *Shirley* (1849). (The narrative tells how the heroine's parents had the name in mind for a possible son, but used it anyway when a girl was born.) Variant spellings include *Sherley* and *Shirlee*, with the most common diminutive *Shirl*, as for the US actress Shirl Conway (b.1914). The name was formerly a male name, and still sometimes occurs as such even now.

US actresses Shirley Booth (1898–1992) (original first name Thelma), Shirley Mason (1900–79) (original name Leona Flugrath), Shirley Ross (1909–75) (original name Bernice Gaunt); Australian athlete Shirley Strickland (b.1925); US film director Shirley Clarke (1925–97); US actress Shirley Temple (b.1928); UK politician Shirley Williams (b.1930); UK businesswoman Dame Shirley Porter (b.1930); UK designer, writer Shirley Conran (b.1932); US actresses Shirley MacLaine (b.1934), Shirley Jones (b.1934); UK actress Shirley Eaton (b.1936); US actress Shirley Knight (b.1937); US swimmer Shirley Babashoff (b.1937); UK singer Shirley Bassey (b.1937); UK actresses Shirley Ann Field (b.1938), Shirley Stelfox (b.1941), Shirley Cheriton (b.1955); Scottish yachtswoman Shirley Robertson (b.1968).

Sholto This is an English form of the Scottish Gaelic name *Sìoltach*, 'sower' (that is, metaphorically, 'fruitful', 'producing many offspring'), in rare and mainly Scottish use from the 19th century. Colonel Sholto Douglas Ashton is the elder brother of the central character, Lucy Ashton, in Walter Scott's novel *The Bride of Lammermoor* (1819), and Sholto Douglas also appears in the same author's *Castle Dangerous* (1831). (In the latter novel the name is explained as being the Gaelic for 'see yon dark grey man'!)

Siân A Welsh form of JANE, pronounced 'Shahn', and often regarded as a feminine equivalent of SEAN. The name has been in mainly Welsh use from the 1940s. It is occasionally written without its accent (indicating a long vowel), as for the US actress Sian Barbara Allen (b.1946). A diminutive is *Siani*.

Welsh actress Siân Phillips (b.1934); Welsh TV weather presenter Siân Lloyd (b.1958); Welsh conductor Siân Edwards (b.1959); UK jewellery designer Siân Evans (b.1963).

Sib see **Sybil**.

Sid An independently adopted diminutive of SIDNEY, in select use among English speakers from the early 20th century. From around the 1970s the name came to denote any ordinary or unremarkable person, the 'man in the street', rather as FRED had been before.

South African-born UK comedians Sid Field (1904–50), Sid James (1913–76) (original first name Sydney); US comedian Sid Caesar (b.1922).

Sidney (m.) An adoption of the surname, historically famous as that of the aristocratic family that included the poet and soldier Sir Philip Sidney (1554–86). The name was taken up increasingly in the English-speaking world from the mid-19th century to the early 20th century, when it began a slow but inexorable decline. It has maintained favour among black Americans, however. Sidney Lorraine is a character in Benjamin Disraeli's novel *Vivian Grey* (1826–7). The variant spelling SYDNEY is in independent use, as is the regular diminutive SID.

US actor Sidney Blackmer (1895–1973); Australian painter Sir Sidney Nolan (1917–92); US actor Sidney Poitier (b.1924).

Sidney (f.) Apparently a female adoption of the male name SIDNEY, perhaps prompted by SIDONIE (or its variant form *Sidony*). The name has been in select use among English speakers from the 19th century. The variant spelling *Sydney* exists, as for the US actress Sydney Fairbrother (1873–1941), while *Sydne* was the preferred form of the US actress Sydne Rome (b.1946). Sydney Fairfield is a character in Clemence Dane's play *A Bill of Divorcement* (1921).

US actress Sidney Fox (1910–42).

Sidonie The name is a French form of the Latin name *Sidonia*, 'woman of Sidon' (the capital of ancient Phoenicia). It has found modest favour among English speakers from the 19th century. The original name of the French novelist Colette (1873–1954) was Sidonie Gabrielle Colette. A spelling *Sidony* occurs, and this may have influenced the adoption of the name SIDNEY.

UK harpist Sidonie Goossens (b.1899).

Sigmund The name represents an Old German name formed from *sigu*, 'victory', and *munt*, 'defender', so 'victorious defender' or 'protector of victory'. It is very occasionally found among English speakers, and may in some cases be a tribute to the Austrian psychiatrist Sigmund Freud (1856–1939). A diminutive *Siggy* occurs.

Hungarian-born US popular composer Sigmund Romberg (1887–1951).

Sigourney From the surname, and gaining favour among some English speakers in the 1990s, mainly thanks to the popularity of the US actress Sigourney Weaver (b.1949). Her original first names were Susan Alexandra. As a teenager she adopted her new name from one of her favourite fictional characters, Sigourney Howard in F. Scott Fitzgerald's novel *The Great Gatsby* (1925). A US bearer of the surname (pronounced '*Sig*erney' rather than 'Si*gour*ney', as now) was the writer Lydia Howard Sigourney (1791–1865), from whom Fitzgerald presumably (in view of the Howard) borrowed the name.

Silas A biblical name, from Latin *Silvanus*, itself from *silva*, 'wood', implying a person who lived in or by a wood. The name was taken up by Puritans in the 17th century and is still occasionally found, although it has never been common. In the Bible Silas is the prophet who accompanies St Paul on his second missionary journey. In literature the name is famous as that of the linen weaver who is the central character of George Eliot's novel *Silas Marner* (1861). It is also that of the villainous central character Silas Ruthyn in Sheridan Le Fanu's novel *Uncle Silas* (1864), and of another central character, a paint merchant, in William D. Howells's novel *The Rise of Silas Lapham* (1885).

Silvester A name of Latin origin, from *silvestris*, 'of the woods', 'rural', a derivative of *silva*, 'wood'. The name has been occasionally taken up by English speakers from the 16th century. It was borne by various early saints, notably the 4th-century St Silvester, bishop of Rome, whose feast day (31 December) is associated with New Year celebrations by Roman Catholics, so giving a suitable name for a child born at or around this time. The variant spelling SYLVESTER is in independent use.

Silvia This name is the feminine form of the Latin name *Silvius*, itself from *silva*, 'wood'. It has been in general use among English speakers from the 19th century but is now much less common than it was. In Roman mythology, Rhea Silvia is the mother of Romulus and Remus. In Shakespeare's *Two Gentlemen of Verona* (1592–3) Silvia is the Duke of Milan's daughter, loved by Valentine. (The play has the famous song 'Who is Silvia?', familiar from Schubert's setting.) In William Congreve's play *The Old Bachelor* (1693), Silvia, the forsaken mistress of Vainlove, marries Heartwell. The variant spelling SYLVIA has now all but superseded the original form of the name.

Simeon A biblical name, from Hebrew *Shim'ōn*, 'he who hears', in select English-speaking use from the 16th century to the early 20th century, when it became increasingly rare. In the Bible Simeon is the name of several people. One of the best known is the second son of Jacob and Leah who was the ancestor of one of the twelve tribes of Israel: 'And she conceived again, and bare a son; and said, because the Lord hath heard that I was hated, he hath therefore given me this son also; and she called his name Simeon' (Genesis 29.33). Another is the 'just and devout' man who blessed Joseph, Mary and the infant Jesus in the temple at Jerusalem (in the words of the 'Song of Simeon' or *Nunc Dimittis*). Simeon Halliday is a Quaker friend of Eliza and George in Harriet Beecher Stowe's novel *Uncle Tom's Cabin* (1852). SIMON is a directly related name.

Simon A biblical name, the English form of SIMEON, with the same Hebrew origin, but popularly also associated with Greek *simos*, 'snub-nosed'. The name was in regular use among English speakers until the early 19th century. It then underwent a decline, only to revive in the early 20th century and win wide popularity in the 1960s and 1970s, after which it sank to a more modest level. The name is that of many people in the Bible, the best known being the two apostles Simon Peter (later just Peter) and Simon the Canaanite (or Simon the Zealot). (Another Simon, a 'brother' or relative of Jesus, has been identified by some with the latter. A fourth, Simon the Pharisee, invites Jesus to his table.) In English history, the name is famously that of the medieval soldier Simon de Montfort, Earl of Leicester, who ruled England from 1264 to 1265. In English literature Sir Simon Darnford is a character in Samuel Richardson's novel *Pamela* (1740–41); Simon Tappertit is an apprentice to Gabriel Varden in Charles Dickens's novel *Barnaby Rudge* (1841); and Simon Legree is the cruel plantation owner who purchases Tom and Emmeline in Harriet Beecher Stowe's novel *Uncle Tom's Cabin* (1852). (This last Simon may have caused the temporary decline in the name.) A more recent literary bearer of the name is the gentleman adventurer Simon Templar, the central character ('The Saint') in many novels (from 1928) by the UK writer Leslie Charteris. Diminutives *Sim* and *Simmy* exist.

UK writer Simon Raven (1927–2001); UK actors Simon Ward (b.1941), Simon Williams (b.1946); UK radio broadcaster Simon Bates (b.1948); UK actors Simon Callow (b.1949), Simon Cadell (1950–96), Simon Jones (b.1950), Simon MacCorkindale (b.1952); UK conductor Sir Simon Rattle (b.1955), UK pop singer Simon Le Bon (b.1958); UK TV presenter Simon O'Brien (b.1965); UK actor Simon Gregson (b.1974).

Simone This name is a French feminine form of SIMON, adopted as an English name from the 1940s, perhaps under the influence of one of the French actresses listed below. A rarish variant form is *Simona*, and the usual diminutives are *Simmie* or *Simmy*.

French writer Simone de Beauvoir (1908–86); French actresses Simone Simon (b.1910), Simone Signoret (1921–85).

Sinclair From the (Scottish) surname, and in occasional favour among English speakers from the late 19th century.

US novelist Sinclair Lewis (1885–1951) (originally middle name, first being Harry).

Sindy see **Cindy**.

Sinead This is the Irish form (properly *Sinéad*) of the English name JANET, pronounced 'Shin*ade*'. It is still mainly in Irish use but has occasionally found favour among English speakers generally from the 1970s, with a more marked popularity from the 1990s.

Irish actress Sinead Cusack (b.1948); Irish pop singer Sinead O'Connor (b.1966).

Siobhan This name is the Irish form (properly *Siobhán*) of the English name JOAN, pronounced 'Shi*vawn*'. It has gained fairly wide favour among English speakers generally from the 1960s, though its prime use is still among the Irish.

Irish actress Siobhan McKenna (1923–86); UK rock singer Siobhan Fahey (b.1957); Scottish actress Siobhan Redmond (b.1959).

Sissy see **Cecilia**, **Cecily**, **Cissie**.

Skeeter An adoption of the nickname, as given to an active or small person (either from *mosquito* or as someone who *skeets*, that is, scoots). Its main English-speaking favour has been in the US, where it was taken up in the early 20th century.

US country singer Skeeter Davis (b.1931) (original name Mary Frances Penick).

Sofia see **Sophia**.

Solomon A famous biblical name, from Hebrew *Shĕlōmōh*, itself from *shālōm*, 'peace', so 'man of peace'. The name has been in regular but select use among English speakers from the 18th century, mainly in Jewish families. In the Bible Solomon is the son of David and Beersheba, and a king of Israel, famed for his wisdom. There was no major war during his reign, so that he justifies his name. The books of Proverbs and Ecclesiastes are ascribed to him, and the Song of Solomon bears his name. In Charles Dickens's novel *Pickwick Papers* (1836–7) Solomon Lucas is a fancy-dress dealer, while in the same author's *Dombey and Son* (1847–8) Solomon Gills is the uncle of Walter Gay. Solomon Grundy ('Born on a Monday') has been a familiar nursery rhyme character since the early 19th century. The regular diminutives are *Sol* and *Solly*, the latter as for the South African-born UK scientist Solly Zuckerman (1904–93).

UK concert pianist Solomon (1902–88) (original name Solomon Cutner); US soul singer Solomon Burke (b.1936).

Sondra see **Sandra**.

Sonia This name is a Russian diminutive of *Sofiya* (English SOPHIA), in select use among English speakers from the early 20th century, with a slight rise in popularity in the 1960s and 1970s. In literature Sonia Dainton is the central character of Stephen McKenna's novel *Sonia* (1917). A variant spelling is *Sonya*, as for the US film writer Sonya Levien (1888–1960).

UK actress Sonia Dresdel (1909–76) (original name Lois Obee); UK artist Sonia Lawson (b.1934); US poet Sonia Sanchez (b.1934) (original name Wilsonia Driver); UK radio presenter Sonia Beesley (b.1936); Brazilian-born actress Sonia Braga (b.1951); Irish athlete Sonia O'Sullivan (b.1969).

Sonny A name that is either an independently adopted diminutive from a name such as SAUL or SOLOMON, or else the borrowing of the general nickname for a young person. It is popularly associated with SUNNY. The name found some favour among English speakers in the 20th century, mainly in the US. Al Jolson's song 'Sonny Boy' in the film *The Singing Fool* (1928) may have encouraged adoption of the name. The variant spelling *Sonnie* exists, as for the UK actor Sonnie Hale (1902–59) (original name John Robert Hale-Monro).

US actor Sonny Tufts (1911–70) (original first names Bowen Charleston); US popular musicians Sonny Terry (1911–86) (original name Saunders Terrell), Sonny Berman (1924–47) (original first name Saul), Sonny James (b.1929) (original name James Loden); West Indian cricketer Sonny Ramadhin (b.1929); US boxer Sonny Liston (1932–70) (original first name Charles); US country musician Sonny Curtis (b.1937).

Sonya see **Sonia**.

Sophia The name, from the Greek word meaning 'wisdom', was adopted in the English-speaking world in the 17th century. It is still found in general use, especially in the US, and became increasingly popular in the UK in the 1990s. The name was first famous from St Sophia, cultivated by the Eastern Orthodox Church, although the saint's name as a whole (Greek *Hagia Sophia*) actually means 'holy wisdom', and serves as a title for Christ regarded as representing the wisdom of God. In Henry Fielding's novel *Tom Jones* (1749) Sophia Western marries Tom, and in Oliver Goldsmith's novel *The Vicar of Wakefield* (1766) Sophia Primrose, daughter of the central character, Dr Charles Primrose, marries Sir William Thornhill. Charles Dickens has the name for Sophia Wackles, who marries Alick Cheggs in his novel *The Old Curiosity Shop* (1840–41), as well as for Miss Pinch's pupil in *Martin Chuzzlewit* (1843–4) and Mr Pocket's housemaid in *Great Expectations* (1860–1). The variant SOPHIE is an independent name, as is the diminutive SONIA. The spelling *Sofia* also exists. The name has aristocratic associations (perhaps partly through its suggestion of *sophisticated*).

US aviator, sports administrator Sophia Heath (1896–1936); UK daughter of Earl Waldegrave, Lady Sophia Schilizzi (b.1908); Italian-US actress Sophia Loren (b.1934) (original name Sofia Scicolone); UK daughter of Marquess of Anglesey, Lady Sophia Keir (b.1954); UK daughter of Marquess of Bute, Lady Sophia Fenwick (b.1956); UK daughter of Duke of Devonshire, Lady Sophia Morrison (b.1957); UK daughter of Earl of Yarborough, Lady Sophia Kinmont (b.1958).

Sophie A French form of SOPHIA, adopted independently, and in English-speaking use from the 19th century, with a considerable increase in popularity from the 1980s. This may have to some extent resulted from the film *Sophie's Choice* (1982), with Meryl Streep in the title role. The variant spelling *Sophy* is also found, as for Sophy Gauntlet in Tobias Smollett's novel *Peregrine Pickle* (1751). The name lacks the aristocratic associations that *Sophia* has, perhaps because it suggests *soft* or *sofa* more than *sophisticated*.

US variety actress Sophie Tucker (1885–1966) (original name Sophia Abuza); US fashion designer Sophie Gimbel (1902–81); UK actress Sophie Stewart (1909–77); UK food writer Sophie Grigson (b.1959); UK actress Sophie Aldred (b.1962); UK sculptor Sophie Ryder (b.1963); UK actress Sophie Ward (b.1964); UK jewellery designer Sophie Harley (b.1965).

Sophronia A Greek name, from *sōphrōn*, 'prudent', 'sensible', in occasional English-speaking use from the 19th century. The name occurs more than once in Charles Dickens: the servant girl (nicknamed 'The Marchioness') who marries Dick Swiveller in *The Old Curiosity Shop* (1840–41) is given the name Sophronia Sphynx by her future husband, and Sophronia Akershem marries Alfred Lammle in *Our Mutual Friend* (1864–5). The diminutive SOPHIE is more usually related to SOPHIA.

Sophy see **Sophie**.

Sorrel (f.) From the plant name rather than the colour, and in occasional use from the 1940s.

Scottish daughter of Earl of Portland, Lady Sorrel Bentinck (b.1942); UK popular journalist Sorrel Downer (b.1961).

Spencer From the surname, associated with the Churchill family, and in select English-speaking use from the early 19th century.

US religious leader Spencer W. Kimball (1895–1985); US actor Spencer Tracy (1900–67).

Spike An adoption of the nickname, either for someone with 'spiky' hair or for any person whose name is otherwise unknown. The name has found some favour among English speakers from the early 20th century.

UK jazzman Spike Hughes (1908–87) (original first names Patrick Cairns); US bandleader Spike Jones (1911–65) (original first names Lindley Armstrong); UK comedian Spike Milligan (b.1918) (original first names Terence Alan); US film director Spike Lee (b.1956) (original first names Shelton Jackson).

Spring A borrowing of the word for the season, the most attractive of the year, or for the well of clear running water. The name has found very occasional adoption among English speakers from the 19th century.

US actress Spring Byington (1893–1971).

Stacey (f.) This name arose either as an independently adopted diminutive of ANASTASIA or, more likely, as a female borrowing of the male name STACY. It has enjoyed increasing favour among English speakers from the 1960s. Variant spellings include *Staci*, *Stacie* and *Stacy*, this last as for the UK actress Stacy Dorning (b.1958) and US pop singer Stacy Lattisaw (b.1966). A diminutive is *Stace*.

Stacy (m.) From the surname, itself a derivative of EUSTACE. The name has found some favour among English speakers from the 19th century. The variant spelling *Stacey* also occurs.

UK fiction writer Stacy Aumonier (1887–1928); US actor Stacy Keach (b.1941) (originally middle name, first being Walter).

Stafford From the surname, famous as that of the dukes of Buckingham, and in select use among English speakers from the mid-19th century.

UK statesman Sir Stafford Cripps (1889–1952) (originally middle name, first being Richard); UK opera singer Stafford Dean (b.1937).

Stan An independently adopted diminutive of STANLEY, in select use among English speakers from the early 20th century. Stan Emery is loved by Ellen Thatcher Oglethorpe in John Dos Passos's novel *Manhattan Transfer* (1925).

UK-born US comedian Stan Laurel (1890–1965) (original name Arthur Stanley Jefferson); US baseball player Stan Musial (b.1920); UK politician Stan Orme (b.1923); US jazz saxophonist Stan Getz (1927–91); UK actor Stan Stennett (b.1927); UK novelist Stan Barstow (b.1928); UK actors Stan Richards (b.1930); Czech-born Canadian ice hockey player Stan Mikita (b.1940).

Stanley From the surname, that of the earls of Derby, and in fairly regular English-speaking use from the 18th century, with a period of widespread adoption from the 1880s to the 1920s, after which the name fell from favour. Doubtless the initial popular interest in the name stemmed from the UK explorer Sir Henry Morton Stanley (1841–1904), who made historic contact with Livingstone in Africa in 1871. Stanley Graff is a salesman in Sinclair Lewis's novel *Babbitt* (1922), and Stanley Poole is a character in J.B. Priestley's novel *Angel Pavement* (1930). The regular diminutive is STAN, in independent use.

UK prime minister Stanley Baldwin (1867–1947); UK comedian Stanley Holloway (1890–1982); UK painter Stanley Spencer (1891–

1959); UK comedian Stanley Lupino (1893–1942); UK bandleader Stanley Black (b.1913); US film director Stanley Kramer (1913–2001); UK footballer Stanley Matthews (1915–2000); UK actors Sir Stanley Baker (1927–76), Stanley Baxter (b.1928); US film director Stanley Kubrick (1928–99).

Stef, Stefanie, Steffie see **Stephanie**.

Stella The name, from Latin *stella*, 'star', was taken up by English speakers in the 18th century and was in more or less regular use until the 1920s, after which it gradually fell from favour. It was made famous in literature by Sir Philip Sidney's sequence of sonnets and songs *Astrophel and Stella* (1582), in which he was 'Astrophel' (Greek, 'star lover') and she, in reality Penelope Rich, was 'Stella' (Latin, 'star'). The same conceit lay behind Jonathan Swift's diaries *Journal to Stella* (1710–13), addressed to Esther Johnson, whose first name means 'star' (see ESTHER). In J.B. Priestley's novel *The Good Companions* (1929), Stella Cavendish is the actress wife of Courtenay Brundit. ESTELLE is a directly related name.

UK writer, traveller Stella Benson (1892–1933); US actress Stella Adler (1901–92); UK author Stella Gibbons (1902–89); Polish-born US athlete Stella Walsh (1911–80) (original name Stanislawa Walasiewicz); US actress Stella Stevens (b.1936) (original name Estelle Eggleston); US country singer Stella Parton (b.1949).

Stephanie This name is a French form (properly *Stéphanie*) of the Latin name *Stephania* or *Stephana*, the feminine equivalent of *Stephanus* (English STEPHEN). It has been in English-speaking use since the late 19th century, and after a fairly moderate period of favour from the 1950s to 1980s suddenly rose in popularity in the 1990s. Variants include *Stefanie*, as for the US actress Stefanie Powers (b.1942) (original name Stefania Federkiewicz), while diminutives include *Stef*, *Steffie*, *Steph* and *Stevie*, the last as for the Welsh feminist writer Stevie Davies (b.1946) and US rock singer Stevie Nicks (b.1948).

The UK poet Stevie Smith (1902–71), born Florence Margaret Smith, was so nicknamed for the jockey, and adopted the name.

US actress Stephanie Bachelor (b.1924); UK actress Stephanie Beacham (b.1947); US soul singer Stephanie Mills (b.1957).

Stephen As a biblical name, this is the English form of the Greek name *Stephanos*, meaning 'garland', 'crown'. It was in regular English-speaking use from medieval times to the early 20th century. It then fairly quickly climbed to a period of high popularity in the second half of the 1950s, since when it has gradually declined to a more moderate level. In the Bible Stephen is the first Christian martyr, falsely accused of blasphemy and stoned to death. Stephen is a character in Ben Jonson's comedy *Every Man in his Humour* (1598), and in George Eliot's novel *The Mill on the Floss* (1860) Stephen Guest, in love with the central character, Maggie Tulliver, as is his brother Tom, marries Lucy Deane. In later literature Stephen Dedalus is a schoolmaster in James Joyce's novel *Ulysses* (1922). The variant spelling STEVEN is in independent use, as is the regular diminutive STEVE.

US writer Stephen Crane (1871–1900); UK poet Sir Stephen Spender (1909–95); UK actor Stephen Murray (1912–83); US composer, lyricist Stephen Sondheim (b.1930); US horror novelist Stephen King (b.1947); UK comedian, writer Stephen Fry (b.1957); UK actor Stephen Rashbrook (b.1958); Scottish snooker player Stephen Hendry (b.1969).

Sterling From the surname, with its suggestion of *sterling* in the sense 'excellent value'. The name has been in select English-speaking use, mainly in the US, from the early 20th century. The spelling STIRLING is in independent use.

US actors Sterling Holloway (1905–92), Sterling Hayden (1916–86).

Steve An independently adopted diminutive of STEPHEN or STEVEN, in fairly popular English-speaking use from the 1930s. The usual diminutive is *Stevie*, as for US pop singer Stevie Wonder (b.1950) (original first name Steveland).

US actors Steve Cochran (1917–65) (original first name Robert), Steve Brodie (1919–92) (original name John Stevens); UK pianist, broadcaster on music Steve Race (b.1921); US TV entertainer, writer Steve Allen (1921–2000); US actor Steve McQueen (1930–80); UK TV presenter Steve Jones (b.1945); UK pop musician Steve Winwood (b.1948); UK motor-racing driver Steve Soper (b.1952); UK athlete Steve Ovett (b.1955); UK snooker player Steve Davis (b.1957); US jockey Steve Cauthen (b.1960); UK athlete Steve Cram (b.1960); UK comedian Steve Coogan (b.1965).

Steven An independently adopted variant of STEPHEN, at first more popular in the US than the UK in the 20th century, but by the 1980s found almost equally in all parts of the English-speaking world. The *v* reflects the pronunciation.

US film director Steven Spielberg (b.1946); UK actors Steven Pinner (b.1961), Steven Pinder (b.1963); US film director Steven Soderbergh (b.1963); UK actor Steven Woodcock (b.1964).

Stevie (m.) see **Steve**.

Stevie (f.) see **Stephanie**.

Stewart A name that either represents the (Scottish) surname or evolved as an independently adopted variant of STUART. It enjoyed modest English-speaking use from the early 19th century to the 1950s, when it picked up somewhat only to decline gradually from the 1970s. Diminutives *Stew* or *Stu* exist.

UK radio commentator Stewart MacPherson (1908–95); UK actor Stewart Granger (1913–93) (original name James Lablanche Stewart).

Stirling This is an adoption either of the surname or of the common variant of STERLING, in select use among English speakers from the early 20th century, and the preferred form of the name in the UK.

US film writer Sterling Silliphant (1918–96); UK racing driver Stirling Moss (b.1929).

Storm A borrowing of the standard word, perhaps implying a romantically passionate nature. The name has found some occasional adoption among English speakers from the early 20th century.

UK novelist Storm Jameson (1891–1986) (originally middle name, first being Margaret).

Stuart From the (Scottish) surname, itself a French form of the surname that gave the identical first name STEWART. This form of the surname was introduced to Scotland in the 16th century by Mary Stuart, Queen of Scots, who was raised in France. The name has found general favour among English speakers from the early 19th century, and became increasingly popular from the 1950s to the 1980s, after which it gradually waned. The usual diminutives are *Stew* or *Stu*.

UK radio announcer Stuart Hibbert (1893–1983); UK footballer Stuart Pearce (b.1962); UK actor Stuart Wolfenden (b.1970).

Sue An independently adopted diminutive of SUSAN or (less often) SUSANNAH, in general use among English speakers from the late 19th century. Sue Bridehead (full first name Susanna Florence Mary) is the cousin and lover of Jude Fawley in Thomas Hardy's novel *Jude the Obscure* (1894–5). The spelling variant *Su* is increasingly common, as for the UK actresses Su Douglas (b.1942) and Su Pollard (b.1949).

UK actress Sue Lloyd (b.1939); South African-born UK radio presenter Sue MacGregor (b.1941); UK actresses Sue Johnston (b.1943), Sue Nicholls (b.1943); US actress Sue Lyon (b.1946); UK writer Sue Townsend (b.1946); UK TV presenters Sue Lawley (b.1946), Sue Cook (b.1949), Sue Robbie (b.1949); UK actress Sue Holderness (b.1949); UK artist Sue Arrowsmith (b.1950); UK TV newsreader Sue Carpenter (b.1956); UK actress Sue Devaney (b.1968).

Sukie, **Suky** see **Susan**.

Sunday An adoption of the day name, in rare 20th-century use among English speakers. The name is suitable for a child conceived or born on this day.

UK actress, broadcaster Sunday Wilshin (Sunday, 16 February 1905–91).

Sunny (m.) A borrowing of the ordinary word or nickname, implying a cheerful ('sunny') personality, but also influenced by SONNY. The name has found some favour among black Americans in the 20th century, but less often elsewhere in the English-speaking world. The name is frequently given to, or adopted by, a person named James, from the popular nickname 'Sunny Jim' (or 'Sonny Jim'), itself associated with the commercial character 'Sunny Jim' who has advertised Force breakfast cereal from the early 20th century.

US musician Sunny Murray (b.1937) (original first name James).

Susan This popular name arose as a shortened form of SUSANNAH, adopted independently. It has been in general use among English speakers from the 18th century, then generally declined until suddenly experiencing a huge rise in popularity in the 1950s. This then tailed off fairly sharply from the 1970s, so that now the name is at a very modest level. An early literary bearer of the name is Susan Mountford in Thomas Heywood's tragedy *A Woman Killed with Kindness* (first performed 1603). Susan Pearson is a character in Charlotte Brontë's novel *Shirley* (1849). The many diminutives include SUE, SUSIE and SUZY, all in independent use, as well as *Sukie* and *Suky*. SUZANNE relates more to SUSANNAH.

US suffragist, editor Susan B. Anthony (1820–1906); US actress Susan Hayward (1918–75) (original name Edythe Marrener); US writer Susan Sontag (b.1933); US actress Susan Strasberg (1938–99); UK actress Susan Hampshire (b.1938); UK writers Susan Howatch (b.1940), Susan Hill (b.1942); US actress Susan Sarandon (b.1946); UK actresses Susan

Brown (b.1948), Susan George (b.1950), Susan Penhaligon (b.1950); US actress Susan Dey (b.1952); UK actresses Susan Gilmore (b.1954), Susan Wooldridge (b.1956), Susan Tully (b.1967).

Susannah A biblical name, from Hebrew *Shūshannāh*, 'lily', in use among English speakers from the 16th century, although in decline from the 18th century, when it was mostly superseded by the shortened form SUSAN. In the Apocrypha Susannah is the beautiful and devout wife of Joachim, falsely accused of adultery by the elders. A character of the name occurs in Laurence Sterne's novel *Tristram Shandy* (1759–67). The most common variant is *Susanna*, as for the US opera singer and actress Susanna Foster (b.1924) (original name Suzan Larsen), and as in the Stephen Foster song 'O, Susanna' (1848), while *Suzanna* is also found, as for the UK actress Suzanna Hamilton (b.1960). The French variant SUZANNE is in independent use, with diminutives as for SUSAN, including the independently adopted SUSIE and SUZY.

UK actress Susannah York (b.1941); UK TV, radio presenter Susannah Simons (b.1948); UK actress Susannah Fellows (b.1956) (mother is Suzanne); UK actress Susannah Harker (b.1965).

Susie An independently adopted diminutive of SUSAN or SUSANNAH, in English-speaking use from the mid-19th century. In J.B. Priestley's novel *The Good Companions* (1929) Susie Deane is a comedienne in the 'Dinky Doos' concert party. The name was popularized by songs such as 'If You Knew Susie' (1925), 'Wake up Little Susie' (1957), and by the dance of the 1930s known as the Susie-Q. Variant spellings *Suzi* and *Suzie* exist, as respectively for the US pop singer Suzi Quatro (b.1950) and the central character of R.L. Mason's novel *The World of Suzie Wong* (1947). The variant spelling SUZY is in independent use.

UK potter Susie Cooper (1902–95); US singer Susie Allanson (b.1952).

Suzanne This is a French form of SUSANNAH, taken up by English speakers from the early 20th century. Diminutives are mostly as for SUSAN.

US opera singer Suzanne Adams (1872–1953); US actress Suzanne Somers (b.1946); UK actress Suzanne Bertish (b.1953); UK artist Suzanne O'Driscoll (b.1955); US pop singer Suzanne Vega (b.1959); UK gymnast, TV presenter Suzanne Dando (b.1961); UK actress Suzanne Packer (b.1962); UK TV weather presenter Suzanne Charlton (b.1963).

Suzi, **Suzie** see **Susie**.

Suzy An independently adopted spelling of SUSIE, as a diminutive of SUSAN, SUSANNAH or SUZANNE, taken up by English speakers from the early 20th century.

US actress Suzy Parker (b.1932) (original first name Cecelia); UK fashion editor Suzy Menkes-Spanier (b.1943); US children's writer Suzy Kline (b.1943); UK actress Suzy Kendall (b.1944) (original name Frieda Harrison); US actress Suzy Gilstrap (b.1966).

Swithin This is the modern form of the Old English name *Suitha*, based on *swīth*, 'strong', 'mighty', and very occasionally found in English-speaking use. Its best-known bearer was the 9th-century bishop of Winchester, St Swithin, who became associated with the legend that rain will last for 40 days if it falls on his feast day (15 July). Swithin Forsyte is an estate and land agent in John Galsworthy's *Forsyte* sequence (1906–22).

Sy see **Sasha** (m.).

Sybil This is an evolution of the Greek name *Sibylla* or *Sybilla*, generally given to various prophetesses, and itself of obscure origin. The name was in select use among English speakers until the 19th century, when it became rather more general. In modern times it is rarely found, however. A famous literary bearer of the name is Sybil Gerard, the central character of Benjamin Disraeli's novel *Sybil* (1845). In Oscar Wilde's novel *The Picture of Dorian Gray* (1891), Sybil Vane is jilted by Gray. The variant spellings *Sibyl* and *Sybille* are sometimes found, the latter as for the UK writer Sybille Bedford (b.1911), while the much rarer form *Cybill* has been made known by the US actress Cybill Shepherd (b.1949). A diminutive *Sib* exists.

UK actress Dame Sybil Thorndike (1882–1976); UK-born US astrologer Sybil Leek (1917–82); South African actress Sybil Jason (b.1929).

Sydne see **Sidney** (f.).

Sydney An independently adopted variant of SIDNEY, in regular English-speaking use from the 19th century but tailing off considerably from the 1920s. In Charles Dickens's novel *A Tale of Two Cities* (1859), the wastrel barrister Sydney Carton is guillotined to save Charles Darnay, while Sydney Herbert is a character in William Faulkner's novel *The Sound and the Fury* (1929). The diminutive *Syd* exists, as for the UK comedians Syd Crossley (1885–1960) and Syd Walker (1887–1945), but is not as common as SID, which is in independent use.

UK film producer Sydney Box (1907–83).

Sylvester An independently adopted variant of SILVESTER, in variable English-speaking favour from the 18th century, but now generally the preferred form of the name. In modern times the name has been humorously popularized by the cartoon cat ('puddy tat') Sylvester who has pursued the canary Tweety Pie since the 1940s. (He may perhaps have been so called from the name's association with woods and trees, from Latin *silva*, 'wood'.) Diminutives *Syl* and *Vester* exist.

Scottish actor Sylvester McCoy (b.1943); US actor Sylvester Stallone (b.1946); US soul singer Sylvester (1946–88) (original name Sylvester James).

Sylvia An independently adopted variant spelling of SILVIA, taken up generally by English speakers from the mid-19th century, but now no longer common after a period of high popularity in the 1930s. Sylvia Robson is the central character in Elizabeth Gaskell's novel *Sylvia's Lovers* (1863), and Sylvia Scarlett is the leading figure in Compton Mackenzie's novels *Sinister Street* (1914), *Sylvia Scarlett* (1918) and *Sylvia and Michael* (1919). The French variant *Sylvie* is sometimes found, as for the French actress Sylvie (1883–1970) (original name Louise Sylvain). The usual diminutive is *Syl*, but the French-style *Sylvette* also exists.

UK political writer Sylvia Pankhurst (1882–1960); US publisher Sylvia Beach (1887–1962); UK novelist Sylvia Townsend Warner (1893–1978); New Zealand writer Sylvia Ashton-Warner (1908–84); US actresses Sylvia Sidney (1910–99) (original name Sophia Kosow), Sylvia Miles (b.1926); US poet Sylvia Plath (1932–63); UK actress Sylvia Syms (b.1934); UK poet Sylvia Kantaris (b.1936); French actress Sylvia Kristel (b.1952); US pop singer Sylvia (b.1956) (original name Sylvia Kirby Allen).

T

Tabitha A biblical name, from Aramaic *Tabhītha*, 'gazelle', taken up by English speakers in the 17th century, but rare today. In the Bible Tabitha is the woman 'full of good works and alms deeds' who was restored to life by St Peter (Acts 9.36–41). Tabitha Bramble is the 'starched, vain, ridiculous' aunt of the central character in Tobias Smollett's novel *Humphry Clinker* (1771), and Tabitha Lark is a character in Thomas Hardy's novel *Two on a Tower* (1882). In the UK the name is traditionally given to cats, especially tabbies, which explains the name of Tabitha Twitchit, the mother cat in Beatrix Potter's children's book *The Tale of Tom Kitten* (1907) and sequels. The US TV series *Tabitha* (1977) was devoted to the adventures of the daughter of Samantha Stephens, the attractive witch in the earlier series *Bewitched* (1964–71) (see SAMANTHA). The stock diminutive is *Tabby*. See also DORCAS.

Tad see **Thaddeus**.

Taffy This is an English form of the Welsh name *Dafydd* (English DAVID), independently adopted as diminutive. The name has been in selective use among the Welsh from the 19th century, especially by those named David (or Dafydd). It has also been used by English speakers generally to apply to a typical Welshman, sometimes in a disapprobatory sense. (Hence the nursery rhyme, dating from the 18th century: 'Taffy was a Welshman, Taffy was a thief, Taffy came to my house', etc.) In George du Maurier's novel *Trilby* (1894), the name occurs for the art student Talbot (Taffy) Wynne. A diminutive *Taff* exists.

Talbot From the surname, that of the earls of Shrewsbury, in select use among English speakers from the 19th century. Through its aristocratic connections the name now has Welsh associations, as for the town and port of Port Talbot. Talbot Twysden is a character in William Makepeace Thackeray's novel *The Adventures of Philip* (1861–2), and Talbot (Taffy) Wynne is an art student in George du Maurier's novel *Trilby* (1894).

Tamar A biblical name, from Hebrew *Tāmar*, 'date palm', in moderate favour among English speakers from the 17th century but from the 1930s superseded by its Russian equivalent, TAMARA. In the Bible Tamar is the name of four women: the daughter-in-law of Judah, a daughter of King David, a sister of Absalom, and a daughter of Absalom. The US poet Robinson Jeffers wrote *Tamar and Other Poems* (1924) on the second of these. In the UK some may associate the name with the River *Tamar*, and therefore with Cornwall. The diminutive TAMMY is now in independent use.

Tamara A Russian adoption of the biblical name TAMAR, with a final feminine -*a*. The name has been in select use among English speakers from the 1930s. The diminutive TAMMY is a name in its own right. The name has aristocratic associations.

Russian-born UK ballerina Tamara Karsavina (1885–1978); Russian-US actress Tamara Shayne (1897–1983); Russian-born UK actress Tamara Desni (b.1913); Russian-born French ballerina Tamara Toumanova (1919–96); Russian-born UK circus owner Tamara Hassani (1928–88); US actress Tamara Dobson (b.1947); Scottish actress Tamara Kennedy (b.1962); UK daughter of Duke and Duchess of Westminster, Lady Tamara Grosvenor (b.1979).

Tammy The name, an independently adopted diminutive of TAMARA, TAMSIN or THOMASIN, was taken up by English speakers in the late 19th century. It enjoyed a modest vogue from the second half of the 1970s, and was popularized by the song 'Tammy' sung by Debbie Reynolds in the US film *Tammy and the Bachelor* (1957), in which Tammy is a backwoods tomboy. Variants *Tammie* and *Tammi* occur, the latter as for US R&B singer Tammi Terrell (1946–70) (original first name Thomasina).

US actress Tammy Grimes (b.1934); US country singer Tammy Wynette (1942–98) (original name Virginia Wynette Pugh); UK country singer Tammy Cline (b.1953); UK hockey player Tammy Miller (b.1967).

Tamsin This name is a contracted form of THOMASIN, adopted for independent use. It has been generally current among English speakers from the 1940s and was in vogue in the 1970s and 1990s. The usual diminutive is TAMMY, now current in its own right, while variants are *Tamzim,* as for the UK actress Tamzin Outhwaite (b.1971) and *Tamasin,* as for the UK writer Tamasin Day-Lewis (b.*c.*1960).

UK actress Tamsin Olivier (b.1963).

Tania see **Tanya**.

Tanith A name that in origin is that of the chief goddess of Carthage, but its meaning is uncertain. It is occasionally found in English-speaking use, where it may have been regarded as a variant of TANYA.

UK children's writer Tanith Lee (b.1947).

Tansy An adoption of the plant name, itself etymologically related to the name *Athanasia*, and in select English-speaking use from the 1940s. The name may have been avoided by some because of its association with cats and donkeys. The diminutive, TAMMY, is in use in its own right.

Tanya An English adoption in independent use of the Russian diminutive of TATIANA. The name was picked up by English speakers in the 1940s, and since the 1960s has been regularly in favour, with its peak of popularity in the 1990s.

The spelling variant *Tania* is also found, as for the UK TV presenter Tania Bryer (b.1962), and for a time enjoyed a greater vogue in the second half of the 1960s. The name has something of an aristocratic cachet.

UK model, fashion consultant Tanya Gordon (b.1945); US country singer Tanya Tucker (b.1958); Scottish daughter of Earl of Dundonald, Lady Tanya Peake (b.1964).

Tara The name is historically associated with Ireland, where the Hill of *Tara* near Dublin is the seat of ancient Irish kings. (The name may actually mean 'hill' or be linked with that of the earth goddess Temair, whose own name is said to mean 'dark one'.) It was this Tara that became well known from Thomas Moore's poem 'The harp that once through Tara's halls' (1807). The name was taken up by English speakers in the 1940s, at first in the US, where its vogue undoubtedly sprang from the film of 1939 based on Margaret Mitchell's novel *Gone with the Wind* (1936), in which Tara is the name of the family estate. In the UK the name has been regularly fashionable since the 1960s, with its new popularity doubtless prompted by the character Tara King, played by Linda Thorson, in the TV series *The Avengers*.

UK actresses Tara Newley (b.1963), Tara Fitzgerald (b.1967), Tara Moran (b.1971).

Tamin The name is probably an alteration of TAMSIN, influenced by JASMINE.

UK pop singer Tasmin Archer (b.1963); UK violinist Tasmin Little (b.1965).

Tatiana A Russian name, itself ultimately from the Roman clan name *Tatius*, of uncertain origin. (Some authorities link it with Greek *tattō*, a form of *tassō*, 'I arrange', 'I set in order'.) The name was taken up by English speakers, mainly in the US, from the 1940s. Its most famous literary bearer is Tatiana Larina in Pushkin's verse novel *Eugene Onegin* (1823–31), familiar from Tchaikovsky's opera of 1879 based on it. The diminutive TANYA is in independent use.

Russian-born US ballerina Tatiana Riabouchinska (1917–2000); Russian actress Tatiana Samoilova (b.1934); US opera singer Tatiana Troyanos (1938–93).

Ted An independently adopted diminutive of EDWARD or (less often) THEODORE, in select use among English speakers from the mid-19th century. Theodore Roosevelt (Ted) Babbitt is the son of the central character, George F. Babbitt, in Sinclair Lewis's novel *Babbitt* (1922). The regular diminutive is TEDDY, which is in independent use.

US bandleader Ted Lewis (1889–1971) (original name Theodore Friedman); UK bandleader Ted Heath (1900–69); UK comedian, violinist Ted Ray (1905–77) (original name Charles Olden); UK playwright, politician Ted Willis (1918–92); UK poet Ted Hughes (1930–98); UK comedian Ted Rogers (1935–2001); UK cricketer Ted Dexter (b.1935); UK powerboat racer Ted Toleman (b.1938); US actor Ted Danson (b.1947).

Teddy An independently adopted diminutive of EDWARD, THEODORE or TED, in select English-speaking use from the 19th century. The name was essentially popularized by the US president Theodore Roosevelt (1858–1919), nicknamed 'Teddy' by the media of his day. (He was a noted bear hunter, and a comic poem about him, with cartoons, was published in the *New York Times* of 7 January 1906, inspiring the launch of a popular new toy, the 'teddy bear'. This was originally known as a 'Roosevelt bear', and the toy bears themselves were at first imported from Germany.) In literature Teddy is the small boy who owns the mongoose Rikki Tikki Tavi in Rudyard Kipling's short story 'Rikki Tikki Tavi' in *The Jungle Book* (1894), and in H.G. Wells's novel *Mr Britling Sees It Through* (1916), Teddy is a secretary to the central character, the art critic Hugh Britling. The spelling variant *Teddie* sometimes occurs.

UK tennis official, fashion designer Teddy Tinling (1910–90) (original first name Cuthbert); Scottish politician Teddy Taylor (b.1937); US soul singer Teddy Pendergrass (b.1950).

Teena see **Tina**.

Tel see **Terry**.

Terence This name is an English form of the Latin name *Terentius*, itself of uncertain origin, but perhaps associated in some way with *terere*, 'to rub', 'to wear out', 'to use up'. The name has been in regular use among English speakers from the late 19th century. Its popularity gradually increased to the 1950s, after which it just as gradually declined. It is historically familiar from the Roman playwright Terence (Publius Terentius Afer) of the 2nd century BC. The spellings *Terrance* and *Terrence* also occur, while the regular diminutive is TERRY, in independent use.

UK actor Terence de Marney (1909–71); UK playwright Terence Rattigan (1911–77); UK actor Terence Alexander (b.1923); UK art historian Terence Mullaly (b.1927); UK designer Sir Terence Conran (b.1931); UK actor Terence Stamp (b.1938); UK playwright Terence Brady (b.1939); US pop singer Terence Trent D'Arby (b.1962).

Teresa An independently adopted variant of THERESA, in origin the Spanish or Italian form of this name. It was taken up by English speakers, especially Roman Catholics, from the 16th century, and in recent times was in vogue in the 1950s and 1960s. The first famous bearer of the name was the Spanish religious, St Teresa of Avila (1515–82). In English literature the name is that of Teresa Alan, a character in E.M. Forster's novel *A Room with a View* (1908). The diminutives TERRY, TESS, TESSA and TRACY are all in independent use.

Albanian-born missionary Mother Teresa (1910–97) (original name Agnes Gonxha Bojaxhiu); US actress Teresa Wright (b.1918); US pop singer Teresa Brewer (b.1931); UK writer Teresa Crane (b.1938); US actress Teresa Graves (b.1944); UK opera singer Teresa Cahill (b.1944).

Teri, **Terri** see **Terry** (f.).

Terrance, **Terrence** see **Terence**.

Terry (m.) This name is either a borrowing of the surname or the independently adopted diminutive of TERENCE. It was taken up by English speakers in the 19th century, and has been in fairly regular use from the 1930s. The usual diminutive is *Tel*.

US boxer Terry McGovern (1880–1918) (original first names Joseph Terrance); UK actor Terry-Thomas (1911–90) (original name Thomas Terry Hoar-Stevens); UK trade unionist Terry Duffy (1922–85); UK actor Terry Scott (1927–94) (original first names Owen John); Irish-born UK TV presenter Terry Wogan (b.1938); UK religious negotiator, hostage Terry Waite (b.1939); US film animator, humorist Terry Gilliam (b.1940); UK theatrical director Terry Hands (b.1941); UK footballer Terry Venables (b.1943); UK writer Terry Pratchett (b.1948); UK footballer Terry Phelan (b.1967).

Terry (f.) The name arose either as an independently adopted diminutive of TERESA or THERESA or as a borrowing of the male name TERRY. It was first in vogue among English speakers in the late 1930s, and became particularly popular in the US. Variant spellings *Terri* and *Teri* exist, as respectively for the US country singer Terri Gibbs (b.1954) and US actress Teri Garr (b.1948).

US writer Terry Morris (b.1914); US actress Terry Moore (b.1929) (original name Helen Koford); UK children's TV producer Terry Marsh (b.1946) (original first name Thérèse); US pop-fiction writer Terry McMillan (b.1951).

Tess An independently adopted diminutive of THERESA or TESSA, in English-speaking use from the early 20th century. Its most famous literary bearer is the central character of Thomas Hardy's novel *Tess of the D'Urbervilles* (1891). Diminutives are usually as for TESSA.

UK artist Tess Jaray (b.1937); UK writer, journalist Tess Stimson (b.1966).

Tessa This name is probably an independently adopted diminutive of THERESA, although some authorities derive it from a different and possibly continental European source. It has been in select use among English speakers from the late 19th century. In literature, Tessa is the contadina (peasant girl) mistress of Tito Melema in George Eliot's novel *Romola* (1863), set in 15th-century Florence, and the same name occurs for the contadina who marries Giuseppe Palmieri in Gilbert and Sullivan's comic opera *The Gondoliers* (1889), set in Venice. Later, Tessa Sanger is the teenage title character of Margaret Kennedy's novel *The Constant Nymph* (1924). The diminutive TESS is in independent use. *Tessie* is also found, as for the UK comedienne Tessie O'Shea ('Two-ton Tessie') (1914–95).

UK interior designer Tessa Kennedy (b.1938); UK restaurateur Tessa Bramley (b.1939); UK actress Tessa Wyatt (b.1948); Jamaican-born UK athlete Tessa Sanderson (b.1956).

Tex A name that originated as a nickname for a person from Texas, perhaps under the influence of names such as TED, DEXTER, LEX and REX. In the English-speaking world its main adoption has been (understandably) in the US, where it was first popular in the early 20th century. It is commonly found for actors in westerns, country and western singers and the like.

US singer, actor Tex Ritter (1905–74) (original first name Woodward); US popular musician Tex Beneke (1914–2000) (original first name Gordon).

Thaddeus A biblical name, perhaps in origin a form of the Greek name *Theodōros* (English THEODORE). The name has found occasional favour among English speakers from the 19th century. In the Bible Thaddeus is one of the twelve apostles and is referred to as 'Lebbæus, whose surname was Thaddeus' (Matthew 10.3). The name is that of the central character in Jane Porter's historical novel *Thaddeus of Warsaw* (1803), in which Thaddeus is a young Polish nobleman. The variant spelling *Thadeus* occurs, with diminutives *Tad* and *Thad*, the latter as for the US popular composer Thad Jones (1923–86).

Thea This name is a diminutive form of DOROTHEA, taken up in its own right, and perhaps regarded by some as a female equivalent of the male name THEO. It has enjoyed select use among English speakers from the 1920s.

Australian writer Thea Astley (b.1925); UK clarinettist Thea King (b.1925); UK fashion designer Thea Porter (1927–2000); Scottish composer Thea Musgrave (b.1928).

Theda see **Theodora**.

Thelma A name of uncertain origin, but possibly evolving from the Greek word *thelēma*, 'will', 'wish'. It has been in select English-speaking use from the late 19th century, with a period of greatest popularity in the 1920s and 1930s. It is now much less common, although it still has some favour among black Americans. It was the original first name of the US actress Butterfly McQueen (1911–95). Its initial adoption may have been suggested by the central character, a Norwegian princess, of Marie Corelli's novel *Thelma* (1887).

UK politician, women's rights campaigner Thelma Cazalet-Keir (1899–1989); US actresses Thelma Ritter (1905–69), Thelma Todd (1905–35); UK writer on social welfare Thelma Wilson (b.1929); UK actress Thelma Holt (b.1933); Irish athlete Thelma Hopkins (b.1936); UK actress Thelma Barlow (b.1937); US film editor Thelma Schoonmaker (b.1940).

Theo (m.) This is an independently adopted diminutive of THEODORE or (less often) THEOBALD. It was first taken up in the English-speaking world in the late 19th century and has remained in very modest favour since, although with something of a rise in popularity in the 1990s. Theo Gilbright is a publisher in Elizabeth Taylor's novel *Angel* (1957).

Theo (f.) see **Theodora**, **Theodosia**.

Theobald This name is the English form of what is ultimately an Old German name, formed from *theud*, 'people', 'race' and *bald*, 'bold', 'brave', so 'brave man', with the first part of the name altered by association with Greek *theos*, 'god', found in other names such as THEODORE and THEOPHILUS. It has found some favour among English speakers from the 19th century. Theobald Pontifex is a character in Samuel Butler's novel *The Way of All Flesh* (1903). The usual diminutive, THEO, is in independent use.

Theodora The feminine form of THEODORE, in select use among English speakers from the 16th century, like its 'reversal', DOROTHEA. The name is familiar from Roman history as that of various empresses, such as Theodora, a beautiful actress of the 6th century, or the Theodora who was the wife of the Emperor Theophilus in the 9th century. Another Theodora was a Roman noblewoman of the 10th century. In English literature Theodora is an Italian patriot in Benjamin Disraeli's novel *Lothair* (1870). Diminutives include the now independently adopted DORA, as well as *Theda* and *Theo*, the former for the US actress Theda Bara (1890–1955) (original name Theodosia Goodman).

UK writer Theodora Benson (1906–68) (mother was Dorothea).

Theodore This is the English form of the Greek name *Theodōros*, formed from *theos*, 'god', and *dōron*, 'gift', so (in Christian terms) 'God's gift' (that is, of a child). It was first taken up on any scale by English speakers in the 17th century, but won wider favour in the US from the late 19th century. It was the name of various saints, but became familiar in modern times from the US president Theodore Roosevelt (1858–1919). The Rev. Theodore Sherlock is a curate in George Eliot's novel *Felix Holt* (1866), and Theodore Roosevelt (Ted) Babbitt is the son of the real-estate agent George F. Babbitt, the central character, in

Sinclair Lewis's novel *Babbitt* (1922). Regular diminutives are TED, TEDDY and THEO, all of which are in independent use.

US actor Theodore Roberts (1861–1928); US novelist Theodore Dreiser (1871–1945); US playwright Theodore Ward (1902–83); US actor Theodore Marcuse (1920–76).

Theodosia A Greek name, composed of *theos*, 'god', and *dōsis*, 'giving', so 'God's gift'. The name was adopted by English speakers in the 17th century, and although it became rather more widespread in the 18th and 19th centuries, is now rather rare. In William Makepeace Thackeray's novel *The Virginians* (1857–9), Theodosia (Theo) Lambert marries George Warrington. The chief diminutives are *Dosia* and *Theo*.

Theophilus A biblical name, in origin a Latin form of the Greek name *Theophilos*, formed from *theos*, 'god', and *philos*, 'friend', so (for Christians) 'one who loves God' or 'loved by God'. The name was adopted by English speakers in the 16th century, as for the English-born US colonist Theophilus Eaton (1590–1658), but it is now much less common. In the Bible Theophilus is the person, presumably a Christian, to whom St Luke's gospel and the Acts of the Apostles are addressed. In Anthony Trollope's novels *The Warden* (1855) and *Barchester Towers* (1857), among others, the Rev. Theophilus Grantly is the archdeacon son of the bishop of Barchester. The usual diminutive, THEO, is in independent use.

Theresa This is a name of uncertain origin. It may have evolved from Greek *tērēsis*, 'guarding', 'watching' (from *tēreō*, 'I take care of') or from *therizō*, 'I mow', 'I harvest' (from *theros*, 'summer', 'harvest'). It was generally adopted by English speakers in the 19th century but was historically familiar some time before this. It was first made widely known in Europe by Marie-Thérèse (1638–83), queen of France and a daughter of Philip of Spain, then by Maria Theresa (1717–80), archduchess of Austria and queen of Hungary and Bohemia. The main variant spelling is TERESA, in independent use, but the French form *Thérèse* is also sometimes found, with or without accents, as for the UK artist Therese Oulton (b.1953). Diminutives now adopted in their own right include TERRY, TESS and TESSA.

US actresses Theresa Harris (1910–85), Theresa Russell (b.1957).

Thom see **Tom**.

Thomas This is a biblical name, representing a Greek form of the Aramaic by-name *Tĕ'ōma*, 'twin'. It has been in regular use among English speakers from medieval times, and after undergoing a gradual decline from the early years of the 20th century, leapt back into favour in the 1990s. In the Bible Thomas is one of the twelve apostles, notorious for doubting the Resurrection until he had seen and touched the wounds of the risen Christ himself. He is referred to as 'Thomas, which is called Didymus' (John 11.16), the latter being the Greek word for 'twin' (from a root word *dis*, 'double'). Thomas Percy, Earl of Worcester, is a historical character in Shakespeare's *Henry IV* (1597), and Thomas is a servant to Sir Anthony Absolute in Richard Brinsley Sheridan's play *The Rivals* (1775). The name is famous in English history as that of the 12th-century archbishop of Canterbury, St Thomas à Becket, murdered for his opposition to the king's endeavours to control the clergy. In US history the name is familiar as that of two presidents, Thomas Jefferson (1743–1826) and Thomas Woodrow Wilson (1856–1924). Regular diminutives are TOM and TOMMY, both in independent use.

UK writer Thomas Hardy (1840–1928); UK opera singer Thomas Allen (b.1944); US-born UK opera singer Thomas Randle (b.1958).

Thomasin A feminine form of THOMAS, in select English-speaking use from the 19th century. The name is found in literature for Thomasin Yeobright, who marries Diggory Venn in Thomas Hardy's novel *The Return of the Native* (1878).

Variants include *Thomasa* and *Thomasina*, while TAMSIN is an independently adopted shortened form of the name.

Thora This is the English form of a Scandinavian name that ultimately derives from *Thor*, the Norse god of thunder. It has been very occasionally adopted among English speakers in the 20th century.

UK actress Thora Hird (b.1913); US actress Thora Birch (b.1982).

Thurston From the surname, and in occasional use among English speakers from the 19th century.

US actor Thurston Hall (1883–1958); UK harpsichordist Thurston Dart (1921–71) (originally second name, first being Robert).

Tiffany This name is an English form of the Greek name *Theophania*, 'Epiphany', given to girls born on this religious festival (6 January). It was taken up by English speakers in the 1960s and has become particularly favoured by black Americans. The name was undoubtedly popularized by the film *Breakfast at Tiffany's* (1961), with Audrey Hepburn in the role of the central character, Holly Golightly. Diminutives *Tiff*, *Tiffie* and *Tiffy* exist.

US actress Tiffany Bolling (b.1947); US pop singer Tiffany (b.1971) (original name Tiffany Darwisch); UK actress Tiffany Chapman (b.1979).

Tilda see **Matilda**.

Tilly This name, an independently adopted diminutive of MATILDA, was taken up generally in the English-speaking world in the 19th century, although occasionally found earlier. It is now rather rare. Henry Handel Richardson's trilogy *The Fortunes of Richard Mahoney* (1917–29) has a landlady's daughter named Tilly Beamish, and the name also occurs in Ian Hay's play *Tilly of Bloomsbury* (1919). The variant spelling *Tillie* exists, as for the US feminist writer Tillie Olsen (b.1913).

Austrian-born UK singer, dancer Tilly Losch (1907–75) (original first name Ottilie); UK actress Tilly Vosburgh (b.1960).

Tim An independently adopted diminutive of TIMOTHY, in select but regular use among English speakers from the mid-19th century. In literature the name is familiar as that of Tiny Tim, the crippled son of Scrooge's clerk Bob Cratchit in Charles Dickens's tale *A Christmas Carol* (1843). A frequent diminutive is *Timmy*, but this tends to be associated more with young boys than grown men.

US actor Tim Holt (1919–73) (original name Charles John Holt III); US popular singer, entertainer Tiny Tim (1930–96) (original name Herbert Khaury); UK politician Tim Renton (b.1932); UK actor Tim Brooke-Taylor (b.1940); UK writer, lyricist Sir Tim Rice (b.1944); UK actors Tim Pigott-Smith (b.1946), Tim Healy (b.1952), Tim Woodward (b.1953).

Timon A name of Greek origin, from *timē*, 'honour', in occasional favour among English speakers in modern times, and perhaps regarded as an 'upper-class' alternative to TIMOTHY. It was borne by the Greek poet and philosopher Timon (320–230BC), who is the subject of Shakespeare's *Timon of Athens* (c.1607).

UK financial journalist Timon Day (b.1951).

Timothy This is a biblical name, representing the English form of the Greek name *Timotheos*, composed of *timē*, 'honour', and *theos*, 'god', so 'honoured by God' or 'honouring God'. It has been in fairly regular use among English speakers from the 18th century, with its greatest recent period of popularity from the 1950s to the 1970s, since when it has slightly fallen from favour. In the Bible Timothy is the companion of St Paul to whom the latter addresses two epistles. In Tobias Smollett's novel *The Life and Adventures of Sir Launcelot Greaves* (1762) Timothy Crabshaw is the squire to the central character, while Timothy Forsyte is a publisher member of the family in John

Galsworthy's *Forsyte* cycle (1906–22). The regular diminutive is TIM, in independent use.

UK actor Timothy West (b.1934); US actor Timothy Bottoms (b.1949); UK actors Timothy Bentinck (b.1953), Timothy Spall (b.1957); US actor Timothy Busfield (b.1957).

Tina This is an independent adoption of the final *-tina* that forms a diminutive of a name such as CHRISTINA, CLEMENTINA or MARTINA. It has been in general English-speaking use from the 19th century, and rose to its peak period of popularity in the 1960s and 1970s, since when it has declined considerably. In literature, it occurs for Caterina (Tina) Sastri, an Italian singer's daughter in George Eliot's tales *Scenes of Clerical Life* (1858). It was popularized to some extent by the UK stage show *Tina* (1915) and the UK popular musical number 'Tina' (1934). The spelling *Teena* also exists, as for the US pop singer Teena Marie (b.1956) (original name Mary Christine Brockert).

US actress Tina Louise (b.1934); US playwright Tina Howe (b.1937); US pop singer Tina Turner (b.1939) (original name Annie Mae Bullock); US film director Tina Rathborne (b.1951); UK magazine editor Tina Brown (b.1953) (original first name Christina).

Tiny A borrowing of the ordinary word or the nickname, given either to a small (or very tall) person, or as a result of some incident. The name has found some favour among English speakers from the early 20th century.

US actor Tiny Sandford (1894–1961) (original first name Stanley); US jazzman Tiny Bradshaw (1905–58) (original first name Myron); UK businessman Tiny Rowland (1917–98) (original name Roland Fuhrhop); US popular musician Tiny Tim (1930–96) (original name Herbert Khaury).

Tish, **Tisha**, **Titia** see **Letitia**.

Titty An independently adopted diminutive of LETITIA, in select English-speaking use from the 19th century, although

now avoided through the colloquial sense of *titty* to mean
'breast'. The name occurs in children's literature for Titty, a
member of the Walker family in Arthur Ransome's novel *Swal-
lows and Amazons* (1930) and sequels. She was based on a real
girl with this name (Titty Altounyan).

Titus A biblical name of uncertain origin, but perhaps from
Latin *titulus*, 'title of honour'. It was taken up by English speakers in the 18th century but by the turn of the 20th century
was not in wide favour anywhere. In the Bible Titus is the companion of St Paul to whom the latter addresses an epistle. The
name is notorious in English history from the Catholic conspirator Titus Oates (1649–1705), who plotted to kill Charles II,
burn London and massacre the Protestants. In Shakespeare
the name is familiar from the central character of his grue-
some tragedy *Titus Andronicus* (1590–94). (The character is not
historical, and has no counterpart in Roman history.) Bernard
Shaw's play *The Devil's Disciple* (1896–7) has a character Titus
Dudgeon, and the name is that of the central character, the
Earl of Groan, in Mervyn Peake's Gothic fantasy trilogy *Titus
Groan* (1946), *Gormenghast* (1950) and *Titus Alone* (1959).

Tobias A biblical name, from Hebrew *Tōbhīyāh*, 'Yah [that
is, Jehovah] is good', in irregular use among English speakers
from the 16th century, and well known from the Scottish novelist Tobias Smollett (1721–71), although now much less prominent. The best-known biblical Tobias is the son of Tobit, in
the Apocrypha, where the story is told of 'Tobias and the
Angel'. (Tobias, a rich Jew, gains the services of the archangel
Raphael to cure his father's blindness.) The Rev. Tobias Tickler
marries Olivia Proudie, daughter of the bishop of Barchester, in
Anthony Trollope's novel *Framley Parsonage* (1861). The regular diminutive, TOBY, is in independent use.

Toby A name that is an independently adopted diminutive
(or variant) of TOBIAS, in regular use among English speakers

from the 19th century, with a slight rise in popularity in the 1980s and 1990s. The name is famous in literature from Sir Toby Belch, the roistering uncle of Olivia in Shakespeare's *Twelfth Night* (1601), as well as from the old soldier Uncle Toby, effectively the main character in Laurence Sterne's novel *Tristram Shandy* (1759–67). In more recent fiction Toby Crackit is a partner of Fagin in Charles Dickens's novel *Oliver Twist* (1837–8), while Toby Tyler is the central character, an orphan who runs away to join a circus, in James Otis Kaler's US children's classic *Toby Tyler* (1881). The name has long been familiar from the dog Toby in the traditional Punch and Judy puppet performances, while the 'toby jug', a beer mug or jug in the shape of a man wearing a three-cornered hat and smoking a pipe, is said to take its name from an 18th-century poem about one 'Toby Philpot'.

UK theatrical director Toby Robertson (b.1928); UK politician Toby Jessel (b.1934); UK actor Toby Cockerell (b.1976).

Todd From the surname, and in select use among English speakers from the late 19th century, with a slight rise in popularity from the 1980s. The variant spelling *Tod* is also found, especially in the US, as for the US actor Tod Andrews (1920–72). The diminutive is usually *Toddy*.

US actors Todd Duncan (1903–98), Todd Armstrong (1939–93); US film director Todd Haynes (b.1961); UK athlete Todd Bennett (b.1962); Irish-born UK actor Todd Carty (b.1963).

Tom An independently adopted diminutive of THOMAS, in regular use among English speakers from the 18th century, gaining its greatest popularity in the late 19th century and showing signs of a revival in the late 20th century. The name is found in literature for several central characters, including the foundling in Henry Fielding's novel *Tom Jones* (1749), the Negro slave in Harriet Beecher Stowe's novel *Uncle Tom's Cabin* (1852) and the small boy in Mark Twain's novel *The Adven-*

tures of Tom Sawyer (1876). The last-named's English counterpart (but hardly equivalent) is the central character of Thomas Hughes's novel *Tom Brown's Schooldays* (1857). The alternative spelling *Thom* is sometimes found, as for the UK-born poet Thom Gunn (b.1929) and the UK fashion writer and broadcaster Thom O'Dwyer (b.1954). The regular diminutive is TOMMY, in independent use.

US actor Tom Mix (1880–1940); UK actor Tom Walls (1883–1949); US pianist, satirist Tom Lehrer (b.1928); UK writer Tom Sharpe (b.1928); UK actors Tom Bell (b.1932), Tom Baker (b.1935), Tom Courtenay (b.1937); UK TV presenter Tom O'Connor (b.1939); Welsh pop singer Tom Jones (b.1940); UK actor Tom Conti (b.1941); US actor Tom Selleck (b.1945); US writer Tom Clancy (b.1947); US golfer Tom Watson (b.1949); US actors Tom Hanks (b.1956), Tom Cruise (b.1962).

Tommy An independently adopted diminutive of THOMAS or TOM, in general English-speaking use from the 1870s, with an upturn in popularity from the 1980s. Tommy Sandys is the central character of Compton Mackenzie's novels *Sentimental Tommy* (1896) and *Tommy and Grizel* (1900). More recently, the name has been popularized by the rock opera *Tommy* (1970). The name is commonly found for comedians, entertainers, sportsmen and the like. The spelling *Tommie* sometimes occurs.

UK radio comedian Tommy Handley (1894–1949); US bandleader Tommy Dorsey (1905–56); UK comedian Tommy Trinder (1909–89); UK footballer Tommy Lawton (1919–96); UK comedian Tommy Cooper (1922–84); UK singer, entertainer Tommy Steele (b.1936); US popular singer Tommy Sands (b.1937); UK cyclist Tommy Simpson (1937–67); UK comedian Tommy Cannon (b.1938); UK radio and TV presenter Tommy Boyd (b.1952).

Toni This name, either an independently adopted diminutive of ANTONIA or a feminine equivalent of TONY, has been in select English-speaking use from the 1930s, mostly in the US, where the suggestion of *tony* (in the sense 'fashionable') may have helped. The spelling *Tony* is sometimes found.

US novelist Toni Morrison (b.1931) (original first names Chloe Anthony); Danish ballerina Toni Lander (1931–85); UK actress Toni Palmer (b.1932); US writer Toni Cade Bambara (b.1939); UK actress Toni Arthur (b.1941); US pop singer Toni Tennille (b.1943); US pop singer Toni Basil (b.1940s); US R&B singer Toni Braxton (b.1968).

Tonia see **Antonia**.

Tony An independently adopted diminutive of ANTHONY or ANTONY, in regular English-speaking use from the early 20th century, and never really out of fashion, but with a brief rise in popularity in the second half of the 1960s. The name is well known in literature from Tony Lumpkin, the loutish country squire in Oliver Goldsmith's comedy *She Stoops to Conquer* (1773), while Tony Jobling is a character in Charles Dickens's novel *Bleak House* (1852–3). The name is particularly common for media and sports personalities, a mere handful of whom are represented below. The diminutive form *Tone* sometimes occurs.

US actors Tony Martin (b.1912) (original name Alfred Norris), Tony Randall (b.1920) (original name Leonard Rosenberg); UK comedian Tony Hancock (1924–68); US actor Tony Curtis (b.1925) (original name Bernard Schwarz); UK actor Tony Britton (b.1925); UK politician Tony Benn (b.1925); US popular singer Tony Bennett (b.1926) (original name Antonio Benedetto); UK actor Tony Beckley (1928–80); UK poet, playwright Tony Harrison (b.1937); UK actors Tony Selby (b.1938), Tony Anholt (b.1941); UK radio presenter Tony Blackburn (b.1943); UK golfer Tony Jacklin (b.1944); Irish-born UK actor Tony Scannell (b.1945); UK actors Tony Haygarth (b.1945), Tony Robinson (b.1946); UK prime minister Tony Blair (b.1953); UK TV presenter Tony Slattery (b.1959); UK actor Tony Pitts (b.1962); UK rugby player Tony Underwood (b.1969).

Tonya see **Antonia**.

Topsy A name, said to derive from *topsail*, that has found irregular favour among English speakers since the 19th century but that has mostly attracted black Americans. It is famous in literature from Topsy, the little black orphan slave girl in Harriet Beecher Stowe's novel *Uncle Tom's Cabin* (1852). Slaves were said to be named for the sails on ships which brought them to America: hence *topsail*. Among whites the name may have evolved as a variant of a similar-sounding name, such as *Totty* (a diminutive of CHARLOTTE or DOROTHY). *Topsey* and *Topsie* are variant spellings.

Tottie, Totty see **Charlotte**.

Tracey (f.) An independently adopted variant of TRACY, taken up by English in the 1950s, soon after the adoption of its source name, and even outstripping it in popularity in the latter half of the 1960s. It has since sunk to a much more modest level. Variant spellings and diminutives are as for TRACY itself.

UK actress Tracey Ullman (b.1959); UK TV presenter Tracey MacLeod (b.1960); Australian swimmer Tracey Wickham (b.1962); UK actress Tracey Childs (b.1963); UK artist Tracey Emin (b.1963).

Tracy (m.) From the surname, and in select but declining use in the English-speaking world from the 19th century. Tracy Tupman is a member of the Pickwick Club in Charles Dickens's novel *Pickwick Papers* (1836–7).

UK soldier, traveller, diplomat Tracy Philipps (1890–1959); US country musician Tracy Schwartz (b.1938); US screenwriter Tracy Keenan Wynn (b.1945).

Tracy (f.) This name is either a borrowing of the male name TRACY or an independently adopted diminutive of THERESA. It was first widely adopted by English speakers in the 1950s and suddenly became very popular in the second half of the 1960s, since when it has gradually faded from favour. It seems to have gained its initial impetus from the young heiress Tracy

Lord in Philip Barry's novel *The Philadelphia Story* (1939), and from the subsequent film (1940) based on it. It was the remake of this film, however, under the title *High Society* (1956), that really sent the name soaring. The heiress, now named Tracy Samantha Lord, was played by the very popular Grace Kelly. (See also SAMANTHA.) Tracy Granger (b.1955), daughter of the UK-born US actress Jean Simmons by her first husband, Stewart Granger, was named for the US actor Spencer Tracy, and he and his name may well have inspired other namers similarly. The variant spelling TRACEY is in independent use. *Tracie* and *Traci* also exist, the former as for the UK actress Tracie Bennett (b.1961) (original first name Tracey). A frequent diminutive is *Trace*.

US country singer Tracy Nelson (b.1944); UK actresses Tracy-Louise Ward (b.1958), Tracy Brabin (b.1961); US tennis player Tracy Austin (b.1962); UK fashion designer Tracy Mulligan (b.1962); UK yachtswoman Tracy Edwards (b.1962); US swimmer Tracy Caulkins (b.1963); US actress Tracy Nelson (b.1963); US rock singer Tracy Chapman (b.1964).

Trevor From the (Welsh) surname, and in gradually increasing adoption among English speakers from the mid-19th century. The name rose to a modest level of popularity in the 1950s, but then gradually fell from favour. The usual diminutive is *Trev*.

US actor Trevor Bardette (1902–78); UK actor Trevor Howard (1916–88); Trinidad-born UK TV newsreader Trevor McDonald (b.1939); UK theatrical producer Trevor Nunn (b.1940); UK journalist Trevor Fishlock (b.1941); UK actor Trevor Eve (b.1951); UK footballers Trevor Francis (b.1954), Trevor Steven (b.1963).

Tricia, Trish, Trisha see **Patricia**.

Tristan A French variant form of TRISTRAM, found in parallel with the other name in medieval literature, and in English-speaking use generally from the 1950s. Its own variant is *Tristam*, as for the UK popular composer Tristam Cary (b.1925).

UK film, TV director Tristan de Vere Cole (b.1935); UK politician Tristan Garel-Jones (b.1941).

Tristram This is a name of uncertain Celtic derivation. It may have evolved from the Pictish Druid name *Drustan*, itself perhaps related to *Druid*, although it has long been popularly associated with Latin *tristis*, 'sad', mainly through the tragic legend of Tristram and Isolde. It has enjoyed modest favour among English speakers from the 19th century. In more recent literature the name is famous as that of the title character of Laurence Sterne's novel *Tristram Shandy* (1759–67) (in which the name is whimsically derived from Latin *Trismegistus*, 'thrice great'). The legendary Tristram also appears in Tennyson's poem 'The Last Tournament' (1859) in *Idylls of the King*, as well as in Algernon Charles Swinburne's poem *Tristram of Lyonesse* (1882). The variant TRISTAN is found in independent use. The diminutive *Tris* occasionally occurs, as for the US baseball player Tris Speaker (1888–1958).

UK painter Tristram Hillier (1905–83); US actor Tristram Coffin (1912–90).

Trixie This is an independently adopted diminutive of BEATRICE or BEATRIX, in select English-speaking use from the 19th century but rare today. The variant spelling *Trixi* also exists.

US actress, singer Trixie Friganza (1870–1955) (original name Delia O'Callahan); US blues singer Trixie Smith (1895–1943).

Troy This is probably a borrowing of the surname, but has been popularly associated with the ancient city of *Troy*. The name has found some favour among English speakers from the 18th century.

UK screenwriter Troy Kennedy Martin (b.1932); US actor Troy Donahue (1936–2001) (original name Merle Johnson); US country singer Troy Seals (b.1938).

Trudy An independently adopted diminutive of GERTRUDE or (less often) ERMINTRUDE, taken up by English speakers from the 1930s but now rather less common. Variant spellings include *Trudi* and *Trudie*, the latter as for the UK actress Trudie Styler (b.1957).

US actress Trudy Marshall (b.1922).

Tudor From the surname, an English form of the Welsh name *Tudur*, itself from an Old Celtic name *Teutorix*, formed from elements meaning respectively 'people', 'tribe' and 'ruler', 'king', so 'people's ruler'. The name has become popularly associated with THEODORE, but that is a different name, of Greek origin. In English history the name is familiar as that of the royal house that reigned from Henry VII to Elizabeth I (1485 to 1603).

Welsh opera singer Tudor Davies (1892–1958); Welsh politician Tudor Watkins (1903–89).

U

Ulysses This name is the Latin form, much altered, of the Greek name *Odysseus*, perhaps related to *odussesthai*, 'to hate'. It is not clear how this particular change came about, although an Etruscan influence has been suggested. The alteration of *d* to *l* is unusual. It has found some favour among English speakers from the 19th century, mainly black Americans. The name is famous from the Greek hero of Troy, the subject of Homer's *Odyssey*, who was noted for his courage and inventiveness. He has appeared in many later literary works, from Shakespeare's *Troilus and Cressida* (1602) to James Joyce's novel *Ulysses* (1922), in which the central character, Leopold Bloom, makes a metaphorical 'Odyssey'.

US president Ulysses S. Grant (1822–85) (original first names Hiram Ulysses); US composer Ulysses Kay (1917–95).

Una This is an Irish name (properly *Úna*), perhaps deriving from *uan*, 'lamb', but also popularly associated with Latin *una*, 'one', and so equated with UNITY. It has been in select use among English speakers from the mid-19th century. In literature Una personifies the singleness of religion in Edmund Spenser's poem *The Faerie Queene* (1590, 1596) (contrasted with the duplicity represented by Duessa). In Rudyard Kipling's novels *Puck of Pook's Hill* (1906) and *Rewards and Fairies* (1910), Una is a central character, together with her brother, Dan. OONA is a related name.

Irish actress Una O'Connor (1880–1959); US literary critic Una Ellis-Fermor (1894–1958); US actress Una Merkel (1903–86); US popular singer, songwriter Una Mae Carlisle (1918–56); UK religious writer, broadcaster Una Kroll (b.1925); UK actress Una Stubbs (b.1937).

Unice see **Eunice.**

Unity An adoption of the standard word, regarded as a sort of virtue. The name was taken up by the Puritans from the 17th century but was never very common among English speakers generally. It occurs in literature for Unity, the servant who marries Martin Cannister in Thomas Hardy's novel *A Pair of Blue Eyes* (1873).

UK socialite Unity Mitford (1914–48).

Urban A biblical name, in origin the English form of the Latin name *Urbanus*, 'from the city', 'urban'. The name has found very occasional favour among English speakers from the 19th century. In the Bible Urban is a Christian who is an active member of the church at Rome. The name was borne by various early popes, doubtless with reference to the city of Rome, which the Latin word *urbs*, 'city', often specifically implied without any direct mention.

Uriah A biblical name, from Hebrew *Ūrīyāh*, 'Yah [that is, Jehovah] is light' (compare URIEL). The name found some favour among English speakers in the early 19th century but is very rare today. In the Bible Uriah is the first husband of Bathsheba, who was seduced by King David while her husband was at war. In literature the name is usually associated with Uriah Heep, the hypocritical and obsequious clerk in Charles Dickens's novel *David Copperfield* (1849–50).

Uriel A biblical name, from Hebrew *Ūrī'ēl*, 'God is light' (compare URIAH). The name has never been anything like common among English speakers but has been taken up in some Jewish families. In the Bible Uriel is the name of two characters merely mentioned in genealogies, but in the Apocrypha it is that of one of the seven archangels sent to Esdras. In both John Milton's epic poem *Paradise Lost* (1667) and Henry Wadsworth Longfellow's dramatic poem *The Golden Legend* (1851) Uriel is an angel of light.

Ursula This is an adoption of the Latin name, itself a diminutive of *ursa*, 'she-bear'. It was taken up fairly widely by English speakers in the 17th century, although it is now in much more modest use. The name's first famous bearer was the 4th-century St Ursula, popularly associated (through a misreading of a Latin text) with 'eleven thousand martyrs'. In Shakespeare Ursula is an attendant of Silvia in *Two Gentlemen of Verona* (1592–3) and of Hero in *Much Ado About Nothing* (1598–9). In Ben Jonson's comedy *Bartholomew Fair* (1614) Ursula is a pig-woman. Dame Ursula Suddlechop is the wife of the barber Benjamin Suddlechop in Walter Scott's novel *The Fortunes of Nigel* (1822). In Henry Wadsworth Longfellow's poem *The Golden Legend* (1851), Ursula is the mother of the central character, Elsie. More recently, Ursula Brangwen is one of two sisters (the other is Gudrun) in D.H. Lawrence's novels *The Rainbow* (1915) and *Women in Love* (1921). Diminutives *Urse* and *Ursie* exist.

UK romantic novelist Ursula Bloom (1892–1984); UK actress Ursula Jeans (1906–73); UK children's writer Ursula Moray Williams (b.1911); UK writer Ursula Torday (b.*c*.1920); UK actress Ursula Howells (b.1922); US science-fiction writer Ursula Le Guin (b.1929); Swiss-born US actress Ursula Andress (b.1936)

V

Val An independently adopted diminutive of VALENTINE, in select use among English speakers from the early 20th century.

UK radio producer Val Gielgud (1900–81); Hungarian-born UK children's writer, illustrator Val Biro (b.1921); Irish popular singer Val Doonican (b.1928); US actor Val Kilmer (b.1959).

Valentine This is the English form of the Latin name *Valentinus*, itself from *valens*, genitive *valentis*, 'healthy', 'strong', in select but regular use among English speakers from the 16th century. The name's best-known bearer is the 3rd-century martyr St Valentine. His feast day (14 February) coincided with the pagan fertility festival that is the source of the modern Valentine's Day. Two characters of the name appear in Shakespeare: as one of the 'two gentlemen' (the other is Proteus) in *Two Gentlemen of Verona* (1592–3) and as a gentleman attending Orsino, Duke of Illyria, in *Twelfth Night* (1601). Valentine Legend is the central character in William Congreve's comedy *Love for Love* (1695), and in J.M. Barrie's play *Quality Street* (1902) Valentine Brown marries Phoebe Throssel. The diminutive VAL is in independent use.

UK actors Valentine Dyall (1908–85), Valentine Palmer (b.1939).

Valeria This is the feminine form of the Roman clan name *Valerius*, itself probably based on *valere*, 'to be healthy', 'to be strong'. The name was taken up by English speakers in the 17th century, but from the late 19th it has been superseded by the French form VALERIE. In Shakespeare's *Coriolanus* (c.1608) Valeria is a friend of Virginia.

Italian actress Valeria Golino (b.1966).

Valerie The name, a French form of VALERIA, has been in English-speaking use from the late 19th century, and gained considerable popularity in the period from the 1930s to the 1950s, after which it noticeably declined. The variant spelling *Valery* is sometimes found, and the usual diminutive is *Val*, as for the UK hockey player Val Hallam (b.1960).

UK actresses Valerie Taylor (1902–88), Valerie White (1916–75), Valerie Hobson (1917–98); US ballerina, choreographer Valerie Bettis (1919–82); UK actress Valerie French (1931–90); UK TV presenter Valerie Singleton (b.1937); UK opera singer Valerie Masterson (b.1937); US actresses Valerie Harper (b.1940), Valerie Perrine (b.1944); UK columnist Valerie Grove (b.1946).

Van This name is either an independently adopted diminutive of EVAN, IVAN or VANCE, or an adoption of the surname *Van* or even the element *van* ('of') in a typical Dutch surname. It has been in select use among English speakers from the early 20th century, mainly in the US.

US actors Van Heflin (1910–71) (original first names Emmett Evan), Van Johnson (b.1916); US pop musician Van McCoy (1944–79); Northern Ireland pop musician Van Morrison (b.1945) (original first names George Ivan).

Vance From the surname, and in occasional English-speaking use from the 19th century.

Australian writer Vance Palmer (1885–1959); US actor Vance Colvig (1892–1967); US writers Vance Packard (1914–96), Vance Bourjaily (b.1922).

Vanessa This name was devised by Jonathan Swift in the 18th century from that of his close friend Esther Vanhomrigh, based on the first part of her surname (*Van-*) and the first part of her Christian name (*Es-*). (The name does not thus mean 'butterfly', as maintained by some, who refer to the scientific name, *Vanessa*, of the red admiral genus. This predates the personal name and probably derives from the name of the Greek goddess *Phānēs*.) The name was popularly taken up in the English-speaking world in the 1920s and has had special 'highs' in the 1950s, 1970s and 1990s. In Swift's poem *Cadenus and Vanessa* (1726), written for Vanhomrigh, the name is that of one of two main characters, the other being Swift himself. (*Cadenus* is an anagram of Latin *decanus*, 'dean', his ecclesiastical title as Dean of St Patrick's, Dublin. Swift had earlier had a close relationship with another Esther; see STELLA.) A later literary bearer of the name is Vanessa Paris, daughter of Judith Paris in Hugh Walpole's historical novels *Judith Paris* (1931), *The Fortress* (1932) and *Vanessa* (1933). The variant spelling *Venessa* is sometimes found, and diminutives include *Nessa*, NESSIE (in independent use) and *Vanny*. The name has something of an aristocratic aura.

UK painter Vanessa Bell (1879–1961); UK singer, actress Vanessa Lee (1921–92); US actress Vanessa Brown (1928–99) (original name Smylla Brind); UK actress Vanessa Redgrave (b.1937); UK daughter of Earl of Yarborough, Lady Vanessa Brown (b.1961); UK TV presenter Vanessa Feltz (b.1962).

Vaughan From the (Welsh) surname and in select but fairly regular use in the English-speaking world from the late 19th century. The variant spelling *Vaughn* also occurs, as for the US bandleader Vaughn Monroe (1911–73).

UK composer Ralph Vaughan Williams (1872–1958).

Venetia The name was perhaps adopted from the Latin name of Venice, in the way that FLORENCE can commemorate the historic Italian city. (Compare also VERONA.) It has been in select use among English speakers from the 19th century, although never common. An early bearer of the name was the noted English beauty Venetia Stanley (1600–33). The name is found in literature for Venetia Herbert, the central character of Benjamin Disraeli's novel *Venetia* (1837). The namer of the planet Pluto on its discovery in 1930 was an eleven-year-old Oxford schoolgirl, Venetia Burney.

UK folklorist Venetia Newall (b.1935).

Vera This is properly a name of Russian origin, meaning 'faith', but it happens to coincide with the Latin word *vera*, the feminine form of *verus*, 'true'. (Russian equivalents of the triple virtues FAITH, HOPE and CHARITY are *Vera*, *Nadezhda* and *Lyubov*. For the second of these see NATASHA.) The name has been in regular use among English speakers from the 1870s, with its peak period of popularity in the 1920s. It is now much less common. The name is familiar in literature from the central character of Elizabeth Von Arnim's novel *Vera* (1921).

UK writer, feminist Vera Brittain (1893–1970); US crime novelist Vera Caspary (1899–1987); US fashion designer Vera Maxwell (1901–95); US actress Vera Vague (1905–74) (original name Barbara Jo Allen); UK popular singer Dame Vera Lynn (b.1917); Norwegian-born US ballerina, actress Vera Zorina (b.1917) (original name Eva Brigitta Hartwig); US dancer, singer Vera-Ellen (1920–81) (original name Vera-Ellen Westmeyr Rohe); US actress Vera Miles (b.1929).

Verena A name that is perhaps a form of VERA, interpreted as 'true' rather than 'faith'. It has been found in occasional use among English speakers from the 19th century. Its earliest famous bearer was the 3rd-century Swiss saint Verena, said to have come from Egypt. In Henry James's novel *The Bostonians* (1886) Verena Tarrant is the beautiful young woman loved by both Olive Chancellor and Basil Ransom.

Vergil An independently adopted variant of VIRGIL, in select use among English speakers from the 19th century, chiefly in the US. In Sinclair Lewis's novel *Babbitt* (1922) Vergil Gunch is a coal dealer.

Verity An adoption of the standard word, treated as a near-virtue (truth), and itself suggesting a variant of VERA. The name was taken up by 17th-century Puritans and has been in modest favour since, with a small rise in popularity in the 1980s.

UK film, TV producer Verity Lambert (b.1935).

Verna This name comes either from Latin *verna*, 'spring' (compare SPRING) or arose as a classical-style feminine equivalent of VERNON. It was in select English-speaking use from the 1880s to the 1960s, after which it fell from such favour as it had.

US actress Verna Felton (1890–1966); US children's writer Verna Norberg Aardema (1911–2000); US actress Verna Bloom (b.1939).

Vernon From the (aristocratic) surname, taken up by English speakers from the early 19th century and enjoying a period of popularity in the 1920s, as well as more general favour among black Americans. The name is famously associated with the English admiral Sir Edward Vernon (1684–1757). In literature Vernon Whitford is a poor, earnest student in George Meredith's novel *The Egoist* (1879). The diminutive *Vern* occurs.

US country musician Vernon Dalhart (1883–1948) (original name Marion Slaughter); UK-born US dancer Vernon Castle (1887–1918); Russian-born US songwriter Vernon Duke (1903–69) (original name Vladimir Dukelsky); UK bassoonist Vernon Elliott (b.1912); UK poet Vernon Scannell (b.1922); US country musician Vernon Oxford (b.1941).

Verona This name appears to be either a shortened form of VERONICA or a commemoration of the town in Italy (compare FLORENCE and VENETIA). It has enjoyed occasional favour among English speakers from the mid-19th century. It occurs in literature for Verona Babbitt, daughter of the central character, George F. Babbitt, in Sinclair Lewis's novel *Babbitt* (1922).

Veronica This is a Latin adaptation of *Berenice* (an earlier form of BERNICE), influenced by the macaronic phrase *vera icon*, 'true image' (of which it is an anagram), referring to the legend telling how St Veronica wiped Christ's face with a cloth on the road to Calvary and found an image of it imprinted afterwards. In modern times it is sometimes linked with the plant name or regarded as a variant (or diminutive) of VERONA.

It has been in general use among English speakers from the mid-19th century, and was quite fashionable from the 1920s to the 1950s, since when it has faded. The central character of H.G. Wells's feminist novel *Ann Veronica* (1909) has the full name Ann Veronica Stanley. The French form of the name, *Véronique*, is sometimes found. Diminutives include NICKY (in independent use, though usually from NICOLA) and *Ronnie*.

UK historian Dame Veronica Wedgwood (1910–97); US actress Veronica Lake (1919–73) (original name Constance Ockleman); UK actress Veronica Hurst (b.1931); US actress Veronica Hamel (b.1943); UK actress Veronica Carlson (b.1944); UK-born US actress Veronica Cartwright (b.1949); UK journalist Veronica Wadley (b.1952).

Vesta An adoption of the Latin name of the Roman goddess of the hearth and of fire, itself from Greek *hestia*, 'hearth' (the shrine of household gods). The name has found occasional favour among English speakers from the mid-19th century. In Theodore Dreiser's novel *Jennie Gerhardt* (1911), Vesta Gerhardt is the daughter of the central character.

UK music-hall artistes Vesta Tilley (1864–1952) (original name Matilda Alice Powles), Vesta Victoria (1873–1951) (original name Victoria Lawrence).

Vic An independently adopted diminutive of VICTOR, in select use among English speakers from the early 20th century. The spelling *Vick* is also found, and a frequent diminutive is *Vicky*.

Austrian-born UK comedian, musician Vic Oliver (1898–1964); US restaurateur Trader Vic (1903–84) (original name Victor Jules Bergeron); UK trade unionist Vic Feather (1908–76); US tennis player Vic Seixas (b.1923); US actor Vic Morrow (1932–82).

Vicki An independently adopted diminutive of VICTORIA, taken up in the English-speaking world from the 1930s. Variant forms of the name include VICKY, in independent use, *Vickie* and *Vikki*, this last as for the US popular singer Vikki

Carr (b.1942) (original name Florencia Bisenta de Casillas Martinez Cardona).

Austrian-born US writer Vicki Baum (1896–1960); UK actress Vicki Woolf (b.1945); UK model, socialite Vicki Hodge (b.1946).

Vicky An independently adopted diminutive of VICTORIA, taken up by English speakers from the 1950s and gradually increasing in favour until the 1990s, when the name tailed off somewhat. A variant spelling *Vickey* exists, as for the UK hockey player Vickey Dixon (b.1959). Other variants are as for VICKI, whose adoption predates it by about twenty years.

Victor This name is a direct adoption of the Late Latin name *Victor*, 'victor', 'conqueror' (compare VINCENT), first generally taken up by English speakers in the mid-19th century. The name enjoyed continuing popularity in the US until the 1950s, but fell from favour rather earlier in the UK, and so is now rarely found in either land. It was the name of various early saints, for whom it symbolized Christ's victory over death. The name was brought before the public to some extent by the French novelist Victor Hugo (1802–85), whose works were widely read in English translation. The diminutive VIC exists in its own right. *Vicky* is also found.

UK actor Victor McLaglen (1883–1959); Canadian actor Victor Jory (1902–82); Danish-born pianist, comedian Victor Borge (1909–2000); US actor Victor Mature (1915–99); UK actors Victor Maddern (1926–93), Victor Winding (b.1929).

Victoria This is the feminine form of the Latin name *Victorius*, strongly influenced by Latin *victoria*, 'victory', and now usually regarded as the female equivalent of VICTOR. It was first taken up in the English-speaking world in the 19th century and after mostly modest favour for the first half of the 20th century suddenly became popular in the 1970s, since when it has remained highly fashionable. The initial popularity of the name sprang exclusively from Queen Victoria (1837–1901), who was herself so named for her German mother, Mary Louisa Victoria of Saxe-Coburg-Gotha. In literature the name occurs for Victoria, a pagan prefect's daughter in Charles Kingsley's novel *Hypatia* (1853). VICKI and VICKY are diminutives in independent use, and others include *Vick*, *Vickie*, *Vikki* and *Vita*.

US feminist, financier Victoria Woodhull (1838–1927); UK poet, novelist Victoria (Vita) Sackville-West (1892–1962); UK novelist Victoria Holt (1906–93) (original name Eleanor Hibbert); US blues singer Victoria Spivey (1906–76); UK writer Victoria Glendinning (b.1937); Australian actress Victoria Vetri (b.1944) (original name Angela Dorian); US actress Victoria Principal (b.1945); UK actress Victoria Tennant (b.1950); UK comedienne Victoria Wood (b.1953).

Vida An independently adopted diminutive of *Davida*, a variant of DAVINA, in select use among English speakers from the mid-19th century. Vida Sherwin is a character in Sinclair Lewis's novel *Main Street* (1920). A diminutive is *Vi*.

Australian feminist Vida Goldstein (1869–1949); UK actress Vida Hope (1918–63).

Vince An independent adoption of the diminutive of VINCENT, in select use among English speakers from the 1950s.

US actor Vince Barnett (1902–77); US actor Vince Edwards (1928–96); UK popular singer Vince Hill (b.1937); US country musician Vince Gill (b.1957); UK pop musician Vince Clarke (b.1961).

Vincent This is either an adoption of the surname or an English form (through French) of the Latin name *Vincens*, genitive *Vincentis*, 'conquering', 'victorious' (compare VICTOR). The name has enjoyed regular if modest use among English speakers, mostly Roman Catholics, from the early 20th century. It was the name of various saints, notably the 3rd-century Spanish martyr St Vincent and the French Roman Catholic priest who founded two charitable orders, St Vincent de Paul (1581–1660). Vincent Crummles is a travelling theatre manager in Charles Dickens's novel *Nicholas Nickleby* (1838–9), and Vincent Gilmore is the Fairlie family's solicitor who is the part narrator in Wilkie Collins's novel *The Woman in White* (1860). The usual diminutive is VINCE, in independent use, but *Vinnie* also exists, as for the UK footballer Vinnie Jones (b.1965).

US actor Vincent Price (1911–93); UK ballet dancer Vincent Redmon (b.1965).

Viola This name was originally a borrowing of the Latin word *viola*, 'violet', but later came to be associated with the plant name and with VIOLET. It was first taken up on any scale by English speakers in the mid-19th century but is now rare. In Shakespeare's *Twelfth Night* (1601) Viola, the central female character, marries Orsino. Beaumont and Fletcher's romantic comedy *The Coxcomb* (1612) also has Viola as its central character. VIOLETTA is a directly related name. A frequent diminutive is *Vi*.

UK novelist Viola Meynell (1886–1956); US film editor Viola Lawrence (1894–1973); US actress Viola Dana (1897–1987) (original name Violet Flugrath); UK actress Viola Lyel (1900–72) (original name Violet Watson).

Violet An adoption of the flower name, and in general use among English speakers from the 1830s. After enjoying considerable popularity in the first quarter of the 20th century, however, the name has now long lost favour. Violet Fane (see listing below) is a character in Benjamin Disraeli's novel *Vivian Grey* (1826–7), and Violet Effingham marries Lord Chiltern in Anthony Trollope's novel *Phineas Finn* (1869). The name VIOLETTA is directly related. The usual diminutive is *Vi*.

UK writers Violet Fane (1843–1905) (original name Mary Lamb), Violet Hunt (1866–1942); UK actress Violet Kemble Cooper (1886–1961); UK politician Lady Violet Bonham Carter (1887–1969); English novelist, socialite Violet Trefusis (1894–1971); UK actress Violet Carson (1905–83); Canadian composer Violet Archer (1913–2000).

Violetta This name, an adoption of the Italian diminutive of VIOLA, was in select use among English speakers from the mid-19th century to the mid-20th, since when it has virtually become obsolete. It may have been helped by the character of Violetta Valery, the beautiful courtesan in Verdi's opera *La Traviata* (1853), especially as sung by the popular soprano Adelina Patti in the 1880s.

Virgil An English adoption of the Roman clan name *Vergilius*, later spelled *Virgilius* by association with Latin *virgo*, 'maiden' or *virga*, 'stick'. The name has been in select use among English speakers, mainly among black Americans, from the 19th century. It is famous from (and adopted by some as a tribute to) the Roman poet of the 1st century BC, whose full name was Publius Vergilius Maro. Virgil Tibbs is a black police detective in John Ball's mystery novel *In The Heat Of The Night* (1964), later made into a successful film (1967) with Sidney Poitier playing Tibbs.

US composer, writer on music Virgil Thomson (1896–1989); US organist Virgil Fox (1912–80); US astronaut Virgil Grissom (1926–67).

Virginia The name arose as a feminine form of the Roman clan name VIRGINIUS (compare VIRGIL), said to derive from Latin *virgo*, genitive *virginis*, 'maiden'. It has been modestly popular among English speakers from the 1870s. In Roman legend Virginia was killed by her father Virginius to save her from the advances of the decemvir Appius Claudius. The story was taken up by later writers, so that Virginia appears in the following: John Webster's (or Thomas Heywood's) tragedy *Appius and Virginia* (c.1603), John Dennis's tragedy of the same name (1709), James Knowles's play *Virginius* (1820) and Thomas Macaulay's poem 'Virginia' in *Lays of Ancient Rome* (1842). A similar account featuring the same Virginia appears in Chaucer's 'The Physician's Tale' in *The Canterbury Tales* (c.1387). Another Virginia is the central character in the popular pastoral romance *Paul et Virginie* (1788) by the French philosopher Bernardin de Saint-Pierre. An early historical bearer of the name was Virginia Dare (b.1587, Roanoke, Virginia), the first child born to English parents in America, and named, like the province, after Elizabeth I, the 'Virgin Queen'. A common diminutive is GINNY, in independent use.

UK novelist Virginia Woolf (1882–1941) (originally second name, first being Adeline); US actress Virginia Valli (1898–1968); UK actress Virginia McKenna (b.1931); US novelist Virginia Andrews (1933–86); UK actress Virginia Maskell (1936–68); UK harpsichordist Virginia Black (b.1943); UK tennis player Virginia Wade (b.1945); UK equestri- enne Virginia Leng (b.1955); US actress Virginia Madsen (b.1963).

Vivian (m.) An English form of the Latin name *Vivianus*, of uncertain origin but perhaps related to *vivus*, 'alive'. Taken up by English speakers in the mid-19th century, it is familiar in literature from the central character of Benjamin Disraeli's novel *Vivian Grey* (1826). The variant spelling VYVYAN is in independent use. The usual diminutive is *Viv*.

UK popular composer Vivian Ellis (1904–96); UK polar explorer Sir Vivian Fuchs (1908–99); West Indian cricketer Vivian Richards (b.1952).

Vivian (f.) A female adoption of the male name VIVIAN, it has been in select English-speaking use from the 19th century. Variant spellings include *Vivianne*, as for the French actress Vivianne Romance (1912–91) (original name Pauline Ortmans), *Viviana*, as for the Italian-born UK ballerina Viviana Durante (b.1967) and, in independent use, VIVIEN and VIVIENNE. The usual diminutive is *Viv*.

US actresses Vivian Oakland (1895–1958), Vivian Vance (1913–79), Vivian Blaine (1921–95) (original name Vivienne Stapleton); UK actresses Vivian Pickles (b.1933), Vivian Brooks (b.1948).

Vivien (f.) The name is a feminine form of the male name VIVIAN, in select English-speaking use from the 19th century. It is famous in legend and literature from Vivian, the mistress of Merlin in the Arthurian romances, who appears as Vivien ('the wily') in Tennyson's poem 'Vivien' (1859), retitled 'Merlin and Vivien' (1870), in *Idylls of the King*. Variant spellings are VIVIAN and VIVIENNE, both in independent use. Diminutives include *Vi*, *Viv* and *Vivie*.

UK artist Vivien John (b.1915); UK actresses Vivien Leigh (1913–67) (original name Vivian Mary Hartley), Vivien Merchant (1929–82) (original name Ada Thomson); UK authority on Edward Lear, Vivien Noakes (b.1937).

Vivienne A French form of VIVIEN, in fashion among English speakers from the late 19th century, though now much less popular. Diminutives include *Vi* and *Viv*.

US actresses Vivienne Segal (1897–1992), Vivienne Osborne (1900–61); UK actress Vivienne Bennett (1905–78); UK fashion designer Vivienne Westwood (b.1941).

Viviette The name is a variant of VIVIENNE with the French diminutive suffix *-ette* as in LYNETTE. It has found some favour among English speakers from the 19th century. Lady Viviette Constantine is a central character in Thomas Hardy's novel *Two on a Tower* (1882).

Vyvyan (m.) From the surname, itself a form of VIVIAN, and in very select use among English speakers from the 19th century.

UK writer, biographer Vyvyan Holland (1886–1967).

W

Wade An adoption of the surname, in use among English speakers from the 19th century. In Margaret Mitchell's novel *Gone with the Wind* (1936), Wade Hamilton is the son of Charles Hamilton, first husband of Scarlett O'Hara. (He is said to have been named after his father's commanding officer, as was then the custom.)

US country musician Wade Mainer (b.1907); UK rugby player Wade Dooley (b.1957).

Waldo This name represents a short form of an Old German name containing *wald*, 'rule', such as WALTER. It has found some modest favour among English speakers from the 19th century and became familiar from the US writer and philosopher Ralph Waldo Emerson (1803–82).

US novelist, critic Waldo Frank (1889–1967); US screenwriter Waldo Salt (1914–87).

Wallace An adoption of the (mainly Scottish) surname, in rarish use among English speakers from the 19th century. The name is historically famous from the 14th-century Scottish patriot William Wallace. The regular diminutive is WALLY, which is in independent use.

US actors Wallace Beery (1885–1949), Wallace Reid (1890–1923); UK actor Wallace Ford (1897–1966) (original name Sam Grundy); US film director Wallace Fox (1898–1958).

Wally An independently adopted diminutive of WALLACE or WALTER, in select use among English speakers from the 19th century, mainly in the US. The use of *wally* as a word for a stupid person has more or less outlawed the name in the UK from the 1970s, although this is not the case in Australia, where there is more acceptable association with *wallaby*, the country's native animal, or with the *Wallabies*, Australia's international rugby team.

US actors Wally Patch (1888–1970) (original name Walter Vinicombe), Wally Brown (1898–1961), Wally Vernon (1904–70), Wally Cox (1924–73); Australian cricketer Wally Grout (1927–68); UK TV entertainer Wally Whyton (1929–97); UK polar explorer Wally Herbert (b.1934); Australian rugby player Wally Lewis (b.1959).

Walt An independently adopted diminutive of WALTER, in select use among English speakers from the 19th century, mainly in the US.

US poet Walt Whitman (1819–92); US film-maker and animator Walt Disney (1901–66).

Walter The English name derives from an Old German name formed from *wald*, 'rule', and *heri*, 'army', so having the overall meaning 'army ruler'. The name, introduced to England by the Normans, was in regular use in the English-speaking world until the 18th century, when it declined. It then revived sharply in the mid-19th century, but again began to fall from favour from the 1930s, since when it has remained at a very low level. Walter Whitmore is a character in Shakespeare's *Henry VI, Part 2* (1590–92), while Walter Shandy is the father of the title character in Laurence Sterne's novel *Tristram Shandy* (1759–67). In Wilkie Collins's novel *The Woman in White* (1860) Walter Hartright is a drawing master and part narrator. Diminutives in independent use are WALLY and WALT (also formerly WAT).

Scottish poet, novelist Sir Walter Scott (1771–1832); US actor Walter Brennan (1894–1974); Canadian-born US actor Walter Pidgeon (1897–1984); UK cricketer Walter Hammond (1903–65); US ballet critic Walter Terry (1913–82); US broadcaster, journalist Walter Cronkite (b.1916).

Wanda A name that is probably of Slavonic origin, related to the ethnic name *Wend*, but in modern times felt to be a variant of WENDY. It has been in select use among English speakers from the 1880s. Historically, Wanda was a legendary 8th-century queen of Poland. In literature it is the name of the central character of Ouida's novel *Wanda* (1883), while in H. Seton Merriman's novel *The Vultures* (1902) Princess Wanda Bukaty loves the diplomat Reginald Cartoner.

Polish harpsichordist Wanda Landowska (1887–1959); US children's writer, illustrator Wanda Gag (1893–1946); US screenwriter Wanda Tuchock (1898–1985); Austrian-born UK actress Wanda Rotha (c.1910–82); US actress Wanda Hendrix (1928–81); US country singer Wanda Jackson (b.1937); UK actress Wanda Ventham (b.1938).

Ward From the surname, and in some favour among English speakers from the mid-19th century.

US actor Ward Bond (1903–60).

Warren From the surname, and found selectively in the English-speaking world from the early 19th century. The name is historically familiar from the UK administrator Warren Hastings (1732–1818), impeached by parliament on charges of corruption. In the US the name was similarly brought before the public by (the surname of) his contemporary, the Revolutionary hero, General Joseph Warren (1741–75). A literary bearer of the name is Warren Forster, father of Adam Paris by Judith Paris, the central character of Hugh Walpole's novel *Judith Paris* (1931).

US actor Warren Hymer (1906–48); UK actor Warren Mitchell (b.1926); US actors Warren Oates (1928–82), Warren Beatty (b.1937), Warren Berlinger (b.1937); UK actor Warren Clarke (b.1947).

Washington From the surname, and in select but declining English-speaking use, mostly in the US, from the 18th century. The name was initially made famous by the first US president, George Washington (1732–99), and was subsequently associated with the US writer Washington Irving (1783–1859), 'the father of American literature'.

Wat An independently adopted diminutive of WALTER, in regular English-speaking use in medieval times and occasionally found since. The name is historically familiar from the English leader of the Peasants' Revolt, Wat Tyler (d.1381). The variant spelling *Watt* sometimes occurs (and gave the surname *Watt*).

Wayne From the surname, and first popularly taken up by English speakers in the 1940s, largely thanks to the US film star John Wayne (1907–79) (original name Marion Michael Morrison), who first appeared on the screen in the late 1920s. The actor himself took his stage name from the US Revolutionary officer 'Mad Anthony' Wayne (1745–96). The name was very fashionable in the 1960s and 1970s but has now significantly declined.

US bandleader Wayne King (1901–85); US politician Wayne L. Hays (1911–89); US actors Wayne Morris (1914–59) (original first names Bert de Wayne), Wayne Rogers (b.1934); US cabaret singer Wayne Newton (b.1942); US actor Wayne Maunder (b.1942); UK pop singer Wayne Fontana (b.1945) (original name Glyn Ellis); UK ballet dancer Wayne Sleep (b.1948); Canadian ballet dancer Wayne Eagling (b.1950).

Webster From the surname, and a name in select English-speaking use from the 19th century. Adoption of the name in the US may have been stimulated by the famous lexicographer Noah Webster (1758–1843) or the politician and orator Daniel Webster (1782–1852).

UK popular singer Webster Booth (1902–84).

Wendell From the surname, and in irregular use among English speakers from the 19th century. The name initially became familiar from the US writer Oliver Wendell Holmes (1809–94) and subsequently from his identically named jurist son (1841–1935).

US vaudeville musician Wendell Hall (1896–1969); US actor Wendell Corey (1914–68); US screenwriter Wendell Mayes (1918–92); US actor Wendell Burton (b.1947).

Wendy The name is popularly said to be the invention of the UK writer J.M. Barrie for the little girl central character of his play *Peter Pan* (1904), derived from the nickname, 'Fwendy-wendy', given him by a child acquaintance, Margaret Henley, but it could equally be an independently adopted diminutive of GWENDOLEN. It has been in general English-speaking use from the 1910s, reaching its peak period of popularity in the 1960s, then gradually declining. (As Barrie was Scottish, the name has been specially favoured in Scotland.) The UK actress Wendy Barrie (see listing below) was Barrie's goddaughter, and named by him for his fictional character. She returned the compliment by adopting his surname as her stage name. The variant spelling *Wendi* is sometimes found, and the usual diminutive is *Wend*.

UK actresses Wendy Barrie (1912–78) (original name Marguerite Wendy Jenkins), Wendy Hiller (b.1912), Wendy Toye (b.1917), South African-born UK art critic Sister Wendy Beckett (b.1930); UK actresses Wendy Craig (b.1934), Wendy Williams (b.1934); UK writer Wendy Perriam (b.1940); UK poet Wendy Cope (b.1945); UK sculptor Wendy Taylor (b.1945); UK actress Wendy Richard (b.1946); UK radio presenter Wendy Jones (b.1949); Northern Ireland radio and TV presenter Wendy Austin (b.1951); Australian tennis player Wendy Turnbull (b.1952); UK athlete Wendy Sly (b.1959); Scottish opera singer Wendy Airey (b.1963); UK actress Wendy Jane Walker (b.1964).

Wesley From the surname, and in modest but fairly regular favour among English speakers from the 18th century. The name originated as a tribute to the English preacher and founder of the Methodist Church, John Wesley (1703–91), and also to his influential brother, Charles Wesley (1707–88). A diminutive *Wes* exists, as for the West Indian cricketer Wes Hall (b.1937).

US film director Wesley Ruggles (1889–1972); US actors Wesley Addy (1912–96), Wesley Snipes (b.1962).

Whitney (m.) From the surname, and in select English-speaking use in the 20th century.

US writer, civil rights leader Whitney M. Young Jr (1921–71).

Whitney (f.) A female adoption of the male name WHITNEY, in select favour among English speakers, especially black Americans, from the 1960s.

US actress Whitney Blake (b.c.1925); US pop singer Whitney Houston (b.1963).

Wilbur From the surname, and in mainly US adoption from the mid-19th century, where the name was originally a tribute to the US aviation pioneer Wilbur Wright (1867–1912).

Zambian-born novelist Wilbur Smith (b.1933).

Wilfred An independently adopted variant of WILFRID, in regular English-speaking use from the mid-19th century, but now much less common. The central character of Walter Scott's novel *Ivanhoe* (1819) is the knight Wilfred of Ivanhoe. The usual diminutive is *Wilf*.

Canadian-born US actor Wilfred Lucas (1871–1940); UK poet Wilfred Owen (1893–1918); UK radio compere, comedian Wilfred Pickles (1904–78).

Wilfrid This represents the Old English name *Wilfrith*, composed of *will*, 'will', 'desire', and *frithu*, 'peace', so 'desirer of peace', 'peace lover'. The name has been in regular use among English speakers, mainly in the UK, from the mid-19th century, but it is now much less frequently found. The variant WILFRED is in independent use and became more popular. The usual diminutive is *Wilf*.

Canadian politician Sir Wilfrid Laurier (1841–1919); UK actors

Wilfrid Lawson (1900–66), Wilfrid Hyde White (1903–91), Wilfrid Brambell (1912–85).

Wilhelmina

This name, a feminine form of the German name WILHELM (English WILLIAM), was introduced to England from Germany in the 19th century but has now mostly been superseded by the independently adopted diminutives MINA and WILMA. It was made familiar to some extent by Queen Wilhelmina of the Netherlands (1880–1962). The anglicized variant *Williamina* also occurs, as for the US astronomer Williamina Fleming (1857–1911).

UK sentimental writer Wilhelmina Stitch (1889–1936) (original name Ruth Collie); Dutch-born US model, business executive Wilhelmina Cooper (1940–80).

Wilkie

From the surname, but popularly felt to be a diminutive of a name such as WILFRED or WILLIAM. It was first taken up by English speakers in the 19th century.

UK novelist Wilkie Collins (1824–89) (originally middle name, first being William); UK actor, cinematographer Wilkie Cooper (b.1911).

Will

An independently adopted diminutive of WILLIAM, in select use among English speakers from medieval times. It is now rare in the UK but still active in the US. In Walter Scott's novel *Kenilworth* (1821) the huntsman Will Badger is a servant of Sir Hugh Robsart, while in Sinclair Lewis's novel *Main Street* (1920) Will Kennicott is the physician who marries Carol Milford. Diminutives *Willie* and *Willy* exist.

US actor Will Rogers (1879–1935); Scottish comedian Will Fyffe (1884–1947); UK actor Will Hay (1888–1949); UK rugby player Will Carling (b.1965).

Willa

An independently adopted diminutive of WILHELMINA, in occasional favour among English speakers from the 19th century.

US novelist Willa Cather (1873–1947) (original first name Wilella); UK writer Willa Muir (1890–1970).

William The present English name has its origins in an Old German name formed from *willo*, 'will', 'desire', and *helm*, 'helmet', 'protection', hence 'one who desires to protect', 'defender'. The modern German form of this is *Wilhelm* (compare WILHELMINA). The name has been in popular English-speaking use from medieval times onwards, and was enormously popular at the turn of the 20th century, but has gradually faded since then. It was introduced to England by the Normans, in the person of William the Conqueror himself. (The fact that he was England's 'Conqueror' does not seem to have hindered its wide adoption by the English 'conquered'.) It has long been a royal name in England, as elsewhere in continental Europe, with four kings bearing the name William from the 11th century to the 19th. It still enjoys royal favour today, and is currently represented by Prince William (b.1982), the first child of Prince Charles and the Princess of Wales. Among the best-known non-royal bearers of the name are the English playwright William Shakespeare (1564–1616) and the English founder of Pennsylvania William Penn (1644–1718). In literature the name is found for William Hammerton, a character in Francis Beaumont's play *The Knight of the Burning Pestle* (1607–8); for Colonel William Morden, the cousin and trustee of the central character, Clarissa Harlowe, in Samuel Richardson's novel *Clarissa* (1748); for Major Wiliam Dobbin and his father, the rich grocer Sir William Dobbin, in William Makepeace Thackeray's novel *Vanity Fair* (1847–8); and for a number of other characters in later literature. The name has been borne by many famous figures over the centuries, and only a handfull of these are listed below. The diminutives BILL, WILL and WILLIE are in independent use.

English poets William Blake (1757–1827), William Wordsworth (1770–1850); US president William H. Harrison (1773–1841); UK writer William Makepeace Thackeray (1811–63); US presidents William McKinley (1843–1901), William H. Taft (1857–1930); Irish poet William Butler Yeats (1865–1939); UK novelist William Golding (1911–93); US writer William Burroughs (1914–97); UK actors William Lucas (b.1925), William Franklyn (b.1926); UK writer William Trevor (b.1928); Canadian actor William Shatner (b.1931); UK actors William Roache (b.1932), William Gaunt (b.1937).

Williamina see **Wilhelmina**.

Willie An independently adopted diminutive of WILLIAM or (less often) some other name beginning *Will-*, in select English-speaking use from the 19th century. It occurs in literature for Robert Burns's poem *Holy Willie's Prayer* (1799). The spelling *Willy* also exists, as for the UK playwright Willy Russell (b.1947).

US bluesman Willie Dixon (1915–92); UK politician Willie Hamilton (1917–2000); US country singers Boxcar Willie (1931–99) (original name Lecil Travis Martin), Willie Nelson (b.1933); UK writer, broadcaster Willie Rushton (1937–96); Scottish jockey Willie Carson (b.1942); UK snooker player Willie Thorne (b.1954).

Willoughby From the surname, and in select but now rarish use in the English-speaking world from the 19th century. Sir Willoughby Patterne is a character in George Meredith's novel *The Egoist* (1879).

Willy see **Willie**.

Wilma An independently adopted diminutive of WILHELMINA, finding occasional favour among English speakers from the 1880s, mainly in the US.

US writer on country music Wilma Smith (b.1926); UK food writer Wilma Holt (b.1937); US country singer Wilma Burgess (b.1939); US athlete Wilma Rudolph (1940–94).

Win see **Winifred, Winnie**.

Windsor From the surname, taken up by some English speakers from the mid-19th century and in the 20th century enhanced to some extent by its association with the royal house name.

Welsh actor Windsor Davies (b.1930).

Winifred This name is an English version of the Welsh name *Gwenfrewi*, itself from *gwen*, 'white', 'fair', 'blessed', and *frewi*, 'reconciliation', so overall 'blessed reconciliation'. The present form of the name was influenced by the components of the Old English male name *Winfrith*, which are *wine*, 'friend', and *frith*, 'peace'. The name, which has been in general English-speaking use since the 16th century, was at its most popular level from the 1880s to the 1930s, after which it fell sharply. Winifred (Win) Jenkins is a servant of Tabitha Bramble in Tobias Smollett's novel *Humphry Clinker* (1771), and Winifred Forsyte is the sister of Soames Forsyte in John Galsworthy's *Forsyte* sequence (1906–22). The diminutives FREDA and WINNIE are in independent use. *Win* is also found.

US social worker Winifred Holt (1870–1945); UK novelist Winifred Holtby (1898–1935); Trinidad-born UK popular pianist Winifred Atwell (1914–83); Scottish politician Winifred Ewing (b.1929).

Winnie An independently adopted diminutive of WINIFRED, taken up by English speakers in the mid-19th century, but now much less common. Winnie Duval is a character in Upton Sinclair's novel *The Metropolis* (1908). The diminutive *Win* exists.

US comedienne Winnie Lightner (1901–71) (original name Winifred Hanson); South African political activist Winnie Mandela (b.1934).

Winona This is an American Indian (Sioux) name traditionally given to a first-born daughter. It is that of a legendary Indian princess and was given to various places in the US, the first of which to be so called (in 1853) was the city of Winona in Minnesota. The name has enjoyed select adoption among English speakers in the US from the mid-19th century, and it is familiar in literature (in the form *Wenonah*) as that of

Hiawatha's mother in Henry Wadsworth Longfellow's narrative poem *The Song of Hiawatha* (1858): 'Fair Nokomis bore a daughter,/And she called her name Wenonah,/As the first-born of her daughters.' The present spelling of the name was further popularized by H.L. Gordon's poem *Winona* (1881).

US actress Winona Ryder (b.1971).

Winston From the surname, and in select English-speaking use in the 20th century, mainly among blacks (West Indians in the UK). The name is famously associated with the UK prime minister Sir Winston Churchill (1874–1965), who continued the name that his family had borne since the 17th century. (The first Winston Churchill, born in 1620, was baptized with his mother's maiden name.) His name is currently borne by his grandson, the politician Winston Churchill (b.1940). (See also RANDOLPH.) The name occurs in literature for Winston Smith, the central character of George Orwell's novel *1984* (1949). The usual diminutive is *Winnie*.

US novelist Winston Churchill (1871–1947); UK writer Winston Graham (b.1911).

Wolf This is either a short form of a German name such as *Wolfgang*, or an adoption of the surname, or even a borrowing of the animal name. It has found occasional favour among English speakers from the 19th century and is that of the history teacher who is the central character of John Cowper Powys's novel *Wolf Solent* (1929).

UK novelist, screenwriter Wolf Mankowitz (1924–98).

Woodrow From the surname, and in mainly US use from the 19th century, where it arose by way of a tribute to the US president Woodrow Wilson (1856–1924) (originally his middle name, his first being Thomas). WOODY is a diminutive that has been adopted in its own right.

UK politician, writer Woodrow Wyatt (1918–97).

Woody An independently adopted diminutive of WOODROW, suggesting an association with woods and forests (as more genuinely do SILAS and SILVESTER). The name has been in select English-speaking use from the early 20th century, mostly in the US.

US folk singers Woody Guthrie (1912–67) (original first names Woodrow Wilson), Woody Herman (1913–87) (original first names Woodrow Charles); US American football coach Woody Hayes (1913–87) (original first names Wayne Woodrow); US actors Woody Allen (b.1935) (original name Allen Stewart Konigsberg), Woody Harrelson (b.1961) (original first names Woodrow Tracy).

Wyatt From the surname, and in rarish use among English speakers from the 19th century.

US lawman Wyatt Earp (1848–1929).

Wyndham From the surname, and taken up by English speakers from the mid-19th century.

US-born UK writer Wyndham Lewis (1882–1957) (originally middle name, first being Percy).

X

Xan see **Alexander**.

Xavier This name has been adopted mainly by Roman Catholics in the English-speaking world in honour of the Spanish soldier who founded the Society of Jesus, St Francis Xavier (1506–52). (His own name comes from the family castle of Xavier in Navarre where he was born. The name itself is a corruption of a Basque name meaning 'new house'.) The name occurs in literature for various priests, monks and other religious characters, such as Father Xavier, the convent confessor in the best-selling novel *Anthony Adverse* (1933) by the US writer Hervey Allen.

Spanish-US bandleader Xavier Cugat (1900–90) (original name Francisco de Asis Javier Cugat Mingall de Bru y Deulofeo); Australian writer Xavier Herbert (1901–84).

Y

Yasmin This name is an independently adopted variant of JASMINE, based on an original Persian or Arabic name with the same meaning. It has been in select use among English speakers from the 1930s and may have owed some of its original impetus to James Elroy Flecker's posthumously published 'Eastern' play *Hassan* (1922), which has a courtesan called Yasmin. In real life it was popularized by Princess Yasmin Khan (b.1949), the daughter of Prince Ali Khan and the US actress Rita Hayworth. The variant spelling *Yasmine* also occurs, and the usual diminutive is *Yas*.

UK model Yasmin Le Bon (b.1965).

Yolande This is a French name, of obscure ultimate origin, although related by some to IOLANTHE. It has been in select use among English speakers since the early 20th century, first among black Americans, then among white Britons. A historical bearer of the name was Yolande (also known as Isabella) of Brienne, an early 13th-century queen of Jerusalem. The usual diminutive is *Yola*.

US actress Yolande Donlan (b.1920).

York From the surname, and in occasional English-speaking use from the 19th century. Its association with the royal title (the various dukes and duchesses of York) may have helped its adoption.

UK composer York Bowen (1884–1961) (originally middle name, first being Edwin).

Yvette This name is a feminine diminutive of the French male name *Yves* (English IVOR), although it has also come to be regarded as a diminutive of YVONNE. It has been in select use among English speakers from the early 20th century.

French diseuse Yvette Guilbert (1865–1944); New Zealand athlete Yvette Williams (b.1929); US actress Yvette Mimieux (b.1942).

Yvonne An independently adopted diminutive of the French male name *Yves* (English IVOR). It was taken up by English speakers at the turn of the 20th century and had its period of greatest popularity in the 1950s and 1960s, since when it has fallen from favour. The fashion for the name may have originally come from one of the French actresses who bore it: Yvonne de Bray (1889–1954), Yvonne Arnaud (1892–1958) and Yvonne Printemps (1895–1977) were all well known outside France. A variant form of the name is *Evonne* (perhaps influenced by EVE but also avoiding the awkward 'Y'), as for the Australian tennis player Evonne Cawley (b.1951). The usual diminutive is *Vonnie*.

Canadian-born US actress Yvonne de Carlo (b.1922) (original name Peggy Middleton); South African actress Yvonne Bryceland (1925–92); UK actresses Yvonne Mitchell (1925–79); Canadian quintuplet Yvonne Dionne (1934–2001); US actress Yvonne Craig (b.1937); Yvonne Romain (b.1938); Australian-born UK opera singer Yvonne Minton (b.1938); UK journalist Yvonne Roberts (b.1948); US popular singer Yvonne Elliman (b.1951); Scottish athlete Yvonne Murray (b.1964).

Z

Zacchaeus A biblical name, from Hebrew *Zakkai*, 'innocent', 'justified', in rare use among English speakers from the 17th century. In the Bible Zacchaeus is an inhabitant of Jericho who, being small, climbs into a tree to see Jesus and then invites him to share a meal in his own home. Diminutives are *Zack* or *Zak*.

Zachariah This is an alteration of the biblical name *Zechariah*, from Hebrew *Zēkharyah*, 'Yah [that is, Jehovah] has remembered', adopted by Puritans in the 16th century. The name was then in fairly regular, but decreasingly popular, use to the 20th century, by which time it had mostly given way to ZACHARY. In the Bible Zechariah is the name of around thirty people, two of the best known being the prophet for whom the Old Testament book is named and the Zechariah who is the husband of Elizabeth and father of John the Baptist. Zachariah Hobson is a character in William Makepeace Thackeray's novel *The Newcomes* (1853–5). Diminutives are *Zack* or *Zak*.

Zachary An English form of the Greek name *Zacharias*, representing the biblical name ZACHARIAH, in occasional use among English speakers from the 16th century and today still active in the US but only rarely in the UK. The name is historically associated with the US president Zachary Taylor (1784–1850). The usual diminutives are *Zach*, *Zack* or *Zak*, the first as for the US baseball player Zach Wheat (1888–1972). US actor Zachary Scott (1914–65).

Zack see **Zacchaeus**, **Zachariah**, **Zachary**.

Zak see Isaac, **Zacchaeus**, **Zachariah**, **Zachary**.

Zandra A name that is either an independently adopted diminutive of ALEXANDRA or a variant of that name's more familiar diminutive, SANDRA. It has found sporadic favour among English speakers in the 20th century.

UK fashion designer Zandra Rhodes (b.1940).

Zara This name is either of Arabic origin, from *zahr*, 'flower', or else represents a rarish variant of SARAH. It was taken up by English speakers in the 1960s and in the UK enjoyed a certain vogue in the 1980s, thanks to the arrival on the royal scene of Zara Phillips (b.1981), daughter of Princess Anne.

Zebedee A biblical name, in origin an English form of *Zebadiah*, itself from Hebrew *Zĕbhadhyāhu*, 'Yah [that is, Jehovah] has given'. It has found occasional favour among English speakers from the 17th century. In the Bible Zebedee is the fisherman father of the disciples James and John. The name was humorously popularized in the UK by the puppet Zebedee in the children's TV series *The Magic Roundabout* (from 1965). (One of the show's catchphrases was 'Time for bed, said Zebedee', which is said to have led to the adoption of the name for a number of babies born at this time.) The diminutive *Zeb* exists.

Zedekiah A biblical name, from Hebrew *Tsidhqīyāhu*, 'Yah [that is, Jehovah] is just', taken up by 17th-century Puritans and finding favour among some English speakers in the years that followed, although it is hardly common today. In the Bible Zedekiah is the name of four people, the most important being the son of Josiah, the last king of Judah. A diminutive *Zed* exists.

Zeke see **Ezekiel**.

Zelda An independently adopted diminutive of GRISELDA, in favour with some English speakers from the early 20th century.

US novelist, wife of F. Scott Fitzgerald, Zelda Fitzgerald (1899–1948); UK film director Zelda Barron (b.c.1933); UK marriage guidance adviser Zelda West-Meads (b.1944).

Zena This name may be either a shortened form of ZENOBIA, an independently adopted diminutive of ROSINA, or (according to some) a form of a Persian word meaning 'woman'. It has found occasional English-speaking use from the 19th century, mainly in the UK.

UK actresses Zena Dare (1887–1975), Zena Marshall (b.1926), Zena Walker (b.1934).

Zenobia This is a Greek name, in origin a feminine form of *Zēnobios*, from *Zeus*, poetic genitive *Zēnos*, 'Zeus' (the greatest of the Greek gods), and *bios*, 'life', so 'life of Zeus'. It is occasionally found in English-speaking use from the late 19th century. A historical Zenobia was a queen of Palmyra in the 3rd century AD. In Nathaniel Hawthorne's novel *The Blithedale Romance* (1852) Zenobia is a passionate, queenly woman who falls in love with the blacksmith Hollingsworth.

Zephaniah A biblical name, from Hebrew *Tsephanyāh*, 'Yah [that is, Jehovah] has hidden', in rarish English-speaking use from the 17th century to the 19th century, but hardly ever found today. In the Bible Zephaniah is a minor prophet with a book named for him. Zephaniah Scadder is a swindler in Charles Dickens's novel *Martin Chuzzlewit* (1843–4), and Zephaniah Timberman is a character in James Fenimore Cooper's novel *The Chainbearer* (1845). A diminutive is *Zeph*.

Zina Apparently a variant form of the rare Greek name *Xenia* ('hospitality'), favoured by black Americans from the 1950s. In the UK the preferred form of the name is ZENA.

US tennis player Zina Garrison (b.1963).

Zoe This name comes from the Greek word meaning 'life'. It was taken up in the English-speaking world in the mid-19th century and suddenly caught on from the 1970s, when it became hugely popular. It has since dropped to a less exalted level but is still widely found. It was first made known by various Christian martyrs of the 2nd and 3rd centuries. In literature Zoe Coleman is a character in Aldous Huxley's novel *Antic Pay* (1923). The spelling with the diaeresis (as *Zoë*) is sometimes found, and *Zowie* is a variant spelling in independent use.

US writer Zoë Akins (1886–1958); Australian actress Zoe Caldwell (b.1933); UK writer Zoë Fairbairns (b.1948); US-born UK actress Zoe Wanamaker (b.1949); UK TV presenter Zoë Ball (b.1970).

Zola This name probably arose as a variant of ZOE, perhaps subconsciously suggested by the surname of the French writer Emile Zola (1840–1902). It has been adopted by some English speakers from the mid-20th century.

South African athlete Zola Budd (b.1966).

Zona This is perhaps an alteration of ZENA. It has found some favour among English speakers, mainly in the US, from the 19th century.

US writer Zona Gale (1874–1938).

Zora This name, perhaps a borrowing of the biblical place name *Zorah*, has occasionally been used by English speakers from the late 19th century. A variant spelling is *Zorah*, found for the professional bridesmaid in Gilbert and Sullivan's comic opera *Ruddigore* (1887).

US writer, folklorist Zora Neale Hurston (1891–1960).

Zowie A name that is apparently a variant of ZOE, with a spelling to reflect the pronunciation. It has found some favour among English speakers from the 1970s.

Zuleika A name of Persian origin, frequently found in poetry, and probably meaning 'brilliant beauty'. It has been occasionally adopted for first-name use among English speakers from the 19th century. In Byron's poem *The Bride of Abydos* (1813) Zuleika is the beautiful daughter of Pasha Giaffir who is destined to marry the elderly Bey of Carasman. The literary use of the name is more familiar from the central character of Max Beerbohm's comic novel *Zuleika Dobson* (1911). (Beerbohm stipulated the name should rhyme with 'beaker', not 'biker'.)

Top 10 Boys' and Girls' Names, 1944–94, England and Wales

1944

BOYS

1	John
2	David
3	Michael
4	Peter
5	Robert
6	Anthony
7	Brian
8	Alan
9	William
10	James

GIRLS

1	Margaret
2	Patricia
3	Christine
4	Mary
5	Jean
6	Ann
7	Susan
8	Janet
9	Maureen
10	Barbara

1954

BOYS

1	David
2	John
3	Stephen
4	Michael
5	Peter
6	Robert
7	Paul
8	Alan
9	Christopher
10	Richard

GIRLS

1	Susan
2	Linda
3	Christine
4	Margaret
5	Janet
6	Patricia
7	Carol
8	Elizabeth
9	Mary
10	Ann

1964

BOYS

1 David
2 Paul
3 Andrew
4 Mark
5 John
6 Michael
7 Stephen
8 Ian
9 Robert
10 Richard

GIRLS

1 Susan
2 Julie
3 Karen
4 Jacqueline
5 Deborah
6 Tracey
7 Jane
8 Helen
9 Diane
10 Sharon

1974

BOYS

1 Paul
2 Mark
3 David
4 Andrew
5 Richard
6 Christopher
7 James
8 Simon
9 Michael
10 Matthew

GIRLS

1 Sarah
2 Claire
3 Nicola
4 Emma
5 Lisa
6 Joanne
7 Michelle
8 Helen
9 Samantha
10 Karen

1984

BOYS

1 Christopher
2 James
3 David
4 Daniel
5 Michael
6 Matthew
7 Andrew
8 Richard
9 Paul
10 Mark

GIRLS

1 Sarah
2 Laura
3 Gemma
4 Emma
5 Rebecca
6 Claire
7 Victoria
8 Samantha
9 Rachel
10 Amy

1994

BOYS

1 Thomas
2 James
3 Jack
4 Daniel
5 Matthew
6 Ryan
7 Joshua
8 Luke
9 Samuel
10 Jordan

GIRLS

1 Rebecca
2 Lauren
3 Jessica
4 Charlotte
5 Hannah
6 Sophie
7 Amy
8 Emily
9 Laura
10 Emma

(Source: Emma Merry, *First Names*, HMSO 1995)

Top 50 Boys' and Girls' Names, 1998–2001, England and Wales

1998

BOYS

1	Jack	25	Nathan
2	Thomas	26	Kieran
3	James	27	Jacob
4	Daniel	28	Ben
5	Joshua	29	Cameron
6	Matthew	30	Aaron
7	Samuel	31	Bradley
8	Callum	32	Christopher
9	Joseph	33	Charlie
10	Jordan	34	Mohammed
11	Connor	35	Jamie
12	Ryan	36	Brandon
13	Luke	37	Robert
14	William	38	Kyle
15	Harry	39	David
16	Benjamin	40	Andrew
17	George	41	Charles
18	Lewis	42	Reece
19	Alexander	43	Edward
20	Oliver	44	Owen
21	Adam	45	Alex
22	Jake	46	Dylan
23	Liam	47	Ethan
24	Michael	48	Jonathan
		49	Sam
		50	Max

GIRLS

1	Chloe	31	Amber
2	Emily	32	Paige
3	Megan	33	Georgina
4	Jessica	34	Danielle
5	Sophie	35	Nicole
6	Charlotte	36	Grace
7	Hannah	37	Natasha
8	Lauren	38	Ella
9	Rebecca	39	Chelsea
10	Lucy	40	Leah
11	Amy	41	Anna
12	Georgia	42	Victoria
13	Katie	43	Phoebe
14	Bethany	44	Zoe
15	Emma	45	Samantha
16	Olivia	46	Alexandra
17	Courtney	47	Jasmine
18	Shannon	48	Amelia
19	Eleanor	49	Louise
20	Jade	50	Lydia
21	Abigail		
22	Ellie		
23	Molly		
24	Laura		
25	Alice		
26	Sarah		
27	Holly		
28	Caitlin		
29	Rachel		
30	Elizabeth		

1999

BOYS

1	Jack	29	Mohammed
2	Thomas	30	Ben
3	James	31	Jamie
4	Joshua	32	Charlie
5	Daniel	33	Owen
6	Matthew	34	Bradley
7	Samuel	35	Brandon
8	Joseph	36	Aaron
9	Callum	37	Kyle
10	William	38	Christopher
11	Ryan	39	Robert
12	Luke	40	Ethan
13	Lewis	41	David
14	Harry	42	Alex
15	Jordan	43	Charles
16	Benjamin	44	Reece
17	Liam	45	Edward
18	George	46	Andrew
19	Alexander	47	Dylan
20	Adam	48	Max
21	Oliver	49	Sam
22	Connor	50	Louis
23	Jake		
24	Cameron		
25	Michael		
26	Nathan		
27	Jacob		
28	Kieran		

GIRLS

1	Chloe	31	Sarah
2	Emily	32	Leah
3	Megan	33	Elizabeth
4	Olivia	34	Amber
5	Sophie	35	Jasmine
6	Charlotte	36	Natasha
7	Lauren	37	Amelia
8	Jessica	38	Phoebe
9	Rebecca	39	Victoria
10	Hannah	40	Anna
11	Bethany	41	Nicole
12	Lucy	42	Paige
13	Georgia	43	Chelsea
14	Amy	44	Georgina
15	Katie	45	Danielle
16	Ellie	46	Zoe
17	Emma	47	Imogen
18	Courtney	48	Niamh
19	Eleanor	49	Lydia
20	Abigail	50	Alexandra
21	Shannon		
22	Molly		
23	Jade		
24	Caitlin		
25	Alice		
26	Ella		
27	Grace		
28	Laura		
29	Rachel		
30	Holly		

2000

BOYS

1	Jack	29	Jacob
2	Thomas	30	Michael
3	James	31	Ben
4	Joshua	32	Ethan
5	Daniel	33	Charlie
6	Harry	34	Bradley
7	Samuel	35	Brandon
8	Joseph	36	Aaron
9	Matthew	37	Max
10	Callum	38	Dylan
11	Luke	39	Kyle
12	William	40	Reece
13	Lewis	41	Robert
14	Oliver	42	Christopher
15	Ryan	43	David
16	Benjamin	44	Edward
17	George	45	Charles
18	Liam	46	Owen
19	Jordan	47	Louis
20	Adam	48	Alex
21	Alexander	49	Joe
22	Jake	50	Rhys
23	Connor		
24	Cameron		
25	Nathan		
26	Kieran		
27	Mohammed		
28	Jamie		

GIRLS

1	Chloe	31	Anna
2	Emily	32	Jasmine
3	Megan	33	Sarah
4	Charlotte	34	Elizabeth
5	Jessica	35	Amelia
6	Lauren	36	Rachel
7	Sophie	37	Amber
8	Olivia	38	Phoebe
9	Hannah	39	Natasha
10	Lucy	40	Niamh
11	Georgia	41	Zoe
12	Rebecca	42	Paige
13	Bethany	43	Nicole
14	Amy	44	Abbie
15	Ellie	45	Mia
16	Katie	46	Imogen
17	Emma	47	Lily
18	Abigail	48	Alexandra
19	Molly	49	Chelsea
20	Grace	50	Daisy
21	Courtney		
22	Shannon		
23	Caitlin		
24	Eleanor		
25	Jade		
26	Ella		
27	Leah		
28	Alice		
29	Holly		
30	Laura		

2001

BOYS

1	Jack	29	Nathan
2	Thomas	30	Jacob
3	Joshua	31	Ben
4	James	32	Charlie
5	Daniel	33	Michael
6	Harry	34	Kieran
7	Samuel	35	Max
8	Joseph	36	Bradley
9	Matthew	37	Brandon
10	Lewis	38	Owen
11	Luke	39	Louis
12	Oliver	40	Aaron
13	William	41	Tyler
14	Benjamin	42	Kyle
15	Callum	43	Reece
16	George	44	Edward
17	Adam	45	Alex
18	Ryan	46	David
19	Jake	47	Robert
20	Alexander	48	Harrison
21	Ethan	49	Christopher
22	Liam	50	Joe
23	Cameron		
24	Connor		
25	Jordan		
26	Mohammed		
27	Jamie		
28	Dylan		

GIRLS

1	Chloe	31	Leah
2	Emily	32	Amelia
3	Megan	33	Elizabeth
4	Jessica	34	Anna
5	Sophie	35	Amber
6	Lauren	36	Lily
7	Charlotte	37	Laura
8	Hannah	38	Sarah
9	Olivia	39	Rachel
10	Lucy	40	Phoebe
11	Ellie	41	Erin
12	Amy	42	Millie
13	Katie	43	Zoe
14	Georgia	44	Abbie
15	Rebecca	45	Nicole
16	Molly	46	Paige
17	Bethany	47	Niamh
18	Emma	48	Daisy
19	Holly	49	Natasha
20	Ella	50	Alexandra
21	Caitlin		
22	Abigail		
23	Grace		
24	Jade		
25	Mia		
26	Shannon		
27	Eleanor		
28	Alice		
29	Jasmine		
30	Courtney		